D1298220

# THE HISTORIOGRAPHY OF THE BRITISH
## EMPIRE-COMMONWEALTH

# THE HISTORIOGRAPHY
# OF THE BRITISH
# EMPIRE-COMMONWEALTH

## TRENDS, INTERPRETATIONS,
## AND RESOURCES

*Edited by* Robin W. Winks

*with twenty-one essays by* George
Bennett, Robert O. Collins, Robert I. Crane,
Edith Dobie, John S. Galbraith, K. W.
Goonewardena, Joseph Jones, William Roger
Louis, Kenneth A. MacKirdy, Robert L.
Middlekauff, Helen F. Mulvey, George
Shepperson, Keith Sinclair, Damodar P.
Singhal, Leonard M. Thompson, Hugh Tinker,
C. Mary Turnbull, D. A. G. Waddell, John
M. Ward, Robin W. Winks, *and*
Harrison M. Wright

*Duke University Press*

*Durham, N. C.*

*1966*

© 1966, Duke University Press
Library of Congress Catalogue Card number 66-15555

Printed in the United States of America
by the Seeman Printery, Durham, N. C.

# CONTENTS

# CONTRIBUTORS

GEORGE BENNETT (M.A., Oxon.) is a Fellow of Linacre House and Senior Lecturer in Commonwealth History at Oxford, a post he has held since 1952. Previously he was Lecturer in History at the School of Oriental and African Studies, London, and Lecturer in History at the University of Toronto. He was Visiting Professor of History at Madras Christian College in the University of Madras in 1957 and at the Institute of African Studies in the University of Ghana in 1965. His publications include *The Concept of Empire* (London, 1953; 2nd ed., 1962); *Kenya, A Political History: The Colonial Period* (London, 1963), and (with Carl G. Rosberg) *The Kenyatta Election: Kenya, 1960-1961* (London, 1961).

ROBERT O. COLLINS (Ph.D., Yale University) is an Associate Professor of History, University of California, Santa Barbara. He is the author of *The Southern Sudan, 1883-1898: A Struggle for Control* (New Haven, 1962), co-author with Peter Duignan of *Americans in Africa: A Preliminary Guide to American Missionary Archives and Library Manuscript Collections on Africa* (Stanford, 1963), and a contributor to numerous African journals. He has also contributed to two forthcoming works, Fred Burke and Stanley Diamond, eds., *The Transformation of East Africa: Studies in Political Anthropology,* and Prosser Gifford and William Roger Louis, eds., *British and German Colonialism in Africa.* Professor Collins has traveled widely in Africa and worked in the British, Belgian, and Sudanese archives.

ROBERT I. CRANE (Ph.D., Yale University) is Professor of History at Duke University, where he has taught since 1961. Earlier he was a member of the faculties of the University of Chicago and the University of Michigan, and in 1962-63 he was Visiting Professor of History in the University of Calcutta. His publications include (as co-author) *Aspects of Economic Development in South Asia* (New York, 1954) and *Asia, Africa, Latin America: A Bibliographical Guide* (New York, 1961); he has edited *A Handbook on Jammu and Kashmir* (New Haven, 1956) and written *The History of India: Its Study and Interpretation* (Washington, 1958). He contributed to *Problems of Historical Writing in India* (New Delhi [1964]); Helen G. Matthew, ed., *Asia in the Modern World* (New York, 1963); Shirley H. Engle, ed., *New Perspectives in World History* (Washington, 1964), and William B. Hamilton, ed., *The Transfer of*

*Institutions* (Durham, N. C., 1965). Professor Crane is a Director of the American Institute of Indian Studies and of the Association for Asian Studies, and is editor of the *Journal of Asian Studies*. He recently has been named a Fellow of the Institute of Historical Studies (Calcutta).

EDITH DOBIE (Ph.D., Stanford University) is Professor Emeritus of History from the University of Washington. She has been a Visiting Professor in the University of Alberta and most recently at Elmira College. In 1963 she renewed her extensive travels in the Mediterranean area. Her publications include *The Political Career of Stephen Mallory White* (Stanford, 1927), and (as editor) *Problems in International Understanding* (Seattle, 1928), as well as numerous articles on British colonial affairs. She was a contributor to *If Men Want Peace* (New York, 1944).

JOHN S. GALBRAITH (Ph.D., State University of Iowa), who was born in Scotland, was Professor of History at the University of California, Los Angeles, from 1948 until 1965. Previously he taught at the State University of Iowa and at Ohio University. He is now the Chancellor of the University of California, San Diego. He has published many articles on Imperial and Commonwealth history and three books: *The Establishment of Canadian Diplomatic Status at Washington* (Berkeley, 1951), *The Hudson's Bay Company as an Imperial Factor* (Berkeley, 1957), and *Reluctant Empire: British Policy on the South African Frontier, 1834-1854* (Berkeley, 1963). He is a Fellow of the Royal Historical Society and a past-President of the Pacific Coast Branch of the American Historical Association.

K. W. GOONEWARDENA (Ph.D., University of London) is Professor of History in the University of Ceylon, Peradeniya. He has published several articles on the Dutch period of Ceylon's history, and a book, *The Foundation of Dutch Power in Ceylon, 1638-1658* (Amsterdam, 1958). He is co-editor of the *University of Ceylon Review*, and in 1961-62 he was a Research Associate of the School of Oriental and African Studies in the University of London.

JOSEPH JONES (Ph.D., Stanford University) is Professor of English at the University of Texas, where he has taught since 1935. He also has lectured at the universities of Illinois and Minnesota, has been a Fulbright Lecturer in American Literature at the university colleges of Auckland and Victoria in New Zealand (1953), and Smith-Mundt Professor of American Literature at the universities of Cape Town and the Witwatersrand in South Africa (1960). He is editor of the *Newsletter* of the Conference on British Commonwealth Literature affiliated with the Modern Language Association of America, and his publications include the following: *The Cradle of Erewhon: Samuel Butler in New Zealand* (Austin, 1959); "Prolegomena to the Study of British Colonial-Commonwealth Literature," *Graduate Journal* (Austin), I (Fall, 1958), 169-181; and the privately circulated *Re-*

*sources for the Study of Commonwealth Literature in English* (Austin, 1959), with R. T. Robertson. A volume entitled *Terranglia: The Case for English as World Literature* (New York) is in press. For 1965-66, Professor Jones has been appointed Fulbright Lecturer in American Literature at the University of Hong Kong.

WILLIAM ROGER LOUIS (D.Phil., Oxon.) is an Assistant Professor of History at Yale University, where he specializes in European colonial problems. He is the author of *Ruanda-Urundi, 1884-1919* (Oxford, 1963) and co-editor with Prosser Gifford, also of Yale, of the forthcoming symposium volume on *British and German Colonialism in Africa*. Professor Louis is on leave during 1965-66 to work on a study of European colonial developments during World War I, and he is exploring the nature of the mandates system for a monograph.

KENNETH A. MacKIRDY (Ph.D., University of Toronto) is Professor of History in the University of Waterloo, Canada. He lectured at the University of Melbourne in 1951-52, served as Research Fellow in Australian History at the Australian National University, 1952-53, and initiated studies in Australian history at the University of Washington (Seattle) in 1957. He has served on the Council of the Canadian Historical Association (1961-64), is co-editor of *Ontario History*, a contributor to John Meisel, ed., *Papers on the 1962 Election* (Toronto, 1964), and in 1965-66 is serving as a Visiting Professor at the University of California, Los Angeles. His publications include numerous articles on Australian topics and comparative studies between Australia and Canada.

ROBERT L. MIDDLEKAUFF (Ph.D., Yale University) is Assistant Professor of History at the University of California, Berkeley. Before taking up his present appointment he taught at Yale University. He is the author of articles on education in colonial New England and of a book, *Ancients and Axioms: Secondary Education in Eighteenth-Century New England* (New Haven, 1963). He has recently edited *Bacon's Rebellion* (New York, 1964), and wrote (with Max Savelle) *A History of Colonial America* (New York, 1964). He is now writing a biography of the Mather family of New England.

HELEN F. MULVEY (Ph.D., Radcliffe College) is Professor of History at Connecticut College, New London, where she has taught since 1946. She has twice visited Ireland in recent years, has written articles on Sir Charles Gavan Duffy for the *Canadian Historical Review* and on W. E. H. Lecky for *Victorian Studies*, and is preparing a biography of Thomas Davis. Her selective bibliographical survey of recent work in Irish history, 1600-1922, prepared for the Conference on British Studies, has been published in *The Historian*, XXVII (August, 1965), 516-59. In 1963 she was in Ireland once again on an American Philosophical Society grant.

GEORGE SHEPPERSON (M.A., Cantab.) is Professor of Commonwealth and American History in the University of Edinburgh and Con-
venor of the Committee of the Centre of African Studies in Edinburgh. He
has frequently visited Africa, as well as the United States, and has taught in
the University of Chicago, Roosevelt University, and Makerere University
College. He has written numerous articles in both of his fields, and on Negro
history, as well as acting as co-author (with Thomas Price) of *Independent
African: John Chilembwe and the Nyasaland Native Rising of 1915* (Edinburgh, 1958). Among his articles are "The Literature of British Central
Africa" and "The Military History of British Central Africa," both in the
*Rhodes-Livingstone Journal*. His latest book is *David Livingstone and the
Rovuma* (Edinburgh, 1965), and he is continuing work on the nineteenth-
century origins of African nationalism and on American Negro connections
with Africa.

KEITH SINCLAIR (Ph.D., University of New Zealand) is Professor
of History in the University of Auckland. His publications include *The Maori
Land League* (Auckland, 1950), *The Origins of the Maori Wars* (Wellington, 1957; 2nd ed., 1961), *A History of New Zealand* (Harmonds-
worth, 1959; 2nd ed., Oxford, 1961), (with William F. Mandle) *Open
Account: The Bank of New South Wales in New Zealand, 1861-1961*
(Christchurch, 1961), and *William Pember Reeves, New Zealand Fabian*
(Oxford, 1965). He also has edited a new edition of John Eldon Gorst, *The
Maori King* (Oxford, 1959), *Distance Looks Our Way* (Auckland, 1961),
and (with Robert McD. Chapman) *Studies of a Small Democracy* (Auckland, 1963) and has contributed to Muriel F. Lloyd Prichard, ed., *The
Future of New Zealand* (Christchurch, 1964). Professor Sinclair has pub-
lished three volumes of poetry, *Songs for a Summer and Other Poems* (Christchurch, 1952), *Strangers or Beasts* (Christchurch, 1954), and *A Time to
Embrace* (Auckland, 1963).

DAMODAR P. SINGHAL (Ph.D., University of London) is Reader
in Asian History in the University of Queensland. Dr. Singhal has written
many articles on problems of Asian historiography, and on India, Pakistan,
and Malaysia. He is the author of two books, *The Annexation of Upper
Burma* (Singapore, 1960), and *India and Afghanistan—A Study of Diplomatic Relations, 1876-1907* (Brisbane, 1963). He has near completion a
major study of cultural intercourse between India and other civilizations from
the earliest times to the present day. Dr. Singhal formerly taught at the University of Malaya in Singapore.

LEONARD M. THOMPSON (M.A., Oxon.; D.Litt., Rhodes
University) is Professor of African History at the University of California,
Los Angeles. Until 1961 he was Professor of History in the University of
Cape Town, where he began teaching in 1946, and in the spring of 1961

was Visiting Commonwealth Professor at Duke University. He was Natal's Rhodes Scholar in 1937. His publications include *The Cape Coloured Franchise* (Johannesburg, 1949); *Indian Immigration into Natal, 1860-1872* (Pretoria, 1952); *The Unification of South Africa, 1902-1910* (Oxford, 1960); "The South African Dilemma," in Louis Hartz, ed., *The Founding of New Societies* (New York, 1964); and *Politics in the Republic of South Africa* (Boston, 1966). After spending the year 1964-65 in Britain, France and Southern Africa on a Fulbright-Hays Award, Professor Thompson is now writing a book on the precolonial history of the Basotho and, with Professor Monica Wilson of the University of Cape Town, editing a two-volume *Oxford History of South Africa*.

HUGH TINKER (M.A., Cantab; Ph.D., D.P.A., University of London) is Professor of the Politics and Government of Asia in the University of London. He was Professor of History in the University of Rangoon, 1954-55, and Professor of Far Eastern Studies at Cornell University in 1959. He toured Southeast Asia most recently in 1963. Professor Tinker's publications include *The Foundations of Local Self-Government in India, Pakistan and Burma* (London, 1954), *The Union of Burma: A Study of the First Years of Independence* (Oxford, 1957; 3rd ed., 1961), *India and Pakistan: A Political Analysis* (New York, 1962), *The City in the Asian Polity* (London, 1964), and *Ballot Box and Bayonet: People and Government in Emergent Asian Countries* (London, 1964). He is a contributor to Ralph Braibanti, ed., *Asian Bureaucratic Systems Emergent from the British Imperial Tradition* (Durham, N. C., in press), and to Philip Mason, *et al.*, *Man, Race and Darwin* (London, 1960).

C. MARY TURNBULL (Ph.D., University of London) was Lecturer in History in the University of Malaya, 1955-63. She also has served in the Malayan Civil Service and now teaches in the University of Singapore. Dr. Turnbull has published several papers in the *Journal of the Malayan Branch, Royal Asiatic Society*, and the *Journal of the South Seas Society* and has written for *Malayan and Indonesian Studies: Essays presented to Sir Richard Winstedt on His Eighty-fifth Birthday* (Oxford, 1964), edited by John S. Bastin and Roelof Roolvink, and for Wang Gungwu, ed., *Malaysia* (London, 1964). She is completing a manuscript on "The Straits Settlements and the Malay Hinterland, 1830-73" for early publication.

D. A. G. WADDELL (D.Phil., Oxon.) is Senior Lecturer in Modern History at the University of Edinburgh. From 1954 to 1959 he was Lecturer in History at the University College of the West Indies, Jamaica, and he is author of *British Honduras: A Historical and Contemporary Survey* (London, 1961) and of various articles, mainly on the history of the Caribbean area. He now is working on a general history of the West Indies and spent the academic year 1964-65 on secondment to the College of Arts and Sciences of the University of the West Indies in Trinidad.

JOHN M. WARD (M.A., LL.B., University of Sydney) has been Challis Professor of History in the University of Sydney since 1949, and was elected Dean of the Faculty of Arts in 1962. Professor Ward was Dominion Fellow at St. John's College, Cambridge, in 1951. In 1957 he lectured in the United States as a Carnegie Traveling Fellow, and in 1963 he was Visiting Professor of History at Yale University. He is the author of *British Policy in the South Pacific, 1786-1893* (Sydney, 1948), *Earl Grey and the Australian Colonies, 1846-1857* (Melbourne, 1958), and numerous articles, and is a contributor to *Trusteeship in the Pacific* (edited by Alexander H. McDonald [Sydney, 1949]) and *The Pattern of Australian Culture* (edited by Alan L. McLeod [Ithaca, 1963]).

ROBIN W. WINKS (Ph.D., The Johns Hopkins University) is Associate Professor of History at Yale University and Advisor to the Yale University Library in Commonwealth History and Literature. He has been Visiting Lecturer in History at the University of Alberta (1959), Smith-Mundt Visiting Professor of History in the University of Malaya (1962-63), and Visiting Professor of History in the University of Sydney (1963). In 1952 he was a Fulbright fellow to New Zealand. His publications include *Canada and the United States: The Civil War Years* (Baltimore, 1960), *Recent Trends and New Literature in Canadian History* (Washington, 1959) and, as editor, *British Imperialism: Gold, God, Glory* (New York, 1963) and (with John S. Bastin) *A History of Malaysia: Selected Readings* (London, in press). He has contributed to Wang Gungwu, ed., *Malaysia* (London, 1964), and Martin B. Duberman, ed., *The Antislavery Vanguard* (Princeton, 1965). He is Chairman of the Committee on Faculty Exchanges with the Commonwealth within the Conference on British Studies.

HARRISON M. WRIGHT (Ph.D., Harvard University) is Associate Professor of History at Swarthmore College, where he has taught since 1957. Professor Wright was a Fulbright scholar to New Zealand, 1950-51, and Ford Foreign Area Training Fellow to England and Ghana, 1961-62. He has written *New Zealand, 1769-1840: Early Years of Western Contact* (Cambridge, Mass., 1959) and edited *The "New Imperialism"—Analysis of Late Nineteenth-Century Expansion* (Boston, 1961). He now specializes in African studies and Commonwealth history at Swarthmore.

# THE HISTORIOGRAPHY OF THE BRITISH
## EMPIRE-COMMONWEALTH

# INTRODUCTION

## *Robin W. Winks*

IN NEARLY ALL FIELDS historians are engaged in an international stock-taking, in pondering how well they have done and after deciding (as historians will) that they have not done nearly well enough, in suggesting how they might do better. Nations newly born are striving to find a national identity through searching the past. Societies not yet nations are using the anvil of their history to beat out their claims to a separate identity. Old and powerful nations alike, with traditions already rich in historical knowledge, are experiencing everywhere an age of re-evaluation. As each field of study is re-examined, its limits spacial and chronological are questioned; periodization, principles of organization, and time-honored generalizations hidden in the shorthand communication of words (gentry, feudal, Puritan, empire, *helot*, frontier) are attacked. Once historians would have echoed the initial certainty of the speaker in Eliot's "Ash Wednesday," "I know that time is always time/And place is always and only place/And what is actual is actual only for one time/And only for one place." Now, less sure of their tools and of their value judgments, many would lament (again with Eliot) the loss of the "glory of the positive hour."

Several historians recently have taken long and sometimes hard looks at British history and historiography,[1] convinced that now is a suitable time, before the mountain of publications grows even higher, to assess what has been done and, by the assessing, perhaps to have some small influence on what may be done in the future. Science, as we know, has grown at an exponential rate, and history cannot be far behind. The number of scientists alive today exceeds the total number of

1. Many articles and *Festschriften* have appeared recently in England. In the United States the Conference on British Studies has sponsored several bibliographical and historiographical articles. Those in print are listed in the *American Historical Review* (Washington), LXVIII (July, 1963), 987, n. 1, and will be published as a book in 1966 by Harvard University Press, Elizabeth Chapin Furber, ed.

scientists who have previously practiced. Similarly, more books by historians are printed each month in the United States and Great Britain alone than once were issued in a year by the combined printing presses of the eighteenth-century Western world. Periodic and frequent examinations of this flood of literature will continue to be necessary.

No one has written a reasonably full examination of the body of historical literature relating to the British Empire and the Commonwealth, and this collection of essays is one effort to begin such an enquiry. The purpose of this book is threefold. These essays attempt to provide, individually and collectively, a critical assessment of the literature now available in the field. Emphasis has been placed on the "recent" literature and on the "newer" interpretations, or in general terms on the period since the beginning of World War II. But the various authors represented here demonstrate that any watersheds of significance differ rather widely from area to area and problem to problem, so that the surveys begin with no common date. All attempt, however, to deal with literature published through 1963.[2]

A second but subordinate purpose of these historiographical essays is to tell why the body of literature developed in the way that it did. Obviously to describe the literature is simpler than to explain it; a multitude of factors would have to be discussed: national attitudes toward education and toward history, the size of libraries, archives and their organization, governmental censorship, language barriers, nationalisms, political ideology, national traditions, questions of who studied with whom, wartime destruction of records, preservation of historical sites, and much more. To pursue the subject fully would require many volumes of this size. Since the chief value of the essays is intended to lie in analytical assessment, the authors chose to limit these explorations in various ways, although all have commented on the problem of how the contours of the field, as they view those contours, were molded.

The third purpose of the essays is to point toward some of the more inviting questions now to be asked. Hopefully, graduate students in search of exciting and significant research subjects, as well as scholars who wish to look into related and comparative areas of Empire-Com-

2. For the most part these essays were written in 1963, and they reflect attitudes held by their authors at that time. While efforts have been made to incorporate some recently published titles into galley proofs, the actual structure of each essay has had to remain as it was when originally sent to the publisher.

monwealth studies, will find in these essays a guide toward uncharted waters. With this purpose in mind each author has written for those generally interested in Empire-Commonwealth history, and none of the essays is intended primarily for a specialist in the specific area to which it speaks. In this way we hope that comparative studies may be strengthened, for if the student of Canadian history finds little that is new in the essay on Canada, his Canadian history is likely to be enriched by some awareness of what has been written about, for example, South Africa.

That this volume is not entirely satisfactory goes without saying; no book from many hands ever is. Any faults in conception and organization lie more with the editor than with the contributors, many of whom set aside other commitments to address themselves to the present task. The chief failing is one which the editor made every attempt to remedy, for another essay is needed to complete the canvas: one which discusses the literature in Russian and non-Western languages concerning British imperialism. Several efforts to establish contact with Russian scholars in the field, in Moscow and Leningrad, failed. Additionally, certain smaller areas—Hong Kong, Aden, the islands of the Indian and Atlantic Oceans—or periods of close economic and social interaction between independent nations and the United Kingdom, have tended to escape our net. Thus important books, ranging from Henry Stanley Ferns' *Britain and Argentina in the Nineteenth Century* (Oxford, 1960) and Alan K. Manchester's *British Preeminence in Brazil, Its Rise and Decline* (Chapel Hill, 1933) to George B. Endacott's *A History of Hong Kong* (London, 1958) have been omitted from these pages.[3]

A few technical points should be mentioned. This volume also is

3. The United Kingdom is intentionally omitted, of course. While many will feel that any description of British Empire-Commonwealth historiography without Britain is *Hamlet* without the Prince of Denmark, practical considerations dictated excluding British history. Obviously no Imperial historian can avoid the wealth of pertinent books, from Elie Halévy (*Imperialism and the Rise of Labor*, the fifth volume of his *The History of the English People in the Nineteenth Century* [2nd rev. ed., 7 vols.; London, 1949-52]) to G. S. R. Kitson Clark (*The Making of Victorian England* [London, 1962]). Particularly useful historiographical articles are John Clive, "British History, 1870-1914, Reconsidered: Recent Trends in the Historiography of the Period," *American Historical Review*, LXVIII (July, 1963), 987-1009, and Henry R. Winkler, "Some Recent Writings on Twentieth-Century Britain," *Journal of Modern History* (Chicago), XXXII (March, 1960), 32-47. Helpful but inconsistent is Charles Loch Mowat, *British History since 1926: A Select Bibliography* (London, 1960), number 61 in the Historical Association's *Helps for Students of History*.

intended to help librarians who wish to build collections in Empire-Commonwealth studies, based on the works discussed here. In order to aid them, in many cases full or "library" forms of authors' names are given in the first instance of each citation. There are exceptions, based on principles that need not be reviewed here, when confusion between two authors of similar names is unlikely to arise. While some authors will not be immediately recognizable (or happy) under the burden of their full names, and while the practice adds density to the essays, the editor felt such citations were necessary in a volume which will serve as a handbook in assessing relative strengths of holdings.[4]

Originally the editor arbitrarily chose a desired length for each essay. This length was meant to reflect the extent of the literature available, not necessarily the importance of the country or area under discussion. As the volume progressed, these arbitrary lengths were abandoned, for authors arrived at their own conceptions of the space necessary to deal with the three questions before them. We believe that the lengths of the essays still reflect in a rough way the relative quantities of the literature as well as the present level of sophistication of that literature.[5]

A third technical adjustment seemed necessary: the Asian nations are dealt with somewhat differently from the African or European. Since there already exist two very useful series of historiographical essays in the Asian field—Cyril H. Philips, ed., *Historians of India, Pakistan and Ceylon* (London, 1961) and D. G. E. Hall, ed., *Historians of South East Asia* (London, 1961)—the present material attempts to do something different. This called for a general and quite interpretative statement on India and more specific and proportionately longer essays on Ceylon, Pakistan, and Malaysia. Readers are referred to the Philips and Hall volumes for more detailed discussions of pre-

4. By reference to the index for authors' names, one may quickly eliminate any remaining confusion. Where multiple places of publication are involved, only the first place mentioned on the title page is given. The place of journal publication is cited in the first instance within each essay and not again. Names of publishers are omitted. Subtitles are given only when they are genuinely helpful to the reader, and ellipses generally are used only for omissions within titles. No attempt has been made to note editions in translation or unrevised reprint editions. The catalogs of the British Museum, the Library of Congress, the School of Oriental and African Studies of the University of London, and the Yale University Library were used as authorities.

5. Where informal readers suggested titles that should be added, these suggestions were passed along to the authors, and final judgment on what to include and exclude was left to them. Inevitably readers will regret the absence of certain titles, just as they will take issue with specific assessments.

European historiography and of the works of specific pre-twentieth-century scholars.[6]

\* \* \*

Where stands Empire-Commonwealth history? And where might it move?[7]

Elsewhere in this volume John S. Galbraith takes to task those scholars who, by early and overspecialization, fail to draw conclusions valid for even a modestly wide range of human experience. As he notes, too often historians have "demonstrated their unawareness of published works which, though not bearing directly on their special subject, would have contributed to a deeper insight." This criticism is not limited to the historian's failure to read peripheral but important books in his field or to look at tangential but related manuscript collections. More damaging has been the fact that apart from students of constitutional problems, or of exploration, few Empire-Commonwealth scholars seem to have engaged in research relating to more than one or at best two societies; and even fewer appear to have compared imperial British administrative, constitutional, or social problems to like problems within other empires.[8] Students of British imperialism have

6. India also has been treated in Upendra Nath Ghoshal, *The Beginnings of Indian Historiography and Other Essays* (Calcutta, 1944); Peter Hardy, *Historians of Medieval India: Studies in Indo-Muslim Historical Writing* (London, 1960); Morris David Morris and Burton Stein, "The Economic History of India: A Bibliographical Essay," *Journal of Economic History* (New York), XXI (June, 1961), 179-207; Mysore Narasimhachar Srinivas, *et al.*, "Caste: A Trend Report and Bibliography," *Current Sociology* (Paris), VIII (1959), whole no. 3, 135-83; Indian Council for Cultural Relations, *Indian Studies Abroad* (Bombay, 1964); Kalikinkar K. Datta, *A Survey of Recent Studies on Modern Indian History* (Calcutta, 1963); J. Michael Mahar, *India: A Critical Bibliography* (Tuscon [1964]); and Bernard S. Cohn, *The Development and Impact of British Administration in India: A Bibliographic Essay* (New Delhi, n.d.). Most useful of all are the essays by Robert I. Crane and John Gallagher in the *Proceedings* of the India International Centre's 1963 seminar on *Problems of Historical Writing in India* (New Delhi [1964]). See, too, Dorothy Mary Spencer, *Indian Fiction in English: An Annotated Bibliography* (Philadelphia, 1960).

7. This Introduction is the responsibility of the editor and is meant to be little more than a speculative, personal essay. The contributors are not necessarily responsive to statements made here or in the Appendix. The editor wishes to thank John S. Bastin, School of Oriental and African Studies, London; Leonard W. Doob, Department of Psychology, Yale University; and Kenneth Robinson, Vice-Chancellor of the University of Hong Kong, as well as the contributors, for comments on earlier drafts of this Introduction.

8. One solution to the problem of dealing with the bewildering variety of different environments which confronts the Empire-Commonwealth historian is the symposium volume, in which experts on different colonies address themselves to a common theme. The comparative conclusions may be left to arise in the mind of the reader, on the basis of the separate arguments, or the conclusions may be made explicit by an

seldom looked closely at the bases for the Imperial structures of other nations under other conditions. Nor have historians utilized as fully as they might the insights provided for them by the social sciences, employing to their own advantage the models by which social scientists organize and interpret their material. Communication, in brief, is slow between area specialists, slow between disciplines—and even slower between scholars of different nationalities.

British scholarship will continue to lead the field, of course, and Americans, Nigerians, or Australians will continue to find their Mecca in Bloomsbury or in Chancery Lane. (Although as archives improve elsewhere, as in Ottawa, or Freetown, or Kuala Lumpur, one may enjoy movable Meccas as well as movable feast days.) It must be admitted that American scholars have not contributed all that they might to Empire-Commonwealth studies and that where their contributions have been truly basic—as with Charles McLean Andrews, or Wallace Notestein, or Robert Livingston Schuyler—they have not been without honor abroad. Of the books mentioned in the essay on Canada, several are by scholars residing in the United States (although frequently Canadian-born), but elsewhere American titles are less frequent. But while we must recognize the failure of Americans to contribute fully to the field, we also must recognize the failure of many of us to be aware of just how much Americans have contributed even outside their own colonial period.

On the whole it does not seem unfair to say that scholars in the United States are relatively alert to the flow of publications and the spark of ideas as they come from the United Kingdom. Indeed, some may feel that American students of the British Empire have, on occasion, become entirely too alert to transatlantic trends, to the detriment of their own national insights into problems of power, authority, race, and empire. But British scholars seem, to Americans (and also possibly to Canadians and Australians), not always sufficiently aware of pertinent research conducted elsewhere.[9]

---

editor's introduction or concluding chapter. Recent examples of this approach to comparative studies are Kenneth Robinson and Albert Frederick Madden, eds., *Essays in Imperial Government Presented to Margery Perham* (Oxford, 1963); Philip Mason, et al., *Man, Race and Darwin* (London, 1960); and the forthcoming volume on *British and German Colonialism in Africa*, edited by Prosser Gifford and William Roger Louis.

9. One well-regarded Commonwealth historical journal in recent years published two articles which already were old news, since books published in the United States before the articles appeared had dealt at greater length with similar subjects. Lack

While the historians of both nations have gone a long way toward joining hands, they can go much further yet. American universities, it must be admitted, still receive far too many overseas guests who apparently feel among the alien corn, for guest speakers from the Commonwealth tend to deliver talks that indicate all too clearly their assumption that few in their audiences will have read their books—and the more famous the speaker the more likely he is to fall prey to this conclusion. Harvard's (and Iowa's) Arthur M. Schlesinger, in his memoirs,[10] tells of one of Britain's leading Imperial historians (indeed, one discussed in this book) who apparently felt Iowa to be a howling wilderness and who refused to shake hands with dinner guests, "instructing them that this was not the English custom." One distinguished British historian has dismissed American scholarship as merely "massed typewriters," while Americans complain of what they regard as the incomplete and unsystematic methods of research and documentation by many European historians and often show an unhealthy defensiveness in the face of overseas scholarship.

These kinds of exchanges will continue to poison the well of Anglo-American scholarly harmony, for two quite different communities are involved with quite different attitudes toward the use and abuse of history. These differences will and perhaps should remain. But the international community of scholars continues to grow, and there must be greater awareness in all nations of how the trends of scholarship are developing elsewhere. The Empire-Commonwealth historian can learn much from a study of the major interpreters of American, or French,

---

of communication between those scholars who write in English and those who do not is even greater, however. René Maunier did not become well known in the United States until Emily O. Lorimer translated and edited his *The Sociology of Colonies: An Introduction to the Study of Race Contact* (London, 1949), and Joseph A. Schumpeter's essay "Zur Soziologie der Imperialismus," which first appeared in 1919, was not widely read until its publication in English in 1951 (*Imperialism and Social Classes* [Cambridge, Mass.], Heinz Norden, trans., Paul M. Sweezy, ed.). Most recently [Dominique] O. Mannoni's *Psychologie de la colonisation* (Paris, 1950) has been translated by Pamela Powesland and introduced by Philip Mason as *Prospero and Caliban: The Psychology of Colonization* (2nd ed., New York, 1964). Yet French and German scholarship are known far better in the English-speaking world than are equally important but less available works from Italy, Portugal, or the Soviet Union. The Soviet Union presents special barriers to communication, and most historians use the journals which abstract Soviet scholarship. See, for example, "Recent Soviet Writing on Burma," *The YUVA Newsletter (Yugo Vostochnaya Aziya)* (London), II (July, 1963), 1-6. *The YUVA Newsletter* abstracts articles on Southeast Asia; *The MIZAN Newsletter* (London) deals with the Middle East and Africa.

10. *In Retrospect: The History of a Historian* (New York, 1963), pp. 70-71.

or Russian history, for example. Scholars should come to feel at home physically and even intellectually in any part of the English-speaking world. There is no good reason why American history should not be taught in an American university by a British historian trained entirely outside the United States, or why one day an American should not hold a chair of Imperial history in Britain (as a Canadian now holds the chair in the University of London).

But this lack of communication between scholars of different nationalities is less serious than the lack of communication, to which Professor Galbraith alludes, between disciplines and between area specialists. The British Empire-Commonwealth historian has a particular obligation to bridge these gaps. He could and should stand central to the growth of interdisciplinary and comparative studies.

Where should we go and what should we study? Which areas and what problems? Everywhere and everything, of course, but not at the same time. Leeds may be no less important than Liverpool, but both surely are less important than London. Every scholar in the field will have his own notions as to the work that we should be doing. Each has his own grindstone, and one need not look abroad for others. But perhaps one may exercise an editor's prerogative to recite one's own peculiar litany of priorities, especially as a sense of urgency for these priorities arises from a reading of the essays in this book.

Empire-Commonwealth history already has a far greater theoretical depth than many realize. Problems abound and systems have been put forth to help us organize the problems.[11] But far more theoretical speculation is needed. Why do empires rise and why do empires fall? Why did Britain exert control over Fiji, or the Niger, or extend its protection over Selangor? Between these two ranges of questions there is room for much fruitful speculation as well as specific documentation.

For example, nations may fruitfully be divided into those that are goal-seeking, those that are goal-sustaining, and those that are goal-creating. The leaders of new nations often define their conscious goals

11. For the diversity of theory on the causes of later British imperialism, see the materials published in Harrison M. Wright, ed., *The "New Imperialism": Analysis of Late Nineteenth-Century Expansion* (Boston, 1961); Robin W. Winks, ed., *British Imperialism: Gold, God, Glory* (New York, 1963); and George H. Nadel and Lewis Perry Curtis, Jr., eds., *Imperialism and Colonialism* (New York, 1964). Since these anthologies appeared D. Anthony Low has written an interesting typology of imperial situations in "Lion Rampant," *Journal of Commonwealth Political Studies* (Leicester), II (Nov., 1964), 235-52.

in terms of the past experience of other nations and their reading of the potentialities of those nations. Some societies—the British and the American, for example—not only have achieved many of their early primary goals, but did so in such a manner as to become goal-creators, objects of imitation for other nations. In their dynamism Britain and the United States continue to create new goals for themselves, to establish value systems that seem worthy of emulation by other societies. Much of Canadian history can be explained only in terms of Canadian responses to the culture of the United States, responses both negative and positive, for Canada is a goal-oriented society which received many (although by no means most, or necessarily the most important) of its goals from interactions with its neighbor. The relationship is one of mutual accommodation, as between Finland and Russia, or Argentina and Chile. The contours of Canadian history can be understood only in terms of the continental pressures which, together with a unique environment, British heritage, and bicultural tradition, have shaped Canada. Thus, a study of the impact of American culture abroad—especially on English-speaking societies—becomes a legitimate, indeed a vital, part of Commonwealth history. Nor is it fanciful to "explain" an often noted paradox in Australian political and social history—that Australian political and social rhetoric is "radical" but that the Australian temper and culture is covertly "conservative" ("when in doubt, vote no")—by suggesting that Australia is now a goal-sustaining society, its energies dedicated to preserving previously achieved goals (the minimum wage, "White Australia," hegemony in the Southwest Pacific) rather than to defining new goals to pursue.

To use this construction in another and obvious context, leadership elites, administrative agencies, labor unions, and instruments of mass media alike recognize that custodial goals (those of the "benign" colonial power) and developmental goals (those of the newly independent nation, or those of the self-interested, "rapacious" colonial power) differ widely. So too, then, do the priority systems of those who control the power. Too often historians seem to write of postindependence developments in a new nation as though they were a natural and organic extension from the period prior to independence. This does not necessarily follow, as the history of Ghana, or of the United States, should indicate. We badly need studies which tell us more exactly than do even such fine books as Archibald P. Thornton's *The Imperial Idea and Its*

*Enemies: A Study In British Power* (London, 1959) or Alfred L. Rowse's *Appeasement: A Study in Political Decline, 1933-1939* (London, 1961), where the power lay at given times. Even more badly we need to know by what systems, rational or irrational, did administrative, custodial, or developmental priorities arise? No historian can fail to benefit from reading Brian Crozier's *The Morning After: A Study of Independence* (London, 1963), which deals with that first awesome moment when demands for nationhood and the techniques of leadership based on agitation from below must quickly give way to demands of a very different sort and leadership of a very different nature. Nor can any Empire-Commonwealth specialist fail to gain from Seymour Martin Lipset's *The First New Nation: The United States in Historical and Comparative Perspective* (New York, 1963), which finds fruitful analogies between Federalist-Jeffersonian America and Sukarno's Indonesia. Again, it is useful to turn to a study of the social ideas of the novelists of empire,[12] of H. Rider Haggard, G. A. Henty, Rudyard Kipling, G. Manville Fenn, Edgar Wallace, John Buchan, and others, to see what course of action and what higher purpose these men, who so influenced the youthful years of those who ruled in the present century, espoused.[13]

12. For attempts in this direction, see Gertrude Himmelfarb, "John Buchan: An Untimely Appreciation," *Encounter* (London), XV (Sept., 1960), 46-53, and Mark Naidis, "G. A. Henty's Idea of India," *Victorian Studies* (Bloomington, Ind.), VIII (Sept., 1964), 49-58, both of which are very good. Susanne Howe, *Novels of Empire* (New York, 1949), offers a promising title but is largely descriptive. Karl W. Deutsch and Norbert Wiener have written an exciting interpretation of "The Lonely Nationalism of Rudyard Kipling," *The Yale Review* (New Haven), LII (Summer, 1963), 499-517. Two urbane and amusing books which demonstrate how popular literature reflects, feeds upon, and nurtures the "Imperial climate" are Richard Usborne, *Clubland Heroes: A Nostalgic Study of Some Recurrent Characters in the Romantic Fiction of Dornford Yates, John Buchan and Sapper* (London, 1953), and O. F. Snelling, *Double O Seven: James Bond, A Report* (London, 1964). A particularly useful example of the survey of a field of fiction rather than of a single figure is William H. Pearson, "Attitudes to the Maori in Some Pakeha Fiction," *The Journal of the Polynesian Society* (Wellington), LXVII (Sept., 1958), 211-38. Charles Edmund Carrington has written on *The Life of Rudyard Kipling* (Garden City, N. Y., 1955) and Morton Norton Cohen has given us *Rider Haggard: His Life and Works* (London, 1960). Archibald Hanna, Jr., has prepared *John Buchan, 1875-1940: A Bibliography* (Hamden, Conn., 1953). We can await the publication of Janet Adam Smith's forthcoming biography of Buchan with confidence. What is needed is a comprehensive study developing some of the points made by John Morton Blum in his *Yesterday's Children: An Anthology, Compiled from the Pages of Our Young Folks, 1865-1893* (Boston, 1959), which is devoted to the childhood literature of the men who became America's leaders in this century. Gordon Stables and R. M. Ballantyne also deserve attention.

13. One such guide is Richard Daniel Altick, *The English Common Reader: A Social History of the Mass Reading Public, 1800-1900* (Chicago, 1957).

Studies, however, need not be so broad-ranging nor so theoretical to contribute in a vital way to the field. Who were the imperialists abroad? We need more work on the middle-range figures, on the "men-on-the-spot" who made the actual decisions. We cannot know enough of Rhodes or Curzon or Raffles or Durham, of course, but we must know more about Lord Monck (a "Father of Canadian Confederation" surely) or W. F. D. Jervois, or Sir Garnet Wolseley, or Thomas Gore Browne.[14] Jervois is, in fact, a Baedeker of the type: an army engineer who served at Woolwich, in South Africa, and in India; who designed Canadian defenses against a feared Yankee invasion during the American Civil War; who made the fateful decisions in the Straits Settlements during the early years of British intervention; who created controversy as Governor of South Australia; and who ended his career as Governor of New Zealand. Such men transmitted ideas and techniques from one part of the Empire to another. Many others await their biographers.

Who were the imperialists at home? We need many more close studies of the composition of crucial committees and a far greater understanding of how these committees operated. Rowse has directed our attention to All Souls. We have seen how important David Hartley, or Lord Liverpool, or Henry Taylor could be. We are being shown now the importance of Sir Edward Mallet or Lord Lothian or Sir Ralph Furse.[15] In American diplomatic history we know of the ubiquitous Alvey Adee. Where are the more recent British counterparts—or the Canadian, or Australian, or Kenyan equivalents? What of the influence of the returned colonial administrator, or of those who remained after independence, of the returned missionary, of the returned and retired soldier?

14. Several dissertations and articles have begun the recognition of Monck's rôle. Brian Dalton of New England University, Armidale, New South Wales, has near completion a study of Gore Browne. The present author is continuing research for a biographical sketch of Jervois. On Wolseley see Joseph H. Lehmann, *All Sir Garnet: A Biography of Sir Garnet Wolseley* (London, 1964). The Boston edition's title is *The Model Major-General: A Biography of Field-Marshal Lord Wolseley* (1964). Especially fine is James de Vere Allen, "Two Imperialists: A Study of Sir Frank Swettenham and Sir Hugh Clifford," *Journal of the Malayan Branch, Royal Asiatic Society* (Singapore), XXXVII (i/1964), 41-73.

15. See J. R. M. Butler, *Lord Lothian (Philip Kerr): 1862-1940* (London, 1960); William Roger Louis, "The Philosophical Diplomat: Sir Arthur Hardinge and King Leopold's Congo" (forthcoming in *The Journal of British Studies* [Hartford]); and Robert Heussler, *Yesterday's Rulers: The Making of the British Colonial Service* (Syracuse, 1963), on Furse.

In writing biography why should we not avail ourselves more of the insights of sociology and psychology?[16] There are obvious dangers, of course: it is difficult for a person to be an economist and an historian, for example, for the sheer weight of the data (as well as the research tools) of the economist may pull down the more humanistically oriented historian. Some economic historians forget that *economic* is meant to be an adjective. But a cautious and limited use of psychology (and especially of rôle psychology)—as shown by the better essays in Bruce Mazlish, ed., *Psychoanalysis and History* (Englewood Cliffs, N.J., 1963)—or of sociology, as shown in one or two of the generally dangerous (for the historian) essays in Maurice Stein and Arthur Vidich, eds., *Sociology on Trial* (Englewood Cliffs, N.J., 1963), would grant us many new paths to the present. John A. Garraty has explored some of the ways in which the biographer might legitimately make use of psychology and sociology in *The Nature of Biography* (New York, 1957), and a psychologist, Leonard W. Doob, in *Patriotism and Nationalism: Their Psychological Foundations* (New Haven, 1964), has written with lucidity and wit a book which all historians should read. In *Studies in Applied Anthropology* (London, 1957), Lucy P. Mair has shown convincingly that anthropology is of great use in historical research. Why do the Polynesians, and notably the Maori, have such a strong sense of time, history, myth, and tradition, while their neighbors, the Melanesians, have very little sense of history? This may be an anthropologist's question,[17] but the historian who wishes to use even present-day native or indigenous records to study the impact of comparative British or French administrations in the Pacific also must be able to evaluate these differences.[18] As the essays

16. Not discussed in this introduction is the special problem which autobiography poses for the historiographer. Bibliographically to be treated as a primary source, the autobiography serves quite a different function for the historiographer, who wishes to ask, In what ways do the autobiographies of a generation reflect that generation's unconscious assumptions? Ultimately the only successful autobiography is one in which the author has taken a voyage of discovery while writing, one in which he emerges a different man precisely because of the act of writing. See Roy Pascal, *Design and Truth in Autobiography* (Cambridge, Mass., 1960), a book which reminds one of Goldwin Smith's confession ("Style! I have no style. I merely wait for the mud to settle"), but which illumines with exceptional insight the many ways by which the historian may more fruitfully approach autobiography.

17. Edward E. Evans-Pritchard, *Anthropology and History* (Manchester, 1961), pp. 6-11.

18. One is struck by the contrast between the historical awareness in the records of the *poutikanga* of the Maori Ringatu Church, for example, and the confused and yet patterned data that may be obtained from a Fijian newspaper of the twentieth century.

in the present volume demonstrate, African history in particular cannot exist without the anthropologist and the archaeologist, without tools for dealing with oral traditions.[19]

A greater use, then, of the techniques and insights of the social scientists may be desirable. There are great problems in this for the historian, of course, but up to now he has approached the social sciences as though he were a naïve innocent, about to be seduced by the social scientists away from his native purity, a kind of scholarly *beau savage* who cannot cope with these at once newer, rougher, and more sophisticated disciplines. This is nonsense, for the historian need only remember his own training and be true to his own insights; the very tools of his discipline are all that he needs to retain his wise innocence.

Unfortunately, where historians have dared to tread they also have not uncommonly fallen. We grasp potentially useful but untried theoretical constructions, heralded in popular works, and fail to note from the periodical literature that the construction already has been discarded by the professionals. Historians discover Robert Redfield or Talcott Parsons in their original form just as anthropologists and sociologists modify them. But there are theoretical constructions surely which historians can use to great benefit provided they use them with caution.

Two such theories may illustrate this point. A political scientist, Karl W. Deutsch, has argued that political change—the rise of nationalism, for example—takes place through highly intricate and yet detectable patterns of social communication, communication which ultimately creates a "security community" or nation, and in *Nationalism and Social Communication* (Cambridge, Mass., 1953) he provides us with several valuable tools. The processes Deutsch describes cannot be used to analyze the rise of national feeling in Kenya, or Malaya, or Canada with equal facility, but they can at the very least provide us with principles by which we can organize our data for closer and more systematic scrutiny, and the categories he establishes help draw our attention to

19. The point is made even clearer by a reading of Daniel F. McCall, *Africa in Time-Perspective: A Discussion of Historical Reconstruction from Unwritten Sources* (Boston, 1964), Jan Vansina (an anthropologist), *Oral Tradition: A Study in Historical Methodology* (London, 1964), and Alfred Louis Kroeber, *An Anthropologist Looks at History* (Berkeley, 1963). Particularly fine is Philip D. Curtin's historiographical essay on *African History* (Washington, 1964). For another area, see Wendell Bell's *Jamaican Leaders: Political Attitudes in a New Nation* (Berkeley, 1964), the work of a sociologist.

several neglected aspects of national sentiment. In *Crowds and Power* (London, 1962) Elias Canetti also is concerned with man's desire for security, and he redirects us toward an understanding of the national (or crowd) will to survive, to command, and to transform. American "Manifest Destiny," Russian Communism, and the Imperial contention that British institutions must be spread, and would be easy to spread, because they were superior (an argument that rolls back upon itself, empire being a positive way to preserve the power and prestige of England, itself worth preserving at all costs because England was morally superior)—these were ideologies that were circular, closed, complete. To transform, Canetti argues, to make in our image and likeness, is to make the world safe for us. Obvious, yes, but Canetti gives the drive for metaphysical security an unusual and provocative statement. As parliamentary government, once presumed to be Britain's major legacy to the Empire, appears to be increasingly unattractive to the new African nations, one wonders whether we have not misread the legacy of empire: the Africans do not want what the British most eagerly gave, and without the excesses of nationalism they apparently cannot have what the British gave least, a sense of historical security, of historical worth.

Historians do, of course, read a great amount of social science. In John Clive's summary of the historiography of British history, 1870-1914, all of the initial titles he discusses are by social scientists. Nonetheless, other historiographical assessments show considerably less concern for the social sciences. These include Wesley Frank Craven, "Historical Study of the British Empire," *Journal of Modern History* (Chicago), VI (March, 1934), 40-69; Lowell J. Ragatz, *The Literature of European Imperialism, 1815-1939: A Bibliography* (Washington, 1944), and "Must We Rewrite the History of Imperialism?" *Historical Studies: Australia and New Zealand* (Melbourne), VI (November, 1953), 90-98; Charles F. Mullett, *The British Empire-Commonwealth: Its Themes and Character. A Plural Society in Evolution* (Washington, 1961); Mullett, "The Commonwealth," in Shirley H. Engle, ed., *New Perspectives in World History: The National Council for the Social Studies' Thirty-Fourth Yearbook* (Washington, 1964); and two bibliographies, William Parker Morrell, *British Overseas Expansion and the History of the Commonwealth: A Select Bibliography* (London, 1961), and James G. Allen, *The British Em-*

*pire and Commonwealth: A Syllabus and Guide to Reading* (3rd ed., Boulder, Colo., 1953), which emphasize archivally-oriented books. But while the pursuit in the archive should remain one of our chief professional delights, historians too can conduct field work. Surely any study of the Maori Wars is enhanced by a year among the Maori or by intensive study of Maori acculturation problems. Surely one can gain some knowledge of nuance if one looks down upon London Town from St. Paul's or climbs the great, bold steps of Sigiriya. We must see the visible symbols of our past: we must go to Eureka, we must go to Batoche.

Yet another area for much inquiry is the history of race relations or, more properly, of racial accommodation. Most of the histories of European-native contact deal either with the history of racial conflict—military history, as it were—or with the history of race legislation. The historian still approaches racial history with his traditional tools: the *Hansard's*, the military maps, the papers of administrators and to a lesser extent of missionaries. But one may pose fruitful questions relating to race history in other ways: what was the Maori response to Christianity and to what degree did the Maori Ringatu Church, with its Quadritarian concept of a fourth figure within the Godhead to speak uniquely for the Maori spirit, for *Maoritanga*, fill the racial void created by Christianity? Did the fugitive American Negro slaves who made their way to Canada in the 1850's encounter, or create, a pattern of prejudice in Canadian society similar to that present in American society? Why has Malayan cultural pluralism, which has allowed each major ethnic group in Malaya—Malay, Chinese, Indian, and European—to police its own sexual mores, begun to break down in recent years? These are valid questions historically, and they deal neither with legislation nor with wars. There are, of course, many such studies relating in particular to India and to Africa, but we need many more. Race history, properly defined, may well be the main problem of the history of the future, as harmonious racial relations surely will be the future's major challenge.

The list of subjects which need exploration can be added to at length. We need more comparative studies of the effects of the administrations of different European powers, as Francis West has given us for Fiji, American Samoa, and Tahiti.[20] We need more comparative

20. Francis James West, *Political Advancement in the South Pacific: A Comparative Study of Colonial Practice in Fiji, Tahiti, and American Samoa* (Melbourne, 1961).

studies of differing racial groups, or of widely divergent colonies of the same power. We need more comparative studies between formal and informal units of the Empire—Canada and Argentina can be compared to mutually useful effect,[21] as can the American and Canadian Wests.[22] We must have many more case studies of why the British presence was made manifest in given areas at given times, in the pattern of Charles Donald Cowan's *Nineteenth-Century Malaya: The Origins of British Political Control* (London, 1961) or Ronald Robinson, John Gallagher, and Alice Denny's *Africa and the Victorians: The Official Mind of Imperialism* (London, 1961). We could use a host of essays on how the British image of empire, or of a given area within it, was created, not only along the lines of Philip D. Curtin's admirable *The Image of Africa: British Ideas and Action, 1780-1850* (Madison, 1964),[23] but also in terms of how scientists' and travelers' accounts created impressions—impressions upon which public attitudes often turned and upon which policy statements were sometimes based—of Borneo, or Sierra Leone, or Hyderabad. Bernard William Smith, in *European Vision and the South Pacific, 1768-1858: A Study in the History of Art and Ideas* (Oxford, 1960), and George Donham Bearce, in *British Attitudes toward India, 1784-1858* (New York, 1961), have begun with exceptional skill what we may regard as a prolegomenon to such an intellectual history of the Empire.[24]

In terms of historiography we need to know far more than the initial and tentative assessments presented here. We need to investigate the genealogy of those generalizations which form a part of intellectual history, that most neglected facet of Empire-Commonwealth

21. See the suggestion in Arthur Preston Whitaker, *Argentina* (Englewood Cliffs, N.J., 1964), pp. 4-7.

22. See especially Paul Frederick Sharp, "Three Frontiers: Some Comparative Studies of Canadian, American, and Australian Settlement," *The Pacific Historical Review* (Los Angeles), XXIV (Nov., 1955), 369-77.

23. See also his "The White Man's Grave: Image and Reality, 1780-1850," *Journal of British Studies*, I (Nov., 1961), 94-110.

24. As a comparative study, see Patrick J. O'Farrell, "The Russian Revolution and the Labour Movements of Australia and New Zealand, 1917-1922," *International Review of Social History* (Amsterdam), VIII (ii/1962), 178-97; or for a weak but suggestive essay in the direction of a study of image-bearing and image-creating authors, see Leslie Reid, "Victorian Naturalists in the Tropics," *The Quarterly Review* (London), CCCI (July, 1963), 283-92. At quite a different level, consult Robert L. Tignor's excellent "Lord Cromer: Practitioner and Philosopher of Imperialism," *The Journal of British Studies*, II (May, 1963), 142-59, and Bernard Semmel, "Sir Halford Mackinder: Theorist of Imperialism," *Canadian Journal of Economics and Political Science* (Toronto), XXIV (Nov., 1958), 554-61.

studies. D. K. Fieldhouse and Richard Koebner recently have explored the many meanings that lay behind two of our basic terms, *imperialism*[25] and *empire*,[26] and the evolution of the meaning of *race* has been traced within the United States;[27] but many other examinations must be written. Do we yet understand the genesis of indirect rule, of the mandate system; can we follow the changing connotations of *Commonwealth* or even of *colony*?[28] We must continue to reconsider the problem of periodization for both the Western and non-Western world, as several scholars already have done for European history in general terms. Our task is one of transmitting dissimilar findings with similar language, and we may have to find new terms if we wish to draw our distinctions fine. An unnecessary suspicion of the special language of the social scientist has helped inhibit our search, for historians do not invent terms lightly. But we must find additional ways to make our meanings clearer and more flexible.

Finally, we must stop assuming that it is exceptionally difficult for Asian scholars to write sound European history, or for European scholars to understand Asia in its historical dimensions. The British and the nationalist interpretations of the history of a newly emergent nation are not, despite much quarreling over a K. M. Panikkar (or a Michel Brunet), necessarily erroneous or even in conflict. Such divergent interpretations are directed to two different problems and concerned with two different goals. To say that one historian has omitted something is not to say that he has overlooked it, for it may have nothing to do with the question he is attempting to answer. "Did colonies pay?" does not involve any recognition of whether colonies benefited the colonized. Generalizations have been used differently, for different purposes, and fictitious feuds have been generated, feuds which have led some to feel that they cannot carry out research involving both

25. "'Imperialism': An Historiographical Revision," *Economic History Review* (London), 2nd ser., XIV (Dec., 1961), 187-209. For a more recent treatment, see Richard Koebner and Helmut Dan Schmidt, *Imperialism: The Story and Significance of a Political Word, 1840-1960* (Cambridge, 1964).

26. *Empire* (Cambridge, 1961).

27. Thomas F. Gossett, *Race: The History of an Idea in America* (Dallas, 1963).

28. As a beginning to this problem, see two admirably lucid and searching essays, Philip Nicholas Mansergh, *The Name and Nature of the British Commonwealth* (reprint ed., Cambridge, 1955), and S. A. de Smith, *The Vocabulary of Commonwealth Relations* (University of London, Institute of Commonwealth Studies, "Commonwealth Paper" No. 1 [London, 1954]).

Western and non-Western members of the Commonwealth without returning to the common denominators of Whitehall and Westminster.[29]

And there will always be an unending list of specific tales to be told. We need many quiet, thorough monographs on specific topics for there are many subjects on which we do not have more than the most basic facts. While this introduction has emphasized the need for theoretical studies, there is a great need for works which simply tell what happened. Is anyone satisfied with our present knowledge of missionary influence?[30] Archives in Papeete, Suva, and Apia remain little touched; those in Bathurst saw but five visitors in 1964. We must have a new, full-scale history of the Loyalists in North America. A study of the problem of "the England-returned man" should tell us much of the nature of power in British society. Surely there can be few fields of historical study in which so much remains to be done. "Massed typewriters" indeed; we need brigades of the lonely, regiments of the trained, and mission systems of the curious. Most of all, we need to convince others, through our own work, of the vitality, the excitement, and the significance of British Imperial and Commonwealth studies.[31]

29. See John S. Bastin, "The Western Element in Modern Southeast Asian History," in his *Essays on Indonesian and Malayan History* (Singapore, 1961), pp. 1-18; Damodar P. Singhal, "The Writing of Asian History," *Hemisphere* (North Sydney), VII (July, 1963), 9-14; and Harry J. Benda, "The Structure of Southeast Asian History: Some Preliminary Observations," *The Journal of Southeast Asian History* (Singapore), III (March, 1962), 106-38.

30. One of the most neglected areas of Imperial history is missionology and the general problem of the relationship of the missionary to Imperial expansion and contraction. While much work has been done on missionary influence in China, Japan, and India, and while Kenneth Scott Latourette has written his monumental *A History of the Expansion of Christianity* . . . (New York, 1937-45) in seven volumes, there are but a few scholarly monographs in English on the subject of missionary activity as it relates to the Empire; e.g., those by Bennett, Koskinen, Oliver, and Rotberg mentioned elsewhere in this volume. Most studies of the missionary fall into two camps, that of the secular anthropologist who, from the writings of George H. L. F. Pitt-Rivers and Lucien Lévy-Bruhl forward, have been intensely hostile to missionary influence, or that of the pious chronicler, usually church-employed, who wished to recount triumphs for Christ. Since voluminous missionary records are open to the researcher, including those of the Church Missionary Society, the Methodist Missionary Society, the Society for the Propagation of the Gospel, and Friends' House in London; the Propaganda in the Vatican City; and the records of the Presbyterian Church, U.S.A., and the Methodist Church in the United States, together with the Board of American Missions materials at Harvard University and the resources of the Missionary Research Library in New York City, students might well be encouraged to begin a scholarly reassessment of the rôle of the Christian missions. Records of non-British groups should also be consulted, especially in Germany, France, and the Netherlands, since they came into frequent contact with their English brethren.

31. The traditional questions need to be asked again and again, and this introduction does not mean to imply that constitutional issues, or the history of exploration,

Such a field of study will continue to present special problems, dealing as it does with many diverse societies over a long time-span and centering upon some of the modern world's most difficult and emotional issues. Since 1947 alone Britain has withdrawn its rule from 693 million people and helped to create twenty-one new nations. Empire-Commonwealth history is intractable chronologically if one deserts the easy solution of the Whig interpretation, as one must. The problems represented by nationalism, racial antagonisms, oral traditions, and illiterate or semi-literate societies are not readily reducible by the historian's traditional tools and attitudes. Britain ultimately spread cartographer's red across such a wide swath of the globe as originally to make the scholar choose between a London-centric, administrative, Colonial-Office approach in order to find some sense of unity, or an Ottawa-, Cape Town-, Colombo-, or Canberra-centric approach, sacrificing breadth for depth. But the first approach represents an illusory breadth, and the second an equally illusory depth. When the field first developed professionally it was unhesitatingly London-oriented; in the 1940's and '50's it was as strongly driven to its many corners; today once again emphasis is upon London, but a reasonable balance is being struck, if not always by individuals at least by the body of literature as a whole. A revitalizing scepticism, a growing desire to bridge the gaps between nations,[32] disciplines, and specializations, and a willingness to entertain broadly theoretical questions[33] are giving new life to a field which falsely has appeared to be in decline.[34]

---

once two staples of Imperial historians, do not need their own regiments. Indeed, testimony to how much remains to be done in the former of these fields is given by William S. Livingston, ed., *Federalism in the Commonwealth: A Bibliographical Commentary* (London, 1963). After all, less than four decades separate us from Robert Livingston Schuyler's *Parliament and the British Empire* (New York, 1929).

32. In addition to the titles mentioned elsewhere, and in the following essays, there is a thorough and informative *Critical Survey of Studies on Dutch Colonial History* by Willim P. Coolhaas: Koninkljk Institut voor Taal-, Land-, en Volkenkunde, *Bibliographical Series 4* (The Hague, 1960).

33. The most sensible statement of how the historian may best pose such questions is to be found in the Social Science Research Council's *Bulletin* 64 (1954), *The Social Sciences in Historical Study: A Report of the Committee on Historiography* (New York), edited by Hugh G. J. Aitken. Two more recent enquiries of a similar nature are Folke Dovring, *History as a Social Science: An Essay on the Nature and Purpose of Historical Studies* (The Hague, 1960), which is disappointing, and Rollo Handy and Paul Kurtz, "A Current Appraisal of the Behavioral Sciences," section 3, "History, Economics," a whole number of the Behavioral Research Council *Bulletin* (Great Barrington, Mass., 1963), which is a good example of what historians must avoid. Far briefer and more stimulating is William Keith Hancock, *The History of Our Times* (London, 1951).

34. See the Appendix.

All this the scholar recognizes, but perhaps on occasion he fails to convey his recognition sufficiently to his students. One reason more has not been done in Empire-Commonwealth history of a really fundamental, analytical nature has been the long influence of John A. Hobson's *Imperialism: A Study*, first published in London in 1902. We have no final answers today, but for years we thought we had. Here spoke the voice of Authority, and even when scholars felt, as scholars must, that Hobson had supplied only *an* answer, they somehow failed to reveal this assumption as they taught. The fact that one still must fall back upon Parker Thomas Moon's 1926 synthesis, *Imperialism and World Politics* (New York), for much necessary data testifies to the need for synthesizers in the field and to the hold of older authorities and their generalizations. Indeed, that the traditional forms of organization still exercise their authority is demonstrated by this book, for while implicitly it contains a plea for some new syntheses in the organization of Imperial studies, the national orientation of the essays reflects the traditional approach—as a stocktaking must.[35]

Between the polemical, the nationalist, and the *engagé* historians, and the dissecting tools of the dissertation writer and the historically uncommitted man of the mid-century, falls a shadow. With Yeats we may find "the best lack all conviction, while the worst / Are full of passionate intensity." But surely the vitality of the questions that lay within the field, the bearing the study of this particular past has upon our particular present, and the peculiar kind of commitment represented by the historian's craft, will continue to appeal. British Empire-Commonwealth history is exceptionally challenging, staggeringly broad and deep, with a limitless horizon of opportunities for productive research. The historian, the "social engineer," the humanist, the social scientist will find much in the field untouched. The essays here provide some indication of where the major work has been done. Perhaps these chapters will arouse new interest in the field in the United States; hopefully they may redirect some of the research that is being done elsewhere. Such is our intention.

35. Organization by discipline rather than area is represented in Robert A. Lystod, ed., *The African World: A Survey of Social Research* (New York, 1965). Such organization seems even less satisfactory.

# THE AMERICAN CONTINENTAL
# COLONIES IN THE EMPIRE

### Robert L. Middlekauff

SEVENTEENTH-CENTURY ENGLISHMEN were prone to
think of the founding of colonies virtually as an act in nature. Colonies
were plantations; their settlement, planting, in the sense of placing
seeds in the ground. English literature brims with such figures. Thus
John Smith described the "first planting" of Virginia and Richard Hakluyt wrote *A Discourse of Western Planting*. Later in the colonial period men on both sides of the Atlantic commonly referred to England
as the "mother" and the colonies as her "children"; and they sometimes speculated about what the "growth" of these children would yield
in the future. Other terms were also used, of course, but descriptions
that implied that the relationship of England and her colonies was
organic were most frequently employed.

These pleasant metaphors were discarded in 1776 when Thomas
Paine showed in *Common Sense* that behind the smile of the "tender
mother" lurked a "devouring monster." But the old natural figures
have had a persistent way of cropping up in accounts of the colonies and
the Revolution. They have because they appear to be extraordinarily
apt. Historians of early America face the problem of explaining enormous changes, not the least of which is how thirteen small English
settlements transformed themselves into an independent nation. Saying
that the colonies "grew" and "matured" has proved to be a convenient
answer.

Words, we all know, convey thought and the choice of words implies a way of thinking. But words may also control thought. Likening
historical change in the American colonies to developments in nature
has sometimes resulted in such control.

The most recent historians to offer a general interpretation of the
American colonial past, the Imperial school, expressed their views in a

vocabulary deeply indebted to metaphors from nature. The great men of this group, Charles McLean Andrews and George Louis Beer, found the use of these figures especially congenial because they were convinced that society follows the laws of evolution. Society, they insisted, was evolving, slowly producing higher and better institutions and ideas. The study of the past revealed this development; indeed history moved linearly. The Imperial historians customarily charted its direction with such terms as "progress" and "advance." Signs of this movement were especially clear in the American colonial past, where simple, crude beginnings had gradually produced a nation. To be sure, at many points in the accounts of the Imperial historians, their treatment implies no belief that the growth described was morphological. They clearly label much growth in inorganic terms, industrial and economic for example. But the over-all conception rests on a conviction of organic change, a growth as in nature, unresponsive to human control. Thus Andrews wrote of the American Revolution: "[Englishmen] could hardly have been expected to appreciate the fact that the colonies in cutting loose from their mother country were but obeying a law of general evolution of human society toward higher and broader forms of government and social relations."[1]

Andrews and Beer probably were not aware of the control the organic metaphor exercised over their interpretations. But both recognized, as others did not, that earlier historians had failed to think about the colonies in a meaningful context. Some neglected everything except the colonies themselves. Others, like George Bancroft, considered colonial history prefatory to the history of American democracy.[2] Bancroft's approach appeared particularly cramping because it distorted the importance of the Imperial connection to colonial development. The idea that the colonial past was simply a preface to a glorious national story obscured the fascination of the early period.

The Imperial historians insisted that the colonies must be placed

1. Andrews, *The Colonial Background of the American Revolution* (New Haven, 1924; Yale Paperbound, 1961), p. 208. Andrews' greatest work was *The Colonial Period of American History: The Settlements* (3 vols.; New Haven, 1934-37) and *England's Commercial and Colonial Policy* (New Haven, 1938). Beer's chief works were *British Colonial Policy, 1754-1765* (New York, 1907); *The Origins of the British Colonial System, 1578-1660* (New York, 1908); and *The Old Colonial System, 1660-1754* (2 vols.; New York, 1912). These books are mentioned and discussed throughout this essay. Beer's books have recently been reissued by Peter Smith (Gloucester, Mass.).

2. Bancroft, *History of the United States* (10 vols.; New York, 1834-74).

within a different context. Andrews argued that the years of the English connection constituted a period which must be studied by itself, free from "all preconceptions based on later events."[3] The colonies were a part of the Empire, and they must be studied in the context of British expansion. Seeing the colonies in context also involved, according to Andrews, studying them not from within but from "without"— indeed from the vantage point of London. This angle of vision conferred a great advantage: "It brings the mother country into the forefront of the picture as the central figure, the authoritative and guiding force, the influence of which did more than anything else to shape the course of colonial achievement."[4]

Andrews' distinguished student, Lawrence Henry Gipson, is less indebted to the idea that colonial development followed organic lines. Although he agrees that the colonies must be seen within the Imperial setting, he does not believe that London offers the best vantage point. By the middle of the eighteenth century, he says, the mother country influenced the Empire less than local forces. Therefore the historian must "beat the bounds," examining from within every British colony throughout the world.[5]

George Louis Beer, on the other hand, approached British expansion largely through investigation of the old colonial system. The colonies interested him only in so far as they were affected by the system, and his work concentrated on the aspects of colonial life most affected by the system. What he may not have emphasized sufficiently was that the way colonies responded to Imperial forces depended in large part upon local conditions.

Like the conception of growth, the Imperial historians' idea of studying the colonies in the context of British expansion has been enormously influential. It has yielded excellent studies of the conditions in England favorable to colonization, of the first settlements, and of the old colonial system itself. Still, the idea has proved to be of limited value; it has not really offered a way of understanding the character of colonial culture itself. Nor has the idea of growth produced satisfactory explanations of social change. In fact it may have inhibited understanding more often than it aided it.

3. *Colonial Period of American History*, p. xi.
4. *Ibid.*
5. Gipson, *The British Empire before the American Revolution* (10 vols.; Caldwell, Idaho, and New York, 1936-61). Two more volumes are anticipated.

The Imperial historians invigorated interest in the conditions that impelled Englishmen to leave their country for America, but they did not have to stimulate interest in the first men to sail westward, the great explorers, for it had rarely drooped. Indeed the fascination of these men obscured the conditions of England's entrance in maritime enterprise and colonization. Drake and his great contemporaries are romantic figures, and most of the writing about them until fairly recently has been romance. Modern scholars have provided more substantial stuff, retelling the story of English expansion not simply in terms of heroes but as the expression of an emergent commercial capitalism and a new science. The English scholar James A. Williamson was responsible for much of the modern telling. His *Maritime Enterprise, 1485-1558* (Oxford, 1913), though now superseded on many details by later studies, blazed the way to the early history of English commerce and discovery. In his book Williamson attempted to refurbish the claims of Sebastian Cabot to exploration in the Northwest, a subject he pursued further in *The Voyages of the Cabots and the English Discovery of North America* (London, 1929). Although Williamson explained the activities of the Cabots better than anyone else has since, much evidence is still lacking about Sebastian Cabot's voyage of 1509. Williamson's *Sir John Hawkins: The Time and the Man* (Oxford, 1927) and *The Age of Drake* (4th ed., London, 1960) are still the standard books in their fields. About the time Williamson began issuing his work, William R. Scott's *The Constitution and Finance of English, Scottish and Irish Joint-Stock Companies to 1720* (3 vols.; Cambridge, 1910-12) appeared. Scott's work, like Williamson's, has been superseded on some points, but its rich coverage of the trading companies makes it still the most useful general work.

Sir Humphrey Gilbert and Sir Walter Raleigh have been the subject of romance almost as often as Drake and the English seadogs. The best work on their explorations and colonization ventures has been done recently. In his Introduction to *The Voyages and Colonising Enterprises of Sir Humphrey Gilbert* (2 vols.; London, 1940), David B. Quinn showed that unlike much English effort, Gilbert's was not in search of a Northwest Passage, but was undertaken to establish a base for piratical expeditions against Spain. Quinn also related Gilbert's experience in Ireland to his overseas adventures. In his edition of *The Roanoke Voyages, 1584-1590* (2 vols.; London, 1955), Quinn suggested that more documents on the voyages may yet turn up. But it is difficult to imagine anyone improving on his brilliant account of Raleigh's ventures in *Raleigh and the British Empire* (rev. ed., New York, 1962).

Exploration and commercial expansion provide only a partial background for the understanding of England's first colonizing efforts. As George B. Parks pointed out in *Richard Hakluyt and the English Voyages* (New York, 1928), someone had to revise old geographical conceptions and drew together the knowledge of the new world for English merchants and statesmen. The Hakluyts, of course, did just that and much more besides. Their activities are described and carefully assessed in Parks' study. Two studies of the development of English geography should also be consulted: Eva G. R. Taylor, *Tudor Geography, 1485-1583* (London, 1930) and *Late Tudor and Early Stuart Geography, 1583-1650* (London, 1934).[6] An excellent recent review is John Horace Parry's *The Age of Reconnaissance* (London, 1963).

Much of the best work on the explorations was done by English historians; American historians have followed it with intensive study of the settlements. Much of their study was given to the conditions making the founding of the colonies possible. Beer, for example, is responsible for showing the link between the belief that England was overpopulated and the encouragement of emigration. His insight has been challenged recently in an essay by Mildred Campbell, which though careful and thorough does not shake Beer's thesis.[7] Other studies of emigration to the colonies abound. At least two add much to our knowledge of the founding of the colonies: Marcus L. Hansen's *The Atlantic Migration, 1607-1860* (Cambridge, Mass., 1940), which discusses admirably the effects of a variety of colonial policies upon the flow of colonists, and Abbot E. Smith's *Colonists in Bondage: White Servitude and Convict Labor in America, 1607-1776* (Chapel Hill,

6. Two important books which I have not been able to discuss in the text should at least be noted: Arthur P. Newton, *The European Nations in the West Indies, 1493-1688* (London, 1933), and Alfred L. Rowse, *Sir Richard Grenville of the Revenge, An Elizabethan Hero* (London, 1937). See also David B. Quinn, "Sir Thomas Smith (1513-1577) and the Beginnings of English Colonial Theory," *Proceedings of the American Philosophical Society* (Philadelphia), LXXXIX (1945), 543-60.

7. Mildred Campbell, " 'Of People Either Too Few or Too Many,' The Conflict of Opinion on Population and Its Relation to Emigration," in William Aiken and Basil Duke Henning, eds., *Conflict in Stuart England: Essays in Honor of Wallace Notestein* (New York, 1960), pp. 169-201.

1947), which demonstrates the commercial character of the trade in servants.

Although these studies are illuminating, they all fail to match Charles McLean Andrews' *The Colonial Period of American History* in either conception or coverage. Andrews saw English expansion largely as the expression of a growing commercial capitalism. But though he argued his case persuasively and buttressed it with rich detail, he did not really sense that the seventeenth-century mind conceived of colonies in religious as well as commercial terms. Even in the founding of Virginia, Perry Miller tells us in "Religion and Society in the Early Literature of Virginia," a chapter in *Errand into the Wilderness* (Cambridge, Mass., 1956), religion "was the really energizing propulsion." Miller's essay is extravagantly phrased, but the point it insists upon— that seventeenth-century Englishmen did not make nice modern distinctions between religion, politics, and commerce—is a valid one. Andrews' massive work convinces one of the commercial motive in English promoters, but he does not persuade one of its simple purity. Miller's studies of Puritanism, *Orthodoxy in Massachusetts, 1630-1650* (Cambridge, Mass., 1933) and *The New England Mind: The Seventeenth Century* (Cambridge, Mass., 1954), have almost completely reshaped historians' conceptions of the impulses of the founding of New England. Still, Andrews' meticulous reconstruction of the companies' charters, indeed of much of the English commercial side, remains useful. And so, for that matter, is most of his work on other seventeenth-century beginnings. In the last generation other scholars have amplified and modified to some extent portions of his work. On Virginia, Wesley Frank Craven's *The Dissolution of the Virginia Company* (New York, 1932) tells the story of the company's collapse convincingly. Craven's superb *The Southern Colonies in the Seventeenth Century, 1607-1689* (Baton Rouge, 1949) leans on Andrews' account for the beginnings of Carolina and Maryland.

Andrews' work on the beginnings of the middle colonies has also stood up well; even John E. Pomfret's admirable studies, *The Province of West New Jersey, 1609-1702* (Princeton, 1956) and *The Province of East New Jersey, 1609-1702: The Rebellious Proprietary* (Princeton, 1962), do not seriously alter his conclusions about the Jerseys, though they offer much more information. Andrews' account of the founding of Pennsylvania is excellent, but it should be supplemented by several essays in Frederick B. Tolles' *Quakers and the Atlantic Culture* (New York, 1960), and by Catherine O. Peare's *William Penn: A Biography* (Philadelphia, 1957).[8]

In his accounts of the settlements, Andrews devoted more attention to the English conditions surrounding the founding than to the first years of the colonists' desperate struggle to carve out a foothold for themselves. This focus followed from his belief that the colonies represented an expression of British expansion; the source of that expansion, Britain, seemed as important as its shape in the colonies. Like others of the Imperial school, Andrews insisted that even after settlement the colonies continued to feel the force of the British connection; indeed, their membership in the Empire was the key fact of their history.

Obviously, how the Imperial historians describe the Empire is an important matter. Andrews found that England, the center of the Empire, always placed its own interests ahead of those of the colonies. Although he and Gipson agreed that the colonies prospered within the Empire, they did not explain the colonial prosperity in the same terms. Andrews implied that the colonies were lucky: Imperial policy, which was drawn in response to mercantilist imperatives, did not by design favor their interests. Fortunately for the colonies the old colonial system, in establishing some lines of trade and prohibiting several others, encouraged activity that the colonies would have engaged in had restrictions not existed. Even when the idea of the self-sufficient Empire began dominating Imperial thinking, Andrews said, the interests of England remained paramount. Gipson, whose work covers the period in which the idea of the self-sufficient Empire was accepted, insisted that by the middle of the eighteenth century English policymakers recognized an Imperial interest which transcended any narrow concern for the home country. British officials always consulted the

8. There are many other studies of the settlements. See especially Samuel Eliot Morison, *Builders of the Bay Colony* (Boston, 1930); Wesley Frank Craven, *An Introduction to the History of Bermuda* (Williamsburg, 1938); Philip A. Bruce, *Economic History of Virginia in the Seventeenth Century* (2 vols.; New York, 1895), and *Institutional History of Virginia in the Seventeenth Century* (2 vols.; New York, 1910); and Frederick B. Tolles, *Meeting House and Countinghouse: The Quaker Merchants of Colonial Philadelphia, 1682-1763* (Chapel Hill, 1948); Herbert L. Osgood, *The American Colonies in the Seventeenth Century* (3 vols.; New York, 1904-07); Verner W. Crane, *The Southern Frontier, 1670-1732* (Durham, N.C., 1928; Ann Arbor, 1956); and Philip L. Barbour, *The Three Worlds of Captain John Smith* (Boston, 1964).

colonies on questions of policy and attempted to devise plans that benefited as much of the Empire as possible.[9]

Besides disagreeing in their assessments of the purposes of Imperial
policy, Andrews and Gipson also evaluated British leadership differently. Andrews described it as frequently "badly informed" about
the colonies; Gipson found it intelligently concerned about colonial
interests, eager and successful in discovering what the colonies really
wanted. In his careful analysis of administrative agencies, Andrews
suggested that their performance was uneven: the Customs Service,
for example, never worked well, but the Vice-Admiralty Courts did.
Although he performed no similar examination, Gipson concluded
that most of the agencies that governed the Empire functioned justly
and efficiently. He rated the service of the Board of Trade much higher
than Andrews did.[10]

Nor did Andrews and Gipson agree on Parliament's rôle in colonial life. Andrews simply dismissed the suggestion that Parliament
interfered with the "internal life or government of the colonies" before
1763 as having no basis in fact. Parliament confined itself to regulating
commerce and navigation. Gipson, on the other hand, professed surprise that the colonies before 1750 did not protest against the series of
parliamentary laws that "amounted in effect to a code held binding on
all." Parliament, he insisted, had interfered with far more than trade
and commerce long before the Revolutionary crisis: it had actually
entered the internal life of the colonies. Beer, whose concern was narrower than Andrews' and Gipson's, provided an analysis substantially
in agreement with Andrews.[11]

These differences should not obscure the fact that the Imperial historians have contributed much to the description of the functioning of
Imperial agencies and to the analysis of English commercial policy. In
a series of graceful books, Beer gave Imperial policy its first systematic
analysis. His first study, *The Commercial Policy of England toward
the American Colonies* (New York, 1893), revealed an interest in the
medieval origins of policy, an interest he sustained throughout his work
but never completely developed. His formal treatment of the begin-

9. Andrews, *Colonial Period*, IV, 7, and *passim*; Gipson, *British Empire* (rev. ed.),
I, 13, and *passim*.

10. Andrews, *Colonial Period*, IV, 221; Gipson, *British Empire*, IX, 3-21, and
*passim*.

11. Andrews, *Colonial Period*, IV, 166; and Gipson, *British Empire* (rev. ed.) III,
274.

nings of policy, *The Origins of the British Colonial System, 1578-1660,* places most of the origins of policy in the seventeenth century. England's economic needs, the financial requirements of the government, and mercantilist theory were the determinants of England's colonial policy. The regulation of the tobacco trade in particular forced the formulation of much policy, and English statesmen tended to generalize from the experience of tobacco regulation. In *The Old Colonial System, 1660-1754* and *British Colonial Policy, 1754-1765* Beer described a fully developed British policy which sought to create a self-sufficient Empire. He emphasized that if self-sufficiency was an ideal, in functioning the system deliberately aimed to protect British interests, and that the economic interest of the colonies always remained "subordinate to that of the mother country. . . ."[12]

Although they are probably richer in the details of the making of policy, Andrews' studies of policy did not significantly alter Beer's conclusions. But Andrews did much that Beer did not: he traced the creation of the administrative apparatus, the commissions, committees, councils, and boards, by which policy was both made and superintended. The faltering beginnings of Imperial administrative agencies appear in *British Committees* (Baltimore, 1908). Andrews expressed his mature ideas in the clear-eyed essay *The Colonial Period of American History: England's Commercial and Colonial Policy* (New Haven, 1938).

Many narrower studies of policy and administration support Andrews' and Beer's view of the intentions and the functioning of the Empire rather than Gipson's. Ralph P. Bieber's *The Lords of Trade and Plantations, 1675-1696* (Allentown, Pa., 1919) suggests that administrative agencies "often failed to grasp the colonial point of view." Lawrence A. Harper's *The English Navigation Laws* (New York, 1939) asserts that the old colonial system was not "designed for the good of the empire as a whole." Similarly Oliver M. Dickerson's *American Colonial Government* (Cleveland, 1912) and Mark Thomson's *The Secretaries of State, 1681-1782* (Oxford, 1932) buttress Andrews and Beer.[13]

12. Beer, *British Colonial Policy,* p. 200. See also the introductory essay by Julius Goebel, Jr., in Joseph H. Smith, *Appeals to the Privy Council from the American Plantations* (New York, 1950). Goebel makes an impressive case for the medieval origins of Imperial policy and Imperial institutions.

13. The complete title of Andrews' book cited in the previous paragraph is *British Committees, Commissions, and Councils of Trade and Plantations, 1622-1675;* of

If all these books aid in assessing the old colonial system each has more specialized uses. Bieber's book, for example, describes the ordinary workings of the Lords of Trade carefully; Harper's account is unrivaled in its analysis of the origins and functioning of the English Navigation Acts.

The metaphor of "growth" has been especially prominent in the Imperial historians' studies of the colonial economy. In this case the metaphor has not impaired understanding but perhaps has increased it. For the components of economic growth are susceptible of description in terms other than those borrowed from nature: in short, economic growth can be analyzed empirically.

Preoccupied by the position the colonies held within the Empire, the Imperial historian attempted to assess the effects of the Acts of Navigation and Trade upon the economic life of the colonies. Gipson, in the latest statement of the Imperial historians' view, suggested that the system of restrictions imposed by Parliament was made less burdensome by the advantages that the Imperial connection conferred. To be sure the colonies paid certain duties, they could manufacture hats and woolens only on a limited scale, they could ship "enumerated" products only to Imperial ports, and they could import manufactures only through Britain. But, he points out, they received drawbacks— or rebates—of many of the duties collected; the restrictions on manufactures were either irrelevant to the facts of colonial production or, as in the case of iron, were ignored; the enumerated goods enjoyed a virtual monopoly of the English market, for foreign competition was prohibited; and the colonies were not much affected by the requirement that they import their manufactures from Britain. All in all, says Gipson, "the opportunities for legitimate financial gain opened up by the trade and navigation system seemed to have more than offset the hin-

---

Harper's, *The English Navigation Laws: A Seventeenth-Century Experiment in Social Engineering*; of Dickerson's, *American Colonial Government, 1696-1765: A Study of the British Board of Trade in Its Relation to the American Colonies, Political, Industrial, Administrative.* The quotation from Bieber is on p. 37, from Harper, p. 59. See also Louise P. Kellogg, "The American Colonial Charter: A Study of English Administration in Relation Thereto, Chiefly after 1688," *Annual Report of the American Historical Association for 1903* (Washington, 1904), I, 185-341; and Philip S. Haffenden, "The Crown and the Colonial Charters, 1675-1688," *William and Mary Quarterly* (Williamsburg), 3rd. ser., XV (July, 1958), 297-311 and (Oct., 1958), 452-66.

drances posed by legal barriers against engaging in certain activities, industrial as well as commercial."[14]

Gipson conceded that several of these conclusions have been disputed, but he does not believe that the general position of the Imperial historians has been shaken: the colonies benefited economically from their connection to the Empire. This contention, it should be observed, rests upon the discoveries that the colonies prospered during the period before the Revolution and that Americans rarely complained before 1764 about parliamentary measures regulating their business activities.

No doubt the Imperial historians are right in insisting that the Americans were prosperous and uncomplaining, but are they justified in assuming that these facts "prove" the beneficial effects of parliamentary regulation? Probably they are, but at least one historian has argued that the costs of the Imperial connection came high to the colonials. Lawrence A. Harper, in "The Effect of the Navigation Acts," suggested that in the late eighteenth century the chief losses were absorbed by planters of tobacco and rice.[15] He calculated the cost of enumeration of tobacco as two and one-fourth cents per pound; in 1773, he says, the total loss must have been between two and three million dollars. Rice planters lost an estimated three shillings a hundredweight, which must have totaled about $185,000 at the least in 1773. The additional charges exacted by the requirement that all manufactures must come through England ran from a half million to three million dollars. The precision of Harper's calculations may be questioned, especially when they depend upon comparisons of commercial activities before and after the American Revolution, yet the evidence he presents of the fact that Americans took some losses seems irrefutable. In his *English Navigation Acts*, Harper showed that the acts wrenched colonial commerce out of its most profitable channel, trade with the Dutch, and compelled exchanges with England. The Dutch appealed to colonials on a number of scores: Dutch credit was cheaper, their manufactures were one-third less, and their freight rates were lower. The commercial habits of the colonials, it seems, were formed

14. Gipson, *British Empire*, III, 292.
15. Harper, "The Effect of the Navigation Acts on the Thirteen Colonies," Richard B. Morris, ed., *Era of the American Revolution* (New York, 1939), pp. 3-39. An excellent study of the failure of Imperial policy on the manufacture of colonial iron is Arthur C. Bining, *British Regulation of the Colonial Iron Industry* (Philadelphia, 1933).

by regulation, and at the beginning of regulation the colonies did complain. Later colonial silence at the requirements of the Navigation Acts may in part have been the result of the old custom of acquiescence.

What especially impressed the Imperial historians about the colonial economy was its growth towards a maturity which almost equaled that of Britain. Tracing the story of the actual working of the colonial economy has been the task of a number of historians less affected by the general conceptional framework than by a number of technical problems. Their answers to many of these problems serve to confirm the Imperial historians' insight into the importance of the Empire to early American life. But it is also clear that colonial economic activity was more complicated than anyone has suspected.

An old study, William B. Weeden's *Economic and Social History of New England, 1620-1789* (2 vols.; Boston, 1891), attempted in a rough way to sketch the interconnections between New England's economy and society. Its diffuseness and limited conception of the sources for the study of economic history decreases its value. Yet Weeden succeeded in at least touching many of the problems later historians have found interesting.

Recently historians have begun to study the economy through the men who made it work, especially the merchants and their families. Seventeenth-century merchants have been treated thoughtfully by Samuel Eliot Morison, Bernard Bailyn, and Viola Barnes.[16] Morison's short biographies of John Hull in *Builders of the Bay Colony* and "William Pynchon," in *Massachusetts Historical Society Proceedings*, LXIV (Boston, 1932), 67-107, show how important it is to give a rounded picture of merchant life. The Hull of Morison's sketch earned a fortune in trade with England and the West Indies. Yet he held medieval economic ideals: he despised "oppression" and usury and welcomed regulation of business by the state. Hull was a Puritan and his social attitudes were those of his society. The transformation of the social type which Hull represented can be followed in Bailyn's *The New England Merchants in the Seventeenth Century* (Cambridge, Mass., 1955). Bailyn exposed the alienation from the old Puritans of

16. Viola F. Barnes, "Richard Wharton," *Publications of the Colonial Society of Massachusetts*, XXVI (Boston, 1925), 238-70. For an exhaustive listing of studies bearing on colonial economic history see Lawrence A. Harper, "Recent Contributions to American Economic History: American History to 1789," *Journal of Economic History*, XIX (March, 1959), 1-24.

a new business community in New England, a community tied together by family as well as interest and oriented toward England, the center of its overseas trade. Bailyn probably claimed a cohesion for this group which it did not possess; at any rate, as he admits, the merchants split badly over the Dominion of New England. But Bailyn's suggestion that the family was an important mechanism in seventeenth-century commercial life seems irrefutable. Friends and relatives in England served as factors for New England merchants or as agents who opened up fresh contacts. Whether kinship continued to be an important commercial institution in the more complex relationships of the eighteenth century remains an open question, though Bailyn seems to assume that it did. There is considerable evidence to support his view. Samuel Rosenblatt's "The Significance of Credit in the Tobacco Consignment Trade: A Study of John Norton and Sons, 1768-1775," *William and Mary Quarterly*, 3rd ser., XIX (July, 1962), 383-99, and Jacob Price's "Who Was John Norton? A Note on the Historical Character of Some Eighteenth-Century London Firms," *ibid.*, pp. 400-407, suggest that family connections served as a means of securing credit and indeed in the organization of the tobacco trade. There is further corroboration in Price's "The Rise of Glasgow in the Chesapeake Tobacco Trade, 1707-1775," *ibid.*, XI (April, 1954), 179-99, an article which goes a long way toward explaining how Scottish factors, resident in Virginia, were able to capture much of the tobacco trade from the consignment houses after 1720.

As important as kinship was in establishing commercial relationships abroad, it was not everything. From several studies of colonial houses one might infer that kinship was important chiefly in connecting colonials to English merchants. In the sizable trade outside these lines, with the Dutch, Spanish, French, and Portuguese ports, family played no important part. Byron Fairchild's *Pepperells*, William T. Baxter's *Hancocks*, James Blaine Hedge's *Browns*, and Philip L. White's *Beekmans* all established close relationships with houses in England and elsewhere, but family played little part in the non-English connections.[17]

The histories of these merchants are rich in their details of com-

17. Fairchild, *Messrs. William Pepperell* (Ithaca, 1954); Baxter, *The House of Hancock: Business in Boston, 1724-1775* (Cambridge, Mass., 1945); Hedges, *The Browns of Providence Plantations, Colonial Years* (Cambridge, Mass., 1952); and White, *The Beekmans of New York in Politics and Commerce, 1647-1877* (New York, 1956).

mercial activity. Ships, cargoes, voyages, exchanges, and the merchants themselves take on a concreteness that can be achieved in written history only through the accumulation of examples. Moreover, the history of each family is a story of change. Thus Hedges' book tells of the simple beginnings of James and Obadiah Brown, who in the 1720's began trading with the West Indies with only a small amount of capital and a single ship. By the end of the colonial period, the sons of James had sent ships as far away as Africa and had branched out into the manufacture of candles and iron. Manufacturing in fact had taken on a greater scale in their enterprises than commerce. Now, in this change the Browns were not typical (though they seem to have been in many other ways) but the variety of their activities was repeated many times throughout colonial ports. Diversified economic activity was a necessity: the merchant could not specialize and still secure the necessary currency and commodities to pay for imports from England. The lack of specie and the small scale of his markets made specialization impossible.

The problems of currency and markets deserve further study. Several careful beginnings have been made on currency, the best being Curtis P. Nettels' *The Money Supply of the American Colonies before 1720* (Madison, 1934), which explains the mechanisms of exchange and the attempts by Americans to collect enough specie to make payments to Europe. All the studies of merchants already cited discuss this problem: White's *Beekmans* is especially fascinating for it shows that when a merchant had a product like flaxseed for export to a large market he experienced little difficulty. Baxter and Fairchild's studies both point up how important government contracts were to merchants —how coveted they were, and how remunerative.

But a flow of trade itself kept the exchange with England open as Richard Pares' *Yankees and Creoles: The Trade between North America and the West Indies before the American Revolution* (Cambridge, Mass., 1956) shows. In search of a way to pay English merchants for imports, the northern colonies sent ships into the West Indies and picked up the sugar (in exchange for foodstuffs, fish, and horses) which English markets demanded. Pares' book tells the story of this roundabout exchange better than it has ever been told before. But it does not sketch the history of the changes in the North America–West Indies trade, changes which occurred but which have never been exploited in the detail necessary.

Pares' study lacks the statistical base which strengthens any history of commerce. Most of the histories of merchants are similarly short on statistics. We need to know in greater precision the lines of trade, the number of ships entering colonial ports over the years, their cargoes and the value of those cargoes, the ownership of the ships, the prices obtained and so on. Recently several such accounts have appeared: Bernard Bailyn's *Massachusetts Shipping, 1697-1714: A Statistical Study* (Cambridge, Mass., 1959), based on Massachusetts shipping registers; Anne Bezanson, *et al., Prices in Colonial Pennsylvania* (Philadelphia, 1935), a detailed history of prices; and Murray G. Lawson's "The Routes of Boston's Trade, 1752-1765," *Colonial Society of Massachusetts Publications,* XXXVIII (1959), 81-120. Many more studies of this sort are needed for a rounded view of colonial economic activity and its relation to the Empire.

As in the investigation of economic activity, the assumptions of the Imperial historians have also provided a rough framework within which colonial politics have been studied. Andrews and Gipson frequently comment on the growth of colonial governments and their "maturity" by the time of the Revolution. Their view merges neatly with a view of colonial political history which insists that sometime in the seventeenth century popular, local, and representative government began challenging Imperial authority. The alignments in this contest are usually assumed to have included rich merchants, grand planters, and royal officials, all led by the royal governor on one side, and opposing this elite the underprivileged, the westerners, the poor debtors, the disfranchised, the lesser merchants and planters, all men on their way up. Their successful grasping of power by 1776 represents the triumph of democracy. More often the struggle is described in terms of institutions; in fact it is seen as being practically synonomous with the "growth" of the lower house of the legislature. This story has been told in Leonard W. Labaree's admirable *Royal Government in America* (New Haven, 1930). Labaree, however, does much more than recount the fight between governor and assembly; his book is a study of almost all aspects of royal government in the colonies. Mary P. Clarke's *Parliamentary Privilege in the American Colonies* (New Haven, 1943) gives depth to a part of the familiar story by showing that by claiming "parliamentary privilege," a set of rights which Parliament exercised, colonial assemblies sought to defend their encroachments on the governor's power by invoking a great tradition.

Recently Jack P. Greene, in "The Role of the Lower Houses of Assembly in Eighteenth-Century Politics," *Journal of Southern History* (Baton Rouge), XXVII (November, 1960), 451-74, has reviewed the whole problem, summarizing his own findings about the southern colonies and those of other scholars about the northern colonies. Greene's article, as well as his book, *The Quest for Power: The Lower Houses of Assembly in the Southern Royal Colonies, 1689-1776* (Chapel Hill, 1963), is curiously dated in its focus upon the activity of the colonial assembly. But in "Foundations of Political Power in the Virginia House of Burgesses, 1720-1776," *William and Mary Quarterly*, 3rd ser., XVI (October, 1959), 485-506, he has examined a single house with a technique which has found increasing favor in the last fifteen years. His study identifies powerful burgesses within the house by analyzing the composition of committees. After showing that a few men dominated the actions of the house, Greene provides information about these men: their educations, occupations, residences within the colony, and length of service.

Studies which make use of similar techniques are altering almost our entire conception of colonial politics. Though the Imperial connection is still considered to be important, it no longer dominates historians' thinking. Indeed their emphasis is upon the local, and upon the anonymous individual, rather than upon the Empire and its royal officials. Perhaps the key book in getting the revision of the older views started was Robert E. Brown's *Middle-Class Democracy and the Revolution in Massachusetts, 1691-1780* (Ithaca, 1955). In this study Brown contends that colonial politics were democratic, and by showing that the franchise was widely held in Massachusetts, offers much, though not compelling, evidence for his thesis. Since his book was published, Brown has found considerable support from Chilton Williamson's *American Suffrage, from Property to Democracy, 1760-1860* (Princeton, 1960), which surveys the right to vote in all thirteen colonies.[18] Brown's latest book, *Virginia, 1705-1786: Democracy or Aristocracy?* (East Lansing, 1964), written with B. Katherine Brown,

18. See also Richard P. McCormick, *The History of Voting in New Jersey: A Study of the Development of Election Machinery, 1664-1911* (New Brunswick, N.J., 1953); and Lucille Griffith, *Virginia House of Burgesses, 1750-1774* (Northport, Ala., 1963).

extends his investigations to Virginia. The book is frankly tendentious—it seeks to demonstrate the democratic character of society and politics in Virginia. The widespread property-holding, the high degree of social mobility, the absence of class, religious, or sectional conflict, the broad franchise, and the equal representation all conspired in favor of majority—that is middle-class—desires, according to the Browns. But the investigation the Browns conducted determined their conclusions, for their inquiry does not permit an adequate assessment of the power of Virginia's gentry; and they reject the results of such an inquiry made by Charles S. Sydnor in *Gentlemen Freeholders: Political Practices in Washington's Virginia* (Chapel Hill, 1952).

A feeling for the way eighteenth-century Virginia politics actually worked is missing in the Browns' study, especially a feeling for the political style of men of family and wealth. Part of the Browns' failure arises from the focus of their interests in the objective political world—the franchise, for example, representation, and the extent of property holding. The subtle manner, so deftly described by Sydnor, in which men of social status got their way in Virginia's politics almost totally escapes the Browns. And so does the complex interplay between the gentry and their constituencies, an interplay marked by a fluidity of power but not of responsibility. Yet the Browns' work is important: it provides significant information, and it forces us to discard many of the old categories in our study of colonial politics.

Much more work needs to be done. We still lack knowledge about many of the purposes and techniques of political life in the colonies. In part our ignorance can be traced to the fact that colonial politics were local, and we have few intensive studies on a small scale. We have also assumed gratuitously that colonial politics resembled modern politics. One notable exception is the late Charles S. Grant's *Democracy in the Connecticut Frontier Town of Kent* (New York, 1961), which examines economic, political, and social opportunity from 1738 to 1800 in a western community. Grant's book provides support of a kind to Brown's thesis by showing that the opportunities for getting wealth were open in Kent. But though the vote was easily obtained, office holding remained a monopoly of the few, a fact Grant does not explain.

Class conflict as described by Roy H. Akagi, *The Town Proprietors of the New England Colonies* (Philadelphia, 1924), did not exist in Kent; proprietors were residents and debtors occupied a variety of places up and down the economic scale. Though it deals with a specific episode, the land bank controversy in Massachusetts, George A. Billias, *The Massachusetts Land Bankers of 1740* (Orono, Maine, 1959), reinforces Grant's finding that class conflict was slight in colonial society. Billias rejects completely the old view of the bank issue in Massachusetts as involving debtors against merchants by showing that merchants led the fight for the bank.

Historians who have stressed the importance of class strife in colonial politics have always found a great gulf (and frequently hostility) between leaders and their constituencies. Two recent studies, Bernard Bailyn, "Politics and Social Structure in Virginia,"[19] and Charles Sydnor, *Gentlemen Freeholders*, mentioned above, reveal that in Virginia, though social status was an important ingredient in political success, the gulf may have been exaggerated. (In New England, where class lines were less distinct than in the southern colonies, the gulf between leaders and constituencies hardly existed outside the cities and large towns.) Bailyn's essay is much more than an analysis of the recruitment of Virginia's leadership. It is an imaginative suggestion about the components of Virginia's politics and the way they should be studied. Sydnor's witty and learned book describes a political situation in which the highly cohesive gentry truly represent the best interests of their electors. The findings of these books, along with Brown's, Grant's, and Billias', suggest a reinterpretation of colonial politics is now underway. Such books reinforce the impression that colonial politics were not primarily Imperial, but local. One suspects that the importance of the royal government and the colonial assembly has been exaggerated. Colonials appear to have been far more interested in concrete and immediate issues than in the struggle for legislative autonomy. Most political issues were settled without any reference to Imperial agencies. In any case, the smallest agencies of colonial government—parishes, counties, and towns—deserve much more attention than they have received.

For the Imperial historians political growth yielded maturity and then ripeness. This American "growth" differed radically from English development. Andrews insisted that the colonies "were far more advanced, politically, socially, and morally, than the mother country"; Beer and Gipson did not suggest that American institutions were supe-

19. Bailyn's essay is in James M. Smith, ed., *Seventeenth-Century America: Essays in Colonial History* (Chapel Hill, 1959), pp. 90-115.

rior to English, but they found them different enough so as to make the American Revolution virtually inevitable.[20]

The existence of the differences raises again the question of the character of the Empire. Indeed one might ask whether by the middle of the eighteenth century the Empire was an entity. Whose allegiance did it enlist? Gipson, who has studied the Empire just before the American Revolution more thoroughly than anyone else, has been so sorely puzzled by these questions that he has given contradictory answers. Colonials, he has written, perceived that their interest lay with the Empire's; in fact the cement of empire was "moral force." But Gipson has also agreed with Beer that fear of the French held America within the Empire before 1763. He says that after the cession of Canada at the end of the French and Indian War the colonies were ripe for rebellion. Economically the colonies had flourished under Imperial protection and regulation. They were free and happy and secure in the Empire. And little wonder! Presiding over this magnificent creation were ministers animated not by the crude considerations of mercantilism but by the ideal of a self-sufficient Empire. These ministers never failed to consult the colonials when decisions which affected them came up; these ministers did not represent the interests of the mother country but of the larger Empire. They are for Gipson the personification of selflessness and wisdom. But the Americans were still restless in the eighteenth century. Not fully aware of the extent of their own strength, and maturity, they remained contented until 1763, when the French were removed from their borders. Then able at last to see themselves in their full strength and liberated from an old fear, they were psychologically prepared for a break. When the British reasonably asked them for contributions for Imperial defense they were seized by "irrational" fear, balked, making absurd distinctions between external and internal taxes and, ignoring the fact that they had long submitted to a virtual code of legislation by Parliament, they suddenly discovered that Parliament lacked the right to legislate for them. And finally after further friction they declared themselves independent.[21]

There are serious flaws in Gipson's account. He misunderstands the character of American politics. Political power, he says, ignoring the revisionist work on the suffrage, was controlled by an elite. Certainly

20. Andrews, *Colonial Background of the American Revolution*, p. 218.
21. Gipson, *British Empire, passim*, and especially X; see also his *The Coming of the Revolution, 1763-1775* (New York, 1954).

American politics were not democratic in any modern sense, but govern-
ing groups were limited by the need to consult their constituencies. Re-
peating the old charge that opportunism governed American political
theory, Gipson describes American protests against Imperial reorganization as shifts of expediency. He characterizes American concern about
the possible extension of taxation at the time of the Stamp Act as "irrational fear," even though the stamp tax was the second statute passed
in two years to collect revenue.[22]

Although Gipson probably has convinced many historians that his
analysis of important Revolutionary questions is correct, he and the
other Imperial historians have failed to persuade the present generation
of American historians that the Revolution was inevitable. The Revolutionary collision, recent accounts suggest, might have been avoided had
British policy taken a different tack after 1763. Few Americans sought
independence until fighting began in 1775. Americans acted only to
defend themselves; and in the process they discovered what they believed about the British constitution and they fashioned a set of beliefs
about the rights of man.

Two books, Edmund S. and Helen M. Morgan's *The Stamp Act
Crisis, Prologue to Revolution* (Chapel Hill, 1953; rev. ed., New
York, 1963), and Oliver M. Dickerson's *The Navigation Acts and the
American Revolution* (Philadelphia, 1951), have shaped recent views
of the Revolution. The Morgans' study has altered our views of colonial constitutional thinking. Older books, most notably Carl Lotus
Becker's brilliant *The Declaration of Independence: A Study in the
History of Political Ideas* (New York, 1922) and Randolph G. Adams'
*Political Ideas of the American Revolution: Britannic-American Con-
tributions to the Problem of Imperial Organization, 1765-1775* (Durham, N.C., 1922; New York, 1958), described a series of shifts
in the colonial position which involved a distinction between internal
and external taxes. The Morgans show that the colonials did not make
this distinction; rather, they agreed in 1765 upon the constitutional
principle "no taxation without representation" and never abandoned
it. Colonials, the Morgans argue, were prepared to fight for their
rights as early as 1765. Their political position was not based upon
"abstract principles," as many historians have interpreted the Morgans; it expressed the colonists' understanding of the inseparability of

22. *British Empire*, X, 365.

liberty and property. Taxation without representation would destroy property and liberty. Had the British government accorded this position the respect that the colonies expected, no Revolution would have occurred in 1776.

But in the years following the Stamp Act the British government demonstrated an insensitivity to colonial rights and interests. The character and effects of British action is nowhere more clearly revealed than in Dickerson's study of the Navigation Acts. While agreeing with the Imperial historians that the old colonial system neither hampered the colonial economy nor provoked colonial resentment, Dickerson shows that after 1767 the creation of an American Board of Customs commissioners led to "customs racketeering," as Dickerson terms the practices of customs officials, which brought grief to merchants, ship owners, and small traders. Dickerson has also shown in "Use Made of the Revenue from the Tax on Tea," *New England Quarterly* (Boston), XXI (June, 1958), 232-43, that the feeding of the tea tax into patronage inserted a new force into American politics and alienated important commercial groups.

Dickerson's book provides an explanation of merchant leadership in the resistance to British measures after 1763. But for the story of the merchants' tangled efforts to oppose the British and at the same time repress the swelling lower-class participation in politics, one must consult Arthur M. Schlesinger's admirable *The Colonial Merchants and the American Revolution* (New York, 1918). Although many recent works demonstrate that group conflict was not as great as Schlesinger thought, his book remains one of the three or four most important books on the Revolution. Support for Schlesinger's views may be found in Carl Lotus Becker's *The History of Political Parties in the Province of New York, 1760-1776* (Madison, 1909).

One particular source of concern to merchants and to many others as well were the Vice-Admiralty Courts. Carl Ubbelohde's *The Vice-Admiralty Courts and the American Revolution* (Chapel Hill, 1960) describes their working and shows that their operating without juries was a persistent threat to liberty in colonial minds. David S. Lovejoy's "Rights Imply Equality: The Case Against Admiralty Jurisdiction in America, 1764-1776," *William and Mary Quarterly*, 3rd ser., XVI (October, 1959), 459-84, explains the American concern with clarity and force.

The intellectual and social background of the American Revolution is now being studied intensively. A pioneer volume which still merits great respect was Moses Coit Tyler's *The Literary History of the American Revolution* (2 vols.; New York, 1897). Three narrower studies have recently appeared. Caroline Robbins' *Eighteenth-Century Commonwealthman* (Cambridge, Mass., 1959) helps explain how radical seventeenth-century political thinking was perpetuated and made available to the American revolutionaries.[23] Robert Brown's study of the franchise in Massachusetts (cited above) suggests that the claims of the Americans that they sought only to defend liberties already obtained had a basis in fact. And Carl Bridenbaugh's studies of cities, *Cities in the Wilderness: The First Century of Urban Life in America, 1625-1742* (New York, 1938), and *Cities in Revolt: Urban Life in America, 1743-1776* (New York, 1955), help clarify the social setting of American protests.

The latest study of Revolutionary ideas is Bernard Bailyn's "General Introduction: The Transforming Radicalism of the American Revolution," in *Pamphlets of the American Revolution, 1750-1776* (Cambridge, Mass., 1965), pp. 1-202. In it Bailyn gives old familiar materials a fresh analysis; his application of Caroline Robbins' discoveries in her *Eighteenth-Century Commonwealthman* is especially rewarding. Perhaps the most original portion of Bailyn's study is the discussion of the American fear of conspiracy in which he shows how this fear becomes embedded in Revolutionary politics and in Revolutionary ideas.

These books, and those by the Morgans, Dickerson, and numerous studies of the coming of the Revolution in the individual states suggest that an intensive study of the American response to Imperial reorganization offers the most revealing approach for an understanding of the coming of the Revolution.[24] The focus in short should be on America,

23. *The Eighteenth-Century Commonwealth, Studies in the Transmission, Development and Circumstance of English Liberal Thought from the Restoration of Charles II until the War with the Thirteen Colonies.*

24. Among the best studies of the states are John R. Alden, *The South in the Revolution, 1763-1789* (Baton Rouge, 1957); Charles Albro Barker, *The Background of the Revolution in Maryland* (New Haven, 1940); Robert J. Taylor, *Western Massachusetts in the Revolution* (Providence, 1954); David S. Lovejoy, *Rhode Island Politics and the American Revolution, 1760-1776* (Providence, 1958); Theodore Thayer, *Pennsylvania Politics and the Growth of Democracy, 1740-1776* (Harrisburg, Pa., 1953); William W. Abbot, *The Royal Governors of Georgia, 1754-1775* (Chapel Hill, 1959); Kenneth Coleman, *The American Revolution in Georgia, 1763-1789* (Athens, Ga.,

not the Empire. The Americans made the Revolution; they must be understood if the Revolution is to be comprehended. Administrative historians who study the origins of colonial policies and the workings of Imperial agencies provide useful information, but they delude themselves when they claim that they explain colonial history, or the American Revolution.

At present no general interpretation of colonial American history commands wide approval. Although the insights of the Imperial school still deserve respect, their general view seems less important than it once did. Colonial historians continue to ask the big questions about early American history, but they seem dedicated to working out their answers on a piecemeal basis. And they perhaps respect fact even more than their predecessors did.

A respect for fact and for the small-scale study are all to the good, but one must also admire the Imperial historians for their willingness to work on the broad scale. They wanted to see things whole; their histories, for all their defects, are impressive for what they attempted. We need today more such attempts, but they should focus more on the colonies themselves and less on the Empire. In particular we need fresh theories of social change; the old metaphors taken from nature are tired. We need theories—not a single theory that pretends to account for change in all the colonies. The local character of American colonial history clearly demands varieties in explanations. If in such explanations the ties to the Empire appear relatively less important than local conditions, we should not entirely forget the great idea of the Imperial historians. It should serve not as a controlling idea but as an inspiration for further attempts to reconstruct the American colonial past.

---

1958); and the volumes of Becker and Brown, previously mentioned. John C. Miller's superb biography, *Sam Adams, Pioneer in Propaganda* (Boston, 1936), adds much to our knowledge of the Revolution in Massachusetts, and his *Origins of the American Revolution* (Boston, 1943) is an able general account. Readers should also consult two recent books: Carl Bridenbaugh, *Mitre and Sceptre: Transatlantic Faiths, Ideas, Personalities, and Politics, 1689-1775* (New York, 1962) for an argument, sometimes overdrawn, about the part colonial fears of an Anglican bishopric in America played in the coming of the Revolution; and Bernhard Knollenberg, *Origin of the American Revolution, 1759-1766* (New York, 1960), which treats the same problem briefly and well, shifting the beginnings of the Revolution to the decade of the 1750's.

# THE EMPIRE SINCE 1783

## John S. Galbraith

ON THE EVE of World War I, James Bryce, comparing the British and the Roman Empires, found no evidence of serious internal or external threats which could portend that the British Empire might soon suffer the fate of Rome.[1] Just before World War II, in the environment of the Munich agreement, Robert Briffault pronounced *The Decline and Fall of the British Empire*.[2] Bryce's optimism proved excessive, for war altered the character of the world and weakened the vitality of the British society; Briffault's announcement of the Empire's decease, on the other hand, was premature. But both found it appropriate to associate Imperial Britain with Imperial Rome.

The British, like the Romans, were law-givers. The political empire might disintegrate, but the law remained; and, said Bryce, "the world is, or will shortly be, practically divided between two sets of legal conceptions of rules, and two only."[3] In the nineteenth and twentieth centuries the Empire transformed itself into the British Commonwealth of Nations, and after World War II, when Great Britain released her hold upon India and other dependencies in Asia and Africa, they with few exceptions chose to remain in the community. This feat of legerdemain almost universally evoked admiration in the Western world; the genius may not have been exclusively British, and the changes were dictated by the realities of life, but the achievement was impressive. Since this translation of an empire into a commonwealth was accomplished by constitutional means, students of the Empire naturally have been preoccupied with analysis of changing constitutional relationships within the Commonwealth association. The dominant emphases have been the development of free institutions in the col-

1. Bryce, *The Ancient Roman Empire and the British Empire in India: The Diffusion of Roman and English Law throughout the World* (London, 1914), p. 76.
2. New York, 1938.
3. Bryce, *The Ancient Roman Empire and the British Empire in India*, p. 132.

onies, the growth of the Dominions to autonomy, and the establishment of a multicentered Commonwealth. The great names—Durham, Laurier, Smuts, Balfour—have related to these developments.

Since the "commonwealth idea" developed first in relation to colonies dominated by European settlers, nineteenth-century prophets of a "Greater Britain" thought of people of European and primarily of English-speaking origin. Charles W. Dilke's Greater Britain was the expansion of the "Saxon race," embracing not only the colonies but the United States.[4] John R. Seeley in his *The Expansion of England* (London, 1883) wrote that India could not be part of Greater Britain in the same sense as the "tens of millions of Englishmen" who lived outside the British Isles. James Anthony Froude's *Oceana* (London, 1886) was inhabited by Europeans, most of whom spoke English. Constitutional and legal historians of the twentieth century also have been concerned primarily with the empire of settlement, since nationalism in the self-governing colonies was producing changes in the structure of the Empire.

Before World War II a number of excellent studies appeared on the evolution of the British Empire to the Commonwealth of Nations. Alexander Gordon Dewey, *The Dominions and Diplomacy: The Canadian Contribution* (2 vols.; London, 1929), though it stressed the rôle of the statesmen of one Dominion, is nevertheless an excellent analysis of the changing character of the Commonwealth, in which Canada played a leading part. The theme is the conflict between the centralizers represented by Joseph Chamberlain and others, and the nationalists whose spokesmen were Laurier and Borden with varying degrees of support from other Dominions, and the eventual triumph of decentralization. Alexander Brady's *Democracy in the Dominions* (Toronto, 1947; 3rd. ed., 1958) likewise described a commonwealth dominated by men of European origin.

The legal characteristics of this "white commonwealth" also attracted considerable attention. Perhaps the most erudite, certainly the most prolific, of the prewar legal historians was Arthur Berriedale Keith. Keith's learning was awesome and his productivity prodigious, but his concentration on the legalities provided little insight into the essential

4. Dilke, *Greater Britain* (London, 1868) and *Problems of Greater Britain* (London, 1890). Comparisons between the two volumes are revealing not only of fundamental changes in Dilke's thinking on the Empire but of the attitude of British society generally. In both, however, the preoccupation is with colonies of settlement.

nature of the Commonwealth association. Since the passage of the Statute of Westminster there have been a large number of works on the constitutions of the Commonwealth and its internal political relationships. Kenneth C. Wheare's *The Statute of Westminster and Dominion Status* (Oxford), first published in 1938, has now reached five editions (the latest published in 1953), each embodying recent changes in the Commonwealth. Significantly in the latest edition Wheare has added a chapter titled "The End of Dominion Status," in which he states that the word "dominion," once a symbol of freedom, has now lost favor as implying the status of an adolescent rather than an adult.

This loss of caste for a designation formerly in high repute coincided with the transformation of the Commonwealth into a multiracial association in which the member states seemed to have few significant substantive or symbolic ties. The layman might wonder if the community had not transformed itself out of existence; not so the legal metaphysician who with impressive acumen explained the Commonwealth in the new era. Among the most valuable analyses of the postwar Commonwealth are Wheare's *The Constitutional Structure of the Commonwealth* (Oxford, 1960), and several works by Sir (William) Ivor Jennings. *Constitutional Laws of the Commonwealth*, Volume I: *The Monarchies*, was published in 1957 (London); a second, on the republics, has not yet appeared. The extent of the change in the Commonwealth is reflected in the contrast between this volume and the first edition, published in 1938 with the collaboration of Miss Charlotte M. Young under the title *Constitutional Laws of the British Empire*. Jennings also, in *Problems of the New Commonwealth* (Durham, N.C., 1958),[5] provides an analysis of recent developments in India, Pakistan, and Ceylon, interspersed with comments on the general character of British rule and its legacy to the Asian communities. Other works by Jennings of particular interest are *The Commonwealth in Asia* (Oxford, 1951) and *The Approach to Self-Government* (Cambridge, 1956). A series of special value for students of the laws of individual Commonwealth states is *The British Commonwealth, The Development of Its Laws and Constitutions*, under the general editorship of George W. Keeton. Ten volumes have been published. The first to appear (though Volume II in the series) was George W. Paton, ed., *The Commonwealth*

---

5. Jennings' volume is one of a series of studies on the Commonwealth and its member states published under the sponsorship of the Commonwealth-Studies Center at Duke University.

of *Australia* (London, 1952) and the latest is Taslim Olawale Elias, ed., *Ghana and Sierra Leone* (London, 1962). Other volumes consider the evolution of law in the United Kingdom, Canada, New Zealand, South Africa, India, Pakistan, and Malaya and Singapore.

(Philip) Nicholas Mansergh in *The Commonwealth and the Nations* (London, 1948) provides a succinct account of the changes produced in the Commonwealth by World War II. Another significant constitutional study is Geoffrey Marshall's *Parliamentary Sovereignty and the Commonwealth* (Oxford, 1957), an analysis of the effects of the Statute of Westminster on the legislative authority of the Imperial and Dominion parliaments. A noteworthy study of recent Commonwealth developments which might be described either as contemporary political analysis or history is John D. B. Miller, *The Commonwealth in the World* (Cambridge, Mass., 1958).

Since World War I and particularly since the Statute of Westminster there has been increasing reason to question whether the community known as the British Commonwealth of Nations and, later, merely the Commonwealth of Nations, was in fact a community. The "barrel without hoops," some argued, had ceased to be a barrel. The Balfour Report of 1926 had described the association as "united by a common allegiance to the Crown" and founded on "positive ideals." But was there a common purpose? Lionel Curtis had warned in 1916 that if the Imperial Commonwealth were broken into a number of states, each pursuing its own foreign policy, the survival of the Empire, and indeed of each of its member states, was in jeopardy. Curtis contended that had statesmanship preserved the community with the North American colonies, Napoleon could never have aspired to dominion over Europe, and if the British Empire had established an effective organization before 1914, the Germans would not have broken the peace of the world. The next ambitious tyrant, he warned, might also be tempted by manifestations of Imperial disunity; and he might not fail.[6] But the fragmentation which Curtis feared had become a reality in the 1920's. The late Vincent T. Harlow has pointed out in a recent essay that analyses of the Commonwealth and World War I have been in fact examinations of international relations, with aspects of the policies of each of the member states being selected and compared.[7] Gerald Palmer's

6. Curtis, *The Commonwealth of Nations*, Pt. I (London, 1916).
7. Harlow, "The Historiography of the British Empire and Commonwealth since

handbook, *Consultation and Co-operation in the British Common-wealth* . . . (London, 1934), though a description of methods and mechanisms of communication, provides striking evidence of the domination of decentralizing tendencies after 1887. Gwendolen M. Carter, *The British Commonwealth and International Security: The Role of the Dominions, 1919-1939* (Toronto, 1947), and Charles A. W. Manning, *The Policies of the British Dominions in the League of Nations* (London, 1932), demonstrate that Dominion opposition to general or regional security agreements contributed to weakening the League of Nations as an instrumentality of world order. Nicholas Mansergh's masterly volumes further delineate the distinctive attributes and aspirations of the members of the Commonwealth.[8] Unquestionably the focus of attention among historians of the twentieth-century Commonwealth has been on the distinctive national histories of the member states. Those who have sought to deal with the Commonwealth as a whole have been concerned almost entirely with constitutional or diplomatic issues.

Restrictions imposed by the Official Secrets Act, the fifty-year rule on public documents, and other limitations on access to the documents force the historian of the twentieth century to depend primarily upon printed materials. Tantalizing hints of what may be in store when the archives are opened appear when excerpts from a statesman's private papers are published; such a glimpse was provided by John W. Pickersgill's edition of the diaries of William Lyon Mackenzie King in *The Mackenzie King Record*, I: *1939-1944* (Toronto, 1960), and more insights may be gained from H. Blair Neatby's *William Lyon MacKenzie King, 1924-1952: The Lonely Heights* (Toronto, 1963) and in Sir William Keith Hancock's biography of Smuts—*Smuts, the Official Biography*, I: *The Sanguine Years, 1870-1919* (Cambridge, 1962) and his edition of the Smuts papers. But for long, much of the essential documentation will continue to be enveloped in government secrecy.

Despite the limitations of the available sources, Hancock, in his

---

1945," *Rapports* V, *Histoire Contemporaine*, International Committee of Historical Sciences, Stockholm, August 21-28, 1960 (Uppsala, 1960), 11.

8. Mansergh, *Survey of British Commonwealth Affairs: Problems of External Policy, 1931-1939* (London, 1952); *Survey of British Commonwealth Affairs: Problems of Wartime Co-operation and Post-War Change, 1939-1952* (London, 1958); *Documents and Speeches on British Commonwealth Affairs, 1931-1952* (2 vols., London, 1953).

*Survey of British Commonwealth Affairs* (2 vols.; second in two parts, London, 1937-42), broke away from established patterns and by applying a different approach to the study of the Empire and Commonwealth gave a fresh interpretation of Imperial history. Rather than attempting to "cover" all events in the Commonwealth in general terms, or merely to concentrate on particular aspects, he chose to select certain areas and problems which he analyzed in depth; these specific studies provide insights into the complexities of Imperial history which would not have been possible by any other method. In his second volume, *Problems of Economic Policy*, Professor Hancock provides a brilliant analysis of the various factors affecting the expansion of the British Empire and suggests new directions in scholarship.

Hancock, in the words of Vincent T. Harlow, "achieved 'holism' by selectivity." Philip Curtin in a recent article has suggested that a broad synthesis of Imperial history in the nineteenth and twentieth centuries is probably out of the question. The Empire, he says, "is not only an ungainly beast, but one that constantly changes its size and shape with the passing of the years," and no historian can be a master of all of its aspects.[9] Certainly the characteristics of scholarship thus far document the truth of his observation. Some historians describe colonial policy during certain periods or in particular areas; some are preoccupied with the development of self-governing institutions at particular times or in particular colonies; some focus their attention on the administrative machinery, some on the economic aspects, some on the metropolis, others on the overseas dependencies. A synthesis, if it is ever written, must certainly be far distant, for the study of British Imperial history is still in its infancy and the problems to be considered are complex.

In various aspects of nineteenth-century Imperial history excellent monographic studies have already appeared upon which historians can build. A pioneer work in the administrative history of the Empire is Helen Taft Manning's *British Colonial Government After the American Revolution, 1782-1820* (New Haven, 1933). After thirty years her description of the machinery of government in Britain and the colonies remains a basic contribution to the administrative history of the Empire. Other first-rate histories of Imperial administration have ap-

9. Philip Curtin, "The British Empire and Commonwealth in Recent Historiography," *American Historical Review* (Washington), LXV (Oct., 1959), 72.

peared recently. Ralph B. Pugh's chapter in *The Cambridge History of the British Empire*, III: *The Empire Commonwealth, 1870-1919* (Cambridge, 1959), on "The Colonial Office 1801-1925," is the best account yet produced of the changing characteristics of the office. Some of the most useful analyses of the structure and functions of the Colonial Office have appeared in articles in scholarly journals rather than in book form. Two of the best are John C. Beaglehole, "The Colonial Office, 1782-1854," and E. Trevor Williams, "The Colonial Office in the Thirties," both of which were published in *Historical Studies: Australia and New Zealand* (Melbourne).[10]

Henry L. Hall's *The Colonial Office* (London, 1937), while of some value, suffers by comparison and is marred by a plethora of errors. Dallas McMurray Young, *The Colonial Office in the Early Nineteenth Century* (London, 1961), should be read as a supplement to Manning and Pugh, covering as it does the period 1801-1830. The development of the Colonial service has not yet received the attention of a careful historian, though Charles Jeffries, *The Colonial Empire and Its Civil Service* (Cambridge, 1938), is an excellent general account by an official of the Colonial Office. Anton Bertram, *The Colonial Service* (Cambridge, 1930), surveys the characteristics of the contemporary service rather than its evolution. There is need for studies of other departments of government which had relation to colonial policy, in particular the Treasury, and of the development of the Colonial Office itself in the period after that studied by Manning and Young.

Since sea power has been the basis for British survival and for the security of Imperial trade, maritime history has engaged the attention of many scholars, and some of the classic works in the English language—Mahan, Corbett, and others—have dealt with the rôle of the navy in the history of the British Empire. But in the twentieth century the study of maritime history has taken on new dimensions. It concerns itself not only with sea fights and with strategy and tactics, but with the interrelationships of sea power with technological developments, commercial policy, and Imperial expansion. Among those who have contributed most to broaden the scope of the study of maritime history is Gerald S. Graham. In an essay on "The Maritime Foundations of Imperial History," Graham pointed out that sea power was an artificial creation rather than an expression of "natural aptitude," and that

10. Beaglehole, I (April, 1941), 170-89; and Williams, II (May, 1943), 141-60.

the contributions of statesmen consequently were of fundamental importance—"Britannia's sceptre was largely a product of Whitehall and Westminster." In the nineteenth century much of British expansion was the fortuitous result of the dominance of the Royal Navy rather than of deliberate national policy.[11] Graham's *Sea Power and British North America, 1783-1820* (Cambridge, Mass., 1941), and *Empire of the North Atlantic* (Toronto, 1950), analyze the implications of British sea power in the North Atlantic world. Another study, with its focus on the Indian Ocean, is now in progress. As the works of Graham illustrate, most scholarship in maritime history has been concerned with particular regions of oceans and land masses. Among the most rewarding of such books are Winston F. Monk's *Britain in the Western Mediterranean* (London, 1953) and Cyril Northcote Parkinson's *Trade in the Eastern Seas, 1793-1815* (Cambridge, 1937). The importance of the Navy in forcing open the channels of trade is emphasized in a superb book by John King Fairbank, *Trade and Diplomacy on the China Coast: The Opening of the Treaty Ports, 1842-1854* (Cambridge, 1953), a model of scholarship drawn from English and Chinese sources. Also noteworthy are the works of Arthur J. Marder. *The Anatomy of British Sea Power* (New York, 1940) is a study of British naval policy in the pre-dreadnought era. Its sequel, *From the Dreadnought to Scapa Flow*, I (London, 1961), utilizes documents not previously available to any non-official historian in describing the British aspect of Anglo-German naval rivalry during the "Fisher era" and World War I to the scuttling of the German fleet in June, 1919. Marder has also published selections from the correspondence of Admiral Fisher in *Fear God and Dreadnought* (3 vols.; London, 1952-59).

The implications for the British Empire of the transition from sail to steam and in the revolutionary changes in the construction of war vessels have been examined by maritime historians, but the broader problems of the influence of technological developments such as the cable and the wireless on the character of Imperial policy and the structure of the Empire have received relatively little attention. Fifty years ago Sir Charles P. Lucas wrote a brief sketch on "The Influence of

11. Graham, "The Maritime Foundations of Imperial History," *Canadian Historical Review* (Toronto), XXXI (June, 1950), 113-24.

Science on Empire,"[12] but no historian has yet undertaken an exhaustive examination of this important subject.

The study of British colonial policy in the nineteenth century has been characterized at one extreme by monographs dealing with specific geographical areas and with restricted periods of time, involving two or three decades, and on the other by highly imaginative syntheses based on scanty documentation. Works in the first category relate primarily to the period from the American Revolution to the 1870's, and in the latter to the "Age of Imperialism" which followed. Vincent T. Harlow's *The Founding of the Second British Empire, 1763-1793* (London), the first volume of which appeared in 1952, suggested that the conventional chronological compartments of "first" and "second" Empires were a product of historians' parochialism, that the "second" Empire, which directed its energies toward the Eastern trade, began before the "first" Empire had ended. No studies of comparable scope have appeared in relation to the subsequent period. Probably the closest approach to such a broad synthesis was William Parker Morrell's *British Colonial Policy in the Age of Peel and Russell* (Oxford, 1930), which after more than thirty years still stands as an essential work on the motives and characteristics of British policy in the early Victorian era. But there are few studies which can be classed with Morrell's and Harlow's in terms of imaginative scholarship based upon intensive research.

The restrictions which confine historians of nineteenth-century British colonial policy are in part related to the mass of the documents, but to a considerable extent they have been imposed by the limitations of the historians themselves. Much error has been perpetuated and dignified by age and unquestioning dependence upon previous authority; and much distortion has been produced by the narrowness of specialists who in their concentration on their own little universes have ignored the wider context within which their special interests should be understood. Obviously no man, however diligent, can review all of the documentary collections relating to the British Empire in the nineteenth century. But in too many instances scholars have demonstrated their unawareness of published works which, though not bearing directly on their special subject, would have contributed to a deeper insight.

12. Lucas, in F. J. C. Hearnshaw, ed., *King's College Lectures on Colonial Problems* (London, 1913), pp. 109-39.

These comments apply with particular force to the sphere of Imperial policy, where hoary generalizations have stood for years unchallenged because they have not been subjected to critical analysis. Only within the last few years have scholars begun to make a reassessment, and the results of recent investigations suggest that a radically new approach to British Imperial history is likely to emerge. When historians accept without question "facts" which are demonstrably untrue, it is not surprising that they should repeat unsound generalizations. An illustration of the hazards of pyramiding on previous authority is the perpetuation of the assumption that James Anthony Froude incorrectly described Adelaide in his *Oceana*, an error which was a manifestation of "Froude's disease," first diagnosed by Edward Freeman. The oracles on the weighing of historical evidence, Langlois and Seignobos, cited H. A. L. Fisher on this subject; and Allen Johnson in his book, *The Historian and Historical Evidence* (New York, 1926), taking his illustration from Langlois and Seignobos, warned young scholars to avoid Froude's inaccuracy, as did James Ford Rhodes in an address to the American Historical Association in 1900. None of them had examined the facts; if they had done so they would have found that Froude was substantially correct and his detractors in error.[13] Likewise, historians of British colonial policy long accepted a framework of ideas established by Arthur P. Newton, Hugh E. Egerton, and others of their generation.[14] This orthodoxy included in its terminology such concepts as "the old colonial system," "mercantilism," "the Manchester School," Little Englanders, Liberal Imperialists, Colonial Reformers, Prestige Imperialists, and Imperialists devoid of any prefix. The interpretation of Imperial history has been greatly influenced by the viewpoints expressed by Edward Gibbon Wakefield and his associates. The clear vision of the Colonial Reformers and the shortsightedness of their opponents was the *leitmotif*.[15] The villains were "Little Englanders" and the "Colonial Office bureaucracy," in particular the permanent undersecretary, James Stephen. Largely as a result of the research of Paul Knaplund, embodied in his *James Stephen and the British Colonial System, 1813-1847* (Madison, 1953), Stephen's character and in-

13. For a discussion of this matter, see Andrew Fish, "The Reputation of James Anthony Froude," *Pacific Historical Review* (Glendale, Cal.), I (June, 1932), 179-92.

14. See for example, Egerton, *A Short History of British Colonial Policy, 1606-1909*, revised by Newton (12th ed., London, 1950).

15. This tradition is illustrated by Egerton, "The Colonial Reformers of 1830," in Hearnshaw, ed., *King's College Lectures on Colonial Problems*, pp. 143-80.

fluence have been reassessed, and it has been demonstrated that the permanent undersecretary was an enlightened and devoted public servant, with no resemblance to the dusty, myopic "Mr. Mothercountry" described by Charles Buller. But much of the framework established by the Wakefieldians has remained, and the magic of Wakefield continues to exercise its spell. Paul Bloomfield, *Edward Gibbon Wakefield: Builder of the British Commonwealth* (London, 1961), describes "this strange far-sighted man" as the "founder of an Empire" whose accomplishments included saving Australia from being a semi-tropical Siberia and inspiring the Durham Report. In the best Wakefieldian tradition, Bloomfield castigates historians who do not share his enthusiasm.

One of the most influential books in the older tradition has been Carl A. Bodelsen, *Studies in Mid-Victorian Imperialism* (Copenhagen, 1924). There has been a continuing demand for this book, which has become a standard authority; it has recently been reprinted (London, 1960). Bodelsen's appraisal of the nineteenth-century Empire was similar to that of Egerton, Newton, and Charles P. Lucas. Like them, Bodelson relied primarily upon published writings and speeches as reported in Hansard; like his progenitors he was concerned primarily with the political relations between Britain and the colonies of settlement. Thus his "imperialism" is in the sense of Seeley and Froude rather than John A. Hobson and V. I. Lenin.

Bodelsen saw the conflicts in Imperial policy during the middle years of the nineteenth century in terms of the clash between Little Englanders and Liberal Imperialists. The distinguished American historian Robert Livingston Schuyler adopted a similar approach to the nineteenth-century Empire. In an article in 1921 he stated that "many of the leading statesmen of England and the officials most closely concerned with colonial administration" contemplated the break-up of the British Empire "with feelings ranging from resignation to pleasure" and that during the decade 1861 to 1870, "a critical period in British imperial history," the doctrines of the Manchester School reached the height of their influence.[16] Schuyler's *The Fall of the Old Colonial System: A Study in British Free Trade, 1770-1870* (New York, 1945), based on four articles published between 1917 and 1922, develops this

---

16. Schuyler, "The Climax of Anti-Imperialism in England," *Political Science Quarterly* (New York), XXXVI (Dec., 1921), 537-60.

theme of the retreat of mercantilism before the advance of the free-trade movement and the ascendancy of Little England before 1870.

Writers of the old school, although they wrote of economic phenomena, were political in their orientation. Their narratives were of party conflicts, parliamentary debates, cabinet caucuses, and government decisions. But even appraised in their own terms, these historians were subject to attack for drawing unwarranted conclusions. Paul Knaplund, for example, in *Gladstone and Britain's Imperial Policy* (New York, 1927), argued persuasively that Gladstone was no "Little Englander" but a prophet of a commonwealth based upon sentiment and interest rather than coercion.

Of course Gladstone during a long career adopted positions on specific issues not easily reconcilable with each other, and any attempt to force his words and actions into a particular concept of Empire expressed in a word or a phrase must involve distortion. The efforts of historians to label statesmen as protagonists of this view or that usually reveal more of the characteristics of the historian than they do of the statesmen. One book which warns against the tendency to construct an artificial consistency from the speeches and writings of politicians responding to events in particular places and particular times is Klaus E. Knorr, *British Colonial Theories, 1570-1850* (Toronto, 1944), one of the most perceptive analyses of the assumptions underlying British colonial policy. George R. Mellor's *British Imperial Trusteeship, 1783-1850* (London, 1951), though it does not escape entirely the temptation to oversimplify, is a work of sound scholarship which points up the fact that Imperial policy might be very different in enunciation than in execution—" exhortations from Downing Street, transmitted through the medium of colonial proclamations and Ordinances, failed to evoke golden conduct from those with leaden instincts."

The second volume of the *Cambridge History of the British Empire* (Cambridge, 1940), concerned with "The Growth of the New Empire, 1783-1870," appeared at a time when the structure of interpretation represented by Schuyler and others was yet virtually unchallenged. Hrothgar J. Habbakkuk, discussing "Free Trade and Commercial Expansion, 1853-1870," accepted the view that in the middle years of the century there was a "tacit assumption among moderate and reasonable men that colonial separation was inevitable and desirable." But there was already evidence of restiveness in some contributors to this volume with the Wakefieldian dichotomy of enlightened Colonial Reformer and benighted Little Englander and with the excessive concentration on narrow political interpretation. Charles R. Fay called attention to the growth of the empire of commerce extending beyond the empire of the flag. Earlier, in his *Imperial Economy and its Place in the Foundation of Economic Doctrine, 1600-1932* (Oxford, 1934), he had coined the phrase "informal empire" to describe the expansion of Britain's commercial and financial power beyond the bounds of political jurisdictions. Habbakkuk also probed deeply into organization of Imperial trade and finance. The broader and deeper context within which these historians appraised the Empire suggested a radically different approach to the study of Imperial policy, as did Hancock in the second volume of his *Survey of British Commonwealth Affairs*. Further impetus was provided for reinterpretation by John Gallagher and Ronald Robinson in an article in 1953.[17] With refreshing irreverence they attacked earlier interpreters of mid-Victorian Empire as narrowly racial and legalistic, blindly ignorant of much which was obvious but inconvenient and unable because of the limitations of their analyses to comprehend the basic character of the phenomena they attempted to describe. To Gallagher and Robinson the middle years of the nineteenth century were the golden age of British expansion. The extension of formal political control was a last resort—ministers desired to avoid the responsibilities and expense of colonial administration—but early as well as late Victorian ministries were prepared to support by appropriate means the interests of British commerce when those interests were threatened by obstruction or disorder. As is often true of revisionists they may have overstated their case in an effort to demolish old stereotypes and their analysis may have been too symmetrical, but they performed a significant service by forcing historians of the Empire to re-examine their assumptions. Their thesis has provoked a strong rebuttal by Oliver Macdonagh, who, in an article titled "The Anti-Imperialism of Free Trade,"[18] argues effectively that Gallagher and Robinson have been guilty of the sin of oversimplification for which they have taxed the earlier orthodoxy.

During the past decade there has been a marked increase in the intensity of controversy regarding the nature of Victorian Empire. Not

17. "The Imperialism of Free Trade," *The Economic History Review* (Utrecht), 2nd ser., VI (Aug., 1953), 1-15.

18. *Ibid.*, XIV (April, 1962), 489-501.

only have there been revisionists but revisionists of revisionists. David S. Landes, while accepting much of Gallagher and Robinson's thesis, contends that their analysis can account for only part—though a major part—of the phenomenon they describe, and that in particular it does not explain the occupation of large overseas areas for non-economic reasons.[19] John S. Galbraith in a recent article calls attention to the importance as a factor in British expansion of the "man on the spot" and the problem of the "turbulent frontier" with which he had to contend: "In India, Malaya, and South Africa, governors, charged with the maintenance of order, could not ignore disorder beyond their borders, turbulence which pulled them toward expansion."[20] The same author has further developed this theme in a book, *Reluctant Empire: British Policy on the South African Frontier, 1834-1854* (Berkeley, 1963). Bernard Semmel, accepting the view that the "Little England era" was a myth,[21] makes a convincing case for the contention that the Benthamite Radicals were advocates of empire rather than anti-colonial in their thinking.[22] The traditional conception of "the Manchester School" as the spokesman of laissez faire and Little England has been demonstrated to be largely fiction. William D. Grampp, *The Manchester School of Economics* (Stanford, 1960), shows that after the abolition of the Corn Laws the "school" had no cohesion beyond admiration for Cobden and Bright, that admiration did not imply commitment to the policies of these two men, and that there was no consistent or comprehensive body of doctrine to which the "Manchester School" gave allegiance. Helen Taft Manning, in "Colonial Crises before the Cabinet, 1829-1835," *Bulletin of the Institute of Historical Research* (London), XXX (May, 1957), 41-61, demonstrates that there was far greater concern about colonial problems among statesmen of the 1830's than has generally been assumed. "Mercantilism," for so long thought to be the antithesis of laissez faire, has been alleged to have little coherence as a label for any consistent body of doctrine,[23] and

19. Landes, "Some Thoughts on the Nature of Economic Imperialism," *Journal of Economic History* (New York), XXI (Dec., 1961), 496-512.

20. "The 'Turbulent Frontier' as a Factor in British Expansion," *Comparative Studies in Society and History* (The Hague), II (Jan., 1960), 168.

21. See my article "Myths of the Little England Era," *American Historical Review*, LXVII (Oct., 1961), 34-48.

22. Semmel, "The Philosophic Radicals and Colonialism," *Journal of Economic History*, XXI (Dec., 1961), 513-25.

23. See, for example, Charles Wilson, "'Mercantilism': Some Vicissitudes of an Idea," *Economic History Review*, 2nd ser., X (Dec., 1957), 181-88.

even laissez faire has been described as a "myth."[24] No part of the old orthodoxy has been safe from the attacks of iconoclasts.

Confronted by flatly contradictory interpretations, the recent initiate to the study of British Empire history is understandably perplexed. The ancient landmarks are in ruins, and no new structure has been established to replace them. The study of the nineteenth-century British Empire is in a phase akin to that of American history at the beginning of the twentieth century. As Frederick Jackson Turner struck at the heart of traditional interpretations, so also have a number of recent scholars in the Imperial field. Within the past ten years there has been a revolution in the characteristics of research on the British Empire. Some of the attacks on the old orthodoxy are unsound or exaggerated, but from the debate they engender a deeper understanding of the Empire is likely to develop.

This prospect is apparent in the study of the later Victorian Empire, "the Age of Imperialism." Here the heritage of the old orthodoxy has been characterized by an excess, not a lack, of imagination. Analyses of the "Little England era," whatever their defects, were usually based on industrious scholarship, at least in printed sources; interpretations of "imperialism" have been subject to no such earthbound restrictions. In no other era of British Empire history has so much dogmatism rested on so little evidence.

Professor Hancock in 1940 anathematized "imperialism" from the lexicon of scholars as a word which confused rather than communicated. "It does not convey a precise meaning," he said. "It is like a stage-screen from behind which may step the most oddly assorted figures—Lord Durham and Mr. Joseph Chamberlain and Mr. Asquith and Mr. R. B. Bennett and David Livingstone and Signor Mussolini."[25] Certainly this condemnation of the inexactitude of the label is as justified today as it was then. "Empire" also has been shown to be a word of uncertain meaning unless related to time and place. Richard Koebner's *Empire* (New York, 1961) demonstrates with impressive erudition the transmutations in the meaning of the word since the days of Imperial Rome. The first volume, published posthumously, ends with the Napoleonic period. A second, which carries the theme to

24. John Bartlet Brebner, "Laissez-Faire and State Intervention in Nineteenth Century Britain," *The Tasks of Economic History*, Supplement VIII, *Journal of Economic History* (1948), pp. 59-73.

25. Hancock, *Survey of British Commonwealth Affairs*, II, Pt. I, 1-2.

the present, has been prepared from Koebner's drafts and notes by Helmut D. Schmidt: *Imperialism: The Story and Significance of a Political Word, 1840-1960* (1963). Koebner contends that the usage of the term "British Empire" in the Tudor-Stuart era had little relation to "colonies." The modern implication developed after the union of England and Scotland, but even on the eve of the American Revolution, "empire" was being used with a variety of connotations.

Hancock and Koebner provide a salutary warning against the use of words with high emotional content and vague meaning. Even when applied to a particular era and a particular phenomenon "imperialism" has until recently been no word for scholars. The influence of the economic determinists has dominated the interpretation of the scramble for Africa. Koebner in 1949 described the "international *communis opinio*" for which the economic interpretation was "accepted fact."[26]

Standard textbooks in American universities, such as Parker T. Moon's *Imperialism and World Politics* (New York, 1926) and Mary Evelyn Townsend and Cyrus H. Peake's *European Colonial Expansion since 1871* (Chicago, 1941), described European diplomacy of the late nineteenth century as the superficial expression of imperialist rivalries which in turn were founded on the economic requirements of capitalist society in an industrial age. The schemata of their interpretations were generally beautifully simple, unmarred by vexing exceptions, reservations, or doubts. The economic interpretations from which such books were derived embraced several schools of thought. Some followed Hobson[27] in the assumption that the financier was the governor of the Imperial engine. Others found the explanation in the essence of monopoly capitalism—there were many variations of the theme. But it was an article of faith among these economic determinists that the motive-power of "imperialism" was the materialist drive of the bourgeoisie (non-Marxists might substitute another term) of the metropolitan power, who used the machinery of the state to advance their interests. This assumption has retained remarkable vitality in non-Marxist as well as in Marxist literature, despite its patent absurdity when applied to the area to which the term "imperialism" usually refers. As David S. Landes has pointed out, "Nothing fits the economic interpretation so poorly as the partition of Africa (South Africa and the Congo ex-

26. Koebner, "The Concept of Economic Imperialism," *Economic History Review*, 2nd ser., II (1949), 1-29.
27. John A. Hobson, *Imperialism: A Study* (London, 1902).

cepted)—that frantic scramble of industrial, industrializing, and pre-industrial European countries for some of the most unremunerative territory on the globe."[28]

A mass of documentation has demonstrated that Africa is a peculiarly inappropriate scene for a simple financial-commercial explanation of Imperial expansion. Leland Jenks, Herbert Feis, George Paish, Alexander K. Cairncross, and many others have driven this myth from the realm of scholarship.[29] Eugene Staley, *War and the Private Investor* (Garden City, 1935), has shown that businessmen were often the tools of governments rather than being themselves the manipulators. In a highly sophisticated analysis, *Studies in British Overseas Trade, 1870-1914* (Liverpool, 1960), Samuel B. Saul demonstrates that the rate of growth of British exports was greater in the two decades after 1870 than since, and probably before that time, and that the character of international finance has been greatly misrepresented by those who have sought an explanation of expansion in financial terms. Nowhere, Saul states, were the conditions contributing to expansion more complex than in West Africa, the alleged classic example of "imperialist exploitation." Mark Blaug, referring to the fact that the old stereotypes of economic imperialism are widely accepted in the new states of Africa and Asia, points out that, contrary to popular belief, the yield of capital is generally higher in a capital-rich economy than in a less-developed country and that "other things being equal," investors prefer to place their capital at home rather than abroad.[30] D. K. Fieldhouse, after analyzing various economic interpretations, concludes that imperialism owed its appeal not to the sinister influence of capitalists but to its inherent attractions for the masses, that it cannot be explained in terms of economic theory and the nature of financial capitalism, and that in its mature form it can most appropriately be described as a sociological rather than an economic phenomenon—"it can properly be understood only in terms of the same social hysteria that has since given birth to other and more disastrous forms of aggressive nation-

28. Landes, "The Nature of Economic Imperialism," p. 498.

29. Jenks, *The Migration of British Capital to 1875* (New York, 1927); Feis, *Europe, the World's Banker* (London, 1930); Paish, "Great Britain's Investments in Individual Colonial and Foreign Countries," *Journal of the Royal Statistical Society* (London), LXXIV (Jan., 1911), 167-87; Cairncross, *Home and Foreign Investment, 1870-1913* (Cambridge, 1953).

30. Blaug, "Economic Imperialism Revisited," *Yale Review* (New Haven), L (Spring, 1961), 335-49.

alism."[31] Observing the repeated explosions of the economic theory by learned authors in scholarly journals, one may wonder whether they are not attacking a target already obliterated, since the thesis they seek to demolish has few if any adherents among non-Marxist scholars, and the mythology which lives on among non-scholars is probably immune to demolition by facts. But zestful attacks on an outmoded theory may produce new error by overcorrection. The economic interpretation, as Landes asserts, "is not a figment of doctrinaire imagination. It casts light upon an important causal relationship, and the effort of certain anti-Marxists to dismiss it completely has only compelled them to erect other myths in its place." Further, mere denial of the economic interpretation or avowal that the causes were complex does not explain late Victorian expansion. Such an interpretation must be based on a profound understanding of the characteristics not only of British but of European society and of the interrelationships of that community of competitors. One effort to make an analysis in depth is George W. F. Hallgarten's *Imperialismus vor 1914* (2 vols.; Munich, 1951). Although much of the book is concerned with German expansion, it is a study not merely of German imperialism but of the entire European international system before World War I. Hallgarten's thesis is that every action of political significance was the result of an "aggregate" of interests. These "interests" were primarily but not exclusively economic; they were associated with the dynamic of the society of which they were a part. Landes in the essay referred to above describes "imperialism as a multifarious response to a common opportunity that consists simply in disparity of power." Whatever the policies of the imperial nation, Landes states, its citizens—businessmen, missionaires, soldiers of fortune—exploited on their own initiative the opportunities offered. Imperialism was only "the last phase of a millennial explosion," expressing "a fundamental and continuing shift in the balance of power between Europe and the rest of the world."[32]

In the study of the late-Victorian Empire, there are encouraging indications that scholarship can produce significant interpretations based on sound research. Earlier it had seemed that the minds pregnant with glittering generalizations and those loaded with facts belonged to different worlds and that never the twain would meet. A brilliantly

31. Fieldhouse, " 'Imperialism': An Historiographical Revision," *Economic History Review*, 2nd ser., XIV (Dec., 1961), 187-209.

32. Landes, "The Nature of Economic Imperialism," pp. 498, 510, 512.

argued and impressively documented new interpretation of British policy in Africa during the scramble is provided by Ronald Robinson and John Gallagher (with Alice Denny) in *Africa and the Victorians* (London, 1961). Subtitled *The Official Mind of Imperialism*, this book is based upon intensive research in official archives and private papers.

To an extent the authors support a thesis first enunciated by Joseph R. Schumpeter in *Imperialism and Social Classes* (1919; reprinted, Oxford, 1951) that imperialism was not a product of the requirements of industrial-financial capitalism but of the characteristics of a ruling class which was becoming an anachronism. The men who made the basic decisions, the authors point out, were representatives of an aristocratic tradition extending back for generations. Salisbury and others in positions of power at Whitehall were imbued with the conviction that statesmanship must be dedicated to the preservation of national security and power, not the advancement of special interests within the society, economic or otherwise. In the halcyon days of British imperialism before the 1870's, British interests had generally been advanced without the necessity of annexation, and there had been no impulse to extend political control in Africa. But in the 1880's the sea route was threatened by the collapse of the Khedive's government. Security could no longer be maintained by informal influence; Gladstone's government was driven to an occupation from which it was unable to extricate itself. That occupation was not dictated by bondholders but by the necessity of protecting the Canal. British intervention in Egypt precipitated the "scramble" of the European powers in Africa. An embittered France retaliated by annexations in West Africa; and Germany, primarily for diplomatic rather than for trading purposes, acted aggressively in both the east and west. No longer could private trade in Africa be conducted by influence alone. In general, however, the authors maintain, the partition of tropical Africa preceded rather than followed the development of trade. The extension of territorial claims required commercial expansion rather than the reverse, as has usually been assumed. The causes of expansion in South Africa were different from those in the north and central areas. In the south, Britain was compelled to intervene, not by the disintegration of a native government, but by the growth of Transvaal power. But the objectives of British policy there as elsewhere were primarily political rather than economic. The partition of Africa was not a manifestation of a revolution in the characteristics of European economic life; the "Age of Imperialism" was produced by strategic and diplomatic considerations, not by a new economic mandate.

In its emphasis on Egypt, the Robinson and Gallagher interpretation is akin to that of William L. Langer's *The Diplomacy of Imperialism, 1890-1902* (2 vols.; New York, 1935), which also stressed the importance of the occupation of Egypt in providing an impetus to expansion, but they go much further than did he in the emphasis on Egypt as the great proximate cause for imperialism in Africa. Robinson and Gallagher, in their zeal to demolish old myths and to document their thesis, may have been led to oversimplification. Certainly there were manifestations before 1882 of a new European aggressiveness not only in Africa but in Asia and the Pacific, which their analysis does not sufficiently take into consideration. But they have produced a book which must stimulate the re-examination of the "Age of Imperialism."

Another new work on European expansion in Africa, based on intensive research in French and British archives, is John D. Hargreaves, *Prelude to the Partition of West Africa* (London, 1963). Hargreaves' study relates to the period ending in 1885, by which time "claims had been established in the coastal regions which to a considerable degree determined the pattern of interior penetration and conquest." The author avoids high-flown generalizations, but he argues convincingly that expansion in West Africa, at least so far as Britain and France were concerned, was basically influenced by "the tactical needs of their complex European policy." Hargreaves brings an additional dimension to his research by his analysis of the objectives of African rulers in relation to Europeans. He shows that though these rulers sometimes were tools of Europeans they often were successful in using Europeans for the advancement of their own objectives—elimination of commercial rivals, enhancement of personal power, or safeguarding the independence of their kingdoms.

Bernard Semmel, *Imperialism and Social Reform* (London, 1960), approaching pre-World War I British society from a different perspective, describes the characteristics of British "social-imperialism," which, he contends, was different in many respects from the continental phenomenon. It expressed itself in less strident tones, and it lacked the aggressiveness and the xenophobia of continental social-imperialism.

British social-imperialism was animated by "a pragmatic, balance sheet tone of defence." Semmel argues that Schumpeter and the Marxists were alike unjust and inaccurate in their assumptions that social-imperialism was an attempt by the imperialist classes to dupe the working men. Imperialism was immensely popular with the lower class. "The democracy," Austen Chamberlain observed, "wants two things: imperialism and social reform." Joseph Chamberlain and the tariff reformers combined social reform with tariff protection and Imperial preference; the imperialists of free trade also linked their imperialism with social reform. The neo-mercantilist tariff reformers regarded trade as war; Britain must organize her Imperial resources in order to survive; the free traders conceived Britain to be a part of an international economy. There were socialists—George Bernard Shaw, the Webbs, Robert Blatchford, and others—who shared much of Chamberlain's imperialist outlook though they and working-class leaders could not support his view that the whole population, including the working class, should pay for social benefits. Organized labor before 1914 chose the older free-trade imperialism and its program of social reform which put "the Biggest Burden on the Broadest Back."

It can be said of the Victorian Empire as did Lytton Strachey of Victorian England that the investigator must seek to analyze an ocean from the contents of a little bucket.[33] Vast manuscript resources remain virtually unexamined and great problems await the attention of scholars possessing intelligence, imagination, energy, and patience. One such problem is the reincarnation of chartered companies in the 1880's. Several studies have been made of individual companies—Kennedy G. Tregonning described the antecedents and developments of the British North Borneo Company in *Under Chartered Company Rule: North Borneo, 1881-1946* (Singapore, 1958). Marie de Kiewiet Hemphill wrote a doctoral thesis, as yet unpublished, at the University of London on the Imperial British East Africa Company; and John E. Flint dealt with the Royal Niger Company in *Sir George Goldie and the Making of Nigeria* (London, 1960). But no comprehensive study has yet been made of the factors which impelled the Imperial government to utilize the instrumentality of the chartered company; and no scholar has so far analyzed the antecedents of the grant of a charter

33. Giles Lytton Strachey, *Eminent Victorians* (1918; Penguin Edition, Harmondsworth, 1948), p. 6.

to the British South Africa Company. For this avoidance of perhaps the most glamorous of the chartered companies two explanations have been offered—the greater glamour of its moving spirit Cecil Rhodes and the destruction of the Company's records by bombing or otherwise. But there still remain great masses of documentation in public and private archives. Many other problems of comparable magnitude remain unexplored. W. Keith Hancock in a paper delivered before the American Historical Association in December, 1952, outlined several "headings for research" on the Empire, most of which remain *terra incognita* a decade later.[34] There is no adequate study, for example, of the revolutionary changes in British philosophy during the last generation with regard to Imperial responsibility for colonial "social welfare" programs. Lucy P. Mair's *Welfare in the British Colonies* (London, 1944) was a good brief survey of the social policy of British and colonial governments, with particular emphasis on education, labor, and health. But she wrote before the vast expansion of postwar assistance programs.

In the reassessment of British Imperial policy it is essential that there be comparative studies. Imperial historians have generally been prisoners of their parochial interests. Scholars of the British Empire know little of the characteristics of French or German expansion. Their conceptions of the motives of Britain's rivals are usually based on British sources. To these historians French and German motivations consequently appear as seen through the eyes of British diplomats. This deficiency cannot be attributed entirely to the narrowness of scholars of the British Empire. Those who seek enlightenment by reading works on French and German imperialism soon discover there has been little archival research on the expansion of those states. Until such studies are undertaken, there will be a great deficiency in the understanding not only of French and German but of British expansion, for though the actions of each state were in part attributable to conditions peculiar to itself, they were also the result of forces affecting Europe generally. Perhaps eventually there will emerge scholars of European expansion in the nineteenth century. At this stage, when so few monographic studies have appeared on the policies of individual nations, the prospect of such broad interpretations seems remote.

Economic historians usually admit the relevance of non-economic

---

34. Hancock, "Agenda for the Study of the British Imperial Economy, 1850-1950," *Journal of Economic History*, XIII (Summer, 1953), 257-73.

factors and then proceed to ignore them. One recent book which has contributed to a broader understanding of British imperialism as a social phenomenon is Archibald P. Thornton's *The Imperial Idea and its Enemies* (London, 1959). Thornton is particularly effective in his analysis of the Victorian and Edwardian ethos which gave to the British Empire its distinctive characteristics. Biography has also given deeper insights into the British culture. Especially noteworthy among recent works with a biographical emphasis are Margery Freda Perham, *Lugard* (2 vols.; London, 1956-60); Roland A. Oliver, *Sir Harry Johnston and the Scramble for Africa* (London, 1957); John Flint, *Sir George Goldie and the Making of Nigeria*; Philip Woodruff (Philip Mason), *The Men Who Ruled India* (2 vols.; London, 1953-54); and James Rutherford, *Sir George Grey, K.C.B., 1812-1898: A Study in Colonial Government* (London, 1961).

The study of Imperial history has been greatly affected by the disintegration of the Empire into a congeries of sovereign states, each intent on demonstrating its national identity. Within the Commonwealth the growth of interest in national history has been paralleled by a decline in emphasis on the history of the Empire and the Commonwealth. But the best of these national histories are not parochial but demonstrate an awareness of a wide context.[35] Within the past generation the study of the British community of nations has developed far greater profundity and sophistication than was characteristic in an earlier period of most historical writing on the British Empire. The present recognition of the vast gaps in our knowledge and understanding is in a sense the measure of this maturing, for an earlier generation devoted less attention to historical problems beyond a narrow compass of political constitutional history. Today historians are at least sensitive to their inadequacies as economists, sociologists, or anthropologists, though they may not repair this deficiency by attempting to master the relevant literature of these fields. The study of the British Empire has entered a new phase; scholars are not only searching for new answers to old questions but are posing new questions. It is a young field of scholarship. Youth is associated with brashness, and sometimes with irreverence, but it exudes vitality. All of these characteristics are to be found in abundance in the recent historiography of the Empire.

35. For a fuller discussion, see Curtin, "The British Empire and Commonwealth in Recent Historiography," pp. 72-91.

# CANADA

## Robin W. Winks

CANADIAN HISTORIOGRAPHY[1] occupies a position roughly midway between the highly developed and self-conscious historiographical traditions of the United States, Germany, or the Soviet Union, and the almost totally undeveloped historiography of Pakistan or Malaysia. But among members of the Commonwealth of Nations, the extent of the Canadian literature of historical self-examination is second only to that of the United Kingdom itself. Most of this body of literature is straightforward "history of history," bibliographical rather than historiographical, in the nature of a census.[2] And since

1. The present essay is based closely upon my own *Recent Trends and New Literature in Canadian History* (Washington, 1959). I am grateful to the Service Center for Teachers of History and to the American Historical Association for permission to reprint portions of that booklet.

2. The following references extend, support, and contradict this essay: Gustave Lanctôt, "Past Historians and Present History in Canada," *Canadian Historical Review* (Toronto) (hereafter *CHR*), XXII (Sept., 1941), 241-53; Donald Grant Creighton, "Towards the Discovery of Canada," *The University of Toronto Quarterly* (Toronto), XXV (April, 1956), 269-82; and his "Presidential Address," Canadian Historical Association (hereafter C.H.A.) *Report* (1957) (Toronto), pp. 1-12; William Menzies Whitelaw, "Canadian History in Retrospect," C.H.A. *Report* (1956), pp. 38-44; Reginald George Trotter, "Historical Research in Canada," *CHR*, XX (Sept., 1939), 251-57; George McKinnon Wrong, "The Beginnings of Historical Criticism in Canada: A Retrospect, 1896-1936," *ibid.*, XVII (March, 1936), 1-18; William Lewis Morton, "Clio in Canada: The Interpretation of Canadian History," *University of Toronto Quarterly*, XV (April, 1946), 227-34, and "History, Writing and Teaching of," *Encyclopaedia Canadiana* (Ottawa, 1958), V, 129-33; Crawford Brough Macpherson, "The Social Sciences," in Julian Park, ed., *The Culture of Contemporary Canada* (Ithaca, 1957), pp. 181-221; David Corbett, "The Social Sciences in Canada," *Queen's Quarterly* (Kingston), LXVI (Spring, 1959), 56-72; Michel Brunet, "Coexistence, Canadian Style: A Nationalistic View," *ibid.* (Autumn, 1956), pp. 424-31; William A. Mackintosh, "Adam Shortt," in Robert Charles Wallace, ed., *Some Great Men of Queen's* (Toronto, 1941), pp. 115-33; Chester Bailey Martin, "Professor G. M. Wrong and History in Canada," in Ralph Flenley, ed., *Essays in Canadian History* (Toronto, 1939), pp. 1-23, and "Fifty Years of Canadian History," The Royal Society of Canada, *Fifty Years Retrospect: Anniversary Volume, 1882-1932*, XX (Ottawa, [1932]), 63-69; Hilda Marion Neatby, "The Dangers of History," *La Nouvelle revue canadienne* (Ottawa), I (July, 1951), 21-33; Hugh McDowell Clokie, "Canadian Contributions to Political Science," *Culture* (Quebec), III (Dec., 1942), 467-74; William Thomas Easterbrook, "Trends in Canadian Eco-

Canadians see their history, and hence their historiography, as insep-
arable from the historiographies of Britain, France, and the United
States, the relevant titles range well into the thousands. One may argue
that the quality of writing about South Africa is better or one may
demonstrate that, relative to time span and size, more has been written
of New Zealand than of any other Commonwealth nation, but one
cannot dismiss the sheer bulk of the literature of Canadian history. As
a result of early revisionism, a longer history, and impinging and
pertinent historiographies, Canada also has a richer historical literature than any other Commonwealth nation, but this richness depends
in great measure upon an awareness of how Canada has drawn upon
other historiographies. Canadian historiography is thus far less nationalistic than that of India, or Ireland, or indeed of Australia. This in
itself is revealing of the nation, for one often learns more about a
people from the history they write than from the history they have
made.[3]

nomic Thought," *South Atlantic Quarterly* (Durham, N.C.), LVIII (Winter, 1959),
91-107; John Manning Ward, "Commonwealth Historiography in Canada and
Australia," *Lock Haven Review* (Lock Haven, Pa.), I, no. 5 (1963), 72-81, and
Alexander Brady, "Federalism in Canada," in William S. Livingston, ed., *Federalism
in the Commonwealth: A Bibliographical Commentary* (London, 1963), pp. 11-28.
The growth of history teaching in Canada is recounted by Richard Arthur Preston in
his "Presidential Address," C.H.A. *Report* (1962), pp. 1-16.
    3. The standard bibliography of Canadian history is Reginald George Trotter,
*Canadian History: A Syllabus and Guide to Reading* (rev. ed., Toronto, 1934). A
new bibliographical manual is being prepared by Richard Walden Hale, Jr., and John
Hall Stewart. William Kaye Lamb, "Seventy-five Years of Canadian Bibliography,"
Royal Society of Canada, *Proceedings and Transactions* (Ottawa), 3rd ser., LI, sec. 2
(June, 1947), 1-11, surveys bibliographical tools, as does Raymond Tanghe, comp.,
*Bibliography of Canadian Bibliographies* . . . (Toronto, 1960). Standard references
include Philéas Gagnon, *Essai de bibliographie canadienne* (2 vols.; Quebec, 1895-
1913), Reginald Eyre Watters, *A Check List of Canadian Literature and Background
Materials, 1628-1950* . . . (Toronto, 1959); William Matthews, *Canadian Diaries
and Autobiographies* (Berkeley, 1950); Marie Tremaine, *A Bibliography of Cana-
dian Imprints, 1751-1800* (Toronto, 1952); Dorothea D. Tod and Audrey Cording-
ley, *A Check List of Canadian Imprints, 1900-1925* (Ottawa, 1950); Henry Harrisse,
*Notes pour servir à l'histoire, à la bibliographies, et à la cartographie de la Nouvelle-
France* . . . *1545-1700* (Paris, 1872); Bruce Braden Peel, *A Bibliography of the
Prairie Provinces to 1953* (Toronto, 1956), with a *Supplement* (1963); Clodaugh
M. Neiderheiser, comp., *Forest History Sources of the United States and Canada* . . .
(Saint Paul, 1956); and Gertrude M. Boyle, ed., *A Bibliography of Canadiana*
(Toronto, 1960).
    To keep abreast of new materials, one may consult the regular bibliographies in
*The Canadian Historical Review* (Toronto, 1920———), in *Canadian Literature* (Van-
couver, 1959———), and in the excellent annual survey of Letters in Canada which
has appeared in *The University of Toronto Quarterly* (1931———) since 1936; or
Canadian Library Association, *Canadiana* (Ottawa, 1951———), a monthly list, and
*Atlantic Provinces Checklist* (Halifax, 1958———).

## THE BEGINNINGS[4]

The milestones which the traveler observes often depend upon his destination and upon his awareness of the distance to be traveled. Canadian historiography has passed many milestones since it began in 1609 with the publication, in Paris, of *L'Histoire de la Nouvelle France* by Marc Lescarbot. In 1744 Father Pierre François-Xavier de Charlevoix became the "Founder of Canadian History," by writing his *Histoire et description général de la Nouvelle-France . . .* (6 vols.; Paris).[5] Since defeated nations often excel in historical productivity, it is not surprising that the first indigenous Canadian historian was of French descent, Michel Bibaud, who in 1837 published his *Histoire du Canada sous la domination française* (later extended to 3 vols., Montreal, 1837-78), or that the first Canadian to devote his full energy to the pursuit of Clio was François-Xavier Garneau, whose *Histoire du Canada* (3 vols., Quebec, 1845-48; 8th ed., in 9 vols., Montreal, 1944-46)[6] became holy writ to many subsequent French-Canadian historians. Garneau's concern was with the survival of the French-Canadian "nation," and while French Canadians have viewed him as the founder of "scientific history" in Canada, he was more interested in the didactic than the analytical qualities of history. Since his time French-Canadian

4. The writer would like to thank R. Craig Brown, Gerald M. Craig, William L. Morton, Kenneth MacKirdy, Cameron Nish, Mason Wade, and Kenneth S. Inglis for their criticisms of early drafts of this essay. They are, of course, in no way responsible for any errors which remain.

5. Most recently reissued as *History and General Description of New France*, trans. by John Gilmore Shea (6 vols.; Chicago, 1962). See William F. E. Morley, "A Bibliographical Study of Charlevoix's *Histoire et Description Générale de la Nouvelle France*," *Papers of the Bibliographical Society of Canada* (Toronto), II (1963), 21-45. Other early histories of considerable importance include Pierre Boucher, *Histoire véritable et naturelle des moeurs et productions du pays de la Nouvelle France* (Paris, 1964), translated by E. L. Montizambert as *Canada in the Seventeenth Century* (Montreal, 1883); François du Creux, *Historiae canadensis* (Paris, 1664), which for those who, with the present writer, do not read Latin, is available as *The History of Canada, or New France* (2 vols.; Toronto, 1951), ed. and trans. Percy James Robinson and James B. Conacher; Nicholas Denys, *Geographische en historische beschrijving der kusten van Noord-America* (Amsterdam, 1688), trans. and ed. William F. Ganong, *The Description and Natural History of the Coasts of North America (Acadia)* (Toronto, 1908); Louis Armand de Lom d'Arce, Baron de Lahontan, *Nouveaux voyages de M*[r] *le baron de Lahontan, dans l'Amérique Septentrionale* (3 vols.; La Havre, 1703); and similar earlier works, all since translated, by François Dollier de Casson, R. P. Chrestien Le Clercq, and Gabriel Théodat Sagard.

6. Andrew Bell translated Garneau's work as *History of Canada, from the Time of Its Discovery til the Union Year 1840-1* (3 vols.; Montreal, 1860). See Gustave Lanctôt, *Garneau: Historien national* (Montreal [1926?]).

historians often have written to win with the pen that which their fore-fathers lost with the sword.

From 1843 to the early 1940's French-Canadian historiography, when it ventured away from genealogy, tended to dwell upon the theme of *survivance*. Such history was polemical, not fully re-searched, and dogmatic, which is made only partially understandable by the fact that no professional historical training was offered in French-Canadian universities until 1945. Most of the works written prior to that time are representative of history used and abused and, while there is an occasional contribution of merit which speaks from the French language, many, such as those of Abbé Lionel-Adolphe Groulx and Jean Bruchési,[7] often are histories for a coterie, valuable within their own framework of assumptions but mystifying and discouraging to the outsider. Like their Old World counterpart, Alphonse de Lamartine, in combining poetry with their history they lost the best of both. Such works are now among the primary materials for a study of French-Canadian cultural nationalism, but they are not histories. However, Groulx's contribution is to be measured in terms of his students as well as from his writings, and by encouraging Robert Lionel Séguin, Michel Brunet, and Guy Frégault to return to the sources, he set the new generation of French-Canadian historians upon the proper path.

One result of French-Canadian preoccupation with self was that much of French-Canadian historiography left the mainstream of Cana-dian history. This is not to say that English-Canadian historiography was less didactic or dogmatic during the nineteenth century and cer-tainly not less dull—witness William Canniff's *History of the Settle-ment of Upper Canada (Ontario)* . . . (Toronto, 1869)—but simply that it tended to be broader in scope. True, the first English histories contained their own parochial limitations, and the first classic history of Canada written by a Canadian writing in English, Robert Christie's *A History of the Late Province of Lower Canada* . . . (6 vols.; Quebec, 1848-55), established one of the principal biases of Canadian histori-

7. See *Temoignages d'hier: Essais* (Montreal, 1961) for a sampling of Bruchési. Groulx continued to write, without any apparent change in his point of view. See *La Canada français missionaries: Une autre grande aventure* (Montreal, 1962), and his pamphlet, *Dollard: Est-il un mythe?* (Montreal, 1960). The answer is, No. On Groulx, see Vaclav Mudroch, "The Abbé Groulx: History as a Weapon," *Queen's Quarterly*, LXIII (Summer, 1956), 179-87. See also the work of Thomas Chapas, especially *Le marquis de Montcalm (1712-1759)* (Quebec, 1911), and of Henri Raymond Casgrain.

ography: that the "parliamentary and political" history of "the Canadas" (present-day Ontario and Quebec) was the history of Canada. A better book, and one which may be read with profit today, was Duncan Campbell's *History of Prince Edward Island* (Charlottetown, 1875), which followed his *Nova Scotia, in Its Historical, Mercantile and Industrial Relations* (Montreal, 1873) by two years, and barely preceded the other two provincial foundation stones of Canada's early political history, James Hannay's *The History of Acadia . . .* (Saint John, 1879), and Donald Gunn's and Charles Richard Tuttle's *History of Manitoba from the Earliest Settlement to 1835* (Ottawa, 1880). Finally George Bryce provided something of a milestone with *A Short History of the Canadian People* (London, 1887), which, as its title implies, was social as well as political history.

The last decade of the nineteenth century saw the first concerted efforts to analyze rather than merely to relate the Canadian story. At the time the outstanding event of the decade in historical writing probably seemed to be the completion of William Kingsford's *A History of Canada* (10 vols.; Toronto, 1887-98), which revealed both what was right and what was wrong with Canadian historiography: it was diligent but dull, packed with a mass of undigested material (often inaccurate) which overwhelmed the reader while undeniably telling him that energetic excavation and construction work was in progress. As an engineer Kingsford represented the continuing tradition of amateurism in Canadian history.[8]

Looking back, with little regard for national boundaries, one suspects that at least three other events of the same decade were of greater significance for Canadian historiography. Francis Parkman, who remains unsurpassed as an historian who wrote literature on a Canadian theme, died in 1893 leaving a legacy of eighteen volumes, nine of which had the title *France and England in North America* (Boston, 1865-92). Because of their style, their use of incident and character, and their grand theme, few books have done more to direct attention to Canadian history. *A Half-Century of Conflict* (1892), *Montcalm and Wolfe* (1884), and *Pioneers of France in the New World* (1865), are perhaps the most enduring, but one should not overlook *The Jesuits in North America in the Seventeenth Century* (1867), *The*

8. See J. K. McConica, "Kingsford and Whiggery in Canadian History," *CHR*, XL (June, 1959), 108-20.

*Old Régime in Canada* (1874), or *Count Frontenac and New France under Louis XIV* (1877), despite their proven inaccuracies and unquestionable anti-Catholic bias. Even *The Conspiracy of Pontiac* (10th ed., rev., 1913), while no longer accepted as history, remains a uniquely stirring reading experience.[9]

In 1895 Pierre-Georges Roy, then twenty-four, became editor of the first durable Canadian historical journal, *Le Bulletin des recherches historiques* (Lévis, 1895-1956), and went on to write and edit over two hundred books and pamphlets, including the useful *Les Petites choses de notre histoire* (6 vols.; Lévis, 1919-31). One year later, in 1896, George McKinnon Wrong, an ordained Anglican clergyman who never had a parish, introduced modern Canadian history to the University of Toronto—which, until his appointment in the previous year, had taught no Canadian history past 1815.[10] Wrong began the *Review of Historical Publications Relating to Canada*, which was the forerunner of the *Canadian Historical Review*, thus launching the first truly professional Canadian history on its way. He was typical of the earlier generation of Canadian historians in that he shifted about from "field" to "field" as academic exigencies demanded or interests dictated. These historians were not to provide us with a shelf of monographs, and they "covered" fewer topics, "contributed" fewer "seminal" articles, and left nothing "definitive," as the professional jargon would have it, but since they wrote out of wide experience with human nature rather than from the techniques of dissertation construction, their writings often have a force and clarity (albeit, at times an undesirable

9. Parkman continues not only to be read but studied. See (H.) Mason Wade, *Francis Parkman: Heroic Historian* (New York, 1942); Wade, ed., *Journals of Francis Parkman* (New York, 1947); Otis Arnold Pease, *Parkman's History: The Historian as Literary Artist* (New Haven, 1953); William John Eccles, "The History of New France According to Francis Parkman," *The William and Mary Quarterly* (Williamsburg), 3rd ser., XVIII (April, 1961), 163-75; William Robert Taylor, "A Journey into the Human Mind: Motivation in Francis Parkman's *LaSalle*," *ibid.*, XIX (April, 1962), 220-37; Howard Doughty, *Francis Parkman* (New York, 1961); Samuel Eliot Morison, ed., *The Parkman Reader* (Boston, 1955); and David Levin, *History as Romantic Art: Bancroft, Prescott, Motley and Parkman* (Stanford, 1959). Eccles quite properly rapped this writer's knuckles for having implied, in 1959, that Parkman had obviated the need for further research. This view—that any subject can be "researched out"—is demonstrably false, and it was not what I had meant to imply. In any case, I was wrong in 1959 and I would be even more wrong in 1965, for several good volumes, not the least from Eccles' own hand, have demonstrated that there is much yet to be done.

10. Abbé J. B. A. Ferland did teach the history of New France at Laval University between 1854 and 1865. See Richard Arthur Preston, "Presidential Address," C.H.A. *Report* (1962), pp. 5, 8-9.

because dogmatic clarity) lacking in those of the more urgent "publish or perish" generation. Wrong, who well might be a subject for a biographer, was to write three works which were basic in their time: *The Earl of Elgin* (London, 1905), *The Rise and Fall of New France* (2 vols.; New York, 1928), and *Canada and the American Revolution: The Disruption of the First British Empire* (New York, 1935).

The period between Canada's participation in the Boer War and the settlement at Versailles[11] was one in which the Dominion made considerable strides toward nationhood. Whether these strides were taken despite or because of Great Britain remains one of the key debates in Canadian historiography. It is significant that at the end of this period William Stewart Wallace wrote his brief account of "The Growth of Canadian National Feeling" for the *Canadian Historical Review* (I [June, 1920], 136-65), and doubly significant that he chose to write of "feeling" rather than of "character," for his was not a study of nationalism.[12] During these same years John Castell Hopkins filled a shelf with the first of many co-operative works on the Dominion, *Canada: An Encyclopaedia of the Country* . . . (6 vols.; Toronto, 1898-1900); another major co-operative venture, "Canada and Its Provinces . . ." (22 vols.; Toronto, 1914-16), under the editorship of Adam Shortt and Sir Arthur George Doughty, introduced economic and cultural history to Canadian studies; and the first history expressly for consumption outside Canada, the *Tercentenary History of Canada, from Champlain to Laurier* . . . (3 vols.; Toronto, 1908), was prepared by Frank Basil Tracy. Yet in looking back none of these enterprises seems quite as important as Wallace's slim, relatively superficial excursion into a search for a Canadian identity. If Canadian historiography since 1920 has shown tendencies toward a greater awareness of the rôle of the United States in Canadian history, has given new emphasis to social, economic, and cultural phenomena, and has leaned heavily to co-operative ventures, its clearest trend has continued to be the

11. The Canadian response to the Boer War is examined by Norman Penlington in *Canada and Imperialism, 1896-1899* (Toronto, 1965). On Versailles, see (George) Gaddis Smith's forthcoming study of the period 1914-19, which promises to be nearly definitive.

12. Wallace expanded his article into a book with the same title (Toronto, 1927). In an essay in the now defunct *Canadian Magazine* (Toronto), "The Growth of Canadian National Feeling," XLV (Aug., 1915), 273-81, C. M. Warner had anticipated Wallace's title, and in 1875 William Canniff quite prematurely had anticipated both in *Canadian Nationality, Its Growth and Development* (Toronto).

political, with a conscious striving to invent, to discover, or to define *Canadianism.*

The decade of the 1920's, like the 1890's, was one of exceptional importance to Canadian historiography. During these years the first works of many of present-day Canada's elder statesmen of history appeared, the first hints of revisionism became apparent, and a host of monographs, to which the first edition of Reginald George Trotter's *Canadian History: A Syllabus and Guide to Reading* (Toronto, 1926) attested, reflected the new canons of a stricter scholarship, at once more objective and less readable. In 1922 the Canadian Historical Association was established, two years after the appearance of the first issue of the *Review.* Of the names which have a prominent position in the first volume of the *Review* only those of Fred Landon and W. P. M. Kennedy furnish an immediate tie with the present, but most—such as those of Wrong, Doughty, Shortt, and William Renwick Riddell— represent a generation of scholars who have but recently passed from the scene.

The period 1920-39 is something of a base period for Canadian historiography, a period of changing interpretations to which writers in subsequent years have looked, a period which may be taken to represent the new dogma upon which the post-World War II revisionists have labored.

## CHANGING INTERPRETATIONS TO 1939

For years Canadian history had the reputation of being dull. This was owing in part to the fact that it leaned heavily to political and constitutional history, burying the individual. When the individual was made the focus of study through biography, he was buried in quite another way, in what Donald G. Creighton has referred to as "fat funereal volumes." However, Canadian history has experienced a genuine flowering since the 1940's and, invigorated by considerable aid from the social sciences, now is among the most challenging of national historiographies within the Commonwealth.

Many leading contributions to Canadian historiography have been made by men whose primary training was in economics or political science, not in history. For years Canadian historians refused to avail themselves of the tools furnished by the methodologies of anthropology, economics, political science, or sociology, possibly because of the exaggerated claims which these "social sciences" at first made for themselves. Anthropology was a servant not allowed at the dinner table. Sociology remained ill-established in Canada until the 1950's, and this was not entirely because of the difficulties presented by its professional jargon.[13] Until recently there was no equivalent in Canada of the interdisciplinary "American studies" approach, and the insights which one field might bring to bear upon another were less than immediately evident.

The earlier tradition of Anglo-Canadian historiography, as represented by Kingsford or James Hannay, placed emphasis upon Canada's supporting rôle in the larger scene of British Imperial development. Canadian history, the history of Yorkshire, or the study of New South Wales, were but minor aspects of a vastly more important story. In reaction to this transatlantic view, a nationalist school of historians—pro-British but in search of an emerging Canadian nationhood—began to trace the growth of responsible government and dominion status. Daniel Coit Harvey, in several articles on confederation in the Maritime Provinces; Reginald George Trotter in a key monograph with a significant subtitle, *Canadian Federation, Its Origins and Achievement: A Study in Nation Building* (Toronto, 1924); Chester William New in his biography of *Lord Durham* . . . (Oxford, 1929); and Chester Bailey Martin in *Empire and Commonwealth: Studies in Governance and Self-Government in Canada* (Oxford, 1929), also emphasized the rôle, negative and positive, of the United States in influencing Canadian development.

Writers with nationalist leanings also tended to identify growing freedom from British control with the rise of a Canadian nationality, underemphasizing how Great Britain itself had encouraged the growth of autonomy and forgetting that negative factors alone do not make a nation. John Wesley Dafoe, a distinguished journalist,[14] in his *Canada: An American Nation* (New York, 1935), *Laurier: A Study in Canadian Politics* (Toronto, 1922), and *Clifford Sifton in Relation to His Times*

13. See David Spring, "History and Sociology: A Plea for Humility," *CHR*, XXX (Sept., 1949), 211-26.
14. Histories written in English by qualified journalists are not as numerous in Canada as in Britain or the United States. However, one should not overlook the several books of (William) Bruce Hutchison, mentioned below, of Edgar Andrew Collard (*Canadian Yesterdays* [Toronto, 1955]), or of Pierre Berton (*The Mysterious North* [New York, 1956], and *The Klondike Fever: The Life and Death of the Last Great Gold Rush* [New York, 1958]). Ralph Allen, Fred Landon, and Wilfrid Eggleston, discussed in the text, also were journalists.

(Toronto, 1931), compounded Canada's particular Whig interpretation of history and emphasized a broadly North American rather than an Imperial view of Canada. Oscar Douglas Skelton, a political scientist who served as Undersecretary for External Affairs from 1925 until his death in 1941, showed how the Canadian Fathers had obtained their measure of independence of Great Britain through evolutionary means, in two giant authorized biographies, *The Life and Times of Sir Alexander Tilloch Galt* (Toronto, 1920), and *The Life and Letters of Sir Wilfrid Laurier* (2 vols.; Toronto, 1921). The predominantly Whiggish view in Canadian historiography already had been given its most precise expression by Sir John Stephen Willison, another journalist, who in *Sir Wilfrid Laurier and the Liberal Party: A Political History* (2 vols.; London, 1903) compiled the history of the liberal party in Canada as though it were the history of the Canadian nation.

This liberal interpretation of Canadian history was strengthened by the emergence of a western school of writers, initially under the guidance of the so-called frontier thesis as outlined by Frederick Jackson Turner, and as first explicitly applied to the Canadian scene by Walter Noble Sage in his paper "Some Aspects of the Frontier in Canadian History" (C.H.A. *Report* [1928], pp. 162-72). Turner's thesis was one of environmentalism, teaching that American democracy was "forest-born," not brought from Europe, and that democracy resulted naturally from the availability of free land. The immediate effect of the Turner thesis, as reworked and sometimes overextended by his students, was to create a continental approach which emphasized the similarities between Canada and the United States and by implication the differences between Canada, Great Britain, and Europe.[15]

The Turner thesis was invoked to explain the uprising of 1837, George Brown and the Clear Grits, and the farmers' revolt in the West. Sage, Arthur Silver Morton, to a lesser extent Arthur R. M. Lower, and most recently William Lewis Morton documented the sense of grievance in and the exploitation of the frontier society. Frank Hawkins Underhill applied the frontier test to "The Development of National Political Parties in Canada" (*CHR*, XVI [Dec., 1935],

15. For some of the literature on Turner as applied in Canada and elsewhere, see Morris Zaslow, "The Frontier Thesis in Recent Historiography," *CHR*, XXIX (June, 1948), 153-67. Sage's essay was reprinted in his *Canada from Sea to Sea* (Toronto, 1940), pp. 17-32.

367-87), and between 1934 and 1940 a series of volumes on "Canadian Frontiers of Settlement" elaborated the Turnerian approach. In 1940 Alfred LeRoy Burt applied the theory to "The Frontier in the History of New France" (C.H.A. *Report*, pp. 93-99), and sociologist Samuel Delbert Clark showed how the frontier created social problems in a pioneer study of *The Social Development of Canada: An Introductory Study with Select Documents* (Toronto, 1942).[16]

Again deriving their stimulus from American historiography, Canadian scholars subjected the Turner thesis to a searching review.[17] American scholars demonstrated that Jacksonian democracy was as much a product of an urban-labor environment as it was a product of the edge of free land. Underhill, who had shown that the Toronto *Globe* was Jacksonian, now demonstrated how the urban liberals under George Brown had modified frontier demands ("Some Reflections on the Liberal Tradition in Canada," C.H.A. *Report* [1946], pp. 5-17). J. M. S. Careless countered with a demonstration of how Brown and the Reform groups reflected the Victorian urban reforms of Bright and Cobden in England,[18] and Gerald M. Craig restored the balance by reassessing "The American Impact on the Upper Canadian Reform Movement before 1837."[19]

During these years another Canadian scholar, Arthur R. M. Lower, was ranging over an amazing amount of material, writing on Canadian religion, relations with the Far East, economic history, political theory, and historical geography. Lower's work is difficult to categorize, although his few documented research efforts tended to form part of the Liberal canon. His *Settlement and the Forest Frontier in Eastern Canada* (Toronto, 1936) was of the Turner school, but his interest in geographical determinants made it possible for him to make contributions in other areas as well. His views were stated most completely in *Colony*

16. Portions of this book were reprinted with more recent essays in Clark's *The Developing Canadian Community* (Toronto, 1962).

17. This review began much later in Canada, just as the original discovery of Turner also was later. The entire Canadian approach to the Turner thesis illustrates the flow of organizing concepts from the United States to Canada and the cultural lag in the acceptance, and later rejection, of these concepts. As late as 1945 a Canadian scholar could say, ". . . not enough attention has been given to the Turner thesis as applied to Canada" (in the discussion, p. 13, following Walter Noble Sage's address, "Where Stands Canadian History?" C.H.A. *Report*, pp. 5-13). In the same year Fred A. Shannon "hammered the nails into Turner's coffin" south of the border.

18. "The Toronto *Globe* and Agrarian Radicalism, 1850-67," *CHR*, XXIX (March, 1948), 14-39.

19. *Ibid.*, (Dec., 1948), pp. 333-52.

*to Nation: A History of Canada* (Toronto, 1946; 4th ed., 1964), a highly individualistic and interpretative work which underscored the schism between the English and French within Canada.

One difficulty with the North American approach, once one had left the period of exploration behind, was that it did not meet the still felt need for a history of a Canadian nation. If one fled from the Scylla of Britain one was in the Charybdis of the United States. Canadian historiography thus seemed derivative from American or British history. In the 1920's and 1930's Canadian historians felt the need to read as much of the history of the United States as they did that of their own country.[20]

The need for a Canadian interpretation of Canadian history was met not by an historian but by an economist, Harold Adams Innis, who together with Donald Grant Creighton, created what usually is referred to as the Laurentian school. Innis, probably the least readable, and Creighton the most readable, of Canadian scholars, substituted a Canadian-rooted environmentalism, which looked back to England for its primal inspiration, for the American-rooted concept of Turner. Innis developed the Laurentian hypothesis which geographer Marion Isabel Newbigin had first suggested in *Canada: The Great River, the Land and the Men* (New York, 1926). Contrary to the North American school, which insisted that Canada was a nation despite its geography, Innis asserted that Canada was a nation because of its geography. Rather than being a series of regions each of which had more natural affinity with a similar region in the United States, Canada was a unit forged out of an east-west line of Imperial communications based on the St. Lawrence River and the western trails.

First glimpsing this view in his early work, *A History of the Canadian Pacific Railway* (Toronto, 1923), Innis revealed it more fully in *The Fur Trade in Canada: An Introduction to Canadian Economic History* (New Haven, 1930; rev. ed., Toronto, 1956), and argued that Canada was not created in reaction to American expansionism but that it emerged because of English dependence upon a geographically determined staple trade. As Frank H. Underhill has noted, Innis was

20. From the extreme left there have been few contributions to Canadian historiography, for Canadian scholars reflect their nation in being essentially liberal-conservatives. However, Stanley Bréhaut Ryerson has attempted a Marxist interpretation of Canadian history in *1837—The Birth of Canadian Democracy* (Toronto, 1937); *French Canada, A Study in Canadian Democracy* (Toronto, 1943); and *The Founding of Canada: Beginnings to 1815* (Toronto, 1960; rev. ed., 1963).

interested in how man conquered—and was conquered by—space and time in terms of communications, a theme particularly evident in one of Innis' last works, *Empire and Communications* (Oxford, 1950). He demonstrated how trade routes and other lines of communication helped shape political entities,[21] and he made the study of staple production a necessity for every student of Canadian history. In rough chronological order, the Canadian economy has been based on fishing, furs, lumbering, wheat, and minerals. In *The Cod Fisheries: The History of an International Economy* (New Haven, 1940; rev. ed., Toronto, 1954), Innis showed how competition between Nova Scotia and New England for fisheries caused the two areas to draw apart and how from 1783 Nova Scotians struggled to keep New England fishermen out of the West Indian markets, to gain entrance to the American market, and to protect their territorial waters from American fishermen. As the subtitle stated, the cod fisheries were part of an international economy, and while they separated the Maritime Provinces from New England they bound the former closer to Great Britain and to Europe. The St. Lawrence was but an extension of the Atlantic water bridge to Britain, thus bringing the international economy to the heart of the continent.[22]

In *The Commercial Empire of the St. Lawrence, 1760-1850* (Toronto, 1937; rev. ed., 1956) Donald Grant Creighton, later to be Innis' biographer, added to the Laurentian interpretation by demonstrating how geography, and the trade routes determined by geography, had shaped society. Creighton's history was more than geographical determinism, however, for he illuminated the strife between the two societies of the St. Lawrence—the acquisitive urban Protestant society and the rural Catholic society. In later works Creighton further challenged the Whig interpretation by emphasizing Great Britain's important place in preparing Canada for nationhood, pointing out that Canada had not wrested its independence from Britain but that Britain had fostered Canadian independence while protecting the provinces from the

---

21. For a more sophisticated and far-reaching application of a similar point of view, see Karl Wolfgang Deutsch, *Nationalism and Social Communication: An Inquiry into the Foundations of Nationality* (Cambridge, Mass., 1953).

22. See also Innis, *The Bias of Communication* (Toronto, 1951), and *Changing Concepts of Time* (Toronto, 1952). The latter reflects Innis' increasing anti-Americanism. On Innis, see Donald Grant Creighton, *Harold Adams Innis: Portrait of a Scholar* (Toronto, 1957), and John Bartlet Brebner, "Harold Adams Innis as Historian," *C.H.A. Report* (1953), pp. 14-24.

United States. Together Innis and Creighton showed how Canada was built upon its communications systems, systems which were but extensions of the St. Lawrence.[23]

Out of an interest in urban dominance over a rural hinterland, which was analogous to Imperial dominance over a colony, came another interpretation of Canadian history, that of metropolitanism. Creighton and Innis made indirect contributions here as well. While not the first statement of its tenets, J. M. S. Careless' article, "Frontierism, Metropolitanism, and Canadian History,"[24] was the most succinct. In 1922 a Canadian, N. S. B. Gras, in his *Introduction to Economic History* (New York), developed certain working assumptions about the rôle of metropolis in the rise of Western civilization. Donald Campbell Masters, his first Canadian convert, who already had demonstrated himself an able economic historian, wrote *The Rise of Toronto, 1850-1890* (Toronto, 1947), which applied Gras's theories to the Canadian scene. Since then the metropolitan approach has been developed in several monographs and articles. Most notably, Arthur R. M. Lower has employed the concept to bolster his thesis on "Two Ways of Life: The Primary Antithesis of Canadian History" (C.H.A. *Report* [1943], pp. 5-18), and Morris Zaslow is applying the hinterland concept to the Canadian north with rewarding results.

As a natural complement to the metropolitan approach there remains the possibility of an increasingly sophisticated use of regionalism. Like metropolitanism, however, regionalism has not been fully exploited in Canada. To a certain extent the older school of historians who wrote of the North American family used a regional approach without the conceptual tools of the social scientists. Howard W. Odum, the American pioneer of the regional concept, attempted to show that there is a difference between a region and a section, but his definitions lacked clarity. But another American, Paul Frederick Sharp, made use of regionalism to good advantage. In *The Agrarian Revolt in Western Canada: A Survey Showing American Parallels* (Minneapolis, 1948), he traced the rise of farm organizations after 1900 and showed, through the Nonpartisan League, how the international boundary often was ignored by a group which shared a common regional problem. In

23. For a recent re-evaluation, especially useful because of its bibliography, see D. A. Farnie, "The Commercial Empire of the Atlantic, 1607-1783," *The Economic History Review* (Utrecht), 2nd ser., XV (Dec., 1962), 205-18.
24. *CHR*, XXXV (March, 1954), 1-21.

*Whoop-Up Country: The Canadian-American West, 1865-1885* (Minneapolis, 1955), Sharp told of international communications along the line of "whiskey forts" in Alberta, Saskatchewan, and Montana.[25] And Kenneth A. MacKirdy has drawn interesting contrasts between Canadian and Australian federalism by using a regional approach.[26]

One of the most significant and eclectic studies to emerge during these years of shifting interpretations was a product of the growing awareness, during World War II, of the interdependence of Great Britain, Canada, and the United States. When John Bartlet Brebner began to write his survey history of Canadian-American relations as the final volume to the Carnegie Endowment for International Peace series, he discovered that Great Britain kept impinging in such a way as to become unavoidable. The result was *North Atlantic Triangle: The Interplay of Canada, the United States and Great Britain* (New Haven, 1945), which was, in some ways, an effort to have the best of both worlds, for it shared the Conservative conviction that Britain had not been the devil to Canadian history and combined it with the Liberal assertion that Canada was an American nation. Brebner thus played the rôle of the great compromiser.

## LONG-RANGE PROBLEMS AND PROSPECTS

Canadian emphasis on environmentalism, especially of the fairly severe Turnerian variety, limited the development of intellectual and cultural history in the Dominion.[27] But Innis' economic history paved

25. The most logical province to which regionalism may be applied is British Columbia. Most studies of the Canadian West omit this province, which to Canadians is not of the West but of the Pacific. Regionally it is of the Pacific Northwest. Yet no study of that region has included British Columbia in any adequate way. The best general history, Dorothy O. Johansen and Charles M. Gates, *Empire of the Columbia: A History of the Pacific Northwest* (New York, 1957), omits British Columbia after the period of exploration and uses regional and sectional concepts interchangeably. Two other studies of this region, less distinguished on the whole but more adequate in a regional sense, are Otis Willard Freeman and Howard Hanna Martin, eds., *The Pacific Northwest: An Overall Appreciation* (2nd ed., New York, 1954), and Benjamin Hamilton Kizer, *The U.S.-Canadian Northwest* . . . (Princeton, 1943). Lancaster Pollard, who states that the Pacific Northwest is "pulled together by a river," nonetheless ignores the province through which the river flows for half its length ("The Pacific Northwest," in Merrill Jensen, ed., *Regionalism in America* [Madison, 1951]).

26. Most notably in "Problems of Adjustment in Nation Building: The Maritime Provinces and Tasmania," *The Canadian Journal of Economics and Political Science* (Toronto), XX (Feb., 1954), 27-43.

27. The most sweeping attempt at a social and intellectual history of Canada is

the way for a rediscovery of the importance of the European background, and as historians came to see that ideas indeed were weapons, themselves "controlling factors," interest developed in the changes in these ideas as they grew in Canadian soil. Nonetheless, intellectual history remains Canada's weakest branch of the discipline, partially because such history requires an extremely flexible, analytic, and whole mind, wherever practiced, and partially because intellectual history is, as James C. Malin has remarked, like nailing jelly to a wall. Numerous students of sociology and theorists of nationalism have argued that English-speaking Canada has no nationality in a cultural sense apart from Great Britain and the United States. Thus it is that in many respects the analysis of American character made by David Morris Potter in *People of Plenty: Economic Abundance and the American Character* (Chicago, 1954), is valid for Canada as well. Potter shows why a modified application of Turner's thesis still has vitality for the present, for Turner's "free land" was but one expression of abundance, an abundance which the continent continued to share after the closing of the frontier. It was, after all, a Canadian-born economist, John Kenneth Galbraith, who analyzed the mutually *Affluent Society* (Boston, 1958). One cannot, despite the Imperial and Laurentian schools' obvious dislike for treating Canada as a "normal American community," do otherwise when her sociologists, such as John R. Seeley, R. Alexander Sim, and Elizabeth Wyeth Loosley, in *Crestwood Heights: A Study of the Culture of Suburban Life* (New York, 1956), have demonstrated that this is what much of Canadian society appears to be.[28] Just so long as

---

Arthur R. M. Lower's *Canadians in the Making: A Social History of Canada* (Toronto, 1958). Brash and idiosyncratic in its judgments, provocative, but given to phrasemaking (such as "the great god CAR and his associates") which reminds one of a scholarly Vance Packard, Lower's book is nonetheless of considerable significance. In its emphasis on religion (or piety) in shaping the early Canadian community, it resembles another recent national history, Charles Manning H. Clark's *A History of Australia*, I: *From the Earliest Times to the Age of Macquarie* (Melbourne, 1962).

28. However, deviations within a normal pattern are common, just as there are major deviations within the American republic. To conclude that because Canada and the United States shared a common environment they were led to similar behavioral patterns is mistaken. Samuel Delbert Clark, in *Movements of Political Protest in Canada, 1640-1840* (Toronto, 1959), seriously overemphasizes the link between radicalism and the frontier and again gives evidence of the lag between theoretical scholarship in the United States and application of these theories in Canada. The present writer feels that the theories on nationalism and social communication, stemming from the work of a political scientist, Karl Wolfgang Deutsch, and a sociologist, Seymour Martin Lipset, may be quite fruitful models to follow in studying Canada. Few Canadian historians appear to know of Deutsch's work, or of Elie Kedourie, who in *Nationalism* (rev. ed., New York, 1961) points out that the Canadian state cannot

Canadian historiography continues to be a fight over one's in-laws will it fail to develop intellectual, cultural, and even social history far beyond the early stages reflected in the old "Canada and Its Provinces" series.

For the most part recent Canadian historiography unabashedly fills out the skeleton. Very little of it is revisionist, for so many areas lack the fundamental studies upon which revisionists work. The truly interpretative histories stand out by contrast. But the interpretative histories must be based upon books which make no further claim than being gap-fillers, holding actions against the chaos of the unrecorded. The shift from non-professional to professional history, with the resultant growth of monographic literature, and the increase in doctoral dissertations on post-confederation history, have produced dozens of highly competent studies which pretend to do no more than to tell a story which has not been told so fully before.

One problem in Canadian historiography is that its material is intractable chronologically. It often seems to be the history of Upper or Lower Canada writ large, as a lack of comparable primary materials on the Maritimes and the West has forced some national historians to generalize on the basis of records which tell a story valid only for Ontario or Quebec. Hardly any of the older general histories of Canada reflect a sense of wholeness, a telling of the Canadian story in its geographical entirety, and while more recent histories strive for balance they still tend to write of each province as an isolated entity, to the benefit of the provincially minded and to the cost of chronology or any understanding of the interlocking nature of Canadian history. The Canadian West, to read most Canadian histories, had no history other than that of exploration and trade until the time of Louis Riel, when suddenly the West was born. The Indian, whom the historian might well study as part of Canadian history, remains the particular concern of the anthropologist.

The older Canadian history often seemed to be history with a grievance, and perhaps in this sense it was highly interpretative. French-Canadian historiography was especially so, but economic histories of the Maritimes, political histories of the West, and religious histories of Ontario and Quebec were only less so. One noticeable

---

be understood in terms of "nationalist logic." Lipset's most interesting statement appeared in the *Canadian Review of Anthropology and Sociology* (Edmonton), I (Dec., 1964), as "Canada and the United States—A Comprehensive View."

development in recent Canadian historical writing has been a decline in such apparent historical participation in the events described.

Canadian historiography also shows a tendency to be cynosural. There is very little on European-native relations because of an obsession with Riel and the *métis* uprisings. There is too little on the evolution of provincial-dominion relations and a very evident obsession with confederation. There is entirely too little on Canadian nationalism as expressed, or not expressed, in Canadian literature (was it not Stephen Leacock who once promised to boot the Americans out of Canada?) and too much on the Fenian raids. There are volumes of studies on the drawing of the Canadian boundary and very few adequate works on Canadian universities. There is virtually nothing on the history of science in Canada, historical geography remains largely untouched except in the journals, and only three provinces (British Columbia, Manitoba, and New Brunswick) can claim to have adequate one-volume histories, while shelves can be filled with the literature on military operations in the War of 1812. There is no good account of Canada's relations with other Commonwealth nations despite an appeal by Alfred LeRoy Burt in his presidential address to the Canadian Historical Association in 1950 to stop writing domestic history and to probe the problems of the Commonwealth. John Bartlet Brebner has written that the years between the two world wars were rare ones in Canada, when "the Canadian spirit of enterprise found an unprecedented amount of intellectual and aesthetic expression." No one has written to document this assertion, nor has anyone written an adequate history of Canadian art, although several books on specific Canadian artists have been published. There are practically no histories of the Indians of Canada, little history of Eskimo-white relations, and nothing of importance on the conservation movement.

Even Canadian biography leaves many gaps to be filled. Canadian history grew as biography, for it is through the life of an individual that the less sophisticated reader can best learn of "the times." There are, of course, hundreds of biographies of Canadian figures and yet, on the whole, until recently biographical writing cannot be said to have flourished in Canada. Some, best represented by Donald Grant Creighton's two volumes on John A. Macdonald and J. M. S. Careless' two-volume study of George Brown, are thorough, interpretative, and well-written, but few pre-1939 biographies can meet these three requirements. Most of the Fathers of Confederation need new biographies and some have yet to receive their first. Given the Canadian obsession with confederation, nothing could better indicate the parlous state of Canadian biography.

If many gaps remain unfilled, this is but a challenge to Canadian historians, and if interpretations sometimes become tendentious, they but testify to the Canadian historian's sense of participation. Historians continue to help Canadians in their search for a nationality, and even works of a non-political nature often have such an implicit theme. In the final analysis a milestone which might best represent a point of departure for "recent" historiography was passed in 1937. In that year André Siegfried wrote what then was regarded as the best popular interpretation of *Canada* (London), and one can measure how far Canada and Canadian historiography have come by the subtitle which he appended to the revised edition in 1949: *Canada: An International Power* (London). Also in 1937 the Canadian Institute of International Affairs, which had been established four years earlier, began an ambitious publishing program which has continued to the present time, and Creighton saw published his *Empire of the St. Lawrence*, which, like the river it describes, is deep, broad, and challenging, further removing the stigma of dullness from his subject. Yet, although many such works of art have been created for Canada, as W. Kaye Lamb, Dominion Archivist and a past president of the Canadian Historical Association, has observed, "There is hardly a corner of the canvas where there are not details to be filled in."

Even so, the Canadian canvas has far fewer open spaces than the Australian or Malaysian. One explanation for the greater outpouring of solidly based research from Canada may be found in the early establishment of archives. The Public Archives of Canada was founded in 1872, and under the expert guidance of Douglas Brymner, Arthur Doughty, and most recently Lamb, the archive has become the finest in the Commonwealth outside Britain. Collections are well-organized and calendared, access policies are comparatively liberal, and the harried and hurried visitor from far away may work through the night if he wishes, since the Archives building is open twenty-four hours a day. Some of the provinces also have exceptional archival facilities: Nova Scotia, Ontario, Saskatchewan, and British Columbia. Strong collections of Canadiana exist outside Canada, notably in Britain, and—at Dartmouth, Harvard, Minnesota, Rochester, and Yale—in the United States as well.[29]

The Manuscript Division of the Public Archives of Canada has published several preliminary checklists of manuscript holdings, including lists of manuscripts deposited with local bodies.[30] In 1963 there were, in addition, 124 local historical societies in Canada, several of them with quite important archives.[31] These societies also have encouraged publication of findings by sponsoring, among them, no less than 62 journals. While many of these journals have lapsed, they remain important sources of data. Provincial journals, notably *Ontario History* (Toronto, 1899——), also add to this flood.[32] Finally, scholars well removed from archival centers may begin their research by using the many Canadian newspapers now available on microfilm through the Canadian Library Association.[33]

## HISTORICAL LITERATURE SINCE 1939

### General Histories

The report of the Royal Commission on Dominion-Provincial Relations, published in 1939-40, is one of the most important documents

---

29. E.g., see William Inglis Morse, *et al.*, eds., *The Canadian Collection at Harvard University* (6 vols.; Cambridge, Mass., 1944-[49]); and Robin William Winks, "Canadiana at Yale: A Report," *The Yale University Library Gazette* (New Haven), XXXVI (Jan., 1962), 97-118.

30. In addition to these guides, other aids include J. Russell Harper, *Historical Directory of New Brunswick Newspapers and Periodicals* (Fredericton, 1961) and Richard Walden Hale, Jr., *Guide to Photocopied Historical Materials in the United States and Canada* (Ithaca, 1961).

31. These are listed in [Clement M. Silvestio and Sally Ann Davis, comps.], *Directory of Historical Societies and Agencies in the United States and Canada, 1963* (Madison, 1963). Additional societies are listed in *Ontario History* (Toronto).

32. Other serials which students of Canadian history must consult include *Queen's Quarterly* (Kingston, 1893——), *Canadian Journal of Economic and Political Science* (Toronto, 1935——); *L'Actualité économique* (Montreal, 1925——); *The Beaver* (Winnipeg, 1924——), published by the Hudson's Bay Company; *Saskatchewan History* (Saskatoon, 1948——); the publications of the Hudson's Bay Record Society (London, 1938); the Champlain Society *Publications* (Toronto, 1907——), and the *Transactions* of the Royal Society of Canada (Ottawa, 1882——); *Culture* (Quebec, 1940——), *The Dalhousie Review* (Halifax, 1921——), *International Journal* (Toronto, 1946——), *Public Affairs* (Halifax, 1937-53), *La Nouvelle revue canadienne* (Ottawa, 1951——), *Revue de l'Université Laval* (Quebec, 1946——), *Revue de l'Université d'Ottawa* (1931——), *Canadian Forum* (Toronto, 1920——), *Atlantic Advocate* (Fredericton, 1910——), *Saturday Night* (Toronto, 1887——); *Manitoba Arts Review* (Winnipeg, 1930——), *Canadian Geographical Journal* (Montreal, 1930——), *Cité Libre* (Montreal, 1950-), *Revue d'histoire de l'Amerique Française* (Montreal, 1947-), and *Canadian Magazine* (Montreal, 1893-1933).

33. These are listed in *Canadian Newspapers on Microfilm* (Ottawa, 1959——).

in Canadian history. Consisting of a lengthy survey of Canadian development since confederation, it marks a stock-taking from which "recent Canadian historiography" may most conveniently be dated. The core of the Rowell-Sirois Commission's enquiry concerned public finance, but the entire report, together with its appendixes and supplements, constitutes an excellent history of Canada.[34] Twenty additional studies were prepared by a corps of experts, and while some of the studies are relatively technical, others—William A. Mackintosh on the *Economic Background of Dominion-Provincial Relations*, Donald Grant Creighton on *British North America at Confederation*, and Stanley Alexander Saunders on *The Economic History of the Maritime Provinces* . . .—are valuable interpretative works. The entire series, some of whose appendixes appeared only in mimeographed form, is an epitome of Canadian historiography.

One of the best recent surveys of Canadian history is Edgar Wardwell McInnis' *Canada: A Political and Social History* (New York, 1947; rev. and enl., 1959). Despite its title the book is heavily political but well balanced chronologically. Donald Grant Creighton's *Dominion of the North: A History of Canada* (Boston, 1944; rev. ed., with subtitle elevated to title, 1958) is extremely well written, as is his shorter *The Story of Canada* (Boston, 1960). The long awaited volume by John Bartlet Brebner, *Canada: A Modern History* (Ann Arbor, 1960), published posthumously with a concluding chapter by Donald Campbell Masters, is below Brebner's usual high standard. Three shorter, less interpretative histories are George P. de T. Glazebrook, *A Short History of Canada* (Oxford, 1950); J. M. S. Careless, *Canada: A Story of Challenge* (Cambridge, 1953; rev. ed., 1964); and Gerald Sanford Graham, *Canada: A Short History* (London, 1950). Carl Frederick Wittke, *A History of Canada* (New York, 1928), remains important historiographically, for it was the first general history to place emphasis on the post-1759 period. A more recent general account, William Lewis Morton's *The Kingdom of Canada*, will be discussed elsewhere.

Concerned with a somewhat more limited approach to the Canadian scene, but still descriptive of the nation as a whole, are Chester

34. A helpful abridgment of Book I of the report may be found in Donald V. Smiley, ed., *The Rowell-Sirois Report* . . . (Toronto, 1963). Appendix III of the report has been reissued as William Archibald Mackintosh, *The Economic Background of Dominion-Provincial Relations* (Toronto, 1964), ed. by John Harkness Dales.

Bailey Martin, *Foundations of Canadian Nationhood* (Toronto, 1955), which brilliantly analyzes Canadian political development through confederation, and two studies of the machinery of government in Canada, Robert MacGregor Dawson, *The Government of Canada* (Toronto, 1947; rev. ed., 1954), and Hugh McDowell Clokie, *Canadian Government and Politics* (Toronto, 1944). In *Canada in the Making* (Seattle, 1953) George Williams Brown brought together several of his articles which throw light on diverse aspects of Canadian nationalism and in particular on Canadian religious development. Two very readable but uneven love poems to Canada have been written by a journalist, Bruce Hutchison: *The Unknown Country: Canada and Her People* (New York, 1942), and *Canada: Tomorrow's Giant* (New York, 1957). A superb historical atlas, edited by Donald G. G. Kerr, was published in 1960: *An Historical Atlas of Canada* (Toronto). Also valuable is Marcel Trudel, *Atlas historique du Canada Français: Des origines à 1867* (Quebec, 1961). Still indispensable is William Stewart Wallace, *The Dictionary of Canadian Biography* (2 vols.; rev. ed., Toronto, 1945), which was first issued, without its present useful reference lists, in 1926.[35]

*Collective and Co-operative histories*

The "Makers of Canada" series (21 vols.; Toronto, 1906-11), edited by Duncan Campbell Scott, Pelham Edgar, and W. D. LeSieur, beginning with Narcisse-Eutrope Dionne's brief life of *Champlain* and ending with James Hannay's life of *Sir Leonard Tilley*, was the first co-operative history to be written in Canada. In 1916 the publisher added James Wilberforce Longley's life of *Sir Charles Tupper* to the series, and in 1926 a new edition, which included new works on three of the figures and biographies of *Lord Strathcona*, *Sir William Van Horne*, and *Sir Wilfrid Laurier*, appeared. Between 1914 and 1917 Glasgow, Brook and Company of Toronto published twenty-three volumes on "Canada and Its Provinces . . . ," edited by Adam Shortt, the

35. Reissued in 1963 as *The* Macmillan *Dictionary of Canadian Biography* (3rd ed., rev. and enl., London). In 1959 work began on a bilingual "Dictionary of Canadian Biography," under the general editorship of George Williams Brown. Volumes will be organized chronologically, with the first to contain some 500 articles and notes on the period up to 1701. Professor Brown's death in 1963 has delayed publication of the first volume. Since Wallace's *Dictionary* is deficient on the French regime, one also has reason to be grateful for Louis Marie le Jeune, *Dictionnaire général de biographie, histoire, littérature, . . . institutions politiques et religieuses du Canada* (2 vols.; Ottawa, 1931).

father of economic history in Canada, and Sir Arthur George Doughty. The series' subtitle, *A History of the Canadian People and Their Institutions by One Hundred Associates,* indicated a new approach to Canadian history, and the lengthy sections on "currency and banking," "public finance," and "missions, arts, and letters," were genuine departures. Between 1914 and 1916 the same publisher produced the *Chronicles of Canada* under the editorship of George Mackinnon Wrong and Hugh Hornby Langton. This series began with Stephen Butler Leacock's *Aboriginal Canada,* a work of no particular merit, and ended with Oscar Skelton's *The Railway Builders.* In between lay thirty volumes, six by William C. H. Wood on military matters. Confederation came in Volume XXVIII and the final fifty-five years of Canadian history were treated in two volumes.[36]

In the third and fourth decades of the present century two excellent series of scholarly monographs were published. Most challenging in its approach was the "Canadian Frontiers of Settlement" series (Toronto, 1934-40), under the editorship of William Archibald MacKintosh and W. L. G. Joerg, which explored questions of social structure, geography, and agricultural economics. In *The Settlement of the Peace River Country: A Study of a Pioneer Area* (1934), Carl Addington Dawson and Robert Welch Murchie made able use of statistical data and information obtained directly from farmers. Again employing statistics to good effect, sociologist Dawson wrote of *Group Settlement: Ethnic Communities in Western Canada* (1936), describing Doukhobor, Mennonite, Mormon, German-Catholic, and French-Canadian groups. Dawson showed how the transportation revolution broke down the group and raised the question of how separatist communities, which contribute stability to a frontier region because of their cohesion, can contribute to a national unity as well. Joint-editor Mackintosh explored the *Economic Problems of the Prairie Provinces* (1935) and described *Prairie Settlement: The Geographical Setting* (1934). Murchie summarized *Agricultural Progress on the Prairie Frontier* (1936) and Dawson and Eva R. Younge analyzed the problems of *Pioneering in the Prairie Provinces: The Social Side of the Settlement Process* (1940). Harold Adams Innis rather disjointedly described *Settlement and the Mining Frontier* (1936), examining the Yukon Territory, the

36. Parallel to this, and to the "Makers of Canada" series, was the "Makers of Canadian Literature" series (Toronto), edited by Lorne Albert Pierce and Victor Morin. Of forty-one volumes originally planned, fourteen titles were issued from 1926.

Kootenay region, and northern Ontario. Indirectly this work was a contribution to metropolitanism as well. Historians contributed three of the best volumes: Arthur Silver Morton traced the *History of Prairie Settlement* (1938) to 1925, while Chester Bailey Martin revealed the inadequacies of the Canadian homestead policy and explored the problem of administration of natural resources in *"Dominion Lands" Policy* (1938). Arthur R. M. Lower documented the waste of such resources and described lumbering activities in *Settlement and the Forest Frontier in Eastern Canada,* previously mentioned.[37]

The "Canadian Frontiers of Settlement" series was written by Canadian scholars under the inspiration of an American research foundation, was published in Canada, and was first suggested by an American, Isaiah Bowman, President of the American Geographical Society and of The Johns Hopkins University. Another series prepared at this time, "The Relations of Canada and the United States," written by Canadian and American scholars, was published in both nations (New Haven and Toronto, 1936-45), and was first suggested by two Canadians resident in the United States, John Bartlet Brebner and James Thomson Shotwell. This series, sponsored by the Carnegie Endowment for International Peace, ran to twenty-five volumes under the general editorship of Shotwell, Director of Economics and History for the Endowment, and was concluded by Brebner's work on the *North Atlantic Triangle*. Once projected to thirty-four volumes, as the Brebner Papers at Columbia University show, the series was rather spotty as published, ignoring much of importance.

The seven volumes which told chronologically the story of Canadian-American relations were all written by Americans or by Canadians resident in the United States, while the remaining eighteen volumes were more evenly divided between the two countries. Max[well] H. Savelle traced the gradual diplomatic retreat of France in *The Diplomatic History of the Canadian Boundary, 1749-1763* (1940), a work which he has extended in several more recent articles. In *The United States, Great Britain, and British North America, from the Revolution to the Establishment of Peace after the War of 1812* (1940), Alfred LeRoy Burt revised the revisionists, rejected Julius W. Pratt's thesis that the War of 1812 was caused by land-hungry western ex-

37. Although nine volumes were planned for the series, only eight were published, for "The History of Immigration Policy and Company Colonization," to have been written by Duncan A. McArthur and William A. Carrothers, never was completed.

pansionists, demonstrated why suspicions that the British were foment-
ing Indian attacks were unjustified, and restored the impressment
controversy and neutral rights to their place among the causes of the
war.[38] The late Albert Bickmore Corey filled in many gaps on the
rebellion of 1837, the *Caroline* affair, and the Webster-Ashburton
Treaty, in *The Crisis of 1830-1842 in Canadian-American Relations*
(1941). Lester Burrell Shippee wrote an uneven treatment of the
middle period in *Canadian-American Relations, 1849-1874* (1939),
and Charles Callan Tansill emptied his filing cabinets upon his
readers' heads as he described negotiations over the fisheries,
pelagic sealing, and the Alaskan boundary controversies in *Canadian-
American Relations, 1875-1911* (1943). (Tansill's work must nonetheless be supplemented with Charles Soutter Campbell, Jr., *Anglo-
American Understanding, 1898-1903* [Baltimore, 1957]). Lewis Ethan
Ellis analyzed the interest groups which defeated the treaty of *Reciprocity, 1911: A Study in Canadian-American Relations* (1939). Brebner's work synthesized these volumes as well as those of a more topical
nature and fixed the completion of the triangle at 1910-17.

On economic interrelations Innis' work on *The Cod Fisheries* gave
meaning to the North Atlantic community concept, and Creighton's
volume on the *Commercial Empire of the St. Lawrence*—both originally in the series—showed how trade projected this concept inland.
George P. de T. Glazebrook described the *History of Transportation
in Canada* (1938) without showing how his subject was part of Canadian-American relations, and John Archibald Ruddick, William Malcolm Drummond, R. E. English, and John Ernest Lattimer examined, among many things, American influence on *The Dairy Industry in Canada* (1937). Lower continued his earlier study in *The North
American Assault on the Canadian Forest: A History of the Lumber
Trade between Canada and the United States* (1938). (Not included
in the series but a logical adjunct to it was Elwood S. Moore, *American
Influence in Canadian Mining* [Toronto, 1941]). Herbert Marshall,
Frank Allan Southard, Jr., and Kenneth Wiffin Taylor examined
*Canadian-American Industry: A Study in International Investment*

38. Recently a number of new studies of the causes of the War of 1812 have
appeared. Most important are Bradford Perkins, *Prologue to War: England and the
United States, 1805-1812* (Berkeley, 1961), and Reginald Horsman, *The Causes of
the War of 1812* (Philadelphia, 1962).

(1936). Volumes on labor relations and railroad connections also were included.

The rest of the series does not fall so easily into categories. In one of the best of the volumes Fred Landon discussed regional interrelations between *Western Ontario and the American Frontier* (1941), while John Perry Pritchett demonstrated how the Northwest Company tried to prevent Lord Selkirk's settlement in *The Red River Valley, 1811-1849:A Regional Study* (1942). Frederic William Howay, Walter N. Sage, and Henry Forbes Angus rather inconclusively looked at *British Columbia and the United States: The North Pacific Slope from Fur Trade to Aviation* (1942), adding to the small shelf of regional literature. Marcus Lee Hansen and Brebner traced *The Mingling of the Canadian and American Peoples* (1940), a superior study in immigration which was bolstered by two volumes of statistical interpretations by Robert Hamilton Coats, Murdoch C. MacLean, and Leon E. Truesdell. (Much recent work on immigration has led to substantial revisions and additions. Notable are the articles of Karel Denis Bicha, especially "The Plains Farmer and the Prairie Province Frontier, 1897-1914," *The Journal of Economic History* [New York], XXV [June, 1965], 263-70, and his forthcoming monograph on the same subject [Philadelphia].) Gustave Lanctôt directed a co-operative study of *Les Canadiens français et leurs voisin du sud* (Montreal, 1941), which dealt well with problems of Americanization, and Percy Ellwood Corbett analyzed *The Settlement of Canadian-American Disputes: A Critical Study of Methods and Results* (1937), which included much material which was not but should have been in the chronological volumes. Henry Forbes Angus edited *Canada and Her Great Neighbor: Sociological Surveys of Opinion and Attitudes in Canada Concerning the United States* (1938), a collection of relatively ineffective essays on what Canadians have thought of Americans.

To a certain extent this last-named volume indicates the weaknesses of the entire series. It seemed to be a collection of worthwhile essays without any apparent over-all plan of exactly what should be included in order to cover adequately the subject at hand. Several of the volumes in the series gave the impression of having been added simply because they were about to be published anyway. Few of the volumes exhausted their subjects and nearly all left tantalizing hints of dozens of books which remained to be written. There was no unity, no basic principle to the series, that was apparent other than that it is a good thing to know more about Canadian-American relations, and the final volume, Brebner's, actually departed from the series to begin what well could become an entirely new series.[39] In the twenty-five volumes there was practically nothing on the influence of American education in Canada, next to nothing on religion at the international level, the post-1911 period generally was ignored, and even in the chronological volumes there were several gaps.

Since the end of World War II three new scholarly series have been launched. The first of these, under the editorship of the late Robert MacGregor Dawson, is the "Canadian Government" series (Toronto, 1946——), at present consisting of fourteen volumes in history and political science. Particularly valuable to historians are John Edwin Hodgetts, *Pioneer Public Service: An Administrative History of the United Canadas, 1841-1867* (1955); James Murray Beck, *The Government of Nova Scotia* (1957), which reveals how little we know of localism in the Maritimes before and after confederation; John Tupper Saywell, *The Office of Lieutenant-Governor: A Study in Canadian Government and Politics* (1957), a pioneer work which is at once administrative history and political theory; and Norman Ward, *The Public Purse: A Study in Canadian Democracy* (1962), which shows how a new environment forced change upon the traditional office of auditor general. James Alexander Corry, *Democratic Government and Politics* (1946), is a comparative study of the governments of the North Atlantic Triangle, which together with editor Dawson's own *Government of Canada*, mentioned previously, comprised a two-volume introduction to the series.[40]

A second series, and the first to be completed, consists of studies on "Social Credit in Alberta: Its Background and Development" (10 vols.; Toronto, 1950-59) under the editorship of a sociologist, Samuel Delbert Clark. Almost uniformly excellent, written by sociologists, historians, and economists, this series is an exciting new contribution to Canadian scholarship. In *The Winnipeg General Strike* (1950) Donald

---

39. Since the several volumes of each series are discussed in the context of the series themselves, the volumes will not, with a few exceptions, be mentioned again in the topical sections which follow.

40. Of less interest to historians are Norman Ward, *The Canadian House of Commons: Representation* (1950); Frank MacKinnon, *The Government of Prince Edward Island* (1951); Hugh Garnet Thorburn, *Politics in New Brunswick* (1961); and Murray S. Donnelly, *The Government of Manitoba* (1963).

Campbell Masters shows that the strike of 1919 was not a Bolshevist movement but was a British-rooted, locally induced protest over the problem of collective bargaining. In *Next Year Country: A Study of Rural Social Organization in Alberta* (1951), Jean Burnet uses the single community of Hanna to analyze the tensions of the 1920's and '30's which gave rise to Social Credit. In *Democracy in Alberta: The Theory and Practice of a Quasi-Party System* (1953), Crawford Brough Macpherson makes a contribution to intellectual history and presents the thesis that a province kept in colonial status by economic dominance from the East, and guided by a *petit bourgeois* society, can develop no true two-party system. Another study with implications beyond the province is James Russell Mallory, *Social Credit and the Federal Power in Canada* (1954), which uses Alberta's Social Credit laws as a case study for the central government's use of the power of disallowance. An important contribution to Canadian religious history as a whole is William Edward Mann, *Sect, Cult, and Church in Alberta* (1955), which shows how religion takes on class colorations in Protestant frontier communities. Vernon Clifford Fowke, in *The National Policy and the Wheat Economy* (1957), demonstrates that the lack of a consistent national agricultural policy has prevented finding a solution to the wheat farmers' problems. The series arrives at its stated goal in John A. Irving's excellent *The Social Credit Movement in Alberta* (1959), which should be read after Lewis Gwynn Thomas' important party history, *The Liberal Party in Alberta: A History of Politics in the Province of Alberta, 1905-1921* (1959). For historians, however, the most interesting of the volumes in the series are the first, *The Progressive Party in Canada* (1950), by William Lewis Morton, probably the best history of a Canadian party yet written; and *Movements of Political Protest in Canada*, by Clark, the ninth volume.[41]

41. Thomas Bertram Costain edited a new "Canadian History" series (5 vols.; Toronto, 1954-61), which is designed for "the general reader." The earlier volumes— Costain, *The White and the Gold: The French Regime in Canada* (1954); Joseph Lister Rutledge, *Century of Conflict: The Struggle between the French and British in Colonial America* (1956); and Thomas Head Raddall, *The Path of Destiny: Canada from the British Conquest to Home Rule, 1763-1850* (1957)—do little that was not done better by Francis Parkman, Henry Adams, and Lawrence Henry Gipson. The best account of the military phases of the War of 1812 still is to be found in Adams' *History of the United States of America during the Administration of James Madison* (2 vols.; New York, 1930), which is Volumes V through IX of his *History of the United States of America* . . . (New York, 1889-91). But the most recent volume in the Costain series, Ralph Allen's *Ordeal by Fire: Canada, 1910-1945* (1961), while prone to minor errors, is exciting and generally reliable reading on World War I.

A third project, which promises to be the most important venture in co-operative history since the war, will be "The Canadian Centenary Series" (Toronto, 1963———), in seventeen volumes. Announced in 1957, under the editorship of William Lewis Morton and Donald Grant Creighton, this new series evidently will be the Canadian equivalent of *The Oxford History of England*. Since the latter series is to cover over 2,000 years in fourteen volumes, the Canadian series has more room for specialized works. It begins with a study which has been received badly, on *Early Voyages and Northern Approaches, 1000-1632* (1963) by Tryggvi J. Oleson. The series reaches confederation in volume twelve, *The Critical Years: The Union of British North America, 1857-1873* (1964) by Morton. Gerald M. Craig's cool and concise *Upper Canada: The Formative Years, 1784-1841* (1963) appeared first, followed by William John Eccles' fine *Canada Under Louis XIV, 1663-1701* (1964), and if these three speak for things to come, Canadian historiography is to be greatly enriched.

## The Struggle for North America

In 1959 this writer offered the opinion that "Little that is new has been said about the Old Regime in North America." Such a statement was based upon a solid foundation of ignorance. Indeed, much that is new has been said if perhaps sometimes said in old ways, and much remains to be said. While a number of French-Canadian books continue to be wearisome catalogues of factual material, or secular echoes of St. Matthew 1:1-16, the most recent works of French-Canadian scholarship, especially those by Guy Frégualt, Gustave Lanctôt, and Marcel Trudel, are very much a part of the mainstream of Canadian historiography. M. Frégault, in *La Guerre de la conquête* (Montreal, 1955), has shown that the French defeat in Canada was a cultural as well as a military defeat. Frégualt also has given us a lengthy, passionate, personal argument with previous historians in his paean to *Iberville le conquérant* (Montreal, 1944) and has written a forthright life of *François Bigot, administrateur français* (2 vols.; Montreal, 1948). His best work is *La Civilisation de la Nouvelle France (1713-1744)* (Montreal, 1944), followed by *Le Grand marquis: Pierre de Rigaud de Vaudreuil, et la Louisiane . . .* (Montreal, 1952). M. Lanctôt, in his *Histoire du Canada, I: Des origines au régime royal* (Montreal, 1959 [1960]), has written an outstanding history from discovery to 1663. A second volume, published in 1964, moves to the Treaty of Utrecht, and M. Lanctôt is now carrying his work forward to other volumes.[42]

Much important work on the French period and the conquest continues to be done by historians whose first language is English. One needs only to think of Alfred LeRoy Burt's *The Old Province of Quebec* (Minneapolis, 1933) to recognize this contribution, or of the excellent series of linked essays which constitutes a fundamental and hostile reassessment of *Frontenac, the Courtier Governor* (Toronto, 1959), by William John Eccles. But the chief speaking voices for this particular period of the Canadian drama clearly have become French, as demonstrated by John C. Rule in a superb article, "The Old Regime in America: A Review of Recent Interpretations of France in America," *William and Mary Quarterly*, 3rd ser., XIX (October, 1962), 575-600. Rule suggests that "historians will find among the writings of the French-Canadian school some of the most impressive work being published in North America today" and discusses many books and articles which, for that reason, need not be included in this essay.[43] Nor can one overlook the general histories of the French Empire, for if British history has its Gipson, Andrews, Osgood, Beer, and Savelle, then French history has its Charles-André Julien, Georges Hardy, Henri Blet, Hubert Deschamps, and Marcel Giraud—all of whom are intelligently discussed by Rule.[44]

Several excellent biographies of explorers and missionaries have been contributed in recent years. Nellis Maynard Crouse has written a good life of *Lemoyne d'Iberville: Soldier of New France* (Ithaca, 1954), and also has told of *La Verendrye, Fur Trader and Explorer* (Ithaca, 1956). The best biography of Champlain is Morris Bishop, *Champlain: The Life of Fortitude* (New York, 1948), and an excellent general biography, not scholarly but useful, is Francis Xavier

---

42. Volume one translated into English by Josephine Hambleton (Cambridge, Mass., 1963) and volume two by Margaret M. Cameron (Cambridge, Mass., 1964).

43. But one must not relegate to the limbo of books too numerous to mention at least Trudel's *L'Eglise Canadienne sous le régime militaire, 1759-1764*, I: *Les Problèmes* (Ottawa, 1956) and II: *Les Institutions* (Quebec, 1957); and Roland Lamontagne, *La Galissonière et le Canada* (Montreal, 1962). Important volumes in English include Percy J. Robinson, *Toronto during the French Regime, 1615-1793* (Toronto, 1933), and Cameron Nish, ed., *The French Regime* (Scarborough, Ont., 1965), a collection of documents.

44. Other guides are Gustave Lanctôt, in his *L'Oeuvre de la France en Amérique du Nord: Bibliographie sélective et critique* (Montreal, 1951); and Richard M. Saunders, "History and French-Canadian Survival," C.H.A. *Report* (1943), pp. 25-34.

Talbot, *Saint Among the Hurons: The Life of Jean de Brébeuf* (New York, 1949). Father Talbot also has written of *Saint among Savages: The Life of Isaac Jogues* (2nd ed., New York, 1935). None of these works claims to do more than tell a story which needed telling.[45] On the other hand, in *Caesars of the Wilderness: Medard Chouart, sieur des Groseilliers, and Pierre Esprit Radisson, 1618-1710* (New York, 1943), Grace Lee Nute unravels, to the discredit of her two central figures, their background and gives us what amounts to a definitive, and revisionist, history of their work, replacing the romantic *King of the Fur Traders: The Deeds and Deviltry of Pierre Esprit Radisson* (Boston, 1940), by Stanley Vestal (Walter Stanley Campbell). Still the best synthesis on continental exploration is John Bartlet Brebner, *The Explorers of North America, 1492-1806* (London, 1933).[46]

The great work of Lawrence Henry Gipson on *The British Empire before the American Revolution* (Vols. I-III [Caldwell, Idaho, 1936]; Vols. IV-X [New York, 1939-61]) marches on, now in its tenth volume. The entire series is indispensable reading, but especially pertinent for Canadian history are Volumes III and V through IX. These books, together with Howard Harvey Peckham, *Pontiac and the Indian Uprising* (Princeton, 1947), render obsolete some but by no

45. Extremely useful is *Black Gowns and Redskins: Adventures and Travels of the Early Jesuit Missionaries in North America, (1610-1791)*, edited by Edna Kenyon (London, 1956), drawn from the 73-volume edition of *Jesuit Relations and Allied Documents: . . . 1610-1791* (Cleveland, 1896-1901), edited by Reuben Gold Thwaites. Also important is *An Autobiography of Martyrdom: Spiritual Writings of the Jesuits in New France*, edited by François Roustang and translated by Sister M. Renelle (St. Louis, 1964) from *Jésuites de la Nouvelle-France* (Bruges, 1961).

46. It will be apparent that this essay omits, on the whole, the history of exploration. North Americans have had a vast continent to explore and have been fascinated with its exploration for 350 years, and the literature of discovery is voluminous. Much of it, like Brebner's volume, is continental, with Canadian content but not Canadian focus. Many books, such as Leslie H. Neatby's *In Quest of the North West Passage* (London, 1958) or Glyndwr Williams' *The British Search for the Northwest Passage in the Eighteenth Century* (London, 1962), are more a part of general Imperial history than of Canadian. Yet others—Bern Anderson's *Surveyor of the Sea: The Life and Voyages of Captain George Vancouver* (Seattle, 1960), or John E. Parsons' excellent triangulation of the Canadian-American boundary survey of 1872-75, *West on the 49th Parallel: Red River to the Rockies, 1872-1876* (New York, 1963), or the accounts of overland exploration, as in Walter Sheppe, ed., *First Man West: Alexander Mackenzie's Journal of His Voyage to the Pacific Coast of Canada in 1793* (Berkeley, 1962) or William Kaye Lamb, ed., *The Letters and Journals of Simon Fraser, 1806-1808* (Toronto, 1960)—are central to the Canadian story. Particularly valuable is John Warkentin's collection of source materials, *The Western Interior of Canada: A Record of Geographical Discovery 1612-1917* (Toronto, 1964). Space must have its victims, however, and this must be one of several themes in Canadian history that is left, perhaps to some future symposium volume devoted solely to Canadian historiography.

means all of Parkman. A preview of the two volumes yet to come in Gipson's *magnum opus* can be obtained from his *The Coming of the Revolution, 1763-1775* (New York, 1954), and a survey of his ideas is available in his inaugural lecture at Oxford in 1951, *The British Empire in the Eighteenth Century: Its Strength and Its Weakness* (Oxford, 1952). Jack M. Sosin, *Whitehall and the Wilderness: The Middle-West in British Colonial Policy, 1760-1775* (Lincoln, Neb., 1961), supports Reginald Coupland's classic *The Quebec Act* (Oxford, 1925) and provides important modifications to Gipson on the Proclamation of 1763. For a critical assessment of Gipson's work, see Arthur R. M. Lower, "Lawrence H. Gipson and the First British Empire: An Evaluation," *The Journal of British Studies* (Hartford), III (November, 1963), 57-78. Unfortunately, Gipson shares Parkman's bias against the necessary full use of French sources and literature.

Gerald Sanford Graham, who wrote *British Policy and Canada, 1774-1791: A Study in 18th Century Trade Policy* (London, 1930), has carried his study of maritime history on with *Sea Power and British North America, 1783-1820: A Study in British Colonial Policy* (Cambridge, Mass., 1941), and *Empire of the North Atlantic: The Maritime Struggle for North America* (Toronto, 1950). Two more specialized studies are John Bartlet Brebner, *The Neutral Yankees of Nova Scotia: A Marginal Colony during the Revolutionary Years* (New York, 1937), which is a sequel to his *New England's Outpost: Acadia before the Conquest of Canada* (New York, 1927). Both tell the history of Nova Scotia as part of New England, and the former ascribes the colony's failure to join in the Revolution to its isolation and the power of the London merchants.[47]

On the War of 1812, in addition to Burt's analysis and the volumes by Raddall, Adams, Perkins, and Horsman, mentioned above, there are four more specialized, military studies. Glenn Tucker has explored the life and personality of Tecumseh in an imaginative biography, *Tecumseh: Vision of Glory* (Indianapolis, 1956), and Alec Richard Gilpin has written a brief and rather unsatisfactory military

47. Another answer to the same riddle is given by Wilfred Brenton Kerr, *The Maritime Provinces of British North America and the American Revolution* (Sackville, N.B., 1941), who credits poor communications and oligarchic controls in the Maritimes for Nova Scotia's failure to join the rebellious colonies. An able re-examination is George A. Rawlyk's article, "The American Revolution and Nova Scotia Reconsidered," *Dalhousie Review*, XLIII (Autumn, 1963), 379-94.

account, *The War of 1812 in the Old Northwest* (East Lansing, 1958). Henry Lewis Coles, *The War of 1812* (Chicago, 1965), is quite brief. For rousing accounts of the blood-letting involved, one can read Tucker's *Poltroons and Patriots: A Popular Account of the War of 1812* (2 vols.; Indianapolis, 1954). A fuller picture of the war may be obtained from a convenient collection of otherwise often obscure articles, *The Defended Border: Upper Canada and the War of 1812* (Toronto, 1964), edited by Morris Zaslow and Wesley B. Turner.

There is a comparatively large literature on the 1837 rebellion and, of course, an even larger literature on the Durham Report. Canadians often argue that theirs is the central Commonwealth historiography constitutionally, for so many of the precedents in the steps toward independence within the Commonwealth were set in Canada: the Durham Report is but one rung in a ladder that ascends via the Reciprocity Treaty of 1854, Galt's tariff of 1859, confederation, the refusal of double dissolution, the Halibut Treaty, independent representation abroad, the League of Nations, and a freely given declaration of war upon Germany in 1939. To a degree this view is correct: whether correct or not, it accounts for an early preoccupation with constitutional history and, in particular, with the Durham Report. French Canadians have had their own reasons to pursue 1837, and the polemical literature in particular is great. Recently an American scholar, Helen Taft Manning, has brought order into the years just prior to the rebellion in *The Revolt of French Canada, 1800-1835: A Chapter in the History of the British Commonwealth* (New York, 1962). Sir Charles Prestwood Lucas prepared the standard commentary on Durham,[48] and George Earl Wilson in the *Life of Robert Baldwin. . .* (Toronto, 1933) and Chester W. New in *Lord Durham* provided solid biographies from which all recent work must depart. Gerald M. Craig's *Upper Canada*, previously mentioned, recasts the period of the rebellion with scholarly preciseness, while Leonard Cooper, in *Radical Jack: The Life of the First Earl of Durham* (London, 1959), provides us with an entertaining but not fundamentally new point of view. A genuinely brilliant book is William Kilbourn's *The Firebrand: William Lyon MacKenzie and the Rebellion in Upper Canada* (Toronto, 1956; rev. ed., 1964). But many questions remain unanswered, and studies of

48. *Lord Durham's Report on the Affairs of British North America* (3 vols.; Oxford, 1912).

decision-making, alternative policies, and specific factions still may be written to advantage.

### Constitutional and Political History

Recent political histories of Canada tend to fall into three groups: fairly traditional studies of the development of dominion status, administrative histories, and histories of the newer political parties of Canada. Many studies of Canada's growing independence continue to stem from Robert MacGregor Dawson's *The Development of Dominion Status, 1900-1936* (London, 1937), a collection of documents (which included South Africa, Australia, and New Zealand) preceded by a lengthy and incisive constitutional history. Maurice Ollivier, *Problems of Canadian Sovereignty from the British North America Act, 1867, to the Statute of Westminister, 1931* (Toronto, 1945), presents a nationalist viewpoint which is especially strong in its analysis of the rôle of the governor-general. Ollivier disagrees with Eugene Alfred Forsey, who in *The Royal Power of Dissolution of Parliament in the British Commonwealth* (Toronto, 1943), maintains that Lord Byng acted both correctly and wisely in 1926 in refusing to dissolve Parliament at the request of Mackenzie King. Both treatments are interesting to contrast with William Lewis Morton's account in *The Progressive Party in Canada* and Australian Herbert Vere Evatt's analysis in *The King and His Dominion Governors* (London, 1936). In *The Road to Nationhood: A Chronicle of Dominion-Provincial Relations* (Toronto, 1946), Wilfrid Eggleston shows how the original intentions of the Fathers of Confederation were modified, especially in fiscal matters.

Dominion-provincial relations have been examined most recently in Arthur R. M. Lower, *et al.*, *Evolving Canadian Federalism* (Durham, N.C., 1958), a series of five addresses, and in J. H. Aitchison, ed., *The Political Process in Canada: Essays in Honour of R. MacGregor Dawson* (Toronto, 1963), which is more informative than most *Festschriften*. Alexander H. McLintock, in *The Establishment of Constitutional Government in Newfoundland, 1783-1832: A Study of Retarded Colonisation* (London, 1941), shows how the wars of the French Revolution helped free Newfoundland of a fishing monopoly based on English ports and how the colony obtained some measure of responsible government by 1832 from the English Reform Parliament. Charles Perry Stacey, in *Canada and the British Army, 1846-1871: A*

*Study in the Practice of Responsible Government* (London, 1936; rev. ed., Toronto, 1963), and in several subsequent articles, has forcefully recounted British efforts to induce Canada to assume the burden of local self-defense. Harold Gordon Skilling, *Canadian Representation Abroad: From Agency to Embassy* (Toronto, 1945), describes the machinery but not the policy of an independent department of external affairs and traces the evolution of representation from the establishment of an immigration agent in London in 1868. Concerned with the preconfederation period, Duncan Hugh Gillis, *Democracy in the Canadas, 1759-1867* (Toronto, 1951), surveys Canadian politics and Oscar Arvle Kinchen's rather slight *Lord Russell's Canadian Policy: A Study in British Heritage and Colonial Freedom* (Lubbock, Texas, 1945), shows how Lord Russell attempted to inaugurate a regime of "moderation and harmony" in British North America. Hilda Marion Neatby, *Administration of Justice Under the Quebec Act* (London, 1937), remains one of the most important and provocative political studies of the pre-Revolutionary period.

A number of generally excellent books on recent political parties in Canada have been written since the war, with American-based scholars contributing a considerable share. John Ryan Williams has presented a concise survey, lacking in interpretation, of *The Conservative Party of Canada, 1920-1949* (Durham, N.C., 1956), while Dean Eugene McHenry has told the story of *The Third Force in Canada: The Cooperative Commonwealth Federation, 1932-1948* (Berkeley, 1950). Seymour Martin Lipset, in *Agrarian Socialism: The Cooperative Commonwealth Federation in Saskatchewan, A Study in Political Sociology* (Berkeley, 1950), focuses brilliantly upon a single province. Lipset shows that the C.C.F. had little significance as a philosophy of government or of socialism but after the party reached office in 1944 it ably represented the wheat farmer. The series on the Social Credit movement in Alberta provides a thorough analysis of a movement which also appeared in New Zealand. Herbert Fuylong Quinn, *The Union Nationale: A Study in Quebec Nationalism* (Toronto, 1963), tells of the party's rise to power, of its policies, and of opposition to it through the election of 1960.[49] Catherine Lyle Cleverdon has written

49. Several electoral studies, influenced by work at Nuffield College, have been coming out of Australia, New Zealand, and Africa in recent years. One Canadian example is John Meisel, *The Canadian General Election of 1957* (Toronto, 1962). An extremely useful collection of essays on *Party Politics in Canada* (Toronto, 1963) has been brought together by Hugh Garnet Thorburn.

of *The Woman Suffrage Movement in Canada* (Toronto, 1950), a movement which represents quite recent history since women did not receive the vote in Quebec until 1940. But the histories of the major Canadian parties, Liberal and Conservative, are yet to be written in the light of political developments since 1957.[50]

Political biography may provide a better entree to the intricacies of political history, in any case, than studies of individual parties. Who could understand twentieth-century Australian political development, for example, in terms of party structure alone? Success in politics depends upon clearly realized systems of priorities, and it is individual leaders and not amorphous parties that define and then pursue priority goals. One of the most striking trends in Canadian historiography in the 1960's is toward the political biography.

William Lyon Mackenzie King is the F.D.R. or Winston Churchill of Canadian historiography around whom controversy is inevitable. The best one-volume life remains the popular account by (William) Bruce Hutchison, *The Incredible Canadian: A Candid Portrait of Mackenzie King* (London, 1952), while Henry Reginald Hardy, *Mackenzie King of Canada* (London, 1949), is also serviceable. Both are written in the Liberal vein. A third biography, *The Age of Mackenzie King: The Rise of the Leader* (London, 1955), by Henry Stanley Ferns and Bernard Ostry, is less laudatory. Ferns and Ostry have written, as their subtitle indicates, only a partial life, carrying King to his election in 1919. The work is not as well documented as it should be and has been severely criticized by some reviewers, but the authors' only sin and major contribution is to show that King was self-seeking and ambitious and, in effect, a superb politician. King's private secretary, Fred A. McGregor, has added to the years when King was out of politics, chiefly serving Rockefeller in the United States, in *The Rise and Fall of Mackenzie King, 1911-1919* (Toronto, 1962). In all four of the books their authors' biases are quite evident, and while this may be a protection for the unsophisticated reader, they leave the serious student dissatisfied.

The authorized biography of King was assigned to Robert Mac-Gregor Dawson, a leading Canadian political scientist of generally liberal persuasions. There were to be three volumes, but Dawson died

---

50. Received too late for examination was Leo Zakuta, *A Protest Movement Becalmed: A Study of Change in the C.C.F.* (Toronto, 1964).

after completing the first, *William Lyon Mackenzie King: A Political Biography, 1874-1923* (Toronto, 1958), which carried King to the Imperial Conference of 1923, when he was forty-nine. Dawson was able to draw freely upon the King papers—over two million pages of documents in all—and upon King's copious, self-revealing diaries. The result is more analytical than narrative, as befitting a political scientist. Upon this all agreed, but upon the merit of the biography—and upon its objectivity—scholars have disagreed. Nothing is more informative than comparing Donald Grant Creighton's discussion of Dawson's achievement with Arthur R. M. Lower's assessment.[51] Dawson's conclusions became even more apparent in a brief book, published posthumously, that drew upon the King diaries to present his side of *The Conscription Crisis of 1944* (Toronto, 1961). Conscription was a central, emotional issue that threatened to divide French-speaking from English-speaking Canadians,[52] and King was able to maneuver his way through his greatest challenge, at the cost of principle, time, and his defense minister. But although Dawson's biography has seemed too laudatory to some, perhaps he (and King) have reminded us that novelists hold no monopoly on the corridors of power. If some reviewers appeared ready to play Leavis to Dawson's Snow, others recognized that Dawson—like Snow—was committed to explanation in the first person.

However, the best picture of this exemplar of Victorian virtues (and passions) came from King's own hands, as laid upon John Whitney Pickersgill, who edited the *Mackenzie King Record, 1939-44* (Toronto, 1960), the first of two volumes from the diaries. King emerges as one of the most fascinating figures in the history of the English-speaking world. The publication of Herbert Blair Neatby's successor volume to Dawson's work, *William Lyon Mackenzie King: The Lonely Heights* (Toronto, 1964), deepens this fascination.

There is no scholarly biography of Robert Borden, although Henry Borden has edited his uncle's papers in *Robert Laird Borden: His Memoirs* (2 vols.; Toronto, 1938). Leslie Roberts has given us *C.D., The Life and Times of Clarence Decatur Howe* (Toronto, 1957), which is something of an interim report. One of the most interesting

51. Creighton in *The University of Toronto Quarterly*, XXVIII (Jan., 1959), 197-200, and Lower in *Queen's Quarterly*, LXVI (Spring, 1959), 146-50.

52. Theodore Ropp's forthcoming study of conscription throughout the Commonwealth should give added perspective to this issue.

biographies is A. H. U. Colquhoun, *Press, Politics, and People: The Life and Letters of Sir John Willison, Journalist and Correspondent of the Times* (Toronto, 1935), which puts flesh on the bones of a strangely inconsistent figure who had great influence as editor of the Toronto *Globe*. Robert Rumilly has written a long and useful life of *Henri Bourassa* (Montreal, 1944), the great French-Canadian nationalist, a biography which is best read in conjunction with Elizabeth Howard Armstrong, *The Crisis of Quebec, 1914-18* (New York, 1937), which shows how Bourassa's attacks upon imperialism, together with the French-language question in Ontario schools and enforcement of conscription, produced the riots of March, 1918. Leslie Roberts, *The Chief: A Political Biography of Maurice Duplessis* (Toronto, 1963), and Peter Charles Newman, *Renegade in Power: The Diefenbaker Years* (Toronto, 1963), are lively journalistic accounts, both hostile. There is still no biography of William Aberhart, prime mover of Social Credit in Alberta, but the agrarian revolt can be seen through *Henry Wise Wood of Alberta* (Toronto, 1950), by William Kirby Rolph, which describes Progressive party activities in the 1920's and the establishment of the Alberta Wheat Pool in 1933. The politics of principle, commitment, and defeat in the C.C.F. is ably viewed through the eyes of *A Prophet in Politics: A Biography of J. S. Woodsworth* (Toronto, 1959), by Kenneth McNaught. Also of great importance in terms of the C.C.F., of Canadian liberalism, and of Canadian historiography in general is a fascinating, always witty, sometimes sharp-tongued, nearly autobiographical collection of the previously published essays of Frank Hawkins Underhill, *In Search of Canadian Liberalism* (Toronto, 1960).

Canadian political figures have been reticent about writing their memoirs, and when they have done so they often have produced apologias of little significance. Four exceptions which are readable and informative are *Public Servant: The Memoirs of Sir Joseph Pope* edited by Maurice Pope (Toronto, 1960), which covers the period from 1854 to 1925; Robert James Manion, *Life Is an Adventure* (Toronto, 1936), by a minister of railways during the depression years; and Harold Adams Innis' edition of *The Diary of Alexander James McPhail* (Toronto, 1940), which tells of the co-operative movement among wheat farmers in the West. Perhaps the best—certainly the most informative—is *What's Past Is Prologue: The Memoirs of Vincent Massey* (New York, 1964).

Four of the Fathers of Confederation recently have been the subjects of new biographies. The most outstanding of the Fathers has received the most outstanding of the biographies, *John A. Macdonald: The Young Politician* (Toronto, 1952), and *John A. Macdonald: The Old Chieftain* (Toronto, 1955), by Donald Grant Creighton. These two volumes are an unabashed "life and times," written with wit, vigor, and occasional beauty. The second volume is more important, for it tells of the building of a nation, but the first volume is more interesting, for it tells of the building of a man. Neither renders obsolete Sir Joseph Pope's older memoirs and collection of Macdonald's letters,[53] but the readability and scholarly merit of Creighton's volumes make them perhaps the best Canadian biography ever written. Properly, Creighton's two volumes on Macdonald have nearly been matched by J. M. S. Careless' two-volume life of *Brown and the Globe: The Voice of Upper Canada, 1818-1859*, and . . . *Statesman of Confederation, 1860-1880* (Toronto, 1959-63). Careless' skill matches that of Creighton, and were it not for the fact that George Brown, often Macdonald's greatest foe, was personally less colorful than the Kingston lawyer, these volumes would rival Macdonald in a way that even Brown did not.

The other Fathers have fared less well. In *The Ardent Exile: The Life and Times of Thomas D'Arcy McGee* (Toronto, 1951), Josephine Phelan tells a good story but does not displace Isabel Murphy Skelton's soporific but more thorough *The Life of Thomas D'Arcy McGee* (Gardenvale, P.Q., 1925). James Alexander Roy, in *Joseph Howe: A Study in Achievement and Frustration* (Toronto, 1935), sometimes strains to prove either achievement or frustration but gives us the fullest and surely the most human portrait of the Nova Scotian that we have. The rest of the Fathers still await their first modern biographers.

Other political biographies of considerable merit are Ronald Stewart Longley's *Sir Francis Hincks: A Study of Canadian Politics, Railways and Finance in the Nineteenth Century* (Toronto, 1943), which shows the interrelations of business with politics, and Dale C. Thomson's skilful delineation of the man who was Prime Minister from 1873 to 1878, *Alexander Mackenzie: Clear Grit* (Toronto, 1960). For the recent period William Roger Graham has published the first two (of three)

53. Pope, *Memoirs of the Right Honourable Sir John Alexander Macdonald . . .* (2 vols.; Ottawa, [1894]), and *Correspondence of Sir John Macdonald . . .* (Toronto, [1921]).

volumes in his sensible and measured life of *Arthur Meighen: The Door of Opportunity, 1874-1920*, followed by *And Fortune Fled, 1920-1927* (Toronto, 1960-63). There is no biography of Edward Blake's Canadian years, and the student must be content with Margaret A. Banks, *Edward Blake, Irish Nationalist: A Canadian Statesman in Irish Politics, 1892-1907* (Toronto, 1957), which reveals something of his character, and Frank Hawkins Underhill's articles. Nor is there a full scholarly biography of John W. Dafoe, although George Victor Ferguson wrote an intimate portrait, *John W. Dafoe* (Toronto, 1948), for the general reader, and in *The Politics of John W. Dafoe and the Free Press* (Toronto, 1963) Ramsay Cook has analyzed the ideas of a western liberal nationalist who appears to have been a Canadian Wilsonian.[54]

There also is need for biographies of several of the governors-general of Canada. Donald G. G. Kerr, with the aid of James Alexander Gibson, has told of *Sir Edmund Head: A Scholarly Governor* (Toronto, 1954), and William Stewart MacNutt has given us *Days of Lorne: Impressions of a Governor-General* (Fredericton, 1955), both of which are brief, attractively written contributions. Many other lives remain to be reviewed, however, in particular those of Lord Monck, who also was a Father of Confederation in his own way, Lord Aberdeen, Lord Byng, and Lord Tweedsmuir.[55]

## Ethnic and Religious History

Church history is not flourishing at the scholarly level in Canada, but there is an abundance of amateur and particularistic works. Subliterary histories of religious groups proliferate by the evangelical

---

54. For the only life of a man who "died with his name a byword for corruption," see the late Barbara Fraser's "The Political Career of Sir Hector Louis Langevin," *CHR*, XLII (June, 1961), 93-132. Recent lesser biographies which are nonetheless important are Pierre Laporte, *The True Face of* [Maurice] *Duplessis* (Montreal, 1960), a bitterly critical attack; Raymond Tanghe, *Laurier: Artisan de l'unité canadienne, 1841-1919* (Paris, 1960), which provides a useful addition to earlier studies; and W. H. Graham, *Tiger Dunlop* (London, 1962), on William Dunlop, a colonization agent for the Canada Company.

55. Two of these men are well on the way to assuming their proper place in the literature of Canadian history. John Tupper Saywell has edited *The Canadian Journal of Lady Aberdeen, 1893-1898* (Toronto, 1960) and has written, in the introduction, a fine beginning for the political history of the period. Tweedsmuir, John Buchan, has spoken for himself in *Memory Hold-the-Door* (London, 1940), of course, and Janet Adam Smith is nearing completion of her authorized biography. A lesser but significant figure is examined by James K. Chapman in a very able study, *The Career of Arthur Hamilton Gordon, First Lord Stanmore, 1829-1912* (Toronto, 1964).

nature of the subject. Nonetheless, a few recent contributions to church history have begun to fill in the Canadian canvas. The most important books are Samuel Delbert Clark, *Church and Sect in Canada* (Toronto, 1948), which recounts the history of a number of dissenting groups from the Great Awakening in Nova Scotia to the urban Great Revival at the beginning of the present century; and Henry Horace Walsh, *The Christian Church in Canada* (Toronto, 1956), which is a survey by a member of a Faculty of Divinity. The total scope of Christian life in Canada is included, with an excellent chapter on the Roman Catholic Church. Recent studies of Jesuit history are Léon Pouliot's *Études sur les relations des jésuites de la Nouvelle-France (1632-1672)* (Montreal, 1940), and Father Talbot's life of Brébeuf. Maurice Whitman Armstrong's *The Great Awakening in Nova Scotia, 1776-1809* (Hartford, 1948), is a needed gap-filler, while John Sargent Moir has dealt with the thorny issues of the Clergy Reserves and the church in education in *Church and State in Canada West: Three Studies in the Relation of Denominationalism and Nationalism, 1841-1867* (Toronto, 1959). Several of the volumes in the Social Credit series show the evangelical background of that movement. More recently Father Pouliot has been exploring the life of Monseigneur Ignace Bourget in a series of articles and a monograph.

One religious group which has been well served in Canada is the Methodist, on which a number of fairly solid older histories already exist. To them now may be added John Henry Riddell, *Methodism in the Middle West* (Toronto, 1946), and Goldwin French, *Parsons & Politics: The Rôle of the Wesleyan Methodists in Upper Canada and the Maritimes from 1780-1855* (Toronto, [1962]). The latter is particularly good on Methodist attitudes toward responsible government. Charles Bruce Sissons, *Egerton Ryerson: His Life and Letters* (2 vols.; Toronto, 1937-47), is the finest biography of a Canadian religious leader yet available. Because of Ryerson's wide range of activities, Sisson's biography encompasses much that is not religious history. Sissons also has edited *My Dearest Sophie: Letters from Egerton Ryerson to His Daughter* (Toronto, 1955), which covers 1858-81. Much less adequate is Sisson's *Church and State in Canadian Education: An Historical Study* (Toronto, 1959).

Other groups have been less well served. There is no general history of Canadian Baptists, although Stuart Ivison and Fred Rosser,

*The Baptists in Upper and Lower Canada before 1820* (Toronto, 1956), is a good start. The two authors cover the interval between the American Revolution and their terminal date and emphasize religious ties with the new United States. Vladimar J. Eylands, *Lutherans in Canada* (Winnipeg, 1945), is rather trivial. Thomas Reagh Millman, *Jacob Mountain, First Lord Bishop of Quebec: A Study in Church and State, 1793-1825* (Toronto, 1947), reveals the problems of organizing a dominant church in a land where the majority of the people are opposed to it.[56] Emerick K. Francis, *In Search of Utopia: The Mennonites in Manitoba* (Glencoe, Ill., 1955), is an excellent analysis, while James F. C. Wright, *Slava Bohu: The Story of the Dukhobors* (New York, 1940), and Harry Bertram Hawthorn, ed., *The Doukhobors of British Columbia* (Vancouver, 1955), tell the popular and scholarly stories, respectively, of this difficult sect. Simma Milner Holt, in *Terror in the Name of God: The Story of the Sons of Freedom Doukhobors* (Toronto, 1964), attacks the radical wing of the group with a reform journalist's vigor.

There are two studies of Judaism in Canada, Benjamin Gutelins Sack, *History of the Jews in Canada from the Earliest Beginnings to the Present Day*, the first of a two-volume work (Montreal, 1945), and Louis Rosenberg, *Canada's Jews: A Social and Economic Study of the Jews in Canada* (Montreal, 1939). The subliterature in Canada concerning the Jewish community best finds its expression in novels—notably in Mordecai Richler and Adele Wiseman—of city life, often opening with an "arrival scene," a subjective view of the Canadian landscape as seen by a newly arrived immigrant. One autobiographical book, Norman Levine's fascinatingly repellent *Canada Made Me* (London, 1958), in effect is a running series of such arrival scenes. Two obviously neglected groups are the Mormons in the West and the Jehovah's Witnesses in Quebec, and little has been written on the Quakers since Arthur Garratt Dorland, *A History of the Society of Friends (Quakers) in Canada* (Toronto, 1927). For many aspects of the Canadian story one can still turn to the fifth volume of Kenneth Scott Latourette, *A History of the Expansion of Christianity* (7 vols.;

56. Despite its date of publication, the writer was unable to obtain T. C. B. Boon's *The Anglican Church from the Bay to the Rockies: A History of the Ecclesiastical Province of Rupert's Land and Its Dioceses from 1820 to 1950* (Toronto, 1962) in time to review it.

New York, 1937-45),[57] and for the problem of religious freedom in Canada one may begin with D. A. Schmeiser, *Civil Liberties in Canada* (London, 1964), a legal history rather than a study of the Canadian civil rights movement.

Ethnic history often is the history of immigration. Several works in the Carnegie Endowment and "Canadian Frontiers of Settlement" series are important in this respect. The best study of policy is Norman Macdonald, *Canada, 1763-1841, Immigration and Settlement: The Administration of the Imperial Land Regulations* (London, 1939), while the best study of a single group is Paul Yuzyk, *The Ukrainians in Manitoba: A Social History* (Toronto, 1953), which surveys the fourth largest national grouping in the Dominion. John Kosa, *Land of Choice: The Hungarians in Canada* (Toronto, 1957) is adequate. Charles William Dunn, *Highland Settler: A Portrait of the Scottish Gael in Nova Scotia* (Toronto, 1953), is a pioneer study in folk culture. There are two substantial studies of German immigration to Canada: Winthrop Pickard Bell, *The "Foreign Protestants" and the Settlement of Nova Scotia: The History of a Piece of Arrested British Colonial Policy in the Eighteenth Century* (Toronto, 1961), about the Germans of Lunenburg County, and George Elmore Reaman, *The Trail of the Black Walnut* (Toronto, 1950), which brings the "Pennsylvania Dutch" trekking to Ontario. That the Negro has had a place in Canadian history has been recognized in several journal articles, notably by Fred Landon and William Renwick Riddell, and in *L'Esclavage au Canada français* (Quebec, 1960) Marcel Trudel throws much light into a dark corner of New France (the majority of slaves were not Negroes, however, but *panis* or Indians). The present writer's *The Negro in Canada* (New Haven, forthcoming) is a general study of the Canadian Negro from slavery to the present time. Canadian racial problems also are explored in the exhaustive study of *Le Métis Canadien: Son rôle dans l'histoire des provinces de l'ouest* (Paris, 1945), by Marcel Giraud; in Auguste Henry de Trémaudan, *Histoire de la nation métisse dans l'ouest canadien* (Montreal, 1936); and in Donatien Fremont, *Les Français dans l'ouest canadien* (Winnipeg, 1959). Midway between general policy and a particular group is Helen I. Cowan, *British Emi-*

57. A mixed bag of generally good sectarian summaries with emphasis on cultural diffusion is John Webster Grant, *The Church and the Canadian Experience: A Faith and Order Study of the Christian Tradition* (Toronto, 1963).

*gration to British North America: The First Hundred Years* (rev. ed., Toronto, 1961), an ably presented analysis of the period to 1860.

There is little on the Indian in Canada. Gontran Laviolette, *The Sioux Indians in Canada* (Regina, 1944), is a generally unsatisfactory pioneer effort. A sociological work, *Tribe under Trust: A Study of the Blackfoot Reserve of Alberta* (Toronto, 1950), by Lucien Mason Hanks, Jr., and Jane Richardson Hanks, recounts the more recent history of the Blackfeet, while in the first half of *The Micmac Indians of Eastern Canada* (Minneapolis, 1955), Wilson Dallam Wallis and Ruth Sawtell Wallis mingle considerable historical material with their anthropology. Archibald (later Sir Archibald) Grenfell Price, in *White Settlers and Native People: An Historical Study of Racial Contacts between English-speaking Whites and Aboriginal Peoples in the United States, Canada, Australia, and New Zealand* (Melbourne, 1949), concludes that Canada has treated her aboriginal population better than the other nations under consideration. Anthropologists have made important contributions in the field of race relations and culture contact, and *The Bella Coola Indians* (2 vols.; Toronto, 1948), by Thomas Forsyth McIlwraith, and the many books and articles of Charles-Marius Barbeau, on totem poles, Indian myths, and folk songs, are of great interest. Three combinations of anthropology and history which meet in that evolving field, ethnohistory, are Alfred Goldsworthy Bailey, *The Conflict of European and Eastern Algonkian Cultures, 1504-1700: A Study in Canadian Civilization* (Sackville, N.B., 1937); George T. Hunt, *The Wars of the Iroquois: A Study in Intertribal Trade Relations* (Madison, 1940); and Bernard G. Hoffman, *Cabot to Cartier: Sources for a Historical Ethnography of Northeastern North America, 1497-1550* (Toronto, 1961). Of particular concern to the historian are the two works of Frank Gilbert Roe, *The Indian and the Horse* (Norman, 1955), and *The North American Buffalo: A Critical Study of the Species in its Wild State* (Toronto, 1951).

## French-Canadian Historiography

In recent years several French-Canadian historians have broken from the Groulx approach and have been writing fully as objectively as their English-speaking colleagues. But Mason Wade's huge *The French Canadians, 1760-1945* (Toronto, 1955) remains an indispensable book on the subject, for unlike most studies of French Canada,

Wade concentrates on recent political history and does not ignore economic and cultural matters. He finds post-World War II French Canadians more eclectic and liberal, less inclined to look to France for cultural nurturing, but also more divided among themselves because of these developments.[58] *The Spirit of French Canada: A Study of the Literature* (New York, 1939), by Ian Forbes Fraser, is a book of readings on how French-Canadian historians and *littérateurs* have viewed *survivance* of the French-Canadian "nation." Robert Rumilly, *Histoire de la province de Quebec* (33 vols.; Montreal, 1942- ), consists of short volumes, primarily political, on the years since confederation. Volume V is devoted to the impact of Louis Riel's uprising in 1885 on thought in the province and makes interesting collateral reading to the works on Riel mentioned below.

Sociologists have provided us with some of our most valuable insights into recent Quebec. Two "classics" were reissued, with new introductions, in 1963. The first, Horace Mitchell Miner's ethnological case study of a single rural community, *St. Denis: A French-Canadian Parish* (Chicago, 1939), generated a major controversy. St. Denis (which exists on any map) was matched by Cantonville (which exists only as a fictitious name for an industrial town), the creation of Everett Cherrington Hughes in *French Canada in Transition* (Chicago, 1943). Hughes, a sociologist who avoids jargon in order to "tell the news," wanted to call his book "Jean-Baptiste Comes to Town"—an excellent summary of its purpose. Jean-Charles Falardeau, in several essays on contemporary Quebec, also has sought to explain this tradition-oriented society. Miner, Hughes, and Falardeau, among others, have been attacked by Philippe Garigue for seeing French-Canadian life as family-dominated, isolated, and akin to Robert Redfield's rural folkways (which resulted in a peasant economy). Garigue argues that Quebec was, in fact, urban and commercial in its traditional orientation.[59] Recently a particularly fine collection of essays on *French-Cana-*

58. Wade, *The French-Canadian Outlook: A Brief Account of the Unknown North Americans* (New York, 1946), shows why and how the French Canadians emphasize *survivance*. A warmly sympathetic, but judiciously critical statement, this brief book is meant for the general reader. Wade also has edited *Canadian Dualism: Studies of French-English Relations* (Toronto, [1960]) and has written a provocative article, "The Politics of Partition: Partition in North America," *Journal of International Affairs* (New York), XVIII (ii/1964), 234-40.

59. This controversy is nicely summarized in Hubert Guindon, "The Social Evolution of Quebec Reconsidered," *Canadian Journal of Economics and Political Science*, XXVI (Nov., 1960), 533-51. See also Norman W. Taylor's "French Canadians as

*dian Society*, I: *Sociological Studies* (Toronto, 1964) has been brought together by Marcel Rioux and Yves Martin.

A related debate has turned upon the nature of the early seigneurial system, "feudalism," and the rise of a local bourgeoisie. Sigmund Diamond, in "An Experiment in 'Feudalism': French Canada in the Seventeenth Century," *William and Mary Quarterly*, 3rd ser., XVIII (January, 1961), 3-34, argued that a Colbertian feudal society could not exist in New France because "the need to recruit a *voluntary* [italics added] labor force was the mother of liberty." The eventual fall of New France meant that the rising local bourgeois class was destroyed by the English entrepreneur, and French Canada never recovered. This argument—ably presented by Guy Frégault is *La Guerre de la conquête*, mentioned earlier, and by Michel Brunet in *Canadians et Canadiens: Études sur l'histoire et la pensée des deux Canadas* (Montreal, [1955])—has been questioned by Fernand Ouellet in several articles and by Jean Hamelin in *Economie et société en Nouvelle-France* (Quebec, 1960).[60]

But French-Canadian historical writing remains more introspective than English, and it is not surprising that a full volume of historiographical essays on the *Situation de la recherche sur le Canada français* (Quebec, 1962) should have appeared while there is, as yet, no book-length examination from the English-Canadian side. Fernand Dumont and Yves Martin edited the results of a revue of *recherches sociographiques* at Laval University: the volume ranges over all of the social studies and contains particularly good essays by André Vachon on the *ancien régime*,[61] Ouellet on the nineteenth century,[62] and

---

Industrial Entrepreneurs," *The Journal of Political Economy* (Chicago), LXVIII (Feb. 1960), 37-52; and Cameron Nish, "Une bourgeoisie coloniale en Nouvelle-France: Une hypothèse de travail," *L'Actualité économique*, XXXIX (Sept., 1963), 240-63. In another context, see Nish's useful "Bibliographie sur l'histoire économique du Canada français: Textes manuscrits et imprimés," *ibid.*, XL (June, 1964), 200-209, and his "Documents relatifs à l'histoire économique du régime français," *ibid.* (Dec., 1964), 630-66, on the budget of New France, 1743.

60. See Ouellet, "M. Michel Brunet et le problème de la Conquête," *Bulletin des recherches historiques*, LXII (June, 1956), 42-101; and Brunet, "The British Conquest: Canadian Social Scientists and the Fate of the *Canadiens*," *CHR*, XL (June, 1959), 93-107.

61. An oblique and interestingly related view of this subject may be found in René Herval, "Le Premier évèque de Québec: François de Laval-Montigny (1623-1708)," *Mélanges de science religieuse* (Lille), XIX (1962), 69-99.

62. Particularly able is Ouellet's recent extension of his analysis in "Le Nationalisme canadien-français: De ses origines à l'insurrection de 1837," *CHR*, XLV (Dec., 1964), 277-92. Ouellet's thesis is not widely accepted, however.

Marc-Adélard Tremblay on *les Acadiens*. Vachon is particularly convincing in his argument for a greater use of *"des greffes des notaries, des documents seigneuriaux, des livres de comptes des communautés et des particuliers, et des archives portuaires de France."*[63] But few serious scholars in Canada today dispute the need for multi-archival research, and M. Vachon appears to be pushing upon an open door. Indeed, the very full research shown by Marcel Trudel in his *L'Esclavage au Canada français*, mentioned earlier, and in his continuing *Histoire de la Nouvelle-France*, I: *Les Vaines Tentatives, 1524-1603* (Montreal, 1963), provides two of several examples of the present multi-archival projects now under way by French Canadian historians.

## Intellectual History

Intellectual history often is so amorphous and yet so embracing as to defy classification, and for this very reason it is among the most challenging aspects of the historian's craft. The major problem of intellectual history is that it often leaves the impression that rational activity is man's dominant activity, an impression which the events of recent years would belie. The particular merit of the field is in the new light it throws on traditional political and economic history by showing how ideas have helped shape the present condition of political, economic, military, or diplomatic affairs. There is no synthesis of cultural and intellectual history for Canada, however, and only a few fairly unadventurous works, usually not by historians, have been attempted. This depressing view of the position of intellectual history in Canada is reinforced indirectly in *Royal Commission Studies: A Selection of Essays prepared for the Royal Commission on National Development in the Arts, Letters and Sciences* (Ottawa, 1951).[64]

Two volumes in the series on "Canada and Its Provinces," edited by Shortt and Doughty, and bearing the title *Missions, Arts and Letters*, were the beginning of Canadian cultural history. The only general series of inquiries since 1914 was edited by Julian Park: *The Culture of Contemporary Canada* (Ithaca, 1957), con-

63. Vachon has made a beginning at following his own advice in his brief statement on the *Histoire du notariat canadien, 1621-1960* (Quebec, 1962), p. 15.

64. Albert Alber Shea, *Culture in Canada: A Study of the Findings of the Royal Commission on National Development in the Arts, Letters and Science (1949-1951)* (Toronto, 1952), summarizes the formal report and its 146 recommendations.

taining twelve essays of almost uniformly high quality on all aspects of Canadian culture with the notable omission of religion. Park's volume serves as an intellectual history of twentieth-century Canada, and together with several excellent articles on the cultural history of French Canada by Richard M. Saunders, and Lower's *Canadians in the Making*, is the full canon of overt cultural history. One must turn to fragments of the intellectual life of Canada and prepare one's own mosaic.

The first attempt at a complete history of Canadian education, Charles Edward Phillips, *The Development of Education in Canada* (Toronto, 1957), is based primarily on printed materials and concentrates heavily on the provincial public school systems. There are histories of several universities but only a few throw light beyond their particular ivy.[65] Frederick William Rowe, *The Development of Education in Newfoundland* (Toronto, 1964), briefly shows how the religious question has plagued the province's chaotic school system. Franklin Arthur Walker, *Catholic Education and Politics in Upper Canada* . . . (Toronto, 1955), throws more light on Egerton Ryerson and the general problem of the separate-school controversy, with conclusions favorable to the church. An excellent work in a highly controversial field is Louis-Philippe Audet, *Les Systéme scolaire de la province de Québec* (Quebec, 1950——), projected to eleven volumes with six now available, while Lionel Adolphe Groulx, *L'enseignement français au Canada* (2 vols.; Montreal, 1931-33) is a standard authority.

Another means of education is through the press. Mark Edgar Nichols, *(CP): The Story of the Canadian Press* (Toronto, 1948), is well told and fills an obvious gap, for despite several articles by James John Talman and W. H. Kesterton the full history of Canadian journalism is yet to be written. Elisabeth Wallace, *Goldwin Smith: Victorian Liberal* (Toronto, 1957), reveals the contradictions in a well-known polemicist and historian; and a journalist, Léopold Lamontagne, has written the first life of *Arthur Buies: Homme de lettres* (Quebec, 1957). The biographies of Dafoe, Willison, and

65. The exceptions are Delano Dexter Calvin, *Queen's University at Kingston: The First Century of a Scottish-Canadian Foundation, 1841-1941* (Kingston, 1941); Charles Bruce Sissons, *A History of Victoria University* (Toronto, 1952); William Lewis Morton, *One University: A History of the University of Manitoba, 1877-1952* (Toronto, 1957); and the older *A History of the University of Toronto, 1827-1927* (Toronto, 1927), by William Stewart Wallace.

Brown, mentioned previously, are also contributions to the history of Canadian journalism, as are the works of Séraphin Marion.[66]

Several attempts have been made to write the history of Canadian literature, but none has been entirely successful. To a certain extent English Canadian literature is American literature, at least at the popular level, as an examination of any list of best sellers in Canadian bookstores or most-in-demand books at Canadian public libraries will show. After reading William Edwin Collin's efforts in *The White Savannahs* (Toronto, 1936) to preserve the memory of several Canadian poets, one must agree with Edward Alexander McCourt, who concludes in *The Canadian West in Fiction* (Toronto, 1949) that no Canadian has written a book (or poem) which will "become part of the permanent literary heritage of mankind." Even the novelists of the Canadian West have failed to tell adequately the story of the prairie region, McCourt adds. In *The Frontier & Canadian Letters* (Toronto, 1957) Wilfrid Eggleston ascribes the lack of any substantial body of Canadian literature to the values of a frontier society which were and are unfavorable to a literary tradition. In Park's volume, noted above, Roy Daniells' eighty-page essay on "Poetry and the Novel" summarizes most succinctly the Canadian contribution to world literature. W. C. Desmond Pacey, *Creative Writing in Canada: A Short History of English-Canadian Literature* (Toronto, 1952; 2nd ed., rev. and enl., 1961) was the standard work on the subject until the publication in 1964 of Karl F. Klinck, ed., *Literary History of Canada: Canadian Literature in English* (Toronto). Edward Killoran Brown, *On Canadian Poetry* (Toronto, 1943; rev. ed., 1947), is a valuable "critical essay" which examines the work of Archibald Lampman, Duncan Campbell Scott, and E. J. Pratt. Also of general value are W. C. Desmond Pacey, *Ten Canadian Poets* (Toronto, 1958); R. E. Rashley, *Poetry in Canada: The First Three Steps* (Toronto, 1958), and John Pengwerne Matthews, *Tradition in Exile: A Comparative Study of Social Influences on the Development of Australian and Canadian Poetry in the Nineteenth Century* (Toronto, 1962). Few Canadian writers have been the subjects of full-length biographies or critical studies, although *Canadian Literature* consistently proves Canadian writing to be interesting when ex-

66. See *Les Lettres canadiennes d'autrefois* (9 vols.; Hull, P. Q., 1939-58), and *The Quebec Tradition: An Anthology of French-Canadian Prose and Verse* (Montreal, 1946), translated by Watson Kirkconnell.

amined at article length. Elsie M. Pomeroy has written the standard life of *Sir Charles G. D. Roberts: A Biography* (Toronto, 1943); Ralph L. Curry in *Stephen Leacock, Humorist and Humanist* (Garden City, 1959) tells an unhumorous story of a mildly humorous man; and James Cappon prepared an undisciplined melange of material on one of Canada's most widely known poets, *Bliss Carman and the Literary Currents and Influences of His Time* (Toronto, 1930). The best of the Canadian novelists—Hugh Maclennan, Morley Callaghan, Mordecai Richler, Gabrielle Roy—are still writing and they await full-length studies in English. Indeed, to many commentators Canadian literature begins as recently as 1941, with Hugh Maclennan's *Barometer Rising*, and serious study of national literature in Canadian universities is quite new. Ironically, it was a German scholar using the Canadian collections at the Universities of Hamburg and Marburg, the latter especially good, who wrote the first extended explanation of Maclennan as a nationalist: Paul Goetsch, *Das Romanwerk Hugh Maclennans: Eine Studie zum literarischen Nationalismus in Kanada* (Hamburg, 1961), a well-documented study.

Recently French-Canadian literature has begun to attract a readership outside French Canada, as attested to by the informative, opinionated, sometimes school-bookish, and yet valuable articles by Edmund Wilson, "O Canada: An American's Notes on Canadian Culture."[67] Jane M. E. Turnbull, *Essential Traits of French-Canadian Poetry* (Toronto, 1938) and Fraser's previously mentioned *The Spirit of French Canada* also are useful, older introductions. Both contain excellent bibliographies. A leading figure in the literature of French Canada has not received his due in *Louis Hémon: Sa vie et son oeuvre* . . . (Paris, 1936), by Allan McAndrew. Marcel Trudel, *L'Influence de Voltaire au \Canada* (2 vols.; Montreal, 1945), is an excellent example of how intellectual history can be written. M. Trudel explores the influence of the man who considered

67. *The New Yorker*, XL (Nov., 14, 21, 28, 1964), 63-140, 64-140, 143-201. Only the second article is devoted exclusively to French-Canadian literature, and it is the best of the three. The publication of these three well-researched articles in a leading American magazine, by a highly regarded American critic, provided further illustration of a common Canadian reaction to America's attempts to contribute to Canadian studies. Wilson, critics pointed out, omitted certain writers, dealt in well-known facts, and although he attempted to understand Canada, failed. These criticisms may well be true, but they seem rather ungracious, since Wilson has made thousands of Americans aware of Canadian literature where but hundreds read before. The essays have recently been published as a book (New York, 1965).

Canada but a "few acres of snow" and gives us a fascinating history of anticlericalism in French Canada.

The history of Canadian art and architecture has not been written, and Graham Campbell McInnes' standard introductory survey, *A Short History of Canadian Art* (Toronto, 1950), is now badly out of date. William G. Colgate has surveyed *Canadian Art: Its Origin & Development* (Toronto, 1943) for 1820 to 1940, and Donald W. Buchanan traces *The Growth of Canadian Painting* (Toronto, 1950). There still is little on Lawren Harris, one of the most influential of Canadian landscape artists, although Frederick Broughton Housser's short *A Canadian Art Movement: The Story of the Group of Seven* (Toronto, 1926) helps meet this need. An autobiography tells of British Columbia's leading artist: *Growing Pains: The Autobiography of Emily Carr* (Toronto, 1946). In *The Old Architecture of Quebec: A Study of the Buildings Erected in New France from the Earliest Explorers to the Middle of the Nineteenth Century* (Toronto, 1947), Ramsay Traquair, author of numerous articles on architectural history, has written the first really adequate account of French-Canadian architecture and has given us excellent illustrations of the outward signs of an inward grace. Alan Gowans, *Looking at Architecture in Canada* (Toronto, 1958), and Marion Macrae and Anthony Adamson, *The Ancestral Roof: Domestic Architecture of Upper Canada* (Toronto, 1964), are helpful and pleasant. On music, one may consult Helmut Kallman, *A History of Music in Canada, 1534-1914* (Toronto, 1960). Most utilitarian of all is Malcolm Mackenzie Ross, ed., *The Arts in Canada: A Stocktaking at Mid-Century* (Toronto, 1958).

Henry Marshall Tory, ed., *A History of Science in Canada* (Toronto, 1939), began the examination of one of the most neglected aspects of Canadian history. Tory's collection surveys nine fields of science and contains a particularly informative essay on physics, while the ten essays on the history of science in Canada in William Stewart Wallace, ed., *The Royal Canadian Institute Centennial Volume, 1849-1949* (Toronto, 1949), provide a factual summary a decade later for the same fields plus anthropology. On the history of medicine the most valuable contribution is Hugh Ernest Mac-Dermot, *Sir Thomas Roddick: His Work in Medicine and Public Life* (Toronto, 1938). Sir Thomas was dean of the faculty of medicine at McGill University, champion of the Canadian Medical Act of 1906, and cofounder of the Canadian medical field service. James Lennox Kerr, *Wilfrid Grenfell: His Life and Work* (Toronto, 1959), does not fill the need for a scholarly study of the famous Labrador doctor.

## Economic History

In terms of quantity, economic and diplomatic history have dominated Canadian historiography, for they reflect the two common assumptions of Canadians: that their nation must be created by economic means, as expressed in the tariff, the railroad, and controlled land settlement—the National Policy—and must be protected from its huge neighbor, the United States. In 1956 William Thomas Easterbrook and Hugh G. J. Aitken completed the first survey of *Canadian Economic History* (Toronto) since Mary Quayle Innis' rather unbalanced *An Economic History of Canada* (Toronto, 1935; rev. and enl., 1943). Easterbrook and Aitken express the major attitudes of the field by dwelling at length on the staple trade and contributing far less to business history. C. D. W. Goodwin also has written an important synthesis, *Canadian Economic Thought: The Political Economy of a Developing Nation, 1814-1914* (Durham, N.C., 1961). Still comparatively neglected are small business, conservation, and finance, and there are only a few adequate works on the Canadian labor movement. There are no adequate histories of the tourist trade in Canada or of the building of the Trans-Canada or Alcan highways, although Edward A. McCourt has written on the former road in an overpraised guide-cum-history, *The Road Across Canada* (Toronto, 1965).

The classics of Canadian economic history remain the works of Harold Adams Innis, but his thesis has come under attack recently. The staple theory, as developed by Innis, Creighton, Easterbrook, and Aitken, and as put into practice through John A. Macdonald's national policy of public support to "national" sectors of the economy, producing Canada's "mixed enterprise" system and the Canadian nation as well, has been sharply challenged by an economist, John Harkness Dales. He argues that Canada became a nation in the face of, not because of, Macdonald's policies. Hopefully Dales has begun what may become a wholesale reassessment of Canadian development in his "Some Historical and Theoretical Comment on Canada's National Policies," *Queen's Quarterly*, LXXI (Autumn, 1964), 297-316. The staples hypothesis also has been reconsidered by Peter D. McClelland in an unpublished paper read at the 1965 annual meeting of the Economic History Association, "The New Brunswick Economy in the Nineteenth Century."

On transportaton the basic studies remain those of Glazebrook and Innis, described above, and the several books and articles of Archibald William Currie, in particular *Economics of Canadian Transportation* (Toronto, 1954) and *The Grand Trunk Railway of Canada* (Toronto, 1957). The latter is a monumental study which describes the building and financing of eastern Canada's leading preconfederation railway, while the former contains pioneering sections on highways and highway transport, a chapter of Canadian economic history yet to be written. George Roy Stevens, *Canadian National Railways* (2 vols.; Toronto, 1960-62), an "official history," will be a standard work for years to come, as is James Blaine Hedges, *Building the Canadian West: The Land and Colonization Policies of the Canadian Pacific Railway* (New York, 1939). Howard Allbright Fleming, *Canada's Arctic Outlet: A History of the Hudson Bay Railway* (Berkeley, 1957), shows how the western wheat lands were given a direct sea route to England while Hugh G. J. Aitken, *The Welland Canal Company: A Study in Canadian Enterprise* (Cambridge, Mass., 1954), and Robert Ferguson Legget, *Rideau Waterway* (Toronto, 1955), contribute to the growing literature on Canada's canal transport. Aitken's study in particular is an excellent history of entrepreneurship. Frank H. Ellis, *Canada's Flying Heritage* (Toronto, 1954), by a pre-World War I pioneer flyer, very capably brings this important aspect of Canadian transportation and settlement to World War I. Gerald M. Craig, ed., *Early Travellers in the Canadas, 1791-1867* (Toronto, 1955), makes readily available selections from twenty-nine travelers' accounts and discusses reasons for their coming.

Although there is no full survey of the history of Canadian agriculture, this aspect of economic history, especially with respect to the wheat farmer, has grown considerably since the war. In *Canadian Agricultural Policy: The Historical Pattern* (Toronto, 1946), Vernon C. Fowke, an economist, has argued that agriculture is not Canada's basic industry, that it can be understood only in terms of more insistent needs—defense, provisioning the staple trades, and providing opportunities for investment—and that the federal government has been responsive to the farmer only in proportion to agriculture's rôle in promoting other interest groups. Thus, the power of farm organizations has been of less importance than the farmer has supposed. Confederation was merely a means by which the old province of Canada could re-create an agricultural frontier, a frontier defined in terms of investment opportunities. Fowke also has written an excellent volume in the Social Credit series, noted above, and with George Edwin Britnell he co-authored *Canadian Agriculture in War and Peace, 1935-50* (Stanford, 1962), a disappointing book for the historian, since it emphasizes governmental policy without showing how the farmers responded.

Wheat has been of major concern to historians and economists just as it has been a problem for farmers and government policy-makers. George Edwin Britnell, *The Wheat Economy* (Toronto, 1939), traces the decline of the wheat farmer, while Duncan Alexander MacGibbon's two volumes, *The Canadian Grain Trade* (Toronto, 1932), and *The Canadian Grain Trade, 1931-51* (Toronto, 1952), are excellent works which, particularly in the latter, show how the government's laissez-faire attitude toward marketing and production was eroded away until, through the Wheat Board and an acreage-reduction program, the farmer became dependent upon government aid. Agriculture in the east is described in an excellent monograph by Robert Leslie Jones, *History of Agriculture in Ontario, 1613-1880* (Toronto, 1946); in several articles in *Agricultural History* (Urbana); and in Andrew Hill Clark, *Three Centuries and the Island: A Historical Geography of Settlement and Agriculture in Prince Edward Island, Canada* (Toronto, 1959). There is little outside the Social Credit and Carnegie Endowment series on such mundane but surprisingly interesting aspects of the economy as hog-raising, dairying, or wine-making.

*In Metals and Men: The Story of Canadian Mining* (Toronto, 1957), Donat Marc Le Bourdais has made fascinating reading of a difficult subject. His *Sudbury Basin: The Story of Nickel* (Toronto, 1953), is somewhat less satisfying, possibly because it was underwritten by a mining company. A popular business history which tells of the gold-copper mines of northwestern Quebec is Leslie Roberts, *Noranda* (Toronto, 1956), but easily the best business history written in Canada is William Kilbourn's lively and scholarly *The Elements Combined: A History of the Steel Company of Canada* (Toronto, 1960). Elwood S. Moore's work on mining was mentioned above. An economist, Eric John Hanson, has explored the Albertan oil boom from 1946 to 1956 in *Dynamic Decade: The Evolution and Effects of the Oil Industry in Alberta* (Toronto, 1958), but a general history of oil in Canada, to include earlier strikes in Alberta and efforts in Ontario, is badly needed. Victor Ross and Arthur St. L. Trigge, *A History of The Canadian Bank of Commerce, with an Account of the Other Banks which Now Form Part of Its Organization* (3 vols.; Toronto, 1920-34), is the standard introduction to the history of Canadian banking, but a more convenient and readable summary appears in Bray Hammond, *Banks and Politics in America from the Revolution to the Civil War* (Princeton, 1957). One of the most formidable but important recent studies is John Harvey Perry, *Taxes, Tariffs and Subsidies: A History of Canadian Fiscal Development* (2 vols.; Toronto, 1955), which deals with the postconfederation years. Orville John McDiarmid, *Commercial Policy in the Canadian Economy* (Cambridge, Mass., 1946), is a detailed treatment of policy questions and administration. Wilfrid Eggleston's account of federal-provincial fiscal relations was mentioned earlier.

Literature on the labor movement or the rôle of management in Canada remains slight. Samuel Delbert Clark has revealed how one pressure group works in *The Canadian Manufacturers' Association: A Study in Collective Bargaining and Political Pressure* (Toronto, 1939), while Harold Amos Logan has written an introduction to *The History of Trade-Union Organization in Canada* (Chicago, 1928) and has proceeded to fill in part of the longer story in *Trade Unions in Canada: Their Development and Functioning* (Toronto, 1948), which devotes considerable space to a history of the individual unions grouped by industries. The most significant recent study is a co-operative effort by nine authors, four of whom are professors of economics: Pierre-Elliott Trudeau, *et al.*, *La Grève de l'amiante: Une étape de la révolution industrielle au Québec* (Montreal, 1956). This is a detailed, overly-long inquiry into the six months' asbestos miners' strike in Quebec in 1949. The book's thesis is that the strike heralded a new stage in provincial history, for a Roman Catholic syndicate, with local church support, called and sustained a lengthy strike despite intervention by provincial police and the use of strike-breakers.

Other aspects of Canadian economic history fall into no convenient group. Gilbert Norman Tucker, *The Canadian Commercial Revolution, 1845-1851* (New Haven, 1936), shows the effects of repeal of the Corn Laws and documents Canada's need for reciprocity with the United States. Donald Campbell Masters, *The Reciprocity Treaty of 1854: Its History, Its Relation to British Colonial and Foreign Policy and to the Development of Canadian Fiscal Autonomy* (London, 1937), replaces Charles Callan Tansill's older work[68] and shows how the provinces fared under the treaty until its abrogation in 1865. At least a dozen doctoral dissertations have been written in recent years on reciprocity in Canadian-American relations, none of which have been published, but the subject is not exhausted.

Books on the Hudson's Bay Company are, or should be, at once economic, Imperial, and political histories. Douglas McKay, *The Honourable Company: A History of the Hudson's Bay Company* (Indiannapolis, 1936; rev. ed., Toronto, 1949), by an employee who early received access to the Company's archives, is the best one-volume survey of company policies. In *Sir George Simpson: Overseas Governor of the Hudson's Bay Company, A Pen Picture of a Man of Action* (Portland, Ore., [1944]), Arthur Silver Morton lets us see a devoted company official at work, but a full-scale biography is badly needed, despite Morton and Frederick Merk, eds., *Fur Trade and Empire: George Simpson's Journal . . . 1824-1825* (Cambridge, Mass., 1931). D. Geneva Lent, *West of the Mountains: James Sinclair and the Hudson's Bay Company* (Seattle, 1963) is readable, disappointing, and erroneous. *The North West Company* (Toronto, 1957), by Marjorie E. W. Campbell, attacks Lord Selkirk for his policies in the Red River settlement and presents an interesting contrast to the conclusions of John Perry Pritchett in *The Red River Valley, 1811-1849*, noted above, and to John Morgan Gray's *Lord Selkirk of Red River* (East Lansing, 1964). Another slim volume of interest is Murray G. Lawson, *Fur: A Study in English Mercantilism, 1700-1775* (Toronto, 1943).

One impediment to research on the H.B.C. (said to mean "Here

68. Tansill, *The Canadian Reciprocity Treaty of 1854* (Baltimore, 1922).

before Christ") is that the bulk of the Company's archives at Beaver House, London (with microfilm copies in Ottawa and Winnipeg), are restricted. But an able staff under Alice Johnson helps remove this barrier somewhat, and two studies of the highest significance have been published in recent years. John Semple Galbraith, *The Hudson's Bay Company as an Imperial Factor, 1821-1869* (Berkeley, 1957), shows how the Company acted as a factor for the mercantile class, from which expansion stemmed, and argues that the Company won its favorable competitive position by virtue of performance rather than through its chartered rights and privileges. And in 1959 Edwin Ernest Rich completed his two-volume study, *The History of the Hudson's Bay Company, 1670-1870* (London, 1958-59), for the Hudson's Bay Record Society. These volumes deserve the much overworked term "magisterial." Rich had access to the Company's records and his work represents the fullest account now possible.[69] Galbraith and Rich have thoroughly replaced George Bryce's older account.[70]

An aspect of history which has been almost totally ignored by academicians in Canada is that of conservation and the historic and scenic preservation movement, a movement in which Canada lags seriously behind Britain and the United States. There is nothing on the national park system in Canada, and although several historians serve on the National Historic Sites Board none has seen fit to tell the story of how Canada has preserved, or more correctly, has failed to preserve, the visible symbols of its past. Two books—Ronald L. Way, *Ontario's Niagara Parks: A History* (Niagara Falls, Ont., 1946), and Audrey Saunders, *Algonquin Story* (Toronto, 1948)—tell of the movement in Ontario. Lower's works, noted previously, and portions of Anthony Scott, *Natural Resources: The Economics of Conservation* (Toronto, 1955), which is not primarily Canadian in focus, are virtually the only books presently available on conservation history.

69. It has been reissued in three volumes by McClelland and Stewart (Toronto, 1959).

70. *Remarkable History of the Hudson's Bay Company, Including that of the French Traders of North-Western Canada and of the North-West, XY, and Astor Fur Companies* (Toronto, 1900). Our understanding of the history of the fur trade has been greatly increased by Innis and by the various publications of the Hudson's Bay Record Society and the Champlain Society. Notable among the latter are William Stewart Wallace, ed., *Documents Relating to the North West Company* (Toronto, 1934) and George P. de T. Glazebrook, ed., *The Hargrave Correspondence, 1831-1843* (Toronto, 1938).

*Foreign Affairs*

Since Canadian nationhood is real while a Canadian nationality may not be, Canadian diplomatic history tends to fall between two schools. Much of it is in the vein of the "newer diplomacy" as written by A. J. P. Taylor in England and Thomas A. Bailey in the United States, so that G. M. Young might seldom have occasion to accuse Canadian scholars of merely writing of "what one clerk has said to another clerk" —sometimes to the detriment of sound diplomatic history. The only full survey is George P. de T. Glazebrook, *A History of Canadian External Relations* (Toronto, 1950), which incorporates his earlier *Canadian External Relations: An Historical Study to 1914* (London, 1942), and brings the account up to 1945. Robert Alexander MacKay and Evan Benjamin Rogers, *Canada Looks Abroad* (London, 1938), while now out of date, was an earlier survey which included material on Latin America,[71] the Far East, and the U.S.S.R.

The importance of the United States in Canadian affairs is attested to by four surveys of Canadian-American relations in addition to the lengthy Carnegie Endowment series. Edgar Wardwell McInnis, *The Unguarded Frontier: A History of American-Canadian Relations* (Garden City, 1942), is the soundest and most complete, showing how Canada has maintained its British connection despite gravitational pull to the south. Hugh Llewellyn Keenleyside and Gerald Saxton Brown, *Canada and the United States: Some Aspects of Their Historical Relations* (New York, 1952), is a revision of Keenleyside's pioneer 1929 book with a slightly altered title. It treats topically selected aspects of their relations. Both books virtually replace James Morton Callahan, *American Foreign Policy in Canadian Relations* (New York, 1937), a badly written history of negotiations. Bruce Hutchison, *The Struggle for the Border* (Toronto, 1955), is readable, misleading, and riddled with errors. Mason Wade and Gerald M. Craig have new surveys in progress.[72]

Several monographs have appeared outside the Carnegie Endowment series. Goldwin Albert Smith, *The Treaty of Washington, 1871:*

71. The only other source of information on Canada's Latin American policy, or lack of it, is Marcel Roussin, *Le Canada et le système interaméricain* (Ottawa, 1960). Roussin argues that French Canadians feel they are part of a broader Latin community, but English Canada has shown little interest in the Pan-American Union or the Organization of American States.

72. See also Robert Mills Clark, ed., *Canadian Issues: Essays in Honour of Henry F. Angus* (Toronto, 1961).

*A Study in Imperial History* (Ithaca, 1941), relates a brief story well, while Roger Hamilton Brown, *The Struggle for the Indian Stream Territory* (Cleveland, 1955), tells of a dispute over northern New Hampshire between 1796 and 1842. Oscar Arvle Kinchen, *The Rise and Fall of the Patriot Hunters* (New York, 1956), complements Corey on the troubled years of the 1830's and 1840's. William D'Arcy, *The Fenian Movement in the United States: 1858-1886* (Washington, 1947), ought to have put an end to further studies of the Fenian raids. Robert Warren James, *Wartime Economic Co-operation: A Study of Relations between Canada and the United States* (Toronto, 1949), recounts the success and failure of the Hyde Park Agreement of April, 1941. John Semple Galbraith, *The Establishment of Canadian Diplomatic Status at Washington* (Berkeley, 1951), again shows the importance of the United States in the development of Canadian independence. It should be read with Skilling's volume on Canadian representation abroad. In "The Myth of the Unguarded Frontier, 1815-1871," *American Historical Review* (Washington), LVI (October, 1950), 1-18, Charles Perry Stacey has brilliantly demonstrated that the so-called undefended border was not, in fact, without its defenses. Leonard Bertram Irwin, *Pacific Railways and Nationalism in the Canadian-American Northwest, 1845-1873* (Philadelphia, 1939), shows how the Northern Pacific Railway in particular attempted to create a single economic region to pull the Canadian West into the American union.

In the *St. Lawrence Waterway: A Study in Politics and Diplomacy* (Madison, 1961), William R. Willoughby provides a thorough, carefully researched account of an important joint Canadian-American undertaking. A lesser-known act of co-operation is investigated by (George) Gaddis Smith in *Britain's Clandestine Submarines, 1914-1915* (New Haven, 1964). The essential activities and dynamics of the wartime Permanent Joint Board on Defence are examined in Stanley W. Dziuban, *Military Relations between the United States and Canada, 1939-1945* (Washington, 1959). And the fact that an earlier war was of continental proportions is documented in Robin William Winks, *Canada and the United States: The Civil War Years* (Baltimore, 1960). This volume shares a point of departure with Donald Frederick Warner, *The Idea of Continental Union: Agitation for the Annexation of Canada to the United States, 1849-1893* (Lexington, 1960), which surveys not so much the "idea" of union as congressional machinations and economic pressures that promoted continentalism. Robert Craig Brown, *Canada's National Policy, 1883-1900: A Study in Canadian-American Relations* (Princeton, 1964), is the nearly definitive volume for its period. An astringent and hard-headed study is James George Eayrs, *In Defense of Canada: From the Great War to the Great Depression* (Toronto [1964]).

Pioneer accounts of Canada's western face are Henry Forbes Angus, *Canada and the Far East, 1940-1953* (Toronto, 1953), and Arthur R. M. Lower, *Canada and the Far East—1940* (New York, 1940). The former is especially valuable since it includes the Korean War. Canada's relations with the nations of the Far East have yet to be fully described, and studies of the Dominion's policy toward Orientals are needed. In this respect Forrest Emmanuel La Violette, *The Canadian Japanese and World War II: A Sociological and Psychological Account* (Toronto, 1948), is of particular importance. Studies with a postwar perspective which follow *Canada and the Orient: A Study in International Relations* (Toronto, 1941), by Charles James Woodsworth, also would be useful. Accounts of Canadian relations with the Asiatic members of the Commonwealth and especially with India should prove of great value, since many Canadians believe that Canada has acted as an interpreter between India and the United States.

Within the Commonwealth little has been done by Canadian scholars, although Alexander Brady, *Democracy in the Dominions: A Comparative Study in Institutions* (Toronto, 1947; rev. ed., 1952) is an outstanding work rapidly becoming a classic in a framework larger than diplomatic history. The lectures of Frank Hawkins Underhill, *The British Commonwealth: An Experiment in Co-operation among Nations* (Durham, N.C., 1956), while brief, are a beginning. Frederic Hubert Soward has written several articles on Canada's relations with nations other than the United States and with Edgar Wardwell McInnis has placed *Canada and the United Nations* (New York, 1956) in perspective. Glazebrook has told of *Canada at the Paris Peace Conference* (London, 1942). The Canadian Institute of International Affairs has sponsored a continuing series of volumes on *Canada in World Affairs* (London, 1941——) to the present total of nine, which are thorough, factual, and analytical accounts of the years preceding World War II through 1957.[73] James George Eayrs has been both the most prolific and the most searching of the students of Canada's present-day rôle in world politics, and in addition to his books cited elsewhere, he has written on the *Northern Approaches: Canada and the Search for Peace* (Toronto, 1961) and has edited *The Commonwealth and Suez: A Documentary Survey* (Toronto, 1964).

## Military History[74]

Military history arises from the failures recounted by diplomatic historians; it also is Imperial history when broadly conceived as in the work of Charles P. Stacey, Gerald S. Graham, and Richard A. Preston. Stacey, former head of the Canadian Army Historical Section in World War II, has presented the major events of Canada's participation in the war in *The Canadian Army, 1939-45: An Official Historical Summary* (Ottawa, 1948). One of the best craftsmen practicing in Canada, Stacey also has written two of the volumes in the Army's series, *Six Years of War: The Army in Canada, Britain, and the Pacific* (1955) and *The Victory Campaign: The Operations in North-West Europe, 1944-1945* (1960), while Gerald W. L. Nicholson has told of *The Canadians in Italy, 1943-1945* (1956), and of an earlier war in *Canadian Expeditionary Force, 1914-1919: The Official History of the Canadian Army in the First World War* (1962). In *Canada's Soldiers, 1604-1954: The Military History of an Unmilitary People* (rev. ed., Toronto, 1960), George F. G. Stanley and Harold McGill Jackson have written the first survey. Gilbert Norman Tucker wrote *The Naval Service of Canada: Its Official History* (2 vols.; Ottawa, 1952). While not strictly a military history, *The North-West Mounted Police, 1873-1893* (2 vols.; Ottawa, 1950), by John Peter Turner, is an adequate official account. In the bicentennial of the fall of Quebec to the British in 1759, a flurry of books and articles of uneven merit attempted to recapture the excitement on the Plains of Abraham. Christopher Lloyd, *The Capture of Quebec* (London, 1959), and Charles Perry Stacey, *Quebec, 1759: The Siege and the Battle* (Toronto, 1959), are the best of these, the latter a model of military history for the lay reader.[75]

73. The chief collection of source materials is Walter A. Riddell, ed., *Documents on Canadian Foreign Policy, 1917-1939* (Toronto, 1962).

74. A most helpful aid is Charles Emil Dornbusch, *The Canadian Army, 1855-1958: Regimental Histories and a Guide to the Regiments* (Cornwallville, N.Y., 1959).

75. Other books are examined in Richard Arthur Preston, "1759," *CHR*, XLI (Sept., 1960), 231-35.

*Regional and Local History*

By its very nature local history seldom is of national importance. Nonetheless, skilful historians can give local matters meaning far beyond the confines of their areas. There are three excellent examples of such history at the provincial level: William Lewis Morton, *Manitoba: A History* (Toronto, 1957), perhaps the best of all provincial records; Margaret A. Ormsby, *British Columbia: A History* (Toronto, 1958); and William Stewart MacNutt, *New Brunswick: A History, 1784-1867* (Toronto, 1963). Robert Alexander MacKay, ed., *Newfoundland: Economic, Diplomatic, and Strategic Studies* (Toronto, 1946), is the most important book on Canada's newest province to appear in many years although it is a series of essays rather than a connected narrative. A model for even more locally reduced history is Charles M. Johnston, *The Head of the Lake: A History of Wentworth County* [Ontario] (Hamilton, 1958). Also rising above purely local questions are Frederick Coyne Hamil, *The Valley of the Lower Thames, 1640 to 1850* (Toronto, 1951); Edwin Clarence Guillet, ed., *The Valley of the Trent* (Toronto, 1957), which was the first volume in the Champlain Society's "Ontario" Series; Edith G. Firth, ed., *The Town of York, 1793-1815* ... (Toronto, 1962), in the same series; Harold A. Davis, *An International Community on the St. Croix (1604-1930)* (Orono, Me., 1950), which shows interaction between Calais, Maine, and St. Stephen, New Brunswick; and Thomas Head Raddall, *Halifax, Warden of the North* (Toronto, 1948; rev. ed., Garden City, New York, 1965).

The history of the West has received so much special attention in recent years that it is virtually a field of its own. The application of the Turner thesis to Canada as well as to the United States, Australia, New Zealand, and Russia,[76] and the continued sense of colonial tutelage and grievance felt in the West, has produced a spate of works. Several of these have appeared in the series on "Canadian Frontiers of Settlement" and "Social Credit in Alberta." Others have been included in the Carnegie Endowment series.

The classic statement of western history remains the giant volume of Arthur Silver Morton, *A History of the Canadian West to 1870-71: Being a History of Rupert's Land (the Hudson's Bay Company's Territory) and of the North-West Territory (including the Pacific*

76. See Ray Allen Billington, *The American Frontier* (Washington, 1958).

*Slope)* (London, 1939).[77] Charles Cecil Lingard, *Territorial Government in Canada: The Autonomy Question in the Old North-West Territories* (Toronto, 1946), is a study of the establishment of the provinces of Alberta and Saskatchewan in 1905, in which the author shows how the territorial premier, F. W. G. Haultain, who fought for responsible government at Regina from 1891 to 1905, deserves to be called one of the "Makers" of Canada. Lewis Herbert Thomas, *The Struggle for Responsible Government in the North-West Territories, 1870-97* (Toronto, 1956), also tells the story of Haultain and demonstrates how the western provinces came to their sense of grievance through their often-thwarted efforts to achieve responsible government. In the two works of Paul Frederick Sharp, mentioned previously, and his article, "When Our West Moved North," *American Historical Review,* LV (January, 1950), 286-300, we have an account of how the Canadian West became the new American frontier by 1890. Several works on western farming are listed under "economic history," above.

Canadian historians continue to write of Louis Riel, and he remains a center of controversy. Questions of race, colonial policy, relations with the United States, land settlement, and religion swirl about him, so that nearly everyone who writes of the West, or of the years between 1870 and 1885, must come to grips with him and his cause. In *The Birth of Western Canada: A History of the Riel Rebellions* (London, 1936; new ed., 1961), George F. G. Stanley maintains that the struggle with the Indians and the *métis* was not a racial or religious clash, but one between a primitive and a civilized people, following the pattern of such clashes throughout the world. He views Riel as a legitimate fighter for constitutional rights for his people, and he has given added fervor to this argument in his biography, *Louis Riel* (Toronto, 1963). Joseph Kinsey Howard, *Strange Empire: A Narrative of the Northwest* (New York, 1952), has written an emotional, deeply moving, heart-convincing story of the *métis* struggle for survival. Reluctantly, only the mind refuses to agree with Howard's impassioned appeal. Creighton, in his biography of John A. Macdonald, contests these favorable views of Riel with considerable force. The story is told through different eyes in Donation Frémont, *Les Secrétaires de Riel: Louis Schmidt, Henry Jackson, Philippe Garnot* (Montreal, 1953). Jules Le Chevallier, *Batoche, les missionaires du Nord-Ouest pendant*

77. A new edition is being prepared by Lewis Gwynne Thomas.

*les troubles de 1885* (Montreal, 1941), is an excellent account of the attempt of the Oblate Fathers to maintain peace during the second Riel rebellion.[78]

## Conclusions: The Present

Today Canadian historiography turns even more self-consciously than before upon a desire to identify the uniqueness of the Canadian experience. In the late 1950's and early 1960's Canadians seemed to be undergoing a *crise de conscience*, entering upon a great national debate as to whether Canada had evolved a value system of its own, and thus a genuine identity, or whether its value system now was so derivative from other sources, chiefly in the United States, that it virtually was an "other-directed" nation, to use the jargon of the sociologist. Two volumes appeared as this essay went to press which explored and were symptoms of this soul searching. George Parkin Grant, in *Lament for a Nation: The Defeat of Canadian Nationalism* (Toronto, 1965), pessimistically inquired into the political traditions of Canada and a sociologist, John Porter, demonstrated how effective, often unfortunately, the Canadian quest for a cultural mosaic of ethnic groups had been in his very important work, *The Vertical Mosaic: An Analysis of Social Class and Power in Canada* (Toronto [1965]). These questions of identity had been present, of course, in the work of Innis and Creighton. The Laurentian school was one answer to the continentalism of the Turner school. But national identification had not been the primary thrust to this earlier and still predominant body of literature. Creighton and Stacey, for example, had been more interested in the effects on Canada of certain fundamental changes in the so-called second British Empire, and their early volumes were closely linked in this sense. But by the late 1950's interest in cultural interaction between Britain and Canada was matched by interest in cultural interaction between Canada and the United States. Jean-Charles Falardeau posed the new, yet old, questions with sophistication in his Alan B. Plaunt Lectures in 1960, *Roots and Values in Canadian Lives* (Toronto, 1961). The old Carnegie Endowment series on Canadian-American relations had demon-

---

78. Three other volumes which center on Riel are Robert E. Lamb, *Thunder in the North: Conflict over the Riel Risings, 1870-1885* (New York, 1957); William Lewis Morton, ed., *Alexander Begg's Red River Journal and Other Papers Relative to the Red River Resistance of 1869-1870* (Toronto, 1956); and James Joseph Hargrave, *Red River* (Montreal, 1871).

strated that these questions lay close below the surface, but the series had been chiefly institutional. The most recent histories were now more alert to imponderables, to public opinion, and to what loosely falls into the category of intellectual history.

Four ways of approach to the problem of the Canadian identity have become dominant during the last ten years. The first was in a heightening of interest in the period of confederation, an interest that has been one of the constants in Canadian historiography. This interest was stimulated not only by the self-conscious quest for an internationally recognizable identity. General postwar concern with world government and especially with federalism encouraged political scientists to look at 1861-71 again. The approach of the one hundredth anniversary of confederation engendered many acts of memorializing piety, just as the centennial of the American Civil War quickened the already flooding rivers of American historiography for the same decade. A new "Canadian Centenary Series," already referred to, was direct fruitage, while the announcement of a project to prepare a Union List of manuscripts in Canadian repositories, under the direction of the Dominion Archivist and National Librarian, W. Kaye Lamb, was an indirect result. The superb biographies of Brown and Macdonald by Careless and Creighton attested to interest in the confederation period, while articles in the historical journals began to provide mortar for the edifice. Walter Ullman, in "The Quebec Bishops and Confederation," *CHR*, XLIV (September, 1963), 213-34, moved on to comparatively new ground, but the most significant single new study, apart from Creighton, Careless, and a revised edition of Stacey's work, was Peter Busby Waite, *The Life and Times of Confederation, 1864-1867: Politics, Newspapers, and the Union of British North America* (Toronto, 1962).[79] Waite emphasized the importance of public opinion and of the press as both an expression and a molder of that opinion. Paul Grant Cornell's careful *The Alignment of Political Groups in Canada, 1841-1867* (Toronto, 1962) provided the first real guide to many of the lesser figures in the drama of confederation, and James K. Chapman's *The Career of Arthur Hamilton Gordon, First Lord Stanmore, 1829-1912* (Toronto, 1964), drew upon the Gordon papers in New Brunswick

79. Waite also edited *The Confederation Debate in the Province of Canada, 1865* (Toronto, 1963), and Creighton again wrote exceedingly well of *The Road to Confederation: The Emergence of Canada, 1863-1867* (Toronto, 1964).

to give an unusually clear picture of a colonial administrator of the times.[80]

A second path to the present was by way of biography. Historians seemed to be seeking out archetypal Canadian figures, as shown by a genuine blossoming of first-rate studies, as noted, of Frontenac, Macdonald, Mackenzie, Brown, King, Meighen, Woodsworth, and Riel.[81] Canadians were in search of a national hero, and although handicapped by the fact that two languages divided them, that Champlain was not "the father of Canada" to all, and that Macdonald could scarcely be a unifying figure for those who looked to Riel, Canadians continued to seek their own mythic giant, a generator of legends.

But two other paths of inquiry lay open. One was an heightened interest in Canadian-American relations, a subject which virtually became a subfield of its own. The most recent listing of graduate school dissertations on Canadian history showed 65 doctoral manuscripts in preparation at Canadian universities, and no less than 59 in the United States.[82] Although most of the latter were not in diplomatic history as narrowly defined, the number alone was evidence of an intellectual discovery of Canada south of the border, not unlike Australia's recent intellectual discovery of the United States.

Several books joined those already published. Hugh Llewelyn Keenleyside, et al., The Growth of Canadian Policies in External Affairs (Durham, N.C., 1960), contains eight good essays, with especially useful contributions on the period 1914-18 by (George) Gaddis Smith and 1931-39 by James George Eayrs. David R. Deener, ed.,

80. Additional information on colonial administration at the time of confederation appears in Arvel B. Erickson, Edward T. Cardwell: Peelite (Philadelphia, 1959), in Transactions of the American Philosophical Society, n.s., XLIX, Pt. 2, but Erickson claims far too much for Cardwell.

81. But surprisingly the only project to publish the papers of a Canadian statesman was the rather tentative foray into the King papers. As the papers of Franklin, Washington, Jefferson, the Adams family, Madison, Calhoun, Clay, Douglas, Lincoln, Theodore Roosevelt, Wilson, Franklin D. Roosevelt, and others poured from scholarly presses in the United States, the riches of the Macdonald, Borden, Laurier, and Dafoe papers remained in archives.

82. The major figures for doctoral dissertations, as listed in CHR, XLV (Sept., 1964), 256-62, were: University of Toronto, 51; Harvard University, 10; Duke University, 9; and the University of Michigan and Oxford University, 8 each; Stanford University, 7; the Universities of Chicago and Rochester, 6 each; and Columbia University, the University of London, and Yale University, 5 each. Equally significant is the fact that the United States Department of State, Bureau of Intelligence and Research, External Research bulletin: Western Europe, Great Britain and Canada (Spring, 1964), shows 27 independent research projects relating to Canadian history in progress by postdoctoral scholars in the United States.

*Canada-United States Treaty Relations* (Durham, N.C., 1963), contains ten essays which examine the ways in which treaties have worked to promote trade, military co-operation, and international waterways. Edgar Wardwell McInnis in *The Atlantic Triangle and the Cold War* (Toronto, 1959), and Melvin Conant in *The Long Polar Watch* (New York, 1962), examine the stresses placed on Canadian-American relations by nuclear-power realities. An Australian, Frederick Alexander, in *Canadians and Foreign Policy* (Toronto, 1960) informally examines policy in relation to public opinion, while Eayrs, in possibly the best book of all, writes of *The Art of the Possible: Government and Foreign Policy in Canada* (Toronto, 1961).[83] Trade and investment ties were examined at length in a mounting periodical literature, best caught in mid-flight by Hugh G. J. Aitken, *et al., The American Economic Impact on Canada* (Durham, N.C., 1959) and Aitken's *American Capital and Canadian Resources* (Cambridge, Mass., 1959). Evidence of this growing interest in Canadian-American relations, in intellectual history, and in the transfer of ideas across international frontiers was shown early in 1964 when the Yale and McGill university presses announced their joint intention to publish a new multivolume series of studies of the North Atlantic Triangle, with emphasis upon social communication and cultural interaction. In the same year The American Assembly turned to a similar theme, and John Sloan Dickey edited, in *The United States and Canada*, the resulting essays by American and Canadian authors (Englewood Cliffs, N.J.).

But the clearest evidence of all that Canadians were seeking new definitions was shown in two significant volumes by William Lewis Morton which together virtually constituted an exposition for a new school, a school loosely to be labeled "Northernism." The titles of the books are sufficient to reveal their basic contentions: *The Canadian Identity* (Madison, 1961) and *The Kingdom of Canada: A General History from Earliest Times* (Toronto, 1963). In the first Morton asserted the existence of a distinct Canadian national character, neither American nor British, which was emerging from a northern rather than a continental environment. This environment shapes the Canadian but in turn is reshaped by Canadian institutions, especially by the fact that Canada is a monarchy. Environment and institutions have inter-

83. [F. J. Boland, ed.], *Sixth Seminar on Canadian-American Relations at University of Windsor* (Windsor, Ont., [1965]), containing the proceedings of the 1964 conference of that title, with its predecessors, also is indicative of this growth in interest.

acted to give Canada a set of distinctive characteristics, an identity of its own, Morton argued. In *The Kingdom of Canada* he committed himself to one or another position in several historiographical controversies,[84] but most important, in "The Realization of the Kingdom of Canada, 1922-1960," he concluded with an affirmation of Canadian maturity which seemed especially sound to many.

If some sceptics south of the border (and within Canada as well) felt that this Canadian identity was more asserted than proved, or that Canadian characteristics remained broadly continental, others continued to feel that neither physical environment nor political institutions, but the continuing fact of "the two races,"[85] gave Canada its uniqueness. If some historians turned their backs upon the grand interpreters to toil in the vineyards of local history, others chose to be neither the fly nor the flybottle. The continuing debate served to demonstrate the vitality, indeed the maturity, of Canadian historiography. Canada, first of the Dominions, had some right to claim to be first in its historiography as well. And historians of Canada seemed to have chosen as their motto the words of a fellow Canadian—a student of another Blake, not Edward but William—Northrop Frye. "Anything may be; nothing must be, and what has produced [such literature] is not an experience. . . but a creative imagination. . . ."[86] Perhaps all history is intellectual history in the long run; assuredly, historiography is such.[87]

84. The chapter title, "The Emergence of the Canadian Bourgeoisie, 1662-1685," shows such commitment, since one body of thought holds that there was no bourgeoisie at this time.

85. The dual society is given a fresh and succinct analysis by Kenneth Douglas McRae in "The Structure of Canadian History," *The Founding of New Societies: Studies in the History of the United States, Latin America, South Africa, Canada and Australia* (New York, 1964), ed. Louis Hartz. See also an important article by Stanley R. Mealing, "The Concept of Social Class and the Interpretation of Canadian History," *CHR*, XLVI (Sept., 1965), 201-18.

86. Frye, *Fables of Identity: Studies in Poetic Mythology* (New York, 1963), p. 96.

87. This essay attempts to discuss historical writings about Canada in English and French and, to the extent that senior scholarship exists, in German. Readers may wish to know of the special collections of Canadiana held by the University of Marburg, and of the interest which has been shown at the University of Upsala. For the former, there is a catalog of library holdings, and for the latter, a modest monograph, *Canadian Studies in Sweden* (Upsala, 1961) by S. B. Liljegren.

# AUSTRALIA

## Kenneth A. MacKirdy

THE CHILDREN OF ISRAEL grumbled when they were required to make bricks without straw. The historians of Australia confront a task of similar difficulty. Australia's past is in large part devoid of those events which infuse cohesiveness and drama into other national histories. There have been no invasions since the British settlements were established. The aboriginal inhabitants were too few and too ineffectively organized to resist the settlers as did the natives of New Zealand, North America, or southern Africa. There is no counterpart to the conflict of language, religion, and culture that has exacerbated relations between Briton and Boer in South Africa or Canadian and *Canadien* in British North America. There is no war of independence, no freedom movement of the Indo-African variety, and the major battles of its constitutionally respectable counterpart, "The Struggle for Responsible Government," were fought in British North America. The insulating effect of the Royal Navy during the periods of Australian settlement and development, which coincided with the *Pax Britannica*, lessened the importance of foreign relations as a major factor in the continent's history until recent years.

A suggestion of the themes which could most effectively be explored by historians of Australia was made by William Keith (later Sir Keith) Hancock in his review of A. C. V. Melbourne's *Early Constitutional Development in Australia: New South Wales, 1788-1856* (London, 1934). Hancock praised the industry and scholarship of the author of a book which still holds its place as a standard authority (2nd ed., ed. by R. B. Joyce, Brisbane, 1964), and which represented the most ambitious project undertaken by an individual Australian professional historian to that time. But he then questioned the wisdom of stressing constitutional history.

Even for the Australian student interested primarily in his own country the most important of modern constitutional documents is the Durham Report. Because the central issues were decided elsewhere, it is not necessary for the majority of Australian students to study at great length the detail of constitutional development in Australia. They may, therefore, keep free a fairly large proportion of their time for those economic and geographic aspects which chiefly constitute the individuality of Australian history.[1]

The Australian story contains an important element of conflict suggested in the phrase, "the economic and geographic aspects." It is the struggle of European man to adapt himself and his domesticated plants and livestock to a strange, dry environment, and to discover and wrest its mineral treasures from what is geologically the oldest of continents.

The first aspect of the theme of man against the elements to be investigated was, understandably, the record of discovery and exploration, a theme common to all new lands containing obvious elements of adventure and interest. Furthermore many of the leading Australian explorers, helpfully, left full accounts of their activities. The generations of Australian school children who were exposed to Ernest Scott's *A Short History of Australia* (1st ed., London, 1916; 7th ed., Melbourne, 1947), with its six chapters on exploration by sea and land, might well be excused if they concluded that the history of their country was largely a chronicle of exploration.

Sir Ernest Scott can be considered the first significant figure in the development of professional Australian history, that branch with which this essay is primarily concerned.[2] This former journalist with no uni-

---

1. *English Historical Review* (London), LI (April, 1936), 372.

2. Excluded by this definition are the works of Arthur W. Jose, who had terminated his brief Australian academic career as an acting professor of modern literature and returned to journalism before he published his series of books sprinkled with stimulating insights, from *A Short History of Australasia* (Sydney, 1899) to *Australia: Human and Economic* (London, 1932).

In recent years a number of writers have reported on the state of Australian historical research from various vantage points. Among those not mentioned elsewhere in this essay are: John A. La Nauze, "The Study of Australian History, 1929-1959," *Historical Studies: Australia and New Zealand* (Melbourne) (hereafter, *Historical Studies*), IX (Nov., 1959), 1-11; Raymond Maxwell Crawford, "History," in Sir Archibald Grenfell Price, ed., *The Humanities in Australia: A Survey with Special Reference to the Universities* (Sydney, 1959), pp. 148-60; Frederick Alexander, "Survey of Recent Research, Australia," *Quarterly Journal of the Indian School of International Studies* (New Delhi), II (April, 1961), 425-45; and Russel B. Ward, "The Main Trends of Australian History, 1788-1901," *Cahiers d'histoire mondiale* (Neuchâtel), VII (iii/1963), 817-27. The most thorough treatment of the subject by an historian is John Manning Ward, "Historiography," in Alan L. McLeod, ed., *The Pat-*

versity training was employed as a shorthand reporter for the Commonwealth *Hansard* at the time of his nomination to the new chair of history at the University of Melbourne in 1914. His primacy among active research scholars in Australian history had been demonstrated in *Terre Napoléon: A History of French Explorations and Projects in Australia* (London, 1910); *The Life of Lapérouse* (Sydney, 1912); and *The Life of Captain Matthew Flinders, R.N.* (Sydney, 1914), the products of his spare-time activity.

History, equated with the study of past events in Europe, had been taught at the University of Melbourne long before a separate chair was established for its profession. When the university commenced operations in 1855 a professor of modern history, literature, political economy and logic was one of the original four faculty members. The older University of Sydney could boast of having the first professor of history *solus* on the island continent when George Arnold Wood was named to the Challis chair in 1891. Although Wood thus enjoyed seniority in appointment over Scott, he was not what in American academic jargon would be called "a productive scholar." Not until 1922 was his first book, also on the theme, *The Discovery of Australia* (London), published.

The concept of the university as a center for research in the humanities and social sciences was slow in gaining acceptance in Australia, and facilities which an American academic would consider adequate for translating the concept into practice are only now becoming available. The 1964 volume of *The Commonwealth Universities Year Book* (London) (all volumes report lists of the previous year) shows a history department at the University of Sydney with nineteen members over the rank of tutor. In contrast, Wood was responsible for all instruction in history from his installation in 1891 until an assistant was appointed in 1916.[3]

Measured against North American standards, the lecture load of an

---

*tern of Australian Culture* (Ithaca, 1963), pp. 195-251. Trevor R. Reese indicated concern over his colleagues' failure to express themselves effectively in "The Historian's Task," *Meanjin Quarterly* (Melbourne), XIX (Sept., 1960), 291-94, and Brian Fitzpatrick gave his assessment of the battle which some commentators see between the ancient radicals and the modern conservatives in "Counter Revolution in Australian Historiography?" *ibid.*, XXII (June, 1963), 197-213.

3. The volume for 1937 showed the University of Melbourne department to be by far the largest in Australia, with five full- and part-time staff and two evening lecturers. The 1964 volume reported twenty-three members in the Department of History and six in a separate Department of Economic History.

Australian academic in the interwar period was not excessive. More serious obstacles to research appear to have been the need to cover too many fields, the absence of associates whose research interests overlapped sufficiently to permit mutual criticism and encouragement, the lack of library and secretarial facilities, and the administrative demands on senior faculty. The postwar expansion in faculty, permitting specialization in lecturing, the development of graduate studies, and the improvement in libraries and archives have had more influence in promoting a favorable attitude toward research than has any lessening of the lecture load.

Scott's achievements as a pioneer author of professional history, and, along with Wood at Sydney, as teacher of many of the next generation of historians, appear all the brighter against such a background. Yet it was not until 1927 that he initiated the first full course in Australian history to be given at the university level.[4]

By instilling in his undergraduate students in British and European history his own "love of the historical document"[5] and discussing problems of historiography and historical method as an integral part of their course work, he laid the basis of the "Melbourne school," which his successor has so ably developed.[6] His own contribution to facilitating the accessibility of documents is his two volumes on *Australian Discovery by Sea* and . . . *by Land* (London, 1929), and on historiography, *History and Historical Problems* (Melbourne, 1925). His major publications of the period are his chapters in the Australian volume of the *Cambridge History of the British Empire*, VII (Cambridge, 1933), for which he served as Australian advisor as well as principal contrib-

4. Prior to this date he had stressed Australian themes in his course on British Empire history, as had Wood in his course on the expansion of Europe. C. M. H. Clark discusses this development in his review of *Australia: A Social and Political History* in *Historical Studies*, VII (Nov., 1955), 95. It is noteworthy that in 1963 the University of Sydney still was not offering a full course in Australian history. In the opinion of the department, neither the quality of secondary writing available nor the importance of the subject warranted fuller treatment.

5. Raymond Maxwell Crawford, "The Late Professor Sir Ernest Scott" in *Historical Studies*, I (April, 1940), 3.

6. Examples of the fruit of the Melbourne school's concern with theory and method are: Raymond Maxwell Crawford, *The Study of History: A Synoptic View* (Melbourne, 1939); D. A. T. Gasking, "The Historian's Craft and Scientific History," *Historical Studies*, IV (May, 1950), 112-24; and A. L. Burns, "Ascertainment, Probability and Evidence in History," *ibid.*, IV (May, 1951), 327-39. Glimpses into the development of a Melbourne approach are provided by Crawford in "The School of Prudence or Inaccuracy and Incoherence in Describing Chaos," *Melbourne Historical Journal*, No. 2 (1962), pp. 3-16.

utor, and *Australia during the War* (Sydney, 1936), the story of the home front during World War I.[7] Although by present standards Scott's scholarship can be criticized for erratic citations and a tendency to trust his memory instead of rechecking sources, his was a major contribution to Australian history.

During the first eleven years of Scott's professional career the Library Committee of the Commonwealth Parliament was making source material for Australian history more readily available. Between 1914 and 1925 thirty-three substantial volumes of *The Historical Records of Australia* appeared. These represent but a portion of the original ambitious project.[8] Seven volumes of *The Historical Records of New South Wales* (Sydney), edited by Frank M. Blaton and Alexander Britton, dealing with events from the discovery of the continent to 1811, were published between 1893 and 1898. Discrepancies, resulting from transcription errors and unindicated deletions, will be found in documents which are duplicated in the two series. An ambitious "Australian Project at the Public Record Office" is making most documents relating directly to Australia in the great London repository readily available on positive microfilm to any purchaser.

It has been argued that the relative economy of microfilming the original documents and the emancipation this form of reproduction gives the research scholar from a copyist's errors and editing, now justify the termination of the *Historical Records* project. The deciphering of manuscript records, however, remains the task of the specialist. Those who enjoy the convenience and ready accessibility of the printed volume can be excused if they lament the fact that no equivalent of Canada's Champlain Society[9] or South Africa's Van Riebeeck Society[10] has been organized in Australia to publish source material of general interest. The absence of such an organization, one of the most notable shortcomings of Australian historical scholarship, possibly reflects

7. It was Vol. XI of C. E. W. Bean, ed., *The Official History of the War of 1914-1918* (12 vols.; Sydney, 1921-42).

8. Seven "series" were projected, but volumes appeared in but three of them: Series I, despatches between the Governor of New South Wales and the Secretary of State, 1787-1848, 26 volumes; Series III, material dealing with the foundation of the other colonies, 1803-1830, 6 volumes; and Series IV, early legal history, 1 volume. J. Frederick Watson was the general editor.

9. See pp. 88, 130.

10. See p. 215.

Australian reliance on state instrumentalities to provide for such needs.[11]

It is also noteworthy that Australian historians have not formed a distinct national body akin to the American Historical Association. In 1911 historians were invited to join Section E of the Australian and New Zealand Association for the Advancement of Science, the geographers' section. The historians made it their own, the geographers later retiring to form Section P. This institutional arrangement satisfies the academic and social needs for periodical meetings. On the other hand, the arrangement limits the effectiveness of historians as an organized group striving to further ends connected with their discipline between such meetings. That no professional historical journal appeared in Australia before 1940 can, in part, be attributed to the lack of a national organization which would incorporate a subscription to the journal into its membership fee. *The Economic Record* (Melbourne) appeared in 1925 with the organization of the Economic Society of Australia and New Zealand.

Since its establishment in 1928 *The Australian Quarterly* (Sydney) has published valuable historical articles, especially relating to events in this century, and the journals of the Royal Australian Historical Society[12] and the state societies have been open to the professional historian. Not until 1940, however, was there a journal edited by and for the professional, *Historical Studies: Australia and New Zealand.* Two issues a year appeared until early 1944. Only two more issues were published before February, 1949, when the Department of History of the University of Melbourne assumed full responsibility for the journal. Since that date it has maintained a regular twice-yearly output. *The Australian Journal of Politics and History,* sponsored by the University of Queensland, Brisbane, made its debut in November, 1955. Since then it has maintained its planned schedule of two issues a year, and, thanks to its regular feature, a detailed chronicle of federal

11. Though their present range of interest is narrowly circumscribed, the decision of the Royal Australian Historical Society to join in the sponsorship of a project to reprint the journals of participants in the foundation of Sydney is, in these circumstances, commendable. Captain Watkin Tench's *A Narrative of the Expedition to Botany Bay* and *A Complete Account of the Settlement at Port Jackson,* with an introduction and annotations by L. F. Fitzhardinge and published under the title *Sydney's First Four Years* (Sydney, 1962), inaugurated the series.

12. An association composed largely (but not exclusively) of lay enthusiasts residing in and around Sydney. The Society was organized in 1901. Permission to add the prefix "Royal" was granted in 1918.

and state politics, its files already have become a useful historical reference.

The existence of such journals mark a growing maturity of Australian historical scholarship, but in order to set present accomplishments in their proper perspective we must turn our attention again to earlier events. Although the universities did not offer undergraduate courses in Australian history until the late 1920's, they provided other incentives for the production of books on Australian historical themes.

In the early 1920's the adults enrolled in the evening classes of the Workers' Educational Association, with which the universities were associated, were requesting courses in Australian topics for which adequate texts were not available. The W.E.A., the major agency for adult education in Australia as in Britain during this period, arranged to commission and publish such books. The most obvious direct product of the lectures was Herbert Heaton's *Modern Economic History, with Special Reference to Australia* (Adelaide, 1921; rev. 1925),[13] which remained the standard text on the subject for university and tutorial classes in Australia until it went out of print about 1930. The "special reference" the then director of tutorial classes at the University of Adelaide gave to Australia occupied about one-quarter of the text. It was W.E.A. sponsorship which made possible the publication in book form of Henry Bournes Higgins' *A New Province for Law and Order* (Sydney, 1922). This discussion of the function of the Commonwealth Court of Conciliation and Arbitration by its most influential president is a historical document of permanent importance.[14] Another of their publications, James Thomas Sutcliffe's *A History of Trade Unionism in Australia* (Melbourne, 1921), still deserves to be read as an impartial and informed assessment of the formative period of the movement.

13. I am indebted to Herbert Heaton for calling my attention to the importance of the W. E. A. in Australian historiography in his review article, "The Progress of Historical Studies in Australia," in *The Journal of Modern History* (Chicago), XV (Dec. 1943), 303-10. In a personal letter to the author (April 29, 1962) Heaton mentioned that the material for his *Modern Economic History* first appeared in 1918 in the Adelaide Labor daily as a verbatim report of the lectures based on a script which he provided the day before the lecture. The paper in return agreed to supply the W. E. A. with the printed lecture in the form of an eight-page pamphlet with wide margins for note-taking.

14. The most prolific writer on the history and law of industrial arbitration is Orwell de R. Foenander. The author's progression from an evening lecturer in history to a professor of industrial relations can be traced in the tendency toward technical specialization in the works which followed his *Towards Industrial Peace in Australia: A Series of Essays in the History of the Commonwealth Court of Conciliation and Arbitration* (Melbourne, 1937).

Sutcliffe's reference in his preface to the fact that he had been awarded the Harbison-Higginbotham scholarship for his manuscript in 1919 by the University of Melbourne reminds us of another stimulus to research in Australian themes. Australian universities were offering prizes for works embodying original research or requiring such research in the terms of their scholarships. The Tinline scholarship, established at the University of Adelaide in 1908, for instance, required the holder to "prepare a thesis on a historical subject, the work to be based on a study of original documents."[15] As few such studies would be acceptable to commercial publishers, the establishment of the University of Melbourne Press, which brought out its first book, Myra Willard's *History of the White Australia Policy*, in 1923, is a significant landmark.[16] Stephen H. Roberts' *History of Australian Land Settlement (1788-1920)* (1924) and his *The Squatting Age in Australia, 1835-1847* (1935), are other early publications which had noteworthy effects on Australian scholarship. Later investigators, dealing with more restricted periods, have demonstrated so many errors in the first of Roberts' books that it should now be used with caution. *The Squatting Age*, with its description of the pastoral society which dominated the eastern mainland before the discovery of gold, has survived the scrutiny of later researchers better. An earlier and still useful study into an important aspect of the problem of government policy with respect to land settlement was Richard C. Mills' *The Colonization of Australia (1829-42): The Wakefield Experiment in Empire Building* (London, 1915).

15. George H. Pitt, "South Australia Archives," in *Historical Studies*, I (April, 1940), 46. A list of Tinline theses held by the University of Adelaide library appears in *ibid.*, VII (Nov., 1956), 353.

16. It is noteworthy that she was a student of Wood at Sydney. Although her book remains the standard reference for the topic, a number of recent articles should also be consulted. These include: from *The Australian Quarterly*, Carlotta Kellaway, " 'White Australia'—How Political Reality became National Myth," XXV (June, 1953), 7-17; Bruce E. Mansfield, "The Origins of 'White Australia,' " XXVI (Dec. 1954), 61-68; Kenneth M. Dallas, "The Origins of 'White Australia,' " XXVII (March, 1955), 43-52; Russel B. Ward, " 'An Australian Legend': An Historical View of the White Australia Policy," *Journal and Proceedings of the Royal Australian Historical Society* (Sydney), XLVII (Dec., 1961), 335-51; A. T. Yarwood, "The Dictation Test —Historical Survey," XXX (June, 1958), 19-29; and Yarwood, "The 'White Australia' Policy: A Re-interpretation of its Development in the Late Colonial Period." in *Historical Studies*, X (Nov. 1962), 257-69. Yarwood's *Asian Migration to Australia: The Background to Exclusion, 1896-1923* (Melbourne, 1964) would appear to provide a summary of the more recent research. All Melbourne University Press books have their place of publication given as "Melbourne" rather than the strictly accurate "Carlton" before mid-1959, or "Parkville" thereafter.

In short, with some notable exceptions such as Scott, Melbourne, Roberts, Archibald Grenfell Price (to whom reference will be made later), and G. V. Portus (whose neglect in this essay is hereby admitted), few of the holders of academic appointments were publishing the results of historical research beyond that required for their graduate degrees. A contributing factor, though not a determining one, as current conditions demonstrate, is the absence in Australia of large-scale co-operative publishing ventures similar to those which stimulated two generations of historical research in a sister Dominion, *Canada and its Provinces*, *The Chronicles of Canada*, *Canadian Frontiers of Settlement*, or *The Relations of Canada and the United States*.[17] Australian Royal Commissions have also not shown the readiness of their Canadian counterparts to engage academics to prepare historical studies relating to the problems they were appointed to investigate.

The Australian government had commissioned a twelve-volume history of Australian participation in World War I. The general editor of this series, C. E. W. Bean, was a journalist,[18] as were most of the authors. As the volumes appeared between 1921 and 1942 it was apparent that the work was well done—given the opportunity, Australians can write, as well as fight, a good war, as was further confirmed by the next generation both of servicemen and historians. The access to records and freedom from official interference which Bean secured for his writers established a notable precedent which simplified the task for authors of the official histories of World War II, possibly not only in Australia.[19] The other notable co-operative work of the period was the Australian volume of *The Cambridge History of the British Empire* (1933). That it still is so frequently consulted reflects the absence of detailed up-to-date compendia of Australian history. It followed the familiar format, and factual rather than interpretative approach, of the series. Its bibliography of primary sources is still useful, while the lists

17. See pp. 75, 90-95.

18. His *On the Wool Track* (Sydney, 1910; rev. ed., 1925), based on a series of articles done for the Sydney *Morning Herald* in 1909, describes life on the sheep stations on the fringe of settlement. It remains one of the best accounts of the continuing element of conflict in the settlement of Australia, man's struggle with, and adaptation to, an inhospitable environment.

19. "In 1918 the idea of a contemporary history by a historian who was paid by the state and given access to all the papers, yet left unfettered, was vastly more unorthodox than it is now; and the Australian history of the war of 1914-18 was produced under probably a greater degree of freedom than any companion history." Gavin Long, "The Australian War History Tradition," *Historical Studies*, VI (Nov. 1954), 250.

of secondary sources reflect the state of historical scholarship at that time.

The endowed lecture series assumes an increased importance in a country lacking other agencies encouraging the organization of original material in a publishable form. Since their inauguration in 1928, the John Murtagh Macrossan lectures at the University of Queensland have yielded valuable bibliographic fruit. The first series by John G. Latham, *Australia and the British Commonwealth* (London, 1929), records the opinions of the man who had been Attorney-General of Australia since late in 1925, and thus remains a significant record of influential Australian opinion when the intra-Imperial relations that were to be given statutory definition in the Statute of Westminster, 1931, were being worked out. Two other studies, Archibald (later Sir Archibald) Grenfell Price, *The History and the Problems of the Northern Territory* (Adelaide, 1930) and A. C. V. Melbourne, *The Life and Times of William Charles Wentworth* (Brisbane, 1934), made no pretense at being the definitive works on their topics, but they are useful, *faute de mieux*.

The lecturer for 1937, Justice Herbert Vere Evatt of the High Court of Australia, demonstrated the value of court records to students of history in his discussion of a controversial event in early Australian history, the arrest and deposition of Governor William Bligh, formerly commander of *H.M.S. Bounty*. His material appeared in revised and expanded form as *Rum Rebellion: The Story of the Overthrow of Governor Bligh by John Macarthur and the New South Wales Corps* (Sydney, 1938). This book, still the subject of controversy,[20] was the second of three notable contributions which Evatt made to Australian history during his sojourn on the High Court bench. His earlier *The King and His Dominion Governors* (London, 1936) is an important constitutional study, inspired by the dismissal of Premier J. T. Lang of New South Wales, of the actual authority of the local agents of the symbol of Imperial unity in whose name government business is transacted. His third major contribution, *Australian Labour Leader: The Story of W. A. Holman and the Labour Movement* (Sydney, 1940; abridged ed., 1954) would have been important if it were only a first rate political biography, then a rare product in Australia, but, as a study

20. E.g., Malcolm H. Ellis, "The Great 'Rum Rebellion' Debate: Dr. Evatt and Others *v.* M. H. Ellis," *The Bulletin* (Sydney), LXXXV (Feb. 2, 1963), 22-24.

of the problems of leadership with the Australian Labor party, it is more than this.

Evatt gives a sympathetic and informed[21] discussion of William Holman, an early leader in the Australian Labor party who became Premier of New South Wales in 1913. Like Prime Minister William M. Hughes on the national level, Holman was unable to carry his party when he advocated conscription in World War I. He continued in office with the suspicious support of his former opponents until the latter felt themselves safe to jettison him. Evatt's own political career following his resignation from the High Court in 1940, particularly the stormy period of his leadership of the federal Labor party from 1951 to 1960, offers ample material for further studies on the same theme.

Those who wish to identify a watershed in Australian historiography might well define it somewhere between 1936 and 1940, the years of Evatt's historical publications. But it is the work of two other writers, professionally trained historians who were not, however, employed in university teaching, that illustrates more clearly the coming of age of Australian historical scholarship. Characteristics of this maturity are a more sophisticated use of source material and an appreciation of the interdependence of developments in Australia with those abroad. They are evident in the Rev. Fr. Eris O'Brien's *The Foundation of Australia, 1786-1800: A Study in English Criminal Practice and Penal Colonization in the Eighteenth Century* (London, 1936), prepared originally as a thesis for the University of Louvain. O'Brien added the bonus of a literary artist's narrative skill to his ability to place his country's history in perspective and to his thorough research.

The other major accomplishment of the period was in economic history, one of the fields whose cultivation Hancock had commended to Australian historians. The first government statistician of New South Wales, Timothy A. Coghlan, whose statistics were to provide basic data for most economic historians until recent years,[22] published in his retirement a four-volume study of *Labour and Industry in Australia, from*

21. Evatt served for a time as Holman's secretary.
22. E.g., his *Wealth and Progress of New South Wales* (Sydney, 1887 *et seq.*) and his *Statistical Account of the Seven Colonies of Australia* (Sydney, 1896 *et seq.*). The service has been continued since 1907 by the annual editions of the Commonwealth Bureau of Census and Statistics' *Official Year Book of the Commonwealth of Australia*, which, judged by comprehension of coverage and editorial arrangement, ranks among the best of national statistical year books.

*the First Settlement in 1788 to the Establishment of the Common-
wealth in 1901* (London, 1918). This massive study of "labour and
industry" was also to prove to be a quarry for later students. Far from
the comparatively richer library and archival resources of the east,
Edward O. G. Shann of the University of Western Australia produced
*An Economic History of Australia* (Cambridge, 1930), a sprightly and
outspoken defense of private enterprise which has retained its popular-
ity in a community whose history is dominated by state intervention
in all phases of economic activity. The economic historians of the new
school who carp at Shann's superficial research could well study and
strive to emulate his effective presentation.

In 1939 the first of two volumes subjecting the continent's economic
development to a searching examination from a leftist vantage point
appeared. Brian C. Fitzpatrick's *British Imperialism and Australia,
1783-1833* (London, 1939) and his sequel, *The British Empire in
Australia: An Economic History, 1834-1939* (Melbourne, 1941) confirmed the indications of Eris O'Brien's work that Australian scholars
were now capable of sustained, meticulous research on which to base a
sophisticated interpretation of the significance of their national development in a larger context. Later commentators, who did not share
Fitzpatrick's politico-economic views, have praised the work as the greatest individual contribution to Australian historical literature.[23]

Recent studies based on revised statistical series[24] have outdated
some of his material and conclusions, based as they are on Coghlan's
data. Until a comparable synthesis incorporating the new material appears, these works will remain in regular service, though they should
be used with caution.

By the outbreak of World War II there existed in Australia a small
but competent group of professional historians, no "publish or perish"
tradition, and considerable documentary material available for the
early period of European settlement, the period in which most of the
serious research work was being done.

The Pacific phase of World War II provided a traumatic experience
to most Australians. The fall of Singapore and the destruction of
British naval power in the Indian Ocean revealed to all that the agen-

23. Raymond Maxwell Crawford and G. F. James in Clinton Hartley Grattan, ed.,
*Australia* (Berkeley, 1947), p. 421; and Alan G. L. Shaw, *The Story of Australia*
(London, 1955), p. 289.
24. See below, p. 169.

cies which had insulated them from the harsh realities of the world were no longer effective. Australians had to adjust to a world with new centers of power, and with their northern neighbors in the throes of national self-assertion. Immigration from continental Europe was encouraged to an Australia which must "populate or perish." As a result, research into Australian history acquired a more obvious national function. An emigrant Briton going to "the colonies" assumed the right to take his history with him, an attitude which was rarely challenged by the fellow overseas Britons among whom he settled. The "foreigner," however, has to be assimilated, and, as American experience has shown, one effective method is the exposure of the young immigrant, or the children of immigrants, to the host nation's history in the schools.

In other respects, too, the intellectual climate in which Australian history has been written after 1941 differs significantly from that of the earlier period. Strong American influences appear, though these are being directed against a fairly mature, British-oriented tradition. It is in this context that the importance of the "coming of age" of Australian historical scholarship in the late 1930's can be appreciated. There was also the growing national self-awareness. One of the institutional manifestations of the latter development was the establishment by the federal government of the Australian National University at Canberra, a step which has had major repercussions in academic studies in Australia generally.

Between 1852, when the University of Sydney received its first students, and 1913, when the University of Western Australia opened its doors, one university had been established in the capital city of each of the six Australian states. These and two university colleges, Canberra (1930, affiliated with Melbourne) and New England at Armidale, N.S.W. (1938, affiliated with Sydney), constituted the sum and total of institutions offering university instruction in Australia prior to the expansion of facilities in the post-World War II era. Each was primarily dependent on state funds for its support. None of the Australian universities, however, could afford adequate facilities for postgraduate instruction comparable to the high quality of their undergraduate training. The best Australian students had gone abroad, usually to Britain. Many of them stayed abroad after completing their training.

Sir William Keith Hancock's autobiography, *Country and Calling* (London, 1954), illustrates the dilemma of the Australian scholar in the interwar period. A brilliant student of Scott at Melbourne, he then went on to Oxford, where he specialized in nineteenth-century Italian history. He returned to the chair of History and Political Science at the University of Adelaide in 1926, and while there was commissioned by an English publishing house to write the Australian volume in their "Modern World" series. His *Australia* (London, 1930) is the most brilliant expository essay on the Australian community and its collective personality that has yet been produced. In insights, if not in analysis, it provides on a smaller scale for the smaller community what Lord James Bryce's *American Commonwealth* does for the United States. Unfortunately, some of his insights have become the clichés of later authors. Neither Adelaide nor the other universities in Australia could offer Hancock professional opportunities comparable to those which lured him back to Britain. The claims of his calling overrode those of his country and not until his return to Canberra in 1957 were the two reconciled.

In an effort to stanch this hemorrhage of talent, to lure back the established expatriate Australian scholar, and to reverse the flow by attracting overseas students and teachers to a first-rate research center, the Commonwealth Parliament in 1946 authorized the creation of the Australian National University. It was to be an institute of postgraduate research concentrating on fields where specialized Australian applications were deemed to be in the national interest. Many faculty members of the state universities viewed the establishment of the new institution with misgivings. Their hopes of expanding graduate instruction in their own departments, with the stimulus and challenge such work offers, seemed threatened by the new rival in Canberra, enjoying the sponsorship of the richer federal treasury. It is now apparent that these fears have not been substantiated. Graduate enrollment and facilities for graduate instruction have increased in all Australian universities at a rate few could have believed possible in the immediate postwar years. Although many of the abler graduates still seek their higher degrees abroad, with American universities now competing with the British for the best of them, it is now a two-way traffic with postgraduate students from overseas coming to Australia. Supervision of graduate research seems to have stimulated interest in the faculty. The faculty member who continues his research and publication beyond that required or facilitated by his own graduate work has ceased to be the exception.

The assessment of recent writing in Australian history can most conveniently be made by considering general studies before moving to the particular. There was a need for a popular up-to-date survey of Australian history in the immediate postwar years when migrants, many with a lively curiosity to learn about their new homeland, flocked into the country. That the demand was met was due largely to the enterprise of overseas publishers who required that the authors treat the subject at an adult, yet at an introductory, level. The American with the longest sustained interest in Australian topics, Clinton Hartley Grattan, whose *Introducing Australia* (New York, 1942; rev. ed., 1947) can still be read with profit, brought together an impressive group of Australian specialists in the volume he edited for the United Nations Series, *Australia* (Berkeley, 1947). Only four of its twenty-eight chapters dealt specifically with the nation's history, and the postwar developments have outdated many of the other essays. More critical and up-to-date assessments of Australian cultural achievements can be found in Peter Coleman, ed., *Australian Civilization* (Melbourne, 1962), written for domestic consumption, and in Alan L. McLeod, ed., *The Pattern of Australian Culture* (Ithaca, 1963).

So many publishers have initiated series of national surveys that an observer might complain that of the making of such books there appears no end. Three which merit attention are Raymond Maxwell Crawford's *Australia* (London, 1952; rev. ed., 1960), A. G. L. Shaw's *The Story of Australia* (London, 1955; rev. ed., 1960), and Douglas Pike's *Australia: The Quiet Continent* (Cambridge, 1962). Crawford's interests in the era when the pastoralists dominated Australian society and in the development of an Australian cultural tradition, introduced in his survey, are further, but still not fully, expounded in his *An Australian Perspective* (Madison, 1960), the text of three lectures he gave while serving as Paul Knaplund Visiting Professor of Commonwealth History at the University of Wisconsin. Shaw's is the largest of the three surveys (320 pages). His success in achieving a "reasonably popular" style, yet combining this with sufficient scholarly concern to append a twelve-page bibliographical essay, are attractive features. He underplays economic themes in this volume but his earlier *The Economic Development of Australia* (London, 1944; rev. ed., 1960), professedly an attempt to steer a middle course between Fitzpatrick and Shann, can be regarded as a supplement.

The distinctive characteristics of Pike's book are his stress on the Australian settlers' achievement in mastering an environment so different from that of Europe, and his attempt to redress the excessive emphasis which other Australian historians have placed on the events which have transpired in the southeastern corner of the continent. Unfortunately, 242 pages provide insufficient space to accomplish his worthy aims. A proper appreciation of the triumphs of peace which he attempts to convey still requires a more detailed description to permit the reader to understand the magnitude of the settler's achievements. There is as yet no shorthand method by which a writer can allude to their victories or reverses, confident that he has evoked the desired emotional response in his reader. The story of the extension of the wheat frontier inland has not been invested with the same aura of romance and adventure as has that of wresting the American West from the plains Indians. The Australian conquest as yet has no phrase similar to "Little Big Horn" which connotes the cost of a temporary setback in the process. Similarly, the combatting of the invasion of prickly pear does not carry the obvious drama inherent in an account of the repulse of human invaders.

Most histories which purport to treat the whole country display a southeastern metropolitan bias. The problems and the achievements of Queensland, South Australia, Tasmania, and Western Australia are ignored, roughly in that order of ascending neglect. Comparable charges, of course, can be made of the historical writing of other geographically large nations. Although those interested in the peripheral areas can make a strong case that their states have been neglected, the fact remains that it was the events in the southeastern corner of the continent which had the major influence in determining the course of Australian development. The discussion of these events can be compressed only to a certain point to permit inclusion of material from other regions if the end product is to be meaningful in an introductory history to be read abroad, as Pike's was intended to be. A history which attempts to be fair to all significant portions of Australia would have to be a substantial volume. Such a volume, written with this intent, has yet to appear.

The first and, at the time of the writing of this essay, still the only book produced primarily for use as a text for university courses in the subject, *Australia: A Social and Political History* (Sydney, 1955), was the product of multiple authorship under the editorial direction of Gordon Greenwood. The priority given "social" in the title is not maintained in the text but a juster balance is evident than in the earlier, larger, co-operative project for the Cambridge History series, although, like its predecessor, it is of uneven quality. A comparison of the two books indicates the extent of the broadening of historical knowledge in the intervening quarter-century. Accounts of the exploits of explorers and of land legislation are curtailed but more meaningfully integrated into the fuller story of Australian development. The general bibliography of Greenwood's book has consciously been made a supplement to that of the older work, listing only books published after 1928.

Australian topics occupy about half of the space of the first and one-third of the second volume of Clinton Hartley Grattan's *The Southwest Pacific to 1900* and . . . *Since 1900* (Ann Arbor, 1963). Writing from a vantage point in the northern hemisphere for a northern-hemisphere audience the author has not stressed the Australian involvement in the affairs of the islands to the extent that would be expected of an antipodean writer. As a result the Australian portions could be extracted and, with very little editing, be combined into a single volume of some five hundred pages. The familiar Grattan style is apparent in the clearly presented, judicious synthesis of recent monographic material. The excessive emphasis on the political scene in the second volume can, perhaps, be attributed to the dearth of other available material.

The start of a more ambitious project is Charles Manning H. Clark's *A History of Australia*, I: *From the Earliest Times to the Age of Macquarie* (Melbourne, 1962). It is a highly subjective study in which early European interest and settlement of the continent are viewed as projections of the Reformation, Counter-Reformation, and the Enlightenment. Themes from classical tragedy are evident as the author readily identifies the tragic flaw in the characters of all the principal participants in his somber story. This un-Australian approach has aroused controversy. The factual errors of the author have been catalogued.[25] It is easy to note his excesses. The imperfection of man-

25. E.g., Malcolm H. Ellis, "History Without Facts," *The Bulletin*, LXXXIV (Sept. 22, 1962), 36-37.

kind is sufficiently well known that his frequent references to the discrepancy between the protestations of the pious and their actions lose their effectiveness. Certainly the author will have to modify his emphasis on individuals to treat adequately the more populous Australia to be dealt with in subsequent volumes. Nevertheless, the work leaves the reader with the impression that a new interpretative dimension has been added to Australian historiography.[26]

Another need which Clark's initiative filled earlier was a compilation of readings in primary source material. Clark excluded the narratives of explorers from his *Select Documents in Australian History, 1788-1850* and . . . *1851-1900* (Sydney, 1950 and 1955; with the assistance of L. J. Pryor) on the ground of their ready availability elsewhere, but he deals with a broad spectrum of other topics. The material is drawn from a wide range of official and unofficial sources, including some verse—a literary form more frequently cited by Australian historians than by those from the other Dominions of the "Old Commonwealth." The volumes reflect the older tradition of "selected readings" which Australian lecturers had used in other branches of history at least from 1914. The "problems" approach, so fashionable in the United States, has produced no Australian bibliographical fruit as yet.

For a wider, more popular audience, to which the "World's Classics" series caters, Clark prepared a smaller, livelier collection covering the period from the foundations to 1919. This volume, *Sources of Australian History* (London, 1957), includes a larger proportion of social commentary, frequently represented by bush ballads. A companion volume, treating the records of overland travelers, *Australian Explorers* (London, 1958), was edited by Kathleen Fitzpatrick.

If the lay reader could be interested in source material he should also be interested in survey histories. He is unlikely, however, to be attracted to the same type of history as is the student. The professional has been so exposed to abstractions and generalizations throughout his training that he is likely to forget how important the individual remains

26. His paperback, *A Short History of Australia* (New York, 1964), has appeared since the lines above were written. In it his irony, more disciplined, perhaps by space restrictions, is more effective, and his stress on representative individuals, most of whom fall short of the author's moral standards, is continued. It is a highly commendable study but one which, like the larger work, would have been improved by a more careful scrutiny of the manuscript for factual slips. Another recent survey which reflects its author's distinctive approach is Russel B. Ward's *Australia* (Englewood Cliffs, N. J., 1965).

to those who have not been similarly initiated. History which stresses people, which describes the reactions of recognizable individuals, is more readily understandable than is history without names, or which mentions names but does not attach faces or characters to them. Hence, despite its exaggerated emphasis on the southeastern mainland and other sins of omission and commission on which academic reviewers have dwelt, Marjory Barnard's *A History of Australia* (Sydney, 1962; 2nd ed, 1964) performs the useful function of presenting a large-scale history to the general public in an understandable form. Her favored technique of letting the eyewitnesses speak through direct quotation or paraphrase is most effective in the early decades of settlement. To this era she devotes an undue portion of the book, perhaps since it is a period she had covered successfully in her earlier impressionistic *Macquarie's World* (Sydney, 1941).

Possibly the best Australian biographer is Malcolm H. Ellis of the Sydney *Bulletin*, another non-academic. His first and most satisfactory study is of the last of the autocractic governors, *Lachlan Macquarie: His Life, Adventures and Times* (Sydney, 1947; rev. ed., 1953). His slimmer *Francis Greenway: His Life and Times* (Sydney, 1949) treats one of Macquarie's clients, the unsuccessful forger who was also an architect of ability, if not of genius. In his *John Macarthur* (Sydney, 1955), his best constructed book, he turns his attention to the founder of the Australian wool industry, the enemy of governors, the destroyer of Bligh's regime, and the foe of Macquarie. He moves into the next generation with his unpublished (at the time of writing) study of William Charles Wentworth, first significant colonial-born Australian and leader in the movement for local self-government. Although Ellis did not achieve the same identification with Greenway and Macarthur as he did with Macquarie, these books reveal by contrast how shallow are most attempts at biography by academically trained historians. The frequent failure of such historians to produce satisfactory full (in contrast to "political") biographies is a condition not unique to Australia, of course. Too often our training tends to stultify rather than discipline and direct the imaginative qualities required in the literary re-creation.

On the other hand, the historian's talents are also required by the biographer. One of Australia's leading poets, Judith Wright, has received wide critical acclaim for her imaginative re-creation of life in Queensland and northern New South Wales during the closing decades of the last century in *The Generations of Men* (Melbourne, 1959). It is a major literary achievement, but, although it is based on the diaries and reminiscences of her grandparents, it lacks the precision and the relating of events to the larger scene which the historian desires. A number of studies of pioneer families which meet these criteria are now available. Amongst these are Mary Durack's account of the activities of her ancestors in *Kings in Grass Castles* (London, 1959) and Marnie M. Bassett's *The Hentys: An Australian Colonial Tapestry* (Melbourne, 1954). Thomas Henty and his seven sons were associated with the start of the Swain River settlement in Western Australia in 1829, with Van Diemen's Land when it was still the second most populous of the Australian colonies, and they were among the first of the unauthorized settlers of what became the colony of Victoria. Tracing the fortunes of this family, who, more consciously than most, were seeking the most profitable investment of their capital and skills at a time when colonial policy regarding land grants and settlement was in flux, provides an excellent introduction into the social, economic, and political history of the period.

It was of the district where the Hentys finally settled that Margaret Kiddle wrote her posthumously published *Men of Yesterday: A Social History of the Western District of Victoria, 1834-1890* (Melbourne, 1961). The author knew well the descendants of those of whom she was writing, the successful proprietors of some of the richest pastoral land in Australia, who had evolved the closest antipodean approximation to the life and attitudes of the British landed gentry. Her explanations of the social and political machinations required to secure their position in the new country expand the scope of her study beyond the strict bounds of social history, making it the standard against which future district histories will be judged. When this work is compared to her *Caroline Chisholm* (Melbourne, 1950), a useful study of the public career of a remarkable woman who inaugurated a private emigration and welfare service in the early nineteenth century, the extent of the growth of her professional competence becomes apparent. So does the loss to Australian historical studies resulting from her early death.

Very few good district or state histories have been produced in the past half century in Australia. Western Australia, more isolated than the others, and hence more self-conscious, has been the best served. Events of the nineteenth century were discussed from a provincialist viewpoint by the state public librarian, James Sykes Battye, in his *Western Australia: A History from Its Discovery to the Inauguration of the Commonwealth* (Oxford, 1924). A more recent work, devoting almost two-thirds of its text to events of this century, is Frank K. Crowley's *Australia's Western Third* (London, 1960). The title is a proper Westralian reminder to easterners of the extent of the state they tend to overlook. Work is underway on similar histories of other states. In Geoffrey Serle's *The Golden Age: A History of the Colony of Victoria, 1851-1861* (Melbourne, 1963) we have, at last, a satisfactory exposition of the decade in which the gold rush and the establishment of responsible government followed close on the separation of Victoria from the mother state. Serle has promised to cover the remaining four decades of the colony's pre-federation history in two more volumes.

The early years of South Australia have been re-examined in Douglas Pike's *Paradise of Dissent: South Australia, 1829-1857* (London, 1957), which performs the same function of relating social and political developments at "Home" to experiments in colonization for the respectable early South Australians as Eris O'Brien's book did for those consigned to Botany Bay. It is a much more thorough exercise in research and scholarly reporting than was Archibald Grenfell Price's *The Foundation and Settlement of South Australia (1829-1845)* (Adelaide, 1924). The meticulous scholarship, so evident in Pike's work (but not, alas, as evident in his survey history referred to earlier), reveals some errors in the older book, but, for the period which it covers, Price's volume still offers the better integrated presentation of the formative period of the settlement. It does not, however, carry the story on to the granting of responsible government as does the later work.

One of the major contributions to Australian historiography in recent years is John Manning Ward's *Earl Grey and the Australian Colonies, 1846-1857: A Study of Self-Government and Self-Interest* (Melbourne, 1958). The Secretary of State for War and the Colonies, Earl Grey, had originally contemplated extending to eastern Australia a system of representative government short of cabinet responsibility which he had introduced in Nova Scotia and Canada in 1848. He associated with the constitutional change the need for some local federal union. One of the first North Americans to display an interest in Australian history, the Canadian Cephas D. Allin, explored this theme in his *The Early Federation Movement of Australia* (Kingston, Ont.,

1907). Ward's study is a much more thorough and far-ranging study than Allin's, which was limited to material available in London. A comparison of their bibliographies and acknowledgments illustrates the greater mobility which improvements in transportation and more generous financial arrangements have given to academics. Ward's ability to view the whole picture, placing the problem of the Australian colonies in the Imperial context, again indicates the extent to which Australian historical scholarship has outgrown earlier manifestations of colonial mentality. The touchy subject of Grey's attempt to reinstitute the transportation of convicts to the eastern mainland colonies, an incident which gives Grey's name a popular connotation in Australia far different from that which it has in Canada, for instance, is dealt with thoroughly and fairly.

Themes relating to the convicts have been sensitive, though fascinating, subjects for the historian. A pleasant and popular interpretation was to stress the harshness of the criminal code and to intimate, at least, that many of the transportees were victims of circumstance or of political reaction.[27] Some defenders of this comforting myth protested vocally when Charles Manning H. Clark subjected it to a critical examination in a paper subsequently published as "The Origins of the Convicts Transported to Eastern Australia, 1787-1852" in *Historical Studies*, VII (May and November, 1956), 121-35, 314-27.

Another cherished myth being subjected to reappraisal concerns the significance of the events associated with the storming of the Eureka Stockade on December 3, 1854. The sound of the shots fired at this time did not carry as far as did those at Concord eighty years earlier, yet myths associated with an armed uprising against constituted but unpopular authority can stimulate the development of national self-consciousness. The editors of *Historical Studies* deferred to the myth by bringing out a special ninety-six page supplement to mark its centenary. The contributors confirmed the present tendency of scholars to deflate the importance of Eureka as a causal factor in shaping the political destinies of mid-nineteenth century Australia while recognizing that the myth itself had become a historical fact that must be taken into account.

This treatment of Eureka is but a part of a general reappraisal of the importance of the gold rushes of the 1850's as a factor in transform-

27. E.g., Scott, *A Short History of Australia* (7th ed.) pp. 54, 60-61.

ing Australian society. Earlier interpreters saw the '50's and the '90's of the last century as epoch-marking decades. The later period was marked by the flowering of the *Bulletin* school of bush ballads and short stories[28] and also saw the emergence of the political labor movement. In *The Legend of the Nineties* (Melbourne, 1954) Vance Palmer, a leading literary critic and author, questioned the validity of emphasizing one decade. His study of key intellectual figures of the decade suggests that the national tradition took form over a much longer period, extending back to mid-century. Other studies followed this lead as more Australians took up the history of ideas. An unsatisfactory but important contribution was made by George Nadel, possibly the first of the promising products of the University of Melbourne to seek his postgraduate training at Harvard rather than Oxford or London. His dissertation was published under the title *Australia's Colonial Culture: Ideas, Men and Institutions in Mid-Nineteenth Century Eastern Australia* (Cambridge, Mass., 1957), a series of insufficiently integrated essays of unequal length. They deal with various themes relating to education in the broad sense and showed a continuity of development between 1830 and 1860; thus they bridge the decade of the gold rush and push back the seedbed of the Australian cultural tradition. In *The Australian Legend* (Melbourne, 1958) Russel B. Ward used folk songs effectively to argue that it was among the pastoral workers of the pre-gold rush period, many of them ex-convicts, that a specifically Australian outlook first emerged. The watersheds of the 1850's and 1890's are thus being eroded by the present trend in interpretation. The Australian ethos is seen as the product of all Australian history.[29]

The difference between the Australian and American frontier legacies on the shaping of national traditions is discussed by Ward in the concluding chapter of *The Australian Legend*. The little man's frontier begets American individualism. The Australian squatter's "big man's" frontier begets a defensive collectivism on the part of the nomad workers who could see little opportunity of moving from the employee

28. The importance of the decade is emphasized in Percy R. Stephensen, *The Foundations of Culture in Australia: An Essay towards National Self-Respect* (Gordon, N.S.W., 1936).

29. James McAuley has expressed doubts regarding the reality of the ethos: "Literature and the Arts," in Coleman, ed., *Australian Civilization*, pp. 123-25. A more subtle approach to the evolution of a generally accepted ideology is to be found in Michael Roe's *Quest for Authority in Eastern Australia, 1835-1851* (Melbourne, 1965). He traces the disruption of the Conservatism of the early Establishment and the substitution of a faith in moral enlightenment.

to the employer class. Although some tentative applications of the Turner hypothesis to Australian conditions had been made earlier, its formal introduction into the interpretation of Australian history can be dated from the delivery by Frederick Alexander of a presidential address to Section E of The Australian and New Zealand Association for the Advancement of Science, later published as *Moving Frontiers—An American Theme and Its Application to Australian History* (Melbourne, 1947). The author's introductory restatement of the thesis suggests that few Australian historians were familiar with it at that time.[30] Popular interest in other aspects of American life had long been evident in Australia, but American history was only being discovered by Australian historians in the 1940's. It was difficult even for the academic to ignore the United States after the arrival of the G.I.'s in 1942 and the invasion of the Fulbright fellows and their associates after the war. It was not an American academic visitor, however, but Harry Cranbrook Allen, an Oxford graduate and Professor of American History in the University of London, who offered the thoughtful comparison of the two frontier legacies in *Bush and Backwoods* (Sydney, 1959). In *Australia's First Frontier: The Spread of Settlement in New South Wales, 1788-1829* (Melbourne, 1963), Thomas M. Perry indicates an interest in providing fuller information on Australian patterns of settlement to test the validity of Turner's thesis.

Investigation into the history of Australian-American relations started in Australia with Gordon Greenwood's *Early American-Australian Relations: From the Arrival of the Spaniards in America to the Close of 1830* (Melbourne, 1944). In *American-Australian Relations* (Minneapolis, 1947) Werner Levi published the fruits of a visiting lectureship in which he covered one hundred and sixty years of increasingly complex relations in exactly the same number of pages as Greenwood used to report his much more thorough investigation of a briefer period of significant contact. A more recent, and generally more satisfactory study, though it stresses 'the recent past and surveys the entire south western Pacific area and Antarctica from an American vantage point, is Clinton Hartley Grattan's contribution to the American For-

30. The assumption of familiarity with the Turner hypothesis made by Norman D. Harper in his presidential address of 1962, "The Rural and Urban Frontiers" (*Historical Studies*, XI [May, 1963], 401-21), indicates the extent of the change. This address also appears in *The Australian Journal of Science* (Sydney), XXV (Feb. 1963), 321-34.

eign Policy Library, *The United States and the Southwest Pacific* (Cambridge, Mass., 1961).

The history of external relations is still a relatively uncultivated field in Australia. The earliest were with the mother country and these Henry L. Hall treated in *Australia and England: A Study in Imperial Relations* (London, 1934). The versatile Archibald Grenfell Price's *Australia Comes of Age: A Study of Growth to Nationhood and of External Relations* (Melbourne, 1945) is a brief, popular, and unreliable survey written when the country was entering the diplomatic field as a distinct entity. The Australian Institute of International Affairs sponsored the production of *Australia in World Affairs, 1950-1955* and . . . *1956-1960* (Melbourne, 1957 and 1963), edited by Gordon Greenwood and Norman D. Harper. Harper and his student, David Sissons, gave perspective to their account of *Australia and the United Nations* (New York, 1959) by including considerable material on the nation's record in the League of Nations.

Americans are responsible for some historical studies of Australian relations with Asia. The most favorable assessment that can be made of Werner Levi's superficial *Australia's Outlook on Asia* (East Lansing, 1958) is that it provides the first general historical survey of this field. A more thorough study of a specific theme over a restricted time span is Richard N. Rosencrance, *Australian Diplomacy and Japan, 1945-1951* (Melbourne, 1962). It covers the period from the defeat of Japan to the exaction of the ANZUS Pact from the United States as a *quid pro quo* for the ratification of the Japanese peace treaty. Australian negotiations with the United States are featured and the author offers some provocative comparisons of Australian and American attitudes toward diplomacy.

It was another American, the Australian-born Donald C. Gordon, who dealt with the background of the agitation for annexation of eastern New Guinea in *The Australian Frontier in New Guinea, 1870-1885* (New York, 1951). As the research was undertaken during the war his sources were limited to those available in the United States. His lack of access to Australian newspapers was particularly unfortunate in a work in which Australian public opinion was a significant factor.[31] The fullest history of modern Papua, the portion of New Guinea which the

31. Microfilm has made it possible for North American libraries to acquire runs of some Australian papers. See "Australian Newspapers on Microfilm, 1962," *The Australian Library Journal* (Sydney), XII (Sept., 1963), 137-40.

British annexed in 1884, is John David Legge's *Australian Colonial Policy: A Survey of Native Administration and European Development in Papua* (Sydney, 1956). A more critical appraisal, lacking the stimulating comparisons between Papuan and Fijian administrative policies which are a feature of Legge's book, is Lucy P. Mair's *Australia in New Guinea* (London, 1948). The administration of Australia's proconsul, criticized by Legge and Mair, is defended by Lewis Lett in *Sir Hubert Murray of Papua* (London, 1949). The foundations of Australian administration in the northeastern portion of the island are described in C. D. Rowley, *The Australians in German New Guinea, 1914-1921* (Melbourne, 1958). Until recently Australians regarded a segment of Antarctica as also being part of their overseas territories and their relations with this region from the days of the whalers are recorded in Robert A. Swan, *Australia in the Antarctic* (Melbourne, 1962).

Australian historians have shown relatively little interest in their domestic history of this century. An interpretative survey of the development of the Australian community since the establishment of the Commonwealth would meet a real need. The one attempt by an Australian to supply such a book, Brian Fitzpatrick's *The Australian Commonwealth: A Picture of the Community, 1901-1955* (Melbourne, 1956), is disappointing. It provides not a picture of the community, but a collection of snapshots, some out of focus, in a series of uneven essays which include some brilliant writing. The general indifference to twentieth-century themes can be explained in part by the British tradition, which places the dividing line between respectable historical research and mere journalistic exercises further into the past than does the American.[32] Nevertheless it was a Briton, Trevor R. Reese, who had returned to his homeland after a six-year sojourn in Australia, who wrote *Australia in the Twentieth Century: A Political History* (London, 1964). The most noteworthy feature of this often superficial study is the stress he places on the nation's rôle in colonial administration in the islands, the Northern Territory, and with respect to the aborigines generally. In his treatment of more conventional themes,

32. Kenneth S. Inglis' account of the rape-murder trial of an aborigine, *The Stuart Case* (Melbourne, 1961), demonstrates that Australian historians can deal with contemporary events, showing the concern for civil liberties and human dignity which we like to believe is characteristic of our discipline.

however, Reese did not make full use of the available monographic material, spotty though it is.

The inaccessibility of recent public records is another factor. The records have been opened to the writers of the war histories. Recognizing his responsibility to his less favored colleagues, Paul Hasluck quoted extensively from these otherwise closed sources in *The Government and the People, 1939-1942* (Canberra, 1952). This frank appraisal of an extremely complicated political situation was to be the first of two volumes dealing with the domestic political scene which Hasluck was commissioned to write.[33] Before completing the companion volume this sometime journalist, civil servant, and history lecturer entered the federal cabinet.

American scholars have made notable contributions in the field of recent history, notably Louise Overacker with *The Australian Party System* (New Haven, 1952). It remains the best introduction to a subject in which it was the pioneer work, but what was perhaps its major significance was its demonstration that a visiting academic could appraise the local situation and undertake the detailed research the project required. An American postgraduate student in political science and a "new Australian" undergraduate, Aaron Wildavsky and Dagmar Carboch, were the authors of the two essays published under the title *Studies in Australian Politics* (Melbourne, 1958). The former dealt with the constitutional referendum of 1926 and the latter with the fall of the Bruce-Page government, both stressing the interplay of pressure groups in political decision-making.

All those who have engaged recently in research into Australian federal politics of the first half of this century have had reason to be grateful to Geoffrey Sawer for his *Australian Federal Politics and Law 1901-1929* and . . . *1929-1949* (Melbourne, 1956 and 1963). This project by the Professor of Law in the Institute for Advanced Studies at the Australian National University stands midway between a history and a lawyer's reference book. It analyzes each of the Commonwealth's parliaments under the following headings: parties, the government acts and bills, budgets, motions of censure, and constitutional issues.

33. To cover the more complicated administration of home-front affairs in World War II, a "Civil Series" of five volumes was authorized in contrast to the single-volume World War I series. The first three to appear are: Hasluck's book, Sydney J. Butlin, *The War Economy, 1939-1942* (1955), and David P. Mellor, *The Role of Science and Industry* (1958).

Political historians of other Commonwealth countries and those working in related disciplines should welcome national counterparts of this useful reference tool.

Another political scientist who has added to our knowledge of Australia in this century is Leslie Finlay Crisp, whose *The Parliamentary Government of the Commonwealth of Australia* (London, 1949; rev. ed., 1961) is the standard work on that subject. His *Australian Federal Labour Party, 1901-1951* (London, 1955) is the best history of an Australian party yet available. The author's own activity within the councils of the party give the study added authority, though his failure to explain adequately the state party organization, upon which the federal party is based, is a weakness of the book. Delving into the historically respectable past, Robin Gollan traces the background and formative years of the Labor party and its relations with middle-class radicalism in *Radical and Working Class Politics: A Study of Eastern Australia, 1850-1910* (Melbourne, 1960). Documents to illustrate the developments of this earlier period have been published under the title *The Australian Labor Movement, 1850-1907: Extracts from Contemporary Documents Selected by R. N[oel] Ebbels* (Sydney, 1960), edited by Lloyd G. Churchward. The other parties have not received as much attention. Another active partisan, Ulrich Ellis, contributed *The Country Party: A Political and Social History of the Party in New South Wales* (Melbourne, 1958), and *A History of the Australian Country Party* (Melbourne, 1963). No history has as yet appeared of the other anti-Labor party which, since 1909, has used the names of the Liberal, National, United Australia and, again, Liberal party.

Although there have been sufficient political controversies to provide reasonable assumption that disgruntled Australian politicians would "tell all," as a group they have been notably reticent. One useful apologia is William M. Hughes' *The Splendid Adventure: A Review of Empire Relations within and without the Commonwealth of Britannic Nations* (London, 1929), written by the former Prime Minister when he was still in the political wilderness and explaining how intra- and extra-Imperial affairs revolved around his activities between 1915 and 1923. His later autobiographical works, *Crusts and Crusades: Tales of Bygone Days* (Sydney, 1947) and *Policies and Potentates* (Sydney, 1952), are chatty and unreliable reminiscences composed after he had been recalled to his party's front bench. Sir Earle Page, the prime agent forcing Hughes out of office in 1923 and long-time leader of the Country party, has provided the fullest and most useful of Australian political autobiographies in his *Truant Surgeon: The Inside Story of Forty Years of Australian Political Life* (Sydney, 1963). A former Premier of New South Wales and stormy petrel of the Labor party, John Thomas Lang, has written two useful volumes, *I Remember* (Sydney, 1956), and *The Great Bust* (Sydney, 1962). Sir Frederic W. Eggleston, state cabinet minister, senior public official, and diplomat, has drawn upon his long career to reflect on public ownership, political parties, foreign policy, and to write the biography of a colleague in state politics.[34] Though all were subjective, he did not write an autobiography. The other worthies who have written autobiographies have generally been uncommunicative on the big questions where they could have contributed to the answer.[35]

The man who was possibly the greatest of all Australian statesmen, Alfred Deakin, planned to write a full autobiography. Partly as a means to amass preliminary material for this project he took the unusual step of serving as the regular but anonymous Australian correspondent of the London *Morning Post* from 1900 to 1914 while holding high public office, including the prime ministership on three occasions.[36] He was denied the mental vigor in his retirement to complete the task, but two fragments completed earlier in his career have recently been published: *The Federal Story: The Inner History of the Federal Cause* (Melbourne, 1944; revised and enlarged ed., 1963), a self-effacing account of the federal movement, and *The Crisis in Victorian Politics, 1879-1881* (Melbourne, 1957). The latter book, and the second edition of the former, were edited by John A. La Nauze, who has

34. The works, in the order of reference above, are *State Socialism in Victoria* (London, 1932); *Reflection of an Australian Liberal* (Melbourne, 1953); *Reflections on Australian Foreign Policy* (Melbourne, 1957); and, with Edward H. Sugden, *George Swinburne: A Biography* (Sydney, 1931).

35. These include Sir George Reid, Premier of New South Wales, equivocal advocate of federation, and prime minister, *My Reminiscences* (London, 1917); Sir George Pearce, who had long service in both Labor and anti-Labor cabinets, *Carpenter to Cabinet* (London, 1951); and Sir Robert R. Garran, active in the federation movement and senior Commonwealth civil servant, *Prosper the Commonwealth* (Sydney, 1958). One outspoken author, whose books provide insights into the spirit of the organizers of Australian trade unions, is William G. Spence. His *Australia's Awakening: Thirty Years in the Life of an Australian Agitator* (Sydney, 1909) and *History of the A.W.U.* [Australian Workers' Union] (Sydney, 1911) have been republished in a single volume (Sydney, 1961).

36. John A. La Nauze, "Alfred Deakin and the *Morning Post*" in *Historical Studies*, VI (May, 1955), 361-75.

been issuing occasional progress reports while working on a full biography of Deakin. One such report is the slim booklet *Alfred Deakin: Two Lectures* (Brisbane, 1960), which also is a reminder that the John Murtagh Macrossan lectures are still functioning, though they are now playing a less significant rôle in Australian historiography. In the somewhat larger *The Hopetoun Blunder* (Melbourne, 1957) La Nauze views the confusion surrounding the formation of the first ministry of the Australian Commonwealth through Deakin's eyes.

The first Prime Minister of the Commonwealth, and later Justice of the High Court, is the subject of a biography by John Reynolds, *Edmond Barton* (Sydney, 1948). Although the extant Barton papers were used for the first time in its compilation, and, as Sir Henry Parkes' designated successor, he was the leading figure in the successful federation movement, the volume casts little fresh light on the political integration of Australia. Deakin has been more informative. The publicity which surrounded the discussion associated with the framing of the Australian constitution[37] and with its acceptance by popular referenda, created the impression that the constitution was an open covenant, openly arrived at. Only in recent years has a reappraisal, laying greater stress on economic motivation and pressure groups, of the early, and admirable, accounts of the movement[38] been undertaken. It is still in the stage of journal articles, a flurry of them being precipitated by R. S. Parker's "Australian Federation: The Influence of Economic Interests and Political Pressures" in *Historical Studies* (IV [November, 1949], 12-24.)[39]

37. The full debates of the constituent assemblies were published and are readily available: *Official Record of the Proceedings and Debates of the Australasian Federation Conference* (Melbourne, 1890); *Official Record of Debates of the National Australasian Convention* (Sydney, 1891); and the successful convention, *Official Record of Debates of the Australasian Federal Convention* (Adelaide, 1897; Sydney, 1897; 2 vols., Melbourne, 1898).

38. An extensive historical introduction to the federal movement prefaced John Quick and Robert R. Garran, ed., *The Annotated Constitution of the Australian Commonwealth* (Sydney, 1901). Quick was a member of the convention and Garran was its secretary. Garran also contributed the chapter on the federation movement to the Australian volume of *The Cambridge History of the British Empire*, the work being based on the earlier material. Another book by a participant in the movement and member of the convention is Bernhard R. Wise, *The Making of the Australian Commonwealth, 1889-1900* (London, 1913).

39. It is noteworthy that the immediate reply was written by an undergraduate, Geoffrey Blainey, "The Role of Economic Interest in Australian Federation—A Reply to Professor R. S. Parker" in *Historical Studies*, IV (Nov., 1950), 224-37. Other articles which have appeared in this journal on the general theme include: John S. Bastin, "Federation and Western Australia: A Contribution to the Parker-Blainey Discussion,"

A leading personality of the early stages of the federation movement, Sir Henry Parkes, has acquired a modern biographer in Alan W. Martin, whose preliminary assessment of the giant of late nineteenth-century politics has appeared as two chapters in *Melbourne Studies in Education 1960-61* (Melbourne, 1962). The papers of prime ministers who guided Australia through the greater part of the two World Wars, William M. Hughes and John Curtin, are now in the hands of Laurie F. Fitzhardinge[40] and Lloyd Ross respectively. The first volume, *William Morris Hughes: That Fiery Particle, 1862-1914* (Sydney, 1964), traces his career and the development of the Labor party down to the outbreak of the war which was to estrange him from the party he helped to mould. Other popular biographies of the colorful "Billy" Hughes are in print, but they provide little insight into his complex character.

The familiarity gained by active membership within the Labor party, which gave authority to Leslie Finlay Crisp's history of that institution, arouses suspicion when the same author writes *Ben Chifley: A Biography* (London, [1961]). It appears as an admirer's tribute to the ideal Labor Prime Minister, whose colleagues could regard him "as father, brother and mate all at one time." Though Crisp possibly was too close to his subject to provide the desired perspective—there being no severing of common political loyalties as occurred between Evatt and Holman—the work must be accepted as a superior contribution to this branch of Australian historical scholarship.

The project for a multi-volume *Australian Dictionary of Biography*, publicly announced in 1960, was thus launched at an opportune time, catching a scholarly interest in biography on the upsurge. It was planned as a co-operative venture of university historians with co-ordination and central office facilities being provided by the Australian National University. This ambitious project, the first major enterprise in co-operative scholarship undertaken by Australian historians, with Sir

---

V (Nov., 1951) 47-58; Alan W. Martin, "Economic Influences in the 'New Federation Movement,'" VI (Nov., 1953), 64-71; and W. G. McMinn, "George Reid and Federation: The Origin of the 'Yes-No Policy,'" X (May, 1962), 178-89. The articles of Parker, Blainey, Bastin, and Martin have been reprinted in J. J. Eastwood and F. B. Smith, eds., *Historical Studies: Selected Articles* (Melbourne, 1964).

40. Fitzhardinge was the principal author of *Nation-building in Australia: The Life and Work of Sir Littleton Ernest Groom* (Sydney, 1941). As Sir Littleton occupied public office during much of the second and third decades of this century, this biography remains a good introduction to the politics of the era and deserves to be reprinted.

William Keith Hancock as general director and Douglas Pike as general editor,[41] does not enjoy the financial sponsorship of corporate or private benefactors such as made possible similar dictionaries of biography in Britain or the United States, or the project now under way in Canada.

Some sponsorship has been obtained by the economic historians, who, possibly as a result, are displaying an increasing interest in business history. The contribution which the nationally owned Commonwealth Bank of Australia made toward the publications costs of Sydney J. Butlin's massive *Foundations of the Australian Monetary System, 1788-1851* (Melbourne, 1953) elicited frequent favorable comment by the reviewers, an indication of its novelty at the time. The assistance accorded by a commercial concern, the Mount Lyell Mining and Railway Company, to Geoffrey Blainey's *The Peaks of Lyell* (Melbourne, 1954) now appears to have marked the opening of a new phase in the writing of Australian history. Australian companies had been notably reluctant to open their archives, or their public relations funds, to historians. Most Australian historians, on the other hand, tended to underestimate the importance of mercantile and industrial concerns as positive factors in building the nation. Although there are large companies in Australia there are no enterprises comparable to the Canadian Pacific Railway or the British South Africa Company which cannot be ignored by those working on the history of the areas where they operated. The situation has changed over the last decade. Since the mid-1950's The Business Archives Council, composed of businessmen and economic historians, has been encouraging this previously neglected field. Blainey, while engaged in a general history of mining,[42] declared further bibliographical dividends such as *Mines in the Spinifex* (Sydney, 1960), and, treating another industry, *Gold and Paper: A History of the National Bank of Australasia Ltd.* (Melbourne, 1958). Commercial banks, concerned, perhaps, with the resurgence of the political fortunes of the Labor party, and mindful of the bank-nationalization crisis of 1947, are commissioning scholars of stature to prepare histories which make substantial contributions to our knowledge while also refurbishing the institution's public image. Another such study is Sydney J. Butlin's

41. The editors of the useful, though sometimes frustrating, ten-volume *Australian Encyclopaedia* (Sydney, 1958) made less use of academic contributors than is normal in major national encyclopedias.

42. This has now been published under the title, *The Rush that Never Ended: A History of Australian Mining* (Melbourne, 1963).

less imaginatively titled, but more satisfactory, *Australia and New Zealand Bank: The Bank of Australasia and the Union Bank of Australia Limited, 1828-1951* (Melbourne, 1961).[43] The rapprochement between the Australian historian and private enterprise has also produced biographies of entrepreneurs, as is illustrated by Alan Barnard's study of the nineteenth-century financier and pioneer of the frozen-meat industry, *Visions and Profits: Studies in the Business Career of Thomas Sutcliffe Mort* (Melbourne, 1961). The transformation of the *Bulletin of the Business Archives Council of Australia* into *Business Archives and History* in 1961 as a twice-yearly journal with editorial offices in the Department of Economics at the University of Sydney confirms the new trend. A notable project recently completed is the editing of the documents of a pioneer land company active in Van Diemen's Land and Tasmania, Philip L. Brown's *The Clyde Company Papers* in five volumes (London, 1952-63).

Another notable tendency among Australian economic historians has been an interest in recovering more accurate statistical data than those supplied by Timothy A. Coghlan. Noel G. Butlin has been a leading spirit of this enterprise, producing new statistical series with such titles as *Private Capital Formation in Australia: Estimates, 1861-1900* (Canberra, 1955). His first interpretative monograph incorporating this material is *Investment in Australian Economic Development, 1861-1900* (Cambridge, 1964).

Microstudies with a bias toward theoretical problems are fashionable among the new school of Australian economic historians. In his preface to *The Economic Development of Van Diemen's Land, 1820-1850* (Melbourne, 1954) R. Max Hartwell explained that he had undertaken this detailed study of a small unit over a short but significant time span because his theoretical studies into the Australian trade cycle before 1850 had been hampered by the dearth of published material. A notable exception to this trend is Edgars Dunsdorfs' *The Australian Wheat-growing Industry, 1788-1948* (Melbourne, 1956), a work which is also noteworthy as the first major contribution to Australian historical literature by a post-war immigrant from continental Europe. The one-time Professor of Economics at the University of

43. Another aspect of banking development is traced in Lyndhurst Folkine Giblin, *The Growth of a Central Bank: The Development of the Commonwealth Bank of Australia, 1924-1945* (Melbourne, 1951), a notable blending of accounts of an institutional transformation and of changing economic concepts of the rôle of the bank.

Riga, who joined the faculty of the University of Melbourne in 1948, understates in his text the range of research required in this account of the country's second most important industry, which he views as an economic, technological, and social process. The continent's major source of foreign exchange is treated over a briefer period and in a narrower fashion by Alan Barnard in *The Australian Wool Market, 1840-1900* (Melbourne, 1958).

The postwar immigration program which brought Dunsdorfs to Australia has stimulated interest in assimilation and related processes. Much of the work undertaken by the Department of Demography at the Australian National University is historical in approach. The head of this department, Wilfrid David Borrie, treats two of the larger non-British immigrant groups in *Italians and Germans in Australia: A Study of Assimilation* (Melbourne, 1954). The importance of understanding the European background of the immigrants becomes apparent to anyone who engages in such studies. A just balance between the European and Australian phases of the migration process is maintained in Charles A. Price's most recent study, *Southern Europeans in Australia* (Melbourne, 1963).

The "New Australians" are influencing the writing of history more than the oldest Australians. Historians, generally, have been content to leave the study of the aborigines to the anthropologists, and then to ignore the anthropologists.[44] Native policy, an aspect of white administration, is another matter. An example of the southeastern bias in some Australian histories is provided in Edmund J. B. Foxcroft's title, *Australian Native Policy: Its History, Especially in Victoria* (Melbourne, 1941), the non-Victorian sections of which must be treated with caution. A more thorough study of the policy in the colony which had a larger aboriginal population is provided by Paul Hasluck in *Black Australians: A Survey of Native Policy in Western Australia, 1829-1897* (Melbourne, 1942). A final solution to the native problem, which was achieved early in Tasmanian history, has been outlined by Clive Turnbull in *Black War: The Extermination of the Tasmanian Aborigines* (Melbourne, 1948). Another pioneering work by Archibald Grenfell Price, that frontiersman of Australian historians who opens up

44. For evidence that this is not entirely true, see D. J. Mulvaney, "The Australian Aborigines, 1606-1929: Opinion and Field Work," *Historical Studies*, VIII (May and Nov., 1958), 131-51, 297-314. These articles have been reprinted in Eastwood and Smith, cited above.

new fields and leaves their cultivation to others, is *White Settlers and Native Peoples: An Historical Study of Racial Contacts between English-speaking Whites and Aboriginal Peoples in the United States, Canada, Australia, and New Zealand* (Melbourne, 1949).

The comparative study is a useful device to broaden the horizons of both the author and the reader. Normally the comparisons with Australia have been drawn from the United States, or from Canada, where the smaller discrepancy in wealth and population and common membership in the Commonwealth provide a wider range of topics lending themselves to the comparative treatment. The possibilities of looking to the Argentine, where fruitful comparisons exist on the development of the pastoral industry, have not as yet been explored by Australian historians. These would include early land grant practices, the impact of refrigerated shipping on diversifying the marketable products of the grasslands, and the competition of the two countries in the British market as producers and as borrowers. The social and economic implications of the development of the self-sufficient *hacienda* in one country and of cash economy of the squatter's station in the other, the tension between metropolis and hinterland—be it "the country" or "the camp"—are other possibilities.

A comparative study of an aspect of literary history has been made by John Pengwerne Matthews in *Tradition in Exile: A Comparative Study of Social Influences on the Development of Australian and Canadian Poetry in the Nineteenth Century* (Melbourne, 1962). The fruit of years of study is to be found in Henry Mackenzie Green's two-volume *History of Australian Literature: Pure and Applied* (Sydney, 1961), which covers the period from the first settlements to the early 1950's and includes eight chapters on history and related subjects. One flippant comment, which takes two notable scholarly achievements in vain, suggests that Green was trying to rival the bibliographic work of John A. Ferguson. The reference is to the four substantial volumes of *The Bibliography of Australia* (Sydney, 1941-55), in which the bibliophile jurist lists all works relating to Australia published separately between 1784 and 1850. The first of three more volumes giving selective coverage until 1900 appeared in 1963. The magnitude of this remarkable work, and its importance to historians, is obvious.

Other arts have also found their historians. In *Australian Painting, 1788-1960* (Melbourne, 1962) Bernard Smith traces the development of Australian painting with more detail than he was able to in his earlier *Place, Taste and Tradition: A Study of Australian Art since 1788* (Sydney, 1945). In *European Vision and the South Pacific, 1768-1850: A Study in the History of Art and Ideas* (Oxford, 1960) he broadens the geographic field while restricting the time range. In these studies his main theme is the difficulty artists experienced in adapting their European training and canons to a new and different environment. The European musical tradition has been accepted by Australians with a less obvious sea-change. A survey, *Music in Australia: More Than 150 Years of Development* (Melbourne, 1952), is by William Arundel Orchard, who, as conductor, composer, and university lecturer, has done much to further that development. Similarly, a leading architect has written the most popular history of architecture in Australia. This is Robin Boyd, who, in *Australia's Home: Its Origins, Builders and Occupiers* (Melbourne, 1952) traces the development of the single-family house, the most common type of housing in Australia, from the first days of settlement, displaying in the process a delightful gift for humor.

Space restrictions preclude consideration of church history, a field so often dominated by the amateur and the zealot. It has attracted an increasing number of trained and competent scholars,[45] enough to support *The Journal of Religious History*, launched in 1960, and edited by Bruce E. Mansfield, in the Department of History at the University of Sydney. The relation of Church and State in education has been a matter of lively dispute in Australia as elsewhere. A useful introduction to the subject is provided by Albert Gordon Austin in *Australian Education, 1788-1900: Church, State and Public Education in Colonial Australia* (Melbourne, 1961).

And so lacunae are being filled in. Whether the undirected interests and enthusiasm of individual scholars should be relied on to locate and satisfy the more obvious of those remaining or whether these can best be dealt with by co-operative ventures similar to the undertaking of the *Australian Dictionary of Biography* is a question which must soon be faced. Collectivism is a highly important force in Australian history, yet Australian historians have remained individualistic. Their failure

45. A useful reminder to his fellow non-Roman Catholics of the importance of and divergence of interpretation among writers of Roman Catholic history is Kenneth S. Inglis' "Catholic Historiography in Australia," *Historical Studies*, VIII (Nov., 1958), 233-53.

to obtain the financial support to undertake co-operative research on related problems which would result in the publication of a series of monographs remains an unsatisfactory characteristic of the scholarly scene.

Yet never has history been in such a healthy state in Australia. The profession is better staffed and enjoying better equipment than ever before. The Mitchell Library of Sydney (physically attached to the Public Library of New South Wales) and the Commonwealth National Library at Canberra remain the fullest repositories for prefederation and postfederation records respectively, but the archival holdings of all state public libraries are being made more accessible and are being enlarged, as the notices of acquisitions of manuscripts, reported regularly in *Historical Studies*, illustrate. The university libraries are also increasing their holdings, although only the Fisher Library of the University of Sydney has approached the minimum size a North American visitor would expect to find at a major university. Possibly because the original universities were located in the state capital cities and have been financed very largely by state grants, it was natural in earlier days to depend on the state public libraries to serve as the research respositories and to limit the holdings of the university libraries largely to material required for undergraduate instruction. With sabbatical leaves and travel grants readily available, and with the visitor from overseas no longer a novelty in the senior common rooms, Australia is no longer isolated. The growing cosmopolitanism is being reflected in the writing of the third generation of Australian professional historians, who are now coming into their maturity. These students of the students of Sir Ernest Scott and George Arnold Wood come into a goodly inheritance. The technique of writing the history of a "quiet continent" is being worked out. They have the assistance of those abroad who have become interested in Australia's history. From those to whom so much has been given more will be expected.[46]

46. Any bibliographical essay is out-of-date before the fair copy is typed. Those interested in Australian topics are fortunate in having the *Australian Book Review* (Adelaide, 1961———) as one guide to new publications.

# NEW ZEALAND

## Keith Sinclair

NEW ZEALAND'S HISTORIOGRAPHY is briefer than its history, but not much. The fact that an article can be written[1] on the historical literature of a country settled by literate people for only a hundred and fifty years, for which written records exist for not much longer, is eloquent testimony to the importance of historical self-explanation to modern civilized man.

Only a small proportion of the very considerable number of books written on New Zealand history, however, are of scholarly interest. Most of them have been inspired by a local or ancestral piety and written by amateurs. Most have been amateurish: their authors lacked the background knowledge and training necessary to see their subjects in perspective or to scrutinize evidence critically. Academic history is quite new. Until the 1920's virtually no thorough research had been carried out, and a negligible number of detailed studies had been published. Almost all of the first generation of professional historians are still living. The breed is still scarce, though increasing: there are now more historians at the University of Auckland (some sixteen) than there were in the country twenty-five years ago.

Brief as is the record of serious historical study, it is already possible to discern certain trends, and to point to distinguishing, if minor, characteristics. The search for national identity and the availability of local records have both directed attention to events within New Zealand rather than to the British origins: to the actual process of settlement, for example, rather than to the English colonizing companies as such. The development of New Zealand as an independent state has led to a new interest in foreign policy, as opposed to Imperial

1. The only previous article on the subject appears to be Trevor G. Wilson's "The Writing of History in New Zealand," *Landfall* (Christchurch), IX (Sept., 1955), 213-33.

or Commonwealth history in general.[2] The attention to Maori history, to racial relations (a novel feature of New Zealand history), arises both from the desire to probe the meaning of the term "New Zealander" (a Pacific man) and from the objective importance of the Maoris in the country's short history. This essay attempts to trace New Zealand historiography, mainly since 1940, and to indicate some recent trends.

## EARLY HISTORICAL LITERATURE

The first history of New Zealand was written in 1859 (nineteen years after the country was annexed by Great Britain) by an army doctor, Arthur S. Thomson. *The Story of New Zealand* (2 vols.; London) necessarily dealt mainly with the Maoris, though it contains some information of interest on the early governorships because Thomson had access to unpublished official records. On the controversial question of the merits of the New Zealand Company he was fairly impartial, unlike his successors for many years.

Most of the valuable early literature on New Zealand history consists of the reminiscences of settlers or travelers. Some of these are of interest to students as well as research workers. The best edited of these is Eric H. McCormick's edition of Edward Markham's entertaining *New Zealand, or Recollections of It* (Wellington, 1963). John Eldon Gorst's *The Maori King* (London, 1864; 2nd edition, ed. Keith Sinclair, Hamilton, N.Z., 1959) is a remarkable account of the growth of the King movement and of racial relations 1860-63. Charlotte Godley's *Letters from Early New Zealand* (private ed., Plymouth, Eng., 1936; 2nd ed., ed. John R. Godley, Christchurch, 1951) and Lady Mary Anne Barker's *Station Life in New Zealand* (London, 1870; 2nd ed., Christchurch, 1951) and *Station Amusements in New Zealand* (London, 1873; 2nd ed., Christchurch, 1954), paint intimate pictures of the life of early settlers. But the majority of such books necessarily need to be read sceptically, especially such works of propaganda as Edward Jerningham Wakefield's *Adventure in New Zealand* (London, 1845). The second edition of this work (Christchurch, 1955) has been uncritically edited and abridged by Joan Stevens.

2. See Philip D. Curtin, "The British Empire and Commonwealth in Recent Historiography," *American Historical Review* (Washington), LXV (Oct., 1959), 72-91, an article which touches on New Zealand historiography.

George William Rusden's three-volume *History of New Zealand* (London, 1883; 2nd ed., Melbourne, 1895) was violently pro-Maori and anti-settler. His allegations about the conduct of John Bryce (later a minister of the Crown) during the Maori Wars involved him in a libel case. He had to pay heavy damages and delete some passages in a second edition. Though this book is a mass of ill-written melodrama, it was based on wide reading of newspapers and official papers. The conspiracies he detected were not always figments; in particular, he came close to the truth about events leading to the Taranaki War in 1860. This book and his *Aureretanga: Groans of the Maoris* (London, 1888) contain much valuable material on the Maoris. Alfred Saunders' two volume *History of New Zealand* (Christchurch, 1896-99) may be regarded as a valuable source for the study of politics in the 1870's and '80's, but it is flawed by violent personal prejudices and a unique penchant for judging politicians by the canons of phrenology.

## WILLIAM PEMBER REEVES AND THE TRADITION

Very little prepared the way for William Pember Reeves's *The Long White Cloud* (London, 1898), a quite outstanding example of an intelligent, eminently readable "short history." A poet, journalist, cabinet minister, and scholar, he had incomparable advantages and produced a book still in print, though weakened by chapters by Angus John Harrop (4th ed., London, 1950). This work, and Reeves's two-volume *State Experiments in Australia and New Zealand* (London, 1902), which has not been superseded as a survey of the radical legislation of the '80's and '90's, crystallized what have been the main traditions of New Zealand historical interpretation.

The tradition starts from a slightly sentimental yet genuine respect for the Maori people. It is interesting that, though Reeves believed the Polynesians could navigate, there is no Kupe, no Toi, and no Maori "fleet"—ingredients added to the story as it developed, and now much questioned. Reeves merely says, "It will be safe to say that the Maori colonists landed at different points and at widely different dates."

Secondly, an exaggerated importance was given to Edward Gibbon Wakefield and the New Zealand Company as the authors both of annexation and settlement. Like much else in Reeves's book, this emphasis may be related to his own experience. He grew up in Canterbury—a "Wakefield" settlement—and knew some of the first settlers. More significant, he was much impressed by Wakefield's *Adventure in New Zealand,* from which source New Zealand Company propaganda passed into our historical writing. For instance, he condemns Hobson's choice of Auckland for the capital (ignoring the reasons for it).

Ancestor worship, and the accompanying assumption that Imperial expansion was meritorious, were scarcely compatible with, indeed with difficulty reconciled with, sympathy for the Maoris. Reeves achieves this reconciliation by blaming Governor Thomas Gore Browne for the Maori Wars: he sees the Waitara purchase as "a blunder worse than a crime." But he scarcely sees the land conflict and wars as arising from colonization itself. In attacking government policy leading to the wars, he echoes the view of the Lyttelton *Times,* which his father owned and he edited for a time. The Vogel borrowing policy is defended (Reeves's father was in Vogel's cabinet). The "continuous ministry" (Reeves's political opponents) are treated with respect but labeled "conservative," while the radical legislation of the '90's, which Reeves helped to pass, is praised and emphasized. Reeves was more fair-minded than might be expected of a politician fresh from battle, less partial than this summary suggests. But the important thing is that he provided an intelligent and intelligible, a coherent and widely acceptable, interpretation of the Colony's history which was scarcely questioned for many years.

Reeves's views were not only parroted and embellished by local writers, but substantially accepted by visitors who wrote the most significant commentaries on the country about 1900. André Siegfried was a political scientist whose accurate insights into New Zealand life derived much from Alexis de Tocqueville. Siegfried's *La Démocratie en Nouvelle-Zélande* (Paris, 1904; E. V. Burns, trans., London, 1914) remains an important study. Henry Demarest Lloyd, an American reformer, wrote *A Country without Strikes* (New York, 1900) and *Newest England* (New York, 1901) to prove a point in the United States: the value of "state socialism." Both these writers, and Albert Métin in *Le Socialisme sans doctrines* (Paris, 1901), followed Reeves in remarking the central rôle of the state in New Zealand society.

## The Beginnings of Research

New Zealand historiography offers a cheering if minor prospect for the historian, because it is evident that the major source of changing emphasis and interpretation has not been the conflicting viewpoints within society, but the progress of research itself. After World War I the process of research (though "search" would be a more accurate term in this case) began. It was conducted by young men, trained in history in New Zealand and British universities. All of them except Johannes S. Marais, a South African, were New Zealanders. Their writings illuminated (if that does not suggest too dazzling an achievement) the 1920's, which were in general dim years in New Zealand literature.

The first scholarly monograph published on New Zealand history was probably Angus John Harrop's *England and New Zealand: From Tasman to the Taranaki War* (London, 1926), which was based on research in French and British archives. He questioned the view, which the New Zealand Company had promulgated, that there had been an Anglo-French race for New Zealand. William Parker Morrell's *The Provincial System in New Zealand*, which appeared in London in 1932, had been written a decade earlier. It has not been superseded. *The Colonisation of New Zealand* (London, 1927), by Johannes S. Marais, was critical towards the evangelicals and government "Maori-phile" policy, and tended to regard events up to 1840 through the eyes of the New Zealand Company agents, but was much less favorable in its judgment of the Company's policies in the Colony itself. It remains a mine of information and one of the most useful books on New Zealand history. John C. Beaglehole's *Captain Hobson and the New Zealand Company* (Northampton, Mass., 1928) was another pioneering monograph. Morrell's *British Colonial Policy in the Age of Peel and Russell* (Oxford, 1930) (which deals partly with New Zealand) and Raymond W. Firth's *Primitive Economics of the New Zealand Maori* (London, 1929; 2nd ed., *Economics of the New Zealand Maori*, Wellington, 1959) remain authoritative works.

Another important scholarly work of this period was John B. Condliffe's *New Zealand in the Making* (London, 1930). The latter was, in several respects, the most important book on New Zealand since *The Long White Cloud*. Though not based on exhaustive research (it dealt with the country's development since European discovery), it rested on a vast amount of work on certain topics, and carried forward the critical study of economic history which had been pioneered by Guy Hardy Scholefield in *New Zealand in Evolution* (London, 1909). A second edition of Condliffe's book (London, 1959) is not an improvement, for he had lost touch with recent work.

This respectable stream broadened and deepened towards 1940, a year which saw a centenary flood of books, good, bad, and indifferent, to commemorate the annexation of the country. It had not washed away the Reevesian dykes of historical dogma, but they were being undermined.

## POINTS OF VIEW

The emphasis laid on the influence of impartial research on the understanding of New Zealand history is justified. New Zealand has not been permanently rent by social division, such as that between Boer and Briton, that might have produced two scarcely compatible views of history. But such divisions as there are have clearly influenced historical interpretation. New Zealand historians have not been mechanical brains, soullessly digesting data and regularly extruding packaged history.

Politically, it might be fair to say, there has been almost complete unanimity, not because there are no differences of opinion, but because conservatives have allowed their opponents to win by default. New Zealand historical literature has been in its political attitudes, rather radical. I think Neville C. Phillips of the University of Canterbury coined the phrase "The Long Pink Cloud" to underline this fact. The conservatives of the 1890's and 1930's produced neither a thinker nor a writer. Harold Miller's brief *New Zealand* (London, 1950) comes nearest of recent books to presenting a conservative view, but it is only mildly and unconventionally conservative. On the other hand, the majority of historians are not very radical. The best-known left-wing histories have been written from a Labour party (or earlier, Liberal party) and trade union point of view, like William B. Sutch's *The Quest for Security in New Zealand* (Harmondsworth, 1942). Books written by Communists are, as far as scholarship is concerned, not worth mentioning.

One reason for the radicalism of much of the country's historical writing has been the traumatic experiences of the depressions of the 1880's and early 1930's. Comfortable complacency suffered shocks which stimulated radical thought about the country's social and economic structure, thought which found expression in verse, fiction, and histories such as those of Reeves and John C. Beaglehole's brilliant essay, *New Zealand: A Short History* (London, 1936). The preoccupation of most historians with such problems as the balance of payments and government debt arises from the same sense of insecurity in a country a third of whose history has been depressions.

Another respect in which New Zealand experience has created a point of view for the country's historians may be detected in their emphasis on racial relations. The importance of the Maoris in the North Island is reflected, perhaps magnified, in the literature. The historians have always, unlike their Canadian, Australian, or American colleagues, placed the history of the Maoris and Maori-European relations in, or near, the center of their focus. Some have been influenced by anthropology. This is probably the most striking feature of the country's historical writings. Like some other Polynesians, the Maoris became literate almost as soon as they emerged from the Stone Age. Their letters (written in Maori) and speeches have added a novel element to the country's historical sources and writings: the voices of a primitive people experiencing the pangs of "culture contact." Consequently their community has interested historians as much as anthropologists.

One further point of view from which New Zealand development has come to be observed (a circumstance not unexpected to historians) is that of local national sentiment, which may be detected first in Reeves's writings. Not until the 1930's did nationalism much influence New Zealand literature, for though the majority of Europeans here were native-born in Reeves's time, the majority over the age of fifty-five (the group which presumably "ran" the country) were immigrants until the '30's.[3] In 1935 William Parker Morrell sought, in his book *New Zealand* (London, 1935), to interpret the country's history as the rise of a nation. In John C. Beaglehole's *New Zealand: A Short History*, published a year later, the imprint of national feeling is clear, though he denied that his compatriots were "with any deep feeling, a nation." In two recent histories the change from a colonial to a national

3. A fact noted by Frank Rogers in an essay, "The Influence of Political Theories in the Liberal-Labour Period: Henry George and John Stuart Mill," in *Studies of a Small Democracy* (Auckland, 1963), eds., Keith Sinclair and Robert McD. Chapman.

outlook is unmistakable, though not, perhaps, complete. It is, at least, the belief of the present writer that nationalism is written large on every page of his *A History of New Zealand* (Harmondsworth, 1959; 2nd ed., Oxford, 1961). In William H. Oliver's *The Story of New Zealand* (London, 1960) its influence is perhaps everywhere assumed, as something no longer needing special attention, though his book concludes with a fine passage expressing something of the pride that sustains nationalism. Speaking of New Zealand writers, he says:

> The imperatives of the habitat are no longer ignored; the heritage of England and Europe has ceased to be an overpowering substitute for independent thought. . . . The spiritual pioneer is beginning to populate the land; he is restless because he knows himself to be part-stranger, part-intimate; he is demanding, not security, but understanding.

Perhaps the endeavor of a new nation to understand, and be understood, partly explains an unusual characteristic of New Zealand historians. Many of them, from Reeves to Oliver, have been poets, not major poets, but not mere poetasters. Perhaps it would be more fitting to say that many of the country's poets have been historians. Others have at least been attracted, at times, to historical subjects. Verse and history have seemed adjoining doors to understanding and expression.

## CURRENT DEBATES

In 1945 it was still true that most books on New Zealand history were the result of amateur enthusiasm and fell far short of the stricter standards of scholarship, that little hard research had been carried out and few monographs published, and those mainly on the early events of European government and settlement. Good use had been made of British public records, but little of the resources in New Zealand libraries, whether newspapers, pamphlets, public archives, or private manuscripts. The main inheritance of the serious young student (such as the present writer) was a tradition of good writing (that of the English historian), kept alive notably by Reeves and Beaglehole, and a suitcase of books.

The change since the war has been remarkable (though it has not, perhaps, amounted to the dialectical quantitative to qualitative change). After the present writer compiled a reading list on New Zealand history in 1959, he noticed that more of the books he thought worth listing had been written since World War II than before. Even more encouraging to the academic, there has been a tremendous increase in the number of monographs (and unpublished theses) based on a thorough search of primary sources. And scholarly controversy, the wine of scholars, has begun to flow in learned journals and theses.

Some of the principal current disputes have involved a reappraisal of the traditions of historical writing in the light of new evidence or attitudes. Some cherished myths or legends now look sadly battered by fact. It is no longer possible to assert, as it was in 1914 by James Hight and Harry D. Bamford, in *The Constitutional History and Law of New Zealand* (Christchurch), that England owed New Zealand to Wakefield's (probably apocryphal) ride to Plymouth (see James W. Davidson's article, "New Zealand 1820-70: An Essay in Re-interpretation," in *Historical Studies: Australia and New Zealand*).[4] Indeed the traditional story of New Zealand's annexation has been rewritten by several historians who place more emphasis on events in New Zealand and New South Wales than in London. The Australian influence has recently been surveyed (not in a very stimulating way) by Edwin J. Tapp, *Early New Zealand: A Dependency of New South Wales 1788-1841* (Melbourne, 1958). The New Zealand Company appears more as a group of anxious speculators than benevolent colonizers in *The New Zealand Bubble: The Wakefield Theory in Practice*, by Michael Turnbull (Wellington, 1959), a short book inadequately summarizing a thesis. In John Miller's *Early Victorian New Zealand: A Study of Racial Tension and Social Attitudes, 1839-1852* (London, 1958), though the "Wakefield System" appears implausibly as "a product of hard reasoning," the Company's agents appear in New Zealand as swindling "land sharks."

The accepted view of previous historians that the government was in the wrong in the policies that led to the Maori Wars has not been shaken by recent work, but we now know more clearly how wrong it was. It has been shown that some of the principal arguments advanced by government officials in defense of their actions were quite false—for example, by Keith Sinclair in *The Maori Land League* (Auckland, 1950). We now know a great deal about government native policy, and Governor Robert FitzRoy, who has been pilloried by some his-

---

4. *Historical Studies: Australia and New Zealand* (Melbourne), V (May, 1953), 349-60.

torians, including Reeves, has found a defender in John Miller. A start has been made in the thorough study of nineteenth-century Maori history, with some unexpected results. Maurice P. K. Sorrenson, for example, has questioned the view, repeated in most general histories, that the Maoris retreated into "sullen isolation" after the Maori Wars.[5]

One of the main disputes among historians today is about the nature of politics in the 1870's and '80's. Reeves's "Whig" (or, more strictly "Liberal") interpretation was assailed by J. D. N. McDonald in an article in 1952,[6] and, more recently, it has come under a cross-fire of facts aimed by graduate students. Some of the conclusions reached in masters' thesis have been summarized in articles by William J. Gardner[7] and Edmund Bohan.[8] Other historians, including Trevor G. Wilson in *The Grey Government, 1877-9* (Auckland, 1954) and *The Rise of the New Zealand Liberal Party, 1880-90* (Auckland, 1956), persist in the view that Reeves's political opponents were conservatives. David A. Hamer, in an important article in *Historical Studies*, reveals the early "Liberals" and their friends in a new guise by uncovering the private business interests concealed and cared for beneath their public phrases and legislation.[9]

Other revisions of established views will be mentioned in the next section of this summary. Quite as important are the results of new emphases, of the investigation of fields scarcely touched on previously. Some of these, such as studies of intellectual history and foreign relations, will be noticed in the following survey of recent literature, but one deserves particular attention.

A new dimension has recently been added to New Zealand history—a pre-history of a thousand years or more—by the work of archae-

5. Sorrenson, "Land Purchase Methods and Their Effect on Maori Population, 1865-1901," *Journal of the Polynesian Society* (Wellington), LXV (Sept., 1956), 183-99.

6. McDonald, "New Zealand Land Legislation," *Historical Studies: Australia and New Zealand*, V (Nov., 1952), 195-211.

7. Gardner, "Some Recent Theses on New Zealand History," *Historical News* (Christchurch), II (March, 1961), 10-11.

8. Bohan, "The 1879 General Election in Canterbury," *Political Science* (Wellington), XII (March, 1960), 45-61.

9. Hamer, "The Agricultural Company and New Zealand Politics," *Historical Studies: Australia and New Zealand*, X (May, 1962), 141-64. A contribution by the present writer to this controversy, "The Significance of the Scarecrow Ministry, 1887-91," appears in *Studies of a Small Democracy*.

ologists, which has shown that the country was inhabited from one end to the other by the twelfth century. The standard book on the subject, now out-of-date, is Roger Duff's *The Moa-Hunter Period of Maori Culture* (Wellington, 1950; 2nd ed., 1956). A major recent article is Jack Golson's "Culture Change in Prehistoric New Zealand," in *Anthropology in the South Seas: Essays Presented to H. D. Skinner* (John D. Freeman and William R. Geddes, eds., New Plymouth, N.Z., 1959). The alleged tradition that the Polynesians were able to navigate, and migrated here intentionally in a fleet of canoes, has been challenged by Charles Andrew Sharp's *Ancient Voyagers in the Pacific* (New Plymouth, 1956; 2nd ed., Harmondsworth, 1957; revised ed., *Ancient Voyagers in Polynesia* [London, 1963]), a work which touched off a long and emotional argument, mainly in the *Journal of the Polynesian Society*. The debate is unfinished; suffice it to say, for the moment, that the legends about the Maori founding fathers have been regarded by historians as no more sacrosanct than those of the *pakeha* (Europeans).

RECENT LITERATURE: FROM 1940

*Documents*

Very few volumes of New Zealand historical documents have been published since Robert McNab's *Historical Records of New Zealand* (2 vols.; Wellington, 1908-14), an incomplete collection of records up to about 1840. The most important in recent years are *The Richmond-Atkinson Papers* (Guy H. Scholefield, ed., Wellington, 1961), two large volumes including a mass of material on politics, racial relations, and settlement. The transcription is not very accurate, but it is an important source book. Lawrence M. Rogers' *The Early Journals of Henry Williams 1826-1840* (Christchurch, 1961) supplements John R. Elder's *Letters and Journals of Samuel Marsden* (Dunedin, 1932) and *Marsden's Lieutenants* (Dunedin, 1934) on missionary history. *Early Travellers in New Zealand* (Oxford, 1959), edited by Nancy M. Taylor, is a scholarly collection of the journals of explorers. There are other minor collections such as *The Torlesse Papers 1848-51* (Peter B. Maling, ed., Christchurch, 1958), which relates to the Canterbury settlement.

*General Histories*

Some of the numerous short histories already have been mentioned. The two most recent are Keith Sinclair's *A History of New Zealand* and William H. Oliver's *The Story of New Zealand,* both of which draw on the results of much recent research and aim at presenting a coherent interpretation of their country's development to students and the general reader. *A History of New Zealand Life* by William Parker Morrell and David O. W. Hall (Christchurch, 1957) is more severely factual and is aimed principally at the secondary schools. So, too, is Michael Turnbull's *A Changing Land* (London, 1960) and *A Short History of New Zealand,* by John B. Condliffe and Willis T. G. Airey (9th ed., Christchurch, 1960), recent editions of which have been completely revised and rewritten by Airey. There is no large, detailed history of the country, *The Cambridge History of the British Empire* (Vol. VIII, Pt. II, "New Zealand," James Hight, ed. [Cambridge, 1933]) being out-of-date. There are some useful surveys of New Zealand history and life, particularly the United Nations volume, *New Zealand* (Berkeley, 1947) edited by Horace Belshaw, and Frederick L. W. Wood's *This New Zealand* (rev. ed., Hamilton, N.Z. 1958; American edition, *Understanding New Zealand* [New York, 1949]). *Distance Looks Our Way* (Auckland, 1961) is a series of lectures, edited by Keith Sinclair, discussing the effects of isolation on New Zealand. It includes several interpretative historical articles. Jack Golson discusses the Polynesian settlement; Sinclair concludes that pioneer European society in New Zealand was "provincial" but not, in fact, "isolated"; and Robert McD. Chapman compares modern New Zealand politics with those in other English-speaking countries. *Studies of a Small Democracy: Essays in Honor of Willis Airey,* ed. Robert McD. Chapman and Keith Sinclair (Auckland, 1963), is a *festschrift* containing detailed articles on several aspects of New Zealand history.

*Discovery and Settlement*

The authoritative works on the European explorers are John C. Beaglehole's *Discovery of New Zealand* (Wellington, 1939; 2nd ed., Oxford, 1961) and *The Exploration of the Pacific* (London, 1934; 2nd ed., 1947), which have been followed by his superb edition of *The Journals of Captain James Cook on His Voyages of Discovery* (2 vols.; Cambridge, 1955-61), and *The* Endeavour *Journal of Joseph Banks,*

*1768-1771* (2 vols.; Sydney, 1962). Eric H. McCormick's *Tasman and New Zealand, A Bibliographical Study* (Wellington, 1959) should also be noted. William G. McClymont, *The Exploration of New Zealand* (Wellington, 1940; 2nd ed., London, 1959) and Nancy Taylor's *Early Travellers,* mentioned above, discuss the exploration of the interior.

Mission history is traced in many books that reveal more piety than wit. Several, such as Eric Ramsden's *Rangiatea: The Story of the Otaki Church Its First Pastor and Its People* (Wellington, 1951), contain material for the critical history that has not been written. Church history, too, has been neglected in recent years, though there are early, scarcely inspiriting accounts.

For the study of European settlement, the books by John Miller, Michael Turnbull, and Johannes S. Marais, mentioned already, are essential. In addition, the provincial histories should be consulted. *A History of Canterbury,* I (Christchurch, 1957), written by George Jobberns, Carl R. Straubel, and Leicester C. Webb is useful, though it contains little on the life of the settlers. Alexander H. McLintock's *The History of Otago* (Dunedin, 1949) is a scholarly volume of perhaps excessive length. Another useful contribution to provincial history is Allister D. McIntosh's *Marlborough* (Blenheim, N.Z., 1940). There are a few good local histories which should not be ignored, particularly the following: Ruth Allan, *The History of Port Nelson* (Wellington, 1954); Basil H. Howard, *Rakiura* (Dunedin, 1940), which deals with Stewart Island; Hensleigh C. M. Norris's *Armed Settlers* (Hamilton, N.Z., 1956) and *Settlers in Depression: The Story of Hamilton, 1875-94* (Hamilton, N.Z., 1964) on Hamilton; and William J. Gardner's *The Amuri* (Culverden, N. Z., 1956), which gives the history of a north Canterbury pastoral county.

## Early Government

The period of New Zealand history most discussed in recent books is the first twenty years of settlement after 1840. A good many studies deal with the early governorships, government policy, constitutional questions, racial relations, and Maori history.

The late James Rutherford examines the precise moment when the country became legally British in *The Treaty of Waitangi and the Acquisition of British Sovereignty in New Zealand* (Auckland, 1949).

The story is then taken up in *New Zealand's First Capital* (Wellington, 1946) by Ruth M. Ross. Alexander H. McLintock surveys the early governorships, with emphasis on constitutional development up to 1852, in *Crown Colony Government in New Zealand* (Wellington, 1958), the first volume of the New Zealand parliamentary history, which has been criticized for accepting the settlers' (and the New Zealand Company's) views with too little qualification. It is, however, quite indispensable for the study of the structure of early government. So too, is James Rutherford's *Sir George Grey* (London, 1961), which also deals with Grey's second governorship in the sixties.

## Racial Relations and Maori History

Early trade and settlement, and their impact on the Maoris, are most recently and adequately treated in Harrison M. Wright's *New Zealand, 1769-1840: Early Years of Western Contact* (Cambridge, Mass., 1959), which makes good use of anthropological insights. Its principal shortcoming is the undue concentration on the Bay of Islands area. The development of Maori opinion, leading to the election of the Maori King and the Maori Wars, is discussed in Keith Sinclair's *The Origins of the Maori Wars* (Wellington, 1957), a detailed study which also (like Rutherford's and McLintock's books just mentioned) examines government Maori policy. Angus John Harrop's *England and the Maori Wars* (London, 1937) consists largely of undigested gobbets of public records. James Cowan, *The New Zealand Wars* (2 vols.; Wellington, 1922-23; 2nd ed., 1955-56) has not been superseded. Robin W. Winks' article, "The Doctrine of Hau-Hauism" in the *Journal of the Polynesian Society*, 1953,[10] discusses an important phase of Maori opinion in the '60's. The following years are examined in Maurice P. K. Sorrenson's article (previously mentioned) in the same journal. A number of histories based mainly or entirely on Maori traditions, such as John Te H. Grace, *Tuwharetoa* (Wellington, 1959) (a history of the Taupo Maoris) and Leslie G. Kelly's *Tainui* (Wellington, 1949), must be treated with great caution, and regarded as picturing what Maoris now believe about the past rather than the past itself. The dangers are well-illustrated in Pei Te Hurinui's (P. Te H. Jones's) *King Potatau* (Auckland, 1960), which relies on a Maori

10. LXII (Sept.), 199-236.

document (written long after the events described) as the source for an account of the King movement in the 1850's and 1860's. It can be shown, from newspapers and other contemporary sources, that this document is quite unreliable in its factual details such as dates; it is, indeed, confused and misleading. How far much older traditions are reliable is at present conjectural. Finally, on the Maoris in recent years, several books are of value: *The Maori People Today*, edited by Ivan L. G. Sutherland (Auckland, 1940), and Ernest and Pearl Beaglehole's *Some Modern Maoris* (Wellington, 1946) analyze the Maori situation in the late 1930's and '40's. James E. Ritchie's *The Making of a Maori* (Wellington, 1963) is a study of a rural community in the 1950's, written in the tradition of the Beagleholes' work, which derives from Freud and Margaret Mead. Alice Joan Metge's *A New Maori Migration: Rural and Urban Relations in Northern New Zealand* (London, 1964), is a thorough and very valuable study of urban and rural Maori communities in the same decade, written, in part, in the Raymond Firth tradition of social anthropology. These four books present a vivid portrait of modern Maori life.

*Politics*

Political history is surveyed briefly in Leicester C. Webb's *Government in New Zealand* (Wellington, 1940), and in Leslie Lipson's *The Politics of Equality* (Chicago, 1948), a somewhat pretentious book marred by many errors of detail which is, nevertheless, the most substantial one on the subject. Morrell's *Provincial System in New Zealand* has not been superseded, though a large number of theses on provincial politics that remain unpublished provide a basis for a quite different attack on the subject. Some of the work of the late David G. Herron has appeared in summary in periodicals.[11] His Ph.D. thesis, "The Structure and Course of New Zealand Politics, 1853-58" (Otago University), is a major contribution to New Zealand history. Trevor G. Wilson's two bulletins on the Liberals have been mentioned. No substantial work on the subject has appeared recently, though three articles, by Richard T. Shannon, David A. Hamer, and Robert McD.

11. Herron, "The Franchise and New Zealand Politics, 1853-8," *Political Science*, XII (March, 1960), 28-44; and "Sir George Grey and the Summoning of the First New Zealand General Assembly," *Historical Studies: Australia and New Zealand*, VIII (May, 1958), 364-82.

Chapman are important.[12] The Reform party awaits an historian, though recent articles by William J. Gardner are a useful contribution.[13] His essay "The Reform Party" and Robert McD. Chapman's "The Decline of the Liberals," in a short symposium, *Ends and Means in New Zealand Politics*, edited by Chapman, echo a current dispute about whether there have been genuine conservatives in New Zealand politics. In the same publication, Willis T. G. Airey discusses "The Rise of the Labour Party"—another subject discussed in some excellent unpublished theses. The growth of the Labour movement is treated, not exhaustively, in James D. Salmond's *New Zealand Labour's Pioneering Days* (ed. Desmond Crowley; Auckland, 1950). Bruce M. Brown's *The Rise of New Zealand Labour: A History of the New Zealand Labour Party from 1916 to 1960* (Wellington, 1962) is a scholarly survey of the subject. Several Labour leaders wrote books (or memoirs) about Labour politics. John A. Lee's *Socialism in New Zealand* (London, 1938), Walter Nash's *New Zealand: A Working Democracy* (New York, 1943; London, 1944) and John T. Paul's *Humanism in Politics* (Wellington, 1946) are worth reading, though disappointing, because they are polemical rather than autobiographical. John A. Lee's vigorous *Simple on a Soap-Box* (London, 1964) is an exception to this generalization. None of Labour's enemies has published a book. Other books of interest to historians are Raymond J. Polaschek's *Government Administration in New Zealand* (Wellington, 1958), and *Welfare in New Zealand* (Wellington, 1955, ed. Kenneth J. Scott). A rather slight, psephological study exists—*The New Zealand General Election of 1960*, by Muriel Lloyd Prichard and James Bruce Tabb (Auckland, 1961). *New Zealand Politics in Action: The 1960 General Election*, by Robert McD. Chapman, William Keith Jackson, and Austin V. Mitchell (London, 1962) is the first substantial work on New Zealand psephology. It is essential reading for the student of modern politics. Kenneth J. Scott's *The New Zealand Constitution* (Oxford, 1962) is a useful constitutional analysis. *Industrial Conciliation and Arbitration in New Zealand* (Well-

12. Shannon, "The Liberal Succession Crisis in New Zealand, 1893," *Historical Studies: Australia and New Zealand*, VIII (May, 1958), 183-201; Chapman, "The Decline of the Liberals," in *Ends and Means in New Zealand Politics* (Auckland, 1961), ed. Chapman; Hamer's article appears in *Studies of a Small Democracy*.

13. Gardner, "The Rise of W. F. Massey, 1891-1912," *Political Science*, XIII (March, 1961), 3-30; and "W. F. Massey in Power," *ibid.* (Sept., 1961), 3-30.

ington, 1963) by Noel S. Woods is a survey of a central feature of industrial relations.

*Economic History*

The most important work on economic history since John B. Condliffe's *New Zealand in the Making* is Colin G. F. Simkin's *The Instability of a Dependent Economy* (Oxford, 1951), which discusses economic fluctuations up to 1914. Condliffe's *The Welfare State in New Zealand* (London, 1959) contains much useful material. The contemporary scene is also analyzed in Cornelis Westrate's *Portrait of a Modern Mixed Economy* (Wellington, 1959). Anthony E. C. Hare's *Report on Industrial Relations in New Zealand* (Wellington, 1946) is now out-of-date but has not been replaced by a comparable work. William Parker Morrell's *The Gold Rushes* (London, 1940; New York, 1941) has a section on New Zealand. Philip Ross May, *The West Coast Gold Rushes* (Christchurch, 1962) and John H. M. Salmon, *A History of Goldmining in New Zealand* (Wellington, 1963) are detailed studies of this topic. Three recent books deal with banking history. The most substantial, Sydney J. Butlin's *Australia and New Zealand Bank* (London, 1961), contains a valuable section on early banking in New Zealand. *Open Account: A History of the Bank of New South Wales in New Zealand, 1861-1961*, by Keith Sinclair and William F. Mandle (Wellington, 1961), outlines economic development as seen through the eyes of bank officials. The history of the country's largest bank, the *New Zealand Banker's Hundred: A History of the Bank of New Zealand, 1861-1961* by Norman McM. Chappell (Wellington, 1961), is uncritical and not always reliable, but contains much useful detail. There are a few histories of other businesses, but they are of little value to historians.

*External Affairs*

New Zealand's external relations are summarized in Frederick L. W. Wood's *New Zealand in the World* (Wellington, 1940). His interpretation is, in part, questioned by Keith Sinclair in *Imperial Federation: A Study of New Zealand Policy and Opinion, 1880-1914* (London, 1955). A symposium edited by John C. Beaglehole in 1944, *New Zealand and the Statute of Westminster* (Wellington), contains the most important discussions of New Zealand's attitude towards the development of dominion status. The most significant work on New Zealand's foreign relations is Frederick L. W. Wood's *The New Zealand People at War* (Wellington, 1958), which treats rather of high policy than of the people. Bernard K. Gordon's *New Zealand Becomes a Pacific Power* (Chicago, 1960), is quite inferior to Wood's book, and has been severely handled by reviewers in New Zealand. Thomas C. Larkin, ed., *New Zealand's External Relations* (Wellington, 1962), is an informative symposium. Books on the history of the armed forces in the World Wars are legion, and would require a separate essay. Neville C. Phillips's *Italy*, I (Wellington, 1957) and Daniel M. Davin's *Crete* (Wellington, 1953) are of particular scholarly interest. Angus Ross, *New Zealand Aspirations in the Pacific in the Nineteenth Century* (Oxford, 1964), is an important scholarly survey of the evolution of New Zealand "sub-imperialism."

*Biography*

There are many biographies of New Zealanders, few worthy of note. Probably no political biography rivals Antony Alpers' *Katherine Mansfield* (New York, 1953). Randal M. Burdon's *King Dick: A Biography of Richard John Seddon* (Christchurch, 1955) provides a lively and convincing portrait. *William Pember Reeves, New Zealand Fabian* (Oxford, 1965), by Keith Sinclair, is a new biography of another Liberal leader. James Rutherford's *Sir George Grey*, as its subtitle indicates, is *A Study of Colonial Government* rather than a "life." Austin G. Bagnall and George C. Petersen's *William Colenso* (Wellington, 1948) is a scholarly study of a remarkable man. Charles E. Carrington's *John Robert Godley of Canterbury* (Christchurch, 1950) is brief, lively, and interesting. The sweeping claims made for his subject by Paul Bloomfield in *Edward Gibbon Wakefield* (London, 1961) are sufficiently indicated by the subtitle, *Builder of the British Commonwealth*. His enthusiasm is not tempered by a knowledge of all the recent research. *Sir Robert Stout* by Waldo H. Dunn and Ivor L. Richardson (Wellington, 1961) has been reviewed unfavorably as being based on inadequate knowledge of Sir Robert's life and his political background alike. Some other lives of politicians are of interest, including Randal M. Burdon's *Life and Times of Sir Julius Vogel* (Christchurch, 1948); Leonard J. Wild's *Life and Times of Sir James Wilson of Bulls* (Christchurch, 1953); William Downie Stewart's *The*

*Right Honourable Sir Francis H. D. Bell* (Wellington, 1937) and *William Rolleston* (Christchurch, 1940). James Thorn's *Peter Fraser* (London, 1952) and Lillian G. Keys's *The Life and Times of Bishop Pompallier* (Christchurch, 1957) are products of different pieties. *Harry Holland: Militant Socialist* (Canberra, 1964) by Patrick J. O'Farrell is a recent scholarly biography of the Labour party leader before he came to power in 1935. *The Dictionary of New Zealand Biography* (2 vols.; Wellington, 1940), edited by Guy Hardy Scholefield, is indispensable for reference though not always reliable on details.

*The Arts, Education, Science*

Popular intellectual or cultural history has not been tackled on the lines adopted in the United States, and recently in Australia, though most historians realize that philosophy does not require a philosopher. But there are many books on the arts and education. Eric H. McCormick's *Letters and Art in New Zealand* (Wellington, 1940), *New Zealand Literature* (London, 1959), and *The Expatriate: A Study of Frances Hodgkins* (Wellington, 1954) stand alone as scholarly and well-written books to be read by anyone studying painting or writing in New Zealand. Joan Stevens has written a brief survey, *The New Zealand Novel, 1860-1960* (Wellington, 1961). Guy Hardy Scholefield's *Newspapers in New Zealand* (Wellington, 1958) pioneers the history of journalism.

A number of books discuss the history of some aspects of New Zealand education. John C. Beaglehole's *The University of New Zealand* (Wellington, 1937) and *Victoria University College* (Wellington, 1949) provide an urbane assessment of the growth of higher education. The New Zealand Council for Educational Research has published many books on educational history, such as John H. Murdoch's *The High Schools of New Zealand* (London, 1943), and Alan H. Thom's *The District High Schools of New Zealand* (Wellington, 1950). There is also the UNESCO volume by Arnold E. Campbell, *Compulsory Education in New Zealand* (Paris, 1952).

Two fairly popular surveys of the work of New Zealand scientists may be consulted: Sidney H. Jenkinson, *New Zealanders and Science* (Wellington, 1940) and Francis R. Callaghan, ed., *Science in New Zealand* (Wellington, 1957).

## THE PRESENT SITUATION OF THE NEW ZEALAND HISTORIAN

Twenty years ago New Zealand history was generally considered a very dull subject. As the result of recent work it now appears in fuller detail, incomparably richer, less black-and-white or gray. But there is no justification either for smugness or for the supposition that the country's industrious scholars have completed their task—caught up with present time, as it were. It is easy to point out historical zones that have scarcely been mapped. Much work remains to be done, though a good start has been made in a score of theses on provincial politics before 1876. There is no adequate published work on New Zealand politics in the present century, though much research has been carried out, particularly by Robert McD. Chapman and his students at Auckland, into voting habits. There is no scholarly history of a trading company other than banks. Nor is there an adequate social history, though a number of books have made a start (notably John Miller's *Early Victorian New Zealand*). Little has been published on historical geography outside the pages of the *New Zealand Geographer* (Christchurch), though there is a useful pioneering contribution to the subject from the United States in Andrew Hill Clark's *The Invasion of New Zealand by People, Plants and Animals* (New Brunswick, N.J., 1949). Relatively little has been published on constitutional history. There is little scholarly work on immigration, existing works such as Ng Bickleen Fong, *The Chinese in New Zealand* (Hong Kong, 1959) or Reuel Lochore's *From Europe to New Zealand* (Wellington, 1951) making questionable assumptions when not frankly propagandist. There is no good critical study of missions. Most politicians lack biographers. But the list of those things that have been left undone would exceed that of what has been done—if not of what ought not to have been done.

Because of the small market, few monographs on New Zealand history are published and the pressure on historians is to write even more general histories. It is still true, as the present writer proclaimed in 1950, that we need "a generation of pedants" to toil at minutiae. The pedants exist, but their work largely goes unpublished. It is truer of New Zealand's than of most history that its public appearance is a visible iceberg, capping submerged depths of theses and dissertations.[14]

14. Masters' theses written in the New Zealand universities are presented in con-

Consequently, anyone embarking on a study of some aspect of the subject should enquire from the four universities what work has already been done. Some very substantial works of considerable merit lie there unread by anyone except the aspiring authors of the next row of unpublished theses.

The existence of hundreds of unpublished theses points to the main reason for the recent upsurge in historical writing: the rapid growth of the universities. Also, after a hundred and fifty years of European settlement, it is becoming more possible to take New Zealand history seriously. Before World War II, where it was taught at universities at all, it was as a part of courses on British Imperial history. Now both undergraduate and graduate courses on New Zealand history, independent of those on British Commonwealth history, are taught at the four universities. A parallel growth of libraries and archives has made research more feasible. Most important has been the organization of the National Archives in Wellington in 1926, but two libraries in its vicinity, the Alexander Turnbull and the General Assembly, also contain many important collections of manuscripts relating to New Zealand history, such as the papers of Sir Donald McLean, Sir John Hall, and other politicians. The Hocken Library in Dunedin also deserves special mention. Other libraries in Auckland and Christchurch have fewer but still important manuscript collections.

At present historical research is mainly confined to New Zealand or Pacific history, or to topics the sources for which are published or available on microfilm. Though there are several valuable collections of old books, they are rarely adequate for original work on British or European history. Moreover, though each main town has two or three very substantial libraries, there are no great libraries in the country.[15] It follows that the research historian must be prepared to work in several of the cities.

---

junction with several written papers (four at present). The theses are based on six months' to a year's full-time research (sometimes more) and the best in recent years approximate in length and merit to doctoral dissertations. Since many of them are on subjects scarcely touched on in published works, they form a major contribution to New Zealand historiography. No one who has not read the best theses can pretend to expert knowledge of New Zealand history. There are, however, few doctoral dissertations. Most New Zealand doctoral candidates in history go to universities abroad for their final degree.

15. The holdings of the major libraries are (1960):

| | |
|---|---|
| National Library Service, Headquarters collection | 155,000 |
| National Library Service, including schoolbooks, etc. | 1,800,000 |

Books on the country's history sell surprisingly well in New Zealand, but the market is nevertheless small. One consequence is that a very large proportion of the histories are still published in England, and English publishers are more likely to be interested in general histories, or works relating to colonization, than in—say—a book on provincial politics. Many of the historical works appearing in New Zealand have been published by the Government Printer, a few by private firms and local bodies. Only three or four private publishing houses at present publish serious historical books, and these are sometimes subsidized by the State Literary Fund. The main hope in the near future appears to lie in the growth of the university presses. The New Zealand University Press closed down when the universities became independent in 1962, but the four universities have begun to expand their own lists of publications.

Facilities for the publication of articles are little better. The main scholarly journal, *Historical Studies: Australia and New Zealand*, is published in Melbourne and dominated, naturally enough, by the more numerous Australians. Several New Zealand journals, especially *Political Science*, published at the Victoria University of Wellington, and the *Journal of the Polynesian Society*, occasionally publish historical articles. The history department at the University of Canterbury puts out a useful journal, *Historical News*, designed mainly for teachers.

If there is now a need for a local historical journal, the need for a national association of historians is equally evident. Its absence may be explained by the fact that there were only a handful of historians twenty years ago, but that is no longer true. A consequence of this lack, perhaps, is that the work of research students is not always well-directed: there is little planning, except by isolated individual teachers,

| Auckland University | 150,000 | (1962) |
|---|---|---|
| Victoria University of Wellington | 130,000 | ( " ) |
| Canterbury University | 140,000 | ( " ) |
| Otago University (includes Hocken Library but not the medical library) | 165,000 | ( " ) |
| Auckland Public Library | 330,000 | |
| General Assembly Library, Wellington | 255,000 | |
| Wellington Public Library | 230,000 | |
| Dunedin Public Library | 171,000 | |
| Department of Scientific and Industrial Research | 101,000 | |
| Alexander Turnbull Library, Wellington | 100,000 | |
| Total | 3,726,000 | |

of the lines of attack. In view of the shortcomings of the organization of New Zealand historical study and the problems facing historians, it is appropriate to conclude this survey with the thought, not of recent achievements, but that the job has only been begun. But if the task may still be called pioneering, there is the encouragement that there is a vast amount of material, published and unpublished, to be cultivated, material promising rich rewards to the industrious and imaginative scholar.

# THE BRITISH TERRITORIES
# IN THE PACIFIC

## John M. Ward

THERE ARE FEW good histories of the British territories in
the Pacific. Historians in Britain, who have near to hand some of the
best sources for the task, have shown little interest in writing the history of the distant, scattered islands that comprise the British territories referred to in this essay. They have preferred to study places
nearer to home, places wealthier, more populous and altogether more
significant in the world's notice, such as the West Indies and, more
recently, Africa. As a result, most of the important contributions to
the history of the British territories in the Pacific have been made by
scholars in Australia, New Zealand and, in a small degree, the United
States of America. Because the historical professions in Australia and
New Zealand emerged so recently, systematic study of the British
territories in the Pacific has begun only in the last thirty years or so.

The interest of Australian and New Zealand historians in the Pacific
is thoroughly consonant with the course of island history since the
British first settled in Australia in 1788. Whalers, sealers, traders, adventurers, missionaries, and officials went out from Sydney, and later
from other ports in Australia and New Zealand as well, to win profits,
save souls, or keep order among the unruly white men resorting to the
islands. Pressure from New South Wales was partly responsible for
the British decision to annex New Zealand. Australia and New Zealand
both developed their own commercial enterprises and missionary organizations in the islands. Many times during the nineteenth century,
colonists in those countries demanded that Britain extend her rule
over the whole of the South Pacific in order to strengthen the Empire
and keep out foreign powers that might disturb the British predomi-
nance that was so convenient to Australia and New Zealand.

During the years in which Britain could have annexed most of the Pacific Islands, had she thought them worth the trouble, other powers became active there. The Americans traded in the South Pacific almost as soon as the British did. The arrival of the French and later the Germans produced some international friction. In the history of what are now the British territories in the Pacific, strands of American history, French history, and German history are often mingled with the records of British and colonial action and the rôle of the indigenous inhabitants. As a result, the historian who works on the British territories in the Pacific may need sources from many countries.

A major obstacle to writing the history of the British islands in the Pacific is the complexity and extent of the sources that have to be studied for a region of inconsiderable land area and small population. The British official records in London and elsewhere, the private papers of British politicians and officials, British missionary and company records, and a great variety of British books, newspapers, and periodicals are obviously indispensable. Similarly the historian may need to use the Australian and New Zealand collections, such as the Mitchell Library in Sydney, the Alexander Turnbull Library in Wellington, and the Australian National Library in Canberra. Recently historians have gained access to another source, whose riches are not yet fully understood. The Central Archives of Fiji and the Western Pacific High Commission in Suva include records that are fundamental to understanding how British rule operated in Fiji and other islands, together with valuable material on the indigenous societies before they passed under British rule. So far none of the scholarly histories of the Pacific Islands has surmounted the problems of the sources with masterly success. Even an historian equipped with the languages, time, patience, and knowledge to master the conventional documentary sources would still need to call on the methods of sociology and anthropology to interpret and supplement his material. Progress has been slow.[1]

1. The standard bibliography of the Pacific Islands, now several years old (but in process of revision) is Clyde R. H. Taylor, *A Pacific Bibliography, Printed Matter relating to the Native Peoples of Polynesia, Melanesia and Micronesia* (Wellington, 1951). It has been supplemented by Floyd M. Cammack and Shiro Saito, *Pacific Island Bibliography* (New York, 1962), which was based on a selection of materials in the Pacific collection of the Gregg M. Sinclair Library of the University of Hawaii, and included books printed since Taylor's work was published, together with manuscripts, typescripts, microfilms, and microcards held in the library. An older bibliography that may be consulted is *Islands of the Pacific: A Selected List of References* (Washington, 1943), compiled by Helen F. Conover under the direction of Florence

## The Landmarks of the British Record

A New Zealand scholar, Guy Hardy Scholefield, wrote a pioneering study of the Pacific Islands as part of a work that included also the Pacific borderlands. *The Pacific: Its Past and Future, and the Policy of the Great Powers from the Eighteenth Century* (London, 1919) was uneven in quality and faulty in proportions, but it was a notable achievement when written and is still cited. Little further progress was made until Ernest Benians contributed a chapter on "The Western Pacific, 1788-1885" to the *Cambridge History of the British Empire*, Volume VII, Part 1, *Australia* (Cambridge, 1933). As a joint editor of the volume, Benians wrote this chapter in the absence of other scholars qualified and willing to do so. It was a perceptive study, recognizing the rôles of the traders, the missionaries, the kidnapers of native labor, the colonists of Australia and New Zealand, and the officers of the Royal Navy. It was weak on the islands themselves.

Two other books that illuminated some important aspects of the British record in the islands were *International Rivalry in the Pacific Islands, 1800-1875* (Berkeley, 1941) by Jean Ingram Brookes and *Early American-Australian Relations: From the Arrival of the Spaniards in America to the Close of 1830* (Melbourne, 1944) by Gordon Greenwood. Although Dr. Brookes did not strain history to fit her title, an analysis that was based on international rivalry was not a rewarding one to adopt for the Pacific Islands in the first three quarters of the nineteenth century. Nevertheless, historians of the Pacific have been indebted to her careful use of diplomatic sources. Greenwood referred to Australian and American interests up to 1830 in the trading, sealing, and whaling of the Pacific Islands. These were prolific sources of wealth and crime.

Since World War II two historians[2] have written general accounts of long periods of British history in the Pacific Islands. John Manning Ward of the University of Sydney built directly on the foundations

S. Hellman of the Division of Bibliography, Library of Congress. James W. Davidson's article, "The Literature of the Pacific Islands" (*The Australian Outlook* [Sydney], I [March, 1947], 63-79) is still interesting. See also Ida Leeson, ed., *A Bibliography of Bibliographies of the South Pacific* (Melbourne, 1954).

2. Professor James W. Davidson of the Australian National University had written his Ph.D. dissertation, "European Penetration of the South Pacific, 1779-1842," before either of the works referred to here had been published. It is available in the Cambridge University Library.

laid by Benians and Brookes when he wrote *British Policy in the South Pacific, 1783-1893* (Sydney, 1948). William Parker Morrell of the University of Otago, twelve years after Ward, produced an extensive, largely authoritative survey entitled *Britain in the Pacific Islands* (Oxford, 1960).

Ward's book, confessedly a pioneering study, was the work of a young scholar who used only the sources available in Sydney and Canberra. It tried to trace British policy toward the South Pacific Islands before they were brought under the rule of the powers. Ward managed to blaze a rather rough trail, usually in the right direction, but leaving formidable tasks of rectification and discovery to his successors. The early chapters on Australian relations with the islands (including New Zealand) still have some value. So does the analysis of the legal aspects of British policy through the whole period of the book. From 1786, when Britain decided to found a colony in eastern Australia, giving the governor power over the "adjacent" islands in the Pacific, down to 1893 when the Western Pacific High Commission was formally reconstituted, British policy toward the islands was as likely to be formulated in legal terms (such as acts of Parliament, orders in council, and official memoranda on problems of international law) as in any other way. Using this kind of evidence, Ward was able to find greater continuity in British policy than any other historian working on the same subject.

Morrell's book was the work of a mature scholar, whose reputation as an interpreter of British Imperial policy was of long standing. Writing on the Pacific, he found little evidence of any continuous British policy at all and in this respect differed sharply from Ward. His book was better founded in the sources than Ward's, but had some defects of its own in this respect. The brute mass of printed and manuscript material proved overwhelming, and Morrell's book was less extensive in time (only an epilogue on the twentieth century) and in area (Hawaii and New Zealand excluded) than he had originally intended. After 1878 he appears to have relied more exclusively on printed sources than for earlier periods; as the official documents in print omitted much that was significant, his treatment of the 1880's and '90's is less authoritative than his account of earlier periods. In general Morrell's book is by far the best, most comprehensive, and most reliable history of Britain in the islands up to 1900. Regrettably it has no bibliography.

Morrell and Ward were both aware of the active rôle played by Australians and New Zealanders in the Pacific. Neither of them studied it profoundly. Clinton Hartley Grattan, whose *The Southwest Pacific to 1900* and *The Southwest Pacific since 1900* (both Ann Arbor, 1963) covered the modern histories of Australia, New Zealand, the Pacific Islands, and Antarctica, stressed the need for a "book on the activities and aspirations of the Australians and New Zealanders in the islands." Grattan himself summed up the existing state of knowledge with quiet authority. A year after his two books were published Angus Ross brought out a scholarly, authoritative study entitled *New Zealand Aspirations in the Pacific in the Nineteenth Century* (Oxford, 1964). The title is significant, for Ross's book emphasizes New Zealand rather than the islands. A comparable book on Australia would be very welcome.

## The Twentieth Century

There are no good general histories of Britain in the Pacific Islands during the twentieth century. Popular works, not mentioned here, abound. Felix Maxwell Keesing, a prolific writer on the islands, summed up their condition just before the war in *The South Seas in the Modern World* (New York, 1941). There were some useful references to the islands in *Trusteeship in the Pacific* (Sydney, 1949), edited by Alexander Hugh McDonald for the Australian Institute of International Affairs. Douglas L. Oliver's *The Pacific Islands* (Cambridge, Mass, 1951; rev. ed., New York, 1961) was a readable introduction to the island peoples and the Australian aborigines, showing their reactions to the coming of Western men and alien civilizations. Cyril S. Belshaw's *Island Administration in the South West Pacific* (London, 1950) discussed government and reconstruction in New Caledonia, the New Hebrides, and the British Solomon Islands. William E. H. Stanner founded *The South Seas in Transition: A Study of Post-War Rehabilitation and Reconstruction in Three British Dependencies* (Sydney, 1953) on anthropological theory and wide experience in the field. Delays in publication allowed the scepticism of some of his judgments on New Guinea, Fiji, and Western Samoa to be supported by events before the book was in print. *Political Advancement in the South Pacific* (Melbourne, 1961), by Francis James West, compared British policy in Fiji, French policy in Tahiti, and American policy in Eastern Samoa, using theoretical foundations that could be applied to almost any of the important British territories. The official war histories of Great Britain, the United States, Australia, and New Zealand have many volumes on the Pacific Islands campaign that need independent treatment of a kind not possible here.

## DISCOVERY AND EXPLORATION

The most successful advances in writing the history of the British territories in the Pacific have been made in the study of discovery and exploration. Public interest has ensured that the original journals of some explorers have been available in one form or another from quite early times. The modern scholar has to use all the records of the voyages, trying to decide where the explorers went and what discoveries they made. Before modern methods of navigation seamen were commonly doubtful of their position, and their records can be very difficult to interpret even with the aid of all the records, the best maps, and close inspection of the places thought to have been visited.

George Cockburn Henderson, who held a chair at Adelaide University and was later Research Professor of History at the University of Sydney, based his *The Discoverers of the Fiji Islands* (London, 1933) on seven years' research in libraries and at sea. "No student will ever do justice to the character and achievements of the old navigators in Fiji or any other dangerous archipelago of the Pacific unless his historic sense has been quickened by reflection on the prevailing conditions of the seafarer's life in days gone by," he wrote. Henderson has been credited with having traced the first sighting of almost every island in the Fiji group.

For a masterly study of the subject as a whole there is still no better book than John C. Beaglehole's *The Exploration of the Pacific* (London, 1934; 2nd ed., 1947), which summarized the political and geographic background of exploration and gave perspective to the story with its clear summaries of the main voyages. A far-reaching judgment on the significance of the discoveries was attempted by Vincent T. Harlow in the early chapters of *The Founding of the Second British Empire, 1763-1793,* I, *Discovery and Revolution* (London, 1952).

The latest general contribution to the subject has been *The Discovery of the Pacific Islands,* by Charles Andrew Sharp (Oxford, 1960), an annotated list of voyages with notes on some ships and islands. Sharp has included much that was published elsewhere, adding, however, important material from Spanish and Portuguese sources. He does not appear to have exhausted the whole of the manuscripts. Some of his identifications of islands differ in conclusion and in method from those made a little earlier by Harry Evans Maude in his article "Spanish Discoveries in the Central Pacific: A Study in Identification" (*Journal of the Polynesian Society* [Wellington], LXVIII [December, 1959], 282-321). Another article by Maude on "Post-Spanish Discoveries in the Central Pacific" (*ibid.,* LXX [March, 1961], 67-111) contained some interesting assessments of British voyages. Sharp also has written "Early Spanish Discoveries in the Pacific" (*ibid.,* LXIX [June, 1960], 29-91).

Thanks partly to the Hakluyt Society[3] several important voyage journals have been published in modern, scholarly editions. John C. Beaglehole was responsible for the society's edition of *The Journals of Captain James Cook on His Voyages of Discovery,* I: *The Voyage of the* Endeavor, *1768-1771* (Cambridge, 1955) and II: *The Voyage of the* Resolution *and the* Adventure, *1782-1795* (Cambridge, 1961). Two more volumes have still to appear. Editing on the grand scale, with the assistance of James A. Williamson, James W. Davidson, and Raleigh A. Skelton, Beaglehole has provided an admirable text, good notes, and elaborate essays on such subjects as the history of the Pacific Islands, the circumstances of the voyages, and Tahitian social structure. Beaglehole has also edited *The* Endeavor *Journal of Joseph Banks, 1768-1771* (2 vols.; Sydney, 1962) for the Trustees of the Public Library of New South Wales, in association with Angus and Robertson Ltd. A significant reassessment of an important part of British exploration in the eighteenth century has been made by Robert E. Gallagher in his edition of *Byron's Journal of his Circumnavigation, 1764-1766* (Hakluyt Society, Cambridge, 1964).

3. See Hakluyt Society, *Prospectus with List of Publications and Maps* (3 vols.; London, 1915-58).

## MISSIONARIES

The records of discovery possess a primacy of time and a wealth of fascination that has put them well ahead of other branches of Pacific Islands history. The British missionaries, however, whose labors in the islands began before the eighteenth century was ended, have never lacked commemorators, apologists, advocates, and detractors. They have had few scholarly historians.

The general histories of the great missionary societies, such as Eugene Stock's *The History of the Church Missionary Society: Its Environment, Its Men and Its Work* (4 vols.; London, 1889-1916), are still useful. So are several of the histories written by the men in the field, whose opinions so often differed from those at headquarters. A particularly valuable early record by a man on the spot is John Davies' *The History of the Tahitian Mission, 1799-1830*, edited by Colin W. Newbury for the Hakluyt Society (Cambridge, 1961). Davies spent fifty years in Tahiti and the neighboring islands. An honest, intelligent observer, he did not pervert the record of missionary achievement and he did understand some of the cultural changes that followed the coming of white men and Christianity to Tahiti. Unfortunately, Newbury has omitted Davies' own introduction that stated his religious interpretation of history and helped to explain missionary thinking. William Ellis' *Polynesian Researches, during a Residence of Nearly Six Years in the South Sea Islands* (2 vols.; London, 1829) was dedicated to the London Missionary Society. Some of its comments on native customs and political developments after the coming of Europeans are shrewdly perceptive. Very many other missionary journals were published in the nineteenth century and some later. Most have interest to the historian.

The best of the early attempts at a scholarly history of Pacific missions was Kenneth L. P. Martin's *Missionaries and Annexation in the Pacific* (London, 1924), which has been largely replaced by later studies. George Cockburn Henderson's scholarly edition of *The Journal of Thomas Williams, Missionary in Fiji, 1849-1853* (2 vols.; Sydney, 1931), was supplemented by his valuable book *Fiji and the Fijians, 1853-1856* (Sydney, 1931), which elucidated the journal and did much else besides. The only systematic study of the missionary impact as a whole was made by Aarne A. Koskinen in *Missionary Influence as a Political Factor in the Pacific Islands* (Helsinki, 1953). Although it had little new to say, this was a significant book because it summed up the state of knowledge contained in works written in five different languages. Koskinen was rather uncritical of his sources and tended to exaggerate missionary influence as a political factor, especially in writing on the British Colonial Office.

The best recent contributions to missionary history have been made by Morrell in *Britain in the Pacific Islands* (already discussed) and in some essays and articles that show anthropological interests. W. Neil Gunson discussed the first of the early millenarian movements in the islands in his "Account of the Mamaia or Visionary Heresy of Tahiti, 1826-41" (*Journal of the Polynesian Society*, LXXI [June, 1962], 209-43). A similar development in Samoa was analyzed in John D. Freeman's chapter on "The Joe Gimlet or Siovili Cult" in *Anthropology in the South Seas: Essays Presented to H. D. Skinner* (ed. Freeman and William Geddes, New Plymouth, N.Z., 1959). "The Great Samoan Awakening of 1839" by Alan G. Daws (*Journal of the Polynesian Society*, LXX [September, 1961], 326-37) also should be mentioned.

Voyages of British warships in the Pacific were recorded as fully by contemporaries as were the labors of the missionaries, whom the naval officers had to visit and assist. Ship after ship that was dispatched to protect British subjects, punish British criminals, or put down the objectionable traffic in Pacific Islands laborers, had a commander with a lively pen and a good story to tell. Among the best of the "cruise" books are John Elphinstone Erskine, *Journal of a Cruise among the Islands of the Western Pacific* (London, 1853) and Julius Lucius Brenchley, *Jottings during the Cruise of the* Curacoa *among the South Sea Islands in 1865* (London, 1873). Several others deserve mention as well.

Thomas Dunbabin's collection of stories about the labor traffic, *Slavers of the South Seas* (Sydney, 1935), is readable but does not provide a systematic history of the labor traffic. A detailed account of British policy towards the labor traffic has now appeared in Owen W. Parnaby's *Britain and the Labor Trade in the Southwest Pacific* (Durham, N.C., 1964).

## REGIONAL HISTORIES

By far the most populous and economically important of the British territories in the Pacific is Fiji. British traders ventured there from 1804; it has been under British rule since 1874. The sources for the study of its history, at least since the coming of the Europeans, are better preserved and more readily available than for any other island group. Three important problems have stimulated historians' interest in Fiji—the reasons for the cession of the group to Great Britain, the policies adopted by the British immediately after the session (land policy especially), and the difficulties presented by the large Indian population, who are the descendants of Indians brought there as plantation workers in the period 1879-1916, and who now outnumber the Fijians.

Several journals of early residents in Fiji are of historical importance. The Hakluyt Society has published the very valuable *The Journal of William Lockerby, Sandalwood Trader in the Fijian Islands during the Years 1808-1809* (London, 1925), edited by Sir Everard F. im Thurn and Leonard C. Wharton. Lockerby's narrative teemed with insolent acts of uncomprehending tyranny, robbery, and exploitation that brought the sandalwood trade in Fiji to an end by 1813. William Thomas Pritchard's *Polynesian Reminiscences; or Life in the South Pacific Islands* (London, 1866) was the work of a British consul in Fiji, whose vigorous temperament led him to exceed his powers in dealing with the problems of white planters at a time when no strong government existed. The first governor of Fiji, Sir Arthur Hamilton Gordon (later first Lord Stanmore), a man of great enterprise, printed privately most of the important despatches relating to his work there, together with private correspondence. *Fiji: Records of Private and Public Life, 1875-1880* (4 vols.; Edinburgh, 1897-1910) was marked "Private and Confidential." While still in Fiji Gordon printed privately two volumes of letters to and from members of his staff under the title *Letters and Notes Written during the Disturbances in the Highlands (Known as the "Devil Country") of Viti Levu, Fiji, 1876* (Edinburgh, 1879). These were vivid and forceful, a very unusual record of administration. Sir Basil Home Thomson, who gave valuable service to Fiji as Native Lands Commissioner, wrote *The Fijians, A Study of the Decay of Custom* (London, 1908), a substantial and fascinating study. Gordon himself has now been the subject of a detailed work by James K. Chapman, *The Career of Arthur Hamilton Gordon* (Toronto, 1964). Chapman has studied Gordon's record in his six governorships and has careful chapters on Fiji and on the Western Pacific Islands.

The first modern history of Fiji to be published was the work of a devoted amateur who lived in the islands. Ronald Albert Derrick's *A History of Fiji* was incomplete when he died. Volume I, published in Suva in 1946, was a detailed narrative of Fijian history to 1874, with a useful bibliography. A work that may be mentioned along with Derrick's is *The Evolution of Government in Fiji*, a collection of documents edited by George C. Henderson (Sydney, 1935). *Fiji* by Sir Alan C. Burns (London, 1963) combines a brief general history with a survey of current problems considered from the points of view of administrators and policy-makers.

The achievement of John David Legge's *Britain in Fiji, 1858-1880* (London, 1958) was that it rested on close, careful use of the principal sources in Britain and Australia. The sources now available in Suva permit closer attention than Legge gave to the events within Fiji that led up to the cession. His treatment is perhaps too favorable to Sir Arthur Gordon, who is credited by Legge with greater novelty in policy-making than he really possessed.

Legge was able to use the important article on "The Colonial Office and the Annexation of Fiji" by Ethel Drus (*Transactions of the Royal Historical Society* [London], 4th ser., XXXII [1950]). Dr. Drus has made some further observations on the same subject in her edition of *A Journal of Events during the Gladstone Ministry, 1868-1874, by the First Earl of Kimberley* (Camden Series, XXXI, Royal Historical Society [London, 1958]). W. David McIntyre of the University of Nottingham has written two recent and good articles on the cession. In "Anglo-American Rivalry in the Pacific: The British Annexation of the Fiji Islands in 1874" (*Pacific Historical Review* [Glendale, Cal.], XXIX [November, 1960], 361-80), he pointed out that the Colonial Office had watched the development of American interests in the Pacific with great care and had duly assessed the strategic advantages of Fiji. In "New Light on Commodore Goodenough's Mission to Fiji, 1873-1874" (*Historical Studies: Australia and New Zealand* [Melbourne], X [November, 1962], 270-88) he used to advantage the full text of the journal of Commodore James G. Goodenough, R.N., who, while senior officer on the Australian station, was charged with important duties in Fiji. The edition of his journal published by his widow[4] some ninety years ago omitted important political material for good personal reasons. Goodenough now appears in a very different light.

The use of Indian laborers in Fiji was attacked bitterly by the Reverend Charles Freer Andrews and William W. Pearson in *Indentured Labour in Fiji* (Madras, 1917). Andrews returned to the topic in *India and the Pacific* (London, 1937). There is now a scholarly assessment of the whole story in *Fiji's Indian Migrants: A History to the End of Indenture in 1920* (Melbourne, 1962), by Kenneth L. Gillion.

Western Samoa was placed under League of Nations mandate to New Zealand after World War I. James W. Davidson of the Australian National University has undertaken a study, "Samoa mo Samoa: The Making of the Independent State of Western Samoa," which he can write as a participator in events as well as an historian. The book will emphasize the years 1946-62 but will include chapters on the traditional political system and the political development of Samoa since 1830. Sylvia Masterman's *Origins of International Rivalry in Samoa, 1845-1884* (Stanford, 1934) and the scholarly work of George Herbert Ryden, *The Foreign Policy of the United States in Relation to Samoa* (New Haven, 1933) both made important references to British policy. Ryden's account is especially interesting for the period that ended in the partition of Samoa in 1899. Robert Louis Stevenson's famous study, *A Footnote to History: Eight Years of Trouble in Samoa* (London, 1892), will always be useful to historians, if only for its treatment of Brandeis, the adventurous Bavarian soldier, who tried to be a good premier to King Tamasese.

The independent Kingdom of Tonga, which has been under British protection since 1900, has not yet been the subject of a scholarly modern history. There are, however, some fascinating nineteenth-century accounts. William Mariner's *An Account of the Natives of the Tonga Islands, in the South Pacific Ocean* (compiled by John Martin, 2 vols.; London, 1817) is equally fascinating to historians and to anthropologists. At the other end of the century there is much to be learned

4. Victoria Hamilton Goodenough, ed., *Journal of Commodore Goodenough, during his Last Command as Senior Officer on the Australian Station, 1873-75, Edited with a Memoir by His Widow* (London, 1876).

from Basil Thomson's *The Diversions of a Prime Minister* (Edinburgh, 1894), a light-hearted but shrewdly observant work. Thomson helped King George of Tonga solve the problems arising from the long premiership of Shirley Baker, a former Wesleyan missionary, who had won for himself a position of extraordinary political power. Another work by Thomson, *Savage Island: An Account of a Sojourn in Niué and Tonga* (London, 1902), should also be noted.

Of the other territories only Pitcairn (and that because of the *Bounty* mutiny) has gained much attention from historians so far. Many of the books on Pitcairn are merely popular; others are more relevant to anthropologists than to historians. The best studies of Pitcairn history that have been published are two articles by Harry E. Maude, "In Search of a Home, from the Mutiny to Pitcairn Island" and "Tahitian Interlude, The Migration of the Pitcairn Islanders to the Motherland in 1831" (*Journal of the Polynesian Society*, LXVII [June, 1958], 104-31, and LXVIII [June, 1959], 115-40). William Keith (later Sir Keith) Hancock's *Politics in Pitcairn* (London, 1947) has an illuminating "morality essay" on the history of Pitcairn.

Up to 1840 Hawaii, like most of the other islands, could have been annexed easily enough by the British. Later Britain had to watch Hawaii pass under American rule. The process is one that should be noted by any scholar trying to understand British policy towards the Pacific Islands before they were annexed to or protected by the powers. In addition to *The Hawaiian Kingdom, 1778-1854* (Honolulu, 1938), by Ralph S. Kuykendall, there are two articles written by Merze Tate in the *Pacific Historical Review*—"British Opposition to the Cession of Pearl Harbor" (XXIX [November, 1960], 381-94) and "Great Britain and the Sovereignty of Hawaii" (XXXI [November, 1962], 327-48).

## GENERAL

In his inaugural lecture, *The Study of Pacific History* (Canberra, 1955), Professor James W. Davidson of the Australian National University gave reasons for thinking that the Pacific Islands provided "an almost ideal opportunity" for studying a great many of the problems of European expansion into areas with a non-European population. "In respect of the characteristics of their indigenous cultures, the range of their natural resources, and the extent of their contact with the west," he declared, "the islands present a wide variety of conditions." David-son did not limit himself to the British islands, but the proposition would certainly hold good for them alone. It is possible to study their histories, not merely as part of Imperial expansion, but also as societies on which alien institutions have been imposed. Their responses to contacts with Western men have varied according to the nature of their indigenous institutions, the characters of leaders, and other circum-stances. The changes so wrought have in turn affected the policies of the ruling powers.

Historians who are to undertake this kind of study need the help of anthropology. Co-operation between the disciplines is not easy to attain and the luxury of joint projects, even if they could be organized, might easily turn out to be frustrating to both parties. There are books by anthropologists from which historians may learn some of the prob-lems of investigating the impact on native society of the coming of white men. Two interesting examples are Raymond W. Firth's *Social Change in Tikopia* (London, 1959) and H. Ian Priestley Hogbin's *Experiments in Civilization: The Effects of European Culture on a Native Community of the Solomon Islands* (London, 1939). The monograph by Ernest Beaglehole, *Social Change in the South Pacific: Rarotonga and Aitutaki* (London, 1957) was designed to combine the conventional methods of historical inquiry with the fieldwork methods of sociology. More experiments of this kind are needed.

Sir Archibald Grenfell Price has drawn attention to another valu-able approach to island history in a chapter on "Sojourner Colonisation" in his latest book, *The Western Invasions of the Pacific and its Con-tinents: A Study of Moving Frontiers and Changing Landscapes, 1513-1958* (Oxford, 1963). Price has shown some of the rich possibilities awaiting a scholar with the learning and the skill to combine the re-searches of historians, economists, anthropologists, geographers, and medical scientists. He has modestly described his conclusions as tenta-tive and as a basis for later research.

There has been little study so far of the impact of the Pacific Islands on Western culture, although the theme is a promising one. The out-standing contribution has been Bernard Smith's *European Vision and the South Pacific, 1768-1850: A Study in the History of Art and Ideas* (Oxford, 1960). This beautifully illustrated work showed how the islands had appeared to and had influenced European painters. Smith may have exaggerated the extent of Pacific influences on European art, but he has certainly made a significant contribution to intellectual history.

Davidson and Ward have both pointed out that there were Pacific Island influences on legal doctrines.[5] Another subject that could be taken up from the same point of view would be general literature. What sort of account of the islands was presented in imaginative writings from the eighteenth century onwards? Was there any influence from island experiences on Western cultures as expressed in literature? The Pacific Islands have always had a strong appeal to imagination, and never more so than before their geography and character were known. Daniel Defoe founded the *Life and Adventures of Robinson Crusoe* (1719) on the experiences of Alexander Selkirk, who was marooned for some years on Juan Fernandez in the southeastern Pacific. Jonathan Swift made Gulliver an early visitor to the Pacific by putting Lilliput and Brobdingnag there. Since the islands have become known, Herman Melville, Robert Louis Stevenson, (George) Louis Becke, and, to a smaller extent, Joseph Conrad have written stories that would be excellent material for the sort of inquiry now suggested.

In the immediate future the most rapid progress will probably be made in studying the history of government. This is to be viewed, not merely as an enquiry into British policy in London and in the islands, but also a study of the way in which the indigenous social institutions adjusted themselves to the impact of traders, missionaries, planters, settlers, naval officers, consuls, and other representatives of alien civilization. Studies of this kind require a profound integration of understanding so as to perceive how political events in London, the characters of men on the spot, indigenous institutions and customs, pressures from Australia or New Zealand, the necessities of oceanic trade, and a host of other factors may have influenced an apparently simple situation. Increasingly the history of the British territories in the Pacific will be written as studies in the problems that have arisen from Western expansion into areas with non-Western populations.

5. Davidson, *Pacific History* p. 22 n. 9; Ward, *British Policy in the South Pacific*, chap. viii, *passim*.

# SOUTH AFRICA

## Leonard M. Thompson

THE HISTORIOGRAPHY of South Africa reflects the divisions which have always existed in South African society. The first attempts to establish outlines of South African history were made by British educators who wrote textbooks, for use in the public schools of the Cape Colony in the nineteenth century, from an assumption of the superiority of British ideals, British institutions, and British officials and settlers.[1] Afrikaner historiography may be said to have started in 1877, when Stefanus J. du Toit, a Cape colonial predikant, made the Afrikaner people the hero of *Die Geskiedenis van ons Land in die Taal van ons Volk* (Paarl, 1877), the first book to be published in the Afrikaans as distinct from the Dutch language. By the end of the century a third approach was being formulated by George McCall Theal, a Cape colonial civil servant, who sought in his *History and Ethnography of Africa South of the Zambesi* (11 vols.; London, 1897-1919) to reconcile the points of view of the white settlers of British and Afrikaner stocks. In the 1920's a fourth approach was adopted by William M. Macmillan, who, using missionary sources, dealt sympathetically with the Coloured people and the Africans in *The Cape Colour Question* (London, 1927) and *Bantu, Boer, and Briton* (London, 1929). And finally, in recent years there has begun to emerge a non-white historiography.

One may therefore distinguish five different schools of thought among historians of South Africa. The British school, which was dominant a century ago, reached a crescendo during and after the South African War of 1899-1902 and waned thereafter. Nevertheless, its influence is to be detected in the important works of Eric A. Walker and in the studies of British settlement in Natal by A. F. Hattersley, and it is pronounced in recent attempts to vindicate Lord Milner's

---

1. E.g., Alexander Wilmot and John C. Chase, *History of the Colony of the Cape of Good Hope* (Cape Town, 1869).

South African policy.[2] The Afrikaner school has flourished since the Afrikaner cultural movement was launched soon after the South African war. Gustav S. Preller (1875-1943), a journalist, was a prolific writer of history which was both anglophobic and negrophobic. This trend reached an extreme form in the doctoral dissertations of J. Albeit Coetzee, *Politieke Groepering in die Wording van die Afrikanernasie* (Johannesburg, 1941) and P. van Biljon, *Grensbakens tussen Blank en Swart in Suid Afrika* (Cape Town, [1947]). Today the Afrikaner school is firmly rooted in the Afrikaans-medium universities—the University of Stellenbosch, the University of Pretoria, the University of the Orange Free State, and Potchefstroom University for Christian Higher Education—and also among the predominantly Afrikaner faculty of the University of South Africa. The focus remains upon the history of the Afrikaner people, but there is a wide variation in the degree of bias in the handling of the subject. Some works of Petrus J. van der Merwe, such as *Die Trekboer in die Geskiedenis van die Kaapkolonie, 1657-1842* (Cape Town, 1938), and Floris A. van Jaarsveld, such as *Die Afrikaner en sy Geskiedenis* (Cape Town, 1959), are distinguished and objective studies, though they lack the illumination which might have come from a consideration of the experiences of analogous communities outside South Africa.[3] The settler school is no longer strongly represented in the universities, but Theal's works continue to exert a strong influence in secondary and primary education, for most of the textbooks are derived from them and reiterate Theal's failure to take cognizance of the points of view of the Coloured and African peoples. Macmillan, who may be regarded as the founder of a liberal school, based his major works too narrowly upon the papers of Dr. John Philip of the London Missionary Society. His successors, notably Cornelius W. de Kiewiet, a master of the illuminating generalization and the broad analysis, as in *A History of South Africa: Social and Economic* (Oxford, 1941), and Johannes S. Marais, a scrupulous unraveler of particular problems, as in *The Cape Coloured People, 1652-1937* (London, 1939), have achieved a greater breadth in dealing sympathetically, but dispassionately, with all the human elements

2. E.g., Edward Crankshaw, *The Forsaken Idea: A Study of Viscount Milner* (London, 1952); Sir Evelyn Wrench, *Alfred Lord Milner, the Man of No Illusions, 1854-1925* (London, 1958).

3. For a critical survey of the more extreme trends in Afrikaner historiography, see Leonard M. Thompson, "Afrikaner Nationalist Historiography and the Policy of Apartheid," *Journal of African History* (Cambridge), III (i/1962), 125-41.

in their involvements in the clashes as well as the harmonies which are the warp and woof of South African history. This approach has now permeated the English-medium universities—the University of Cape Town, the University of the Witwatersrand, the University of Natal, and Rhodes University—and though its influence in non-academic circles in South Africa is limited, it is probably the closest of the schools to the mainstream of modern historiography elsewhere.[4] Very few non-whites in South Africa have yet had the opportunity of receiving an historical training or indulging in sustained historical research and writing, so that it is still too early to predict what will eventually emerge from non-white historians. Such historical works as we do have from non-whites vary considerably in approach.[5]

Individual historians, of course, are attached in varying degrees to the schools of thought which have been distinguished above. The classifications of historians like Cecil Headlam,[6] J. Albert Coetzee, George McCall Theal, and William M. Macmillan are clear enough, but others do not fall exclusively into a single category. If, for example, Eric A. Walker is to be regarded as a member of the British school, there is more than a hint of the liberal approach in his works; and if Johannes S. Marais is to be regarded as a member of the liberal school, his latest book, *The Fall of Kruger's Republic* (Oxford, 1961), shows some convergence with the Afrikaner school; while some historians, such as J. A. I. Agar-Hamilton, author of *The Native Policy of the Voortrekkers* (Cape Town, 1928) and *The Road to the North: South Africa 1852-1886* (London, 1937), are difficult to place in this system of classification. Nevertheless, the distinctions which have been drawn have considerable validity in the substance of South African historiography and they tend to be perpetuated by the institutional cleavage in South African higher education, for there is scarcely any mobility and

4. For criticism of some liberal historians from the settler point of view, see Lewis H. Gann, "Liberal Interpretations of South African History," *Rhodes-Livingstone Journal* (Lusaka), XXV (June, 1959), 40-58.

5. Examples of historical works in English by Africans are S. M. Molema, *The Bantu, Past and Present* (Edinburgh, 1920), and *Chief Moroka: His Life and Times* (Cape Town, n.d.). John H. Soga, who was of part-African and part-European descent, wrote a useful study of *The South-Eastern Bantu* (Johannesburg, 1930). There are several historical sketches by Africans in Xosa, Zulu, and Sotho, e.g., R.R.R. Dhlomo's biographies, *uDingane kaSenzangakhona* (Pietermaritzburg, 1935), *uShaka* (Pietermaritzburg, 1935), *uMpande kaSenzangakhona* (Pietermaritzburg, 1938).

6. E.g., in Headlam's editorial commentary in *The Milner Papers (South Africa) 1897-1905* (2 vols.; London, 1931-33) and in his contributions to *The Cambridge History of the British Empire*, VIII (Cambridge, 1936; rev. ed., 1963).

not very much professional contact between the Afrikaans-medium and the English-medium universities.

The South African archival services are well organized. The State Archives in Pretoria contain the official records of the central government since 1910; and there are provincial archives in Cape Town, Pretoria, Bloemfontein, and Pietermaritzburg, containing the official records of the pre-Union colonies and republics as well as of the post-Union provinces.[7] The time rule for access to official documents is forty years. These depositories also contain important collections of private documents. Other major collections of books, pamphlets, and documents are in the Library of Parliament and the South African Public Library (Cape Town), the Public Library and the library of the South African Institute of Race Relations (Johannesburg), the library of Miss Killie Campbell (Durban), and several of the university libraries.

The most valuable series of published documents are George McCall Theal's *Basutoland Records* (3 vols.; Cape Town, 1883), *Records of South-Eastern Africa* (9 vols.; London, 1898-1903), and *Records of the Cape Colony from 1793 to 1828* (36 vols.; London, 1897-1905); the *Kaapse Plakaatboek, 1652-1803*, edited by Mary K. Jeffreys and others (5 vols.; Cape Town, 1944-50); the publications of the Van Riebeeck Society, which include many key documents for the pre-Union period, from the *Journal of Jan van Riebeeck, 1652-1662* (3 vols.; Cape Town, 1952-58) to *Die Konvensie Dagboek van sy edelagbare François Stephanus Malan, 1908-1909* (Cape Town, 1951); Gustav S. Preller's *Voortrekkermense* (6 vols.; Cape Town, 1918-38); John Bird's *The Annals of Natal, 1495 to 1845* (2 vols.; Cape Town, [1885]) and Alan F. Hattersley's *More Annals of Natal* (London, 1936) and *Later Annals of Natal* (London, 1938); and the several series of *South African Archival Records*, published by the archives. The archives also publish yearbooks, containing theses and essays upon South African history.[8] The only single volume of documents covering a long period of South African history is still George W. Eybers, *Select Constitutional Documents Illustrating South African History, 1795-1910* (London, 1918), which may be supple-

7. Colin Graham Botha, *The Public Archives of South Africa, 1652-1910* (Cape Town, 1928).

8. Hereafter, *A.Y.B.*

mented for the post-Union period with Daniel W. Krüger, *South African Parties and Policies, 1910-1960* (Cape Town, 1960). The principal bibliographies are those of Sidney Mendelssohn, George McCall Theal, and Isaac Schapera,[9] the *Grey Bibliographies* produced by the South African Public Library, and the *Hiddingh Bibliographies* on particular topics produced by the library of the University of Cape Town. There is also an extensive bibliography in the South African volume of the *Cambridge History of the British Empire*.

In reviewing the general histories of South Africa one still cannot ignore Theal's eleven volumes, which take the story to 1884, because they summarize a great deal of archival material. They must be used with caution, however, because they lack perspective, are weak in analysis, and have a settler bias which sometimes leads to distortion of fact as well as of interpretation. Eric A. Walker's one-volume *A History of South Africa* (London, 1928), when first published, was the first scholarly synthesis by a trained historian, drawing upon a wide range of sources, especially the British blue-books. In its latest edition, *A History of Southern Africa* (London, 1957), it is still useful as a work of reference; but it is too heavily laden with political detail to be readily digestible, and in some parts it is being superseded by recent research. The South African volume in *The Cambridge History of the British Empire*, VIII (Cambridge, 1936), edited by Arthur P. Newton and Ernest A. Benians with Eric A. Walker as their South African advisor, contains chapters which are still useful, but it has the defects of other collaborative works—a lack of continuity and variations of quality. The revised edition of 1963 is for the most part substantially the same as the first edition. Cornelius W. de Kiewiet's *A History of South Africa: Social and Economic* (Oxford, 1941) is a series of analyses of South African society at successive stages in its development from a liberal standpoint and, since it omits political detail, it is much more readable than Walker's book. Though it was published over twenty years ago, it has stood the test of time remarkably well and it is still the best book to place in the hands of the student who is making his first entry into South African historiography. The major Afrikaans history is A. J. H.

9. Mendelssohn, *Mendelssohn's South African Bibliography* (2 vols.; London, 1910); Theal, *Catalogue of Books and Pamphlets relating to Africa South of the Zambesi* (Cape Town, [1912]); Schapera, *Select Bibliography of South African Native Life and Problems* (London, 1941).

van der Walt, J. A. Wiid, and Albertus L. Geyer, eds., *Geskiedenis van Suid-Afrika* (2 vols.; Cape Town, 1951). The first volume is a political history of *Die Witman in Suid-Afrika*; and the second contains sections on constitutional history, economic history, the history of native policy, and the cultural struggle of the Afrikaner. The leading Afrikaner historians of a decade ago are all represented, and the work is essential for anyone who wishes to gain an understanding of Afrikaner scholarship. Leo Marquard and Arthur M. Keppel-Jones have written short outlines which are useful introductions to South African history.[10] Under the pseudonym "Mnguni" there is an interesting polemic, *Three Hundred Years* (2 vols.; Cape Town, 1952), which is a diatribe against "the process of the conquest, dispossession, enslavement, segregation and disfranchisement of the oppressed Non-Europeans of South Africa," with a strong Marxist ingredient.[11] The best analyses of South African economic history—other than de Kiewiet's—are Michiel H. de Kock, *Selected Subjects in the Economic History of South Africa* (Cape Town, 1924) and C. G. W. Schumann, *Structural Changes and Business Cycles in South Africa, 1806-1936* (London, [1938]), while S. Herbert Frankel's *Capital Investment in Africa: Its Course and Effects* (London, 1938) has important passages on South Africa. Eric A. Walker's *Historical Atlas of South Africa* (Cape Town, 1922) is the best of its type.

This is not the place for a discussion of the more remote prehistory of South Africa. John Desmond Clark's *The Prehistory of Southern Africa* (Harmondsworth, 1959), which has an excellent bibliography, is a distinguished summary of the present state of knowledge; and there are many relevant articles in the *South African Archaeological Bulletin* (Claremont, Cape) and the *South African Journal of Science* (Cape Town).

There is a wide range of data shedding light on the condition of the non-white peoples of South Africa before they came under white control. Most of the relevant publications are listed in Isaac Schapera, *Select Bibliography of South African Native Life and Problems* (Lon-

10. Marquard, *The Story of South Africa* (London, 1955); Keppel-Jones, *South Africa: A Short History* (4th ed.; London, 1963). For an analysis of some major themes in South Africa history, see Leonard M. Thompson, "The South African Dilemma," in Louis Hartz, ed., *The Founding of New Societies* (New York, 1964).

11. I am privately informed that "Mnguni" is not an African but a white South African.

don, 1941). They include publications of missionary presses, such as *A Compendium of Kafir Laws and Customs*, a valuable compilation edited by John Maclean (Mount Coke, South Africa, 1858); official publications, such as the important *Report . . . of the Government Commission on Native Laws and Customs* (Cape Town, 1883); and historical reconstructions based largely on oral traditions, such as John H. Soga's general account of *The South-Eastern Bantu* and the many histories of particular tribes and clans, including accounts of the Zulu by Alfred T. Bryant, the Tembu by W. D. Cingo, the Basuto by D. F. Ellenberger, the Mfengu by R. T. Kawa, and the Mpondo by Victor P. Ndamase.[12]

In recent years an increasing number of African, European, and American scholars have been devoting attention to the histories of the peoples of tropical Africa. Some of them have been extending our continuum of knowledge backwards from the period when the documentary evidence began to be recorded in significant quantities, by refining the techniques for obtaining historical data from oral tradition, archaeology, linguistics, and other disciplines, and by making the utmost use of the earliest documents.[13] These efforts are not being equaled in South Africa. South African comparative linguistics are not keeping pace with developments further north; oral traditions are not being added to and systematically reanalyzed; Iron Age archaeology is still somewhat neglected, and when it is handled, as by Revil Mason in part of his *Prehistory of the Transvaal* (Johannesburg, 1962), the distinction which marks the work of Roger Summers on the Iron Age in Southern Rhodesia[14] is lacking; and South African historians are not reassessing the existing evidence and relating it to the growing body of knowledge and speculation concerning the history of the peoples of tropical Africa. Consequently, while Isaac Schapera's *The Khoisan Peoples of South Africa* (London, 1930) remains an admirable study of the peoples commonly called Bushmen and Hottentots, its statements concerning their origins warrant reconsideration, and so do the statements concerning the origins of the Bantu-speaking peoples of

12. Bryant, *Olden Times in Zululand and Natal* (London, 1929); Cingo, *Ibali laba Tembu* (Pondoland, 1927); Ellenberger, *History of the Basuto, Ancient and Modern* (London, 1912); Kawa, *I-Bali lama Mfengu* (Lovedale, [1929]); Ndamase, *Ama-Mpondo: Ibali ne-Ntlalo* (Lovedale, [1926]).

13. See the *Journal of African History*, which started publication under the editorship of Roland Anthony Oliver and John D. Fage in 1960, *passim*.

14. E.g., Summers, "The Southern Rhodesian Iron Age," *Journal of African History*, II (i/1961), 1-3.

South Africa in all the existing works, including those written and edited by Schapera and by N. J. van Warmelo.[15]

This neglect of the historical antecedents of the Bushmen, the Hottentots, and, more particularly, the Bantu-speaking South Africans is a result illustrative of the gulf which now exists between the older universities of South Africa and the newer universities of tropical Africa, and of the policy of the South African government. In South Africa today, as was formerly the case in Europe and the United States of America, it is still assumed by most white people that local history started with the arrival of Europeans, so that traditional African cultures are regarded as static phenomena and the reconstruction of the history of African societies before they experienced the impact of Europeans is scarcely regarded as a legitimate task for the scholar. The South African government is also committed to the proposition that Bantu-speaking Africans only began to move southwards across the Limpopo River at about the same time as the Dutch settlement was founded at the Cape of Good Hope. This claim has been refuted by Monica Wilson in an article, "The Early History of the Transkei and Ciskei" (*African Studies* [Johannesburg] XVIII [iv/1959], 167-79), which deals with the chronological aspect of the African occupation of the southeast coast, by summarizing some of the data from archaeology, from oral tradition, and from the journals of Portuguese travelers who were shipwrecked there in the fifteenth and sixteenth centuries; but Professor Wilson's article is almost unique in dealing with such a question. In view of the work which is now being done on the prehistory of other parts of the continent, no aspect of South African history demands more attention than this.[16]

In the *Records of South-Eastern Africa* (9 vols.; London, 1898-1903) Theal has published in English translation, as well as the original, many of the documents of the Portuguese period, but Charles R. Boxer's translation of three of the journals of the survivors of ships that were wrecked on the South African coast, in *The Tragic History*

15. E.g., Isaac Schapera, ed., *Western Civilization and the Natives of South Africa* (London, 1934), *The Bantu-speaking Tribes of South Africa* (Cape Town, 1946); van Warmelo, *A Preliminary Survey of the Bantu Tribes of South Africa* (Pretoria, 1935), and the other ethnographical publications of the South African Native Affairs Department produced under van Warmelo's editorship.

16. In *The Rise of the Zulu Empire*, to be published soon in Edinburgh, it is hoped that Max Gluckman, an anthropologist of South African origin, will provide a systematic historical survey of the Zulu before they came under white control.

*of the Sea, 1589-1622* (Hakluyt Society, Cambridge, 1957), is to be preferred. Portuguese enterprise in southeast Africa has been dealt with at length by Sidney R. Welch and Eric Axelson, on the basis of extensive research in the Portuguese printed sources and archives; but Boxer has shown in a devastating article that the works of Welch are vitiated by such an extreme Portuguese and Catholic bias that they are a "travesty of history."[17] However, since the Portuguese established no bases in the territory of the present Republic of South Africa, the Portuguese period of maritime supremacy in the eastern Atlantic and the Indian Ocean need not detain us further here.

The principal documentary sources for the history of the Cape Colony during the Dutch East India Company period (1652-1795) are the company records in the Netherlands and in South Africa and several accounts by European travelers; but very little documentary material is extant from the hands of the white settlers of this period, except in the official records, and there is virtually nothing from the hands of the non-white inhabitants of the colony. Some of the company records have been published and there are modern editions of several of the travelers' accounts.[18] The Dutch historians of the Company have paid comparatively little attention to the Cape Colony, which was an outlying and somewhat insignificant part of the Dutch East Indian empire.[19]

Afrikaner scholarship has been mainly concerned with the origins of the Afrikaner people. Attention has been paid to the early free burghers, the French Huguenot immigrants and their absorption, administrative institutions, the Dutch Reformed Church, the educa-

17. Welch, *Europe's Discovery of South Africa* (Cape Town, 1935), *South Africa under King Manuel, 1495-1521* (Cape Town, 1946), *South Africa under John III, 1521-1557* (Cape Town, 1948), *South Africa under King Sebastian and the Cardinal, 1557-1580* (Cape Town, 1949), *Portuguese Rule and Spanish Crown in South Africa, 1581-1640* (Cape Town, 1950), *Portuguese and Dutch in South Africa, 1641-1806* (Cape Town, 1951); Axelson, *South-East Africa, 1488-1530* (London, 1940), *Portuguese in South-East Africa, 1600-1700* (Johannesburg, 1960); Boxer, "S. R. Welch and His History of the Portuguese in Africa, 1495-1806," *Journal of African History*, I (i/1960), 55-63.

18. E.g., the *Kaapse Plakaatboek, 1652-1803*, edited by Mary K. Jeffreys and others (5 vols.; Cape Town, 1944-50); and several of the publications of the Van Riebeeck Society.

19. Herman T. Colenbrander, *Koloniale Geschiedenis* (3 vols.; The Hague, 1925-26); Johan K. J. de Jonge, *De opkomst van het Nederlandsch gezag in Oost-Indië* (13 vols.; The Hague, 1862-88); Frederick W. Stapel, *Geschiedenis van Nederlandsch-Indië* (Vol. III, Amsterdam, 1939).

tional services, the origins of the Afrikaans language, and settler agitations for economic and political reforms.[20] The most significant works are those of Petrus J. van der Merwe on the trekboers: *Die Noordwaartse Beweging van die Boere voor die Groot Trek* (The Hague, 1937), *Die Trekboer in die Geskiedenis van die Kaapkolonie, 1657-1842* (Cape Town, 1938) and *Trek: Studies oor die Mobiliteit van die Pioniersbevolking aan die Kaap* (Cape Town, 1945). Van der Merwe explains the evolution of the peculiar loan farm system of land tenure and describes the social, economic, military, and psychological aspects of the trekboer community and the continuation of the trekboer mode of life into the twentieth century.[21] In a monograph entitled *Economic Influences on the South African Frontier, 1652-1836* (Stanford, 1957), Soloman Daniel Neumark, of the Stanford Food Research Institute, argues that the trekboer was more dependent upon an exchange economy than was formerly realized, but the tenor of the facts which he produces was already well known and they do not destroy the established picture of the eighteenth-century trekboers as one of the most isolated and most nearly self-sufficient communities of white frontiersmen that has existed. *The First South Africans and the Laws which Governed Them* (Cape Town, [1949]), by Margaret Whiting Spilhaus, is a balanced description of the colony in the early eighteenth century, based on the *Plakaatboek*, and it includes a new translation of the diary of Adam Tas, the French Huguenot leader of the settler opposition to Governor Willem Adriaan van der Stel. The development of race attitudes among the settlers from 1652 to 1806, both in the agricultural and in the pastoral areas, is traced in detail from the archival material in a valuable pioneer study by a psychologist, Ian D. MacCrone, *Race Attitudes in South Africa: Historical, Experimental and Psychological Studies* (London,

20. E.g., Colin Graham Botha, *The French Refugees at the Cape* (Cape Town, 1919), and *Social Life in the Cape Colony in the 18th Century* (Cape Town, 1927); Anna J. Böeseken, *Nederlandsche commissarissen aan de Kaap, 1657-1700* (The Hague, 1938), *Die Nederlandse Kommissarisse en die 18de Eeuse Samelewing aan die Kaap* (*A.Y.B.*, 1944); P. J. Venter, *Landdros en Heemrade (1682-1827)* (*A.Y.B.*, iv/ 1940); Coenraad Beyers, *Die Kaapse Patriotte, 1779-1791* (Cape Town, 1929); Petrus S. du Toit, *Onderwys aan die Kaap onder die Kompanjie, 1652-1795* (Cape Town, n.d.); Adriaan Moorrees, *Die Nederduitse Gereformeerde-Kerk in Suid-Afrika, 1652-1873* (Cape Town, 1937).

21. Sir William Keith Hancock comments favorably on the works of P. J. van der Merwe in "Trek," *Economic History Review* (London), 2nd ser., X (April, 1958), 331-39.

1937). The relations between the Dutch officials and settlers and the Cape Hottentots in the crucial first decade are analyzed in articles by A. J. H. Goodwin.[22] Cape slavery still needs a historian, though W. Blommaert has published an introduction to the subject, *Het Invoeren van de Slavernij aan die Kaap* (*A.Y.B.*, 1938), and Victor de Kock has written a popular account from archival sources, *Those in Bondage* (London, 1950). Johannes S. Marais's *The Cape Coloured People, 1652-1937* includes a careful analysis of the origins of the Coloured people in miscegenation between slaves, Hottentots, Bushmen, European soldiers and sailors, and white settlers, and a summary of the condition of the non-white inhabitants of the Colony during the company period. Aspects of the early contacts between the Afrikaners and the Bantu-speaking tribes have been expounded from the documentary evidence by Petrus J. van der Merwe in *Die Kafferoorlog van 1793* (Cape Town, 1940) and by Marais in *Maynier and the First Boer Republic* (Cape Town, [1944]). Both writers have found Theal's description of these events deficient, and in his introduction Marais makes a warranted condemnation of Theal's negrophobia. Marais's book describes the effects upon the trekboers of their first meetings with the Bantu-speaking tribes, and the failure of the Company and its successor, the British government, to establish order in the frontier imbroglio of undisciplined trekboers, detribalized Hottentots, and Bantu-speaking tribesmen down to 1802. This is not Marais's best-known or best-written book, but it will remain of the first importance until it is superseded by a study based on anthropological knowledge of the African tribes as well as the documentary evidence.

The private as well as the official sources of South African history become increasingly numerous after 1795, and more particularly after the emergence of a newspaper press in the 1820's; but until well into the present century there is a comparative dearth of documents from the hands of non-white South Africans.[23]

John S. Galbraith in his contribution to this volume shows that many aspects of British colonial policy in the nineteenth century re-

22. Goodwin, "Jan Van Riebeeck and the Hottentots, 1652-1662" *South African Archaeological Bulletin*, VI (March, 1952), 2-53, and VII (June, 1952), 86-91.

23. Probably the first Bantu newspaper, other than the publications of missionary institutions, was *Imvo Zabantsundu*, founded in 1884, published in Kingwilliamstown until 1940 and thereafter in Johannesburg.

quire substantial reconsideration. This is certainly true of British policy in South Africa. The background to the British occupation of the Cape Colony in 1795 is revealed by Vincent T. Harlow in *The Founding of the Second British Empire, 1763-1793*, I (London, 1952), and in *The 1820 Settlers in South Africa* (London, 1934) Isobel E. Edwards has made a careful study of the British purposes and plans for their settlement; while the relevant chapters of William Parker Morrell's *British Colonial Policy in the Age of Peel and Russell* (Oxford, 1930) deal with some aspects of British policy in South Africa in that period. Since Macmillan's works appeared, historians of all schools have tended to accept his proposition that John Philip of the London Missionary Society was a decisive agent of the emancipation of the Cape Hottentots from their legal disabilities in 1828 and of the liberalization of British frontier policy in the 1830's, and to take sides for and against Philip on these issues.[24] In an important new book, *Reluctant Empire: British Policy on the South African Frontier, 1834-1854* (Berkeley, 1963), John S. Galbraith shows that, for the frontier question at any rate, Philip's influence over policy has been greatly exaggerated and that among the complex tissue of considerations affecting British policy "the zeal for retrenchment" was always present and often uppermost. A great deal has been written by Afrikaner historians, most of it condemnatory of Britain, on British policy as a cause of the Great Trek and British policy towards the Voortrekkers. The most systematic and balanced of these works is Christoffel F. J. Muller's *Die Britse Owerheid en die Groot Trek* (Cape Town, [1948?]), which presents, however, a somewhat oversimple analysis. The best biography of a South African governor of the nineteenth century is James Rutherford's *Sir George Grey* (London, 1961), but it is stronger in its handling of the Australian and New Zealand problems which confronted Grey than the South African. Cornelius W. de Kiewiet's first book, *British Colonial Policy and the South African Republics, 1848-1872* (London, 1929), based largely on the minutes written in the Colonial Office on South African despatches, shows how the British government came to reconsider its decision not to intervene north of the Orange River and eventually accepted Moshweshwe's request for the annexation of Basuto-

24. The liberal historians were generally for Philip, e.g., Marais in *The Cape Coloured People*; the settler and Afrikaner nationalist historians were against him, e.g., C. E. G. Schutte, *Dr. John Philip's Observations Regarding the Hottentots of South Africa* (*A.Y.B.*, i/1940).

land and the arguments for the annexation of the diamond fields. De Kiewiet's next work, *The Imperial Factor in South Africa* (Cambridge, 1937), is a fine exposition of Britain's reaction to the still more complex situations with which she was confronted in the 1870's and early 1880's. It may be compared with Cornelis J. Uys's *In the Era of Shepstone* (Lovedale, [1933]), which is more critical of the policy leading to the annexation of the Transvaal in 1877. There remains a need for a systematic reappraisal of British policy in South Africa throughout the period when Britain had no serious European competitors for supremacy—that is to say, from 1806 to the German annexation of Southwest Africa in 1884.

There have been several accounts of the establishment of the British settler communities in the Cape Colony and Natal in the nineteenth century, notably Sir George E. Cory's *The Rise of South Africa* (5 vols.; London, 1910-30), Harold E. Hockly's *The Story of the British Settlers of 1820 in South Africa* (2nd ed., rev.; Cape Town, 1957), Alan F. Hattersley's *Portrait of a Colony: The Story of Natal* (Cambridge, 1940) and *The British Settlement of Natal* (Cambridge, 1950), and John Bond's *They Were South Africans* (Cape Town, 1956). Cory was a professor of chemistry who failed to apply scientific methods to his historical work, and both he and Hockly are extreme examples of the settler school of historiography. Hattersley is an accomplished social historian, but he has refrained from getting to grips with the fundamental issue of the relations between the Natal settlers and the Africans in whose midst they settled. Bond, in a series of able biographical sketches, illustrates the contributions which British settlers made to missionary and economic enterprise. An objective analysis of the manner in which the British settlers adapted themselves to the South African environment, and of their relationships with the Afrikaner, Coloured, African, and Indian communities, would be of great value; and there is also a need for a study of the Uitlanders in the South African Republic at the end of the nineteenth century.

Afrikaner historians have always made the Great Trek the focal point of the nineteenth century and there are many works dealing with its causes, its course, and its aftermath in the creation of the Orange Free State and the South African Republic, including biographies of the leading participants.[25] Many of these works express an Afrikaner nationalist mystique and liken the Great Trek to the escape of the Israelites from the house of bondage to the promised land. The best narrative by a non-Afrikaner is Eric A. Walker's *The Great Trek* (London, 1938), which has great literary merit. The works of Floris A. van Jaarsveld on local government in the South African Republic, on the relations between the Orange Free State and the South African Republic, and on early Afrikaner historiography are comparatively free of the emotionalism which clouds the judgment of many Afrikaner historians.[26] A later book, which is available in an English translation, *The Awakening of Afrikaner Nationalism, 1868-1881* (Cape Town, 1961), dates the emergence of an Afrikaner national spirit to 1881, when the Transvaal Boers took up arms against the British regime and aroused a fellow-feeling among the Afrikaners of the Orange Free State and the Cape Colony. Van Jaarsveld concludes that this national spirit had five ingredients: a sense of injustice suffered at the hands of the British government, an emphasis upon the entire Afrikaner "nation" and its "fatherland," an urge towards group self-preservation, a religious sense of being a chosen people, and an historic sense of being heirs to a great tradition.

Even with van Jaarsveld, however, there are a failure to relate Afrikaner nationalism to similar phenomena elsewhere and a tendency to isolate the Afrikaner people from their context as a minority group in South Africa and thus to understate the effect to which negrophobia as well as anglophobia was an ingredient in Afrikaner nationalism

25. Izak D. Bosman and others, *Voortrekker-gedenkboek van die Universiteit van Pretoria* (Pretoria, 1938); A. J. du Plessis, *Die Republiek Natalia (A.Y.B.,* i/1942); Johan L. M. Franken, *Piet Retief se lewe in die Kolonie* (Pretoria, 1949); Gustav B. A. Gerdener, *Sarel Cilliers* (Pretoria, 1925); Ernest G. Jansen, *Die Voortrekkers in Natal* (Cape Town, 1938); Jan H. Malan, *Die Opkoms van 'n Republiek* (Bloemfontin, 1929); Frederick J. Potgieter, *Die Vesting van die Blanke in Transvaal (1837-1886) met spesiale verwysing na die Verhouding tussen die Mens en die Omgewing (A.Y.B.* ii/1958); Gustav S. Preller, *Piet Retief* (Cape Town, 1920), and *Andries Pretorius* (Johannesburg, 1937); Hendrick B. Thom, *Die Lewe van Gert Maritz* (Cape Town, 1947); Friedrich A. F. Wichmann, *Die Wordingsgeskiedenis van die Zuid-Afrikaansche Republiek, 1838-1860 (A.Y.B.,* ii/1941).

26. The principal works of van Jaarsveld are: *Die Veldkornet en sy aandeel in die opbou van die Suid-Afrikaanse Republiek tot 1870 (A.Y.B.,* ii/1950), *Die Eenheidstrewe van die Republiekeinse Afrikaners,* Part 1, *Pioniershartstogte* (Johannesburg, 1951), *Die Afrikaner en sy Geskiedenis* (Cape Town, 1959), *Die Ontwaking van die Afrikaanse Nasionale Bewussyn* (Cape Town, 1959) (English trans. by F. R. Metrowich, *The Awakening of Afrikaner Nationalism*), *Lewende Verlede* (Johannesburg, 1962), and *The Afrikaner's Interpretation of South African History* (Cape Town, 1964).

from the very beginning. Moreover, when he does touch upon Afrikaner clashes with Africans, he himself reveals a negrophobic bias.

Historians of the liberal school have studied the experiences of
the Coloured people in this period. William M. Macmillan's *The Cape
Colour Question* initiated this entire field of enquiry, making most
effective use of the papers of Dr. John Philip. The changes in the legal
status of the Coloured people between 1828 and 1838 are placed in
broader historical perspective in Isobel E. Edwards, *Towards Emancipation: A Study in South African Slavery* (Cardiff, 1942), which
relates the background to the emancipation of the Cape slaves to the
main story in the West Indies; in George R. Mellor's *British Imperial
Trusteeship, 1783-1850* (London, 1951), which places the changes at
the Cape in the broad stream of British policy; and in Marais' *The
Cape Coloured People*, which reviews them as a phase in the history
of the Coloured people. Nevertheless, it would still be fruitful to
study in depth, not only the problem of the causation of British policy
(which has already been mentioned), but also the social, economic, and
psychological adjustments made by the Coloured people after their
emancipation from legal inferiority. The origins of the Indian population of South Africa have been examined by Leonard M. Thompson
in *Indian Immigration into Natal, 1860-1872* (*A.Y.B.*, ii/1952); and
in *The History of Indians in Natal* (Cape Town, 1957) Mabel Palmer
has written a general history of the Natal Indian community.

Most of the historical works concerning Africans in the nineteenth
century are primarily studies of the policies of the British, the colonial,
and the republican governments, rather than of the historical experiences of the African peoples. There is, for example, an early attempt
at a broad synthesis of native policy made by Edgar H. Brookes in *The
History of Native Policy in South Africa from 1830 to the Present
Day* (Cape Town, 1924), where Brookes expounded a segregationist
point of view which he disavows in *The Colour Problems of South
Africa* (Lovedale, 1934). William M. Macmillan in *Bantu, Boer and
Briton* and H. A. Reyburn in "Studies in Cape Frontier History," *The
Critic* ([Cape Town], III [1934-35], 40-56, 101-9, 148-63, 204-9, and
IV [1935-36], 47-59, 105-16) attacked the settler interpretation of
policy on the eastern frontier of the Cape Colony in the first half of the
nineteenth century; and there are several other studies of policies on

particular frontiers from various points of view.[27] Of the agents of European expansion, it is the missionaries who have attracted most attention from historians, sympathetic in the case of Edwin W. Smith, *The Mabilles of Basutoland* (London, 1939) and *The Life and Times of Daniel Lindley* (London, 1949), and Charles P. Groves, *The Planting of Christianity in Africa* (4 vols.; London, 1948-58), and severely critical in Nosipho Majeke, *The Rôle of the Missionaries in Conquest* (Johannesburg, [1952]), where the missionaries are presented as being essentially the self-conscious agents of British imperialism. There has been no general analysis of the function of the white trader in African societies; but Sheila T. van der Horst, in *Native Labour in South Africa* (London, 1942), deals historically with the introduction of Africans into the modern sector of the South African economy.

In the work of an American, Waldemar B. Campbell, *The South African Frontier, 1865-1885: a Study in Expansion* (*A.Y.B.*, i/1960), the focus is shifted significantly from the study of the formulation of policy (though that is considered) to the study of the frontier itself, which is portrayed in all its complexity (from a wealth of South African and British sources) in the decisive period when African and Griqua polities were crumbling beneath the weight of a combination of alien influences, and the British and colonial governments reluctantly succumbed to the pressures of missionaries, traders, white settlers, and local administrators for the extension of their political responsibilities over Basutoland, the Transkeian Territories, Griqualand West, Bechuanaland, and Walvis Bay. For the inner experiences of the African peoples during and after the imposition of white rule there are several excellent anthropological studies of particular tribes, notably by Edmund Hugh Ashton on the Basuto, Max Gluckmann on the Zulu, W. D. Hammond-Tooke on the Bhaca, Monica Hunter (Wilson) on the Mpondo, Henri A. Junod on the Tonga, Hilda B. Kuper on the Swazi, and Isaac Schapera on the Tswana, and Schapera has also edited two volumes dealing with the Africans as a whole; but these are not primarily

27. E.g., J.A.I. Agar-Hamilton, *The Native Policy of the Voortrekkers* (Cape Town, 1928), and *The Road to the North: South Africa, 1852-1886* (London, 1937); Anthonie E. du Toit, *The Cape Frontier: A Study of Native Policy with Special Reference to the Years 1847-1866* (*A.Y.B.*, ii/1954); J. J. G. Grobbelaar, *Die Vrystaatse Republiek en die Basoetoe-vraagstuk* (*A.Y.B.*, ii/1939); Jacobus J. Oberholster, *Die Anneksasie van Griekwaland-Wes* (*A.Y.B.*, 1945); Jean van der Poel, *Basutoland as a Factor in South Africa Politics, 1852-1870* (*A.Y.B.*, i/1941).

historical works.[28] It is therefore to be hoped that historians of South Africa may take cognizance of the work of anthropologists and embark upon a series of studies of the African tribes, before, during, and after the imposition of white rule. Only when this has been done will our knowledge of the history of the African peoples of South Africa in the nineteenth century become comparable with our knowledge of the history of the Afrikaners and the British settlers.

Much of the historiography of the period from 1884 to 1899 is concerned with the origins of the South African War. Johannes S. Marais' *The Fall of Kruger's Republic* is a scholarly treatment of this question. After an interesting but somewhat brief sketch of political conditions in the South African Republic, it consists mainly of a step-by-step analysis of the diplomacy from June, 1895, when Joseph Chamberlain became colonial secretary, to the outbreak of war. Its main conclusion is that Chamberlain and Alfred Milner believed that British supremacy in South Africa as a whole would have been lost if the Kruger regime had been allowed to persist in its policy of building up an independent source of power in the Transvaal after it had become strengthened by the rise of the gold-mining industry; that they decided that this was to be prevented, if possible by diplomatic pressure, if necessary by force; and that when the Kruger government became convinced that this was so, it declared war. In the final stages it was Milner who forced the pace and Chamberlain who followed and carried Milner's policy in the British cabinet. Marais also goes to some lengths to assess the extent of Chamberlain's connivance in the plot which led to the abortive Jameson Raid, and concludes that it was considerable. This conclusion had already been reached by Jean van der Poel in *The Jameson Raid* (London, 1951), by Ethel Drus in an article based on the Chamberlain papers,[29] and by Richard H. Wilde in *Joseph Chamberlain and the South African Republic, 1895-1899*

---

28. Ashton, *The Basuto* (London, 1952); Gluckmann, "The Kingdom of the Zulu," in Meyer Fortes and Edward E. Evans-Pritchard, eds., *African Political Systems* (London, 1940); Hammond-Tooke, *Bhaca Society* (Cape Town, 1962); Hunter (Wilson), *Reaction to Conquest* (2nd ed., London, 1961); Junod, *The Life of a South African Tribe* (2 vols.; 2nd ed., London, 1927); Kuper, *An African Aristocracy: Rank among the Swazi* . . . (2nd ed., London, 1961), and *The Swazi* (London, 1952); Schapera, *The Tswana* (London, 1953), *Government and Politics in Tribal Societies*, ed. (London, 1956), *The Bantu-speaking Tribes of South Africa* (Cape Town, 1946), and, ed., *Western Civilization and the Natives of South Africa* (London, 1934).

29. Drus, "A Report on the Papers of Joseph Chamberlain, Relating to the Jameson Raid and the Inquiry," *Bulletin of the Institute of Historical Research* (London), XXV (May, 1952), 36-62.

(*A.Y.B.*, ii/1956), in refutation of the attitude adopted by Chamberlain's biographer, James L. Garvin, in *The Life of Joseph Chamberlain*, III, (London, 1934). The origins of the war have been placed in a broader perspective by Reginald I. Lovell in *The Struggle for South Africa 1875-1899: A Study in Economic Imperialism* (New York, 1934), by William L. Langer in *The Diplomacy of Imperialism, 1890-1902* (2 vols.; New York, 1935), and by Ronald Robinson and John Gallagher, with Alice Denny, in *Africa and the Victorians: The Official Mind of Imperialism* (London, 1961); but none of these works is based on an intimate knowledge of the South African historical background like that of Marais, and Robinson and Gallagher are wrong in viewing the war as the product of a clash between Afrikaner and British South African nationalisms, because in so far as there ever was a British South African national spirit it was largely the creation of a representative of the British government, Lord Milner. The aggressive tenor of British policy towards the South African Republic is stressed in several works in Afrikaans, notably Gert D. Scholtz, *Die Oorsake van die Tweede Vryheidsoorlog, 1899-1902* (2 vols.; Johannesburg, 1948-49) and Johann H. Breytenbach, *Die Tweede Vryheidsoorlog* (2 vols.; Cape Town, 1948-49).

There are several studies of particular aspects of the background to the war: the exclusion of the South African Republic from access to the sea, the Uitlander franchise question, education in the republic, the presidential office, and the judicial crisis culminating in the dismissal of Chief Justice J. G. Kotzé.[30] Still lacking are definitive accounts of the government of the South African Republic and of its gold-mining industry; and also definitive biographies of Paul Kruger, Cecil Rhodes, and Alfred Milner, for most of the existing biographies are sycophantic.[31] Eric A. Walker's biographies, *Lord de Villiers and His*

---

30. Daniel W. Krüger, *Die Weg na die See* (*A.Y.B.*, i/1938); Noel G. Garson, *The Swaziland Question and a Road to the Sea, 1887-1895* (*A.Y.B.*, ii/1957); Maria J. Hugo, *Die Stemreg-vraagstuk in die Zuid-Afrikaansche Republiek* (*A.Y.B.*, 1947); Jan Ploeger, *Onderwys en Onderwysbeleid in die Suid-Afrikaanse Republiek onder Ds. S. J. du Toit en Dr. N. Mansvelt* (*1881-1900*) (*A.Y.B.*, i/1952); Jacobus S. du Plessis, *Die Ontstaan en Ontwikkeling van die Amp van die Staatspresident in die Zuid-Afrikaansche Republiek* (*1858-1902*) (*A.Y.B.*, i/1955); Benjamin A. Tindall, introduction to Sir John Gilbert Kotzé, *Biographical Memoirs and Reminiscences*, II (Cape Town, 1941?); Leonard M. Thompson, "Constitutionalism in the South African Republics," *Butterworths South African Law Review* (Durban) (1954), pp. 49-72.

31. The most useful study of Paul Kruger is F. P. Smit, *Die Staatsopvattinge van Paul Kruger* (Pretoria, 1951). Of the many biographies of Cecil Rhodes the most reliable are Arthur Basil Williams, *Cecil Rhodes* (London, 1921), and Sir Lewis Michell

*Times: South Africa, 1842-1914* (London, 1925) and *W. P. Schreiner, a South African* (London, 1937), and *The Life of Jan Hendrik Hofmeyr (Onze Jan)* by his kinsman Jan H. Hofmeyr in collaboration with Francis W. Reitz (Cape Town, 1913), illuminate the history of the Cape Colony during this period and explain the attempts which were made by Cape colonial politicians to avert the war; while Alen Kieser's *President Steyn in die Krisisjare, 1896-1899* (Cape Town, 1939) describes the cementing of the alliance between the two republics.

The two major accounts of the South African War were written by British authors soon after the event and they saw the war mainly through the eyes of the British commanders.[32] Sir William Keith Hancock's *Smuts, the Official Biography,* I: *The Sanguine Years, 1870-1919* (Cambridge, 1962) opens up the possibilities of reconsideration by a military historian, drawing upon the experience which we now have of the military potential of other mobile guerillas operating in friendly countryside against alien forces.

British policy, before, during, and after the war, is ably surveyed by Godfrey H. L. le May in *British Supremacy in South Africa, 1899-1907* (Oxford, 1965). G. B. Pyrah's *Imperial Policy in South Africa, 1902-10* (Oxford, 1955) is somewhat diffuse. The grant of responsible government to the former republics in 1907 has recently been reconsidered, in the light of South Africa's withdrawal from the Commonwealth, by Nicholas Mansergh in *South Africa: The Price of Magnanimity* (New York, 1962). Jean van der Poel's *Railway and Customs Policies in South Africa, 1885-1910* (London, 1933) summarizes the ineluctable economic tensions which persisted between the South African political units, after the war as before, so long as they remained disunited. Leonard M. Thompson's *The Unification of South Africa, 1902-1910* (Oxford, 1960), based mainly on the private papers of South African politicians, describes the movement which culminated in the creation of the Union and the origins of the South African constitu-

---

*The Life of the Rt. Hon. Cecil Rhodes, 1853-1902* (2 vols.; London, 1910) and John Gibson Lockhard and Christopher M. Woodhouse, *Rhodes* (London, 1963); while Felix Gross, *Rhodes of Africa* (London, 1956), is exceptional in being critical. There is an interesting French assessment of Milner by Vladimir Halpérin, *Lord Milner et l'évolution de l'impérialisme britannique* (Paris, 1950) (English trans., with a foreword by Leopold C. M. S. Amery, London, 1952).

32. Leopold C. M. S. Amery, ed., *"The Times" History of the War in South Africa* (7 vols.; London, 1900-1909); Sir John F. Maurice and staff, *History of the War in South Africa, 1899-1902* (4 vols.; London, 1906-10).

tion, laying special stress on the provisions which have had lasting significance—the franchise provisions, the electoral system, and the language section. It also sheds light on South African politics and on British South African policy in this period.

For the history of South Africa since 1910 the most illuminating work is to be found in the relevant sections of Cornelius W. de Kiewiet, *A History of South Africa, Social and Economic*, William Keith Hancock, *Survey of British Commonwealth Affairs* (2 vols. in 3; London, 1937-42), Nicholas Mansergh, *Survey of British Commonwealth Affairs* (2 vols.; London, 1952-58) and Hancock's *Smuts*. All of these are distinguished. The *Surveys* are largely concerned with South Africa's relationship with the Commonwealth. When the second volume of Hancock's *Smuts* is published the biography is to be expected to provide penetrating discussions of many of the crucial issues of South African history (and much else besides) for the entire period of Smuts's public life, from 1898 when he became state attorney of the South African Republic to his death in 1950. In comparison Daniel W. Krüger's *The Age of the Generals* ([Johannesburg], 1958) is a somewhat pedestrian outline of South African politics from 1910 to 1948; but Michael Roberts and A. E. G. Trollip, in *The South African Opposition, 1939-1945* (London, 1947), give a discerning account of Afrikaner political fragmentation and reconsolidation during World War II and a good analysis of the differences between the policies of J. C. Smuts, J. B. M. Hertzog, and D. F. Malan.

The most informative works from the Afrikaner nationalist viewpoint are J. Albert Coetzee's *Politieke Groepering in die Wording van die Afrikanernasie* (Johannesburg, 1941), Gert D. Scholtz's *Die Rebellie, 1914-15* (Johannesburg, 1942), and accounts of the Afrikaans language movement such as Eduard C. Pienaar's *Die Triomf van Afrikaans* (2nd. ed., Cape Town, 1946). Coetzee's thesis is that each nation is "an organic entity with a definite destiny"; and that by the end of the eighteenth century the Afrikaners had become a nation, with the destiny to occupy South Africa, win it for Christian civilization, and exert a mastery over it. But the Afrikaner nation had been continuously obstructed by the British government and the British settlers in South Africa, and some of its own leaders, including Botha and Smuts, had been corrupted by their influence.

No other biography for this period is comparable with Hancock's *Smuts*; but Frans V. Engelenburg's *General Louis Botha* (London, 1929) and Arthur Basil Williams' *Botha, Smuts and South Africa* (London, 1946) shed light on the attempt made by Botha and Smuts to create a single white South African nation in close co-operation with the evolving British Commonwealth; while Christian M. van den Heever's *Generaal J. B. M. Hertzog* (Johannesburg, 1943), Gert D. Scholtz's *Generaal Christiaan Frederik Beyers, 1869-1914* (Johannesburg, 1941), and Daniel F. Malan's posthumous autobiography, *Afrikaner-Volkseenheid en my Ervarings op die pad daarheen* (Cape Town, 1959) are helpful for an understanding of Afrikaner nationalism and the distinctions between its successive phases. Alan S. Paton's *Hofmeyr* (London, 1964) demonstrates the inability of a South African politician to give effect to his liberal inclinations.

Until comparatively recently the central argument of Afrikaner nationalist historiography was directed against Great Britain and the British settlers in South Africa, who seemed to constitute the main obstacles to the realization of the national ideal; but ever since the time of S. J. du Toit Afrikaner nationalist historiography had a negrophobic as well as an anglophobic content, and in the last few decades, as British power in South Africa waned, as anti-colonial sentiment grew in Europe, America, and Asia, and as African nationalism became a potent force inside and outside South Africa, the negrophobic element has become dominant. Gustav S. Preller's later works, notably *Andries Pretorius*, are strongly negrophobic. The thesis of P. van Biljon in *Grensbakens tussen Blank en Swart in Suid Afrika*, which was presented as a doctoral dissertation in 1937 and published in Johannesburg in 1947, is that the genuine white settlers had always sought to apply a principle of territorial separation between themselves and Africans, that it was British commercial imperialism, in league with Exeter Hall and its agents, the missionaries, who forced a breach in that principle in the nineteenth century, and that it would be the duty of an Afrikaner government to restore it. The same thesis is expounded by Geoffrey Cronjé in *'n Tuiste vir die Nageslag: die Blywende Oplossing van Suid-Afrika se Rassevraagstukke* (Cape Town, 1945), which was a blueprint for the policy of apartheid; while Jacob D. du Toit, in "Die Godsdienstige Grondslag van ons Rassebeleid" (*Inspan*, December

1944, pp. 7-17), reasons that separation is the divine teleological principle revealed in the Book of Genesis.

Since 1948, when apartheid became the official policy of the South African government, it has attracted world-wide attention, and learned journals as well as the popular press have contained many articles on the subject. It is not proposed to review this immense literature here, for most of it is in the nature of historical evidence rather than historical writing. From inside South Africa the most revealing account of the historical antecedents of apartheid, as seen by its supporters, is in N. J. Rhoodie and H. J. Venter, *Apartheid: A Socio-economic Exposition of the Origin and Development of the Apartheid Idea* (Pretoria, 1960), which reiterates the thesis of van Biljon in a confused narrative replete with historical error and distortion. This thesis is also to be found in recent publications of the South African government, for example, the "Tomlinson Report" (*Summary of the Report of the Commission for the Socio-Economic Development of the Bantu Areas within the Union of South Africa*, U.G. 61/1955). There have been several studies of South Africa politics since 1948. They include Gwendolen M. Carter's *The Politics of Inequality: South Africa Since 1948* (London, 1958) which contains a great deal of useful data from the mid-1950's, and Leonard M. Thompson's *Politics in the Republic of South Africa* (Boston, 1965). *The Anatomy of South African Misery* (London, 1956) is a dispassionate, brief analysis by a fine historian, Cornelius W. de Kiewiet, who is now an American citizen, but who spent most of his early life in South Africa. *The Peoples and Policies of South Africa* (3rd. ed., London, 1962) by Leopold Marquard, a liberal South African of Afrikaner descent, explains the present position against its historical background; while Hector M. Robertson's *South Africa: Economic and Political Aspects* (Durham, N.C., 1957), G. V. Doxey's *The Industrial Colour Bar in South Africa* (Cape Town, 1961), and Desmond H. Houghton's *The South African Economy* (Cape Town, 1964) are strong on the economic aspect. The publications of the South African Institute of Race Relations (Johannesburg), which include a quarterly *Journal*, many pamphlets, some of them by historians, and admirable annual *Surveys of Race Relations in South Africa* edited by Muriel Horrell, are a mine of accurate information, and should be compared with the publications of the Suid-Afrikaanse Buro vir Rasse-Aangeleenthede, which supports the principle of apartheid. The constitutional crises that have taken place in South Africa recently have evoked some fundamental work by constitutional lawyers and political theorists, notably Geoffrey Marshall, *Parliamentary Sovereignty in the Commonwealth* (Oxford, 1957), half of which is devoted to South Africa, Herman R. Hahlo and Ellison Kahn, *The Union of South Africa: The Development of Its Laws and Constitution* (London, 1960), and articles by Denis V. Cowen and B. Z. Beinart.[33]

Mature historical studies of African life in the twentieth century are few, but the Border districts of the Cape Province have been examined by anthropologists and economists in a series of works which contain data and insights of the first importance to the historian—*The Keiskammahoek Rural Survey*, by Desmond Hobart Houghton and others (4 vols.; Pietermaritzburg, 1952), *Economic Development in a Plural Society*, edited by Houghton (Cape Town, 1960), and *Xhosa in Town: Studies of the Bantu-speaking Population of East London*, by D. H. Reader, Philip Mayer, and Berthold A. Pauw (3 vols.; Cape Town, 1961-63). There is much relevant material among the publications of the South African Institute of Race Relations, including a compendium, *Handbook on Race Relations in South Africa*, edited by Ellen Hellman (Cape Town, 1949). Systematic study of African political activity is impeded by the banning of African organizations and by the fact that most of the evidence is in the hands of the security branch of the South African police. Nevertheless, the history of the African National Congress has been analyzed by Edward Feit, in *South Africa: The Dynamics of the African National Congress* (London, 1962), and ably related by Mary Benson, in *The African Patriots: The Story of the African National Congress of South Africa* (London, 1963); while Leo Kuper's *Passive Resistance in South Africa* (New Haven, 1958) is a powerful sociological analysis of the passive resistance movement of 1952; and Edward Roux's *Time Longer than Rope* (London, 1948; 2nd ed., Madison, 1964) and Albert Luthuli's *Let My People Go* (London, 1962) contain important information about some

---

33. Cowen, *Parliamentary Sovereignty and the Entrenched Sections of the South Africa Act* (Cape Town, 1951), and "Legislature and Judiciary: Reflections on the Constitutional Issues in South Africa," *Modern Law Review* (London), XV (July, 1952), 282-96, and XVI (July, 1953), 273-98; Beinart, "Parliament and the Courts," *Butterworths South African Law Review* (1954), pp. 134-81, "The South African Senate," *Modern Law Review*, XX (Nov., 1957), 549-65, and "The South African Appeal Court and Judicial Review," *Modern Law Review*, XXI (Nov., 1958), 587-608.

phases of African political activity, though they tend to be unreliable beyond the range of their authors' personal experiences. Bengt G. M. Sundkler's *Bantu Prophets in South Africa* (2nd ed., London, 1961) is an important study of separatist churches, and the works by "Mnguni" and Majeke which have already been mentioned are indicative of one strand in recent thinking.

South Africa is a laboratory for the social sciences, with a wide range of data, some readily available, some to be discovered, and an unsurpassed range of problems which cut to the core of human behavior. As has been emphasized in several contexts in this review, the history of the non-white peoples of South Africa has not been explored to the same degree as the history of the whites; but there are also important lacunae in our knowledge of the history of white South Africans. There is need for a series of studies of the history of racial attitudes in South Africa, extending the scope of MacCrone's pioneer study not only to the Afrikaners after 1806 and to the British settlers, but also to the Coloured people, the Asians, and the Africans. The social historian has the task of analyzing the mutations which fragments of European societies have undergone after their transplantation to South Africa, and those which African societies have undergone as their tribal self-sufficiency has been eroded; and also of explaining the subtle and changing balance between those forces which have tended to perpetuate distinctions between endogamous groups and those which have tended to weaken them. The economic historian is confronted with the need to explain the growth and the nature of a peculiar dualistic economy, resting in part upon subsistence production and in part upon the joint endeavors of people of all races in the expanding capitalist sector of the economy. The intellectual historian will find a complex and largely unexplored accumulation of evidence, ranging from serious attempts to create modes of thought appropriate to the realities of the South African situation[34] to various types of group neuroses. The historian of religion has to deal with interesting examples of the relationship between Church and State, and with developments in the social ethic of the Dutch Reformed Church and its relation to the social

34. Notably Reinhold F. Alfred Hoernlé, *South African Native Policy and the Liberal Spirit* ([Lovedale], 1939), and *Race and Reason* (Johannesburg, 1945). See also the publications of the South African Institute of Race Relations, especially the annual Hoernlé Memorial Lectures.

ethic of other Christian churches (including Calvinist churches) inside and outside South Africa, as well as with the changing religious beliefs of Africans. The legal historian is confronted with a rare case of the blending of two different European systems of law—the Roman-Dutch system and the British system—and the coexistence with both of an attenuated form of African customary law. The political historian has to deal, not only with the establishment of white settler communities, the mutual relations of Boer and Briton, and the gradual elimination of the Imperial factor, but also with the transformation of Western institutions in the South African milieu, the responses of non-whites to the imposition and exercise of white supremacy, and the process by which a political system which was analogous to political systems existing elsewhere a few decades ago has now become virtually unique. At the present time we have a few syntheses which illuminate the general trends of South African history and a larger number of studies of specific themes, but most of the latter are connected with the evolution of the Afrikaner people, the policies of the successive rulers of South Africa, and the political struggles within the white community. In relation to the exceptional wealth of historical problems which exist, the historiography of South Africa is still in its infancy. It is to be hoped that it may be matured by penetrating and dispassionate scholarship in the coming generation.

# BRITISH CENTRAL AFRICA

## *George Shepperson*

IT IS CONVENIENT to put together a historiographical essay
in terms of the thesis that each generation or so writes its own history.
In this way, one's thoughts on the changing fashions in historical
perspective can be strung neatly on a chronological thread. But the
writing of history is a literate skill; and where, as in the example of
the Rhodesias and Nyasaland, even a modest degree of literacy is little
more than half a century old, there are few literate generations to give
substance to a cogent chronological approach. It may be true that John
Kirk, on Livingstone's Zambesi expedition in 1860, could write of the
Shire Highlands that "Everyone here knows the name of Karata for
paper and seems to have some idea of the object of writing."[1] There is,
however, a gulf between the appreciation of the power of literacy and
its use in the writing of history. This, indeed, may be said not only of
the Africans in the early days of British administration in Central
Africa but also of many of the white settlers who, with the exception of
the Scots in Nyasaland from a country with a distinctive tradition of
popular education as old as the Knoxian Reformation, came from a
land whose first important Education Act was passed as late as 1870
and whose symbols of popular literary culture were *Tit Bits* and Hora-
tio Bottomley. The gap between literacy and Literature is marked in
all pioneering territories, and where these are such relatively new
settlements as the Rhodesias and Nyasaland, it complicates the use of
the chronological approach in the consideration of their historiography.

Nevertheless, if employed with caution, this approach is justified.
Caution is necessary, however, not only in appreciating that the vertical
time-scale to be used is relatively short but that, if the historiographical

---

1. Sept. 12, 1860: from Kirk's journal in the possession of Reginald Foskett, who
is editing it for publication by Oliver and Boyd (Edinburgh) under the title *The
Zambesi Journal and Letters of Dr. John Kirk*. "Karata" is probably a form of the
Swahili word for "paper."

marks on it are not to be overestimated—or underestimated—this vertical line must be crossed by a number of horizontal ones. Three factors are important here.

The first is the geographical: the fluctuating and often artificial nature of the boundaries of the growth of British influence and power in Central Africa. From the 1850's, when Livingstone and Moffat went up into what is now the Rhodesias, until at least 1922, the year of the Southern Rhodesian referendum on union with South Africa, much of the story of the British in Central Africa is a legitimate part of South African history. This is illustrated in the attention paid to the South African northern frontier in Eric A. Walker's standard work and the change of its title from *A History of South Africa* in the first edition of 1928 to *A History of Southern Africa* in 1957 (both London). On their northwestern flank the British Central African territories display similar problems of geographical continuity: their relations with the Belgian Congo from the days of the no-man's land of Msiri's country in the 1880's when there was a possibility that Katanga might become a British possession to the period after 1899 when the Tanganyika Concessions Limited was formed and a financial frontier of British investment in the Congo began to replace the political dream that the British might edge their way again into the rich rubber and copper country of the Congo. The whole subject of British Central African relations with the Belgian Congo needs detailed exploration. A start has been made by British writers in Ruth Slade's *King Leopold's Congo* (London, 1962) and Roger Anstey's *Britain and the Congo in the Nineteenth Century* (Oxford, 1962), but much more work is needed. To the northeast, there was a kindred problem of political indeterminacy: the fluid boundary until 1894 between what is now Nyasaland and the eastern regions of Northern Rhodesia. Alexander J. Hanna's *The Beginnings of Nyasaland and North-Eastern Rhodesia, 1859-95* (Oxford, 1956) used British archives to outline this problem. Public and private collections in the Rhodesias, however, should add further details. To the southeast, the rivalry between the rising empire of Britain and the declining power of Portugal provided another boundary controversy. Philip R. Warhurst's *Anglo-Portuguese Relations in South-Central Africa, 1890-1900* (London, 1962) is an adequate monograph on the question. But, as a note in its bibliography (p. 163) suggests, further detailed study is impeded by the confidential nature of some of the Portuguese material. Finally, the links between Nyasaland and the East African territories through the slave trade and the migration of its soldiers and workers show the character of the problem of deciding the nature of the boundaries of British influence in Central Africa. The pioneer work of Sir Reginald Coupland on East African slavery provides a starting-point here; and Hubert Moyse-Bartlett's *The King's African Rifles* (Aldershot, 1956) gives additional details on the Nyasa diaspora. But the subject, like the frontier with which it deals, is still wide open for research.[2] And, for those who have a taste for the curiosities of terminology, there is a fascinating historical essay to be written on the elasticity of the term "Central Africa" from the mid-nineteenth century when it was often used to describe parts of what would now be called West Africa and the Sudan; through the days when it shifted south to the Zambesi and there was a time when it seemed that "British Central Africa" might be used to describe the regions to which Cecil Rhodes ultimately gave his name—down to the period between 1891 and 1907 when these words were applied to the little protectorate which is now known as Nyasaland.

The second factor which crosses horizontally, as it were, the vertical time-scale of British Central African historiography is the distinction between the white and the African approach to the past. Even where white writers are sympathetic to African aspirations, they are often influenced by the Hegelian idea that Africa had no history before the coming of the European. At its worst the white conception is highly selective, concentrating on the European element in the Rhodesias and Nyasaland and showing contempt for the African contribution. The African approach to the past, before the emergence of literacy, is well illustrated by Ian Cunnison's *History on the Luapula* (Cape Town, 1951). As this localized, traditional approach begins to give way to the desire for fuller historical knowledge, there are few, if any, African writers available, the attention of those Africans who might produce it being absorbed by the immediate tasks of government and politics. The African element, therefore, in the history of the Rhodesias

2. For some suggestions for research in these fields, see George Shepperson, "The Military History of British Central Africa," *Rhodes-Livingstone Journal* (Lusaka), XXVI (Dec., 1959), 22-33; and Shepperson, "External Factors in African Nationalism, with Particular Reference to British Central Africa," *Phylon* (Atlanta), XXII (Fall, 1961), 207-25.

and Nyasaland has been traced, if at all, by white writers: the missionary chain, for example, in Nyasaland from David Clement Scott's *A Cyclopaedic Dictionary of the Mang'anja Language spoken in British Central Africa* (Edinburgh, 1892) to T. Cullen Young's *Notes on the History of the Tumbuka-Kamanga Peoples* (London, 1932) and beyond; and the officials' contribution, not only in the too often—but not always—perfunctory notes of the "tribal background" variety in governmental reports and handbooks but also in the personal writings of officials, ranging from Sir Harry Johnston's polymath *British Central Africa* (London, 1897) to W. H. J. Rangeley's work on the African peoples of Nyasaland, of which his "The Amacinga Yao" in the *Nyasaland Journal* (Blantyre) (XV [1962], 40-70) seems typical. To date, the slow development of university education for the Africans of the Rhodesias and Nyasaland has delayed the emergence of indigenous historians such as is now a marked element amongst the intelligentsia of West Africa. Their creation is an urgent task for the study of history in these areas today.

Mention of the historical interests of missionaries and government servants draws attention to a third element which complicates the simple chronological approach. This is the division between amateurs and professionals. Admittedly, it is not such a complicating factor as the other two, because there is a sense in which it may be said that the entry of the professional historian, in any substantial fashion, into the field of British Central African history is limited to the last decade and a half. Yet it must be remembered that at least two historians from the universities had turned their attention to this in the 1920's: Basil Williams with his *Cecil Rhodes* (London, 1921) and Reginald (later Sir Reginald) Coupland in his *Kirk on the Zambesi* (Oxford, 1928), the subtitle of which is, significantly enough, *A Chapter of African History*. Furthermore, the use of the term "professional" is itself complicated by two other divisions: the non-academic writer who is employed or encouraged by official agencies to produce such a volume as Hugh Marshall Hole's semi-official *The Making of Rhodesia* (London, 1926); and the anthropologist whose work, both as a piece of contemporary history and as a repository of notes, however imperfect, on the traditional African past, is a clear contribution to history. Where anthropologists have had legal training or have done specific historical research, as in the examples of Max Gluckman with his corpus of writing on the Lozi and other Central African peoples and personalities and James Albert Barnes's *Politics in a Changing Society: A Political History of the Fort Jameson Ngoni* (Cape Town, 1954), their work sometimes seems to belong as much to history as to anthropology, if one insists on a clear differentiation between these two disciplines.

But, for all the complications of the use of the term "professional" in Rhodesian and Nyasaland historiography, there are many writers who are clearly amateurs. To this genre belong, first of all, the local antiquarians: the contributors to the local newspapers and missionary magazines and some of the writers in such periodicals as *N.A.D.A.* (the *Native Affairs Department Annual of Southern Rhodesia*, Salisbury), *The Northern Rhodesia Journal* (Lusaka) and *The Nyasaland Journal*. Beyond the occasional level there may be noted the amateur historians of such monographs as R. H. Hobson's *Rubber: A Footnote to Northern Rhodesian History* (Livingstone, 1960) and Richard Sampson's *They Came to Northern Rhodesia* (Lusaka, 1956), an annotated inventory of all known immigrants up to 1902 which suggests how much research remains to be done in the serious study of emigration from all parts of the world to Central Africa, using the wealth of techniques and comparative materials which forty years of migration studies in North America has produced. Outstanding among the amateurs is Michael Gelfand, with his work on the medical and social history of the British period in Central Africa (for example, *Livingstone the Doctor* [Oxford, 1957], and *Northern Rhodesia in the Days of the Charter* [Oxford, 1961]). If the professionalization, in the strictest sense, of Central African history is obviously to be welcomed, one hopes that it will not discourage the important amateur tradition in these territories. Its faults are apparent—but so should be its contribution. Without it, much of the new historiography which now seems to be opening up in Central Africa would have been impossible; this amateur tradition can still find and furnish into enjoyable narrative scattered materials which the archive- and university-bound professional historian does not readily discover and which, by the competitive and critical atmosphere of scholarship in which he now works, he is often inhibited from turning into readable prose.

Bearing these three complicating factors in mind, the chronological approach to British Central African historiography may be employed.

If one wishes a *vade mecum* for the journey, an admirable little reference book could be put together out of three short studies: James Clyde Mitchell's chapter on "The African Peoples" and Lewis H. Gann's "History of Rhodesia and Nyasaland, 1889-1953" in *Handbook to the Federation of Rhodesia and Nyasaland* (edited by William Vernon Brelsford [Salisbury, 1960], pp. 57-181) and the valuable bibliography by the Librarian of the National Archives in Salisbury, A. R. Taylor's "Recent Trends in Central African Historiography" in *Historians in Tropical Africa* (edited by T. O. Ranger [Salisbury, 1962], pp. 387-400; mimeographed). Four periods may be singled out for examination. If they are periods in the history rather than the historiography of what, at the time of writing, are called the Rhodesias and Nyasaland, they enable not only some of the fashions and problems in their historiography to be examined but, at the same time, offer the opportunity to indicate briefly some of their outstanding historical questions.

The first is the period before 1889. It might seem desirable to give it an exact initial date, such as 1851, when David Livingstone met Sebitwane near the Zambesi River. This would certainly be a convenient time for beginning the study of effective British penetration into Central Africa. Nevertheless, the subsequent history of Britain and Central Africa has been profoundly influenced by two factors of a much earlier date. The first is the nature of the African societies in the pre-European period. This has already been the subject of some fascinating historiographical changes, as the story of the speculations about the Zimbabwe Ruins and the empire of Monomatapa indicates. From the days of Carl Peters' *The Eldorado of the Ancients* (London, 1902), when romance of the King Soloman's Mines variety was the historical *motif*, Gertrude Caton-Thompson's sober standard work, *The Zimbabwe Culture* (Oxford, 1931) and the even more sober carbon dating techniques have stripped much of the colorful away from the story of the Ruins. In case the overarchaeological approach, however, should seem doomed to divest them altogether of their romance, the history of the area from 1050 to 1902, using oral tradition and Portuguese records, which D. P. Abraham is preparing[3] may well restore, on a solider foundation, some of the excitement which the first

---

3. A foretaste is provided by two articles by Abraham: "The Early Political History of the Kingdom of Mwene Mutapa (850-1589)," *Historians in Tropical Africa*, pp. 61-91; and "Maramuca: An Exercise in the Combined Use of Portuguese Records and Oral Tradition," *Journal of African History* (Cambridge), II (1961), 211-25.

Europeans experienced when they saw the Zimbabwe and allied cultures. African nationalism is interested in the outcome of this historiographical struggle because, if there is to be an African government in Southern Rhodesia, there is a possibility that it will change the name of the state to "Zimbabwe." The African nationalists here can look back to a much greater range of scholarship in the search for their myth of origins than the Nyasa nationalists who intend to call their new state "Malawi" after the Maravi,[4] the pre-European people of much of their area. As a few scattered references in Eric Axelson's *Portuguese in South-East Africa, 1600-1700* (Johannesburg, 1960) suggest, the necessary further work on the Maravi culture may find much of its material in Portuguese sources.

The importance of the Portuguese background to the British occupation of Central Africa is a second reason for not providing a mid-nineteenth century date as a starting point for a chronological survey. The announcement recently that a Gulbenkian Foundation grant will at last make possible the much-postponed publication of *The Historical Documents of East and Central Africa*, a co-operative British-Portuguese venture, using the wealth of Portuguese archival material, is encouraging. Without such basic documentary collections, the achievement of an adequate perspective of the Portuguese factor is difficult for the specialist in the British rôle in Central Africa.

It is to be hoped these *Documents* will not be edited on the selective principles of the important Oppenheimer Series of the Central African Archives. The limitations of their approach is revealed in the statement by J. P. R. Wallis in his introduction to one of the volumes in this series, *The Zambesi Journal of James Stewart, 1862-1863* (London, 1952, p. xxvi) that "passages of intimate and personal, rather than of historical reference" have been omitted. It is this principle that has vitiated much of the historical writing on the lives of the pioneers in British Central Africa since William Garden Blaikie produced his *The Personal Life of David Livingstone* (London, 1880). Fortunately, a less narrow approach to the life of Livingstone and the other pioneers is now evident, as is indicated by the editorial labours recently of Isaac Schapera on important new Livingstone manuscripts (for

4. See Thomas Price, "More about the Maravi," *African Studies* (Johannesburg), II (1952), 75-79.

example, *David Livingstone: Family Letters, 1841-1856* [London, 1959]).

It is not so easy to say this about the life of Cecil Rhodes, which dominates so much of our second period: 1889 to 1922. From the days when the British South Africa Company was chartered to the establishment of modern Southern Rhodesia, his activities have been the subject of bitter controversy. A fully rounded biography is still needed. The publication in 1963 of John Gibson Lockhart and Christopher M. Woodhouse's *Rhodes* (London) makes up for some of the deficiencies of existing biographies. Nevertheless it is not the life of Rhodes which presents the man, wart and all, which many scholars had expected. It has been suggested elsewhere[5] that the relations between Cecil Rhodes and his brother, Herbert, who died prospecting in Nyasaland, is one possible key to his drive to the north. This key has yet to be turned. The historiography of Cecil Rhodes vacillates between the adulatory and the denigratory. Even such a sober professional as Basil Williams allows the adulatory note to spoil his biography. Some young modern professional historians find it difficult to restrain the denigratory. It may be that the first fully rounded biography of Rhodes will be the work of the second or third generation of African historians to come, when African historiography may have had time to get rid of the anti-European animus which seems inevitable in its initial stages.

It was in this second period, under the stimulus of Rhodes's creation of a new state, that the first attempts were made at synoptic histories. The very deficiencies of some of these, such as Howard Hensman's *A History of Rhodesia* (Edinburgh, 1900), acted as a challenge to budding historians in the third period: from the division of responsibility for the Rhodesias in 1923 to the creation of the Federation of 1953. It was in these thirty years that the basis was laid for the modern historiography of British Central Africa. At their beginning, one could look back on nearly half a century of effective British influence in these regions. It was a long enough period to supply even the narrowest historians with something of a perspective.

Yet, with the exception of Basil Williams and Coupland in the 1920's, professionals were slow to respond until almost the end of this period. And both Coupland and Williams were more interested

5. "The Literature of British Central Africa," *Rhodes-Livingstone Journal*, XXIII (June, 1958), 12-46, to which reference may be made for suggestions for further research.

in East and South than Central Africa. The focus of attention lay outside the Rhodesias and Nyasaland, which were only incidental to a
larger survey for professional historians who showed any interest in
them until after World War II. Examples of this are provided by the
two American works which paid any serious attention to Central African history: Reginald Ivan Lovell's *The Struggle for South Africa,
1875-1899* (New York, 1934) and Lois C. A. Raphael's *The Cape-to-
Cairo Dream* (New York, 1936).

The 1939-45 war was responsible, to some extent, for creating a
new interest in the British Central African territories. Young servicemen who would later become historians or the potential public for
their work were introduced to the Rhodesias and Nyasaland; others
who were never in these territories became aware of their existence
through meetings with white Rhodesians in the army and air force.
As students or university teachers they returned to civilian life to find
that the opening of a further group of British Public Records to 1902
supplied them with material for answering at least some of the questions they had been asking about the past of these territories. It would,
of course, be wrong to give the impression that the new wave of research sprang from the war alone: the growth of a new interest in
African nationalism and politics, and the inevitable move of the M.A.
and Ph.D. frontiers towards relatively unexplored historical territory,
also had much to do with it.

The beginning of discussions on the federation of the Rhodesias
and Nyasaland in the 1950's had even more. It opened the eyes of
those perfervid students of federalism everywhere, the Americans, to
new possibilities in Central Africa. It stimulated young British scholars
whose researches had begun much earlier to publish and take advantage of the public interest.

The creation, then, of the Federation in 1953 open the fourth and,
certainly, the most fruitful period, to which no end is yet in sight.
Much of the historical writing that has dominated the recent wave of
political historiography has been based on secondary sources or readily
available government documents. Of course, when—and if—the rami-
fied complex of documents about the Federation and its controversies
are available for public inspection, a long vista of historical research
will be opened. Until then, such works as Colin Leys's *European
Politics in Southern Rhodesia* (Oxford, 1959) and the three-volume

history of Southern Rhodesia and the emergence of the Federation which the London Institute of Race Relations has produced must satisfy the curious. Two of the volumes of this work (Philip Mason's *The Birth of a Dilemma* and his *Year of Decision* [London, 1958 and 1960]) show what can be done with secondary sources. The other volume, Richard Gray's *The Two Nations* (London, 1960), which covers the period between the two World Wars, is in a somewhat different category, because Gray was allowed to examine papers not normally available to public inspection and, within the limits imposed upon him, made good use of them. This is fortunate because, as A. R. Taylor in his bibliography referred to above points out, in the political field "the period from 1890 to about 1914, and the post-1953 period are both well-documented. For the period in between there is nothing" much apart from Gray.

Two works may be taken as examples of the richness of documentation which is becoming available for the pre-1914 period: George Shepperson and Thomas Price's *Independent African: John Chilembwe and the Origins, Setting and Significance of the Nyasaland Native Rising of 1915* (Edinburgh, 1958) and Lewis H. Gann's *The Birth of a Plural Society: The Development of Northern Rhodesia under the British South Africa Company, 1894-1914* (Manchester, 1958). Gann has been appointed to write an official history of the territories within the Federation. One hopes that he will bring to it the detailed documentation which distinguishes this and other of his writings.

An important contribution to British Central African history has been made by a writer whose interests are primarily in East Africa: Roland Oliver in the Central African sections of his *Sir Harry Johnston and the Scramble for Africa* (London, 1957) and *The Missionary Factor in East Africa* (London, 1952). Missionary historiography, indeed, continues to engage interest. Since James Williams Jack's *Daybreak in Livingstonia* (Edinburgh, 1901) there has been a constant flow of missionary histories, using, with various degrees of skill, primary public and private sources. In the post-1953 period, Shepperson and Price's work has drawn attention to the complications of the Christian scene in Nyasaland; Robert I. Rotberg's *Christian Missionaries and the Creation of Northern Rhodesia, 1880-1924* (Princeton, 1965), and John V. Taylor and Dorothea Lehmann's *Christians of the Cop-*

*perbelt* (London, 1961) have opened up the study of Northern Rhodesian mission history; and William Cecil Northcott's pioneering biography, *Robert Moffat: Pioneer in Africa, 1817-1870* (London, 1961), has provided a wealth of preliminary detail for the early Southern Rhodesian missionary story. The later history of missions in Southern Rhodesia, however, still awaits concentrated academic investigation.

The obvious political importance of Central Africa has at last turned the academic attention of Marxists to these regions. At the textbook level, the Central African references in Endre Sík's *Histoire de l'Afrique Noire* (Budapest, 1961) show what may be expected. At the more specialist stage, the controversial but highly interesting article by L. D. Yablochkov, "De la consolidation national des peuples dans la Rhodésie du Nord et le Nyassaland" in *Des Africanistes russes parlent de l'Afrique*: (*Présence Africaine* [Paris, 1960]), foreshadows future Soviet historical writing on Central Africa.

Whatever new developments await British Central African historiography, there is now enough serious historical writing available to make possible the production of a reliable and readable one-volume history which would do justice to both the European and African contribution and would strike a balance between constitutional, political, social, and economic factors. The attempt was made in Alexander J. Hanna's *The Story of the Rhodesias and Nyasaland* (London, 1960). It was not successful. An important task thus awaits the adventurous historian. The successful candidate may well find that, in his synthesis, he has provided a perspective that could be the opening of yet another period in the historiography of the territories now called Southern and Northern Rhodesia and Nyasaland.[6]

6. Since this article was written, the achievement of independence by the last two African states has changed the names of these countries to Rhodesia, Zambia, and Malawi, respectively. Also a further one-volume history has been published: Alfred J. Wills, *An Introduction to the History of Central Africa* (London, 1964). While it is, in some ways, an improvement on Hanna's volume (particularly in its bibliography and its attention to specifically African history) it is, largely because of over-hasty compilation, still not entirely satisfactory.

# BRITISH EAST AFRICA

## George Bennett

BRITAIN BECAME INVOLVED in East Africa through her
position in India. The Bombay government was particularly interested in the activities of Seyyid Said of Muscat as he moved in the
first half of the nineteenth century to Zanzibar. That island became
the base for a predominantly British exploration of the East African
mainland but, through the German challenge of 1884-85, the whole
of the area did not fall immediately to Britain. Her strategic interests in the route to India led first to the occupation of Egypt and
then to a desire to control the whole of the Nile Valley. Thus the
Imperial British East Africa Company, chartered in 1888, was urged
to drive for Uganda. When control of this area with the building of
a railway proved to be beyond its resources, the British government
assumed control, proclaiming the Protectorates of Uganda in 1894
and, in 1895, of British East Africa, the later Kenya. The latter appeared to be largely empty. It could not support the railway built up
from Mombasa to Lake Victoria and completed in 1901. For this
reason the British government then encouraged the immigration of
both Europeans and Asians, the former predominantly as farmer-
settlers and the latter to fill jobs as clerks and craftsmen that the local
African population did not then seem capable of performing. This produced the peculiar characteristic of British East Africa: it was a meeting place for people of three continents, Europeans, Asians, and Africans. British control was rounded off by the acquisition of Tanganyika
as a mandate after World War I. This completed Cecil Rhodes's
dream of an all-red route from the Cape to Cairo and caused some, in
the British government and elsewhere, to consider the possibility of
federating the whole British area from the Sudan to South Africa.
Examination by successive commissions[1] showed that East Africa

1. The information in these reports and in their minutes of evidence is of such
fundamental importance to any student of the area as to make them worth listing:
*Report of the East Africa Commission* (Ormsby-Gore) Cmd. 2387 (1925); *Report*

was a separate area. Communications to the south were poor, while the presence of Indians had led to the European settlers' aspirations to control Kenya being checked in 1923 just as the Southern Rhodesian whites were obtaining internal self-government. British East Africa was to develop a different and separate history in which Africans were to play an increasingly important part until Tanganyika's independence in 1961 led the way to full African control.

The controversies over the first stage of British rule, that by a chartered company, led its secretary, P. L. McDermott, to publish an immediate defense of its stewardship, *British East Africa; or IBEA* (London, 1893). Those of the Hobson-Lenin anti-imperialist school regarded the whole affair as a classic case of economic imperialism and it was so explained by Leonard S. Woolf in his *Empire and Commerce in Africa* (London, 1920). Only in 1955 was the Company's history examined academically, and then in a London Ph.D. thesis by Marie Jeanne de Kiewiet. Her dissertation provides the basic material for her chapter on "The British Sphere, 1884-94" in the first volume of the Oxford *History of East Africa* (Oxford, 1963), pp. 391-432.

McDermott's was little more than a turgid, grumbling defense of the Company, but a more exciting personal account came then from one of its main employees, Frederick Dealtry (later Lord) Lugard. The two volumes of his *The Rise of Our East African Empire* (Edinburgh, 1893) not only contributed to the campaign for the retention of Uganda but also began a tradition of former British administrators in East Africa writing about their work. Their accounts have not only been autobiographical in part—and hence valuable source material for the historian—but also often directly historical in approach. In his two magnificent illustrated volumes, *The Uganda Protectorate* (London, 1902), the then recently returned Special Commissioner, Sir Harry Hamilton Johnston, included a brief historical survey covering the story of the coming of the Europeans, first missionaries and then administrators. Johnston's work had an encyclopedic quality, covering all aspects, scientific and historic, of the Protectorate. Other commissioners and governors were more personal in their approach. Both the first two commissioners of the East Africa Protectorate published

---

of *the Commission on Closer Union of the Dependencies in Eastern and Central Africa* (Hilton Young) Cmd. 3234 (1929); and *Report of the Joint Select Committee on Closer Union in East Africa*, H. C. 156 (1931).

accounts of their periods of office. The chapters in Sir Arthur Hardinge's *A Diplomatist in the East* (London, 1928) form part of a wider career but his successor, Sir Charles Eliot, decided, in the flurry over his resignation, to make immediately clear the European paramountcy policy he had adopted in *The East Africa Protectorate* (London, 1905). It was longer before the first two governors of Uganda, Sir Henry Hesketh J. Bell and Sir Frederick John Jackson, produced respectively *Glimpses of a Governor's Life* (London, 1946) and *Early Days in East Africa* (London, 1930). The former underlined the distinction that was to develop between the two Protectorates, for Bell's diary revealed how, between 1905 and 1911, he had laid much of the foundation of the policy of peasant agriculture. Recent access to the Foreign and Colonial Office records has shown that Jackson was more critical of Eliot and of the settler invasion of the East Africa Protectorate than his discreet memoirs allowed us to see.

Other early accounts, in a mixture of personal and historical information, came from the missionaries. Missionary writing has, of course, tended to hagiography, an outlook found in Mrs. J. W. Harrison's account of her brother, *A. M. Mackay* (London, 1890), the famous Church Missionary Society pioneer in Uganda. Buganda was that society's main center of attraction in East Africa in the last quarter of the nineteenth century. To it went an able group of men who laid the foundations not only of missionary work but also of scholarship. Robert Pickering Ashe produced accounts of the kingdom of Buganda in *Two Kings of Uganda* (London, 1889) and *Chronicles of Uganda* (London, 1894), and the historian must not neglect the anthropological material on *The Baganda* (London, 1911), among other tribes, by the missionary anthropologist John Roscoe. Sir Albert R. Cook, who was so largely instrumental in the beginnings of medical work in Uganda, later published his *Uganda Memories* (Kampala, 1945), while Bishop Alfred Robert Tucker, who played a most important part in the signing of the Uganda Agreement of 1900, had earlier published two volumes as *Eighteen Years in Uganda and East Africa* (London, 1908). Of the early missionary figures there is one outstanding biography, *Pilkington of Uganda* (London, 1898) by Charles Forbes Hartford-Battersby. For a contemporary conspectus of the C.M.S. position the reader may also be referred to Eugene Stock's *History of the Church Missionary Society*, III (London, 1891). On the Roman

Catholic side there is a biography of Mackay's antagonist, *La Vie du Père Siméon Lourdel* (Algiers, 1895), by A. Nicq, and a later work, *Black Martyrs* (London, 1941), by John P. Thoonen. The richness of early missionary writing about Uganda is not matched elsewhere, though Bishop Tucker has something to say about the East Africa Protectorate, especially around Mombasa, and there is a lively biography of Bishop Weston by Herbert Maynard Smith: *Frank, Bishop of Zanzibar* (London, 1928).

Of the military men who wrote accounts we may perhaps note Lugard's opponent J. R. L. Macdonald, who published in 1897 *Soldiering and Surveying in British East Africa* (London), and Richard Meinertzhagen, whose *Kenya Diary, 1902-1906* (Edinburgh, 1957) gives a vivid picture of this early period. The military story of East Africa has been most excellently brought out in Hubert Moyse-Bartlett's *The King's African Rifles* (Aldershot, 1956). This book has a dual value: it naturally tells the story of the campaigns, in East Africa and elsewhere, in which the regiment has been involved but, besides this, it shows what an important part army officers often played as the first effective administrators of large parts of British East Africa.

Civil servants who have served in the East Africa Protectorate (or Kenya Colony since 1920) have published some important material. G. R. Sandford's *An Administrative and Political History of the Masai Reserve* (London, 1919) had government support and was based on the records of at least one leading member of the administration; nevertheless, this work is sometimes surprisingly frank in retelling the Masai controversies. The account of Charles William Hobley, who had been with the Imperial British East Africa Company from early days, *Kenya, from Chartered Company to Crown Colony* (London, 1929), appeared pedestrian after the excitements of two highly critical books: Norman Maclean Leys's *Kenya* (London, 1924) and William McGregor Ross's *Kenya from Within* (London, 1927). Dr. Leys had been removed from the East Africa Protectorate and sent to Nyasaland for his part in opposing government action in the second Masai move of 1911, and his book has, therefore, much of an "inside story" value. Its publication drew considerable attention upon the Colony where it appeared then as if the European settlers might gain control. Their influence was further attacked by Ross: while his book is polemical and sensational in tone, it is the work of a man who, while in Kenya, kept his press-clippings and other records carefully. His statements of fact are usually accurate, and he is particularly important for his account of the early African political movements.

Ross's book needs to be read, and the impressions balanced, with Elspeth Joscelin Huxley's two-volume biography of Lord Delamere, *White Man's Country* (London, 1935). Essentially Mrs. Huxley is a novelist. Elsewhere, in *Red Strangers* (London, 1939), she has provided a most valuable imaginative account, based on anthropological work, of the Kikuyu reaction to the coming of the Europeans, while her *Murder in Government House* (London, 1937) is readily recognizable as a picture of Kenya official society, a plan printed with the book being that of Government House, Nairobi. Mrs. Huxley's talent as a novelist enabled her portrait of Delamere as the settler leader to be particularly lively, though perhaps his influence is over-stressed; certainly a judicious use has been made of his speeches and the time-scale is on occasion speeded up to heighten effect.

In complete contrast there appeared two years later Marjorie Ruth Dilley's *British Policy in Kenya Colony* (New York, 1937). Miss Dilley was a young American who worked in the Colonial Office library in London and did not visit Africa until many years later. While it is true that her book lacks atmosphere and smells of the lamp, she achieved something for which all future historians of Kenya must be grateful: she quarried a way for the first time through the vast bulk of material on this colony and set it all out topic by topic. Hers is not a chronological history and the book's poor index is a constant irritant. One topic, treated by Miss Dilley, received at this time an examination in a far wider setting: by William Keith (later Sir Keith) Hancock in the first volume of his *Survey of British Commonwealth Affairs* (London, 1937). His section on Kenya, in the chapter "India and Race Equality," remains the best account of the Indian controversy of the twenties.

During the twenties Professor (later Sir) Reginald Coupland of Oxford became drawn into the constant political discussion about the future of East Africa. Already he had become interested in Sir John Kirk, on whom he published *Kirk on the Zambezi* (Oxford, 1928). His intention was to follow the great British consul's career at Zanzibar and produce a study of his life and work there. As Coupland proceeded with this, he found that Kirk's activity was so central to the whole

East African story in the latter part of the nineteenth century that he finished by writing two volumes which were immediately accepted as the standard works on East African history. For an understanding of the position Kirk found when he arrived at Zanzibar in 1866, Coupland felt compelled to write *East Africa and Its Invaders* (Oxford, 1938), a book which was the story of the East African coast "from the earliest times to the death of Seyyid Said in 1856." It covered, as far as Britain was concerned, the earliest contacts in the sixteenth century before finding a main focus in Britain's continuing action against the slave trade, an earlier and wider interest of Coupland's. The story of Britain's relations with Zanzibar, broached in the first volume, was carried on in the second, *The Exploitation of East Africa, 1856-1890* (London, 1939), until the Anglo-German treaty of 1890.

By the time this book appeared Coupland was projecting a three-volume study on Kenya in which he considered seeking as collaborators to do single volumes Margery Freda Perham, whose work on Nigeria had just appeared, and Charlotte Leubuscher, who was then working on the economic history of Tanganyika.[2] Coupland was the father of academic historical writing in Britain on East Africa, even if all his projects did not prove fruitful. It is to be regretted that nothing then came from Miss Perham except controversial newspaper writing, though this did blossom into a full-scale exchange of letters with Elspeth Huxley which was published as *Race and Politics in Kenya* (London, 1944; 2nd ed., 1956), a volume that provides valuable contrasting material on the previous years.

Another writer who has disappointed on Kenya has been Sir Edward Grigg (later Lord Altrincham), the Colony's important Governor in the twenties; his *Kenya's Opportunity* appeared only in 1955 (London) and was composed of barely more than the most rambling of reminiscences. Of more interest were the memoirs of Sir Philip Euan Mitchell, *African Afterthoughts* (London, 1954), which covers a long period of East African service from Nyasaland in 1913 through Tanganyika and Uganda to conclude as Governor of Kenya in 1952. There is some value also in Sir Charles Cecil E. Dundas' *African Crossroads* (London, 1955), the recollection of another civil servant with a career that took him from Kenya to Northern Rhodesia.

The first scholarly work on Tanganyika was Miss Leubuscher's

2. Correspondence in the papers of Dr. J. H. Oldham, in private possession.

*Tanganyika Territory: A Study of Economic Policy under Mandate* (London, 1944). In comparison with the rest of East Africa, this country has been somewhat neglected by writers. Certainly the most interesting book on it to appear between the two World Wars was *My Tanganyika Service and Some Nigeria* (London, 1939) by Sir Donald C. Cameron. He had, as Governor from 1924 to 1931, developed the policy of indirect rule, and he thus provided the most formative influence upon Tanganyika's development during the whole period of British rule. In view of the paucity of published works, Raymond Leslie Buell's chapter in his great survey *The Native Problem in Africa* (New York, 1928) retains a certain importance—and his chapters on the other East African territories may also be consulted.

Perhaps the most important development for future historical work in respect of Uganda and Tanganyika during the thirties was the appearance of two new periodicals: *The Uganda Journal* (Kampala) in 1934 and *Tanganyika Notes and Records* (Dar es Salaam) in 1936. While neither has been limited to history alone, much new historical work has seen its beginnings in their pages. In them two British officials have made, in articles and in other ways, a considerable contribution: Harold Beken Thomas, who has been almost a guardian angel presiding over the development of the history of Uganda, and Sir John Milner Gray. Thomas also produced with Albert E. Spencer, *A History of Uganda Land and Surveys* (Kampala, 1938) while Sir John's *History of Zanzibar from the Middle Ages to 1856* appeared in 1962 (London).

In the years since World War II serious contributions to East African history have multiplied. A first important book was Roland Anthony Oliver's *The Missionary Factor in East Africa* (London, 1952). Charles Pelham Groves was then producing his four-volume *The Planting of Christianity in Africa* (1948-58), the last two volumes of which provide much other useful material about East Africa against a wider background. Oliver's volume is concerned with local detail in the period from 1844 to 1914 but his final chapter is somewhat different. It turns to the influence on East Africa of missionary activity in Britain, for there, after World War I, Dr. J. H. Oldham, secretary of the International Missionary Council, had a considerable influence on governmental policy-making.

A first study of one Roman Catholic missionary order in one area has now been provided by Hubert Philip Gale in his *Uganda and the Mill Hill Fathers* (London, 1959). Two recent books have carried the story of the missionary impact on to the most recent period: John Vernon Taylor's *The Growth of the Church in Buganda* (London, 1958) and Frederick Burkewood Welbourn's *East African Rebels* (London, 1961). The former discusses only the Anglican Church, but the latter deals with separatist African churches in Buganda and Kikuyuland and is of particular importance in underlining the connection between religion and politics.

Oliver's next contribution to East African history is to be found in his *Sir Harry Johnston and the Scramble for Africa* (London, 1957). This was one of two major biographies of British colonial administrators that appeared about this time—the other being Margery Freda Perham's two-volume *Lugard* (London, 1956-60). In Part III of Volume I Miss Perham produced an authoritative account of Lugard's work in Uganda and also of the subsequent campaign for retention in which the international and diplomatic picture is brilliantly depicted. She then edited, with Mary Bull, *The Diaries of Lord Lugard* (3 vols.; London, 1959), thus enabling us to see the original material for much of Volume I. The second volume contains a discussion of the controversies of the '20's over East Africa in which Lugard played a crucial and important rôle. Unfortunately Miss Perham has only outlined this. A full account of the attempt then at closer union, or federation, a major theme of the period, remains to be written.

In Kenya a number of commercial histories have been produced by Mervyn Frederick Hill and Mrs. Huxley. Hill, the editor of the important and influential *Kenya Weekly News* (Nakuru) was engaged by the East African Railways to write their history. Perhaps it was appropriate that the first volume, *Permanent Way: The Story of the Kenya and Uganda Railway* (Nairobi, 1950) should, in telling the story of Kenya's spinal cord, provide what was in effect a first essay at a history of the Colony, especially for the early years. The second volume, *Permanent Way: The Story of the Tanganyika Railways* (1959), is not so successful in conveying the history of that country under British rule but is interesting on the railway construction and the German period generally. Hill's other commercial volumes appeared in 1956: *Cream Country: The Story of Kenya Co-operative Creameries*

*Limited* and *Planters' Progress: The Story of Coffee in Kenya.* Mrs. Huxley's *No Easy Way: A History of the Kenya Farmers' Association and Unga Limited* was published in 1957 and followed almost naturally from her earlier life of Delamere. One other business history that should be mentioned is Cyril Ehrlich's *The Uganda Company Limited* (Kampala, 1953). With its exception all these books were published in Nairobi, which is doubly appropriate, for Nairobi is the commercial capital of East Africa.

In the postwar years Makerere Hill in Kampala developed as the region's intellectual center. There the college, which started university courses in 1950—together with its East African Institute of Social Research—has gathered scholars who have had at their disposal the rich and well-arranged government records at Entebbe. Its chronicle-history has been written by Margaret Macpherson: *They Built for the Future: A Chronicle of Makerere University College, 1922-1962* (Cambridge, 1964). At the Institute, under the direction of Audrey Isabel Richards, a fruitful collaboration soon developed among social scientists of several disciplines, historians among them, centering in particular on a series of studies, which Dr. Richards organized, of new forms of leadership among Africans. She edited a volume, *East African Chiefs* (London, 1960), subtitled "A Study of Development in Some Uganda and Tanganyika Tribes," which made plain the growing anthropological interest in political organization that made the co-operation so useful to the understanding of the historian. Dr. Richards was succeeded as Director by an American, Lloyd A. Fallers. His *Bantu Bureaucracy* (Cambridge, 1956) has a marked historical approach to the Soga chiefs whose changing position it studied. Another anthropologist who has seen the necessity of tracing the history of the tribe he was studying was John H. M. Beattie, whose *Bunyoro: An African Kingdom* appeared in New York in 1960 and summed up much of his work elsewhere. One other Uganda tribe which received both anthropological and historical treatment was *The Iteso* (London, 1957), this being the title of a work by Jeremy C. D. Lawrance, an administrative officer with long service among them. A Penguin book by Lucy P. Mair, *Primitive Government* (Harmondsworth, 1962), conveniently sums up the present stage of anthropological work in East Africa on this particular subject, and is thus of considerable value to the historian.

The East African Institute's studies were intended to focus on two particular regions, chosen for the social contrasts they provided: Buganda and the Nyanza Province of Kenya. There first appeared, on Buganda and edited by Dr. Richards, *Economic Development and Tribal Change* (Cambridge, 1954), which contained an important historical chapter by Philip G. Powesland. His *Economic Policy and Labour: A Study in Uganda's Economic History* (Kampala, 1957) was published posthumously, after the early and regretted death of this promising young scholar. For Nyanza, Hugh Fearn produced *An African Economy: A Study of the Economic Development of the Nyanza Province of Kenya, 1903-1953* (London, 1961), while a most valuable article has appeared from an African lecturer at Makerere, Bethwell A. Ogot: "British Administration in the Central Nyanza District of Kenya, 1900-60" (*Journal of African History* [Cambridge], IV [1963], 249-73).

From the historical point of view the most valuable work to emerge from the leadership study project was undoubtedly *Buganda and British Overrule: Two Studies* (London, 1960) by Donald Anthony Low and Robert Cranford Pratt. In effect this was the history of Buganda from the making of the Uganda Agreement of 1900 to the return of the Kabaka from deportation in 1955. Buganda's fascination next attracted an American political scientist, David Ernest Apter, for whom it made a clear comparison with the position of Ashanti in Ghana, which he had studied earlier. Apter's *The Political Kingdom in Uganda* (Princeton, 1961) carried further the problem, already broached by Pratt, of the way the chiefly hierarchy in Buganda has effectively foiled the development of Western-style politics, on which more information has now been provided in Lloyd A. Fallers, ed., *The King's Men: Leadership and Status in Buganda on the Eve of Independence* (London, 1964).

In the study of the history of African politics Pratt produced an important article, "Nationalism in Uganda,"[3] but the subject has been taken further by Low in his *Political Parties in Uganda, 1949-1962* (London, 1962). For Tanganyika "An Outline History of Tanu" from its formation in 1954 to independence in 1961 has appeared as an article (*Makerere Journal* [Kampala], no. 7 [1963], pp. 15-32) by George Bennett, the present writer. For Kenya he has set the longer history of African politics there against the background of European and Asian developments in "The Development of Political Organizations

3. *Political Studies* (Oxford), IX (June, 1961), 157-78.

in Kenya,"[4] an article which was heavily drawn on in the *Historical Survey of the Origins and Growth of Mau Mau,* Cmnd. 1030 (London, 1960), a government report by Frank Derek Corfield. The main value of this work, which is certainly not that of a professional historian, remains the information it gives about the Kenya government's view of Mau Mau. Controversy will continue about the connection between Jomo Kenyatta and Mau Mau; on this George Delf's *Jomo Kenyatta* (London, 1961) put an opposing view to that of the government.[5] Kenyatta's *Facing Mount Kenya* (London, 1938) is a strange mixture of anthropology and political tract, with some slight historical reference. L. S. B. Leakey, the anthropologist who has worked most on the Kikuyu, produced at the time of the Mau Mau emergency two books, *Mau Mau and the Kikuyu* (London, 1952) and *Defeating Mau Mau* (London, 1954), of which the former, in particular, has historical material of value. The politics of the post-Mau Mau period have been examined in George Bennett and Carl G. Rosberg, Jr., *The Kenyatta Election: Kenya 1960-1961* (London, 1961), while personal comments of the two leading politicians of the period have appeared in Tom J. Mboya's *Freedom and After* (London, 1963) and Sir Michael Blundell's *So Rough a Wind* (London, 1964). Rosberg is presently completing, with John Nottingham, a study of the development of Kikuyu political movements; Bennett's *Kenya, a Political History: The Colonial Period* (London) appeared on Kenya's independence day in 1963.

The year of Kenyan independence also saw the appearance of a useful study of *The Political Development of Tanganyika* (Stanford) by James Clagett Taylor. This may be read with *Tanganyika and International Trusteeship* (London, 1961) by Barnard T. G. Chidzero, an African from Southern Rhodesia. It remains unfortunate that Margaret Louise Bates's most valuable Oxford D. Phil. thesis has not been published, though it does form the basis for her lengthy and informative chapter, "Tanganyika," in *African One-Party States,* edited by Gwendolen M. Carter (Ithaca, 1962). For Zanzibar the story has been taken to 1913 by Lawrence William Hollingsworth in *Zanzibar under the Foreign Office, 1890-1913* (London, 1953), while its more recent politics are being examined by a young American scholar, Michael F.

4. *Political Studies,* V (June, 1957), 113-30.
5. For detailed references on this, see George Bennett, "Kenyatta and the Kikuyu: Review Article," *International Affairs* (London), XXXVII (Oct., 1961), 477-82.

Lofchie. He has so far produced two interesting articles: "Party Conflict in Zanzibar," *Journal of Modern African Studies* (Cambridge), I (1963), 660-71, and "Zanzibar," in *Political Parties and National Integration in Tropical Africa* (Berkeley, 1964) edited by James Smoot Coleman and Carl G. Rosberg, Jr. On Uganda there is a stock and solid history by Kenneth Ingham, written while he was Professor of History at Makerere: *The Making of Modern Uganda* (London, 1958). He followed this with *A History of East Africa* (London, 1962) in which he made a bold attempt to examine the development of the region as a whole, weaving together in subject chapters, such as the European conquest, politics, and economics, the territorial stories which are usually treated in isolation one from another. The attempt was particularly valuable for, as the East Africa Royal Commission Report indicated in 1955, the territorial boundaries often lead to mutual ignorance in East Africa, and the writing of history has suffered in this way also.

Now, at Oxford, a three-volume *History of East Africa* is appearing. The first volume (1963) treats of the period before European colonial rule, though it does take the story down to 1894 for the British sphere of influence and to 1898 for the German. Its editors, Professor Roland A. Oliver and the Reverend Gervase Mathew, insist on the need for a new approach to the history of East Africa. It must now be attempted from the point of view of the region itself. One effect of the period of colonial rule has been that it has been seen too often from the outside. To understand the work of the colonial administrators it has been necessary to examine the events of East Africa against a wider Imperial background.

The appearance of the Oxford volumes (2nd., 1965), together with Ingham's single volume, does provide a convenient opportunity to assess the progress made in the last quarter of a century, since the publication of Coupland's two volumes. Briefly, there has been an advance in time and space. Coupland's history was basically one of the coast and it did not go beyond 1890. The subsequent advance has focused mainly upon Kenya, where European settlement has provoked much of the writing, and upon the kingdom of Buganda. There, in its capital, the academics at Makerere have, if anything, increased the natural concentration of interest upon this fascinating African kingdom. In contrast one is compelled to note vast untouched areas of East Africa on which detailed historical study might well be carried out. It is, perhaps, surprising that histories of tribes have not been more often attempted. The Chagga in Tanganyika have commissioned a history of themselves (Kathleen M. Stahl, *History of the Chagga People of Kilimanjaro* [The Hague, 1964]), but not many tribes are capable of such action. During the British period Tanganyika was the mainland territory least served by historians but perhaps this is only a comment on its generally peaceful and uneventful development.

Yet it is not only regionally that much remains to be done. The writers on economic history in the Oxford *History of East Africa* break much new ground. The Asian community, which has made such a large and important contribution to East African development, has never been studied by a historian. This may be due in part to the lack of effective economic work but possibly still more to the difficulty European writers have felt in studying this community. The experts on India have not come over to help—though there is some basic material in Chenchal Kondapi's *Indians Overseas, 1838-1949* (New Delhi, 1951)—and no Asian in East Africa has yet emerged as a historian.

More important, Africans themselves must start to reassess their own past as historians. East Africa has not yet produced a counterpart of K. Onwuka Dike in Nigeria, though some have hopes that one may not be long in appearing. The editors of the Oxford *History* have called for the writing of East African history from the focal point of the region itself. We need to go further: to express the hope that Africans will soon give us an internal picture of their history, especially for the period of colonial rule. Attempts have been, and are being, made to probe the African past through the collection of oral traditions; already it is clear that this can have only a limited value for the remote past but surely it would be profitable for Africans to work on the personal memories of people alive today in the hope of evolving a full picture of how colonial rule looked from underneath. Our picture of East Africa is still too European-centered—it has been based so far mainly on European records, governmental, missionary and commercial. We must hope that African writers will be able to remedy this by producing, in the full scholarly tradition, balanced accounts that will display more fully the rich tapestry that must be made of East African history if it is to be a full account of an area which has seen the meeting of peoples from three continents.

# BRITISH WEST AFRICA

## Harrison M. Wright

THE FORMER British West African territories—Gambia, Sierra Leone, Ghana, and Nigeria[1]—present a typical historiographical problem in that they may be studied usefully from many points of view. To the Imperial historian the four territories considered together, although geographically disconnected and in many ways dissimilar, make an appropriate unit of variations on a single theme. To the historian of the now-developing independent states, on the other hand, the local background of the individual territories is far more important than the tenuous British connection which existed among them in earlier years. And to the historian of non-political or of precolonial history the boundaries of the territories themselves often seem arbitrary and irrelevant compared to cultural or natural geographic divisions within West Africa as a whole. Depending upon one's historical perspective, in other words, the four territories may be treated as a unit, or separately, or may be largely disregarded as political entities. Yet while these three as well as other approaches are all perfectly valid ones, historiographical essays have to be restricted in their scope. After considering the general development of historical attitudes toward the four territories, therefore, this essay will concentrate primarily on the period of British contact from the point of view of the histories of the individual countries.

Compared to most other Commonwealth areas British West Africa has an extremely sketchy historical literature, because professional historians and West Africa had only the most incidental connection with each other until after 1945. For perfectly obvious reasons there were virtually no professional historians, either African or British, actually living in West Africa until after World War II. The Africans were too busy with other tasks; there were no British settlers; and

1. Ghana (formerly, the Gold Coast), Nigeria, Sierra Leone, and The Gambia became independent in 1957, 1960, 1961, and 1965 respectively.

the few British visitors who stayed any length of time were occupied with exploration, trade, religion, and administration. The only body of professional historical tradition concerned at all with the area emanated from Britain itself. But the British historians did not spend very much time on West Africa. They were not interested in the indigenous population. Many felt that except for those areas where there had been significant Islamic influence the West Africans had hardly changed for millennia before the time of European contact and that in any case the absence of written sources made uncovering the African past impossible. Nor was there much interest in so far as the British connection with the area was concerned. The West African territories, unlike India or the settlement colonies, were usually not sufficiently in the public eye or considered important enough in their effects on British policy to be studied in detail.

This is not to say that no worthwhile history relating to West Africa was written before the war. In three fairly distinct streams non-historian visitors, Africans, and historians in Britain produced works which variously illuminated different aspects of the West African past. And while much of what they wrote lost its historical "respectability" in the general reassessment of African history which has taken place since the war, each stream foreshadowed and contributed to the new developments.

The non-historians interested in West Africa wrote several kinds of history. Some were explicitly historical in aim, in that a number of civil servants attempted general histories of the territories in which they worked. As might be expected these books were very much alike in their patently British orientation: the areas considered were British administrative units, the time covered was almost exclusively that of European contact, the sources used were European published works combined with occasional eye-witness recollections, and in spite of broad-sounding titles the subject matter was essentially a narrative of European activities and relations with the Africans from a British point of view. William Walton Claridge, a medical officer who had been stationed in the Gold Coast, wrote *A History of the Gold Coast and Ashanti* (2 vols.; London, 1915; 2nd ed., 1964), an extremely lengthy narrative consisting for the most part of nineteenth-century diplomatic and military relations between the British and the Ashanti and coastal peoples. Alan (later Sir Alan) C. Burns, after twelve years in the civil service in Nigeria, in 1929 published his well-known *History of Nigeria* (6th ed., London, 1963), a book much like Claridge's although shorter and slightly more concerned with problems of British administration. John (later Sir John) M. Gray, like Burns, to write history throughout his colonial career, brought out *A History of The Gambia* (Cambridge, 1940) just before the war. Although based on extensive manuscript sources, it was nonetheless essentially similar to the others in its point of view and structure. These books, and many like them, are much criticized today. Yet in spite of their limited scope and typically scissors-and-paste construction, they were written by men of moderate attitudes and considerable sympathy toward the Africans, and they are still useful for students of British colonial activities.

After World War I, when the problems developing out of indirect rule and the new attitudes engendered by the mandate system claimed the attention of social scientists and others, non-historians produced a series of well-known works concerned primarily with administrative policy, in which history was largely a by-product. In 1922 Frederick Dealtry, Lord Lugard published his famous Imperial credo, *The Dual Mandate in British Tropical Africa* (Edinburgh, 1922), which reflected the contemporary changes in colonial theory. Colonial administrators gave support to anthropological research, and government officers such as Rattray in the Gold Coast and Talbot and Meek in Nigeria made detailed studies of existing African societies. In following years anthropologists and social scientists wrote important books analyzing the nature and effects of colonial policy on African ways of life. Raymond Leslie Buell, an American political scientist, provided a mine of information on that topic in his massive work, *The Native Problem in Africa* (2 vols.; New York, 1928). Lucy P. Mair's briefer *Native Policies in Africa* (London, 1936) and Margery Freda Perham's specialized *Native Administration in Nigeria* (London, 1937) followed, both being earnest apologies for indirect rule. Perhaps the most influential of these books was the monumental study directed by William Malcolm, Lord Hailey, *An African Survey, A Study of Problems Arising in Africa South of the Sahara* (London, 1938; rev. ed., 1957), which considered all aspects of European rule in tropical Africa. While these books were often concerned with Africa as a whole, rather than West Africa only, and were an attempt to deal with contemporary rather than exclusively historical problems, they provided the most stimulating West African history written before the war. In their historical sections they dealt not only with European activities but with the interaction between the Europeans and the Africans. Still relying for the most part on the old historical sources, they nevertheless fruitfully combined a new subject matter with non-historical concepts and techniques in a way that professional historians would not undertake seriously until the postwar period.

The histories written by Africans before the war—concerned with African political units, largely based on oral tradition, filled with details of local African history—were in many ways the antitheses of those written by Claridge, Burns, and Gray. They usually reflected a desire to preserve traditional oral histories before they were forgotten. About 1890 the Reverend Carl Christian Reindorf, of Ga-Danish descent and a minister in the Basel mission, published *The History of the Gold Coast and Asante* (2nd ed., Basel, [1951]), covering events to 1856 and showing both a Ga and a Christian bias. The Anglican pastor of Oyo, a Yoruba, the Reverend Samuel Johnson, wrote *The History of the Yorubas, from the Earliest Times to the Beginning of the British Protectorate* (London, 1921) before the turn of the century, a long work emphasizing nineteenth-century narrative. In northern Nigeria, meanwhile, "The Kano Chronicle" was written down in Arabic, later to be translated and published along with similar documents by the Englishman Herbert Richmond Palmer.[2] Of the many other West African chronicles perhaps the best known is Jacob Egharevba's *A Short History of Benin* (3rd ed., Ibadan, 1960), brought out first in 1934. For present-day purposes all of these works suffer from their unsophisticated efforts to deal with oral sources critically, but they are still important in their recording of tradition which might otherwise have been entirely lost and because they represented the first attempts to produce West African history from the perspective of the Africans.

For the prewar professional historians in Britain, West Africa held only a peripheral interest, related to its association with Imperial history as a whole. West Africa was mentioned as an aspect of European exploration, of the slave trade and its abolition, and of late-nineteenth-century European expansion. But in the various books written about different aspects of the slave trade, for example, there was scarcely a

2. In *Sudanese Memoirs* (Lagos, 1928), III, 92-132.

reference to the impact of the trade or its abolition on West Africa itself. Even Elizabeth Donnan's immense and valuable collection of *Documents Illustrative of the History of the Slave Trade to America* (4 vols.; Washington, 1930-35) and Hugh A. Wyndham's scholarly *The Atlantic and Slavery* (London, 1935), both of which had material on West Africa, considered the trade there largely from the European point of view.[3] The few specialized studies on West Africa were similar in this respect. Eveline C. Martin's *The British West African Settlements, 1750-1821: A Study in Local Administration* (London, 1927) compared British administrative activities (but not their effects) in three West African holdings; John W. Blake's *European Beginnings in West Africa, 1454-1578* (London, 1937) discussed the diplomacy of early European rivalry; and Sybil E. Crowe's *The Berlin West African Conference, 1884-1885* (London, 1942) re-examined the European negotiations of that conference in detail. Where the rising historical interest in social and economic questions touched West Africa, a different emphasis—although still within the general Imperial framework—could sometimes be found. Allan McPhee's *The Economic Revolution in British West Africa* (London, 1926) was a pioneer work on recent British activities and their impact. Chapter II, Part II,

3. The works of Donnan and Wyndham are also among the very few which contributed to an understanding of the slave trade during the years when it was at its peak. For the most part the prewar literature on the slave trade was concerned with the British movement for abolition, and it was closely bound up with similar examinations of the campaign against slavery itself and of British humanitarianism in general. The scholarly works on the subject tended to be either broad analyses of British attitudes and activities or biographies of prominent anti-slavery propagandists. Of the former perhaps the best-known and still most useful are Frank J. Klingberg's *The Anti-Slavery Movement in England: A Study in English Humanitarianism* (New Haven, 1926), William Law Mathieson's *Great Britain and the Slave Trade, 1839-1865* (London, 1929), Reginald (later Sir Reginald) Coupland's *The British Anti-Slavery Movement* (London, 1933; 2nd ed., 1964), and Wyndham's more general *The Atlantic and Emancipation* (London, 1937). Of the latter there were such studies as Coupland's eulogistic *Wilberforce, a Narrative* (Oxford, 1923), Charles Booth's brief but balanced *Zachary Macaulay* ... (London, 1934), and Earl Leslie Griggs' *Thomas Clarkson, the Friend of Slaves* (London, 1936). By and large these books presented the traditional view that the anti-slavery crusade was essentially humanitarian in its origins, a view that was vigorously challenged by the important and controversial book of Eric E. Williams, *Capitalism and Slavery* (Chapel Hill, 1944; London, 1964), which emphasized the economic self-interest of the abolitionists. Although valuable from the point of view of general Imperial history, however, none of these works shed much light on West Africa or even on Britain's relation to it. While the study of slavery and its end seemed naturally to involve West Indian as well as British Imperial history, the study of the slave trade did not at this time lead to a comparable interest in West African affairs. Some of the more recent books have done so, however, and are mentioned later in this essay.

of William Keith (later Sir Keith) Hancock's famous *Survey of British Commonwealth Affairs* (2 vols.; London, 1937-42) analyzed current British economic policies in her West African colonies through a detailed study of the effects of past policies on African society. It was a model of economic history. Although on the whole the Imperial viewpoint of the British historians was soon to be outdated and rather condescendingly criticized, this viewpoint was a valid one. And in their application of serious historical techniques, particularly in the early exploitation of manuscript sources, the Imperial historians contributed an indispensable ingredient to postwar developments.

The changes which developed in the attitudes and techniques of West African history after the war resulted from influences similar to those occurring at the same time in other British colonial areas: the commitment to political liberalization with its growing realization of the importance of the Africans themselves; the flood of technicians and scholars to the area resulting from the concomitant interest in social, economic, and intellectual affairs; the rising concern of Americans and others for non-European peoples and their problems. Perhaps the most important development for the study of British West African history was the postwar establishment of university colleges in the Gold Coast and Nigeria and the reorganization of Fourah Bay College in Sierra Leone, actions which not only brought professional historians to West Africa for the first time but also began the local training of African students in history as well as other disciplines.

The need for reassessment of attitudes and techniques was recognized at an early date. John W. Blake's thoughtful "The Study of African History,"[4] for example, decried the obsoleteness of continuing to write African history from a purely European standpoint and pleaded for "an integrated study of African history from the point of view of the Africans." Concern for technique followed naturally from such a change in perspective. Except for manuscripts in the areas influenced by Islam there are few written sources for the study of West African history outside the times and areas of past European contact. And on the coast the European and other manuscripts have been subjected to constant deterioration and loss. The historian who is to study West African history from the point of view of the Africans, in other

---

4. *Transactions of the Royal Historical Society* (London), 4th ser., XXXII (1950), 49-69. The quotation is from p. 69.

words, cannot rely solely on traditional historical methods. He must be able to cope with linguistic, anthropological, and archaeological techniques, and with the evaluation of oral tradition, as well as with the written word.

The period since the war has been concerned primarily with these new problems. To be sure a great deal of West African history has recently been written with a European perspective—partly through the inertia of historians, partly because so much work along those lines still needs to be done, and partly because the overwhelmingly European orientation of most manuscript sources has sometimes shaped the approach of authors in a way they have not intended. But the trend has been toward breaking down the traditional categories of research and subject matter. In the past decade it has been intensified by the political revolution of African independence and by the arrival of the first professional African historians.

The steps taken have been various. Shortly after the war, in the three larger territories, groundwork was laid for the establishment of historical archives. Historians and others started the *Transactions of the Historical Society of Ghana* (Legon)[5] and the *Journal of the Historical Society of Nigeria* (Ibadan) in 1953 and 1956, respectively, while in the former year, *Sierra Leone Studies* (Freetown), a more general magazine, reappeared after a fourteen-year lapse in a new series under historical direction. These three periodicals, with *The Journal of African History*, published by the Cambridge Press since 1960, have helped to fill the crucial need for periodicals in a rapidly developing field. To contribute to the publication of longer works, the Oxford Press began a new "West African History Series," edited by Gerald S. Graham. Meanwhile, the first Conference on African History and Archaeology, held in 1953, and its quadrennial successors have brought together students of different disciplines to review their recent work. There have been begun as well a few interdisciplinary research projects, most notably the elaborate five-year Benin Historical Research Scheme initiated in 1957.

Even for historians concerned with the history of the four individual territories since the early years of European contact, the studies of archaeologists, anthropologists, and linguists are indispensable, if only

5. Until 1957 known as the *Transactions of the Gold Coast and Togoland Historical Society.*

to understand the nature of the African response to European impact. Yet these disciplines have also been adjusting to the African environment and their literature is already enormous, so that only a few works can be mentioned here. *The Ethnographic Survey of Africa*, a series edited by Cyril Daryll Forde and published by the International African Institute in London, provides introductory anthropological studies with extensive bibliographies of many of the important indigenous societies. A number of longer works on individual societies by modern anthropologists consider the crucial problems of culture change in some detail. Anthropological periodicals, such as *Africa* (London), have a wide range of specialized studies. General background can be found in George P. Murdock's highly controversial *Africa, Its Peoples and Their Culture History* (New York, 1959)[6] and in the older but more reliable and more comprehensive book of Hermann Baumann and Diedrich Westermann, *Les peuples et les civilisations de l'Afrique* (Paris, 1948). Joseph Harold Greenberg's *Studies in African Linguistic Classification* (New Haven, 1955) has virtually revolutionized the classification of African languages, and hence the historical deductions which may be drawn therefrom.[7] In the matter of unraveling oral traditions, Jan Vansina's discussion of theory and technique in his *Oral Traditions: A Study in Historical Methodology* (London, 1965),[8] although its examples are drawn largely from the Congo, has, like all such methodological analyses, great relevance for historians of West Africa. Particularly useful discussions of method in general may be found in the reports of the successive conferences on African History and Archaeology, especially that of the conference of 1961.[9] Such

6. For one analysis of Murdock's book, see John D. Fage, "Anthropology, Botany, and the History of Africa," *The Journal of African History* (London), II (1961), 299-309.

7. Revised and expanded as *The Languages of Africa* (The Hague, 1963). For criticism of Greenberg's work see Malcolm Guthrie, "Some Developments in the Prehistory of the Bantu Languages," *The Journal of African History*, III (1962), 273-82.

8. Originally published in French as *De la tradition orale: Essai de methode historique* (Tervuren, Belgium, 1961). A local example of the methodological problems involved in working with oral sources may be seen in Eva L. R. Meyerowitz's volumes about the origins of the Africans in Ghana and in the increasingly devastating criticism these volumes have drawn forth. See, for example, Jack (John) Goody, "Ethnohistory and the Akan of Ghana," *Africa*, XXIX (Jan., 1959), 67-81, and R. W. Wescott, "Ancient Egypt and Modern Africa," *The Journal of African History*, II (1961), 311-21.

9. "Third Conference on African History and Archaeology 1961," *The Journal of African History*, III (1962), 173-374. For the earlier conferences see Robert A.

studies as these are necessary for anyone who wishes to understand and to deal with African subject matter and African materials.

For consideration of some of the broad themes of Imperial activity in British West Africa the prewar books are often still useful, but they have been supplemented recently by works with more emphasis on affairs in West Africa itself. John W. Blake's collection of documents for the Hakluyt Society, *Europeans in West Africa, 1450-1560* (2 vols.; London, 1942), is probably the best source of information on early European coastal activities. Kenneth G. Davies' *The Royal African Company* (London, 1957), though England-oriented, has a very good section on the Company's trade in West Africa, while Christopher Lloyd's *The Navy and the Slave Trade* (London, 1949) is a popularized but still relevant narrative of the suppression of the trade along the African coasts. There are a great many reprints of explorers' journals with historical introductions, Cecil Howard, ed., *West African Explorers* (London, 1951) being a handy one. A. Adu Boahen's *Britain, the Sahara and the Western Sudan, 1788-1861* (Oxford, 1964) deals with British penetration into the interior. *British Policy Towards West Africa: Select Documents, 1786-1874* (Oxford, 1964), a collection of sources edited by Colin W. Newbury, reflects a century of British official policy. Its documents (briefly introduced) are drawn primarily from state papers. For the understanding of British attitudes and policies in general, Philip D. Curtin's *The Image of Africa: British Ideas and Action, 1780-1850* (Madison, 1964) is a significant and highly original contribution. It considers early nineteenth-century British opinion on Africa and the Africans in all its aspects and is, because of the nature of British activity at the time, particularly concerned with West Africa.

For missionary efforts the best introduction is Charles Pelham Groves' *The Planting of Christianity in Africa* (4 vols.; London, 1948-58), supplemented by Kenneth Scott Latourette's works—in particular, Volume V of *A History of the Expansion of Christianity* (New York, 1943)— and the many individual mission histories and biographies. The study of the partition of West Africa has for years required a thorough overhaul, the older general books by Keltie, Johnston, and Lucas being now largely out-of-date. A recent book, *Africa and the Vic-*

Hamilton, ed., *History and Archaeology in Africa: Report of a Conference Held in July 1953 . . .* (London, 1955), and D. H. Jones, ed., *History and Archaeology in Africa: Second Conference Held in July 1957 . . .* (London, 1959).

*torians: The Official Mind of Imperialism* (London, 1961), by Ronald Robinson and John Gallagher with Alice Denny, unfortunately pushes its thesis so hard that it creates serious distortion where West Africa is concerned. The most thorough study at present, although restricted to the years before 1885, is John D. Hargreaves' *Prelude to the Partition of West Africa* (London, 1963), which considers the policies of Britain and France and their relations with West African states. Finally, the history of Africa as a whole has been best treated recently in Roland A. Oliver and John D. Fage's excellent *A Short History of Africa* (Harmondsworth, 1962), which places particular emphasis on pre-European history.

Of the individual territories Ghana has, for its size, been the most thoroughly covered by recent historians. Two general histories reflect some of the changes and difficulties of the postwar period. William E. F. Ward's *A History of Ghana* (2nd ed., London, 1958), first published in 1948[10] (although largely written much earlier), is based on Claridge's work but attempts to supplement it by the addition of new material on internal African history and on social and economic developments. But while advanced for its time, it is still Claridge amended, not Ghanaian history rethought. John D. Fage—whose school text *An Introduction to the History of West Africa* (3rd ed., Cambridge, 1962) is probably the best short introduction to general West African history—recently published the brief but important *Ghana, A Historical Interpretation* (Madison, 1959). This is a stimulating rethinking, certainly, but it nonetheless suffers in turn from a necessary reliance on the inadequate historical research which even Ghana has had to date. It shows such syntheses perhaps still somewhat premature, although the situation has been improving rapidly since 1959.

Changes in interpretation are most effectively resulting today from intensive studies of small areas. Two students in particular have been revising aspects of Ghanaian history in the early period of European contact by their careful use of manuscript materials. Ivor Wilks uses Dutch, Danish, and British sources to bring to life "The Rise of the Akwamu Empire, 1650-1710,"[11] a hitherto largely neglected political unit, while his *The Northern Factor in Ashanti History* ([Legon],

10. The 1948 edition was entitled *A History of the Gold Coast.*
11. *Transactions of the Historical Society of Ghana,* III (1957), 99-136.

1961) traces the little-suspected impact of Islam on Ashanti development. Margaret Priestley's "The Ashanti Question and the British: Eighteenth-Century Origins"[12] pushes back by decades the beginning of significant British-Ashanti relations; and both authors combine in the important article "The Ashanti Kings in the Eighteenth Century: A Revised Chronology."[13]

For the period since 1800 the interest generated by recent political developments combined with the natural bias of the source materials have produced primarily works on political history, to which, as always in Africa, not only historians but scholars in other disciplines have contributed. George Edgar Metcalfe's *Maclean of the Gold Coast: The Life and Times of George Maclean, 1801-1847* (London, 1962) is a solid and impressive biography based on official documents. With wide-ranging materials David Kimble's *A Political History of Ghana: The Rise of Gold Coast Nationalism, 1850-1928* (Oxford, 1963) is a detailed, substantial, and important analysis and narrative of the background to the nationalist movement. Douglas Coombs provides a diplomatic coverage in his *The Gold Coast, Britain, and the Netherlands, 1850-1874* (London, 1963). An older book, by Florence M. Bourret, most recently entitled *Ghana: The Road to Independence, 1919-1957* (Stanford, 1960),[14] typifies the early postwar American interest in Africa, with all its disadvantages of unfamiliarity and all its advantages of detachment. Based on published sources only, it is a balanced but essentially factual coverage. The sociologists Kofi A. Busia's *The Position of the Chief in the Modern Political System of Ashanti* (London, 1951) shows the impact of British administration upon Ashanti political institutions before 1945, while an American political study of great insight but somewhat awkward terminology, David Ernest Apter's *The Gold Coast in Transition* (Princeton, 1955),[15] deals primarily with the first decade of postwar nationalism. A large collection of documents, mostly official, covering a period of one hundred and fifty years, may be found in *Great Britain and Ghana: Documents of Ghana History, 1807-1957* (Legon, 1964), edited by George E. Metcalfe.

12. *The Journal of African History*, II (1961), 35-59.
13. *Ibid.*, I (1960), 83-96.
14. The first (1949) edition was entitled *The Gold Coast: A Survey of the Gold Coast and British Togoland, 1919-1946.*
15. A revised edition (New York, 1963), entitled *Ghana in Transition*, has a chapter interpreting the events of recent years.

For the most recent period more informal books are also illuminating: George Padmore's *The Gold Coast Revolution: The Struggle of an African People from Slavery to Freedom* (London, 1953), a polemical work on the rise of Ghanaian nationalism as one of the actors in the movement saw it; J. Godson Amamoo's *The New Ghana: The Birth of a Nation* (London, 1958), a simple but clear account of the events leading to independence; and *The Autobiography of Kwame Nkrumah* (Edinburgh, 1957), an interesting insight into that leader's motives and activities.[16] The latest and most important work on recent Ghanaian history, however, is the scholarly and detailed political study by Dennis Austin, entitled *Politics in Ghana, 1946-1960* (London, 1964).

Of social and economic history about Ghana there is not yet much. *Pageant of Ghana* (London, 1958), an anthology of comments and descriptions from 1471 to 1957 edited by Freda Wolfson, is a suitable introduction, and Polly Hill has made important contributions to one facet of economic history in *The Migrant Cocoa-Farmers of Southern Ghana* (Cambridge, 1963) and in other studies. But the material is difficult and enormous amounts of work remain to be done.

Historical work on The Gambia and Sierra Leone is also in its infancy and so far largely unaffected by postwar developments. Bella Sidney, Lady Southorn, the wife of a former Governor, wrote *The Gambia: The Story of the Groundnut Colony* (London, 1952), a pleasant but episodic history in the old tradition. *A History of the Gambia* (London, 1964), by Harry A. Gailey, Jr., is a useful and straightforward account emphasizing British policy in the modern period. A. Peter Kup's *A History of Sierra Leone, 1400-1787* (Cambridge, 1961) suffers from lack of coherence and from an essentially European viewpoint for a time when few Europeans were about. In *A History of Sierra Leone* (London, 1962) Christopher Fyfe has produced a lengthy and carefully documented description of life in Sierra Leone from about 1787 to 1900 pegged to the activities of the British governors. Its wealth of detail and documentation make it useful in spite of its unfortunately rather unimaginative conception and organization. A more penetrating analysis of Freetown social history in the nineteenth century is Arthur T. Porter's succinct *Creoledom: A Study of The Development of Freetown Society*

16. For Nkrumah's views at a later date, one should also see his *I Speak of Freedom: A Statement of African Ideology* (London, 1961) and *Africa Must Unite* (New York, 1963).

(London, 1963), which combines historical and sociological techniques, while on the political side John D. Hargreaves has written one of the few biographies of a West African in his *A Life of Sir Samuel Lewis* (London, 1958). Christopher Fyfe has recently edited *Sierra Leone Inheritance* (London, 1964), a collection of documents largely devoted to the period before 1900, but extending to the time of independence.

A considerable amount of history has been written about Nigeria, but because of the size and nature of the country it is still painfully inadequate. As with the three other territories, there is no really satisfactory general history for the country as a whole. Arthur Norton Cook's *British Enterprise in Nigeria* (Philadelphia, 1943), for example, based on printed sources and an out-of-date point of view, should have been long since superseded, but on British policy it can still be helpful. Thomas Hodgkin's valuable *Nigerian Perspectives: An Historical Anthology* (London, 1960) has an excellent short historical chapter in addition to a broad range of selections, but unfortunately ends with the year 1900. The latest contribution, Michael Crowder's *The Story of Nigeria* (London, 1962), is a balanced and straightforward account based for the most part on recent secondary sources.

More specialized studies about Nigeria have followed a pattern similar to Ghana's. The anthropologist R. E. Bradbury's revision, "Chronological Problems in the Study of Benin History,"[17] written with the co-operation of the historian Alan F. C. Ryder, is one of the first fruits of the Benin project. A rare diary of an eighteenth-century African trader can be found in *Efik Traders of Old Calabar* (London, 1956), edited by Cyril Daryll Forde. For the nineteenth century, as usual, the materials available have influenced both subject matter and points of view. Colin W. Newbury's *The Western Slave Coast and Its Rulers* (Oxford, 1961), for example, although it cuts across European administrative boundaries by discussing European contact along a wide stretch of coast, is still almost exclusively based on European sources and concerned with European activity. Several enthusiastic biographies of Mary Kingsley, author of the well-known *Travels in West Africa* (London, 1897) and *West African Studies* (London, 1899), follow the line of least resistance by extolling her personality but neglecting her relation to West African history. In an extreme case, George Taub-

17. *Journal of the Historical Society of Nigeria*, I (Dec., 1959), 263-87.

man Goldie's deliberate destruction of his private papers forced John E. Flint's excellent *Sir George Goldie and the Making of Nigeria* (London, 1960) to broaden into a history of the Royal Niger Company. Margery Freda Perham's impressive biography of *Lugard* (2 vols.; London, 1956-60) uncovers new material of great importance in a warmly sympathetic portrait, although it has little space for the African context within which Lugard's activities took place.

While obviously much of the period of European penetration must be focused at least partially on European activities, it is necessary in Nigeria, as elsewhere, to study also the impact of this movement on the Africans, as the new postwar attitude proclaims. Kenneth Onwuka Dike's *Trade and Politics in the Niger Delta, 1830-1885* (Oxford, 1956) is of great importance not only because it is the first book on British West Africa by a professional African historian but also because it is the first careful examination of nineteenth-century African societies under the influence of European pressure. A similar, if shorter, study is Saburi O. Biobaku's *The Egba and Their Neighbours, 1842-1872* (Oxford, 1957). Although both authors rely heavily on European documents and emphasize diplomatic and commercial relations with the Europeans rather than internal history, the points of view and the social units considered in these books are African at last. Dike, born near Onitsha in Eastern Nigeria, was educated in Ghana and Sierra Leone as well as Nigeria, before going to the British Isles to complete his training. He is now Vice-Chancellor of the University of Ibadan. To many historians his book, in particular, marks the turning point in the new approach to British West African history. His work, for example, was in part the inspiration for an excellent study of the Eastern Delta states before 1885, Gwilym I. Jones's *The Trading States of the Oil Rivers: A Study of Political Development in Eastern Nigeria* (London, 1963), which carries the African perspective a step further in its concentration on internal political development and in its use of oral traditions and anthropological techniques. Two further books reflecting the new techniques and attitudes are James Bertin Webster's sympathetic *The African Churches Among the Yoruba, 1888-1922* (Oxford, 1964) and J. F. Ade Ajayi and Robert Sydney Smith's brief *Yoruba Warfare in the Nineteenth Century* (Cambridge, 1964).

Northern Nigeria, where British control came late, where there was already a venerable tradition of history in Arabic, and where much of the past was linked to the rest of the Sudan, has long been in a class by itself so far as the writing of history is concerned. Long ago Flora L. Shaw (Lady Lugard) in *A Tropical Dependency* (London, 1905) and Edward W. Bovill in *Caravans of the Old Sahara* (London, 1933[18] wrote well-known volumes on the western Sudan with special reference to the periods before 1800. John Spencer Trimingham has recently completed a more technical and up-to-date book with roughly the same subject matter, *A History of Islam in West Africa* (London, 1962), while Yves F. M. A. Urvoy, in *Histoire de l'empire du Bornou* (Paris, 1949), has written a specialized work also of considerable value on the pre-European developments. Although the nineteenth century has not been very well served, Michael G. Smith's *Government in Zazzau, 1800-1950* (London, 1960) is a significant study of changing political administration in Zaria by a social anthropologist who develops new concepts of social process and works with extremely complex sources. Historians should certainly, however, also consider Smith's methods of dealing with oral tradition in his later explanatory article, "Field Histories among the Hausa."[19]

A few works stand out on the history of Nigeria for the past fifty years. The most important is that of an American political scientist, James Smoot Coleman, whose *Nigeria: Background to Nationalism* (Berkeley, 1958) is a pioneer effort both in the utilization of available documents where the fifty-year rule is in effect and in the analysis of Nigerian political development to the early 1950's. Kalu Ezera's *Constitutional Developments in Nigeria* (Cambridge, 1960) is a balanced and sober, if less well-digested, view by a Nigerian sympathetic to both the nationalists and the British. Legal history has been considered by Taslim Olawale Elias in *Groundwork of Nigerian Law* (London, 1954) and in other studies. Finally, in its self-analysis of that important figure, *Awo: The Autobiography of Chief Obafemi Awolowo* (Cambridge, 1960) is one of the most revealing documents on modern Nigerian nationalism. And it has been supplemented by Alhaji Sir Ahmadu Bello's *My Life* (Cambridge, 1962) and by the less satisfactory *Zik: A Selection from the Speeches of Nnamdi Azikiwe*

18. Later rewritten and entitled *The Golden Trade of the Moors* (London, 1958). Lady Lugard's volume was reissued in 1964 (London).

19. *The Journal of African History*, II (1961), 87-101. In this regard see also H. F. Charles Smith's critical "The Dynastic Chronology of Fulani Zaria," *Journal of the Historical Society of Nigeria*, II (Dec., 1961), 277-85.

(Cambridge, 1961), which suffers from the lack of an explanatory text.

In spite of the recent historical efforts in Nigeria and elsewhere, however, it is not too much to say that work on the history of the four British West African territories is only just beginning. A few needs may be sketched. Manuscripts in West Africa are still largely uncatalogued, to begin with, and there are no really adequate bibliographies of published works. Perhaps the best introduction to the latter is H. A. Rydings' pamphlet, *The Bibliographies of West Africa* (Ibadan, 1961), which discusses the strengths and weaknesses of the various bibliographies which existed at that date. The most important bibliography concerned with British West Africa published since then has been Albert F. Johnson's *A Bibliography of Ghana, 1930-1961* (Evanston, 1964), which covers all aspects of Ghanaian life.

In spite of the self-conscious and frequently stated postwar reassessment, subject matter and approach have continued to be weighted toward political history in the modern period and—particularly where the obvious theme of nationalism is not available—with a European administrative point of view. A great deal of work along these lines of course still needs to be done. Guggisberg and Clifford, for example, require biographers. But the impact of the British on African political development has been much more seriously neglected. There should be studies of the nationalist movements in Sierra Leone and The Gambia, comparisons of political growth in the four areas, adequate biographies of Horton, Blyden, Sarbah, Hayford, Ofori Attah, Macaulay, and Azikiwe—to name a few of the projects which are needed.

Social, economic and intellectual history is even less developed. Analyses of the effects of the missionaries and of European trade at different times on African society should be made, beginning with the nineteenth century, where materials are so readily available. The study of the role of social groups, particularly of the prominent families of mixed descent along the coast, would make a valuable contribution to our understanding of the period. Works are needed on the relations between the coastal and interior peoples and on the development of urban communities along European lines. There have been only a few slight studies on the development and impact of Western education. And in all these prospective topics more, and more critical, use should be made of oral sources and of family-held papers.

For those places and times in which European contact was not significant, such as northern Ghana and the interior of Sierra Leone in the nineteenth century, historical studies are still virtually non-existent. The new techniques must be sharpened for these areas. H. F. Charles Smith, in "A Neglected Theme of West African History: The Islamic Revolutions of the 19th Century,"[20] points out the lack of work on purely African subjects even in Northern Nigeria, which is well-documented with written Arabic and Hausa sources.

In addition to gaps in subject matter and to difficulties of technique are problems of motivation and attitude toward the writing of African history which stem from the peculiar position of Africa in the world today. In 1953 Kenneth Onwuka Dike made an earnest and convincing plea in his "African History and Self-Government"[21] that the study of African history was necessary to give Africans self-respect and confidence by providing them with an understanding of their cultural heritage. This is a delicate matter in execution, however, and the temptation has occasionally arisen among non-African and African authors to over-compensate beyond the bounds of historical prudence in the name of political justice. At the same time, the world-wide demand for books on Africa has led popularizers with little apparent historical background to produce a multitude of works on all aspects of the field. Because of the embryonic state of African history, some of these books have had useful material in them, but the historical level is unfortunately not always high.[22]

While research is already in progress on a number of the topics mentioned above, and on other topics,[23] the revolution in the attitude

20. *Ibid.*, pp. 169-85.

21. *West Africa* (London), XXXVII (Feb. and March, 1953), 177-78, 225-26, 251.

22. The authors tend, for example, to be relatively innocent of current trends in general historical thinking (as in their references to European background), to be inconsistent from place to place according to the dramatic needs of particular points being made, to use questionable historical techniques (such as the exploitation of colorful but unrepresentative quotations, the assigning of motives without adequate substantiation, the use of equivocal vocabulary), and so on. The results may be suggestive, but they are also often somewhat unreliable. One of the best volumes of this genre is Basil Davidson's well-known and in many ways illuminating *Black Mother, Africa: The Years of Trial* (London, 1961), on the impact of the slave trade on African society between the fifteenth and nineteenth centuries. It has been published in Boston (1965) under the title *The African Slave Trade: Precolonial History, 1450-1850.*

23. Books, for example, will be published in the near future by Jean H. Kopytoff on "A Preface to Modern Nigeria: Sierra Leonians in Yoruba, 1830-1890" and by J. F. Ade Ajayi on Christian missionaries and their impact on Nigeria, 1841-91.

toward West African history which was announced after the war has, in the last analysis, only just gotten underway. The techniques are difficult, the students few, and much tempting work still needs to be done from the traditional perspectives where sources are familiar. But "an integrated study of African history from the point of view of the Africans" is a worthy goal; and the pursuit of it should add in time great depth and new dimensions to our understanding of the past relations between the four West African territories and Britain.[24]

24. I should like to acknowledge my thanks to the Ford Foundation for a Foreign Area Training Fellowship to Ghana in 1961-62.

# EGYPT AND THE SUDAN

## Robert O. Collins

ALTHOUGH IT IS THE FASHION, if not the duty, for writers of history to differ, past and present historians of Africa, the Middle East, and of the British Empire would agree that the history of the British occupation of the Nile Valley is of vital concern to their specialized studies.[1] Indeed, Ronald Robinson and John Gallagher, with Alice Denny, in *Africa and the Victorians: The Official Mind of Imperialism* (London, 1961), have made Egypt the linchpin of the European partition of Africa, the British occupation of which led inexorably to the creation of much of Britain's African empire. This in-

---

1. There are several useful bibliographies of modern Egypt and the Sudan. For Egypt the reader should consult René Maunier, *Bibliographie économique, juridique et sociale de l'Égypte moderne (1798-1916)* (Cairo, 1918), and the New York Public Library, *Modern Egypt, A List of References to Materials in the New York Public Library*, compiled by Ida A. Pratt under the direction of Richard Gottheil (New York, 1929). The other well-known bibliography of Egypt, Prince Ibrahim-Hilmy, *The Literature of Egypt and the Soudan from the Earliest Time to the Year 1885 . . .* (2 vols.; London, 1886-87), unfortunately has no subject index. Although these bibliographies refer to works in Arabic, the thorough student should consult Carl Brockelmann, *Geschichte der Arabischen Litteratur* (2 vols.; Weimar, 1898-1902), and 3 supplements (Leiden, 1937-42), and Yūsuf Ilyās Sarkīs, *Mu'jam al-Maṭbū'āt al-'Arabīyah wa-l-Mu'arrabah* ("Dictionary of Works in Arabic or Translated into Arabic") (Cairo, 1928-31). For more recent publications Yūsuf As'ad Dāghir, *Maṣādir al-Dirāsah al-Adabīyah: al-Fikr al-'Arabī al-Ḥadīth fī Siyar A'lāmihi* ("The Sources of Literary Study: Modern Arab Thought in the Biographies of its Great Men") (Beirut, 1955), should be supplemented by Charles Kuentz and M.-M. Anawati, *Bibliographe des ouvrages Arabes imprimés en Egypte en 1942, 1943, et 1944* (Cairo, 1949) and the publications of the Egyptian Library at Cairo, Dār al-Kutub, *Al-nashrah al-Miṣīyah li-l-Maṭbū'āt* ("The Egyptian Publications Bulletin"), published triennually since 1956. The Sudan is even better served than Egypt for comprehensive bibliographies. First and foremost is Richard Leslie Hill, *A Bibliography of the Anglo-Egyptian Sudan, from the Earliest Times to 1937* (London, 1939), and its sequel, Abdel Rahman el-Nasri, *A Bibliography of the Sudan 1938-1958* (London, 1962). Although both these bibliographies contain works in Arabic, again the student should consult Brockelmann. For literature concerning the Sudan since 1958, *Sudan Notes and Records* (Khartoum) publishes reviews and book and periodical lists of the latest materials. Hill has also written a stimulating bibliographical essay entitled "Historical Writing on the Sudan since 1820," Bernard Lewis and Peter Malcolm Holt, eds., in *Historians of the Middle East* (London, 1962), pp. 357-66.

terpretation, like others before it, has been challenged, but the controversy rages over the motives of British imperialism, not the importance of Egypt and the Sudan to the expansion of the British Empire.[2] Yet in spite of its consequences, British rule in Egypt and the Sudan has attracted the attention of hardly any established historians and few beginners, and its history still remains largely the product of British proconsuls.

This imbalance of historical inquiry into the British imperium on the Nile is in part understandable. No professional historian of today, who claims his methods to be scientific even if his conclusions are not, would feel confident or comfortable writing about British rule in Egypt and the Sudan without at least a working knowledge of Arabic. More particularly, Empire historians have displayed little interest in British rule in Egypt and the Sudan precisely because these two countries occupied an anomalous position within the British Empire. Except for the few short years between 1914 and 1922 Egypt was never officially a protectorate or a colony, while the Sudan was theoretically ruled as a condominium in which both Britain and Egypt shared sovereignty. Moreover, neither country became part of the Commonwealth upon which so much of the energies of Empire historians has recently been expended. Indeed, one cannot help sympathizing with those historians of the British Empire who wish to avoid the shoals of bitterness that today mark the channel of Anglo-Egyptian relations, preferring to steer through clear water to the more faithful dependencies. Even European and American historians of the Arabs and the Turks have turned from British rule in Egypt, leaving that subject to the Empire historians, who have already abandoned it. How much more exciting for those orientalists to plunge into the intricacies of Ottoman rule in Egypt than to investigate the Westernization imposed by officials from their own and consequently more comprehensible culture. And as for the Sudan, that vast land appears to the historian of the Middle East a dreary subject best left to the Africanists, who, however, are convinced that it belongs to the Arab world and not to what the medieval Muslim geographers called the Bilād al-Sūdān, Land of the Blacks. Like British rule in Egypt, the Anglo-Egyptian Sudan remains an historical backwater, the history of which has been left almost

2. See Jean Stengers, "L'Impérialisme colonial de la fin du XIXe siècle: mythe ou réalité," *Journal of African History* (Cambridge), III (1962), 469-91.

exclusively in the hands of the olympian administrators who ruled the length and breadth of the Nile Valley.

Before the British occupation of Egypt in 1882, the shortest route from London to Cairo frequently passed through Constantinople, where the declining Ottomans played the Great Powers against one another in order to maintain an ever-diminishing claim to Egypt, while their viceroys on the Nile played everyone against everyone else to their own satisfaction and a remarkable degree of independence. Those were the violent years when Muḥammad 'Alī dragged a reluctant Egypt into the nineteenth century and his profligate grandson, Ismā 'īl Pasha, prematurely tried to drag an even more reluctant Egypt into the twentieth. Before 1882 Britain's rôle at Cairo was subordinate to the French, which was surprising for a nation of shopkeepers and sea-men, but the diplomatic intrigues have been brilliantly unraveled by Harold W. V. Temperley, *England and the Near East: The Crimea* (London, 1936), and the more recent but general work of John Marlowe, *A History of Modern Egypt and Anglo-Egyptian Relations, 1800-1956* (New York, 1954; 2nd ed., Hamden, Conn., 1965), while the economic and financial manipulations, which were such a characteristic of power politics in nineteenth-century Egypt, have been given meaning in the wider terms of economic imperialism by David S. Landes, *Bankers and Pashas: International Finance and Economic Imperialism in Egypt* (Cambridge, Mass., 1958). This is all exciting and dramatic history, but history without watersheds, those great divides which delight the historian, guide the student, and frequently distort the truth.

The British occupation of Egypt in 1882 is just such a watershed, for although time has eroded the epic proportions of that event, the destruction of the Egyptian Army at Al-Tall al-Kabīr and the occupa-tion of the country by British forces changed the course of modern Egypt. New ideas and men came from Great Britain to dominate and to transform Egypt, and it is not surprising that historians have lingered over the drama as well as its significance. The best history of the British conquest of Egypt is Robinson and Gallagher's *Africa and the Victorians*—researched, analyzed, and written with depth and power. Its subtitle in the New York edition, "The Climax of Imperialism in the Dark Continent," is less indicative of its theme. No longer able to control at Cairo through influence and prestige as their mid-Victorian predecessors had done, the late Victorians were forced to occupy and to administer Egypt directly in order to protect the strategic routes to the great Indian empire and the East. By so doing, however, they triggered a chain reaction that ended only with the partition of the African continent. Revolving around the strategy of empire, this interpretation is a heady antidote for the many and muddled economic interpretations of imperialism that have captivated the ill-informed and driven to despair more critical men. Robinson and Gallagher have shown, as no others, the attitudes and assumptions of Victorian statesmen seeking to preserve an empire whose very reason for being they have begun to question. New methods of administration were employed to solve old Imperial problems, but few questioned the attitudes and assumptions by which the late Victorians applied those same solutions to a changing and expanding Empire. One who did challenge the assumptions of the official mind was that stormy petrel of the Nile, Wilfrid Scawen Blunt, whose *The Secret History of the English Occupation of Egypt . . .* (London, 1907), *Gordon at Khartoum . . .* (London, 1911), and his later denunciation of British administration in Egypt, *My Diaries: Being a Personal Narrative of Events, 1888-1914* (2 vols.; London, 1919-20), form a triad and a continuous tirade against Britian in Egypt and the Sudan. The most vigorous English advocate of Egyptian nationalism, Blunt was both arrogant and irascible, his works scathing, discursive, and at times utterly ridiculous. Immature and unfair, both he and his writings must be used with caution, but even the dullest of men will come away stimulated if not aroused and with fresh insights to challenge the sometimes smug attitudes of British officials in Whitehall and Cairo. Of course, to them Blunt was anathema if not disloyal and Edward Mallet, the British Consul-General at Cairo from 1879 to 1883, replied to Blunt's charges in his posthumously published *Egypt, 1879-1883* (London, 1909).[3]

To linger in British sources for the history of the establishment of British rule in Egypt may be pleasant, even exhilarating reading—tales of victory are always more exciting than apologies for defeat—but such accounts are usually distorted and one-sided, not only since the British

---

3. The military campaign, so glorious yet so brief, which culminated in the British occupation of Egypt is too episodic for discussion here. For further information, see Thomas Archer, *The War in Egypt and the Soudan* (4 vols., London, 1885), and Sir George C. A. Arthur, ed., *The Letters of Lord and Lady Wolseley, 1870-1911* (London, 1912).

were victors but Westerners as well. From the shattered remains of
Aḥmad 'Arābī's army Egyptian nationalists have long drawn their inspiration and martyrs to feed the fires of nationalism which in the end
consumed the British imperium. Particularly today Egyptian scholars
and the present government of the United Arab Republic have displayed the greatest interest in 'Arābī's revolt. His personal account,
Aḥmad 'Arābī, *Mudhakkirat 'Arābī* ("The Memoirs of 'Arābī"), in
two volumes (Cairo, 1952), has been published, as well as the accounts
of other revolutionaries, Maḥmūd Fahmī, *Al-Baḥr al-Zākhir fī Ta'rīkh
al-'Ālam wa Akhbār al-Awā'īl wa-l-Awākhir* ("The Full Sea: A History of the World from the Earliest Times to the Present") (4 vols.;
Cairo, 1893-94), and that of the editor of the newspaper *Al-Maḥrūsah*,
Salīm Al-Naqqāsh, *Miṣr li-l-Miṣriyīn* ("Egypt for the Egyptians")
(9 vols.; Alexandria, 1884) not to mention collections of the writings
of various revolutionaries, including those of Adīb Isḥāq, editor of the
nationalist paper, *Miṣr* and *Al-Tijārah*, collected and published by his
brother 'Āwnī Isḥāq, as *Al-Durar* ("The Pearls") (Beirut, 1909), or
the memoirs of Al-Nadīm, edited and published by Muḥammad
Aḥmad Khalaf Allāh, *'Abdallāh al-Nadīm wa Mudhakkirātuhu al-
Siyāsīyah* (" 'Abdallāh al-Nadīm and His Political Memoirs") (Cairo,
1956), and 'Abdallāh Fikrī, Minister of Education in 'Arābī's ministry,
whose writings have been collected and published by his son Amīn
Fikrī, *Al-Āthār al-Fikrīyah*, ("The Works of Fikrī") (Cairo, 1897).[4]

The foremost history of British Egypt is that of Evelyn Baring,
Earl of Cromer, *Modern Egypt* (2 vols.; London, 1908), and his
little essay *Abbas II* (London, 1915). *Modern Egypt* is the history
of British administration in Egypt from 1876 to May, 1907, but the
principal Egyptian political events are discussed only to 1892. Cromer's
*Abbas II* fills this gap. These are both great works by a great man.
Where his mid-Victorian predecessors had hoped to reform oriental
regimes by free trade and the samples of Western civilization marked
for export, Cromer set out to regenerate Egypt through scientific administration, sound finance, and applied technology. To the great proconsul progress was the result of pragmatic change, not revolutionary
design, and the reward was political control, granted to Egypt after

4. For a full account of the materials, published and archival, of the 'Arābī
Rebellion, see Robert L. Tignor, "Some Materials for a History of the 'Arābī Revolu-
tion, A Bibliographical Survey," *The Middle East Journal* (Washington), XVI
(Summer), 239-48.

long tutelage under British officials skilled in the craft of government which they had, in turn, inherited from the great political traditions of England. Cromer's histories deeply reflect his views, and although many have interpreted them to mean no political progress if not the permanent British occupation of Egypt, this is to misread Cromer. In an age of rapid modernization Cromer remained the rock of political stability on which the incoming tide of Egyptian nationalism broke into impotent eddies and whirlpools, but the decisive triumph of Egyptian nationalism in this century has cast doubts on Cromer's political wisdom. Today the student remains unsatisfied with his historical analysis, conscious that the age of Cromer still awaits its historian. Nevertheless, Cromer's achievement towered for long above all criticism and dominated those who wrote of his administration. Three proconsuls in their own right, Alfred Milner, Undersecretary for Finance in Egypt, Sir Auckland Colvin, British Comptroller-General in Egypt, and Lieutenant-Colonel P. G. Elgood, who served for many years in the Egyptian ministries of War, Interior, and Finance, have left really excellent accounts of British administrative reforms (Sir Alfred Milner, *England in Egypt* [London, 1892]; Sir Auckland Colvin, *The Making of Modern Egypt* [London, 1906]; and Percival George Elgood, *The Transit of Egypt* [London, 1928]). Like Cromer's works they are proconsular history—a record of impressive reforms with all the pride and prejudice, false assumptions and attitudes of the late Victorian imperialists—yet they remain in every respect superior to the more journalistic account by Sir Valentine Chirol, *The Egyptian Problem* (London, 1920), or the rambling discourse of Edward W. Polson Newman, *Great Britain in Egypt* (London, 1928).

Lord Cromer was succeeded by Sir Eldon Gorst, Lord Kitchener, Sir Henry McMahon, Sir Reginald Wingate, and Viscount Allenby, none of whom ever lived to write the history of his administration in Egypt. Perhaps it is just as well. Gorst could hardly play the rôle of a proconsul when hatless and collarless he would exchange repartee with the Egyptian crowds as he drove his motorcycle alone through the streets of Cairo that had seen Lord Cromer in top hat and frock coat, looking neither to the right nor to the left, pass by in a coach and four. Actually Egypt on the threshold of the twentieth century needed a man like Gorst, but he died only four years after taking up his appointment. Kitchener was every inch a proconsul, and to him

Egypt was but another rung up the ladder of success, yet the fellahin owes to him some of Egypt's most progressive land reform which has moved so biting a critic as Sir Philip M. Magnus, *Kitchener: Portrait of an Imperialist* (New York, 1959), to magnanimity. Even after the outbreak of World War I, a conflict which has exhausted the energies of more than one generation of historians, Egypt has been regarded principally as the headquarters for the dramatic feats of T. E. Lawrence and his Arabs east of Suez, while the British High Commissioner in Egypt, Sir Henry McMahon, remained more concerned with Sharif Ḥusayn and Arab aspirations for independence from the Turk than Egyptian nationalist hopes for independence from Britain. Sir Reginald Wingate succeeded Sir Henry McMahon in 1916. A proconsul of the Cromer era, Wingate is rightly associated more with the Sudan than Egypt, but his long association with the peoples of the Nile Valley had made him sympathetic to the moderate demands of Egyptian nationalism. He himself had intended to write his own history but instead has left behind in the Sudan Archive at Durham University only his papers, the finest and largest collection of private papers of all the political figures in the modern Middle East, from which Sir Ronald Wingate, his son, has produced a short but admirable biography, *Wingate of the Sudan* . . . (London, 1955), in which the great confrontation between Wingate, a proconsul of the Nile, and Lord Curzon, a proconsul of the Empire, is dramatically presented. Viscount Allenby was appointed Special High Commissioner in 1919 to succeed Wingate and remained until the appointment of Lord Lloyd in 1925. The conqueror of Jerusalem, Allenby was more soldier than proconsul, but when it came to politics he managed a not unsuccessful but temporary balance between the demands of the Empire and those of Egyptian nationalism excellently described in the second volume of his biography by Archibald Percival, Lord Wavell, *Allenby in Egypt* (New York, 1944),[5] to which the recent biography by Brian Gardner, *Allenby* (London, 1965), adds illuminating insights and illustrations from Allenby's hitherto unexamined letters to his wife and his mother.

Although good reading, these biographies are not always good history, and the restricted chapters in the life of a man, be he even a proconsul, are no substitute for an analysis of the forces confronting

5. Volume I covering the earlier years of Allenby's career is entitled *Allenby: A Study in Greatness* (New York, 1941).

him. Only P. G. Elgood and Lord Lloyd have left satisfactory histories in English of the British occupation of Egypt during the war. Percival George Elgood, *Egypt and the Army* (London, 1924), is a solid factual account with a great deal of information, but like his later work it is restricted by interpretations derived from assumptions about government, morality, and nationalism acquired as a ruler on the Nile. George Ambrose, Lord Lloyd, *Egypt since Cromer* (2 vols.; London, 1933-34), covers a wider period, from 1907 to 1929, and in many respects lacks the solid information of Elgood. Wealthy, educated at Eton and Cambridge, and formerly Governor of Bombay, Baron Lloyd of Dolobran was the perfect successor to Cromer and Kitchener. A prudent but forceful man and an admirer of Cromer, he was convinced, like Cromer, "that good administration is the first requirement to be fulfilled, and that all other questions are subordinate to it," but since the catastrophe of World War I, the increased strength of Egyptian nationalism, and the abolition of the Protectorate in 1922, Lord Lloyd, unlike Cromer, could never hope to be the rock of political stability which sound administration required.[6] Like Cromer, however, he writes good history but history to defend and to justify as much as to elucidate and to enlighten. He retired from Egypt in 1929 frustrated by his government and not a little confused about the postwar Empire, which is perhaps not an inappropriate ending for the last of the proconsuls.

Although the British rulers of Egypt have understandably written the most authoritative accounts of their occupation, the ruled in turn have produced a host of memoirs, biographies, and general political histories which not only present a different point of view but challenge the testimony of the proconsular histories. First are the memoirs by politicians and nationalist critics of British rule such as Aḥmad Amīn, *Ḥayātī* ("My Life") (Cairo, 1950), or Muḥammad Ḥusayn Haykal, *Mudhakkirāt fī al-Siyāsah al-Miṣriyyah* ("Memoirs on Egyptian Politics") (2 vols.; Cairo, 1952-53). Muḥammad Haykal was the leader of the Liberal Constitutional party and President of the Egyptian Senate, and although much of his work is devoted to justifying his own actions, there are many valuable insights into Egyptian feelings toward Britain and the British. Egyptian attitudes and reactions to British policy can also be found in the briefer narrative by

6. Lloyd, II, 358.

the Egyptian politician and former Prime Minister, Ismā'īl Ṣidqī, *Mudhakkirātī* ("Memoirs") (Cario, 1950) or the writings of al-Sayyid Aḥmad Luṭfī, *Al-Muntakhabāt* ("Selections") (2 vols.; Cairo, 1937-45), and *Ta'ammulāt fī al-Falsafah, wa-al-Adah, wa-al-Siyāsah, wa-al-Ijtimā'* ("Reflections on Philosophy, Literature, Politics, and Society") (Cairo, 1946), and the biography by 'Abbās Maḥmūd al-'Aqqād, *Sa'd Zaghul* (Cairo, 1936), of one of Egypt's foremost nationalists, not to mention the three later works written in defense of the Egyptian Revolution of 1952, Gamal Abdel Nasser, *Egypt's Liberation; The Philosophy of the Revolution* (Washington, 1955), Muhammad Naguib, *Egypt's Destiny* (New York, 1955), and the more autobiographical account by the conspirator Anwar el-Sadat, *Revolt on the Nile* (London, 1957).

The more general Arabic histories of the British imperium in Egypt are dominated by the works of 'Abd al-Raḥmān al-Rāfi'ī, one of Egypt's most prolific historians. Unhappily, the quantity of his work is outweighed only by his bias, but his access to the archives in Cairo (Dār al-Maḥfūzāt, the Egyptian Public Record Office) and the Abdin Palace (Qaṣr 'Ābidīn now al-Qaṣr al-Jumhūrī) has enabled him to write enormously detailed and informative narratives, among which are *Al-Thawra al-'Arābīyya wa-al-Ithtilāl al-Injilīzī* ("The 'Arābī Revolt and the British Occupation") (Cairo, 1937) and his later works *Fī a'qab al-Thawra al-Miṣriyya* ("Aftermath of the Egyptian Revolution") (3 vols.; Cairo, 1947-51), a detailed narrative of Egyptian national history between 1921 and 1951, and his *Thawrat Sanat 1919* ("The 1919 Revolution") (2 vols.; Cairo, 1946), a detailed account of Egypt during World War I and of the causes of the Revolution of 1919. Muhammad Rifaat Bey, *The Awakening of Modern Egypt* (London, 1947), is a more handy one-volume history of Egypt during the British occupation, presenting not only an Egyptian point of view but elaborate and unnecessary praise for the dynasty of Muḥammad 'Alī. The most able analysis of Egyptian politics from independence to mid-century with many shrewd observations of British rule is Marcel Colombe, *L'Évolution de l'Égypte, 1924-1950* (Paris, 1951).[7]

7. The purpose of this essay is not to record all the works which touch on the British in Egypt, for the list would be voluminous, but rather to discuss those significant works of lasting value. There are, however, a number of specialized studies of economic, social, and intellectual life in Egypt, part of which deal with such subjects during the years of British rule. The most important accounts of economic and social development are Arthur Edwin Crouchley, *The Investment of Foreign Capital in*

Yet with the exception of 'Abd al-Raḥmān al-Rāfi'ī's admittedly emotionally partisan works on the British occupation of Egypt, the proconsular histories still remain the most substantial accounts of that vital but transitional period in Egyptian history. Historians in the latter half of the twentieth century will certainly not interpret the events as did the proconsuls at the beginning. More detached, less committed, and less sure of their judgments in a world in which the Arabs and the Africans are no longer content to play a subordinate rôle in the writing of history, future historians will be deeply influenced by the new attitudes and assumptions from areas of the world which in the past were supposed to have none. The impact on the history of the British in Egypt will consequently be great. Equipped with the documents now becoming available, armed with the shield of hindsight, and fresh with ideas derived from interchange with Arab and African scholars, the Empire historians can hope to arrive at more meaningful interpretations and more accurate conclusions than the proconsuls. The British in Egypt still await their historian.

The British in the Sudan, unlike their countrymen in Egypt, have only just ended their history. They too await their historian, and until that time the record of British rule in the Sudan remains, like British Egypt, largely the product of its proconsuls. The early proconsuls were not Imperial administrators at all but employees of the Khedive Ismā'īl—a small, hardy band of British adventurers who thundered against the slave trade and the incompetence of the Egyptian bureaucracy on the middle and upper Nile. Most wrote of their experiences, and a new literate population in England, nurtured on the Harmsworth press, soon devoured the triumphs of these British crusaders against Sudanese slave traders, corrupt Egyptian officials, and ungrate-

_Egyptian and Public Debt_ (Cairo, 1936); Muhammed Ali Rifaat, _The Monetary System of Egypt_ (London, 1935); and the two books by Charles P. Issawi, _Egypt: An Economic and Social Analysis_ (London, 1947; reprinted as _Egypt at Mid-Century_ [London, 1954]), and _Egypt in Revolution: An economic Analysis_ (London, 1963). The intellectual life of Egypt including the impact of the British occupation upon it are dealt with in Charles C. Adams, _Islam and Modernism in Egypt_ (London, 1933); Albert H. Hourani, _Arabic Thought in the Liberal Age, 1798-1939_ (London, 1962); Nadav Safran, _Egypt in Search of Political Community_ (Cambridge, Mass., 1961), and Jamal M. Ahmad, _The Intellectual Origins of Egyptian Nationalism_ (London, 1960). The Suez Canal will remain controversial until the appropriate documents are made available. Until then Hugh J. Schonfield, _The Suez Canal in World Affairs_ (London, 1952), and Donald Cameron Watt, ed., _Documents on the Suez Crisis . . ._ (London, 1957), are competent accounts of the nationalization crisis. See also Compagnie Universelle du Canal Maritime de Suez, _The Suez Canal: Notes and Statistics_ (London, 1952).

ful tribesmen. As standard-bearers of commerce, Christianity, and civilization, in that order, these early proconsuls prepared the English public for the conquest of the Sudan and the extension of the British imperium up the Nile which was to come at the end of the century. The British Vice-Consul at Khartoum, John Petherick, in *Egypt, the Soudan, and Central Africa* (London, 1861) the Governor-General of Equatoria, Sir Samuel White Baker, in *Ismailia* (London, 1874), and his successor, Charles George Gordon, in *Colonel Gordon in Central Africa, 1874-1879* . . ., edited by G. B. N. Hill (London, 1899), and in *The Journals of Major-General C. G. Gordon at Khartoum*, edited by Alfred Egmont Hake (London, 1885), captivated the British reading public with some of the most exciting adventure stories ever written. Unhappily it is not good history. The tales of Baker and the letters of Gordon are great polemics against the iniquities of the slave trade and the corruptness of Egyptian rule as observed through the eyes of a Victorian official in the pay of an oriental potentate. Then suddenly the forces of Mahdism arise, seemingly from nowhere, overwhelm the Egyptian administration in the Sudan, eliminate the European, Christian officials employed by the Khedive, and, by killing Gordon at Khartoum, add a third, and even more heroic, theme to the barbarities of the slave trade and the venality of Egyptian officials. Every martyr has his detractors and his eulogists, and Gordon is no exception. He has certainly received more ill-considered attention than he deserves, ranging from the indiscriminate debunking of Giles Lytton Strachey in *Eminent Victorians* (London, 1918) to exuberant panegyrics of even less value.[8] Bernard M. Allen, *Gordon and the Sudan* (London, 1931), is the most balanced and the best-documented account, but Gordon still eludes his biographers and perhaps always will.

The crusade against the slave trade, the corruption of the Egyptian administration, and the death of Gordon were the beginnings of British involvement in the Sudan. They were nearly the end. The rise of the Mahdist state and the elimination of foreign rule and influence from the Nile south of Wādī Ḥalfā terminated British interests until the establishment of the Anglo-Egyptian Condominium at the turn of the

8. For a description of the literature about General Gordon, see Richard L. Hill, "The Gordon Literature," *Durham University Journal* (Durham), n.s., XVI (June, 1955), 97-103. Only the omniscient could hazard an exact count of the quantity of books about Gordon. At last count, however, an informal reckoning put the number at 323, but the amount is only as impressive as its fallibility.

century. Three books of real merit span this period, known as the Mahdīya, which begins before Gordon's final mission and ends with the Anglo-Egyptian conquest. Mekki Shibeika, *British Policy in the Sudan, 1882-1902* (London, 1952), traces in detail the twists and turns of British policy with thorough documentation if not insight. Alan Buchan Theobald, *The Mahdīya: A History of the Anglo-Egyptian Sudan, 1881-1899* (London, 1951), although concerned primarily with the Sudan, covers much the same ground in a highly readable account. Peter Malcolm Holt, *The Mahdist State in the Sudan, 1881-1898* (Oxford, 1958), is an erudite analysis of the Mahdīya, most valuable to the Empire historian for the elucidation of Sudanese feelings toward Gordon, Britain, and the Anglo-Egyptian invasion. The destruction of the Mahdist state on the plains of Kararī on September 2, 1898, by the Anglo-Egyptian forces under Kitchener is a great landmark in British Imperial history not unlike the occupation of Egypt sixteen years before: Gordon avenged, the Sudanese saved, the Nile waters secured, the British Empire extended. These are all familiar themes still accepted by many today with an astonishing want of discrimination and critical analysis. They are all to be found brilliantly narrated by Winston S. Churchill, *The River War* (2 vols.; London, 1899), or if one prefers them served with even more spicy relish, George Warrington Steevens, *With Kitchener to Khartum* (London, 1898), is hard to surpass.[9]

The Anglo-Egyptian Condominium in the Sudan was in theory a partnership between the English and the Egyptians. In practice the British ruled and everyone else, Egyptian officials as well as the Sudanese population, obeyed. At first the Sudan was administered by military officers who had come with Kitchener's victorious army, but within a few years a new corps of civilian administrators appeared to dominate the Sudan Political Service. These were the administrative technicians who had been reared on stories about the intrepid Baker, the heroic Gordon, and the fanatical Mahdi and who believed, with a passion associated more with Exeter Hall than with British bureaucracy, that by hard work and the application of scientific principles of administration they could, like their counterparts in Egypt, remake the oriental despotism of the Mahdist state into a prosperous and productive land. Not only Gordon, Victorian morality, and Exeter

9. See also chaps. vi and vii in Sir Philip Magnus's *Kitchener*.

Hall but triumphant technology and efficient, incorruptible adminis-tration has conditioned the historical writing of the Anglo-Egyptian Condominium. Dry, factual, enormously informative but usually very personal accounts dominate Sudan proconsular history. The Earl of Cromer in the second volume of his *Modern Egypt* (London, 1908), describes the principles upon which British administration in the Sudan was based, and in *Wingate of the Sudan*, Sir Ronald Wingate, devotes a penetrating chapter (VI) to his father's seventeen years of halcyon rule as Governor-General. But these are sparse materials for that important transitional period before World War I for which the final chapters of Makkī Shibayka (Mekki Shibeika), *Al-Sūdān fī Qarn, 1819-1919* (Cairo, 1947), and the recent publication of two specialized studies only partly compensate. Before World War I Wingate relied on the advice of Rudolf von Slatin Pasha, who had been a prisoner of the Khalifa during the Mahdīya and who, as the Inspector-General of the Sudan, played the role of *éminence grise* during the Condominium. Richard L. Hill, *Slatin Pasha* (London, 1965), has produced a charm-ing, scholarly biography of Slatin who was primarily responsible for relations with the last independent sultan of Dār Fūr, 'Alī Dīnār. The history of 'Alī Dīnār's rule has been scrupulously analyzed by Alan Buchan Theobald, *'Alī Dīnār, Last Sultan of Darfur, 1898-1916* (Lon-don, 1965), to form a happy complement to Hill's biography.[10]

Between the two great World Wars the quantity of books about the Anglo-Egyptian Sudan increases, but they are still very much the products of the proconsuls untempered by critical comments by either the ruled or non-British observers. The long time (1926-34) Civil Secretary of the Sudan government and nephew of Lord Curzon, Sir Harold Alfred MacMichael, *The Anglo-Egyptian Sudan* (London, 1934), provides a plain narrative of the achievements of British rule. The facts speak for themselves, dry statistics of a truly impressive accomplishment with little to stimulate the reader or excite the student. The unspectacular but ever forward march of government is never stalled, at least publicly, by crises or scandals. The Anglo-Egyptian Sudan is orderly, efficient, and progressive. The administrators are still Victorians who in the Sudan never felt the full impact of World War I on their assumptions about the white man's burden and the British

10. For the history of early British administration in the Southern Sudan see the forthcoming account by Robert O. Collins.

Empire. They still believed that civilization was the product of ordered reason in which material progress was advanced by technology and science and in which the spirit was made content by an unshakable belief in God. Indeed, in the closing years of the great war, the journal *Sudan Notes and Records* was founded by a group of government officials to elucidate what they did not know about the Sudan, implying that with time, diligence, and applied technology the mysteries of the Sudan would give way to an ever-unfolding pageant of progress, directed, of course, by British officials. Sophisticated scholars were at first cynically amused by the amateur articles published by political officers, technicians, archeologists, and missionaries in the Sudan about dull and seemingly insignificant subjects, frequently in complete isolation from the greater horizons of the Islamic world to the north or the African cultures to the south. Today we know better. Still published in Khartoum, *Sudan Notes and Records* provides a continuous and impressive wealth of undigested materials about the Anglo-Egyptian Sudan scarcely tapped by the historian. The proconsuls may have had attitudes of empire which today seem quaint, but they were absolutely correct in their assumption that knowledge cannot be advanced without the curiosity and the will to investigate. This is a great tradition for which the imperialists have received little credit and the value of which can best be seen in Uganda and Tanganyika, where comparable journals were begun in emulation, while Kenya and Egypt are the poorer because they failed to do so.

But British officials in the Sudan did not confine themselves to a journal. *The Anglo-Egyptian Sudan from Within*, edited by J. A. de C. Hamilton (London, 1935), is a collection of essays, mostly with historical themes. They are, however, incomplete, leaving the impression that these very knowledgeable men could have written in greater detail without losing the threads of their analysis in a larger fabric. An earlier and fuller treatment of British administration is Percy F. Martin, *The Sudan in Evolution* (London, 1921). Martin was a journalist, and although it is by far the best account of early British administration, he was regarded as an interloper by the proconsuls, one of whom indignantly criticized part of his book for its "deplorable taste." In addition to these two compendiums, there were during the interwar period numerous volumes of personal literature that may swell bibliographical lists but in the aggregate add more knowledge to big game shooting in the Sudan than to the history of British administration. They are, of course, grand reading, full of the spirit of British rule if not the facts, but to the historian all of this is nearly as scanty as the prewar literature. None of it is critical history, let alone interpretative or analytical. The accounts reflect too clearly the attitudes and assumptions of the late Victorian proconsuls. As in Egypt it could not last.

The outbreak of World War II marked the beginning of the end of British rule in the Sudan. A few of the older officials, like Sir Douglas Newbold and Sir James Robertson, who between them held the key post of Civil Secretary from 1939 to 1953, foresaw great changes in British rule even if they were not sufficiently omniscient to see what form those changes would take. The younger officials, who grew up in the spiritual and economic depression of postwar Europe, had come to the Sudan with new attitudes in which the Victorian confidence in European civilization and progress was noticeably absent. This does not mean that they were any less skilled in administration than their predecessors. In fact they were, if anything, better trained in the technology which had transformed the Sudan, but they could no longer preach with conviction about the benefits of a civilization which had nearly destroyed itself on the battlefields of Europe. At that point British rule in the Sudan approached its end, and the proconsuls began to justify, to excuse, and to vindicate before retiring from their outposts on the Nile.

Although late proconsular writings about the Anglo-Egyptian Condominium range from narratives of British administration to personal reminiscences, the theme is the same—British rule was essential to save the Sudanese from the disasters of the Mahdīya and to guard against a recurrence of Egyptian exploitation. The tone is paternal, if not olympian, friendly to the Sudanese, hostile to the Egyptians, and proudly convinced of the material and moral benefits of British Imperial rule. The proconsuls have a strong case, but written at a time when British administration was under heavy attack from Sudanese nationalists, which everyone expected, but also from vicious Egyptian assaults, their defense lacks the perspective, the detachment, and even the facts of good history. Stung by the virulence of Egyptian claims that the Condominium was imposed by Britain and that the only future solution was the unification of Egypt and the Sudan (for everyone was supposed to know that the Sudan could not be a viable state), the proconsuls could hardly permit such a condemnation of their work and intentions to go unrefuted. Sir Harold Alfred MacMichael, *The Sudan* (London, 1954), defended British rule with the precision that so characterized his administration. But Sir Harold left the Sudan before the rising tide of Sudanese nationalism rolled over the breakwaters he had tried to erect. Sir Douglas Newbold was left to channel the rampaging waters into useful spillways. The story is resolutely described in his own words, *The Making of the Modern Sudan*, edited by K. D. D. Henderson (London, 1953). J. S. R. Duncan, *The Sudan: A Record of Achievement* (London, 1952), and *The Sudan's Path to Independence* (London, 1957), take up where Newbold leaves off, combining the personal memories of Duncan with a vindication of his colleagues' administration. This is not proconsular history in the sense of Cromer or even Lord Lloyd. Half a century has elapsed since Cromer's great work, and today there are few men who can match the scholarly detachment of the late Victorians. Duncan is too committed to the Sudanese and too hostile to the Egyptians to remain prudently aloof. As with the writings of another official, Henry Cecil Jackson, *Sudan Days and Ways* (London, 1954), and *Behind the Modern Sudan* (London, 1955), the moral fervor of nineteenth-century imperialism has combined with a passionate belief in twentieth-century scientific administration to provide a defense which is not completely convincing for proconsular rule in the Sudan.[11]

These are familiar and well-worn themes, challengeable interpretations which will certainly not remain inviolate much longer. Indeed, the Sudanese Mekki Abbas, in *The Sudan Question* (London, 1952) foreshadowed a more analytical history of British administration in the Sudan in his general discussion of the Anglo-Egyptian dispute over the Condominium, and a few years later, Saad ed Din Fawzi in *The Labour Movement in the Sudan, 1946-1955* (London, 1957) did much the same in his analysis of the rise of trade unions. Only Peter Malcolm Holt's *A Modern History of the Sudan* (London, 1961) has provided, however, any dramatically new approach to the history

---

11. To list but a few of many personal accounts by British officials in the Sudan, see: D. C. E. ff. Comyn, *Service and Sport in the Sudan* (London, 1911); Major Arthur Radclyffe Dugmore, *The Vast Sudan* (London, 1924); Sir Stewart Symes, *Tour of Duty* (London, 1946); Reginald Davies, *The Camel's Back: Service in the Rural Sudan* (London, 1957); Alexander Cruickshank, *The Kindling Fire: Medical Adventures in the Southern Sudan* (London, 1962); Sir Geoffrey Francis Archer, *Personal and Historical Memoirs of an East African Administrator* (Edinburgh, 1963).

of the Condominium period as a whole. It is, of course, but a brief beginning, the judgments of which have yet to stand the tests of time and scholarship, but it is an important beginning against which future Sudanese and European historians can examine the more specialized themes of British administration—British policy in the Southern Sudan, the pattern of local government, the impact of British culture and technology, the rôle of British political ideas upon the rise of Sudanese nationalism, and the part played during the Condominium by the religious orders. Only when this has been done can proconsular history, with all its national and personal loyalties, be judiciously re-written.[12]

12. I am indebted to Robert L. Tignor of the Department of History, Princeton University, for his advice and assistance in preparing the bibliography of Britain in Egypt.

# GREAT BRITAIN AND INTER-
# NATIONAL TRUSTEESHIP:
# THE MANDATE SYSTEM

*William Roger Louis*


IN 1919 THE PARIS PEACE CONFERENCE created the
mandate system. The purpose of this innovation in colonial rule was
to supervise the administration of the former German colonies in
Africa and the Pacific and in Turkish territories in the Middle East. According to Article 22 of the League of Nations Covenant, these areas
were not to be regarded as colonial possessions but as "a sacred trust
of civilization." The works about Great Britain and the mandate system
deal both with the origins and the application of this idea. Virtually
without exception those writers who have analyzed the proceedings of
the Permanent Mandate Commission and the administration of the
mandated territories have had to rely upon published sources of memoirs and official documents. And it will not be until 1989 (if the
British government maintains the present fifty-year restriction) that
all of the British records through 1939 will be open to public inspection. Those scholars concerned with the establishment of the mandate
system have been more fortunate. In 1942 the United States State Department began publishing the American documents concerning the
Peace Conference.[1] This collection answered many questions that previously had puzzled scholars; but it contained few revelations: practically since the time of the conference itself various writers have had
access to collections of private papers which reveal the main lines of
the colonial settlement of 1919. The scholarly interpretations of the
meaning of a "mandate" have been shaped by these disclosures as well
as by the spirit of the times after the two World Wars.

The first important commentary on the founding of the mandate

1. *Papers relating to the Foreign Relations of the United States: The Paris Peace
Conference, 1919* (13 vols.; Washington, 1942-47).

system appeared in 1922 when the journalist Ray Stannard Baker published *Woodrow Wilson and World Settlement* (3 vols.; New York), based on Wilson's private papers. In a chapter entitled "War Spoils at Paris," Baker scathingly denounced the "wilier diplomats of the old order" who demanded "a division of the spoils." He depicted Wilson as a courageous idealist confronted with diabolical adversaries conspiring to defeat the proposal for a mandate system. The situation was, of course, more complicated than this. But Baker's commentary remains of interest as representative of postwar American disillusionment with the colonial settlement at Paris.

Baker was among the first to raise the question of the origins of the mandate idea. He defined trusteeship as "an idea of national service to the world." He thought that this concept was essentially American: "It had its roots in the traditional principles and policies of the United States. . . ." The immediate origins of the proposal, however, he traced to President Wilson's reading of a pamphlet by General Jan Smuts of South Africa entitled *The League of Nations: A Practical Suggestion* (London, 1918). "President Wilson," Baker wrote, ". . . was greatly impressed by the statesmanlike suggestion of General Smuts . . . but . . . pressed it further than General Smuts ever intended. He universalized it. General Smuts never thought of applying the principle to the former German colonies, but only to the old empires that were to be 'liquidated.' " At Wilson's dogged insistence at the Peace Conference, all of the former German colonies were included in the mandate system. The first full scholarly account of this episode did not appear until 1941, when an American, Paul Birdsall published *Versailles: Twenty Years After* (New York). Birdsall's balanced record, sufficiently recognized in the last year of American neutrality to win a Pulitzer Prize, offsets the "pure melodrama" of Ray Stannard Baker.

Writing in the same year as Baker, an American political scientist, Pitman B. Potter, also emphasized the American rôle in the "Origin of the System of Mandates under the League of Nations," *American Political Science Review* (Baltimore), XVI (November, 1922), 563-83. Following the same interpretation as Baker as to the influence of General Smuts, Potter then traced the invention of mandates to the pre-World War I period:[2]

2. P. 577. See also Potter's "Further Notes," *American Political Science Review*, XX (Nov., 1926), 842-46.

The thing needed to make the [American] open door principle effective was the device of the mandate with general international supervision in connection therewith.

That particular solution of the problem was discovered more than a dozen years before the mandate system was actually established in the League Covenant. It was discovered by an American President and an American secretary of state. It was described and prescribed by them in words which anticipate the action of 1919 in almost every detail.

Potter referred to the Algeciras Act of 1906—which Walter Lippmann in 1915 had called "the most hopeful effort at world organization made up to the present,"[3] and which George Louis Beer (Wilson's colonial adviser) had once observed held a special place in "liberal thought in America."[4] According to Potter the United States in 1906 had pursued an "open door" policy in Morocco.

A mandate scheme was invented to make this effective while providing protection to the natives and also allowing special privileges and authority to the most interested nation, acting under a mandate and subject to international supervision in its acts. This was all put into Articles I-XII of the General Act of Algeciras.[5]

In 1924 another American scholar, Luther H. Evans, published a lengthy article entitled "Some Legal and Historical Antecedents of the Mandatory System," in the *Proceedings of the Fifth Annual Convention of the Southwestern Political and Social Science Association*, V (Austin), 143-61. Arguing that the concept of mandates had "been in existence for a long time," he traced its origins to the *mandatum* of Roman law: "In the mandatory system of the League, the League is the mandator and the backward area the mandant, thus being a deviation from the mandate in Roman Law." He attacked Potter:

While the significance of the Algeciras proposal is great, it would appear that Potter is distinctly in error in calling it 'the most important source of the mandate system, including the use of the very word itself.' . . . A system more closely resembling the mandatory system had been instituted in the British Empire in the type of administrative control set up over New Guinea and certain territories in South Africa. The Algeciras Conference offers just another example of the use of the term and another proposal of some-

3. Walter Lippmann, *The Stakes of Diplomacy* (New York, 1915), p. 149.
4. Beer's diary (typescript copy) deposited at the Library of Congress; quoted in William Roger Louis, "The United States and the African Peace Settlement of 1919: The Pilgrimage of George Louis Beer," *Journal of African History* (Cambridge), IV (iii/1963), 413-33.
5. Potter, "Origin of the System of Mandates," p. 581.

thing similar to the mandatory system for the solution of an international problem arising out of the control of backward areas [p. 159 n. 46]

In the same year still another American, Walter Russell Batsell (then Director of the Reference Service on International Affairs of the American Library in Paris), published an article called "The United States and the System of Mandates," *International Conciliation* (New York), CCXIII (October, 1925), 269-315. Batsell saw "mandates" originating in late nineteenth century diplomatic history:

The word 'mandate' . . . is used by practically every writer to describe the status of Bosnia and Herzegovina between 1878 and 1908 . . . is used repeatedly in the correspondence concerning Egypt after 1880, and . . . [is also used] in the negotiations between the representatives of Great Britain, Germany, and the United States at Washington, June 25–July 26, 1887, to discuss the disposition of Samoa [p. 270 n. 2].

These interpretations mark the beginning of the academic controversy over the origins of the mandate system. What can the present-day historian, who has more sources available to him than his predecessors, add to clarify the history of the founding of the mandate system? Did the inventor of mandates have a specific precedent in mind?

The papers of the British Colonial Secretary in 1919, Lord Milner, are now accessible at New College, Oxford. This important collection reveals that British statesmen at the Peace Conference did discuss historical "antecedents," but they were usually mentioned only in passing. Milner himself once pointed out "that the mandatory principle was not altogether an innovation."

Our administration of Egypt for thirty-five years was carried on on that principle, and subject to innumerable obligations which we consistently fulfilled, at one time even to the extent of giving a decided preference to other nations over ourselves.[6]

By contrast the Prime Minister, David Lloyd George, emphasized the analogy of the Berlin Act of 1885: there was in his opinion "no large

6. British Imperial War Cabinet Minutes, secret, Dec. 20, 1918. Copies of these minutes may be found in several collections of private papers, but are most easily accessible in those of Sir Robert Borden and Sir George Foster, Public Archives of Canada, Ottawa. In the following passages I have drawn on two unpublished articles of mine, "Sir John Harris and the Development of 'International Trusteeship' in Tropical Africa, 1914-1919"; and "The Founding of the Mandates System and the Repartition of Africa." I am grateful to the Cabinet Office for allowing me to publish excerpts from the Milner papers.

difference between the mandatory principle and the principles laid down by the Berlin Conference."[7]

If they were more or less aware of the historical precedents of the mandate system, the British delegates at the Peace Conference nevertheless believed they were making a break with the past. "We are opening a new chapter in International Law," Milner wrote in March 1919.

The mandated territories are to be under the supervision of the League of Nations. But actual authority, in each of these territories, will be exercised by one member of that League, or by some native ruler or rulers guided and assisted by a member of that League. . . . As it seems to me, there will in all mandated territories be in a sense a divided 'sovereignty.'

Juridically the British thus helped to create an anomaly in international law. Milner did not think this was important: "I leave it to lawyers to say, where the 'sovereignty' will in any case reside. . . . What is essential is to get rid of the existing sovereignties."[8]

The legal vagueness of Article 22 has generated practically as much controversy as has the origin of the mandate system. As early as 1922 an English barrister, Thomas Baty, in an article entitled "Protectorates and Mandates," *British Year Book of International Law* (London), II (1921-22), 109-21, caustically commented:

Perhaps there is something to be said, after all, for legal precision in a document intended to create legal relations. . . . It is tolerably obvious that Article 22 of the Covenant, relating to mandates, was drafted with a high regard for Mr. Wilson's supposed announcement that he 'did not want a lawyer's treaty.' Nothing less like a legal instrument than this section can be imagined. It reads like a University Extension lecture. . . . Its language regarding the conditions to be fulfilled by mandatories is so slip-shod that it has given a loophole for the assertion of a right to close the 'Open Door' in the third class of mandate-territory [in Southwest Africa and the Pacific] [p. 119].

In fact these loopholes were deliberate. The Australians and New Zealanders were determined not to admit Japanese influence of any sort in British territories in the Southern Pacific. But Baty was quite right in his inference about British concern for President Wilson's susceptibilities. "Playing up to America," as General Smuts once put it,[9] was one of the principal reasons for Britain's adoption of the mandate system.

7. *Foreign Relations of the United States, 1919: The Paris Peace Conference* III, 750. In this connection see my article, "African Origins of the Mandates Idea," *International Organization* (Boston), XIX (Winter, 1965), 20-36.

8. Milner's memorandum of March 8, 1919, secret, Milner papers.

9. Eastern Committee Minutes, Dec. 2, 1918, secret, *ibid.*

The mandate system offered an expedient solution to a number of problems facing the British government in 1919. Accepting mandates seemed to align British policy with Wilson's slogan of "no annexation." In tropical Africa the mandate system secured equality of commercial opportunity in French and Belgian territories that otherwise might have been sealed off by differential tariffs. But there were disadvantages also. In Southwest Africa and the Pacific, the southern Dominions of South Africa, Australia, and New Zealand regarded the mandate system as a threat to their security. In the Middle East the mandates carried with them the implicit principle (not stated explicitly in Article 22) of self-determination for peoples "not yet able to stand by themselves." A. J. Balfour, the Foreign Secretary, feared that this principle might be applied to the wrong territories. "We must not allow ourselves," he said in December, 1918, "to be driven by that broad principle into applying it pedantically where it is really inapplicable, namely, to wholly barbarous, undeveloped, and unorganized black tribes, whether they be in the Pacific or Africa."[10]

Why did the British adopt the principle of self-determination in the first place? According to Lord Curzon (who as Chairman of the Eastern Committe helped to shape Britain's policy in the Middle East):

I am inclined to value the argument of self-determination because I believe that most of the people would determine in our favour . . . [i]f we cannot get out of our difficulties in any other way we ought to play self-determination for all it is worth wherever we are involved in difficulties with the French, the Arabs, or anybody else, and leave the case to be settled by that final argument knowing in the bottom of our hearts that we are more likely to benefit from it than anybody else.[11]

The early historians of the founding of the mandate system such as Potter, Evans, and Batsell did not have access to records which divulge these frankly opportunistic statements. Nevertheless, their writings will remain valuable not only as attempts to trace the antecedents of the mandate system but also as explanations of American involvement in European colonial affairs at the close of World War I. Their works are historical documents themselves: they reflect the idealistic spirit of the times in which mandates were conceived and which lingered on into the 1920's.

10. Eastern Committee Minutes, Dec. 5, 1918, secret.
11. Ibid.

Of all the forgotten ideals of World War I perhaps the most interesting to the present-day Imperial historian is the one of an Anglo-American colonial alliance. In Lord Milner's view the mandate system would not be "a mere cloak for annexation, but . . . a bond of union . . . between the United States and ourselves."[12] This idea inspired statesmen and scholars on both sides of the Atlantic. In Canada the Prime Minister, Sir Robert Borden, urged "that the United States should be invited to undertake world-wide responsibilities in respect of undeveloped territories and backward races."[13] In the United States Lord Milner found a disciple in Wilson's adviser on colonial affairs, George Louis Beer—whose "dearest wish [was] that America, his America, should work in closest association [with] . . . Britain."[14] Beer believed that the Anglo-American colonial alliance could be cemented by the United States' accepting mandatory responsibility in the Cameroons. The only difficulty, he wrote in 1918, was "that we would probably spend so much money in developing West Africa that the other colonizing Powers could not stand the pace."[15] Beer's scheme for the Cameroons did not materialize, but as head of the colonial section of the American delegation at the Peace Conference he handled the problems confronting him so skilfully that he was invited, at Milner's suggestion, to become the first head of the "mandate section" of the League of Nations. Because of the refusal of the United States to join the League he was unable to accept this position. The action of the United States Senate, combined with Beer's premature death in 1920, ended the prospect of an Anglo-American "colonial alliance."

Beer's memoranda written in preparation for the Peace Conference were edited and published in 1923 by Louis Herbert Gray as *African Questions at the Paris Peace Conference* (New York). This collection of documents is indispensable for a study of colonial problems during World War I; but a better insight into the personalities and issues of the Peace Conference can be gained by reading Beer's manuscript diary, copies of which are deposited at the Columbia University Library and at the Library of Congress. Another important manuscript source for

12. British Imperial War Cabinet Minutes, Dec. 20, 1918, secret.
13. *Ibid.*
14. Alfred E. Zimmern in *George Louis Beer: A Tribute to His Life and Work in the Making of History and the Moulding of Public Opinion* (New York, 1924), p. 63.
15. Beer to Lionel Curtis (copy), July 11, 1918, Lothian papers, box 139 (Scottish Record Office, Edinburgh).

the founding of the mandate system is the Edward M. House papers at Yale University. Important excerpts from this collection were published by Charles Seymour, ed., in *The Intimate Papers of Colonel House* (4 vols.; New York, 1928). Seymour was not, however, especially interested in colonial problems, and it is only recently that a scholar has pointed out "the profound conflict between the views [toward colonialism] of Wilson and House."[16] So far as the mandate system is concerned, House's *Intimate Papers* should be read in conjunction with David Hunter Miller, "The Origin of the Mandates System," *Foreign Affairs* (New York), VI (January, 1928), 277-89. Based on his own meticulous notes taken at the Peace Conference, Miller's essay is perhaps the most important factual commentary on the establishment of the mandate system that appeared between the wars. But it is now more or less superfluous because of the availability of primary sources.

The documents published in David Lloyd George's memoirs, *The Truth about the Peace Treaties* (2 vols.; London, 1938),[17] also have been superseded. But his memoirs are a historical curiosity, written subtly and skilfully. His captions "I propose Mandates," "I attempt conciliation," and Wilson "supports my proposals" give the impression that he alone created the mandate system and that he did so for altruistic reasons. In fact he seized upon mandates mainly because they removed, in his own words, "any prejudice against us of land grabbing." That he published this quotation in his memoirs bears evidence that he tried to fulfil his boast of publishing his account of the Peace Conference without "suppression or distortion of any relevant fact or document." So far as colonial problems are concerned, he seems to have suppressed little.

Lloyd George's motives had already been exposed in 1926 by Parker Thomas Moon's classic *Imperialism and World Politics* (New York). "The clever Welsh statesman," Moon wrote, "was endeavouring to dispel the idea that the allies were fighting for the fulfilment of imperialist secret treaties. . . . Yet he did not abrogate the treaties." This observation is entirely accurate, but, like other passages in his book, smacks of banality. This quality along with contentious inter-

16. (George) Gaddis Smith, "British War Aims and the German Colonies in Africa, 1914-1919," in Prosser Gifford and William Roger Louis, eds., *British and German Colonialism in Africa* (forthcoming).

17. Published in America as *Memoirs of the Peace Conference* (2 vols.; New Haven, 1939).

pretations of "economic imperialism" and curious attempts at humor ("The mandate system may be toothless, but it is not bootless") mar what remains the only satisfactory textbook on imperialism. On the mandate system Moon's comments are perceptive. Few writers have so clearly grasped the essential issue:

The 'old imperialism' and the new 'trusteeship' cannot live together in so small a world as ours. The idea of trusteeship, the public criticism of administration in the mandates, and the careful study by the Mandates Commission of specific policies which benefit or injure the natives, must invariably, though perhaps insensibly, influence the administration of colonies legally outside the mandate sphere . . . [p. 512].

Did the mandate system actually influence colonial administration? Several books written in the late 1920's attempted to answer this question. The main characteristic of these works is one of optimism. According to Aaron M. Margalith in *The International Mandates: A Historical, Descriptive, and Analytical Study of the Theory and Principles of the Mandates System* (Baltimore, 1930), the system was "an improvement over earlier methods of indirect supervision, chiefly because it has behind it the greatest moral force in present day international relations, the League of Nations." In the opinion of an economist, Benjamin Gerig, in *The Open Door and the Mandates System: A Study of Economic Equality before and since the Establishment of the Mandates System* (London, 1930), "the Mandates System is undoubtedly the most effective instrument yet devised to make the Open Door effective." The Attorney-General of Palestine, Norman DeMattos Bentwich, in *The Mandates System* (London, 1930), thought that "the system . . . has on the whole justified the incursion of idealism into the domain of the conqueror." The tone of these useful books is well expressed by Elizabeth van Maanen-Helmer in *The Mandates System in Relation to Africa and the Pacific Islands* (London, 1929): "The mandates system is the principal means by which . . . international coöperation is being developed at the present time. . . . The mandates system has a splendid future."

In 1930 Quincy Wright gave his authoritative opinion about "the value of mandates." In his encyclopedic *Mandates under the League of Nations* (Chicago, 1930) he examined in detail the origin of the mandate system, its organization and administration, and the problem of mandates in international law. To assess the achievement and deficiencies of the mandate system he discussed population statistics, health expenditures, policies toward land tenure and wages, and educational problems. He concluded that the mandate system "has proved a practical method for administering backward areas, more satisfactory than others that have been tried from the standpoint of the natives and from the standpoint of the world in general." Wright's book remains one of the best in the field. Among its many values is that it reflects the "general confidence" in the mandate system that he and others held in 1930.

In the late 1930's British publicists began to fear that the mandated territories might become the object of German aggression. The following titles indicate the prevalent anxiety about the future of the mandate system on the eve of World War II: Benjamin Bennett, *Hitler over Africa* (London, 1939); A. L. C. Bullock, ed., *Germany's Colonial Demands* (London, 1939); Percy Evans Lewin, *The Germans and Africa* (London, 1939), a revision of a book first published in 1915; Neil Macaulay, *Mandates—Reasons, Results, Remedies* (London, 1937); Eric Moore Ritchie, *The Unfinished War* (London, 1940); Granville Roberts, *The Nazi Claims to Colonies* . . . (London, 1939); and George Lowther Steer, *Judgment on German Africa* (London, 1939). The problems of this era were first studied in a scholarly way by Rayford W. Logan, *The African Mandates in World Politics* (Washington, 1948). More recently Wolfe W. Schmokel, in *Dream of Empire: German Colonialism, 1919-1945* (New Haven, 1964), has provided a wealth of new information based upon unpublished German sources.

The German writings of the interwar period, such as Heinrich Schnee, *German Colonization, Past and Future* . . . (London, 1926), aimed mainly at destroying the "German Colonial Guilt Lie." This myth of Germany's "colonial failure" had grown out of British propaganda of World War I, during which time humanitarians and Foreign Office officials alike had "exposed" German "colonial atrocities." During the interwar years the belief in German colonial "turpitude" began to wane, but it was not seriously challenged until 1938. In this year an American, Harry Rudolph Rudin of Yale University, published *Germans in the Cameroons* (New Haven). He wrote: "Germany's colonial accomplishments in thirty short years constitute a record of unusual achievement and entitle her to a very high rank as a successful colonial power. . . ." Rudin's well-argued account contradicts one of the premises on which the mandate system was founded: that the Germans had forfeited their "moral right" to administer colonies as a "sacred trust of civilization."

The transition from the Permanent Mandates Commission of the League to the Trusteeship Council of the United Nations is dealt with fully by Hessel Duncan Hall in *Mandates, Dependencies and Trusteeship* (Washington, 1948). Hall, an Australian scholar who served in the League secretariat, wrote the first part of this work for circulation at the San Francisco Conference of the United Nations Organization of April, 1945. The rest was completed before the tension between Russia and the Western Powers culminated in 1948; nevertheless, his book reveals the most important difference, perhaps, between the founding of the two systems of trusteeship: "The powers were not faced in 1919 (as they were to be in the United Nations) with any conflict in their basic ideology or way of life." The history of both institutions has been heavily influenced by this basic fact. The Permanent Mandates Commission consisted of a tightly knit group of colonial experts mainly from Western Europe. The work of the Trusteeship Council on the other hand has been conducted by spokesmen from all over the world in "an atmosphere of political tension and profound ideological division." The Permanent Mandates Commission was a forum that debated how to improve colonial administration; the Trusteeship Council has been "the battleground for ideological and political conflict"— a conflict initiated by the non-Western Powers to end Western colonialism.

Hall writes with insight and verve and with considerable historical knowledge. His volume will probably remain for some time the best work on the successes and failures of the mandate system. His views may be taken as representative of the conclusions of recent scholarship on the question. Hall concludes that the Permanent Mandates Commission was generally effective in supervising the mandated territories because of "the rapid maturity, the high level and continuity of its membership, the stability of its constitution, and the definiteness and certainty of its procedures." Regarding the most notable failure of the Commission, that of Japan, he writes:

The mandates system was based on an assumption of the League system as a whole. This was the assumption that there existed in the mandatory powers several at least of the fundamental processes of democracy—namely, an active and free parliamentary opposition able to question freely the government of the day, a free press whose reporters would be able to visit and report upon conditions in the territories, free access to the territories by visitors from abroad, and the writing of free books and papers by free students able to investigate the facts and to express freely their opinions. None of these factors existed in the case of Japan.

*Mandates, Dependencies and Trusteeship* was the first important work written in the era of post-World War II scholarship. What new light have other recent works thrown on the question of "international trusteeship?"

A considerable amount of interest in "mandates" has been generated by American political scientists concerned with "international organization." Ernst B. Haas, "The Reconciliation of Conflicting Colonial Policy Aims: Acceptance of the League of Nations Mandate System," *International Organization*, VI (November, 1952), 521-36, provides a good example of a political scientist's analytical approach to the founding of the mandate system. The other outstanding work by an American political scientist is the first full-blown study of the United Nations and colonial problems, James N. Murray, Jr., *The United Nations Trusteeship System* ("Illinois Studies in the Social Sciences," Vol. XL [Urbana, 1957]).

The works written recently by American historians are no less important. Based on a variety of unpublished sources, Lawrence E. Gelfand's *The Inquiry: American Preparations for Peace, 1917-1919* (New Haven, 1963) gives much new information about Wilson's advisory staff. Henry R. Winkler's *The League of Nations Movement in Great Britain, 1914-1919* (New Brunswick, N.J., 1952) contains a chapter entitled "The Idea of Colonial Trusteeship," which is a systematic examination of the development of this idea in the British press during World War I. Seth P. Tillman's chapter "The Opening of the Peace Conference and the Anglo-American Controversy over Colonial Claims and the Mandate Principle," in his *Anglo-American Relations at the Paris Peace Conference of 1919* (Princeton, 1961), is a summary of the negotiations at the Peace Conference based mainly on published sources. Campbell L. Upthegrove's *Empire by Mandate* (New York, 1954) digests the Permanent Mandates Commission's *Minutes*.

Other writers have used the Permanent Mandates Commission's

*Minutes* to discuss the administration of various mandated territories. Regional studies on the mandates in the Middle East began to appear in the interwar years, a good example of which is Jacob Stoyanovsky's *The Mandate for Palestine: A Contribution to the Theory and Practice of International Mandates* (London, 1928). More recent important works include Albert M. Hyamson's *Palestine under the Mandate, 1920-1948* (London, 1950) and Stephen H. Longrigg's *Syria and Lebanon under French Mandate* (London, 1958). Though she is not specifically concerned with the problem, Elizabeth Monroe, in her brilliant work *Britain's Moment in the Middle East, 1914-1956* (London, 1963), tersely discusses "the magic of the word 'mandate'": "It was sufficiently elastic to suggest to the British left that here was a fitting job for the new League of Nations, and to the British right that the essentials of imperial defence would remain safely in British hands." The theme of "strategic trusteeship" also runs through the pages of Alexander Hugh McDonald, ed., *Trusteeship in the Pacific* (Sydney, 1949).

On Africa there are several important works. Barnard T. G. Chidzero's *Tanganyika and International Trusteeship* (London, 1961) is a good study "of the interaction between the most pronounced of the diverse circumstances of Tanganyika, British colonial principles, methods, and practices, and the factor of international trusteeship." The other principal work on the East African mandate is Charlotte Leubuscher, *Tanganyika Territory: A Study of Economic Policy under Mandate* (Oxford, 1944). On West Africa see two works by David E. Gardinier, *Cameroon: United Nations Challenge to French Policy* (London, 1963), and "The British in the Cameroons, 1914-1961," in Prosser Gifford and William Roger Louis, eds., *British and German Colonialism in Africa* (forthcoming). See also Victor T. Le Vine, *The Cameroons from Mandate to Independence* (Berkeley, 1964). Much of the work concerning Southwest Africa is polemical. For a defense of the South African government, see *South-West Africa and the Union of South Africa: The History of a Mandate* (Union of South Africa Government Information Office, New York, 1949). For "the ironic tragedy whereby a League of Nations mandate became an instrument of oppression," see Ruth First's *South West Africa* (Harmondsworth, 1963). Since South Africa's refusal to participate in the United Nations Trusteeship Council and the legal complexities concerning the mandatory status of Southwest Africa will probably continue to generate controversy, perhaps it is of interest to place on record an opinion written by General Smuts in 1919 that the mandate was conferred upon "His Majesty in His Dominion Government."[18]

Sir William Keith Hancock's *Smuts: The Sanguine Years, 1870-1919* (Cambridge, 1962) contains an illuminating discussion of the "realist and idealist" elements of Smuts's mind and of the mandate system itself. This work (which is based on the Smuts archive) is a general history as well as a biography and is a valuable guide to the intellectual currents of World War I and the Peace Conference.

For the work of the Permanent Mandates Commission the most distinguished contribution of recent years, though only briefly touching on the subject, is the second volume of Margery Freda Perham's *Lugard: The Years of Authority, 1898-1945* (London, 1960). Lord Lugard served as British representative on the Permanent Mandates Commission for thirteen years and thus was the most important Englishman connected with "international trusteeship" during the interwar years. Miss Perham's biography is based on Lugard's private papers (of which those after 1919 are still in her possession; the rest are deposited in Rhodes House, Oxford). It is one of the few works, if not the only one, which delineates the personalities as well as the issues of the Permanent Mandates Commission. Discussing Lugard's attitude toward the mandate system, Miss Perham writes that he was "at once a nationalist and an internationalist." Lugard's book itself, *The Dual Mandate in British Tropical Africa* (Edinburgh, 1922), is an important point of departure for the two traditions of national and international trusteeship after World War I.

The distinction between "national" and "international" trusteeship is merely that of national rather than international responsibility for dependent peoples. Both these traditions have commonly been regarded as springing from Edmund Burke's dictum in 1783: "All political power which is set over men . . . ought to be some way or other exercised ultimately for their benefit. . . . Every species of political dominion . . . are all in the strictest sense a trust." This assumption has recently been challenged in a remarkable work of synthesis, Ramendra Nath

18. Buxton to Milner (transmitting Smuts's message), Nov. 15, 1919, tel. no. 10, "Correspondence as to Mandates," secret, Milner papers. Reference to further works on Southwest Africa may be found in a bibliography by C. F. J. Muller, F. A. van Jaarsveld and Theo van Wijk, *A Select Bibliography of South African History* (Pretoria, 1965). Also important is van Jaarsveld's *The Afrikaner's Interpretation of South African History* (Cape Town, 1964).

Chowdhuri's *International Mandates and Trusteeship Systems: A Comparative Study* (The Hague, 1955). "It was the Spanish jurists and theologians of the first half of the sixteenth century," Chowdhuri writes, "and not Edmund Burke, who first conceived the idea of modern Mandates and Trusteeship Systems." Apart from the interesting comparisons and contrasts which he draws between the two institutions under the League and the United Nations, Chowdhuri's work (which has a full bibliography) is valuable as an intellectual history of international trusteeship.

Less has been written on the "national" trusteeship of Great Britain. The most important recent work on this subject is George R. Mellor's *British Imperial Trusteeship, 1783-1850* (London, 1951), which in part is an attempt to refute the economic interpretation of the abolition of the slave trade given by Eric E. Williams in *Capitalism and Slavery* (Chapel Hill, 1944). In this connection see also the balanced comments of John D. Fage in his introduction to the second edition of Sir Reginald Coupland's *The British Anti-Slavery Movement* (London, 1964). By far the best work on "national trusteeship" in the interwar years is Kenneth Robinson's stimulating essay, *The Dilemmas of Trusteeship: Aspects of British Colonial Policy between the Wars* (London, 1965).

Despite these notable contributions, a full history of British trusteeship remains to be written. At present there is no consensus among scholars either about the origins of the idea of trusteeship or about the influence of the mandate and trusteeship systems on colonial administrations. From the nineteenth century to the present "international trusteeship" has meant different things to different Englishmen—as may be gathered by reading passages from Sir Harry H. Johnston's "International Interference in African Affairs," *Journal of Comparative Legislation and International Law* (London), n.s., XVIII (Part 1, 1918), 26-41; and Sir Alan Cuthbert Burns, *In Defence of Colonies: British Colonial Territories in International Affairs* (London, 1957). Yet despite the disagreement about the origin and application of the trusteeship idea, there is one distinct theme running through many of the works on Great Britain and the mandate system. This is that British trusteeship has had a definite impact on the colonial rule of the other European powers. Jack Simmons has recently stated with great force: "It is generally agreed that the idea of 'trusteeship' is one of the most important contributions Great Britain has made to the relations between Europe and its dependencies in the rest of the world."[19] Whatever the truth of this assertion, it may be taken as representative of the present trend in the historiography of the subject.[20]

19. Simmons in his introduction to Mellor's *British Imperial Trusteeship*, p. 7.
20. This paper was presented in modified form at the 1964 meeting of the African Studies Association.

# GIBRALTAR, MALTA, AND CYPRUS

## Edith Dobie

BRITAIN'S COLONIES in the Mediterranean have played significant rôles in every phase of the development of her Empire-Commonwealth. When Gibraltar was acquired from Spain in 1704, during the War of the Spanish Succession, Britain already had begun to concentrate upon world trade. This trade could be won and extended as well—and often better—by ensuring British influence in given areas rather than by establishing political control. Modern historians have called such regions "the informal empire," the extent of which greatly exceeded that of the colonies or formal empire.[1] The eastern part of the informal empire expanded rapidly, with India becoming of vital importance both for its trade and for developing British interests in adjoining parts of Asia.

As the volume of commerce mounted the British began to make some use of the old overland routes from the Mediterranean to the East via Egypt. To protect these routes Malta, which Napoleon had spied out as another Gibraltar, was obtained as a result of Nelson's victory over Napoleon in the Egyptian campaign. A third outpost, Cyprus, gained during the Congress of Berlin in 1878, was to be used to strengthen the Turkish Empire and thus to block Russia's access to the Mediterranean, check her drive toward India, and exclude her from the trade with Syria and other Turkish countries. These three places, Gibraltar, Malta, and Cyprus, as the eastern trade became more and more essential to Britain's continued prosperity, became guardians of what was literally a life-line of Empire.

1. Charles R. Fay, "Movement toward Free Trade," *Cambridge History of the British Empire* (Cambridge, 1940), II, 388-414; John Gallagher and Ronald Robinson, "The Imperialism of Free Trade," *Economic History Review* (London), 2nd ser., VI (Aug., 1953), 1-15.

The history of that Empire from the end of the eighteenth century was largely determined by two policies—pursuit of world trade and development of self-government. The latter had made great advance in the settler colonies by the early twentieth century, but in the dependencies, including the Mediterranean territories, expansion and protection of trade had been given priority and steps toward self-rule were very slow indeed.

World War I, with its slogan of "the consent of the governed," aroused British colonial officials to greater interest in hastening these steps. It also awakened in the people of the dependencies a more earnest desire to share management of their own affairs. Consequently from about 1921 forward the history of Gibraltar, Malta, and Cyprus turned largely on progress in self-government, a progress influenced by cultural relations and religion within the colonies. In the sphere of British government two problems were especially important: how to reconcile internally the right of self-determination with the status of a defense post and how, if this right were achieved, to ensure the unity of the colony and its continued connection with the Empire.

World War I was a kind of watershed dividing the content of historical writing on the three areas. Accordingly, after a necessarily brief and superficial discussion of the history of the route for protection of which these colonies have functioned in the Empire, the scant writings on each colony will be examined separately. Contents of books will be considered on the basis of their treatment of the reason for acquiring the colony; of the introduction and progress of self-government before 1921 and the acceleration of the movement for self-government after that time, together with the way self-government affects and is affected by Britain's purpose in holding her Mediterranean possessions in a rapidly changing world.[2]

2. There is an entire literature concerning the rôle of these outposts in Imperial defense and trade. Few histories of the Napoleonic Wars, of British naval policy, of modern Spain, or of modern Greece and the Near East are without important references and often entire sections on Gibraltar, Malta, or Cyprus. For much of the history of Britain in the Mediterranean one must turn to general works and military accounts. Many historians of eighteenth-century political events treat of the debate in England over the relative merits of Gibraltar and Minorca as a naval base, a debate that continued until Admiral Byng lost Minorca in 1756. To discuss these works would require several times the space available. This essay  is limited, on the whole, to a few selected overviews, to literature relating specifically to the three colonies, and to studies of post-1783 British activities in those colonies. The standard works in the earlier period such as Stetson Conn's *Gibraltar in British Diplomacy in the Eighteenth Century* (New Haven, 1942) are omitted.

GIBRALTAR

Two works are so basic as to deserve to be called, perhaps prematurely, "classics." In *British Routes to India* (Philadelphia, 1928), Halford L. Hoskins described Britain's tentative use of the overland routes from the Mediterranean to the Red Sea and the Persian Gulf. These routes gained extraordinary value by interaction with many factors—British maritime supremacy, the rise of steam navigation, Britain's growing control of India, and the growth of vast business and commercial interests in the eastern sector of this informal empire.[3] Eric A. Walker, "The Routes to the East," in Volume II (1940) of *The Cambridge History of the British Empire* (9 vols.; Cambridge, 1929-59) gave much attention to the diplomacy by which protection of the route was gained and ensured. He also explained the continuing importance of the Cape Route, especially after the discovery of diamonds and gold in South Africa.

There are few scholarly studies of Gibraltar, perhaps because this fortress colony has not attracted sociologically minded investigators interested in adjustments between cultures.[4] The history of Gibraltar differs from that of Malta and Cyprus inasmuch as the presence of two cultures, Spanish and English, and a common religion, Roman Catholicism, have been unifying rather than divisive influences. In addition, advances in self-government have come through Britain's initiative—not after agitation by the colonists—and have been put into effect with little or no friction.

Probably the best work on Gibraltar is an article by a Canadian scholar, Richard A. Preston. In a well documented piece, "Gibraltar, Colony and Fortress," in the *Canadian Historical Review* (Toronto), XXVI (December, 1946), 402-23, Preston recounted how merchants in the community that grew up within the fortress assumed non-political authority by organizing an Exchange Committee in 1817 to facilitate business transactions. The grant of a partially elected city council in 1921 and an executive council advisory to the Governor in the following year was made in advance of any demand by Gibraltarians. During

3. For a recent restatement, see Hoskins, *The Middle East* (New York, 1954), pp. 295-96.

4. Most writers on Gibraltar have made extensive use of Captain John Drinkwater (Bethune), *A History of the Late Siege of Gibraltar, 1779-1783* (London, 1785; reprinted, 1941), and Frederick Sayer's *The History of Gibraltar and Its Political Relations to the Events in Europe* (London, 1862).

wartime suspension of local government, from 1939 to 1945, an Association for Advancement of Civil Rights was formed to express public opinion, and it later exercised some influence in framing a constitution after the war.[5]

Allen Andrews, in *Proud Fortress: The Fighting Story of Gibraltar* (London, 1958), depicted vividly the rôle of Gibraltar in World Wars I and II. In the former it was the base for a convoy system that struck at the effectiveness of German submarines and made possible the eventual landing of American troops in Europe. In World War II a gathering point for ships carrying an invasion force to North Africa, and one means of getting supplies to Malta, Gibraltar also witnessed the improvement and enlargement of its key fortifications. Geoffrey Garratt in *Gibraltar and the Mediterranean* (New York, 1939), adds to Andrews' account by providing an accurate narrative of the history of Gibraltar from 711 to World War I. The second half of the book, more useful as a source than as history, consists of opinions—thought-provoking but supported by little evidence—on the vulnerability of the fortress and its relation to British Imperial interests during the inter-war years. Differing from the works of Preston, Andrews, and Garratt, which are scholarly and place emphasis on the military and political, are the works of journalists and travelers who strive for the colorful and the dramatic. Such books range from José Pfa's *Gibraltar* (London, 1955), a serious exposition of Spain's claim to this fortress site, to Paul Gallico's *Scrubby: A Diversion* (New York, 1962), a witty comedy about the apes of Gibraltar which occasionally rallies the military and the officials.[6]

## MALTA

Malta, on the other hand, gained a rather large measure of self-government in the latter half of the nineteenth century, and as a result

5. In "Citizenship, Parties and Factions in Gibraltar," *Journal of Commonwealth Political Studies* (Leicester), I (May, 1963), 249-65, Arnold J. Hudenheimer has written a perceptive analysis of constitutional and party development, and of social and economic progress, in the years 1945-60. He credits this progress to the Association for Advancement of Civil Rights. A single political party has resulted, thus preventing a division of the colony along religious lines. Loyalty to British institutions and traditions, as well as regard for cultural and family ties to Spain, continues.

6. Alison Yates, assistant editor of *New Commonwealth* (London), in "Gibraltar Still Prospers," XXXVII (June, 1959), 366-68, portrays the colony's political leaders as recognizing the impossibility of independence and working in co-operation with the British government to obtain the substantial share in self-government which they desire while successfully expanding their economy.

historians have primarily considered constitutional interests, and given much less attention to the military. After 1880 some leaders in the elections to the Council of State began to insist that the language and culture of Malta were Italian. They also asserted that English, which the working class wished to learn, was to be used to Protestantize their completely and devoutly Roman Catholic island. They contended, therefore, that those favoring more use of English were enemies of the Church. These fabrications bedeviled the political life of Malta from the late nineteenth century forward, set back self-government in 1903, put an end to responsible government in 1933, and were a factor in a second loss of responsible government in 1958.

The problems of language, religion, and government, together with those of an economy entirely dependent on Malta's strategic position, provided greater scope for the historian than did Gibraltar. Albert V. Laferla, an able Maltese-born scholar, in *British Malta*, I: *1800-1872*; II: *1872-1921* (Malta, 1945-47), traced the fluctuations of self-government and gave an illuminating account of the "language question," its relation to religion, and the way it was used to bring confusion to the life of the island and stalemate to the operation of the government. Harrison Smith, in *Constitutional Development in the Nineteenth Century*, Volume I of his *Britain in Malta* (2 vols.; [Valletta], 1953) also provided a heavily documented narrative of the tortuous course toward self-rule. He examined polemics of local leaders, reports of governors and Royal Commissions, and debates in Parliament, all of which helped to determine the way the movement veered. Much more limited in scope but superior to Smith for the period it covers, is Hilda Lee's "The Development of the Malta Constitution, 1813-1849," *Melita Historica* (Malta), I (1952), 7-18. First given as a lecture before the Royal University of Malta, Miss Lee's article presents a scholarly explanation of advance from rule by a governor to the first stage of representative government. Finally, a case study of a colonial governor gives added point to Miss Lee's work. Willis Dixon's *The Colonial Administration of Sir Thomas Maitland* (London, 1937) revealed the ruthlessness of the first governor in his attempt to establish efficient administration from 1813 to 1824. The benevolent despotism of Sir Thomas gave a handle to all who thereafter sought constitutional advance by representing British rule as tyrannical.

Even now, however, by far the best historical writing on Malta appears in William Keith (now Sir Keith) Hancock's *Survey of British*

*Commonwealth Affairs*, I: *Problems of Nationality* (London, 1937). Hancock discussed responsible government for the period 1919 to 1936 as granted immediately after World War I. After nine years of a reasonable facsimile of parliamentary government, counter charges that religion was being used to promote a political cause and that politics were being used to endanger the Church led to suspension of the election of 1930 and eventually to withdrawal of responsible government. All of this Hancock analyzed with dispassionate thoroughness, revealing the constitutional principles involved.

One other useful study of Malta, by an Australian student of ethnic migrations, Charles A. Price, is *Malta and the Maltese: A Study in Nineteenth Century Migration* (Melbourne, 1954). Price described the close family relations of the Maltese, their love of country, and their intense devotion to the Roman Catholic faith—features of their life which throw light on weak spots in the administration and help to explain the response of the people to political agitation.[7]

Sir Harry Luke, in *Malta: An Account and an Appreciation* (London, 1949), has considered social and economic conditions and problems in a lively resumé of the history of the island. There is a chapter on the impasse with the British government which came about as a result of a plan devised by the head of the Malta Labour party government, Dom Mintoff. In 1955 when most of her remaining dependencies were demanding separation from Britain, he proposed integrating Malta with the United Kingdom. This idea and the storms in its wake were discussed in two articles by Edith Dobie, "Malta and Her Place in the Commonwealth," *The Western Political Quarterly* (Salt Lake City), IX (December, 1956), 873-83; and "Whither Malta," *Parliamentary Affairs* (London), XII (Autumn, 1959), 329-36. The demand for integration is explained as devised to overcome obstacles in the way of dominion status, and the calamitous cultural-religious strife, now revived in new form, was revealed to be an indirect but decisive factor in bringing responsible government to an end and in giving Mintoff an opportunity to demand independence.

7. The only time the village meets as a corporate group is in a religious context, under the leadership of the parish priest. In this way the Church remains basic to the political life of the island. See Jeremy Boissevain, "Maltese Village Politics and Their Relation to National Politics," *Journal of Commonwealth Political Studies*, I (Nov., 1962), 211-22, and Boissevain, *Saints and Fireworks: Religion and Politics in Rural Malta* (London, 1965).

A summary of the position of the leaders of Malta's four political parties is F. I. Watson's "Malta in Transition," *New Commonwealth*, XXXVII (June, 1959), 369-71. They are shown demanding independence, dividing sharply over the conditions on which it is to be attained, and holding out inflexibly against any compromise. "What Prospect for Malta Now?" *New Commonwealth*, XL (April, 1962), 225-28, by Sir Hilary Blood, Chairman of the Malta Constitutional Commission, views the new constitution as freeing the Maltese from terms to which they had strenuously objected and interprets the election of 1962 and its results with reference to the position taken by the Church.

While the body of literature on Malta is more substantial than that on Gibraltar, it is largely to be found in such brief and present-minded journal articles. The lack of local archival collections holds back the development of a genuine Maltese historiography. Local manuscript sources for the period of British rule are limited to the papers of Sir Adrian Dingli, a distinguished jurist and Crown Advocate from 1854 to 1895, recently deposited in the Royal Library of Malta, and the papers of Lord Strickland in the possession of his daughter, the Hon. Mabel Strickland, which cannot be consulted easily. The debates of the Council of Government, later the Legislative Assembly, and files of many short-lived newspapers—all incomplete—are in the Royal Malta Library. Most of the future histories of Malta, despite independence, will therefore have to continue to be written from Colonial Office records in London.

### CYPRUS

A similar archival situation exists in the Republic of Cyprus. There is, however, a fairly substantial body of literature on this small country. When Cyprus came under British control in 1878 one-fourth of the inhabitants were Turks and Moslems, while three-fourths shared Greek culture and were members of the Greek Orthodox Church. The latter were exceedingly proud of their Greek heritage, and even at the time of Britain's occupation their clergy (who were also their political leaders) were proclaiming hope for union, or *Enosis*, with Greece. Within four years William E. Gladstone had granted a comparatively advanced form of self-government, and the clergymen-politicians regarded this step chiefly as a means for realizing their goal. *Cyprus under British Rule* (London, 1917), by Charles W. J. Orr, is a detailed description of the administrative system that resulted from Gladstone's policy. Doubting that the "Hellenic idea" really expressed popular desire, Orr criticized the indifference of Britain to the necessity of making self-government a reality. In questioning Britain's claim to be a "champion of small nations" he offered one of the challenges that soon were to arouse the Colonial Office to a more positive response to requests for self-government.

Arnold J. Toynbee, in a section of his *Survey of International Affairs, 1931* (Oxford, 1932), "Cyprus, the British Empire and Greece," wrote in the tradition of Gladstone[8] and with sincere belief in the proclaimed Allied aims of World War I. He protested that Britain had failed to live up to her obligations. *Enosis,* in his opinion, was a widely supported nationalist movement and it should have been dealt with as such by the British government. Sir Harry Luke also has written briefly of British rule in *Cyprus: A Portrait and an Appreciation* (London, 1957; 2nd ed., 1965). A former official in the island, Sir Harry differed with Toynbee in his conviction that at the time of the 1931 uprising 80 per cent of the villagers wanted to remain under British rule. The violence of the *Enosis* movement after 1955 he attributed to the influence of Soviet Russia, whose threat to the West Britain had to take into account in formulating a policy for Cyprus.

The most scholarly work on Cyprus, however, is George Francis Hill's *A History of Cyprus* (4 vols.; Cambridge 1940-52). In part of Volume IV, *The Ottoman Province: The British Colony,* covering 1571-1948, the author analyzed various aspects of Cyprus life under British rule, including a particularly good study of the agitation against annual payments on a Turkish debt, of the way the Orthodox clergy had been allowed to continue to use their influence in promoting *Enosis,* and of the system of self-government under which the Cyprus Council found that the unofficial majority was made powerless by a combination of the votes of the Turkish and the official members plus the casting vote of the governor. The book also is valuable in that the bibliography found in the footnotes is an exhaustive assembly of sources.

It is evident that political and constitutional history tends to dominate Cypriot historiography. Part of Sir Ronald Storrs' *Orientations*

8. See Gladstone, "England's Mission," *The Nineteenth Century* (London), IV (Sept., 1878), 560-84.

(London, 1937), for example, was an account of his governorship of Cyprus from 1927 to 1932. In an effort to better conditions he persuaded the British government to put an end to the Cyprus payments on the Turkish debt and used the funds made available to improve agriculture, forestry, health, and education. The clergy, whose political activities the Colonial Office would not permit the governor to curb, fearing, so Storrs believed, that economic and social improvements would weaken their influence, instigated the insurrection in 1931. Among the penalties imposed on Cypriots were loss of limited self-government and a belated ban on public demonstrations for *Enosis*, a step condemned by Toynbee but supported by Luke.

A Cypriot, Doros Alastos, who was prominent in the London Committee for Cyprus Affairs, in *Cyprus in History* (London, 1955) traced *Enosis* from 1878. Without rancor he represented it as a reasonable and orderly effort to obtain union with Greece. From his viewpoint, this posed no problem for Britain except putting into effect her fundamental principle of democracy; only when peaceful methods failed did *Enosis* leaders resort to violence. The book depicts only one side of the coin, but gives some aid in understanding the troubled history of Cyprus.

The history of the island was increasingly troubled in the 1950's. The leaders of terrorism in Cyprus were discussed in Wilfred Byford-Jones *Grivas and the Story of EOKA* (London, 1959); *Grivas: Portrait of a Terrorist* (New York, 1960), by Dudley C. Barker; *Cyprus' Guerrilla: Grivas Makarios and the British* (London, 1960), by Doros Alastos, and *Cyprus and Makarios* (London, 1960), by Stanley Mayes. Barker described Grivas as an unintelligent assassin but admitted his skill in obtaining young recruits for the National Organization of Cypriot Fighters (*EOKA*). He wrote with such contempt for Grivas that it is hard to evaluate the book as a means of insight into the Cyprus situation. Alastos, on the other hand, without expressing either approval or disapproval of Grivas, presented him as a successful organizer and guide of a revolution made necessary by stupid obdurance. Mayes was pessimistic about what Makarios would do in the future. He argued that the Archbishop had never shown any evidence of recognizing that Cypriots have any obligations to Britain, and he believed that at best Makarios would set up a feudal theocracy. Recently Charles Foley edited and helped write the *Memoirs of General Grivas* (London,

1964), and Alexander A. Pallis translated *General Grivas on Guerilla Warfare* (New York, 1964) from the Greek.

A brief look at the independent state of Cyprus is available in two articles by Nancy Crawshaw, "The Republic of Cyprus: From Zürich Agreement to Independence," *The World To-day* (London), XVI (December, 1960), 526-40, and "Cyprus: Collapse of the Zurich Agreement," *ibid.*, XX (August, 1964), 338-47. Based on parliamentary papers and other official publications, the articles dealt effectively with the Constantinople-Anglo-Cypriot negotiations, various anti-Makarios movements, the election that brought into existence the Republic of Cyprus, the budget crisis of 1961, and the cease fire of 1964. In *Island in Revolt* (London, 1962) Charles Foley, editor of the *Times of Cyprus* (Nicosia) from 1955 to 1960, wrote of these years with first-hand knowledge. With sympathy and understanding he discussed the dilemma of government and people in the face of terrorism and the difficulties encountered in inaugurating the new republic. Finally, Albert Julius Meyer and Simon Vassiliou, in *The Economy of Cyprus* (Cambridge, Mass., 1962) described the rôle of this colony in World War II when it served as a starting point for Allied guerrillas working against Axis forces in Greece, and demonstrated its new importance as a staging area for British forces after their withdrawal from Palestine and Egypt. Britain's expenditures for troop quartering and construction of bases having given great stimulus to the economy, it was the opinion of the authors that improvement could continue only with the expansion of agriculture and maintenance of "economic neutrality" in wooing the trade of both Israel and the new Arab states.[9]

9. In *The World To-day* (London), XX (March, 1964) 131-37, Anthony Verrier, Defence Correspondent of *The New Statesman*, writes of "Cyprus: Britain's Security Role." He notes decisive factors determining the situation, one being the fact that Cypriot-Turks, comprising one-fourth the population, own approximately one-half the cultivable area. He also explains the great importance of Britain's strategic interests; only on the express understanding that no damage be done to those interests did Britain grant independence to Cyprus. *The United Nations Review* (New York), XI (April, 1964) 5-15, 35-36, gives a detailed account of developments in Cyprus from December, 1963. This includes accounts of the London Conference, charges and counter charges of Greek Cypriot and Turkish Cypriot leaders, discussions in the Security Council, the positions taken by Turkey, Greece, and the Soviet Union and reports and statements from the U. N. Secretary General. In chap. ix of his book *A Start in Freedom* (London, 1964), Sir Hugh Foot gives a vivid account of what went on behind the scenes in the formulation and execution of plans to bring order to Cyprus during his governorship, November, 1957, to August, 1959. Of interest are the positions taken in regard to these policies by the Prime Minister, the Colonial Secretary, and representatives of the Greek and the Turkish government. T. W. Adams and Alvin J. Cottrell,

## The Mediterranean

Many developments since World War I have focused attention of students of the British Empire-Commonwealth on the Mediterranean area as a whole, quite apart from specific issues relating to the area as a route to the East. Several works of this type are worth noting. One of the best historians was the late Winston F. Monk of New Zealand. His book, *Britain in the Western Mediterranean* (London, 1953), was a concise narrative of Britain's control of this region from the eighteenth century through World War II. His account of the economic development of both Gibraltar and Malta is particularly informative. He analyzed with percipience the effort to find, after World War II, a form of self-government for Malta which, consonant with its economic situation and strategic position, would satisfy the desires of the Maltese people.

Among other works primarily concerned with Britain's position in this area was Margret Boveri's *Mediterranean Cross Currents* (London, 1938). The author, then a member of the staff of the *Berliner Tageblatt,* wrote an authoritative and discriminating resumé of the history of all three Mediterranean colonies and shrewdly appraised changes taking place in terms of their strategic value for Britain. In *The Mediterranean in World Politics* (London, 1938), Elizabeth Monroe discussed the Mediterranean route, the character of its trade and the threats to its safety as an arterial highway indispensable for Britain's economy and for Empire-Commonwealth defense, and explained something of the importance for Britain of dominance in the area and of the great value of British investment in the Levant countries, which still were part of the informal Empire in 1939. Most recently she has given us *Britain's Moment in the Middle East, 1914-1956* (London, 1963). In 1958 the Council of Chatham House, London,[10] issued *British Interests in the Mediterranean and the Middle East* (London). Those compiling it maintained that between 1945 and 1957 Britain suffered a major defeat in the area, a defeat which called for fundamental changes in attitudes and policies. The relation of the Mediterranean colonies to Britain no longer was merely a question of self-government

---

"The Cyprus Conflict," *Orbis* (Philadelphia), VIII (Spring, 1964), 66-83, is also helpful.

10. The Royal Institute of International Affairs.

but rather one of international good will. Britain's responsibilities should be shared with the North Atlantic Treaty Organization, but in that body the United States would have to be kept aware of the rights and requirements of British policy. Finally, Stewart C. Easton, in *The Twilight of European Colonialism* (New York, 1960), examined at length Britain's remaining dependencies with reference to progress toward self-rule. He included some discussion of political parties which, in the case of Malta in particular, provided some guidance to one trying to find a way in the maze of that island's political situation.

Two aspects of the historiography of this part of the Empire-Commonwealth that call for comment are the paucity of local histories and the failure of historians of the area to make use of the work of sociologists, anthropologists, psychologists, and other social scientists. The sparseness of writing on local history is due partly to the lack of adequate sources, partly to a general disinclination to pursue critical inquiry, and partly to the unimportance of local events in comparison with the Imperial developments and crises in which these colonies were involved. Limited as the content of local history may be, it offers, particularly in the case of Malta and Cyprus, a fertile field for the study of human behavior and its relation to the forces that have shaped the history of these colonies. It is to be hoped that historians in the future may either collaborate with students in other fields or make use of the ideas and techniques developed by them.

There are small beginnings in this direction. At the time of writing three books which use an interdisciplinary approach had been published. Of special use to the historian is *Malta: Background for Development*, by Howard Bowen-Jones and others (Durham, Eng., 1961). This study, made by geographers of Durham University, considered the community "in the round." One of several conclusions in regard to rural areas in the island is that here the relation of man to the land is astoundingly complete and coherent and that changes must be made with extreme caution. *The Socio-Religious Study of Malta and Gozo,*[11] Report No. 62 of the *Centre de Recherches Socio-Religieuses* (Brussels, 1960), is concerned with changes in the social situation and the way that such changes alter the place of the church in society and culture. It includes studies of such matters as urbanization, birth rates,

11. Gozo is a small island forming one of the electoral districts of Malta.

and age groups, all of which will be of interest to students of Malta's political affairs.

Most recently Diamond Jenness, in *The Economics of Cyprus; A Survey to 1914* (Montreal, 1962), has attempted to show how man has used this small island and what successes have attended his efforts to win a satisfactory livelihood. The study of the British regime of 1878-1914, when, the author thinks, the pattern was laid for all later economic expansion, will prove useful for future historians of that period.

It is to be hoped that in the future much more valid material will be furnished by social psychologists and social anthropologists, but some journalists and former residents of these islands already have written of the hopes and fears of their people with sympathetic insight. Their books describe the environment which helps to form the point of view of the workers and peasants who make up more than 70 per cent of the population of Malta and of Cyprus. They are valuable to an historian endeavoring to interpret those movements for self-government which have come to be directed toward a complete break with Britain. In *Malta and Me* (London, 1926) Eric Shepherd, an Oxford graduate teaching literature in Malta's Royal University, has given amusing accounts of student and public opinion. John Hay Beith's *Malta Epic* (New York, 1943) is one of several tributes to the high courage of the Maltese and their devotion to the cause of Britain in World War II. And towering above the numerous journalists writing about Cyprus is Lawrence Durrell. His book *Bitter Lemons* (New York, 1957) is the work of a poet sensitive to the frustration and despair of a people torn between real affection for England and an undying devotion to the cause of *Enosis*.

The sparseness of historical literature on this area is, perhaps, more apparent than real, for many of the works on Britain in Egypt and the Sudan, on the Suez Canal, and even on the Indian Ocean, as well as literature relating to Palestine-Israel, to the Middle East, and the Balkan frictions, contain peripheral material, often of considerable value and interest, on Cyprus especially, and Malta to a lesser extent. Such works as Thomas E. Marston's *Britain's Imperial Role in the Red Sea Area, 1800-1878* (Hamden, Conn., 1961) and David S. Landes' *Bankers and Pashas: International Finance and Economic Imperialism in Egypt* (Cambridge, Mass., 1958) are examples of the type of research on which British Mediterranean historiography may be said to lean. Nonetheless, there are few works of truly scholarly merit which focus upon this vital region of Empire-Commonwealth studies, and the field as a whole, despite the handicaps under which researchers would and do operate, is open to much future research.

# IRELAND'S COMMONWEALTH YEARS, 1922-1949

## Helen F. Mulvey

IRELAND'S TWENTY-SEVEN YEARS in the British Commonwealth is an episode of much interest and is deserving of more attention than it has received.[1] For students of Irish history it is a reminder of the power of the past; for students of Commonwealth affairs it is at the very center of those developments which move in the 1920's toward the Statute of Westminster, and in the 1930's follow from it. All the work, of course, which deals with Ireland in these years is not oriented solely to Ireland in the Commonwealth. Ireland, the new nation, has an interest all its own, an interest heightened in these days of new nations fiercely independent in spirit if not in power, and aggressively neutral in disposition.

For Ireland's Commonwealth history, certain large themes command the attention. Was Lloyd George's hope of reconciling Irish national aspirations with membership in the British Commonwealth foredoomed to failure? If India could so easily be accepted within the Commonwealth as a Republic in 1949, why, even allowing for twenty-five years difference in experience, was de Valera's "external association," or something like it, so impossible in 1921? How significant was Ireland's responsibility for pushing the Commonwealth toward a sharper definition of status and function? These questions suggest the force of Irish nationalism existing in the new context of the Common-

1. This essay is based on a selection of books which are important for interpretation or information. For all the sources which bear on any one of the subjects mentioned, the student will have to turn to British as well as Irish materials. An essay on Ireland in the Commonwealth cannot be the same kind of essay as one on Canada. The prelude would be a more extensive essay on British and Irish affairs than is possible here. For a recent interpretive essay see James C. Beckett, *The Study of Irish History: An Inaugural Lecture* . . . *13 March 1963* (Belfast, 1963). For bibliography on Irish internal history, see my "Modern Irish History Since 1940: A Bibliographical Survey (1600-1922)," *The Historian* (Allentown, Pa.), XXVIII (August, 1965), 516-59.

wealth, and they remind us that all the men who voted for the Treaty of 1921 did not necessarily think of it as a final settlement. Kevin O'Higgins, fated to play a significant rôle in Commonwealth history, saw the Treaty as an instrument for progress and reconciliation, a means whereby Ireland's full claims could be won "by peaceful political evolution."[2] Nor should Arthur Griffith's response to those bound too closely both to the distant and to the immediate past be forgotten: "Is there to be no living Irish nation? Is the Irish nation to be the dead past or the prophetic future?"[3]

To recall Griffith's words is to suggest that the episode of Ireland's membership in the Commonwealth can be only imperfectly understood without something more than a superficial knowledge of Irish history. Nor, as the student soon learns, is a knowledge of the immediate past enough. For the purposes of this essay, however, attention will be given by way of introduction to a few recent books which add to our knowledge of the forces and events which in the half century or so before 1922 were making modern Ireland and creating the nation that was to enter the Commonwealth. General histories can be mentioned first. Most students know Edmund Curtis's *A History of Ireland* (6th ed., London, 1951), a famous and distinguished work which concludes its story in 1922. Two good recent surveys which carry the story to the present are James C. Beckett's *A Short History of Ireland* (rev. ed., London, 1958), and Brian Inglis' *The Story of Ireland* (London, 1956). Inglis, in an introductory chapter, presents the contemporary scene, and in a concluding section, "After the Treaty," gives a compact and thoughtful statement on Irish affairs since 1922. Beckett's last chapter has some interesting observations on the "arrested development" of Irish politics, North and South, since 1922.

For the Irish nineteenth century there has been no Lecky, and the "great history" remains to be written. Three fairly recent books, however, alike in nothing except the period they study (roughly 1800-1922) and in the light they throw on Irish national aspirations, are important. Patrick S. O'Hegarty's *A History of Ireland under the Union, 1801-1922*[4] (London, 1952) might better have been called

---

2. Dáil Eireann, Official Report: *Debate on the Treaty between Great Britain and Ireland Signed in London on 6 December 1921* (Dublin, 1922), p. 47.

3. *Ibid.*, p. 338.

4. The full title is *A History of Ireland Under the Union, 1801-1922, with an Epilogue Carrying the Story Down to the Acceptance by de Valera of the Anglo-Irish Treaty of 1921.*

"Materials towards a History of Ireland, 1800-1922." O'Hegarty was a participant in the events described in the latter part of his book, which is therefore valuable for the period 1916-22. O'Hegarty supported the Treaty and calls the settlement of 1921 a "magnificent deed."[5] He makes the controversial judgment that the treaty killed England's "will to Empire."[6] The historical part of this book is rich in quotation from the literature on Irish nationalism—books, pamphlets, and newspapers. A quite different book is Nicholas Mansergh's *Ireland in the Age of Reform and Revolution: A Commentary on Anglo-Irish Relations and on Political Forces in Ireland, 1840-1921* (London, 1940). An analysis, not a narrative, this book looks at the Irish question from the point of view of Italian nationalists, of Marxists, and of various British statesmen. The author sees economic history as illuminating Anglo-Irish relations, not explaining them. The Irish question was a problem in politics, and a most serious charge against English statesmanship was its failure to help forward an inevitable new order in Ireland. The last chapter suggests that Irish nationalism, despite the intensity of its feeling, has been deficient in political ideas, a deficiency which has had, Mansergh suggests, a real effect on the failure to solve the problem of partition. Eric Strauss, in *Irish Nationalism and British Democracy* (New York, 1951), has also written an analysis, not a history, but his book stresses economic forces and class relationships. Economic interpretation dominates, but this fact does not prevent the ideas from being fresh and interesting. Strauss is especially good on Ireland's influence on nineteenth-century Britain, an influence which he sees continuing after 1922 in the wider sphere of the British Commonwealth.

A new work, filling a long-standing gap in Irish history, is a reminder that the more dramatic events of nineteenth-century Ireland have received a disproportionate share of attention: Robert B. McDowell's *The Irish Administration, 1801-1914* (London, 1964), a study of the duties and organization of government departments functioning in Ireland, is, it hardly needs saying, valuable for general history, and for an understanding of the administrative inheritance of the Free State in 1922.

Irish economic history has not received in any period enough atten-

5. O'Hegarty, *Ireland under the Union*, p. 773.
6. *Ibid.*, p. 774. For O'Hegarty's views in more detail, see his *The Victory of Sinn Féin: How It Won It, and How It Used It* (Dublin, 1924).

tion. Two recent books, even though their subject matter lies within the nineteenth century, and although they may not seem immediately relevant to the subject of this essay, should nevertheless be studied. *The Great Famine, Studies in Irish History, 1845-52*, edited by Robert Dudley Edwards and Thomas Desmond Williams (Dublin, 1956), is the work of several scholars. It is thorough in its research and generous in its judgments. The book will interest students of any part of the nineteenth century, but its central concern is with the famine itself. It raises some important questions about Ireland in the age of British laissez faire. Interestingly related to some of the themes of *The Great Famine* is R. D. Collison Black's *Economic Thought and the Irish Question, 1817-1870* (Cambridge, 1960). Black's book is a contribution to intellectual, economic, and Irish political history, even though politics is not its chief concern. A foreword by Jacob Viner suggests the interest which nineteenth-century Ireland should have for students of "colonialism," "economic imperialism," and "economic development." Two older works on Irish economic history are John E. Pomfret's *The Struggle for Land in Ireland, 1800-1923* (Princeton, 1930), and Jesse Dunsmore Clarkson's *Labour and Nationalism in Ireland* (New York, 1925). Clarkson argues that "the national aspirations of Ireland have derived their motive power from the driving force of social oppression."[7] His special vantage point is the Irish urban labor movement. A good half of Clarkson's work is devoted to the twentieth century. A last chapter, "Labour and the Free State," carries the story to 1925. Another survey which is not strong on historical background but which sets out in a clear and comprehensive manner the problems and rearrangements connected with Irish land legislation is Elizabeth R. Hooker's *Readjustments of Agricultural Tenure in Ireland* (Chapel Hill, 1938). It covers the period 1870 to 1938.

Irish events from 1886 and again from 1914 raise for the student many reflections. Suppose, for example, the Home Rule Act of 1914 could have operated with the co-operation of Ulster. What would have been the political evolution of Ireland and its relation to the Commonwealth? A book on the Free State published in 1940 suggests that the development of Ireland might have been toward Commonwealth status, that the 1914 act would have been outgrown with time.[8] This

7. Clarkson, p. 22.
8. Donal J. O'Sullivan, *The Irish Free State and Its Senate: A Study in Contemporary Politics* (London, 1940), p. 1.

view raises large questions and invites close study of the years from Parnell to 1916. Several recent books have added much to our understanding of that era. In *Parnell and His Party, 1880-1890* (Oxford, 1957), Conor Cruise O'Brien has written a study of as much interest to the political scientist as to the historian. He sees Parnell's whole course as one of reconciliation between "Irish national and English imperial traditions." A united, self-governing Ireland living in harmony with Britain was undoubtedly Parnell's desire. How would such an end, one must surely ask, ultimately have arranged itself in institutional form? This fascinating book is outstanding for its research, its use of new materials, and its clear style.

The details of Parnell's fall are the subject of an important work by Francis S. L. Lyons, *The Fall of Parnell* (Toronto, 1960). Lyons has used fresh manuscript materials and has shed new light on the last year of Parnell's life.[9] In an essay, "The Economic Ideas of Parnell," *Historical Studies II, Papers Read Before the Third Conference of Irish Historians* (London, 1959), Lyons has some interesting things to say on Parnell's attitudes towards agriculture and industry and on the ideas in his speeches made during the last year of his life. In *The Irish Parliamentary Party, 1890-1910* (London, 1951), Lyons had earlier studied Irish politics after the fall of Parnell. Not a general history, the book is a close study of the inner workings of the Parliamentary party itself. For the Parnell era and earlier, a famous work, which belongs as much to Irish as to English history, has recently been reissued with a new introduction by M. R. D. Foot: John LeB. Hammond, *Gladstone and the Irish Nation* (London, 1938; 2nd ed., Hamden, Conn., 1964). The most recent study on the Gladstone-Parnell era, which attempts to look at the Irish question from the Conservative side, is Lewis P. Curtis, Jr.'s *Coercion and Conciliation in Ireland, 1880-1892: A Study in Conservative Unionism* (Princeton, 1963). The author examines the rationale of Conservative opposition to Home Rule, studies government policy in Ireland from 1885 to 1892, and investigates the relation of the Irish question to Conservative political tactics and ideas.

A volume of much interest for the years before 1916 is *The Shaping of Modern Ireland*, edited by Conor Cruise O'Brien (Toronto,

9. For an important study of this book and the questions which it raises, see Robert Dudley Edwards, "The Fall of Parnell: 1890-1: Seventy Years After," *Studia Hibernica* (Dublin), I (1961), 199-210.

1960). A group of distinguished contributors discuss such figures as Stephens, Devoy, Clark, Hyde, Carson, Griffith, and Redmond. Full of interest as these biographical sketches are, they do not collectively provide a history of Ireland between 1891 and 1916. What they do suggest is the need for a quite different book which would examine the interaction of all the forces which were making modern Ireland before 1916: not only political, economic, literary, and cultural developments in Ireland itself, but British policies, for instance, on land, education, and local government. An important figure in pre-1914 Ireland on whom no separate essay appears in this volume is now the subject of a full length study by Emmet Larkin, *James Larkin, Irish Labor Leader, 1876-1947* (London, 1965).

On the period 1916-22, there is a large polemical literature; it will be possible here to mention only works which attempt to assess these years as a whole or which add seriously to our information on events or personalities. The most recent study is Edgar Holt's *Protest in Arms: The Irish Troubles, 1916-1923* (London, 1960). Although not a work of original research, Holt's book is an interesting and useful account of these years. An earlier, quite different, but partisan account is Dorothy Macardle's *The Irish Republic . . .* (London, 1937; 4th ed., Dublin 1951). Miss Macardle calls her book a "documented chronicle." There is in this nearly thousand-page work a wealth of quotations from a great variety of important documents. Miss Macardle's bias is pro-Republican and anti-Treaty, but no student of the period should neglect her work.

A famous book on the Treaty is Frank F. A. Pakenham's *Peace by Ordeal: An Account, from First-Hand Sources, of the Negotiation and Signature of the Anglo-Irish Treaty of 1921* (London, 1935). Writing in 1935, in the midst of de Valera's quarrels with the British government, Pakenham was on the Irish side, and he saw a time when historians, writing de Valera's biography and the history of the Irish Republican movement, would find for both a stronger case than he had himself made. His own view, expressed in the epilogue of his book, is one of agreement with the Republicans in 1921 who were prepared to co-operate with, but not be "inside," the British Commonwealth. It is essentially de Valera's formula of "external association." Whatever his own bias, Pakenham's sympathies are wide and he has been able to include within them both the men who opposed the Treaty, and those who supported it. Argument there has been and will be about this book; it remains an outstanding contribution to the history of the Treaty.[10] An older book is Walter Alison Phillips, *The Revolution in Ireland, 1906-1923* (London, 1923). The viewpoint is Unionist. Surprisingly, Phillips arrived at the opinion that the British government, having granted all it did in 1921, might have gone further to placate Republican sentiment along the lines suggested by de Valera's Document No. 2.[11] For a recent brief account of these events in their setting of postwar Britain there are the first two chapters of Charles L. Mowat's *Britain between the Wars, 1918-1940* (Chicago, 1955). The reader can follow some of the controversial literature in Mowat's most useful footnotes. In two vivid chapters (XIV and XV) in *The World Crisis: The Aftermath* (London, 1929), Winston Spencer Churchill, one of the negotiators of the Irish Treaty, gives his account of that event.

For more specialized studies on this period, a few largely recent contributions should be mentioned. In "Eoin MacNeill on the 1916 Rising," in *Irish Historical Studies* (Dublin), XII (March, 1961), 226-71, the Reverend F. X. Martin has made, in his analysis of two memoranda written by MacNeill, a scholarly addition to our knowledge of the 1916 rebellion. His lengthy notes discuss some of the literature on the rising. On Padraic Pearse there is an older book, Louis N. Le Roux, *Patrick H. Pearse*, translated by Desmond Ryan (Dublin 1932), but there is need of a new work. The most recent book on Connolly is C. Desmond Greaves, *The Life and Times of James Connolly* (London, 1961). Padraic Colum in *Ourselves Alone* . . . (New York, 1959) has done a sympathetic study of Arthur Griffith. In *Michael Collins* (London, 1958), Rex Taylor, an Englishman, has written a biography based to some extent on new materials, Collins'

10. For a critical discussion of Pakenham, see Desmond Fitzgerald, "Mr. Pakenham on the Anglo-Irish Treaty," *Studies* (Dublin), XXIV (Sept., 1935), 406-414. This important review suggests that Pakenham had not correctly interpreted the situation in Dublin among the Republicans and stresses the greatness of Collins and Griffith against the Republican extremists.

11. Phillips, p. 250. "It is possible to regret that the British Government having once made up its mind to surrender, did not frankly recognize the Irish Republic on some such terms as these. To have done so would not have exposed the Crown to any greater humiliation than it has suffered, nor Great Britain to any dangers from which the actual treaty preserves her. . . ." The text of de Valera's Document No. 2 can be found in Dorothy Macardle, *The Irish Republic: A Documented Chronicle of the Anglo-Irish Conflict and the Partitioning of Ireland* (London, 1937), pp. 959-63.

papers and letters made available to him from private sources.[12] Chapter XII contains some interesting material on dominion status and Collins' views on it. Collins emerges from this book, as he had from earlier studies, as a generous and intelligent moderate. On Collins' career the two older works are Piaras Béaslaí, *Michael Collins and the Making of a New Ireland* (2 vols.; London, 1926), and Frank O'Connor (Michael O'Donovan), *The Big Fellow* (London, 1937). In *The Black and Tans* (London, 1959), Richard L. Bennett has written on the Irish war of independence. For some of the special atmosphere and quality of this era, there is Desmond Ryan's *Remembering Sion* (London, 1934), a brilliant book difficult to put in any category. For the constitutional story and its end, Denis R. Gwynn's *The Life of John Redmond* (London, 1932) is important as is also a more recent book of history and reminiscence by John J. Horgan, *Parnell to Pearse* (Dublin, 1948).[13] Two biographies of Lord Carson may also be noted here: the first, Edward Marjoribanks and Ian Colvin's *The Life of Lord Carson* (3 vols.; London, 1932-36), and the more recent, Hanford Montgomery Hyde's *Carson* (London, 1953).

The critical literature on Ireland during the Commonwealth years is not large; one hopes eventually for more biographies, for more studies on the economic and cultural life of the state. These undoubtedly will appear after more time has passed. Ireland is only forty years away from an intense civil war, and many of the participants in that struggle are still involved in the public life of the country. A brief summary of some of the materials which will be useful can perhaps be made here before works of history and analysis are examined.

First, the debates on the Treaty must be read by any student attempting to understand the period 1922-49.[14] The Dáil and Senate debates speak for themselves. It would be useful if some speeches could be collected, those of Kevin O'Higgins for example. One such collection has been made by Donald R. Pearce in *Senate Speeches of W. B. Yeats* (Bloomington, Indiana, 1960). There are summaries of Dáil debates in *Journal of the Parliaments of the Empire* (London), 1922-1948. The relevant sources on Commonwealth matters can be found in

12. In Appendix K Taylor discusses the Collins materials. The name of but one of the four persons who gave him documents could be divulged.

13. On Horgan's book and for some interesting observations on post-Treaty Ireland, see Terence De Vere White, "An Aspect of Nationalism," *Studies*, XXXVIII (March, 1949), 8-14.

14. See footnote 2.

Sir Arthur Berriedale Keith, *Speeches and Documents on the British Dominions, 1918-31: From Self-government to Sovereignty* (London, 1932), and in Nicholas Mansergh, *Documents and Speeches on British Commonwealth Affairs, 1931-1952* (2 vols.; London, 1953). There is also Irish documentary material in *The Development of Dominion Status, 1900-1936* edited by Robert MacGregor Dawson (London, 1937).

Among periodicals, the *Round Table* (London) is an important source. The Irish articles cover current affairs, parliamentary debates, and Ireland's relations to the Commonwealth. The articles are not without a point of view, a fact which in no way lessens their value. *Studies*, a Dublin quarterly, gives space to history and current affairs. *Irish Historical Studies* (Dublin), founded in 1938, appears twice yearly. It reviews important books on Irish history and once a year publishes current bibliographies. The economic story can be followed to some extent in the *Economist* (London). The *Bell* (Dublin, 1940-54) is useful occasionally for political and economic, as well as for literary and cultural matters. Among newspapers the *Irish Times* (Dublin) is to be recommended. It was the former Unionist paper, and a study of its editorial views during Ireland's Commonwealth years would be an interesting subject in itself. A recent work of autobiography, by one who had professional associations with this famous newspaper, has interesting material on its post-1922 history: Brian Inglis, *West Briton* (London, 1962). For the various slants of party politics, the *Irish Press* (Dublin) and the *Irish Independent* (Dublin) will be of interest.

In discussing special books on Ireland's Commonwealth years, general accounts for the whole period had best be mentioned first, although there is no single historical account that covers the years 1922-1949. Pride of place must be given to two chapters, "Saorstat Eireann" and "Ireland Unappeased," in William Keith (later Sir Keith) Hancock's *Survey of British Commonwealth Affairs, I: Problems of Nationality, 1918-1936* (London, 1937). These chapters carry the story from 1922 to 1936 and are together a brilliant if brief history of the period; it is impossible in a few phrases to convey their high quality. The author gets at the minds and hearts of the men involved in Irish events before and after 1922; he can judge them, but with generosity. Hancock's narrative takes account not only of constitutional and economic matters but of the irrationalities of feeling. At the end of his account, written in the midst of the Anglo-Irish disputes of the 1930's, the author speaks not of Ireland and the Commonwealth, but of Ireland and Great Britain, an emphasis to be noted. The greater forces, he concludes, were working for co-operation and reconciliation between the two countries. It should be added that these chapters emphasize Ireland as a "problem in nationality" within the Commonwealth; they are not all the history of these years.

Hancock's work is brilliantly continued by Nicholas Mansergh in two volumes of the *Survey of British Commonwealth Affairs: Problems of External Policy, 1931-1939* (London, 1952, and : *Problems of Wartime Cooperation and Post-War Change, 1939-1952* (London, 1958). They cover the de Valera "revolution," Ireland at the League of Nations, the de Valera-Chamberlain agreement of 1938, Irish neutrality in the war, and the withdrawal from the Commonwealth. On this last, crucial subject Mansergh has written in considerable detail, and he has examined carefully the nuances of Irish domestic politics and their bearing on what occurred. In a "perspective view" of the years 1921-49, Mansergh calls it one of the "ironies of Commonwealth history" that de Valera's cherished "external association" was repealed while de Valera was out of power, and just before India remained within the Commonwealth as a republic.[15] Finally, the author suggests that the fundamental fact in these years was Ireland's relations with Great Britain, not with the Commonwealth, which for Ireland "was never more than a superstructure."[16]

One aspect of Ireland's contribution to the twentieth-century Commonwealth is discussed by Ridgway Shinn, Jr. in an unpublished Columbia University Ph.D. dissertation, "The Right of Secession in the Development of the British Commonwealth of Nations" (1958).[17] The thesis is concerned with South Africa as well as with Ireland, and includes material on India and on British opinion as it reacted both to Irish and to South African claims before and after the Statute of Westminister. Shinn argues that the right of secession, admitted before 1939, operated after the war as a constructive, not a disruptive force, enabling Britain to meet the emerging claims to independence of Asian and African states.

15. *Survey of British Commonwealth Affairs: Problems of Wartime Cooperation and Post-War Change,* p. 295.
16. *Ibid.,* p. 304.
17. I should like to thank Professor Ridgway Shinn of Rhode Island College for permission to read this thesis.

Two chapters on Ireland, which also deal with these years as a whole, are included in Nicholas Mansergh's *The Commonwealth and the Nations* (London, 1948). Chapter VII, "Political and Social Forces in Ireland, 1916-48," is a brief survey with important comment. It is not as helpful on social as on political matters. Chapter VIII, "The Implications of Eire's Relationship with the British Commonwealth of Nations," is a discussion which no student of the Commonwealth episode in Irish history can afford to miss. To try to summarize this compact, perceptive, and brilliant discussion would be difficult. The initial mistake, Mansergh suggests, was made in 1921 with the application of dominion status to Ireland. Once a member, Ireland "strengthened greatly the fissaperous tendencies" in the Commonwealth in the years 1926-31 and, it is "probable," hastened Commonwealth developments which "in any event" Canada and South Africa would have demanded. A better solution more in harmony with "psychological realities" would, after all, have been something resembling de Valera's "external association," applied imaginatively from the beginning. Writing in 1948, Mansergh saw lessons to be drawn from the Irish experience in handling the nations of Africa and the East as they won their freedom and entered the Commonwealth. Like Ireland, they would be sensitive about history, tradition, and symbol; and these intangibles, insufficiently recognized in 1921, must be considered. In view of all that has happened since, this essay is of extraordinary interest. One or two questions suggest themselves. Should there not be more study on the possibilities really open to the British government in 1921? If Irish dominion status was in retrospect a mistake, could that mistake, considering everything, have been avoided?

A fairly recent book, not devoted solely to Commonwealth matters, contains important material. This is Alfred G. Donaldson's *Some Comparative Aspects of Irish Law* (Durham, N.C., 1957). In Chapter III, "Ireland and the Commonwealth, Dominion Status and International Law," the author judges Ireland's contribution to the Commonwealth to have been "considerable" in the development of dominion status, in the use of public international law, and in the application of private international law rules. The volume has excellent bibliographies for legal and constitutional matters. A second chapter, "Constitutional History," is a useful summary of a field for which no comprehensive work as yet exists.

One of the few books which deal with a special aspect of domestic history for the entire period, 1919-49, is a recent study of politics by John L. McCracken, *Representative Government in Ireland: A Study of Dáil Eireann, 1919-1948* (London, 1958). The most original part of the book is the analysis of the educational and vocational background of Dáil members. The accompanying tables of statistics are most valuable. McCracken has also studied the Dáil member from the point of view of parliamentary experience, age, and length of political service. The book assembles material not easily available and should be indispensable to anyone working on other aspects of this period.

For brief surveys on various aspects of Irish life since 1921, the December, 1951, issue of *Studies* (XL) should be consulted. The entire number is devoted to the thirty years since the Treaty. Four of these essays are especially pertinent: Vincent Grogan, "Irish Constitutional Development," pp. 385-98; Robert C. Geary, "Irish Economic Development since the Treaty," pp. 399-418; John O'Donovan, "Trends in Agriculture," pp. 419-27; and Seamus O'Farrell, "The Changing Pattern of Irish Life," pp. 428-36. There are briefer articles on education, Irish letters, the theater and drama, and the arts.[18] Geary's essay suggested that the most disappointing features of Irish economic life since 1921 have been the failure of Irish agriculture to develop, and the continued migration from the land to Dublin and to the cities of Great Britain and the United States.

Three books which are valuable for Irish internal affairs may be mentioned together, although they treat of quite varied matters. Joseph Johnston surveys the problems of agriculture in these years in *Irish Agriculture in Transition* (Oxford, 1951). He is concerned with those aspects of former land policies which explain the mid-century difficulties of Irish farming, and he diagnoses the problems as social and technical as well as agricultural. He includes material on the Anglo-Irish economic war of the '30's. For the administrative side of Irish government, *Public Administration in Ireland*, edited by Frederick C. King (3 vols.; Dublin, 1944-54) should be consulted. A book which is significant and interesting is Percy Arland Ussher's *The Face and Mind of Ireland* (London, 1949). Part I has some political material and a brief

18. The other essays are: Sean O'Cathain, "Education," pp. 437-56; Lorna Reynolds, "Thirty Years of Irish Letters," pp. 457-68; Roger McHugh, "Tradition and the Future of Irish Drama," pp. 469-74; and Thomas McGreevy, "Development in the Arts," pp. 475-78.

estimate of de Valera. Two articles written in the '50's are useful on certain aspects of Irish affairs since 1921, although they are looking at the contemporary scene. These are by John V. Kelleher, "Can Ireland Unite?" *Atlantic Monthly* (Boston), CXCIII (April, 1954), 58-62; and "Ireland—And Where Does She Stand?" *Foreign Affairs* (New York), XXXV (January, 1957), 485-95.

On the Cosgrave era there are several important books. Leo Kohn in *The Constitution of the Irish Free State* (London, 1932) is concerned with the legal development of the constitution of 1922. Nicholas Mansergh, in *The Irish Free State, Its Government and Politics* (New York, 1934), writes a comprehensive analysis of the institutions of the new state. Students of the author's later work, already discussed in this essay, will be interested in the entire work, but particularly in the chapter on "External Relations." Here the author contends that Ireland was "in no small measure" responsible for the development of inter-Imperial constitutional law and practice from 1922 to 1931.[19] William Warner Moss in his *Political Parties in the Irish Free State* (New York, 1933), deals with the working of party machinery, finances, local and national organization, candidates, and campaigns. For a study of the new state at work there is Denis Gwynn's *The Irish Free State, 1922-1927* (London, 1928). Part I discusses dominion status and Part II the work of founding the state and getting its various parts to function. It is Part III which contributes material assembled nowhere else in quite the same way. There are, for instance, chapters on unemployment, agriculture, the Shannon electrification scheme, public credit, education, roads, railways, and the post office. The viewpoint of the book is one of admiration for the solid work of the Cosgrave government.

Especially valuable on the Free State Senate, its founding, its procedures, and its membership is Donal J. O'Sullivan's *The Irish Free State and Its Senate: A Study in Contemporary Politics* (London, 1940). As Clerk of the Senate, O'Sullivan had opportunities to know from a position of "intimate detachment" of all he writes. This book is more than a history of the Senate; it covers the whole range of Free State political history beyond the Cosgrave régime into the de Valera era to 1939, and future students will find it an important source. The author's viewpoint is that of a constitutional nationalist. His sympathies

19. *Irish Free State*, p. 263.

lie with the makers of the Free State, and he is critical of de Valera. He finds his own position in history and tradition. "We are of diverse origin," he writes, "but we are one people" (p. 21). Partition he would end, but in 1939 he saw no way to do it; he believed it would be more easily ended within the Commonwealth than without it. O'Sullivan, looking at the geographical whole of Ireland in 1939, saw membership in the Commonwealth of Nations as the "régime which divides us the least," with many privileges and few remaining obligations (p. 26).

Biographical studies of those whose careers lie wholly within the last forty years are rare, and it is still too soon to expect many. For the history of the Cosgrave government there is, however, one of outstanding significance. This is Terence De Vere White's *Kevin O'Higgins* (London, 1948). The author's materials should be noted. He was given every assistance by O'Higgins' family and had the help of O'Higgins' colleagues who had worked with him at the Imperial Conference of 1926. Leopold Amery read the sections of the book concerned with that conference, and in letters to White suggested that he had overstated the case for O'Higgins' influence on the decisions of 1926. Amery's comments are published as footnotes and will interest students of Commonwealth events in the '20's.

Among articles a few on the Cosgrave period can be noted. Hugh Kennedy, Chief Justice of the Irish Free State, wrote on the "Character and Sources of the Constitution of the Irish Free State" in the *Journal of the American Bar Association* (New York), XIV (September, 1928), 437-45, and on "The Association of Canada with the Constitution of the Irish Free State" in *Canadian Bar Review* (Toronto), VI (December, 1928), 747-58. This second article discusses the "Canadian clauses" in the Free State Constitution. Kennedy hailed Canada as an example of the truth that no man can set bounds to the onward march of a nation "even by a written constitution." Andrew E. Malone's "The Development of Party Government in the Irish Free State" in the *Political Science Quarterly* (New York), XLIV (September, 1929), 363-78 supplements the book of William Warner Moss already mentioned. Three articles in *Foreign Affairs*, each by a famous Irishman, estimate the various achievements and problems of the Free State during the first dozen years of its existence. These are George Russell (A.E.), "Twenty-Five Years of Irish Nationality," VII (January, 1929), 204-20; Sir Horace Plunkett, "Ireland's Economic

Growth," V (January, 1927), 205-18; and Eoin MacNeill, "Ten Years of the Irish Free State," X (January, 1932), 234-49. In "Lord Balfour's Legacy to Ireland," *Nineteenth Century* (London), XCVIII (September, 1925), 361-69, Denis R. Gwynn makes some interesting connections between the old régime and the new. His subject is the congested districts of western Ireland.

For the de Valera period in the '30's, for the links of policy which connect it with the Cosgrave era, and for its constitutional differences with Great Britain, a number of the books of Sir Arthur Berriedale Keith are important. Two will be mentioned here: *Letters on Imperial Relations, Indian Reform, Constitutional and International Law, 1916-1935* (London, 1935); and *The King, the Constitution and the Empire and Foreign Affairs* (London, 1938). These volumes are collections of letters addressed at various times by Keith to the press. He was, from the beginning, realistic about the Irish situation. Indeed, he was asking in 1922 whether the British Commonwealth was not flexible enough to encompass a Republic.[20] In 1933 he said that the Cosgrave government had made many gains towards a fuller sovereignty. Was not the British government, in its quarrels with de Valera, "Straining at a gnat after swallowing a camel?"[21] To be read in conjunction with Keith's books is Henry Harrison's *Ireland and the British Empire, 1937: Conflict or Collaboration?* (London, 1937). The author is critical of certain sectors of British opinion which would have frozen Ireland's position to the Treaty status of 1921, in spite of the Statute of Westminster. Harrison's view is one of friendliness to both countries, of reconciliation based on a recognition of Ireland's full rights. For a later discussion of many of the issues raised by Keith and Harrison the relevant pages on Ireland in Kenneth C. Wheare's *The Constitutional Structure of the Commonwealth* (Oxford, 1960) can be consulted.

For the years between the External Relations Act of 1936 and the war, the account of Mansergh in the *Survey of British Commonwealth Affairs* is the best. There are several useful articles on special matters, a few of which can be mentioned. Arthur Bromage discusses the constitution of 1937 and its background in "Constitutional Development in Saorstat Eireann" and "The Constitution of Eire" in the *American Political Science Review* (Baltimore), XXXI (October and December,

20. *Letters*, p. 34.
21. *Ibid.*, p. 133.

1937), 842-61 and 1050-70. James Hogan, in "Ireland and the British Commonwealth, 1931-7" in *Ireland To-day* (Dublin), II (October, 1937), 11-26, sees the situation with the Commonwealth created by the de Valera government as ending either in secession, or in a new type of relationship. Joseph Johnston has examined de Valera's economic policies in "The Anglo-Irish Economic Conflict," *Nineteenth Century*, CXIX (February, 1936), 187-200.

On Ireland and the war there is Henry Harrison's *The Neutrality of Ireland: Why It Was Inevitable* (London, 1942). Harrison explains Irish neutrality in terms of mistaken British policies, especially in regard to Partition. A different emphasis is found in an important article by R. M. Smyllie, "Unneutral Neutral Eire," *Foreign Affairs*, XXIV (January, 1946), 317-26. The author suggests that Ireland was of "greater assistance to the Allies as an official neutral than she could have been as an active belligerent." He notes also the view that Partition saved the Allied cause because of the importance of Northern Ireland as a military base. For official Irish views of the issues a collection of de Valera's speeches, *Ireland's Stand* (Dublin, 1946), should be consulted.[22] There is a useful and objective account of Ireland's neutrality by Constance Howard in *Survey of International Affairs, 1939-1946: The War and the Neutrals*, IX, Arnold and Veronica Toynbee, eds. (Oxford, 1956), 230-56.

The very full account of Ireland's secession from the Commonwealth in Mansergh's *Problems of War Time Cooperation and Post-War Change* has been noted. The debates in the Dáil and Senate should be followed for all the nuances. The prelude, as it turned out, to the Republic of Ireland Act, was J. A. Costello's Canadian speech, "Ireland in International Affairs," delivered in Toronto in September, 1948. The text is in the *Canadian Bar Review*, XXVI (October, 1948), 1195-1211. Three articles in *International Affairs* (London) which have to do with the situation created by Ireland's withdrawal from the Commonwealth are illuminating in various ways. These are Robert F. V. Heuston, "British Nationality and Irish Citizenship," XXVI (January, 1950), 77-90; Nicholas Mansergh, "Ireland: The Republic Outside the Commonwealth," XXVIII (July, 1952), 277-91; and Sean MacBride, "Anglo-Irish Relations," XXV (July, 1949), 257-73.

22. The full title is *Ireland's Stand: Being a Selection of the Speeches of Eamon de Valera during the War, 1939-1945* (Dublin, 1946).

There have been a number of attempts to estimate the character and career of Eamon de Valera. There is Denis R. Gwynn's *De Valera* (London, 1933); Desmond Ryan's *Unique Dictator: A Study of Eamon de Valera* (London, 1936); Seán O'Faoláin, *De Valera* (London, 1939); M. J. MacManus, *Eamon de Valera, A Biography* (Dublin, 1944); and Mary C. Bromage, *De Valera and the March of a Nation* (London, 1956). This last book has the advantage of later publication but suffers from an unfortunate adulatory tone; narration, not analysis, dominates. Desmond Ryan makes an interesting judgment for 1936 that "on a short view, Mr. de Valera is fallible enough"; however, "on a long view, with very few reservations, he stands out as one of the great figures in Irish history."[23] Mansergh judges that in a certain sense de Valera was a "Commonwealth statesman," and he argues that this description is less "paradoxical" than it at first sounds.[24]

Some brief mention must be made of books which deal with Partition, a question which has been so deeply involved with Irish attitudes to Great Britain and the Commonwealth. For background there is Edward R. R. Green, *The Lagan Valley 1800-1850: A Local History of the Industrial Revolution* (London, 1949). For various aspects of northern Irish history since 1800, two books of essays, *Ulster since 1800: A Political and Economic Survey* (London, 1954), and *Ulster since 1800, Second Series: A Social Survey* (London, 1957), both edited by Theodore W. Moody and James C. Beckett, are very helpful. For the institutions and problems of Northern Ireland there is Nicholas Mansergh, *The Government of Northern Ireland: A Study in Devolution* (London, 1936), and two more recent books, Desmond G. Neill, ed., *Devolution of Government: The Exepriment in Northern Ireland* (London, 1953), and *Ulster Under Home Rule*, edited by Thomas Wilson (London, 1955). One of the essays in Wilson's book is of interest for the war years: "Northern Ireland and the Defense of the British Isles," by Cyril Falls. The official history of Northern Ireland and the war has been written by John W. Blake, *Northern Ireland in the Second World War* (Belfast, 1956). Northern Ireland's part in the battle of the Atlantic was crucial, Blake judges, and her most important contribution to the outcome of World War II.

23. Ryan, pp. 10-11.
24. *Problems of Wartime Cooperation*, p. 264.

For the origins of Partition one should read Denis Gwynn, *The History of Partition, 1912-1925* (Dublin, 1950). Gwynn argues that Partition is so illogical and so harmful that it "cannot continue indefinitely" (p. 10). For another view there is Hugh Shearman, *Not An Inch: A Study of Northern Ireland and Lord Craigavon* (London, 1942). There is a sizable controversial literature on Partition, but there is one most interesting recent book written by a southern Irishman, which with some sympathy attempts to assess the point of view of the North. That is Michael Sheehy, *Divided We Stand: A Study of Partition* (London, 1955). The financial and economic problems of Partition are set out by Labhras O'Nuallain in *Ireland: Finances of Partition* (Dublin, 1952). Recently Marcus W. Heslinga, a Dutch geographer, has addressed himself to the problem of the division of Ireland in *The Irish Border as a Cultural Divide: A Contribution to the Study of Regionalism in the British Isles* (New York, 1962).

One might end this survey with mention of an address given at University College, Cork, in 1957 by Francis, Lord Pakenham, and published as *Forty Years of Anglo-Irish Relations* (Cork, 1958). Considering the possibility of a united Ireland, with Partition ended, rejoining the Commonwealth as a Republic, he ends his speculations on a note "not yet clearly articulated." Already, perhaps, the moment, if there ever was one, for any such Commonwealth arrangement has passed. As for historical writing, there should lie ahead in our century many new perspectives on the theme of "the recession of Empire." The history of Ireland from 1922 to 1949, its rôle in shaping the new Commonwealth, its reconciliation with Great Britain, and its own independent life should be significant parts of that larger story.

# THE BRITISH WEST INDIES

## D. A. G. Waddell

THREE PHASES may be discerned in the historiography of the British West Indies. In the first of these, from earliest times to the beginning of the present century, the writing of West Indian history was in the hands of "amateurs," usually either West Indians of the ruling class, or British sojourners in the West Indies, whose interests were primarily local and whose main qualifications were local knowledge and experience. In the second phase, although local residents continued to contribute, the most important work was done by professional historians from the universities of Britain and America, whose interests usually lay in some wider sphere than the West Indies, and whose basis for writing was extensive use of the records of the British government. The third phase, which may be dated from the early 1950's, and is thus as yet in its very early stages, may be expected to be dominated by the West Indian professional historian.

The first phase, which has already been the subject of a historiographical study by Elsa V. Goveia,[1] need only be outlined here. Historical writing about the British West Indies started very soon after their settlement in the early seventeenth century,[2] and in the eighteenth century some attention was given to the West Indies in works on the history of the British Empire generally. But in the dozen or so seventeenth- or eighteenth-century studies of the British islands, the historical element is rather incidental to what were really either descriptive contemporary accounts or pamphlets advocating, opposing, or justifying contemporary actions or policies. Such distinctions are of course far from clear cut—indeed there is little writing in the first phase that is exclusively historical—and necessarily arbitrary. But it is pos-

[1]. *A Study on the Historiography of the British West Indies to the End of the Nineteenth Century* (Mexico, 1956), on which the following paragraphs are largely based.

[2]. The Spanish discovery and settlement of islands later to become British had already been chronicled before British colonization began.

sible to suggest that the first two important works on the history of the British West Indies were products of the late eighteenth century— Edward Long's *The History of Jamaica* . . . (3 vols.; London, 1774) and Bryan Edwards' *The History, Civil and Commercial, of the British Colonies in the West Indies* (2 vols., London, 1793; enlarged ed., 3 vols., 1801). Both Long and Edwards were identified with the West Indian plantocracy, and reflected its interests and prejudices. In discussing disputes between the colonial legislature and the British government, for example, they were very much on the colonial side; and both defended the institution of slavery, though, where Long justified it on grounds of Negro racial inferiority, Edwards, writing a little later when the humanitarian attack had begun, argued for its retention more on grounds of expediency necessitated by the Negro's cultural inferiority. Though they wrote very much from a West Indian point of view, both Long and Edwards used a wide range of materials with care and skill, and, like other West Indian historians before and after them, did not confine themselves to political narrative, but included lengthy, and in Long's case encyclopedic, analyses and descriptions of such aspects as natural resources, economic development, social structure, and administrative institutions.

None of the productions of the nineteenth century reached quite the level of Long and Edwards, whose works have some claim to be regarded as literature, though several were of interest and importance. Thomas Coke, the founder of Methodist missions in the West Indies, for example, sought to remedy Edwards' neglect of religious history in his *A History of the West Indies, Containing the Natural, Civil, and Ecclesiastical History of Each Island; with an Account of the Missions Instituted in Those Islands from the Commencement of Their Civilization* . . . (3 vols.; Liverpool, 1808, London, 1810-11). Coke's view was wider than that of Edwards, not only in this respect, but also in that he dealt with all of the West Indian islands, rather than just the British ones. In this he was followed by Thomas Southey, a naval officer with much Caribbean experience, whose *Chronological History of the West Indies* (3 vols.; London, 1827) was a simple annalistic compilation of facts, supported by much careful documentation. Neither of these visitors to the West Indies shared the viewpoint of the plantocracy. Coke's position was that of a Christian determinist, while Southey was a humanitarian who favored the abolition of slavery and criticized the planter-dominated colonial governments. On both these grounds he was violently opposed by George Wilson Bridges, an Anglican clergyman, whose *The Annals of Jamaica* (2 vols.; London, 1828) represented the extreme planter attitude, defending slavery on racial grounds and the colonial assembly by traditional constitutional arguments. Much of Bridges' book is of little value, adding nothing to Long, and its main contribution lies in its account of the economic decline of the island since Long's time.

After Bridges, with the defeat of the plantocracy over the emancipation of the slaves in 1833, the plantocrat tradition in West Indian historical writing, which had reached its peak in Bryan Edwards, virtually died out. History continued to be written, however, by public officials, non-conformist clergy, doctors, lawyers, and the like; and a number of competent histories of individual colonies appeared, such as Henry H. Breen's *St. Lucia: Historical, Statistical, and Descriptive* (London, 1844); Henry I. Woodcock's *A Histoy of Tobago* (Ayr, 1867); James Rodway's *History of British Guiana, from the Year 1668 to the Present Time* (3 vols.; Georgetown, 1891-94); and Lionel M. Fraser's *History of Trinidad* (2 vols.; Port-of-Spain, 1896). Two works were rather more than this. Sir Robert H. Schomburgk's *The History of Barbados, Comprising a Geographical and Statistical Description of the Island, a Sketch of the Historical Events since the Settlement, and an Account of Its Geology and Natural Productions* (London, 1848), the work of a European geographer well acquainted with the island, is comparable in its scope and quality of analysis to Long's *Jamaica*; and *A History of Jamaica from its Discovery by Christopher Columbus to the Year 1872* (London, 1873), by William J. Gardner, a Congregationalist missionary of many years' residence in the Colony, combined a dispassionate approach with a comprehensive and careful study of a wide variety of sources, and represents amateur local history at its best.

These writers, and others like them, had usually tried to tell the whole story of their islands. Toward the end of the nineteenth century another group emerged, perhaps more properly described as antiquarians than historians, who tended to content themselves with accumulating and recording facts and were responsible for works such as James H. Lawrence-Archer's *Monumental Inscriptions of the British West Indies* (London, 1875); Vere Langford Oliver's *The History of the Island of Antigua* ... (3 vols.; London, 1894-99)—a largely gene-alogical study; Nicholas Darnell Davis's *The Cavaliers and Round-heads of Barbados* (Georgetown, 1887); and the periodicals *Timehri, Caribbeana,* and the *Journal of the Institute of Jamaica.*[3] In this cate-gory Frank Cundall is outstanding. His work, extending over nearly half a century, in bibliography,[4] in compiling information on Jamaican history,[5] and as librarian in making known and available the resources of the Institute of Jamaica, contributed materially to the ability of others to write West Indian history.

At the opposite end of the scale, no West Indian had presumed to follow in the footsteps of Bryan Edwards. After Southey, the only significant attempts to give a general account of the history of the British West Indies were made by two English writers, Robert Mont-gomery Martin and Sir Charles P. Lucas, as part of larger works on the British Empire as a whole.[6] In this wider view, and in that they were outsiders and at least semi-professionals, Martin and Lucas may be regarded as precursors of the second phase of West Indian histori-ography. On the other hand, their treatment of the whole of the area's history was more characteristic of the first phase, when perhaps writers were influenced less by academic inhibitions and more by literary pre-tensions, and stands in marked contrast to the characteristic production of the second phase, which was the narrower detailed study of a partic-ular period or aspect of West Indian history.

It is, however, from the point of view of Imperial history, implicit in Martin and Lucas, that most of the works of the second phase were written, being conceived both in Britain and America rather as contribu-

3. *Timehri: The Journal of the Royal Agricultural and Commercial Society of British Guiana* (Demerara, 1882-97); *Caribbeana: Being Miscellaneous Papers relat-ing to the History, Genealogy, Topography, and Antiquities of the British West Indies* (London, privately printed, issued irregularly 1909-19); *Journal of the Institute of Jamaica* (Kingston, published irregularly 1891-99).

4. Of which the most important were *Bibliographia Jamaicensis* (Kingston, 1902) and *Bibliography of the West Indies (excluding Jamaica)* (Kingston, 1909).

5. Presented in such works as *Historic Jamaica* (Kingston, 1915); *The Governors of Jamaica in the Seventeenth Century* (London, 1936); and *The Governors of Jamaica in the First Half of the Eighteenth Century* (London, 1937); as well as in articles in the *Journal of the Institute of Jamaica* and elsewhere.

6. Martin's *History of the British West Indies* was Volumes IV and V of his larger work, *The British Colonial Library* (10 vols.; London, 1838-44), and he also dealt with the West Indies in Volume IV of *The British Colonies: Their History, Extent, Condition and Resources* (6 vols.; London, 1851-57). Lucas' *Historical Geography of the West Indies* (Oxford, 1890; rev. ed. by Chewton Atchley, Oxford, 1905) was Volume II of *A Historical Geography of the British Colonies* (8 vols.; Oxford, 1887-1923).

tions to the history of the British Empire than to the history of the British West Indies. Many of the early British works of this period gave much attention to British Imperial policies and the mechanics of their formulation and implementation. Thus Arthur P. Newton's *The Colonising Activities of the English Puritans: The Last Phase of the Elizabethan Struggle with Spain* (New Haven, 1914), although giving a fully adequate account of the Caribbean colony of Old Providence, was equally a contribution to English history and the general history of seventeenth-century expansion; James A. Williamson in *The Caribbee Islands under the Proprietary Patents* (Oxford, 1926) was primarily concerned with the study of the proprietary form of colonial government; and Lillian M. Penson subtitled her *Colonial Agents of the British West Indies* (London, 1924) *A Study in Colonial Administration, Mainly in the Eighteenth Century.* The same approach may be seen in the *Cambridge History of the British Empire,* which did not dignify the West Indies with a volume of their own, but dealt with them in the general volumes[7] along with Imperial policy.

Interest on the American side seems to have emerged as a by-product of the study of American colonial history. The leading scholar in that field at the time, Charles McLean Andrews, saw the British West Indian islands as forming an integral part of colonial America, and treated them as such in his *The Colonial Period of American History* (4 vols.; New Haven, 1934-38), a work which made a significant independent contribution to seventeenth-century West Indian history. Long before this, however, one of Andrews' pupils, Frank Wesley Pitman, had made a major and more specific contribution with *The Development of the British West Indies, 1700-1763* (New Haven, 1917) and other writings.[8] Another American scholar, Lowell J. Ragatz, produced a sequel to Pitman in *The Fall of the Planter Class in the British Caribbean 1763-1833* (New York, 1928), as well as an important bibliography.[9] Pitman's and Ragatz' books were both pri-

---

7. Ernest A. Benians, *et al.,* eds., I, *The Old Empire to 1783* (Cambridge, 1929); II, *The New Empire 1783-1870* (1940); III, *The Empire-Commonwealth 1870-1919* (1959).

8. Especially "Slavery on the British West India Plantations in the Eighteenth Century," *Journal of Negro History* (Washington), XI (Oct., 1926), 584-668, and "The Settlement and Financing of British West India Plantations in the Eighteenth Century," in *Essays in Colonial History presented to Charles McLean Andrews by His Students* (New Haven, 1931), 252-83.

9. *A Guide for the Study of British Caribbean History, 1763-1834, including the Abolition and Emancipation Movements* (Washington, 1932): American Historical Association, *Annual Report, 1930,* III.

marily social and economic studies, and in these respects the West
Indies clearly differed sufficiently from the mainland colonies to call
for such separate treatment. Both authors noted significant variations
between the developments in the different islands, but their concentration on the effects of Imperial legislative measures, and on written
communications between the colonies and the home government as a
major source, enabled them to study the British West Indies as a unit.
Pitman and Ragatz remain two of the major works on the eighteenth
century.

The seventeenth century also received much attention in the 1920's.
In addition to his work on proprietary government already mentioned,
Williamson described the *English Colonies in Guiana and on the
Amazon 1604-1668* (Oxford, 1923); Charles S. S. Higham discussed
*The Development of the Leeward Islands under the Restoration, 1660-
1688: A Study in the Foundation of the Old Colonial System* (Cambridge, 1921); Arthur P. Watts devoted much of his *Une histoire des
colonies anglaises aux Antilles (de 1649 à 1660)* (Paris, 1924) to a detailed account of the British conquest of Jamaica; Vincent T. Harlow
followed his *A History of Barbados 1625-1688* (Oxford, 1926) with
a study of *Christopher Codrington 1668-1710* (Oxford, 1928), besides
editing and introducing a set of documents on *Colonising Expeditions
to the West Indies and Guiana 1623-1667* (London, 1925); and Agnes
M. Whitson examined *The Constitutional Development of Jamaica,
1660 to 1729* (Manchester, 1929). There was, however, little of the
attempt at synthesis that Pitman and Ragatz had made for the eighteenth century, and when a synthesis did appear in Arthur P. Newton's
*The European Nations in the West Indies, 1493-1688* (London, 1933)
it was of a rather different order.

The choice of topics, the way they were handled, and, perhaps,
most of all, the concentration on the seventeenth and eighteenth centuries, reflected the Imperial viewpoint of the historians. The study of
the West Indies was of the period when they were of great importance
to Britain; and the nineteenth century, when the Caribbean degen-
erated into an Imperial backwater, attracted little attention, save for
the one particular subject of the abolition of slavery, where a general
interest in the British humanitarian movement, which produced a
substantial literature, was reflected in William L. Mathieson's *British
Slavery and Its Abolition, 1823-1838* (London, 1926), a superficial

work based on a limited range of printed authorities, as were its two sequels.[10] To say that professional historical writing about the West Indies up to about 1930 was in some sense circumscribed by the Imperial approach is not of course in any way to depreciate the value or significance of the considerable contributions made at this time, nor to minimize the continuing utility of such an approach for the study of some aspects of West Indian history, as evidenced for example in William L. Burn's *Emancipation and Apprenticeship in the British West Indies* (London, 1937), a theme which the author discussed as an experiment in colonial government; in Ruth M. Bourne, *Queen Anne's Navy in the West Indies* (New Haven, 1939); in Frances Armytage's *The Free Port System in the British West Indies: A Study in Commercial Policy, 1766-1822* (London, 1953); and in Archibald P. Thornton's *West-India Policy under the Restoration* (Oxford, 1956).

In the 1930's new approaches were tried. Newton's *European Nations in the West Indies* burst the bounds of British Imperial history and dealt with the whole of the West Indies as an area of European exploitation, settlement, and international rivalry.[11] For the period up to 1688 at any rate Newton seemed sceptical of the usefulness of the British West Indies as a historical unit, and indeed pointed out that the contributions of Williamson, Harlow, and Higham were rather to the histories of individual islands than to that of the British West Indies. A work of popularization rather than of research, innocent of footnotes or bibliography, open to criticism for its concentration on European rather than Caribbean factors, Newton's book is yet significant in West Indian historiography, both for its comparatively long sweep in time, and for the breadth of its scope in area. Shortly afterwards Richard Pares' *War and Trade in the West Indies, 1739-1763* (Oxford, 1936) appeared. While Pares' approach resembled Newton's in that he did not confine his attention to British islands (though it is perhaps worth noting that his original intention was to write a history of the British West Indies), in other respects it differs substantially. *War and Trade* was restricted to a short period, fully documented from original sources, and concentrated much more on West Indian than

10. *British Slave Emancipation, 1838-1849* (London, 1932) and *The Sugar Colonies and Governor Eyre, 1849-1866* (London, 1936).

11. This international approach had to some extent been anticipated in Clarence H. Haring's study of the much narrower theme of *The Buccaneers in the West Indies in the XVII Century* (New York, 1910).

European factors. In attempting to disentangle the intricate pattern of West Indian trade with both Britain and France, Pares revealed West Indian economic history as immensely more complicated than the history of West Indian policy (to which earlier writers had given most of their attention), and in subsequent books and articles,[12] which were based largely on private business and estate papers, he went a long way toward the elucidation of some of the problems he had raised. In the second phase of West Indian historiography Pares' contribution is un-rivaled, not only for its impressive volume and for its qualities of balanced perspective, rigorous scholarship, mastery of detail, and imaginative insight, but also for his demonstration of the fruitfulness both of intensive studies of individual enterprises, and of the use of a wider historical unit than the British West Indies.

Other new approaches were also used in further work on the history of slavery and emancipation. An interesting light was thrown on this subject by the Hon. Hugh A. Wyndham's two volumes on *The Atlantic and Slavery* (London, 1935) and *The Atlantic and Emancipation* (London, 1937); and Charles H. Wesley, writing in the *Journal of Negro History*,[13] investigated West Indian emancipation for lessons bearing on the advancement of the Negro in the United States. The slave trade, rather than its ending, also began to receive some notice. Much material was made available in *Documents Illustrative of the History of the Slave Trade to America*, edited by Elizabeth Donnan (4 vols.; Washington, 1930-35), and Charles M. MacInnes published a summary account, *England and Slavery* (Bristol, 1934). But a definitive treatment of even part of the subject had to await the publication of Kenneth G. Davies' *The Royal African Company* (London, 1957), a work conceived primarily as a contribution to English economic history and restricted to the period 1670-1713. For the later eighteenth century some necessary revision of the conclusions of Gomer

12. The most important were *A West-India Fortune* (London, 1950); *Yankees and Creoles: The Trade between North America and the West Indies before the American Revolution* (London, 1956); "The London Sugar Market, 1740-1769," *The Economic History Review* (Utrecht), 2nd ser., IX (Dec., 1956), 254-70; "A London West India Merchant House, 1740-1769," in Richard Pares and A. J. P. Taylor, eds., *Essays Presented to Sir Lewis Namier* (London, 1956), pp. 75-107; and *Merchants and Planters* (Cambridge, 1960).

13. "The Neglected Period of Emancipation in Great Britain, 1807-23," XVII (April, 1932), 156-79; "The Emancipation of the Free Coloured Population in the British Empire," *ibid.*, XIX (April, 1934), 137-70; "The Abolition of Negro Apprenticeship in the British Empire," *ibid.*, XXIII (April, 1938), 155-99.

Williams' *History of the Liverpool Privateers and Letters of Marque, with an Account of the Liverpool Slave Trade* (Liverpool, 1897) was undertaken by Frances Hyde and others, and the rôle of London in the financing of the trade was explored by R. B. Sheridan.[14] The technique of detailed study of an individual enterprise was successfully applied to illuminate the institution of slavery in J. Harry Bennet, Jr., *Bondsmen and Bishops: Slavery and Apprenticeship on the Codrington Plantations of Barbados, 1710-1838* (Berkeley, 1958), which concentrated on this aspect of the history of the estates of the Society for the Propagation of the Gospel, already the subject of a more general study edited by Frank J. Klingberg, *Codrington Chronicle: An Experiment in Anglican Altruism on a Barbados Plantation, 1710-1834* (Berkeley, 1949). It was the subject of slavery, too, that called forth the first important contribution by a West Indian professional historian, Eric E. Williams' *Capitalism and Slavery* (Chapel Hill, 1944), which dramatically substituted an economic interpretation of emancipation for the prevalent humanitarian one. In suggesting that the slaves were freed for material rather than moral reasons, Williams did more than contribute to the literature of the emancipation movement. In questioning the concept of Imperial trusteeship, he spoke with the authentic voice of contemporary Negro West Indian nationalism. Although Williams chose a well-worn subject and treated it professionally, his point of view was clearly a West Indian one, and his book portended the modification in the orientation and emphasis of West Indian historiography which was to mark the beginning of the third phase.

Although all these professional historians had added enormously to the knowledge of West Indian history, they had left certain areas and periods virtually untouched and had signally failed to produce general histories of either individual islands or the whole area.[15] The

14. Francis E. Hyde, Bradbury B. Parkinson, and Sheila Marriner, "The Nature and Profitability of the Liverpool Slave Trade," *Economic History Review*, 2nd ser., V, no. 3 (1953), 368-77; R. B. Sheridan, "The Commercial and Financial Organization of the British Slave Trade, 1750-1807," *ibid.*, XI (Dec., 1958), 249-63.

15. A possible exception to this generalization is William L. Burn, *The British West Indies* (London, 1951). But this is no more than a brief sketch, although it does constitute an able and lively epitome of much of the work of the second phase, of which its Imperial point of view is typical—the author says (p. 11) that West Indian history "could, no doubt, be written as a narrative of local and provincial happenings," but considers that "a greater interest lies in the opportunity it gives for a survey of the thought and activities of men, and especially of Englishmen, over three centuries." An earlier brief general work, on the constitutional side, was Humphrey Hume Wrong, *Government of the West Indies* (Oxford, 1923).

work of amateur historians, mainly colonial civil servants, went some way to repair the omissions, though few of their attempts were entirely successful. One neglected area was British Honduras, whose governor, Sir John A. Burdon edited (very badly) a selection of documents, *Archives of British Honduras* (3 vols.; London, 1931-35), on which the Reverend Stephen L. Caiger later based his readable but inadequate *British Honduras: Past and Present* (London, 1951).[16] The relative neglect of the nineteenth century meant that the newer colonies of Trinidad and British Guiana had little to show. Gertrude Carmichael's *A History of the West Indian Islands of Trinidad and Tobago, 1498-1900* (London, 1961), an indigestible compilation of facts, did not remedy the former deficiency. More successful, perhaps because narrower in scope, were Sir Cecil Clementi's *A Constitutional History of British Guiana* (London, 1937) and Dwarka Nath's *A History of Indians in British Guiana* (London, 1950).[17] The neglected post-emancipation century in Jamaica was discussed in a highly individualistic way by Sydney, Lord Olivier in *The Myth of Governor Eyre* (London, 1933) and *Jamaica: The Blessed Island* (London, 1937), the latter valuable rather for the author's personal recollections than as formal history. Sir Alan C. Burns's mammoth attempt at the synthesis from which the professionals had shied, *A History of the British West Indies* (London, 1954), seldom rose above the level of compilation and revealed the limitations of the British West Indies as a unit of historical study. The most outstanding work by an amateur was Noël Deerr's *The History of Sugar* (2 vols.; London, 1949-50), which dealt with one of the most important aspects of West Indian history in a world-wide context. Into this amateur category should perhaps also fall Prime Minister Eric E. Williams' *A History of the People of Trinidad and Tobago* (Port-of-Spain, 1962; London, 1964), written to appear on the day his Colony became independent. The ex-professor makes it clear that it is the politician who is writing: "This book is not

16. With the exception of a first-rate professional study of one particular aspect, Robert A. Humphreys, *The Diplomatic History of British Honduras, 1638-1901* (London, 1961), this territory remains ill-served, as was the Bahamas until the appearance of Michael Craton's competent *History of the Bahamas* (London, 1962).

17. It may be noted that Indian immigration was discussed in Edgar L. Erickson, "The Introduction of East Indian Coolies into the British West Indies," *Journal of Modern History* (Chicago), VI (June, 1934), 127-46; and, as part of a wider theme, in Ivy M. Cumpston, *Indians Overseas in British Territories, 1834-1854* (Oxford, 1953).

conceived as a work of scholarship. It is a manifesto of a subjugated people."

The groundwork of the third phase of West Indian historiography, which had been heralded by Williams' *Capitalism and Slavery* in 1944, was laid by increased opportunities after the World War II of higher education for West Indians, both abroad and at the new University College of the West Indies in Jamaica. Its relevance was emphasized by the development of movements for colonial independence, and it may be said to have been fairly launched when the local university introduced a full-fledged undergraduate course in West Indian history in 1952. West Indian history was now being studied by West Indians for its own sake as an integral part of the West Indian educative process, and this was both a reflection of and a stimulus to new attitudes to West Indian historiography. From the start the university course was conceived as not being confined to British territories, but as embracing the whole of the West Indies. In its conception it thus tended to emphasize the unity of the common factors in the region's past, such as the ethnic inheritance of the various waves of European, African, and Asiatic immigration, and the social and economic legacy of the slave plantation system, rather than the diversity of the linguistic, religious, legal, and governmental patterns imposed by the various Imperial authorities. This tendency was well in line with current thinking about the Caribbean. The events of World War II had revealed the geopolitical realities of the Caribbean as a single region and institutionalized them in the international Caribbean Commission. A pamphlet by Eric E. Williams, *The Negro in the Caribbean* (Manchester, 1945), had emphasized both in historical and contemporary terms the whole region's heritage of degradation and poverty—and this was, of course, only one manifestation of the anti-imperialist climate of opinion in the non-European parts of the world, which saw in their common poverty and colonial status fundamental factors transcending the more superficial distinction between the different European cultures imposed on the various Imperial possessions. It is interesting to note that this tendency ran counter to the movement for a political federation of the British West Indian islands, which flourished in the 1950's but failed to survive, at least partly through the lack of development of a feeling of West Indian nationhood. It is possible that this lack may be explained in part by the existence of such concepts, which implied aspirations towards a wider West Indian identity than that of the British colonies.

The immediate historiographical result of these developments was the publication of *A Short History of the West Indies* (London, 1956) by John Horace Parry, the first incumbent of the chair of history at the University College of the West Indies, an Englishman already noted for his work in Spanish colonial history, and Philip M. Sherlock, the university's Jamaican Vice-Principal. Their book was a survey of West Indian history from the West Indian point of view, which constituted a statement, and indeed, as it succeeded so well in telling a meaningful story, a justification of the new approach to West Indian history adopted by the University College. Based almost entirely on secondary authorities, it was a work of interpretation rather than research, which performed extremely well the dual task of synthesizing many of the detailed studies of the previous half-century and indicating the work still to be done, both in filling obvious gaps and in drawing together the histories of the different islands and empires.

Some of these gaps had already been noted, and steps taken to fill them. In particular, the post emancipation period, of little interest from the Imperial point of view, but vital from the West Indian point of view, attracted the attention both of outsiders and West Indian research students. Three significant contributions were made by an American, Philip D. Curtin, a Canadian, Raymond W. Beachey, and a Jamaican, Douglas Hall, with respectively, *Two Jamaicas: The Role of Ideas in a Tropical Colony, 1830-1865* (Cambridge, Mass., 1955), *The British West Indies Sugar Industry in the Late 19th Century* (Oxford, 1957), and *Free Jamaica, 1838-1865: An Economic History* (New Haven, 1959).[18] The eighteenth century was not totally neglected. An

18. Other work on the nineteenth century includes Anton V. Long, *Jamaica and the New Order, 1827-1847* ([Mona], 1956); A. Bruce Hamilton, *Barbados and the Confederation Question, 1871-1885* (London, 1956); Ronald V. Sires, "Sir Henry Barkly and the Labour Problem in Jamaica, 1853-56," *Journal of Negro History*, XXV (April, 1940), 216-35, "Negro Labour in Jamaica in the Years following Emancipation," *ibid.*, (Oct., 1940), 484-97, "The Jamaica Constitution of 1884," *Social and Economic Studies* (Mona), III (June, 1954), 64-81, and "The Experience of Jamaica with Modified Crown Colony Government," *ibid.*, IV (June, 1955), 150-67; and the following unpublished theses by West Indians: Fitzroy R. Augier, "Crown Colony Government in Jamaica, 1865-1884" (Ph.D., St. Andrews, 1954); W. G. Demas, "Trends in the West Indian Economy, 1870-1913" (M.Litt., Cambridge, 1956); Rawle E. G. Farley, "Aspects of the Economic History of British Guiana, 1781-1852" (External Ph.D. [Econ.], London, 1956); C. V. Gocking, "Constitutional Problems in Jamaica, 1850-1866" (D.Phil., Oxford, 1955); Keith O.

American, R. B. Sheridan, wrote on the planters of Antigua,[19] but the Guianese, Elsa V. Goveia, reflected the newer trend by showing more interest in the slaves than their masters.[20] Of particular interest from the historiographical point of view is Goveia's "The West Indian Slave Laws of the Eighteenth Century," *Revista de Ciencias Sociales* (Rio Piedras, P.R.), IV (1960), 75-106, illustrating the differing responses in British, French and Spanish colonies to the common social problem of slave control; and a similar approach was used by Sir Harold Mitchell, in discussing the various ways in which the very recent problems of self-government and economic development have been handled, in his *Europe in the Caribbean: The Policies of Great Britain, France and the Netherlands towards Their West Indian Territories in the Twentieth Century* (Edinburgh, 1963). Further co-ordinating and comparative work of this sort will call for more studies of particular aspects and particular islands. Historians from the West Indies, and from many other countries, have responded enthusiastically to the challenges posed by the new approach to West Indian history, in which the Imperial factor, which dominated the second phase of British West Indian history, is now seen as only one of a number of analytical tools. In the third phase, the historiography of the British West Indies seems more likely to form part of the historiography of the Caribbean than of that of the British Empire and Commonwealth.

---

Lawrence, "Immigration into Trinidad and British Guiana, 1834-1871" (Ph.D., Cambridge, 1958); and Francis X. Mark, "The Rise and Development of Labour Movements in the British Caribbean, with particular reference to British Guiana, Jamaica, and Trinidad" (Ph.D., Edinburgh, 1959). Also relevant are: Gisela Eisner, *Jamaica 1830-1930: A Study in Economic Growth* (Manchester, 1961); George E. Cumper, "Labour Demand and Supply in the Jamaican Sugar Industry, 1830-1950," *Social and Economic Studies*, II (March, 1954), 37-86, and "Population Movements in Jamaica, 1830-1950," *ibid.*, V (Sept., 1956), 261-80; George W. Roberts, *The Population of Jamaica: An Analysis of Its Structure and Growth* (Cambridge, 1957), the work of a Barbadian demographer; Trinidadian Hewan Craig's *The Legislative Council of Trinidad and Tobago* (London, 1952); and *The Approaches to Local Self-Government in British Guiana* (London, 1958) by Allan Young, a Guianese civil servant.

19. "The Rise of a Colonial Gentry: A Case Study of Antigua, 1730-1775," *Economic History Review*, 2nd ser., XIII (April, 1961), 342-57.

20. Both in "Slave Society in the British Leeward Islands, 1780-1800" (Ph.D. thesis, London, 1952) to be published shortly, and in her *Historiography*, which devoted much attention to analyzing the views of the historians on race and slavery.

# INDIA

## Robert I. Crane

AN ENQUIRY into the state of historical writings on India can
serve at least three purposes. It can provide an awareness of the
strengths and limitations of work in the field, the difficulties faced, and
the important gaps which remain to be filled. It can also suggest the
kinds of materials upon which the historian must draw if he is to perfect his knowledge of the subject. This can be helpful both in teaching
and in research. Moreover, it can assist the non-specialist to identify
and locate the most useful volumes for various aspects of Indian history and thus facilitate his work in a field in which he cannot be expected to know the sources thoroughly.

The latter function of an enquiry into the state of historical writings on India is especially relevant because of the underdeveloped
character of the curriculum with regard to India in American higher
education. A basic knowledge of the history of India is seldom available in the college curriculum, while many of the significant publications in the field are hard to find in American libraries. As a result,
educated Americans tend to lack awareness of the framework of Indian
history—a necessary background against which to fit specific items of
information.

The absence of an adequate framework reflects not only the paucity
of materials, the inadequacy of typical college courses on India, and
the exotic character of the Indian tradition as contrasted with our own;
it reflects also the state of knowledge which has been achieved by the
scholars who have published on India. The gaps which have yet to be
filled and the limitations on the kinds of history which have been
written make the understanding of the history of India difficult for the
non-specialist. By and large, the texts have been written within the
confines of a narrow emphasis on political and narrative history, leaving much to the imagination as to the structure and nature of the society

in which the political events took place. In order to understand Indian history, even political history, one needs awareness of the background of Indian society, Indian religion, and Indian thought.

This essay cannot, therefore, be limited to a discussion of recent historical writings. It must include some discussion of materials on Indian society, materials which at first glance may seem to be outside the field of history as a discipline. At the same time, the effort has to be made to illuminate the framework against which the reading of Indian history needs to be placed. This means, in particular, the provision of leads into the understanding of Indian culture and society. If Indian history is to be meaningful, the major characteristics of Indian culture have to be comprehended.

## PROBLEMS OF CONCEPTUALIZATION

Among the many problems in the study or writing of Indian history, problems of conceptualization are, perhaps, the most important. Conceptualization sets the basis for and is deeply involved in the acquisition of an appropriate frame of reference. Europeans have done much of the writing of Indian history and have tended to use concepts which were developed in the writing of European history. This can, of course, lead to a bias in the study of India that is extraneous to Indian culture and development.

Periodization is one of the difficult problems in the conceptualization of Indian history. In writing European history we have in mind a fairly specific set of definitions when we use terms such as medieval or modern. In that context a term such as medieval has meaning and serves as a kind of shorthand to sum up a set of characteristics. When we turn to Indian history there is a tendency to apply the same kind of categorization. Such categorization, useful when it expresses definitions that are agreed upon, may be misleading when applied to a totally different historical experience. The movement of Indian history, its "natural" epochs, and the major characteristics of its ebb and flow may, on careful examination, turn out not to fit our terms.

In European history we speak of a feudal age. This brings to mind a fairly clear picture of the conditions to which the term can properly be applied. It is, therefore, a useful generalization. But the term "feudal" has also been applied to certain periods in Indian history;

such usage seemingly has contributed, not to a clearer understanding of the phenomena of a period in India's past, but to misconstruction and misunderstanding. The reader, coming across a reference to feudal India, may think he knows what is meant.[1] In point of fact, there is good reason to doubt that Indian society ever exhibited the pattern of institutions and relationships which are subsumed in the concept "feudal" in European history.

Another difficult problem in Indian history is that of the level of conceptualization. Though this is a problem faced in the writing of any history, it has special bearing on the history of India[2] for at least two reasons. India has had a "high" intellectual tradition and a "low" intellectual tradition, and we do not know enough about the complex relationships between the two in Indian culture. Moreover, there is room for disagreement over the similarities and dissimilarities between the Brahmanical tradition, which has been the main stem of what we call Hinduism, and the *de facto* local and regional approximations thereto.[3] Many of the Europeans who first studied Vedic thought or the Brahmanical tradition and Hinduism confined themselves to the elaboration in the classical texts. The result has been a comprehensive literature on High Hinduism. What we know in the West about Hinduism is derived from this study of what was essentially the Sanskritic culture of India. Far less is known about the popular Hinduism of the masses or the low intellectual tradition. Even less that is systematic is known of the local and regional variants. One result of this has been genuine difficulty in saying—with any certainty—what Hinduism is. This situation is made more difficult because Hinduism—at any level—has always shown an unusual ability to absorb materials that are diverse or even contradictory.

Nor is the problem of level of conceptualization confined to the understanding of Hinduism. When we look at the effects of European impact on India, we are confronted with the problem of the level at

1. A recent effort to grapple with the use of the concept "feudal" is to be found in Rushton Coulborn, ed., *Feudalism in History* (Princeton, 1956). It includes a section, "Feudalism in India," by Daniel Thorner, which is quite provocative.

2. Levels of conceptualization are lucidly discussed in Yoshio Sakata and John W. Hall, "The Motivation of Political Leadership in the Meiji Restoration," *Journal of Asian Studies* (Ann Arbor), XVI (Nov., 1956), 31-50.

3. For discussion of this problem, see V. Raghavan, "Variety and Integration in the Pattern of Indian Culture," *Far Eastern Quarterly* (Ann Arbor), XV (Aug., 1956), 497-505. Also M. N. Srinivas, "A Note on Sanskritization and Westernization," *ibid.*, pp. 481-96.

which the impact is to be studied. A complex process such as Westernization brought in a variety of elements which touched many aspects of Indian life at different levels. We can talk rather confidently of the effects of Westernization on the graduates of Indian universities, but this means very little with regard to the illiterate peasant in an outlying rural district.

These questions of conceptualization are important because they affect what we mean by Indian history: what we choose to include or to exclude. The concepts we utilize direct our attention—perhaps unwisely —to certain parts of the totality of Indian history to the exclusion of other parts. The writing of Indian history is not unique in this respect, but it is a serious matter. This is especially true because the subcontinent contains a variety of regional, linguistic, and cultural groupings. The treatment of such diversity requires considerable sophistication and self-conscious awareness in conceptualization.

## PROBLEMS OF INTERPRETATION

While the problems just indicated are obviously important in the interpretation of Indian history, other issues of interpretation seem to be logically separate from problems of conceptualization. Interpretation reflects not only the way we conceptualize what we are studying, it also reflects our *use* of the materials of history.

One of the central problems of interpretation of the history of India reflects a polemical difference of opinion between various schools of thought. Perhaps the most basic of these differences of opinion has been between English scholars and writers on the one hand and Indian historians on the other.

Of the published volumes in Indian history probably the largest number have been contributed by English historians. Without the contributions made by English scholars we would today know very little of Indian history. It was the great English Orientalists of the nineteenth century who recovered much of the basic material of India's past. Many of the English scholars who have worked in Indian history, archaeology, and numismatics were academicians of the highest quality, marked by a keen and disinterested search for knowledge. There were, however, certain biases which tended to characterize at least part of the product of English scholarship on India. Part of that bias, doubtless, resulted simply from the importation of European attitudes into work on India's past. Other parts reflected an undue reliance on the high intellectual tradition, a tendency to put too much reliance—especially for the period of British Indian history—upon official sources and official viewpoints, and an emphasis on purely political or quasi-dynastic history. Some of the best-known volumes in the history of India reflect a narrow approach to the subject of history, stressing what the rulers were doing, who fought which battles, when such-and-such a river was crossed.

Although a great number of substantial works have been produced by English authors, there are areas of Indian life and history which have received very little attention. The British government of India had certain preoccupations and for the areas of life affected by those preoccupations the government kept excellent, detailed, and massive records. The historian who wished to rely on official records naturally worked in the areas for which official concern kept the best records. If official interest happened to be slim with respect to native schools, the files might be relatively silent on that topic and the historian might find little encouragement to proceed with it.

It is also clear that there were certain topics, especially after the Indian Mutiny of 1857, into which government was reluctant to delve too deeply or to allow scholars easy access to. The administration had its own difficulties to face, its policies were increasingly under attack by Indian nationalists and even by liberal friends of India in London, and there were topics over which government and its bureaucrats preferred to draw a veil of silence. Alternatively, government often had its own official version of or justification for events. There was a natural desire on the part of the overworked official to get the official explanation into the public record. This too had its effect upon the writing of Indian history.[4]

Increasingly, after the Mutiny, there was a tendency among English writers, many of whom had been officials or had close connections with officials, to act as apologists for the government of India. As Indian nationalism developed and nationalist attacks upon the administration increased in frequency and vigor, there was an almost

4. A valuable publication, Cyril H. Philips, ed., *Historians of India, Pakistan and Ceylon* (London, 1961), reflects a number of these traits of interpretation. The reliance upon official sources and the tendency to write within the official viewpoint are exhibited by many of the historians dealt with in the volume.

perceptible movement by the beleaguered British to close ranks and defend the record. The result was an increase in polemical accounts.

This tendency was accompanied by an understandable failure, by many Englishmen, to comprehend the motives behind Indian attitudes and actions. Usually the Englishman in India had a self-image of tireless devotion to the cause of justice as part of a benevolent if autocratic government. Most often the self-image was quite sincere. Though there was cant in the idea of the "white man's burden," it is clear that many English officials honestly shouldered the burden. Though there were exceptions to the rule, it seems safe to say that no other alien government ever put into the field so sincere, honest, and devoted a band of officials as did the British government in India.

When the Indian nationalist, out of what must have seemed the depths of ingratitude, belabored the civil servant, accused him of evil, and published polemical and exaggerated accounts of the darker side of the record, the civil servant's burden seemed most unjust. The obvious result was an inability to see the other person's point of view—to put oneself in the other man's shoes. Quite frequently in the contest of interpretation of recent Indian history, the two sides have simply not been communicating with each other. They have spoken from different viewpoints, they have misunderstood each other's motives, and what has seemed self-evident to the one has seemed absurd to the other. This is reflected in the writing of modern Indian history; in fact, the situation deteriorated after the Mutiny.

If the English historian of India has suffered from certain biases or from a lack of understanding of the Indian viewpoint, his Indian colleague has not been less free from taint. Among Indians there has been a strong tendency to glorify the alleged virtues of India's past civilization and to deprecate all that the English did. According to this school of thought, there is nothing good among men which was not to be found in Vedic India. Not only has this view been guilty of exaggeration and of over-emotional national pride, it has on more than one occasion been based upon loose or faulty scholarship.[5] As nationalist sentiment waxed, it seemed almost imperative to show that India flowed with milk and honey under the benign reign of enlightened philosopher-kings—before the English came.

5. For an illuminative example of the Indian nationalist interpretation of India's past, see the first chapter of Gorham D. Sanderson, *India and British Imperialism* (New York, 1951).

However understandable, this attitude was not good for Indian historical scholarship and was often accompanied by intemperate and injudicious attacks on almost everything the English had done in India. The Indian could argue that the bland ability of the English to paint with rosy colors their record in India required a counter-effort to set the record straight. The result was often indiscriminate attack, consistent misinterpretation of English motives, and unwillingness to see the record in balanced perspective. Interestingly enough, the average Indian historian seemed to have little more interest than his English counterpart in describing in any systematic fashion the growth of indigenous institutions.

In the West we have, in general, an impressive substructure of solid monographic studies on almost every aspect of the historical record upon which to base more general studies. For India, the more general studies have been written without benefit of access to monographic accounts. This situation has improved in the past decade, but there still remain substantial areas in Indian history which are poorly mined. This is by no means due, in all cases, to the lack of sources. Too much energy was required for polemics to leave much time for hard work.

## SOURCES FOR INDIAN HISTORY

It may, in general, be said that for recent Indian history there is a plethora of available sources. Although a substantial portion of the source materials may be official, they range over wide areas of Indian life and can be used for the most fruitful of studies. Evidences of this have been given in the past few years.[6] The further back we go in Indian history, the more serious the problem of sources becomes. For the Mughal Period sources are adequate though, in certain respects, limited. In the pre-Muslim period the sources are very much more limited and more difficult to use. The climate and active insect life of a semi-tropic environment have conspired to eliminate such records as may have been kept on material of a perishable nature. Fortunately there are ancient rock inscriptions, copper-plate inscriptions, and old coins.

6. As an example of what can be done out of official sources see the study by Kenneth Ballhatchet, *Social Policy and Social Change in Western India, 1817-1830* (London, 1957).

For early India some literary remains have survived intact. Of these some would be classed as belles-lettres, and the author's preface often provides the historian with information about the times and the writer. Some commentaries also survive, containing casual statements on contemporary events. We also have certain biographies of saints which contain some useful information. Another valuable source, if used with discretion, is the old quasi-historical vernacular poems. There are, in addition, a few early chronicles. Literary sources for early Indian history are, of course, quite limited in number and in intrinsic value for the historian. These sources have to be supplemented by the work of the archaeologist, on which a good beginning has been made in India, and by reliance upon epigraphy. The latter field is of special value for Indian history, with substantial numbers of inscriptions having been discovered, collected, and edited.[7]

Another useful source for early Indian history is found in foreign accounts of India. Ambassadors, such as Megasthenes of the Hellenistic kings who came after Alexander the Great, visited India and studied its people and institutions. Megasthenes is, in fact, a valuable source for the period. Similarly, certain Chinese pilgrims and visitors who traveled widely in India left accounts which, when stripped of the legends they accepted, are quite informative. Fa-Hien, Hiuen-Tsang, and I-Tsing are perhaps the best known among such Chinese visitors. Their writings fall in the period between the third and eighth centuries A.D. Not too long thereafter came the first of the Arab visitors to India, to whom our knowledge of the premodern era owes so much. At a still later date Marco Polo traveled in India, soon to be followed by other early European visitors who left accounts of their impressions of the country.[8]

For the Muslim period in Indian history the materials, primary and secondary, are voluminous, but not, however, comprehensive. Again, political and dynastic histories predominate, with less available for social or economic history. During the Mughal era this imbalance was somewhat improved, and more study has been made of the condition of India at that time.

7. For a good, concise discussion of Indian epigraphy and of other sources for early history, see chap. iv of *Historical Method in Relation to Indian History* (Madras, 1956), by Kallidaikurichi A. A. Nilakanta Sastri and H. S. Ramanna.

8. Note the early travelers cited in my article on "Urbanism in India," *American Journal of Sociology* (Chicago), LX (March, 1956), 463-70.

While useful materials are not lacking on the Portuguese in India during the period of their ascendency along the Malabar Coast, much remains to be done. The Portuguese archives in Lisbon contain massive and valuable sources, but their surface has hardly been scratched by historians. Since the Portuguese were prominent only in a few corners of India, this lack does not substantially affect the history of India as a whole. At the same time, the Portuguese established relationships with major kingdoms in India, such as the Vijayanagar empire in the Dekkhan, and our knowledge of Vijayanagar affairs would be enhanced by careful use of the Portuguese archives.

For the era of the East India Company, the situation is quite different. Not only are there records of great volume and broad coverage, but also the records have been widely used. Much remains to be done with the archival materials of the East India Company, especially in connection with the social and economic condition of India under company rule, but enough has been done to give us an excellent picture of the period. The archives of the East India Company, kept in the India Office Library in London, are readily exploitable by professional historians. They include a variety of different kinds of papers, records, correspondence, reports, and other documents. The company archives are supplemented by voluminous government documents and reports. After 1784, the English Parliament took increasing interest in the affairs of the Company, and between 1784 and 1857 a number of important parliamentary papers were produced. Prominent among these papers would be such an item as the *Fifth Report of the Select Committee of the House of Commons on the Affairs of the East India Company* (London, 1812).

In addition to the India Office archives and the relevant parliamentary papers, the National Archives of India, Public Series, in New Delhi, is a valuable documentary source. Moreover, under Company and Crown there were prepared district gazetteers for every district of British India. While uneven in quality, the various district gazetteers are a gold mine of information on local conditions and local history. To date they have been but inadequately used by historians. Through judicious use of these sources the historian could round out our knowledge of local conditions in the Indian empire. In general, it may be said that for the period of the Company and, after the Mutiny, of Crown rule, the sources are voluminous and excellent. Historians face a challenge in the effective use of these records for monographic studies.

### THE TREATMENT OF INDIAN HISTORY IN TEXTBOOKS

Though many of the existing textbooks in Indian history reflect the tendency to follow the official viewpoint, or suffer from the biases mentioned above, or concern themselves with political narrative to the virtual exclusion of a rounded account of Indian life and institutions, a few can be used with profit.

The best single basic textbook on the whole of Indian history available is probably Ramesh Chandra Majumdar, Hemchandra C. Raychaudhuri, and Kalikinkar Datta's *An Advanced History of India* (2nd ed., London, 1950), which combines relative comprehensiveness with something like brevity. Although it is, generally, a balanced account of Indian history, avoiding the pitfalls of the various extremes, and its authors are capable and honest craftsmen, unfortunately, the organization of the book is not ideal. Within a general chronological framework, the authors have used a topical arrangement which detracts from the usefulness of the volume for the novice in Indian history.

Another valuable general text is by Edward I. Thompson and Geoffery T. Garratt, *Rise and Fulfilment of British Rule in India* (London, 1934). Though limited by the fact that it was published thirty years ago and by the emphasis on the British period, it is one of the best in terms of breadth of coverage, balance of judgment, and craftsmanship. Well organized, easy to read, and lucid, it stands as a tribute to English scholarship.

An old standby in Indian history is the well-known *Cambridge Shorter History of India*, edited by Henry Herbert Dodwell (Cambridge, 1943), which covers Indian history from its beginnings up through 1919 in a relatively lucid and solid fashion. Its scope is rather limited because it is par excellence the record of wars, dynasties, palace revolutions, and sundry other political events. For the British period it is, of course, heavily infused with the official viewpoint.

Two other valuable general accounts may be mentioned at this time. The first is Cyril H. Philips' *India* (London, 1949). While this can hardly be called a textbook in Indian history, as it devotes only a few pages to the period prior to the coming of the Europeans, it is one of the best single-volume studies in print. Quite well written and organized, it is a perceptive study based on trenchant judgments. It should be required reading on any list of basic works dealing with India. Equally valuable, though it proceeds from a somewhat different set of emphases and is differently organized, is William Norman Brown's *The United States and India and Pakistan* (rev. ed.; Cambridge, Mass., 1963). Brown devotes much of the book to modern India but includes a brief and most perceptive account of pertinent historical background. He includes a good account of British rule, of the growth of nationalism, and of events leading up to independence and partition. The volume also contains material on postindependence India.

Another text which presumes to cover all of Indian history in a single volume can be recommended, with certain reservations, for the Western reader. The late Kavalam Madhava Panikkar's *A Survey of Indian History* (London, 1947) has a number of attractive qualities. Brief and well written, it includes material on religion, culture, and intellectual history. In some ways it makes a genuine contribution. But it was written for readers who are fairly well read in the subject and makes reference to names and events with which the reader may not be familiar. Easier for the Westerner is the text by William H. Moreland and Atul Chandra Chatterjee, *A Short History of India* (4th ed., London, 1957), which is balanced, lucid, and competent even though its organization leaves something to be desired.

Useful for its discussion of Indian culture and religion, though not a textbook in Indian history, is a recent publication by Humayun Kabir, *The Indian Heritage* (New York, 1955). In this volume, Kabir gives an informative summary of Vedic and Hindu thought, as well as of daily Hinduism and other aspects of Indian culture.

For the pre-Muslim period we are fortunate to have the good text by Gertrude Emerson Sen, *The Pageant of India's History* (New York, 1949). It is well written and presents the early history of India in a manner designed specifically for the American reader. The most recent edition of the *Oxford History of India*, edited by T. G. Percival Spear (3rd ed., Oxford, 1958) is quite good and can be used with confidence.

## The Vedic Period

About 2000 B.C. the so-called Aryan or Indic-speaking peoples began to invade northwest India from a home somewhere in Central Asia. Slow but steady migrations of clans and tribes continued till about 1000 B.C. The invading Aryans were essentially a pastoral people, living off their cattle and organized into clans or federations of clans. Upon arrival in north India they came into conflict with the dark-skinned inhabitants, whom they called *dāsas*, most important among whom were the Dravidian peoples, who spoke one or another of a group of allied Dravidian languages. "They migrated in bands westwards, southwards and eastwards, conquering the local populations, and intermarrying with them to form a ruling class. They brought with them their patrilinear tribal organization, their worship of sky gods, and their horses and chariots."[9] To the pastoralist Aryans, nature was an ever-present and overpowering reality. As their early hymns show, reverence for nature as well as love of nature was basic to their religion. There was, at the same time, fear of nature in its more threatening manifestations. The problem of man was to secure the favor of the supernatural ones by propitiating them and by not offending them. The Aryans conquered the *dāsas*, intermarried with them, borrowed ideas and practices from them, and settled down in peasant villages in their midst.

The Aryans brought to India their own religious beliefs and practices, an important aspect of which was an emphasis on the efficacy of sacrifice in propitiating the gods and securing divine blessings. The chanted hymns which accompanied their various sacrifices comprised the first great religious work of the Aryans, known as the *Rig Veda*. Since the words of the hymns were thought to be as important to the sacrifice as were the actual ritual forms, the Aryan priests—the Brahmins—were enjoined to memorize the thousands of Vedic verses with great care and precision, so that no word or syllable would be lost or distorted.

Closely tied to the basic rituals of the faith in this way, the Vedas and the Brahmins, who alone knew the verses and the ritual performances which went with them, came to hold a most prominent place in

9. Arthur L. Basham, *The Wonder That Was India: A Survey of the Culture of the Indian Sub-continent before the Coming of the Muslims* (London, 1956), p. 29.

Vedic society. Although the Vedic faith was essentially that of the sacrifice designed to propitiate the gods, it was, however, elevated above sacrifice cults by the majesty of the Vedic hymns. The student who wants a closer understanding of Vedic India should therefore dip into collections in translation. Nicol Macnicol has published a handy edition under the title *Hindu Scriptures: Hymns from the Rigveda, Five Upanishads, the Bhagavadgītā* (London, 1938).

The mingling of Vedic ideas with those of the Dravidians and other inhabitants of India in time produced a synthesis that provided the basis for the emergence of classical Hinduism. The transition to classical Hinduism is marked by the appearance of the *Upanishads* and later writings. Frederick Max Muller has what is perhaps the best translation of the *Upanishads* (2 vols.; Oxford, 1879-82), but Swami Prabhavananda and Frederick Manchester have recently put into a Mentor pocketbook a good edition, *The Upanishads: Breath of the Eternal* (New York, 1957).

For the pre-Muslim period of Indian history there is no better text than Arthur L. Basham, *The Wonder That Was India...* (London, 1956). Basham has done a splendid job of providing the latest and most informed summary of scholarship on the period, giving due emphasis to the religion, the political life, the social organization, and the economy of premodern Hindu India. It is doubtful that his volume will be superseded. Two other works, though not so authoritative or comprehensive as Basham's, may be used for the period. The first, by Gertrude Emerson Sen, *The Pageant of India's History*, has been mentioned above. Jawaharlal Nehru, in his *The Discovery of India* (New York, 1946), gives an interesting, sympathetic, and informed exposition. The fact that Nehru wrote *The Discovery of India* while in prison limits its accuracy, for the author was in no position to check his details. Nor would Nehru claim to be a historian by training. Nonetheless, his views on Vedic and classical Hindu society merit attention.

## CLASSICAL HINDUISM

As has been indicated, classical Hinduism evolved out of the older Vedic faith after the latter had been mixed with indigenous cult practices, beliefs, and superstitions. The emphasis in classical Hinduism was rather different from that of the Vedas. The growth of pessimism, the desire to escape from an endless round of rebirths, the proliferation of schools of thought on the best means of escape from life and the rise to prominence of doctrines of salvation (escape) by devotion to a personalized deity were among the major developments in Hinduism as it emerged. By about the fourth century B.C. Hinduism had supplanted the older Vedic faith, and from that time until the Muslims established their first kingdoms in India Hinduism reigned supreme, even though it was for a time challenged by heresies which had themselves grown out of Hinduism—Buddhism and Jainism.

During this period Hinduism—whatever it may have been as a system of religious thought—developed its basic characteristics as a religiously ordained way of life. Central to the Hindu way of life was the belief in the rôle and importance of *dharma*, or the law of the moral order and of the universe. Closely linked to belief in a moral law was the belief in the doctrine of *karma*, or the law of the act *and* its effect. In Hindu thought each class or caste in society, and each individual according to his caste, was governed by the details of a divine order laid down in and operative through the concept of *dharma*. Within his *dharma*, his acts and their effects governed his progress through the endless cycle of rebirths.

These fundamental beliefs gave to Hindu social organization a sanction, rules of behavior, and a justification that were firmly imbedded in the basic religion of the people. The classical statement of this way of life was in the *Manava-dharmasastra*, or the Law Code of Manu. It has been published in translation by Johann G. Bühler under the title *The Laws of Manu* (Oxford, 1886), but there is also a handy edition by John M. Macfie, *The Laws of Manu* (Madras, n.d.). Possibly the most informative discussion of premodern Hinduism, with special reference to its social forms, remains the pioneer work by Max Weber, *The Religion of India: The Sociology of Hinduism and Buddhism* which has been translated by Hans H. Gerth and Don Martindale (Glencoe, Ill., 1958).

Among the most useful of the titles which emphasize one or another aspect of Indian life for the classical period is Vincent Arthur Smith, *Asoka, The Buddhist Emperor of India* (3rd ed., Oxford, 1920). This classic on the life and career of the greatest of Indian rulers sheds considerable light on the society of Asokan times. In his

*Village Communities in Western India* (Oxford, 1929), Anant Sadashiv Altekar has provided valuable information on the structure of the premodern village community. John H. Hutton, in *Caste in India: Its Nature, Function and Origins* (Cambridge, 1946), gives what is believed by many to be the most authoritative account of the caste system. Another account, competent but somewhat dated, is that by Jogendranath Bhattacharya, *Hindu Castes and Sects* (Calcutta, 1896). Bhattacharya's discussion of the origins of the caste system, its structure, and its functions is easy to read and useful as a brief reference volume.

On the Hindu religion a number of titles can be cited. One of the clearest expositions, somewhat biased by the author's viewpoint, is found in John Nicols Farquhar, *A Primer of Hinduism* (London, 1912). A much more recent and more sympathetic study was edited by Kenneth W. Morgan, *The Religion of the Hindus* (New York, 1953).

Education under classical Hinduism, and the inculcation of religiously prescribed knowledge, is discussed in the volume by Sekharipuram Vaidyanatha Venkateswara, *Indian Culture through the Ages*, I: *Education and the Propagation of Culture* (London, 1928). Valuable material on this period and on the Hindu way of life will also be found in Moreland and Chatterjee, *A Short History of India*, mentioned above.

## THE MUSLIM PERIOD

In 1018 A.D. Mahmud of Ghazni invaded India from Afghanistan, marched down the plain of the Jumna River, seized the holy city of Muttra (Mathura), and conquered the kingdom of Kanauj. This was the effective date of Muslim rule in the Indian subcontinent. From that time until 1707 A.D., at the death of the last great Mughal emperor, Aurangzeb, Muslim kingdoms and empires were a prominent if not predominant feature of the life of India. Though generally confined to north India, Muslim rule did on occasion extend into south central India.

Islam was, of course, in many ways a different faith and different way of life from Hinduism. Many of the Muslim rulers who acquired a kingdom in India as invaders from Turkey, Iran, or Central Asia were zealous iconoclasts and stern monotheists. Generally, however, they settled down in India, intermarried with Hindus, and ruled kingdoms the bulk of whose populations remained Hindu. Conversions to Islam took place and this along with the process of intermarriage produced over time a Muslim minority with a Hindu heritage. Despite the orthodoxy of most of the Muslim rulers, long residence in India permitted an almost imperceptible process of mingling of the ideas of the two faiths and produced syncretic beliefs which influence Hinduism as well as Islam. As part of this confrontation of the two cultures there was, in Hinduism, the growth of monotheistic beliefs accompanied by a tendency to de-emphasize caste. At the same time, high caste Hindus adopted the Muslim custom of *purdah* (veiling) for their wives.

Among the Muslims the *sufi* mystics were clearly influenced by Hinduism. In art and architecture Hindu forms and traditions mingled with those of Islam to produce what has been called Indo-Saracenic art. In literature there was the development of Hindustani, a new *lingua franca* that combined the Hindi, Arabic, and Persian vocabularies. The emergence of this new language, spread widely over India, had a healthy effect on Indian vernaculars, which had too long been subservient to the priestly Sanskrit.

The prolific literature of the Muslim period in India includes texts by Muslim contemporaries, accounts by European travelers, and indigenous Hindu sources. A compendious and interesting collection, Sir Henry M. Elliot's *The History of India, as Told by Its Own Historians: The Muhammadan Period*, edited by John Dowson (8 vols.; London, 1867-77), is a gold mine in contemporary Muslim writings on the Muslim period in Indian history. It should, however, be noted that certain of the passages are given in doubtful translation and there are disagreements over some of the texts. Stanley Lane-Poole's work, *Medieval India under Mohammedan Rule, A.D. 712-1764* (London, 1903), another basic source for the Muslim period, though prejudiced in spots, remains one of the better surveys available. Valuable recent studies of the Muslim period include Ashirbadi Lai Srivastava, *The Sultanate of Delhi, including the Arab Invasion of the Sindh, 711-1526 A.D.* (Agra, 1953) and Ishwari Prasad, *History of Medieval India from 647 A.D. to the Mughal Conquest* (Allahabad, 1940). Both of these books give considerable insight into politics and life in Muslim India.

During the period of Mughal ascendency in India, a number of European travelers visited the subcontinent. Some of these men left valuable accounts, frequently written in a most interesting manner, of their travels and experiences. William Irvine translated the *Storia do Mogor* . . . by Niccolao Manucci as *A Pepys of Mogul India, 1653-1708* . . . (London, 1906), while John S. Hoyland has translated *The Commentary of Father* [Antonio] *Monserrate, S. J.* (London, 1922). Use should also be made of the fascinating accounts published in two major collections: John Pinkerton, *A General Collection of the Best and Most Interesting Voyages and Travels in All Parts of the World*, VIII (London, 1811), and Richard Hakluyt, *The Principal Navigations, Voyages, Traffiques and Discoveries of the English Nation* (12 vols.; Glasgow, 1903-1905).

Studies of the Mughal empire are too numerous to list. Among the most helpful are the following: Sir Jadunath Sarkar, *The Mughal Administration* (Calcutta, 1920); Sri Ram Sharma, *Mughal Government and Administration* (Bombay, 1951); William H. Moreland, *From Akbar to Aurangzeb: A Study in Indian Economic History* (London, 1923); and T. G. Percival Spear, *Twilight of the Mughals: Studies in Late Mughal Delhi* (Cambridge, 1951). The Spear volume, though not, in general, recommended for the beginner in Mughal history, contains a chapter on life in the Delhi kingdom that is a classic of descriptive and historical writing. Unfortunately, most of the published volumes in Mughal history concentrate on government and give all too little information on conditions of life among the villagers who formed more than 80 per cent of the total population.

Among the visitors to India during the heyday of the Mughals were the forerunners of what came to be a veritable deluge of Englishmen. Fascinating accounts of the first Englishmen in India are to be found in two good volumes: Edward F. Oaten's *European Travellers in India during the Fifteenth, Sixteenth, and Seventeenth Centuries* (London, 1909), and John C. Locke's *The First Englishmen in India: Letters and Narratives of Sundry Elizabethans Written by Themselves* (London, 1930). In addition, for Mughal India and the coming of the English, use should be made of Sir William Wilson Hunter's *A History of British India* (2 vols.; London, 1899), which remains one of the most balanced, scholarly, and readable surveys in print. In the introduction to his *History*, Hunter makes some incisive comments on the nature of the forces which shaped the character of European enterprise in India.

## The Coming of the Europeans

A number of myths have come to be accepted regarding the purpose and enterprise of the Europeans which led to domination in India. Most of these versions contain more than a germ of truth but tend to beg the issue. It may be comforting to think that the Europeans arrived in India humbly and diffidently and that empire was thrust upon them to their great surprise.[10] There was, however, more to the story than that. The reader will find in C. H. Philips' *India*, cited above, a good chapter describing the coming of the Europeans and their rise to power.[11]

The rise of European power in India cannot be taken out of its context in the rivalry for the rich spice trade. Two recent volumes shed valuable light on the subject. The first is by D. G. E. Hall, *A History of Southeast Asia* (New York, 1955). Chapter XIV of Hall's book deals with the nature of the European contest for trade, in the course of which interest in India arose. The second title, Brian Harrison, *South-East Asia, A Short History* (London, 1960), a revision of an earlier (1954) book, devotes several chapters to the matter, and is concise and lucid. Sir William Wilson Hunter's *History of British India* is most useful for the East India Company.

## The Ascendency of the East India Company

A valuable contemporary account of the rise of British power in India is to be found in Harry Verelst's *A View of the Rise, Progress, and Present State of the English Government in Bengal* (London, 1772). Verelst was a senior official of the Company in Bengal and his

10. In this connection note the version given in C. L. Reid, *Commerce and Conquest: The Story of the Honourable East India Company* (London, 1947), p. 16.

11. Valuable material on the early operations of the English and on the nature of the East India Company will be found in Bāla-krishna, *Commercial Relations between India and England (1601 to 1757)* (London, 1924); Parakunnel Joseph Thomas, *Mercantilism and the East India Trade: An Early Phase of the Protection v. Free Trade Controversy* (London, 1926); and Ephraim Lipson, *The Growth of English Society* (4th ed.; London [1959]), pp. 152 ff. A good general account of early European expansion in Asia is to be found in John Horace Parry, *Europe and a Wider World, 1415-1715* (London, 1949).

volume provides considerable insight into a period which has been rather inadequately treated by later writers. Use should also be made of Sukumar Bhattacharya, *The East India Company and the Economy of Bengal from 1704 to 1740* (London, 1954). Another valuable source is Ramesh Chander Dutt, *The Economic History of India under Early British Rule from the Rise of British Power in 1757 to the Accession of Queen Victoria in 1837* (4th ed., Edinburgh, 1916). Paul E. Roberts, *History of British India Under the Company and the Crown* (3rd ed., London, 1952), one of the best texts on the British period in Indian history, has several good summary chapters on the East India Company. The volume by Thompson and Garratt, cited previously, also has good summary chapters dealing with the Company. A number of other volumes help to give a balanced and accurate view. Some of these tend to concentrate on the Company as an organization; others give space to the rôle of the Company in India and its effects on Indian life. The latter subject is clearly one whose surface has hardly been scratched. The source material is, however, available in London and India, and recent signs indicate a healthy development of scholarship on the subject of changes in India under company rule. Two useful works on the Company are those by Holden Furber, *John Company at Work: A Study of European Expansion in India in the Late Eighteenth Century* (Cambridge, Mass., 1948) and Cyril H. Philips, *The East India Company, 1784-1834* (Manchester, 1940). Though both are quite good, they are relatively specialized and require of the reader a basic knowledge of the history of the Company. An older study, written before the growth of a tendency to minimize criticism of the British, is still quite useful: Robert Montgomery Martin, *The Indian Empire* (3 vols.; London, 1858-61). The growth of English power in India had to face and overcome serious rivalry from the French. While a number of titles already cited discuss the Anglo-French contest for power, use should also be made of a recent substantial study by Siba Pada Sen, *The French in India, 1763-1816* (Calcutta, 1958). Recently there has appeared the volume by Kenneth Ballhatchet, *Social Policy and Social Change in Western India, 1817-1830*. In it Ballhatchet has shown what can be done with official sources for a topic during the period of the Company. Unfortunately, his study covers only a brief span of years and only one part of British India. Moreover, it has little to say that is based upon the Indian view of the changes that were taking place.[12]

Useful and informative material on the pre-Mutiny period will also be found in Sir Percival J. Griffiths, *The British Impact on India* (London, 1952). Griffiths' account, though unsatisfactory in some respects, includes valuable information on economic change in British India. For the life of British officials in India see T. G. Percival Spear, *The Nabobs: A Study of the Social Life of the English in Eighteenth Century India* (London, 1932), or the amusing and informative book by Dennis Kincaid, *British Social Life in India, 1608-1937* (London, 1939). More recently we have Philip Woodruff (Philip Mason), *The Men who Ruled India* (2 vols.; London, 1954-55). Woodruff's material is solid, but he has a tendency to become sententious and to labor the issue that in Britain's relations with India there has been "more reason for pride than for shame."

In 1961 Bernard Cohn published a valuable and informative bibliographic essay entitled *The Development and Impact of British Administration in India* (New Delhi, 1961), which includes trenchant observations on the period of company rule and the literature of that period. It deserves close attention. Another valuable recent addition to the literature on the period of company rule is George D. Bearce's *British Attitudes towards India, 1784-1858* (London, 1961). In it Bearce has categorized the major schools of British thought regarding India and has made a detailed study of the implications of these sets of attitudes. See also Eric Stokes, *The English Utilitarians and India* (Oxford, 1959), for an important evaluation.

## THE MUTINY

Of all the events during the British era in India, none has received more controversial notice than the famous Mutiny of 1857. During the Mutiny men disagreed on its extent and its meaning. After the establishment of Crown rule the argument continued. Later there was a tendency to minimize the Mutiny's significance as anything more

---

12. Two brief introductory articles which try to summarize British impact on Indian society are: Robert I. Crane, "India: A Study of the Impact of Western Civilization," *Social Education* (Washington), XV (Dec., 1951), 365-71, and, by the same author, "Strata Disruption and Social Change in South Asia," *United Asia* (Bombay), VI (March, 1954), 228-34. See also the valuable work by Frederick J. Shore, *Notes on Indian Affairs* (2 vols.; London, 1837).

than a purely military movement and to decry the possibility that it
had included civil disaffection and rebellion. The argument has continued until today, without reaching any agreed-upon interpretation.

Thompson and Garratt, in their *Rise and Fulfillment of British
Rule in India*, not only give a balanced account of the background of
the Mutiny but also comment on its interpretation. In part, they say:

> Many important official documents and some recent histories were writ-
> ten, consciously or unconsciously, with an eye to certain criticisms which
> have been made in India or abroad. The growth of Indian nationalism has
> accentuated a bias which is often unfavorable to Indians. . . .
>
> The mischievous tendency to make historical truth subservient to ad-
> ministrative expediency has been increased by changes in legal practice and
> procedure, which operate as an effective censorship. . . . The freedom with
> which the Mutiny was discussed during the subsequent two decades would
> have led, under present conditions, to innumerable *causes celebres* . . . official
> secretiveness, of which there was litttle before the Mutiny, combined with
> this informal censorship, makes it almost impossible to supply the "penetra-
> tion, accuracy, and coloring" which Dr. Johnson demanded of the historian.[13]

In India today one school of thought asserts that the Mutiny was,
in fact, the first act in a national war for Indian independence. Other
Indians refuse to go so far, but agree that it was more than a military
uprising. The past few years have witnessed an unusually heavy publication on the subject. Though it is difficult to arrive at any satisfactory
judgment on the nature of the Mutiny, it seems fair to say that it
involved more than soldiers, that there were elements of civil rebellion, and that there were Indians, in and out of the Sepoy Army, who
were genuinely alarmed by what seemed to them to be a plan to
undermine their religion and their caste. Moreover, there were those
who had suffered loss of status, or of emoluments, or of traditional
employment through the spread of British power and who wished to
return to the older order of things.

At the same time, it seems clear that there was no organized national conspiracy, no effective co-operation among the various contingents
and local uprisings, and little or no concept of what would be done
if the uprisings were effective and turned the British out. Meanwhile,
a substantial proportion of the population appears to have watched the
struggle passively. The Mutiny did, however, have considerable effect
on the subsequent course of events in British India. This is true be-

13. Thompson and Garratt, *Rise and Fulfilment of British Rule in India*, pp. vii-viii.

cause it alarmed the British and made them suspicious of their Indian subjects, because it poisoned relations between the two communities, and because the "lessons" of the Mutiny influenced subsequent British behavior and policy in India.

The standard account of the Mutiny is, by all odds, the multi-volume study by Sir John W. Kaye and George Bruce Malleson, *History of the Indian Mutiny of 1857-8* (6 vols.; London, 1908-9). The brutality of the Mutiny is sketched in Edward J. Thompson's *The Other Side of the Medal* (New York, 1926). A highly interesting contemporary description of the Mutiny by a correspondent for *The* (London) *Times* has recently been republished, Sir William Howard Russell's *My Indian Mutiny Diary* (London, 1957). A sober and balanced study has been published in India by Surendra Nath Sen, *Eighteen Fifty Seven* (Delhi, 1957). An interesting older account, well worth reading, is by J. J. McLeod Innes, *Lucknow and Oude in the Mutiny: A Narrative and a Study* (London, 1895).

## India under the Crown

With the suppression of the Mutiny, the Company was abolished and British India was placed under the Crown. By the new arrangement a Secretary of State for India, accountable to Crown and Parliament, was in charge of the government of India. This inaugurated a long period of Crown rule which witnessed a multitude of changes in Indian life and eventuated in the transfer of power to the Dominion of India in 1947.

Shortly after the establishment of Crown rule, the opening of the Suez Canal had a dramatic effect upon India. In the first place, it meant that the Indian economy could be effectively linked to the economy of Western Europe and to the world market. In the second place, it meant that communications between India and England became much more rapid. This encouraged travel, brought larger numbers of Europeans to India, and facilitated the movement of Indians to Europe and America for education. Also, the opening of direct telegraphic communications between London and India led to close and continuous scrutiny by the home authorities of the affairs of the government of India.

During the same period the British pushed the development of a rail network throughout India. This helped to give the subcontinent a unity it had never had before. The unity of roads and rails promoted economic unification and heightened the effect of world-market conditions and opportunities on the rural sector of society. Moreover, people could travel in India as never before. At the same time, the government began to expand educational institutions at the college and secondary level, modeled after English colleges and schools. The steady growth of a Western-educated intelligentsia among the upper and middle economic groups in the Indian population was to have profound and lasting effects on the future of India.

Later in the nineteenth century the government began a cautious experiment with the development of representative institutions into which Indians could move. By the end of World War I the evolution of representative forms of government had gone far enough so that Indian ministers in the provincial legislatures were given responsibility for certain areas of government, under British supervision. Thus were parliamentary institutions introduced into the alien soil of India.

This was also the period of the rise of Indian nationalism. In its early phases, about 1885, Indian nationalists were loyal to the British connection, constitutional in their procedures, and moderate in their demands. By the end of the nineteenth century, however, the moderate and strictly constitutional phase had begun to wane in the face of ardent supporters of direct action. Among the extremists some were inclined to terrorism, hoping to drive the British from India by violence. Relations between the British and the Indians became increasingly strained.

During World War I, Indian nationalism secured fresh impetus— among other things from President Wilson's proclamation of the right of self-determination—and tensions increased. At this point the Secretary of State for India announced that it was Britain's intention that India become, sooner or later, a self-governing Dominion. Though the announcement had a good effect on Indian opinion, the effect was not long lasting. Soon the tempo of events outpaced British intentions and renewed violence marred the scene.

In 1920 Mohandas Gandhi came forward as a leader in the nationalist movement and, by the character of his leadership, made the Congress party into a mass national party and drew the attention of the world to India's demand. During the period of intermittent conflict

and truce that followed the growing bitterness of Indian opinion toward Britain cannot be doubted. At the same time the scene in India
was characterized by a steady increase in animosity between the Hindus
and the Muslim minority, or at least between the more vocal elements
of the two communities. Gandhi constantly sought a compromise with
the British over India's progress toward self-government as well as a
compromise with the Muslims over their claims as a political minority.
He was not very successful with regard to the Muslim leadership.

World War II interrupted the course of events in Indian life and
postponed evolution of some form of federal dominion government.
By the end of the war it was clear that—wisely or not—India was
soon to be partitioned into two new nations. The intransigence of the
various parties to the quarrel had by that time grown to such proportions that rational solutions seemed excluded from the realm of
the possible.

With independence in 1947 a national government, manned by the
Congress party, which had led the struggle for independence, came
into office, declared India to be a secular republic, guided a democratic
constitution to adoption, and launched upon ambitious plans for rapid
economic development. For years the Congress had told the masses
that their poverty, disease, and illiteracy were the product of British
rule. Whether this argument was valid or not, it was a conviction
firmly held by those Indians who gave thought to such matters.
Naturally, the Congress party had also promised that political independence would mean the end of exploitation and the termination of
poverty. Promises were easy to make and to believe when working
for independence, but not so easy to implement after independence.
The past decade has witnessed a manful effort by Indian political
leadership to make good the promises of the prewar days.

The period of Crown rule, as has been mentioned, was a period
of many kinds of change in Indian life. Since the opening of the
Suez Canal, India has been progressively more opened to Western
practices, ideas, and values. The Westernized intelligentsia became the
leaders of the nationalist movement. Today many of the leaders may
be said to have become so Westernized in their values that they no
longer speak in the idiom of traditional India, a number of them
having openly indicated their opposition to traditional religious and
social practices enjoined by Hinduism. The fact of change seems ap-

parent on every hand. Unfortunately, much of the history produced during and for the period eschews any serious effort to analyze the factors making for change, the extent of penetration of change-producing situations, and the degree to which changes have been accomplished.

Several basic texts valuable for the modern period have already been indicated. Reference should also be made to a brief but excellent summary by Daniel and Alice Thorner, "India and Pakistan," in Ralph Linton, ed., *Most of the World: The People of Africa, Latin America, and the East Today* (New York, 1949). The article indicates with real penetration the ways in which foreign contact affected traditional Indian life.

Early in World War II, the then Secretary of State for India, Leopold C. M. S. Amery, published a small volume of speeches which set forth British policy for India—*India and Freedom* (London, 1942), which is useful as an authoritative summary of the official viewpoint. If one compares it with earlier statements of a similar variety, one can notice certain shifts in emphasis. A very different interpretation will be found in Charles Freer Andrews' *India and Britain: A Moral Challenge* (London, 1935). Its author, formerly a teacher in India, became an active supporter of Gandhi and argued from the Indian viewpoint against the British position. Andrews' lucid account helps get at Indian sentiment.

For an earlier period in Crown rule and an interesting example of the British point of view, one can use the well-written volume by Elizabeth E. Bulwer-Lytton, Lady Balfour, *The History of Lord Lytton's Indian Administration, 1876 to 1880* . . . (London, 1899). This volume gives information about and insights into one of the most convinced Imperial proconsuls, with special reference to frontier policy and the messy Second Afghan War. For a view of India under British rule that is rather balanced and detailed, see Devadata Ramakrishna Bhandarkar, ed., *India*, which appeared as Volume CXLV of the *Annals of the American Academy of Political and Social Science* (Philadelphia, 1929). With few exceptions this is a good collection of articles on various aspects of Indian life, politics, economic conditions, and education. A recent, solid study sheds valuable light on the period: Hira Lal Singh, *Problems and Policies of the British in India, 1885-1898* (London, 1963).

One of the classics in the field, though written from a position which was clearly British, is Sir Valentine Chirol's *India* (London, 1926). Uneven but worthwhile, it includes a good account of the working of the Indian legislatures under Dyarchy and of the effects of Western education on the Indian intelligentsia.

More polished and lucid is Sir Reginald Coupland's *Britain and India, 1600-1941* (London, 1941), which gives the official viewpoint in a concise, well-argued, and rather authoritative fashion. An earlier but more neutral account of British rule in India is to be found in Cecil M. P. Cross, *The Development of Self-Government in India, 1858-1914* (Chicago, 1922), a solid account of constitutional evolution, well documented though unimaginative. Cross includes a good summary of the development of local self-government in India. His volume, by the way, leans quite heavily upon two famous reports by the government of India.

India had a number of governors-general who were men of substance and interest, though not all had equally eventful careers. One of the most eventful was that of Lord Curzon, the author of the highly controversial partition of Bengal in 1905 and long a most senior figure in Britain's Eastern Empire. There is still disagreement over the magnitude of his rôle in India. An early but solid study of his viceroyalty is that by Lovat Fraser, *India under Curzon and After* (London, 1911). The account contains much useful material and is fairly detailed, though relatively unimaginative. While it is difficult to decide which of the Indian governors-general, after Curzon, merit special attention, there is reason to suggest Lord Minto. Of his career and the important reforms connected with his name, we have the worthwhile study by (Mary Caroline Grey) Countess Minto, *India, Minto and Morley, 1905-1910* (London, 1935). Though not definitive, Countess Minto's book makes use of her husband's correspondence and includes comments drawn from her own diaries. More recently, Sarvepalli Gopal has written two volumes on viceregal careers, *The Viceroyalty of Lord Ripon, 1880-84* (London, 1953), and *The Viveroyalty of Lord Irwin, 1926-31* (Oxford, 1957).

For British policy toward India, there is the authoritative, well-written account based on official sources by Arthur (later Sir Arthur) Berriedale Keith, *Speeches and Documents on Indian Policy, 1750-1921* (London, 1922). Keith has also written a substantial history of the administration of India, *A Constitutional History of India* (London, 1936). There are also lesser summaries such as the one by Walter Elliott Duffett, *India Today: The Background of the Indian Nationalist Movement* (Toronto, 1941), which provides a brief but decent summary of major developments in Indian politics.

An exotic and interesting aspect of British-Indian affairs was the position and prospects of the Indian princes. Prior to independence buckets of ink were consumed in describing them, lauding them, condemning them, or speculating on their future. Most of what was written about them proved, after achievement of independence by India, to have been idle if not sententious. One of the best titles on the princes came from the pen of an official who was sympathetic to their claims, Sir William Lee-Warner: *The Protected Princes of India* (London, 1894). The second edition is *The Native States of India* (London, 1910). These volumes deal with the political position of the princes and with the nature of their relationship to the Crown.

One of the more important activities of the government of India was the establishment and supervision of a system of higher education. Though many titles purport to discuss education in India, the majority are incomplete, unreliable, or prejudiced. One volume is considerably more useful than those which preceded it—Syed Nurullah and J. P. Naik's *A History of Education in India (during the British Period)* (Bombay, 1951). Solid, well-documented and balanced, this is a good account of the progress of education in India with emphasis on the major phases of educational development and systematic information on the education provided. An older volume with good material on Indian education was edited by L. S. S. O'Malley, *Modern India and the West: A Study of the Interaction of Their Civilizations* (London, 1941). This collection of essays covers a variety of topics including education, the economic system, Hindu society, literature, and drama. Though uneven, it is a good introduction to India under British rule. A concise summary of trends in higher education in India will be found in the chapter by Robert I. Crane, "The Transfer of Western Education to India," in William B. Hamilton, ed., *The Transfer of Institutions* (Durham, N.C., 1965), pp. 108-38.

For those who are interested in the dramatic but tangled tale of India's frontier—too often treated in a romantic fashion—Bisheshwar Prasad has provided a scholarly and careful study in *The Foundations of India's Foreign Policy*, I: *1860-1882* (Calcutta, 1955). The volume is well documented as well as lucid. In addition it makes an effort to analyze the mainsprings of policy.

Recognized as a concise and highly informed exposition of the principles of British rule in India is Sir John Strachey's *India; Its Administration and Progress* (4th ed., London, 1911). Strachey was a senior Indian official and his study contains a wealth of information. Another account, also by a senior official, gives a rather different and less comprehensive view of British rule. Septimus S. Thorburn in *The Punjab in Peace and War* (London, 1904), concentrates on the province in which he served, but provides an illuminating discussion of the strengths and weakness of British rule. Thorburn had rather decided views on the economic effects of British policy in India and on frontier policy.

Three works by Englishmen have been reserved for closing reference in this discussion of British rule in India. Each of the three has qualities that set it apart from the run-of-the-mill studies in Indo-British history. The least impressive of the three is Reginald Reynolds, *The White Sahibs in India* (London, 1937), an effective but bitter criticism of British rule in India, well sprinkled with official sources. Its chief value is that it contains material not often found in standard works. The second book is by Edward Penderel Moon, *Strangers in India* (London, 1944), a slim but engrossing volume which digs deeply and thoughtfully in questioning many of the rather complacent asumptions made by British officials. Its author had considerable experience in India and his views command respect even from those who would disagee with his conclusions. The third is by Sir Stanley Reed, who was for years editor of the leading English newspaper in India: *The India I Knew, 1897-1947* (London, 1952). Though written in biographical form, its breadth of understanding and range of interest make it an informal history of India for the years it covers, and in it Sir Stanley provides one of the most discerning accounts available. The chapter on the Indian Civil Service deserves to rank with the classics.

## THE CONDITION OF INDIA

Although a number of the titles already mentioned contain information on the condition of India, it seemed wise to include others which are especially informative on the subject. These titles will be divided into two groups: those which give a general picture of the economic, social, or intellectual milieu, and those which provide information on village life. As the bulk of India's people live in villages, one cannot claim to understand India unless he has studied the Indian village.

One of the best-known titles on the Indian economy, written in scholarly fashion, is Vera P. Anstey's *The Economic Development of India* (London, 1952). Essentially a straightforward economic history, this summary emphasizes the period between 1900 and World War II. A similar effort, probably not so scholarly but covering a wider range of topics and easier to read, is M. Arokiaswami and T. M. Royappa's *The Modern Economic History of India* (5th ed., Madras, 1957). Pramathanath Banerjea also has a respectable text in the field, *A Study of Indian Economics* (6th ed.; Calcutta, 1951).

With this as background one can turn to other titles on various aspects of the condition of India. One of the best available is by John S. Hoyland, *Indian Crisis, the Background* (London, 1943); it has elements of Indian history, a perceptive discussion of Indian living conditions, some lucid passages on Hinduism, and an illuminating but brief discussion of British rule and its effects. Written for the non-specialist, it deserves special attention. Rather more comprehensive is Romesh Chander Dutt, *The Economic History of India in the Victorian Age* (London, 1916). Though dated, it remains one of the best accounts of economic conditions in nineteenth-century India. Another good source on conditions of life is Sir William Wilson Hunter's *The Indian Empire: Its People, History and Products* (3d ed., London, 1893). Dadabhai Naoroji's *Poverty and un-British Rule in India* (London, 1901), represents substantial research on the economic effects of British rule. Naoroji was an outstanding early nationalist leader, and his book presents the nationalist viewpoint. It cannot, however, be discounted simply on that ground. Moreover, it set the tone for later nationalist arguments. A similar volume, also well written, is by G. Subrahmanya Aiyar, *Some Economic Aspects of British Rule in India* (Madras, 1903). For India's foreign trade Parimal Ray's *India's Foreign Trade since 1870* (London, 1934), a solid though dated account, can be used.

Though there exists no comprehensive group of works covering the rural economy of all of India, a few titles of merit do give a substantial view of economic conditions and the working of the agrarian economy in certain regions of India. Among the most helpful are Dhananjaya R. Gadgil, "Problems of Rural Life," in *Annals of the American Academy of Political and Social Science*, CCXXXIII (Philadelphia, 1944); Clark G. Chenevix-Trench, "The Rural Community," in Edward A. H. Blunt, ed., *Social Service in India* (London, 1938); Septimus S. Thorburn, *Musalmans and Moneylenders in the Punjab* (London, 1884); Phillips Talbot, ed., *South Asia in the World Today* (Chicago, 1950); Adrian C. Mayer, *Land and Society in Malabar* (London, 1952); Malcolm L. Darling, *The Punjab Peasant in Prosperity and Debt* (4th ed., Bombay, 1947); and Harold Hart Mann, *Land and Labor in a Deccan Village* (London, 1917).

Recently a few good volumes have appeared concerning village life, village social organization, and the nature of village society in India. The first, a novel, Hilda Wernher's *The Land and the Well* (New York, 1946), is quite informative and perceptive and gives an excellent picture of a typical north India village. Of the more scholarly studies, that by Shyama Charan Dube, *Indian Village* (Ithaca, 1955), may well be the most useful for non-specialists. A recent collection of articles, some quite good and others not, will be found in Mysore Narasimhachar Srinivas, *et al.*, *India's Villages* (Calcutta, 1955).

A valuable collection of village studies is brought together in McKim Marriott, ed., *Village India, Studies in the Little Community* (Chicago, 1955). The most recent publication on the organization of life in an Indian village is the attractive and informative volume by Oscar Lewis, *Village Life in Northern India: Studies in a Delhi Village* (Urbana, Ill., 1958). This study includes an excellent account of the *jajmani* system of mutual service relations in the village. *Jajmani* is an aspect of village life which has received all too little attention, even though it was described some years ago by the missionary William H. Wiser in his classic, *The Hindu Jajmani System*...(Lucknow, 1936). Wiser and his wife, Charlotte, also published an informative and interesting book on village life called *Behind Mud Walls* (New York, 1930). Finally reference must be made to an informal and autobiographical account that is very well written and most informative: Gertrude Emerson Sen's *Voiceless India* (rev. ed., New York, 1944).

## NATIONALISM

Though nationalism in modern India is a product of British rule and of Western education, its development has been a complex process reflecting a variety of urges in Indian society and a set of responses to European domination. Among the nationalist leaders there have been highly Westernized graduates of Oxford; there have also been fiery leaders who, despite a B.A. from an Indian university, spoke in terms of a Hindu revival; and there have been half-educated Hindu lads from orthodox homes who knew too little about the West against which they proposed the use of gun and bomb. There have even been occasional peasant leaders who have had very little contact with things European.

Though all may have agreed on the desire for independence, there were at all times major potential disagreements among them on other issues. Disagreement arose primarily over the best way to get independence, but there was also disagreement over the kind of India that was to develop after independence. Some wanted to return to an idealized Vedic society, some wanted an India organized along lines which would have pleased a nineteenth-century liberal, some worked for a free enterprise system, and others preferred one or another brand of socialist state. Some favored caste; others opposed it. Some wanted more Westernization; others wanted less. Some favored machines; others looked upon them as the very wages of sin. The paradoxes are too numerous to list but should not be forgotten.[14]

A phenomenon as complex as Indian nationalism cannot be understood through any one viewpoint or from any one book. Though a great deal has been published on aspects of Indian nationalism, each volume reflects the special interest or the bias of its author or sponsor. Much of the material on nationalism is particularly polemical in origin or in purpose. The documentary sources for a balanced history of Indian nationalism have not been used very effectively to date, and certain aspects of Indian nationalism have received almost no attention. Even those aspects of nationalism which have been discussed threadbare have seldom received *critical* study. In the past few years some

14. I have published an essay recently which explores some of the divergent trends and groupings within Indian nationalism: "Problems of Divergent Developments within Indian Nationalism, 1895-1905," in Robert K. Sakai, ed., *Studies on Asia, 1961* (Lincoln, Neb., 1961), pp. 1-14.

collections of source materials have been published, but there is reason to fear that these collections have not been edited too well. The situation is improving, however, and source materials which could not be seen before are now beginning to appear in print.

It should also be noted that the nationalist movement contained several parties. The Congress party, though certainly the most important nationalist party, was by no means the only one. The Muslim League, the Indian Liberal Federation, the Indian Association, and the Hindu Mahasabha were nationalist parties and require study along with the Congress party. More has been published on or about the Congress party than about the other, however. The result has been an imbalance which requires correction. The existing imbalance will, of course, be reflected in the literature to be cited here.

One of the better-known attempts by foreigners to assess the nature of nationalism in India, Horace G. Alexander's *India Since Cripps* (Harmondsworth, 1944), is an effort to explain the viewpoint of Indian nationalists in a sympathetic fashion. Brief and quite readable, it covers a limited span of time. Much earlier, Sir Valentine Chirol, *India Old and New* (London, 1921), gave a workmanlike account of the growth of nationalism. Given his bias, the book shows considerable insight and is worth reading.

Less well known but more effective in getting at the viewpoint of the early nationalists is Sir Henry J. S. Cotton, *New India; or, India in Transition* (London, 1907). It is doubtful that anyone could have done a better job of analyzing the major characteristics of the rise of nationalism than Cotton. His successor, Sir Harrington Verney Lovett, in *A History of the Indian Nationalist Movement* (London, 1920), by contrast, has provided an account that reflects official sentiment. Though useful, it is rather inadequate in expressing the nationalist viewpoint.

A most valuable source for the rise of nationalism among educated Indians is Bruce T. McCully's *English Education and the Origins of Indian Nationalism* (New York, 1940). McCully's book includes excellent documentation and a penetrating study of nationalist views. William Roy Smith, *Nationalism and Reform in India* (New Haven, 1938), is rather more comprehensive than McCully but lacks the latter's insights. Sir Francis Younghusband's *Dawn in India: British Purpose and Indian Aspiration* (London, 1930) should also be mentioned. Younghusband displays a justifiable pride in British accomplishments mingled with a sense of the justice and inevitability of the Indian demand.

Well worth noting is the book by Cecil Freer Andrews and Girija Mookerji, *The Rise and Growth of the Congress in India* (London, 1938). It provides a sympathetic, intelligent summary of the growth of nationalism through the end of World War I. The authors place the Congress in its setting in the nineteenth-century renaissance of Indian thought. Another basic source on the growth of nationalism is the autobiography of Sir Surendranātha Vandyopādhyāya (Banerjea), *A Nation in Making, being the Reminiscences of Fifty Years of Public Life* (London, 1925). Banerjea was one of the founders of Indian nationalism and a prominent leader in the moderate wing of the Congress. To this can be added Annie Besant, *Speeches and Writings of Annie Besant* (Madras, 1921). Mrs. Besant, a leading Theosophist, was prominent in Congress circles in the pre-Gandhian era. Another useful volume on early nationalism is Sir Chirranoori Yajneswara Chintamani's *Indian Politics since the Mutiny*...(London, 1940). Chintamani surveys pre-Congress nationalist activities, discusses the leading nationalists, and summarizes the growth of the Congress. John S. Hoyland has provided a valuable account of another Congress leader *Gopal Krishna Gokhale, His Life and Speeches* (Calcutta, 1933).

Several books have recently been published on Bal G. Tilak, the fiery leader of extremist nationalism from Poona. One of the most extensive of these is by Shirrain Lakshinan Karandikar, *Lokamanya Bal Gangadhar Tilak, the Hercules and Prometheus of Modern India* (Poona, 1957). Though quite favorable to Tilak, it is a solid and respectable study of his controversial career. More recently, Stanley A. Wolpert has published his study of two prominent nationalist leaders, *Tilak and Gokhale: Revolution and Reform in the Making of Modern India* (Berkeley, 1962).[15]

A recent contribution to the literature on the early Congress is Haridas and Uma Mukherjee's *The Growth of Nationalism in India, (1857-1905)* (Calcutta, 1957), a valuable supplement to the standard reference work on the Congress, Bhogaraju Pattabhi Sitaramayya's *The*

15. Published too late for examination here were Charles H. Heimsath, *Indian Nationalism and Hindu Social Reform* (Princeton, 1964), Thomas R. Metcalf, *The Aftermath of Revolt: India, 1857-1870* (Princeton, 1964), and Stanley A. Wolpert, *India* (Englewood Cliffs, N. J., 1965).

*History of the Indian National Congress* (2 vols.; Bombay, 1946-47), the official history of the Congress. Sitaramayya's study, though solid and rather well documented, requires careful supplementing. Also valuable for study of the Congress is *Congress Presidential Addresses* (Madras, 1934), a compilation of the annual speeches made to the Congress by the president-elect for the year, which gives the reader considerable insight into the major themes of the Congress as it developed.

Among the titles published by nationalist leaders, some of the most interesting and informative were by Lala Lājpat Rāya (Rai). Two of his works are particularly useful in getting at nationalist opinion: *Young India: An Interpretation and a History of the Nationalist Movement from Within* (New York, 1916), and *Unhappy India, being a Reply to Miss Katherine Mayo's 'Mother India'* (Calcutta, 1928). Whether one agrees with the nationalist arguments or not, it is important that they be understood. Lājpat Rai expresses the nationalist viewpoint effectively and authoritatively. Two valuable recent additions to the literature on nationalism and its leaders should also be noted. The first is by the president of the Republic of India, a long-time leader in the Congress, Rajendra Prasad: *Autobiography* (Bombay, 1957). It contains a wealth of interesting material on his own life, the growth of the Congress, and the setting in which nationalism developed. Another recent book, somewhat comparable, is Frank (Francis) R. Moraes' *Jawaharlal Nehru, a Biography* (New York, 1956), a lucid and provocative account of Nehru's background, education, ideas, and career.

Of all the Congress leaders, Mohandas Gandhi has been the most controversial figure. Seemingly possessed of numerous paradoxes, Gandhi has been analyzed from almost every viewpoint. No single book has managed to encompass him; his own voluminous writings contain interesting contradictions. Of a vast literature on or by Gandhi only a few works are mentioned here. The first was published under the title *Gandhi's Autobiography: The Story of My Experiments with Truth* (Washington, 1948), and is quite revealing. The second, also by Gandhi, *Swaraj in One Year* (Madras, 1921), is valuable as an early statement of his program, method, and basic ideas. Glorney Bolton's *The Tragedy of Gandhi* (London, 1934), a quiet, unassuming, and in some ways light volume, is, nevertheless, well written, interesting, and usually quite penetrating. Another informal but very informative title is Ghanshyam Dass Birla, *In the Shadow of the Mahatma: A Personal Memoir* (Bombay, 1953).

A Congress leader unlike Gandhi or Nehru was Subhas Chandra Bose. During World War II Bose fled India and eventually went to Japan, where he emerged as leader of the Indian National Army, supported by the Japanese military, which was to invade India and drive the British out. Bose died in the last days of the war and a considerable literature has appeared around his name. Before the war he published a substantial book which remains an important source on Indian nationalism, *The Indian Struggle, 1920-1934* (London, 1935); though not comprehensive, it contains useful and interesting material.

Two helpful books are available on other nationalist parties in modern India. One is by Jogesh Chandra Bagal, *History of the Indian Association, 1876-1951*, I (Calcutta, 1953). The Indian Association played an important rôle in the rise of nationalism and its history is informative by contrast with that of the Congress. At the other extreme of the political spectrum was the Hindu revivalistic Rashtriya Swayam Sevak Sangh, or "R. S. S." The volume by Jean A. Curran, *Militant Hinduism in Indian Politics: A Study of the R. S. S.* (New York, 1951), provides a concise but valuable study of the Rashtriya, laying bare its ideology and organization. Finally, one may mention a volume which tries to analyze the background from whence Indian nationalism emerged. Akshayakumar Ramalal Desai's *Social Background of Indian Nationalism* (Bombay, 1948) is a relatively scholarly attempt, based on Marxist assumptions, to set forth the social and economic conditions which influenced the growth of nationalism. Michael Brecher has provided a valuable study of modern Indian nationalism in his volume, *Nehru, a Political Biography* (London, 1959).

## India since Independence

The published materials on India since independence are spotty and generally inadequate. The volume by W. Norman Brown, *The United States and India and Pakistan*, mentioned previously, contains a fair amount of material on the postindependence period and should be used.

On the political side two important publications have recently appeared. Written by a high-ranking Indian civil servant, each is a major contribution. The author, Vapal Pangunni Menon, was intimately involved in the events of which he writes, yet has achieved considerable objectivity. The first, covering the integration of the princely states with what had been British India, *The Story of the Integration of the Indian States* (New York, 1956), includes a laudable summary of the past relationship of the states to India and gives in clear and interesting terms the story of their merger with India. The second describes the complicated events which led to partition and independence: *The Transfer of Power in India* (Princeton, 1957). Both belong on any reading list dealing with modern India.

Jawaharlal Nehru has, of course, made a number of important policy statements since independence. Some of the most interesting of these have been published in a collection, *Independence and After* (Delhi, 1949), which gives the reader excellent insight into Nehru's views on a variety of public issues. Some of the topics touched upon in this volume and in V. P. Menon's *Transfer of Power* are also dealt with, intelligently though informally, in Alan Campbell-Johnson's *Mission with Mountbatten* (New York, 1953), covering the period in office of the last English Viceroy of India.

The government established by the Congress, the nature of the constitution of free India, and the character of its laws are very well discussed in the recent book by Alan Gledhill, *The Republic of India: The Development of its Laws and Constitution* (London, 1951). Gledhill is quite well fitted for the task and has produced a worthwhile study.

Since independence one of the major problems facing the Republic of India has been the achievement of balanced economic growth and improvement of poor living conditions. Of the many books discussing problems of India's economic development only a few can be mentioned here. Sir Percival I. Griffiths' *Modern India* (New York, 1957), though of dubious value in some respects, has a section on economic affairs in independent India which is excellent. It includes a good discussion of India's two five-year plans. Chandulal Nagindas Vakil's *Economic Consequences of the Partition* (Bombay, 1949), provides a handy and relatively concise summary of India's economic position on the morrow of independence and partition. Partition, of course, had a marked short-term effect on the viability of the Indian economy.

Wladimir S. Woytinsky, in *India, the Awakening Giant* (New York, 1956), has provided a compendium of the economic development plans and progress of India. Woytinsky, it should be noted, leans on government sources and data regarding economic performance and appears to accept with light heart many a claim considered optimistic by other observers. Much of the material used by Woytinsky will be found in *Statistical Abstract, India, New Series*, published annually in New Delhi by the Office of the Economic Advisor, Government of India. Recently the Planning Commission, Government of India, has published its own survey of economic growth, *The New India, Progress through Democracy* (New York, 1958). It is basically a reference volume, designed to explain India's economic problems and her approaches to their solution. Sections are included on rural development, industrial development, and social services. The book is well written, indexed for quick use, and informative.

Perhaps too dour, the study of economic development problems in India and other countries of south Asia by Robert I. Crane, *Aspects of Economic Development in South Asia* (New York, 1954), attempted a critical evaluation of the various development plans, their objectives and techniques, and their potentialities. The volume includes a brief discussion, with tables, of conditions of life in south Asia.

India's foreign policy and posture in world affairs is a source of continuous amazement to most Americans. This reflects a number of regrettable facts, one of which is lack of awareness of the Indian point of view and its background. Even though one may not agree with the major tenets of Indian foreign policy, one should try to understand its basis and its character. Three titles can be recommended, each of which will help the foreigner to understand why Indian foreign policy is what it is. These titles will also provide enough information so that the critic will know what he is criticizing and the student will understand the major principles on which India's policy rests.

The most scholarly of the three is Jagdish Chandra Kundra, *Indian Foreign Policy, 1947-1954: A Study of Relations with the Western Bloc* (Groningen, 1955). It will certainly repay careful reading. The work by Kotta P. Karunakaran, *India in World Affairs, August, 1947–December, 1953* (2 vols.; Calcutta, 1952-58), is not so balanced and objective but is nonetheless well worth reading, for it more faithfully mirrors the official policy of the government of India and thus helps the reader to understand that policy; too, it covers a wider range than does the Kundra volume. Finally, it is well written and interesting. The third title, Madusudan Ganju's *Indian Foreign Policy* (Bombay, 1951), is a brief, summary account of some aspects of Indian policy, with emphasis on Indo-Pakistan relations and on India's rôle in the Korean War.

One of the most interesting titles published on independent India happens to be the work of a former United States ambassador to India, Chester Bowles. In his provocative and insightful book, *Ambassador's Report* (New York, 1954), Bowles has provided a solid and reliable interpretation of free India. Somewhat similar as a general study, though not so useful as Bowles' book, is the account by Hugh George Rawlinson, *India, A Short Cultural History* (New York, 1955). Rawlinson gives rather more of India's history than does Bowles, and includes sections on India's geography, cities, rural life, and arts, as well as a good appendix of concise data.

An aspect of the current Indian scene which very few authors have touched is the Indian political party. A recent title, designed for the serious student, contains much valuable information: Myron Weiner, *Party Politics in India: The Development of a Multi-Party System* (Princeton, 1957). It can be read, profitably, in conjunction with Donald Mackenzie Brown, *The White Umbrella: Indian Political Thought from Manu to Gandhi* (Berkeley, 1953), which provides an excellent background in Indian political thought, couched in terms which should make the volume quite useful to the Western reader. A valuable recent volume on Indian politics, edited by Cyril H. Philips, is *Politics and Society in India* (New York, 1962).

Two other volumes may be mentioned which shed light on contemporary India. Th efirst, by Gardner Murphy, *In the Minds of Men: The Study of Human Behavior and Social Tensions in India* (New York, 1953), is an important study. It links basic characteristics of Indian life and the effects of foreign domination with current tensions. The second, by John and Ruth Hill Useem, *The Western-educated Man in India: A Study of His Social Roles and Influence* (New York, 1955), discusses a topic of importance for India's future. The Useem book emphasizes the effects of Western education and cross-cultural contacts on modern Indians in an informative and effective fashion.

Among more recent titles designed to interpret the contemporary scene in India there are a few which are valuable. An illuminating enquiry will be found in Selig S. Harrison's *India, the Most Dangerous Decades* (Princeton, 1960). Harrison is concerned with significant problems such as caste and regionalism, the Communist penetration of Indian politics, and the stresses to which the Indian party system is subjected. Donald Eugene Smith, meanwhile, has concentrated his attention on the difficult issue of the survival of a secular order in free India, *India as a Secular State* (Princeton, 1963).[16]

16. This essay is closely based upon the author's earlier survey, *The History of India: Its Study and Interpretation* (Washington, 1958), which has been drawn upon with the permission of the Service Center for Teachers of History of the American Historical Association. Several additional titles relating to India are discussed in Damodar P. Singhal's essay on Pakistan, in this volume, pages 396-420.

# PAKISTAN

## *Damodar P. Singhal*

HISTORICAL CONSCIOUSNESS and writing of history, in the
sense of interpreting the past and explaining events, are comparatively
modern developments in the Indian subcontinent. It was not until the
expansion of Western concepts and techniques that the process of scientific investigation of history began. In Pakistan traditional ideas of history were varied and often vague. The Muslim historians of the medieval period, who had a keener sense of history than their predecessors,
were mainly concerned with chronicling events without attempting
to find either relationship or meaning in them.[1] Under the stimulus
of national awakening and modernity, however, interest in historical
research grew steadily, and history soon became, as elsewhere, an intellectual discipline as well as an instrument of political propaganda. The
peculiar nature of Indian politics during the modern period, in which
a triangular contest between the Indian National Congress, the Muslim
League, and the British government dominated the scene, emphasized
the need for political theoreticians to seek valid historical arguments
in support of their respective assertions. Consequently there appeared
in rapid succession a variety of inarticulate, tendentious, and superficial
historical publications. Of little historical value, they did help to build
a tradition of research and stimulate criticism. The nationalist urge, if
it stirred historical activity, also, in a way, hampered its natural growth.
As a result the works of serious scholarship were few, and even today
Pakistani historiography remains in a formative stage.

Meanwhile historical writing on Pakistan inevitably reflects, and
suffers from, the peculiar problems inherent in its polity. Pakistan was
created in 1947 on the strength of the Muslim League's insistence that

1. For an introduction to the traditional ideas and attitudes, see the relevant chapters in Cyril H. Philips, ed., *Historians of India, Pakistan and Ceylon* (London, 1961);
and Peter Hardy, *The Historians of Medieval India: Studies in Indo-Muslim Historical
Writing* (London, 1960).

the Islamic culture was distinct from Indian culture and that the Indian Muslims were a nation. Partition of India, however, involved partition of the Muslim community and of the cultural heritage, the repercussions of which continually beset historical writing on Pakistan. It was easy to divide territory but how to divide Muslim consciousness? Muslims of both India and Pakistan share a common Islamic tradition yet belong to two distinct nationalities, whose interests and aspirations are dissimilar, even at times conflicting, and who interpret their past differently. The territorial division, based on population structure, has given rise to overlapping and contradictory interpretations of the cultural past. Whereas India has inherited the principal seat of Mughal power and Islamic culture—the areas of Delhi and Agra—West Pakistan is located in the region of the Indus Valley civilization in which lie deep the roots of Hindu culture. While the former cripples Pakistan's exclusive claim to Islamic lineage, the latter raises temptation to avow descent from a rich and ancient, though un-Islamic, civilization, and together they confuse historical analysis and definition of Pakistani historiography. A discussion of Pakistani historiography in the absence of well-demarcated frontiers must therefore remain partially arbitrary and open to dispute. Should it begin with the ancient land, or the Islamic culture, or the actual physical birth of Pakistan? How is one to evaluate and reconcile the claims of these divergent considerations?

Strictly speaking, an assessment of Pakistani historiography must exclude those writings which deal with the pre-Partition periods of Indian history. Yet no history of Pakistan can be adequate without sufficiently appraising the origins that lie entangled in the complex Indian politics of this century, and without giving some account of the history of Muslims in India. Consequently Pakistani historiography has a large share in all the historical writings on Indian history before 1947. In fact, the prepartition period can be designated as the "Indian period" of Pakistan. But I can include in this essay only such historical works which, written in English, treat the embryonic phases of Pakistan specifically from the Pakistani viewpoint.[2]

2. There is an impressive list of histories, both general and specialist on the medieval period of Indian history; and considerable work is being done in India, especially at the Aligarh and Osmania universities. For a quick reference see Shapuashah Harmasji Hodivala's *Studies in Indo-Muslim History* . . . (Bombay, 1939), which is a commentary on Sir Henry Miers Elliot and John Dowson's *The History of India, as Told by Its Own Historians* . . . (8 vols.; London, 1867-77); Ishwari Prasad's *History of*

Sir Syed Ahmad Khan is generally regarded as the father of Muslim modernism and most thinkers trace the early beginnings of Muslim nationalism to his influence. A contemporary work on his career and ideas is *The Life and Work of Syed Ahmad Khân* (London, 1885), by C. F. I. Graham. More recently Johannes M. S. Baljon, Jr., published *The Reforms and Religious Ideas of Sir Sayyid Ahmad Khân* (Leiden, 1949). Sir William Wilson Hunter's *The Indian Musalmans* . . . (London, 1871) is a valuable study by a British administrator-historian describing the condition of the Muslim community in India after the revolt of 1857. The All-India Muslim League was founded in 1906 and the seed of political separation between Muslims and non-Muslims was sown by the Constitutional Reforms in 1909. But it was the famous poet-philosopher Sir Muhammad Iqbal who is often designated as the spiritual father of Pakistan, and who put forward for the first time the idea of a separate state for the predominantly Muslim areas of northwest India in his presidential address to the Allahabad session of the All-India Muslim League in 1930.[3]

Three years later an Indian Muslim student at Cambridge, Chaudhary Rahmat Ali, coined the word "Pakistan" in a four-page leaflet entitled *Now or Never: Are We to Live or Perish for Ever?* (Cambridge). Although politically inexperienced, Rahmat Ali had remarkably stout faith in Pakistan, and even the contempt of the Muslim League leaders who told the Joint Select Committee of Parliament in 1933 that Pakistan was "only a students' scheme," "chimerical and impracticable," did not deter him from pursuing his ideal. In July, 1934, Rahmat Ali formally founded the Pakistan National Movement and issued another of his political manifestos. Five years later he pub-

*Medieval India* . . . (Allahabad, 1948), and the writings of Sir Jadunath Sarkar, the greatest Indian historian of the Mughal Period, such as *History of Aurangzib* (5 vols.; Calcutta, 1912-24); *Fall of the Mughal Empire* (4 vols.; Calcutta; 1932-52); and *Mughal Administration* (Calcutta, 1920). See also William H. Moreland, *From Akbar to Aurangzeb* (London, 1923); Ashirbadi Lal Srivastava, *The Sultanate of Delhi* (Agra, 1953); and T. G. Percival Spear, *The Twilight of the Mughals* (Cambridge, 1951).

3. For the views of the Aga Khan, who founded the Muslim League and led the famous deputation of the Muslim community of India in 1906 to the Viceroy Lord Minto, see Sultan Mohammed Shah, Aga Khan, *The Memoirs of Aga Khan: World Enough and Time* (London, 1954), and *India in Transition* (London, 1918). Also refer to the much discussed Lady (Mary Caroline Grey) Minto's diary, *India, Minto and Morley 1905-1910* (London, 1935). For Iqbal, see Shamloo, *Speeches and Statements of Iqbal* (Lahore, 1948)—Shamloo is probably a pseudonym of a Muslim writer; Iqbal, *Letters of Iqbal to Jinnah* (Lahore, n.d.); and Iqbal, *The Reconstruction of Thought in Islam* (London, 1939).

lished in England a pamphlet entitled *The Millat of Islam and the Menace of 'Indianism'* (Cambridge). In March, 1940, the Muslim League, under the presidency of Mohammad Ali Jinnah, officially adopted the historic Pakistan Resolution, and seven years later Pakistan came into being. The dream of a student was finally converted into reality. But Rahmat Ali was deeply disappointed, for the Muslim League had accepted an abridged version of the Pakistan he had conceived. In 1948 he left Pakistan for England, where he wrote a pamphlet, *The Great Betrayal* (Cambridge), and died soon afterwards.

The goal of a separate homeland quickly fascinated Indian Muslims, and the movement for Pakistan took long and rapid strides. It was also the period of crises, revolution, and war. Indian politics was charged with precarious negotiations, agitation, and mutual fear and distrust. The story of this Indo-Pakistani period is too deeply involved in prejudices to be recounted dispassionately until memories of physical violence and bitter political relationships have been obliterated with the passage of time. Students of history, therefore, will be best advised to read a variety of books written from different viewpoints and to draw their own individual conclusions.

Apart from the Indian Assemblies' and the British parliamentary papers, reports and debates, newspapers, and other source materials, a variety of selections of documentary materials, including speeches and reports, have been published.[4] Of these the following are most useful, representative, and readily available: Cyril H. Philips, ed., *The Evolution of India and Pakistan, 1858 to 1947: Select Documents* (London, 1962). Compiled in co-operation with two other Indian historians, it draws its extracts from a vast body of both published and unpublished materials, including state and private papers, deposited in British archives. Any selection of documents, however skilfully done, must be somewhat arbitrary, especially when the available materials are enormous and rich as in this case, but this volume has endeavored to cover the various aspects, including social and economic, of the Indo-Pakistani problem with an awareness of the shifting emphasis in the analysis of Indian history from state to society. Another important publication is *Speeches and Documents on the Indian Constitution, 1921-47* (2 vols.; Bombay, 1957), edited by Sir Maurice L. Gwyer and Angadi-

4. A discussion of the sources of Pakistani history is excluded by the nature of this essay, but once the documents are edited and published they are "contaminated" by historical judgment and as such are nearer historical writing than sources.

puram Appadorai. Sir Maurice, the first Chief Justice of the Federal
Court of India, was closely connected with the constitutional discussions
and drafting which culminated in the Government of India Act, 1935.
Those who wish to explore constitutional documents before 1921 will
find rewarding the well-known work of Sir Arthur Berriedale Keith,
*Speeches and Documents on Indian Policy, 1750-1921* (2 vols.; London, 1922).[5] Exclusively devoted to covering Indo-Pakistani documents is *Sources of Indian Tradition* (New York, 1958), compiled by
William Theodore De Bary, *et al.* Arranged by experts in their respective fields, the selection of extracts in this work is sympathetic, wide,
and representative of the local traditions.

Collections of speeches, biographies, autobiographies, and memoirs
of prominent personalities must be considered important reading for a
more realistic appreciation of the wide variety and conflicting attitudes
prevalent in this period. As compared to the enormous quantity of
published material dealing with the Indian nationalist side, publications
focusing on the Pakistani stream of development are very few. A main
reason for this dearth may be that while innumerable leaders of Indian
nationalism emerged in a continuous succession, the Pakistani movement was led almost single-handedly by Mohammad Ali Jinnah, who,
in marked contrast to his Congress adversaries, had himself written
and published practically nothing that could bring us closer to his
thought processes.[6] However, several selections from his speeches have
been published. Of these the best known is *Some Recent Speeches and
Writings of Mr. Jinnah* (2 vols.; 5th ed., Lahore, 1952), edited by
Jamil-Ud-Din. Henry Hector Bolitho's biography, *Jinnah: Creator of
Pakistan* (London, 1954) based on some unpublished material and on
personal interviews with friends and associates of Jinnah, is a standard

5. He also wrote the substantial *A Constitutional History of India 1600-1925* (London, 1936).

6. Some of Jinnah's letters to Jawaharlal Nehru are found in the latter's *A Bunch
of Old Letters* . . . (London, 1960). A few others to Gandhi are in *Jinnah-Gandhi
Talks* (Delhi, 1944). For the nationalist phase of Jinnah, when he was a prominent
leader of the Congress, see Sarojini C. Naidu, *Introduction of Mohamed Ali Jinnah, An
Ambassador of Unity, His Speeches and Writings, 1912-1917* (Madras, 1918). A few
interesting articles on Jinnah are Woodrow Wyatt, "Jinnah," *New Statesman and Nation* (London) XXXVI (Sept. 18, 1948); "In Memory of Jinnah," *The Economist*
(London) CXXXVII, (Sept. 17, 1949), a brief but penetrating analysis of Jinnah's
career; George E. Jones, "Nehru and Jinnah—a Study in Contrasts," *New York
Times Magazine* (Dec. 8, 1946); and Ziauddin A. Suleri, "Mr. Jinnah," *Contemporary
Review* (London), CLXX (July, 1946), an appreciative review of Jinnah's political
career.

work on the subject written with sympathy. It contains an account of the origins of Pakistan. Appreciative biographies of Jinnah written by Muslim writers are Abdur Rauf's *Meet Mr. Jinnah* (Lahore, 1947); Matlubul Hasan's *Saiyid Mohammad Ali Jinnah: A Political Study* (Lahore, 1953); and Anwar Khurshid Ahmad's *Life Story of Quaid-i-Azam* (Lahore, 1955). A. H. Albiruni's *Makers of Pakistan and Modern Muslim India* (Lahore [1950]) is a collection of biographical sketches of Muslim leaders from Sir Syed Ahmad Khan to Laiquat Ali Khan, the first Prime Minister of Pakistan.[7]

The relevance of the memoirs and biographies of the British statesmen concerned with India is as close to Pakistani as to Indian history. It is somewhat of a surprise that often these works are not fully considered by Indo-Pakistani historians. For instance Viscount Templewood's *Nine Troubled Years* (London, 1954), which is profitable reading because of the interesting light it throws on behind-the-scenes activities in the 1930's, has found little reflection in any recent writing on Indo-Pakistani history, although the work was published ten years ago and is well known to British historians. Templewood, as Sir Samuel J. G. Hoare, was the Conservative Secretary of State for India from 1931 to 1935, the period of the famous Round Table Conferences and the making of the vital Government of India Act 1935. His opinions, based on information not readily available to historians (that the Conservative Baldwin was more liberal, in relation to India, than the Liberal Lloyd George, for example, and that but for Winston Churchill's strong and determined opposition, the Act of 1935 would have been adopted two years sooner, influencing thereby the course of Indo-Pakistani history in a most beneficial way) may alter some shades of historical interpretations. Recently published is Vera M. Brittain's biography of *Pethick-Lawrence* (London, 1963), who led the Cabinet Mission to India which made it possible for Mountbatten to work out an acceptable plan for Indian independence. The autobiography of Clement R. Attlee, *As It Happened* (London, 1954) and his conversations with Francis Williams, *A Prime Minister Remembers: The*

7. Albiruni is a pseudonym of a Pakistani I.C.S. (C.S.P.) officer who has mostly written in Urdu. For a biographical account of Liaquat Ali Khan, who was Jinnah's principal coadjutor, consult the following articles: V. S. Swaminathan, "Premier of Pakistan," *Contemporary Review*, CLXXIX (Feb., 1951); Frank Guy Wint, "Liaquat Ali Khan," *Twentieth Century* (London), CL (Nov., 1951), a thoughtful evaluation; and Patrick Lace, "Liaquat Ali Khan," *Commonwealth and Empire Review* (London), LXXXIV (Oct., 1950).

*War and Post-war Memoirs of Earl Attlee* (London, 1961), are an essential part of the reading material on Pakistan. Attlee was not only the Prime Minister of Britain when the transfer of power took place in India, but he also was a member of the important and controversial Simon Commission. John Connell [John Henry Robertson], *Auchinleck* . . . (London, 1959), can also be read with profit. Field Marshal Sir Claude Auchinleck was the commander-in-chief of India on the eve of Partition and after.

For a fuller appreciation of the origins of Pakistan, consideration should be given to the views and attitudes of the principal parties involved.[8] Jawaharlal Nehru's *The Discovery of India* (New York, 1946) is an excellent one-volume introduction to the issues. For an imperialist advocacy of British policy, *Report on the Constitutional Problem in India*, by Sir Reginald Coupland, published in three parts under different titles, *The Indian Problem, . . . 1833-1935* (London, 1942), *Indian Politics, . . . 1936-1942*, and *The Future of India . . .* (both 1943), is outstanding. Extremely well-written, the work has influenced later British nationalist historical writing on India and Pakistan. Coupland's *India—A Restatement* (London, 1945) reproduced the Report in summary form and added the historical background of British rule in India.

The Muslim League, demanding Pakistan, represented the overwhelming majority of the Muslim community. But there were other Muslim organizations and non-Muslim League Muslims whose ideas and activities are particularly significant for the study of the Muslim separatist movement. They expressed themselves in a number of minor and some major publications. Well known of these are *Muslim Politics 1905-42* (Calcutta, 1943), by Humayun Kabir; *Hindu Muslim Cultural Accord* (Bombay, 1949), by Syed Mahmud; and *India Wins Freedom: An Autobiographical Narrative* (Bombay, 1959), by Abul Kalam Azad.[9] An outstanding leader of the Indian National Congress

8. Edward John Thompson and Geoffrey Theodore Garratt's *Rise and Fulfilment of British Rule in India* (London, 1934), and Garratt, ed., *The Legacy of India* (Oxford, 1937) are excellent survey-studies of Indian history and culture respectively. Rajani Palme Dutt's *India Today* (London, 1940), subsequently republished in various editions, is a Marxist interpretation of modern Indian history.

9. Of the biographical accounts of the non-Muslim League Muslim leaders the following are useful: Afzal Iqbal, ed., *My Life: A Fragment—An Autobiographical Sketch of Maulana Mohamed Ali* (Lahore, 1942); Sir Mirza Ismail, *My Public Life* (London, 1954); and Pran Nath Chopra, *Rafi Ahmad Kidwai: His Life and Work* (Agra, 1960). For a Communist interpretation of the proposals for Pakistan, see Gangadhar M. Adhikari, *Pakistan and Indian National Unity* (London [1943]); and

and a renowned scholar of Islamic thought, Azad has made revealing comments on the tactical errors of his intimate friends. A part of his autobiographical narrative, dealing with reflections of a personal nature, has been deposited in the National Library, Calcutta, for publication at a later date.

From the viewpoint of historical analysis and an over-all evaluation of Pakistan, the following works published before the actual Partition of India are of incalculable value. All are major contributions of solid scholarship, analytical and thorough, although not altogether dispassionate. They are *Pakistan or the Partition of India* (Bombay, 1940), by Bhimrao Ramji Ambedkar; *Modern Islam in India: A Social Analysis* (2nd ed., London, 1946), by Wilfred Cantwell Smith; and *India Divided* (Bombay, 1946), by Rajendra Prasad. A Doctor of Science in Economics of the University of London, Ambedkar, in addition to his literary pursuits, worked for the betterment of the depressed classes of the Hindu community, independent of and often in conflict with Gandhi. He was a severe critic of the Indian National Congress. In his work, which was published within a few months of the adoption by the Muslim League of the Pakistan Resolution, Ambedkar made a thorough survey of Indian politics in its communal aspects. To him must go the credit of producing the first authoritative exposition of Pakistan which makes the proposition of a separate Muslim homeland appear plausible at a time when, at best, only vague and varied schemes were being put forward. Such a work was inevitably to invite criticism as well as adulation. Its impact was clear and deep, as is indicated by the fact that before the birth of Pakistan the book had gone into three editions. Rajendra Prasad, a prominent leader of the Congress and a Doctor of Laws, took advantage of his prison sentence from 1942 to 1945 to write his scholarly work from an Indian nationalist viewpoint. While Ambedkar had emphasized the dissimilarities between Hindus and Muslims and the practicability of Pakistan, Rajendra Prasad brought out the unity between the historical traditions and political ideals of the two communities. Analyzing the various schemes, he argued against Partition as politically unnecessary and economically impractical. Based on solid historical research and containing valuable data, *India Divided* also made a great impact on both Indian historical

for a socialist interpretation, Asoka Mehta and Achyat Pata-Vardhana, *The Communal Triangle in India* (Allahabad, 1942).

writing and political thinking. It had gone into three editions before India was partitioned a year after publication. A comparative study of these two works, classics of Pakistani historiography, may be both fruitful and engaging.

While Rajendra Prasad was writing his book, a Canadian lecturer in Islamic history at the Forman Christian College in Lahore, Wilfred Cantwell Smith, now a renowned Harvard scholar of Islamic thought and history, first published (Lahore, 1943) his famous and remarkable study, *Modern Islam in India: A Social Analysis*. In a masterly way Smith described the transformation of the traditional Muslim community into a modern society during the preceding seventy-five years and gave a rich account of its intellectual and political movements. (Three years later the book was revised and published in London, incorporating a pamphlet, *The Muslim League—1942-45*, by the same author.) Smith showed that economic disparity between the Hindus and Muslims, rigidity in Hindu social behavior, and British colonial policy were as important contributing factors to Muslim separatism as was its Islamic cultural content.[10] British authorities did not permit the importation of his book into India. In 1954 a pirated edition was published in Lahore as *Modern Islam in India and Pakistan* without the author's consent or knowledge, with interpolations, and an additional chapter written by someone else.

Much as the movement for Pakistan had gathered momentum by 1946, its attainment was far from certain. The emergence of the Labour government in Britain, with its promise to relinquish power in India by a definite date, followed by brisk Indo-British political negotiations, and increasing unrest in India, including unprecedentedly large-scale communal riots, led finally to the transfer of power to two independent nations, India and Pakistan, in August of 1947. A full understanding of the events of this period is indispensable, since they put the seal on Partition.

Pakistan is as much an accident of history as of persistent political agitation. A host of books and publications deal with this phase of Paki-

10. A few years later Smith called this book, modestly, a youthful work (*Islam in Modern History* [Princeton, 1957]), but seldom can an author match Smith's combination of imaginative understanding, mastery of details, and dispassionate exposition. For a general criticism of British policy, consult Reginald Reynolds' *The White Sahibs in India* (London, 1937), and for a penetrating survey of the Indian scene by an eminent British Labour leader, writer, and thinker, Henry Noel Brailsford, see *Subject India* (London, 1943).

stani history as a part of major studies both on India and Pakistan, many of them quite valuable. Of the few which concern themselves mainly with the vital scene of diplomatic and political activity, *Mission with Mountbatten* (London, 1951), by Alan Campbell-Johnson, and *The Transfer of Power in India* (London, 1957), by Vapal Pangunri Menon, are extremely important studies. Both the authors were employees of the British government who were intimately connected with the political negotiations and decision-making processes. Campbell-Johnson was the Press Attaché of Viceroy Mountbatten and Menon the Constitutional Adviser to the Governor-General from 1942 to 1947. Campbell-Johnson's book mainly records the story from daily notes, letters, and memoranda and provides a graphic description of the eminent political personalities of the period and of delicate diplomatic bargaining. Menon, on the other hand, has woven his personal knowledge of the scene and leaders into a historical narrative, but has refrained from advancing personal opinions.

In contrast to these two books E. W. R. Lumby's *The Transfer of Power in India, 1945-7* (London, 1954) is a library account, based purely on published material, such as White Papers, parliamentary debates, speeches, manifestos, and press comments. Lumby had no personal knowledge of the country and its peoples.[11] He treated the parties involved—the Congress, the League, and the British—as corporate personalities, without concerning himself with their internal conflicts and contradictions and limited himself to their official and publicized reactions. Such a study obviously has limitations of insight but has the advantage of detachment emanating from lack of involvement. Dangerous and difficult though Partition was, he concludes, it was nonetheless inevitable.

More recently a British journalist, Leonard Oswald Mosley, and a former British member of the Indian Civil Service, Edward Penderel Moon, have published a book each on this topic. Mosley's *The Last Days of the British Raj* (London, 1961), is a readable picture of the period containing too sweeping, untenable, and unsubstantiated political and moral judgments. Claiming to be a historical text, it appears to be addressed to a popular audience without due consideration for historical

11. Lumby is perhaps the only writer on this theme who was not personally concerned with the Indian scene and who has written an account purely from official sources. A recent publication dealing with this period is Michael Edwardes, *The Last Years of British India* (London, 1963).

standards of accuracy.[12] Moon's *Divide and Quit* (London, 1962) is somewhat autobiographical, giving us a graphic account of the savage violence prevailing in the state of Bahawalpur, where the author was a minister in 1947. He is frank in his judgments, which are inconsistent and superficial at times. He regards British policies as wholly good and finds the explanation of the chaotic situation in the character of the local peoples and their leaders.[13] But the force and feeling with which the book is written compel attention and heart-searching. It includes an analysis of the causes of Partition and of party-politics in the Punjab.

Looking at the scene from a purely subjective and Pakistani viewpoint is the recent autobiography of Choudhry Khaliquzzaman, *Pathway to Pakistan* (Lahore, 1961), about half of which is devoted to the events of the 1940's. An outstanding leader of the Muslim League and now a prominent leader of Pakistan, the author was closely associated with the political proposals, responses, and developments which he describes in considerable detail. Although published in 1961, the narrative stops in 1947.[14] A. B. Rajput's *Muslim League—Yesterday and Today* (Lahore, 1948) is a typical Pakistani nationalist account written with evident conviction. Concentrating on the modern political scene, Rajput has quoted extensively from political speeches, reports, and proceedings. Earlier Muhammad Numan, the Secretary of the All India Muslim Students Federation, under the inspiration and guidance of Jinnah himself, had published *Muslim India: Rise and Growth of the All India League* (Allahabad, 1942). Fazal Karim Khan Durrani's *The Making of Pakistan* (Lahore, 1944); el-Hamza, *Pakistan, a Nation* (Lahore, 1941); and Syed Hassan Mahmud's *A Nation Is Born* (Lahore, 1958) also deserve attention. K. Sarwar Hasan, a student of Pakistan's foreign relations, wrote *The Genesis of Pakistan* (Karachi, 1956), emphasizing the validity of the stand taken by the Muslim League.

Undoubtedly, with the passage of time, the story of Partition will

12. Reviewing this work, Michael Brecher wrote, "Leonard Mosley has written a nasty and intemperate book" (*Pacific Affairs* [Vancouver], XXXV [Fall, 1962], 295).

13. Another study of somewhat similar nature is Sir Francis Tuker's *While Memory Serves* (London [1950]).

14. Khaliquzzaman, a resident of Lucknow, migrated to Pakistan after Partition and took over the presidency of the Muslim League from Jinnah when the latter became Governor-General. At present (1963) he is again leading the revived Muslim League and (if they are published) his memoirs of the period after 1947 should be of great value.

be unfolded in a variety of ways and approached from various angles. One important method may well be to make a detailed study of the emergence and growth of the Muslim population in different parts of India and of the part they played in the life of Indian villages and cities. There is, however, not much material available on this subject in monograph form. Some of the relevant data is available in the form of documents such as census reports, revenue settlement records, partition plans, gazetteers, etc., but much of the necessary material may be extremely difficult to unearth and collect. A starting point may be O. H. K. Spate, *India and Pakistan* (London, 1954), and Vera Powell Anstey, *The Economic Development of India* (London, 1929).

It is remarkable that all these narratives analyze the Indian Partition in terms of historical inevitability, as the logical outcome of the follies of either one party or the other, or of political developments. The *Evolution of Pakistan* (Lahore, 1963) by Syed Sharifuddin Pirzada, in tracing the development of the movement of Pakistan, highlights the rôle British officials and politicians played from behind the scenes. In a recent study, based on considerable research, *Britain and Muslim India* (London, 1963), Khursheed K. Aziz has endeavored to show that the British influences are extremely important to the understanding of the Muslim demand for a separate state. In spite of the care and work which has gone into this study, it is not unlikely that many readers may find some of Aziz's assumptions unacceptable and conclusions untenable. For instance, his principal assertion that the Muslim case did not receive adequate attention in Britain may well appear unconvincing in view of the British policy of progressive concessions, commencing from the separate franchise in 1909 to a separate homeland in 1947 for Muslims.

The whole episode of Muslim nationalism, including the part played by the British in it, is a vital, though somewhat explosive, area of study for a student of Indo-Pakistani history. In course of time the subject, no doubt, will be tackled from a variety of angles and the results published in multiple monographs. The private papers of Morley and Minto, recently released for public inspection in Britain, made it possible for Syed Razi Wasti to publish *Lord Minto and the Indian Nationalist Movement, 1905-1910* (Oxford, 1964), throwing new light on some of the questions which touch the core of the problem, especially on the part played by Minto in working out the constitutional proposals of 1909.

Writing on the same theme and using the same set of private papers, an Indian scholar, M. N. Das, has recently published *India under Morley and Minto* (London, 1964). While Wasti exonerated Minto from any complicity in the politics of "divide and rule," Das sees in the policies of the ingenious Minto a firm determination and ingenuity to maintain Brtish hold over India indefinitely. No doubt a good deal more will be said and written on this subject, but, meanwhile, a study of these two works will constitute a rewarding pursuit.

Having made Pakistan a reality, its people were confronted with multiple tasks of nation-building. Prophecies of gloom were not uncommon, but the enthusiasm and pride of the Pakistanis were evident. It was therefore expected that scientific studies especially by Pakistani scholars, would appear in quick succession, not only by way of stock-taking of the ordeals, sacrifices, and errors of their people but also to focus world attention on Pakistan and to give her a new sense of purpose. A good many publications did come out, but only a few measure up to the required historical standards. Most of the better-known works have been produced by Western scholars, largely British, who (with notable exceptions) were inspired more by their previous association or nationalist sentiment rather than genuine interest in historical research. Soon after, as a result of the growing American interest in Asia, including Pakistan, American scholars also entered the field.

The first foreign scholar who published a work of pure historical interest bearing the title of Pakistan, *Five Thousand Years of Pakistan: An Archaeological Outline* (London, 1950), was Sir R. E. Mortimer Wheeler, a former archaeological adviser to the government of Pakistan. The book was an account of the Indus Valley civilization which in 3000 B.C. was located in the area in which West Pakistan stands today.[15] Wheeler has published other scholarly books and articles on the same theme under similar titles, for example his *Early India and Pakistan: To Ashoka* (London, 1959). The lead given by Sir Mortimer has not been followed with the persistence which could be expected once the national imagination was aroused, but attempts have been made to blend the ancient Hindu-Buddhist past with the Islamic

15. For the general background of the ancient Indian culture and civilization, see Arthur L. Basham, *The Wonder That Was India* ... (London, 1956), a work of remarkable scholarship.

cultural heritage of Pakistan. It is too early to foresee the eventual outcome of this tendency. Following Wheeler a few years later, *The Cultural Heritage of Pakistan* (London, 1955) was published under the joint editorship of Sheikh Mohammad Ikram, a member of the Pakistani Civil Service, and T. G. Percival Spear, the British nationalist historian of the Indian subcontinent. It is a collection of articles by Pakistani scholars, except one by Wheeler, on a variety of themes ranging from archaeology to modern intellectual movements. Many of the contributors are relatively unknown and the work is of mixed quality. It is useful, however, for so few publications are available on this very important subject. A two-volume work entitled *Pakistan Miscellany* is also a collection of articles on cultural topics by a number of scholars. Surprisingly the editorship is not indicated on either of these volumes—the first published in 1952 and the second in 1958 (Karachi). Another collection of somewhat overlapping material is *Crescent and Green: A Miscellany of Writings on Pakistan* (London [1955]).[16] These articles were selected and reproduced from the *Pakistan Quarterly* (Karachi). *Pakistan: Society and Culture* (New Haven, 1957), edited by Stanley Maron, carries articles by non-Pakistani scholars on some aspects of Pakistan's anthropology, including one by Zekiye Suleyman Eglar, a Turkish Muslim, who three years later published *A Punjabi Village in Pakistan* (New York, 1960), a case study of the traditional social customs, especially of women, in West Pakistan.

Realizing the value of history for the new nation, and, perhaps, the relative inadequacy of historical works, the government of Pakistan established the Pakistan History Board for "recasting the history syllabi and preparing standard books on history." Under the sponsorship of the board a number of publications have appeared including *A Short History of Hind-Pakistan* (Karachi, 1955). This is a corporate work of a number of Pakistani scholars setting out a standard version of their own past. Much as a discerning critic would disagree with certain interpretative narratives reflecting national pride, this work could, as is intended, set the pattern of the teaching of history and, no doubt, will affect the writing of history in Pakistan. The government

16. Also see Kenneth W. Morgan, ed., *Islam, The Straight Path: Islam Interpreted by Muslims* (New York, 1958); Harald Ingholt, *Gandharan Art in Pakistan* (New York, 1957); Sheikh Mohammad Ikram, *History of Muslim Civilization in India and Pakistan* (Lahore, 1961) and Mahomed A. Shushtery, *Outlines of Islamic Culture* (2nd ed.; Bangalore, 1954).

of Pakistan also appointed a board of editors in 1952 "to prepare an authentic History of the Freedom Movement of the Muslims in the Indo-Pakistani sub-continent covering the period from the death of Emperor Aurangzeb in 1707 to the establishment of Pakistan in 1947." To date four volumes have been published, bringing the narrative to 1928.[17] A work of collective scholarship of this nature, unless subjected to ruthless editing, must suffer from overlapping discussions, unevenness of quality, and gaps. The tone of this work is set by Ishtiaq Husain Qureshi, who in a lengthy introductory chapter provides a résumé of Indian history and interprets it in terms of Muslim superiority, both in arms and faith. Those who are tutored in conventional techniques of historical investigation and writing will find the narratives somewhat alien and the interpretations overstretched. For them, at least, much of its value as scholarship has been inhibited by its heavily nationalist slant.[18] These books have been published by the Pakistan Historical Society (Karachi), which also publishes the annual *Proceedings* of the Pakistan History Conference and the quarterly *Journal of the Pakistan Historical Society* (1953—).

Of the survey-studies by individual scholars, which are few, Khalid Bin Sayeed's *Pakistan: The Formative Phase* (Karachi, 1960) excels them all. A brilliant example of penetrating and mature scholarship by a Pakistani political scientist, the book covers both phases of Pakistani history, before and after 1947, in almost equal detail. Beginning by tracing the origins and growth of Pakistan from the middle of the nineteenth century, Sayeed has brought his story up to the 1958 military revolution. The book is based mainly on published material but also on the unpublished diary of Sir George Cunningham, his fortnightly reports to Jinnah, and on numerous personal interviews including talks with Mohammad Zafrulla Khan and Shaheed Suhrawardy. Although both parts of the book are equally valuable, it may well be remembered chiefly for its balanced survey of Pakistan's historical

17. There are three volumes but the second was published in two parts. Originally the series was projected in four volumes. The first volume was published in 1957 (Karachi) and Vol. III, pt. 1, the latest which I have seen, in 1961. The period covered by the last published volume as announced on the title page (1936) is incorrect and misleading.

18. The government of India has also commissioned *A History of the Freedom Movement in India*, a volume of which, dealing with eighteenth-century India, was published under the authorship of Tara Chand in 1961 (Delhi). It should be engaging to compare the two approaches and narratives and their historicity. Two more volumes are to be published.

background. Before Sayeed, Richard Symonds had brought out *The Making of Pakistan* (London, 1950), giving a brief account of the origins and development of Pakistan together with an appendix on "The Culture of Pakistan" by Ahmad Ali. Symonds had been engaged in relief work in the Punjab in 1947 and later with the United Nations Commission for India and Pakistan. To his view, the Partition of India took place because the Indian Muslims, dissatisfied with the inadequacy of the constitutional safeguards, felt that they were Muslims first and Indians afterwards. Pakistan was, therefore, inevitable and Jinnah merely provided timely and competent leadership to the movement. Symonds' historical analysis is sympathetic to Muslim aspirations but it is the British who come out best, for they are exonerated from complicity in any policy of "Divide et impera."[19]

Ishtiaq Husain Qureshi held high academic as well as public positions, including a cabinet ministership from 1949-1954. Before the Partition he was an ardent advocate of Muslim separatism. Until the formation of Pakistan his main historical work was *The Administration of the Sultanate of Delhi* (Lahore, 1942), which had grown from his Cambridge doctoral thesis. In this work Qureshi had taken a definite Muslim nationalist approach. In recent years he has contributed articles widely to a variety of publications on the development of Pakistan and two books: *The Pakistani Way of Life* (New York, 1957) and *The Muslim Community of the Indo-Pakistani Sub-continent (610-1947): A Brief Historical Analysis* (The Hague, 1962). The first of these is a small study of Pakistan for the general reader written for the Way of Life series sponsored by UNESCO. The second is a more solid piece of work dealing with the Muslim intellectual, social, and political movements in India. Qureshi has unfolded the story of the Indian Muslims in terms of religious conflict. His main thesis is that Islam spread into various parts of India through persuasion, not coercion, and influenced Indian society in a most beneficial way. The decline of the Muslim power, therefore, was injurious to Indian interests. This decline was brought about by the meek submission of the Hindus to the British, by the misguided deeds of the unorthodox Muslim sects, such as Shias and Ismailis, and by Akbar, who practiced

19. Herbert Feldman, who had written *A Constitution for Pakistan* (Karachi, 1955), dealing with the vagaries of constitutional politics until Choudhury Mohammad Ali became Prime Minister in 1955, published later *Pakistan: An Introduction* (London, 1960).

a policy of religious toleration. Once the Muslims were dislodged from their political supremacy, Hindu intolerance made it inevitable for the Muslims to seek and secure a separate homeland. Written in a fluent style and filled with laboriously compiled details of names and places, the historical value of this solid work is much marred by its obvious partisanship for Muslim orthodoxy, sweeping generalizations, and untenable assertions. Another study by a Pakistani scholar, Hafeez Malik, is *Moslem Nationalism in India and Pakistan* (Washington, 1963). In this study, Malik has traced the history of Indian Muslims with special reference to Hindu-Muslim differences, bringing out historical justification for the establishment of Pakistan.

It is useful to read Qureshi's and Malik's books along with some of the writings of the Indian Muslims who have written on the same theme, which after all is of their past too. For example, Humayun Kabir's *The Indian Heritage* (Bombay, 1955), Abid Husain's *National Culture of India* (Bombay, 1956) and *Indian Culture* (New York, 1963), Yusuf Husain's *Glimpses of Medieval Indian Culture* (Bombay, 1957), containing an account of social and economic conditions, and Muhammad Yasin's *A Social History of Islamic India, 1605-1748* (Lucknow, 1958), based mainly on Islamic sources and contemporary European accounts, are important in this light.

About thirty-four years ago Murry T. Titus published a religious history of Islam in India, which has been recently revised under a new title, *Islam in India and Pakistan* . . . (Calcutta, 1959). Titus, excluding his theological discussion, concentrated his attention on the advent and expansion of Islam and its various sects in the Indian subcontinent.[20] Muslims of the Shià sect, who had been very capable commanders and administrators at the successive courts of the Muslim kings in India, and who are commonly regarded as important nationalists in India, also have been discussed by John Norman Hollister in *The Shià of India* (London, 1953).

A somewhat neglected but important school of Islamic thought which deeply influenced Indian Muslims was the Deoband movement. Founded after the great revolt of 1857 by a group of *Alims* who had actively participated in the uprising, Deoband attracted renowned and

20. Also see *Indian Muslims: A Political History (1858-1947)* (Bombay [1959]), by Ram Gopal, an Indian journalist who, having re-examined recently the causes of Muslim alienation, restates that religion itself was not the dividing factor but its exploitation was.

able men, built a distinctive and dynamic tradition, and produced a succession of brilliant people who were devoted to Islam and Indian independence. Ziya-ul-Hasan Faruqi has published *Deoband and the Demand of Pakistan* (Bombay, 1962), examining Muslim intellectual response to the British conquest of India and to Muslim separatism. Originally written as a postgraduate thesis for McGill University, it is a competent work which will encourage further and more comprehensive studies.

The post-Partition history of Pakistan is a story of recurrent crises and of a search for stability. Unhappily, Pakistan's past is wrapped in prejudices and its present in predicaments. Both have a crippling effect on historiography. Before Khalid Bin Sayeed's book, Keith Callard, a Canadian scholar (whose promising career was cut short recently by his untimely death), had published a major study of contemporary Pakistan and its political background entitled *Pakistan: A Political Study* (London, 1957). Based on sound research and field work, this book was the first serious and systematic analysis of Pakistan's politics written with understanding of her aims and aspirations. The work is somewhat dated now since Pakistan has had a few more political convulsions since Callard wrote. Two years later, in a brief but sharp study, *Political Forces in Pakistan, 1947-1959* (New York, 1959), Callard analyzed the political scene in terms of "a continual struggle between the forces of authority and the pressures of political groups claiming to represent the will of the people."[21] At the same time, Golam Wahed Choudhury, a Pakistani scholar who has contributed numerous articles on Pakistan politics to various learned journals, published an extended version of his Ph.D. thesis for Columbia University, incorporating material from his earlier articles under the title *Constitutional Development in Pakistan* (Lahore, 1959). Somewhat narrower in scope than Callard's book, it is a useful survey of the constitutional processes and problems from 1947 to March, 1956. Following up this work, Choudhury has now published *Democracy in Pakistan* (Vancouver, 1963) in which he re-examines the working of parliamentary democracy in Pakistan and its transformation first to authoritarianism and, later, to constitutional government. He strikes a note of optimism about the re-emergence of fully liberal and free political institutions. A Pakistani journalist, Mushtaq Ahmad, also published *Government*

21. Callard also contributed chapters on Pakistan's history and politics to *Major Governments of Asia* (Ithaca, 1958), edited by George McT. Kahin.

*and Politics in Pakistan* (Karachi, 1959), covering the same ground. A painstaking, laborious, and mammoth work discussing the theory of constitutionalism and its application to the 1956 Pakistani constitution, *Fundamental Law of Pakistan* (Karachi, 1958), by Allahbukhsh K. Brohi, was almost stillborn because the constitution it had sought to analyze had been abrogated by the time it was published. Alan Gledhill's *Pakistan: The Development of Its Laws and Constitution* (London, 1957) is a major work on the 1956 Pakistani constitution and legal system. The 1956 constitution has long been dead but the legal system still survives. While several studies were published dealing with the constitution and its associated politics, no major work has yet come out on the 1962 constitution. The current constitution is too young and perhaps too unstable to invite the labors of a full-length study. The past experience of scholars does not inspire much confidence for such an undertaking. Politics in Pakistan change so rapidly, even periodical articles become out of date by the time they are published.[22]

Specialist studies, competent and full length, dealing with specified themes are too few. Sir William Ivor Jennings' *Constitutional Problems in Pakistan* (Cambridge, 1957) is perhaps the most notable. Jennings, a British authority on constitutional law and a former constitutional adviser to Pakistan, discusses decisions of the Pakistan Federal Court concerning four important constitutional cases. Khurshid Ahmed, ed., *An Analysis of the Munir Report* (Karachi, 1956), is very useful to the specialist interested in the communal rioting in West Pakistan in 1953. Various political administrations, political parties, and pressure groups, the October Revolution, martial law administration, regional politics, and the problem of minorities are some of the many themes awaiting exploration.[23] Even the working of basic democracy has not received the

22. Some recent articles of worth are: K. Sarwar Hasan, "The New Constitution of Pakistan," *Parliamentary Affairs* (London), XVI (Spring, 1963); Damodar P. Singhal, "The New Constitution of Pakistan," *Asian Survey* (Berkeley), III (Aug. 1962); Latif Ahmed Sherwani, "The Constitutional Experiment," *ibid.;* K. J. Newman, "The Constitutional Evolution of Pakistan: A Study in Analysis" *International Affairs* (London), XXXVIII (July, 1962); T. G. Percival Spear, "The Political Evolution of Pakistan," in Saul Rose, ed., *Politics in Southern Asia* (London, 1963); Khalid Bin Sayeed, "Pakistan's Constitutional Autocracy," *Pacific Affairs*, XXXVI (Winter, 1963-4); and Stephen P. Cohen, "Arms and Politics in Pakistan," *India Quarterly* (New Delhi), XX (Nov., 1964).

23. Some recent articles on these topics are Khalid Bin Sayeed, "Martial Law Administration in Pakistan," *Far Eastern Survey* (New York), XXVIII (May 28, 1959), an informative account of the composition and functioning of the new martial law regime in Pakistan; Charles B. Marshall, "Reflections on a Revolution in Pakistan," *Foreign Affairs* (New York), XXXVII (Jan., 1959), a critical and very able essay on

concerted treatment of a full-length study. Masud-ul-Hasan's *Law and Principles of Basic Democracies* (Lahore, 1960) is merely a theoretical enunciation containing unassimilated data.[24] Another Pakistani scholar, Mohamed Samin Khan, published *An Introduction to Basic Democracy* (Karachi, 1960), arguing strongly in favor of the system as being in accordance with the Pakistan ideology.

Religion has played a major rôle in both the origins and growth of Pakistan, and no doubt will continue to influence her future. Pakistan may be called the first modern nation which has seriously strived to become an Islamic state. It is therefore only natural that relatively greater attention should have been paid by scholars to the Islamic content of Pakistan's politics. Wilfred Cantwell Smith's *Modern Islam in India*, already mentioned, supplemented by his *Islam in Modern History*, provides a competent and comprehensive analysis of the problem. Smith's *Pakistan as an Islamic State* (Lahore, 1951) is superseded by his *Islam in Modern History*, which contains two excellent chapters on Islam in India and Pakistan. Leonard Binder's *Religion and Politics in Pakistan* (Berkeley, 1961) is a work of substantial research based on documentary material, field work, and personal interviews. Describing the various concepts of Islamic states in their historical setting and the processes which determined their practical application, Binder focuses his attention on the impact of politics on the Islamic ideology in Pakistan. He traces in considerable detail the interaction on the constitutional developments in Pakistan of the Ulama, the politicians, and the Jama-at-i-Islami. Although definitions of philosophical abstractions are seldom precise or unanimous, Binder's thesis on the development

the political process in Pakistan by a former adviser (1955-1957) to prime ministers of Pakistan; K. J. Newman, "Pakistan's Preventive Autocracy and Its Causes," *Pacific Affairs*, XXXII (March, 1959), an historical account of the breakdown of political democracy in Pakistan; Frank Guy Wint, "The 1958 Revolution in Pakistan," in Raghaven Iyer, ed., *St. Antony's Papers No. 8: South Asian Affairs*, No. 1 (London, 1960), and M. Mohammad Ayub Khan, "Pakistan Perspective," *Foreign Affairs*, XXXVIII (July, 1960), by Pakistan's President.

24. S.M.Z. Rizvi, ed., *A Reader in Basic Democracies* (Peshawar, 1961), is an official publication of an introductory nature. The following articles are, however, analytical and helpful: Stanley Maron, "Basic Democracies in Pakistan," *Foreign Policy Bulletin* (New York), XXXIX (Feb. 1, 1960); K. J. Newman, "Basic Democracy as an Experiment," *Political Studies* (Oxford), X (April, 1962); Harry J. Friedman, "Pakistan's Experiment in Basic Democracies," *Pacific Affairs*, XXXIII (June, 1960); R. L. Mellema, "The Basic Democracies System in Pakistan," *Asian Survey*, I (Aug., 1961); and for the part played by women in the political life of Pakistan, Begum Ikramullah, *From Purdah to Parliament* (London [1963]).

of Islamic political ideology is open to various objections. Even the accuracy of his historical analysis has been questioned. But on the whole the work compels attention and thought. Two shorter studies, Ervin Birnbaum's *Some Theoretical and Practical Aspects of the Islamic States of Pakistan* (Karachi, 1956) and Javid Iqbal's *The Ideology of Pakistan and Its Interpretation* (Lahore, 1959), are worth consulting.[25]

No outstanding and comprehensive study analyzing Pakistan's foreign policy, its principles, institutions, and instruments, has been published. Golam Wahed Choudhury and Parvez Hasan's forty-nine page exposition, *Pakistan's External Relations* (Karachi, 1958), could hardly be expected to attract attention outside Pakistan even if the bare outline laid out were neat and complete. Certain aspects of the theme, however, especially Kashmir, have been the subjects of a few widely known books. Jyoti Bhusan Das-Gupta's *Indo-Pakistan Relations, 1947-1955* (Amsterdam, 1950), Michael Brecher's *The Struggle for Kashmir* (New York, 1933), Mushtaq Ahmad's *The United Nations and Pakistan* (Karachi, 1955), Christopher Bromhead Birdwood's *Two Nations and Kashmir* (London, 1956), and Josef Korbel's *Danger in Kashmir* (Princeton, 1954) are useful for historians but they need to be reconsidered in the light of subsequent happenings. William Norman Brown's *The United States and India and Pakistan* (Cambridge, Mass., 1953), which includes a rather long historical background, has recently been revised. Pakistan's expert on foreign affairs, K. Sarwar Hasan, who has often represented his country at the United Nations, wrote a full-length study entitled *Pakistan and the United Nations* (New York, 1960), a substantial part of which is devoted to the discussion of the Kashmir dispute, which indeed has been Pakistan's chief occupation at the U.N. This work, prepared under the auspices of the Pakistan Institute of International Affairs, which publishes a quarterly journal, *Pakistan Horizon* (Karachi), is inadequate in some ways, but it is useful since there is so little literature available on this topic. On Kashmir there are a good many local

25. Some useful articles on this theme are Muhammad Zafrulla Khan, "Interrelation of Religion and Government in Pakistan," in Richard Nelson Frye, ed., *Islam and the West* (The Hague, 1957); A. A. A. Fyzee, "The Impact of Islam upon Political Conduct in Recent Times (A Brief Survey)," Harold Dwight Lasswell and Harlan Cleveland, eds., *The Ethic of Power: The Interplay of Religion, Philosophy and Politics* (New York, 1962); and Wilfred Cantwell Smith, "The 'Ulama' in Indian Politics," in Cyril H. Philips, ed., *Politics and Society in India* (London, 1963).

publications, but they hardly measure up to historical standards, although it is not always possible to demarcate between historical writing and political pamphleteering. Liaquat Ali Khan's *Pakistan, Heart of Asia* . . . (Cambridge, Mass., 1951) is a collection of speeches which the first Prime Minister of Pakistan delivered on his tour of America in 1950. Aslam Siddiqi's *Pakistan Seeks Security* (Lahore, 1960) is an attempt to vindicate Pakistan's foreign policies with reference to her membership in military pacts for mutual defense.[26]

One of the most dangerous problems of Pakistan, which constantly hangs over her politics, is her territorial division into two almost equal and dissimilar parts—West and East Pakistan. A serious investigation of this situation is yet to be undertaken, but *Pakistan One and Indivisible* (Karachi, 1960) by Fazlur Rahman, a prominent politician of Pakistan and her first education minister, is a plea for a united nationhood. In this small volume are collected some of Rahman's speeches, in which the ideals that inspired the movement for Pakistan are recalled and a unitary form of government for the two halves is suggested.[27]

Equally surprising is the problem of Pahktunistan—the movement disputing the continued validity of the Durand Line and demanding an independent state of the Pushtu-speaking people in the northwestern areas. This dispute has damaged Pak-Afghan relations for years, and yet it has escaped the attention of Pakistani historians.[28]

26. Some further material on external relations: Mohammed Ahsen Chaudri, *Pakistan and the Regional Pacts* (New York, 1959), a concise account of Pakistan's participation in SEATO and the Baghdad Pact with introductory chapters on "Pakistan in Perspective" and "Pakistan and the Great Powers"; K. Sarwar Hasan, *The Strategic Interest of Pakistan* (Karachi, 1954); Keith Callard, *Pakistan's Foreign Policy* (New York, 1959)—a brief interpretation of the main trends and motivating factors up to the beginning of the Ayub administration; B. C. Rastogi, "Alignment and Non-Alignment in Pakistan's Foreign Policy, 1947-60," *International Studies* (Bombay), II (Oct., 1961), 159-80; and Prem Nath Bazaz, *The History of Struggle for Freedom in Kashmir, Cultural and Political, from the Earliest Times to the Present Day* (New Delhi, 1954). Bazaz is the leader of the Kashmir Democratic Union and a prominent writer on Kashmiri politics. A recent publication on the subject is A. G. Noorami, *The Kashmir Question* (Bombay, 1964).

27. Some articles are Richard D. Lambert, "Factors in Bengali Regionalism in Pakistan," *Far Eastern Survey*, XXVIII (April, 1959), a sociological exploration of the nature of economic and social variables which underline Bengali regionalism in Pakistan; Stanley Maron, "The Problem of East Pakistan," *Pacific Affairs*, XXVIII (June, 1955); Nikhil Chakravarty, *Black-Out in East Pakistan* (Delhi, 1954), an Indian Communist's interpretation of economic and political changes, and Rehman Soghan "The Problem of Regional Imbalance in the Economic Development of Pakistan," *Asian Survey*, II (July, 1962).

28. For the Afghan viewpoint, see *Pahktunistan* (London, n.d.) : Dorothea S. Franck,

Although a few articles have appeared analyzing the problem, there is no major study. However, Sir Olaf K. Caroe, who was the last governor of the Northwest Frontier Province before Partition, has published a full-length account of the Pathans which is informative but subjective: *The Pathans, 550 B.C.-A.D. 1957* (London, 1958). For the historical background and the actual delimitation of the Durand Line one should see the well-known study of Cuthbert Collin Davies, *The Problem of the North-west Frontier, 1890-1908, with a Survey of Policy since 1849* (Cambridge, 1932), and a recent study by Damodar P. Singhal based on official documents and private papers, *India and Afghanistan—A Study in Diplomatic Relations, 1876-1907* (Brisbane, 1963).

Lately, three well-known British writers have published books on Pakistan. Hugh Tinker's *India and Pakistan—A Short Political Guide* (London, 1962) is a critical survey of the workings of political institutions, parties, and groups in these two countries. L. F. Rushbrook Williams' *The State of Pakistan* (London, 1962) is so sympathetic an account of contemporary Pakistan that the work may well be considered by critical historians as one of advocacy rather than of exposition. Williams, however, has been closely associated with the Pakistan government, has frequently visited the country, and has known her leaders intimately. Ian Melville Stephens' *Pakistan* (London, 1963), similarly sympathetic, is better written and covers a much wider period, from 1857 to November, 1962.[29] A former editor of the *Statesman* (Calcutta), Stephens earlier had published a travelogue on Pakistan entitled *Horned Moon* (London, 1955), describing in some detail the frontier areas. An American scholar, Wayne Ayres Wilcox, has also recently published a monograph entitled *Pakistan: The Consolidation of a Nation* (New York, 1963). This study, based on published materials, including Pakistani government publications and newspaper reports, and on field work, mainly strives to describe the difficult pro-

"Pahktunistan—Disputed Disposition of a Tribal Land," *Middle East Journal* (Washington) VI (Winter, 1952); "The Implication of 'Pahktunistan': Prospects for Pakistani-Afghan Relations," *World Today* (London), XI (Sept., 1955), provides much historical background necessary for an understanding of the present situation; and Peter Mayne, *Journey to the Pathans* (New York, 1955). The author was a former member of the Indian Civil Service who served in the Northwest Frontier Province.

29. Recently *The* (London) *Times* issued a supplement on Pakistan's Independence Day of articles from British and Pakistani writers on Pakistan's national life (Aug. 14, 1963).

cesses and efforts made in search of a democratic and stable government in Pakistan. This work approaches the subject from a somewhat unusual angle, looking at the political development in Pakistan as a struggle between the traditional systems, as embodied in the princely states, and the pressures of modernization, as represented by the central government. Donald N. Wilber's *Pakistan: Yesterday and Today* (New York, 1964) and Richard V. Weekes's *Pakistan: Birth and Growth of a Muslim Nation* (Princeton, 1964) are two recent American publications deserving attention.

The foregoing description, brief as it is, clearly reveals that there are few works of sound historical scholarship on Pakistan. Without the rich variety of interpretation to be found for many other Commonwealth nations, the historical literature may well appear uninspiring. Even if allowance is made for the fact that Pakistan is a developing country, and that more literature will flow in increasingly each year, the sum total of research and writing is not impressive. Almost the entire field with its distant horizons is open to be explored. Specialist studies are rare, and even general survey works are in many ways inadequate. The two views of history, the bird's eye view and the worm's eye view, must be properly synchronized for its rapid and smooth advancement. One cannot expect sound and well-considered over-all assessment of a period unless it is preceded by a multiplicity of monographs which have independently and thoroughly investigated its areas and layers. At best Pakistani historiography has explored some regions of political history; it has yet to expand into the fields of social, economic, and local histories, and to acquire familiarity with the newer tools of historical investigation, such as archaeology and anthropology. The history of art is at least known but that of science is completely neglected. These historical disciplines cannot be pursued in separate compartments; they require constant co-ordination.

Much of what has been written on Pakistan has come from non-Pakistani authors, many of whom are not trained historians. Not academic interest, but past political association or perhaps desire to capitalize on a virgin land, has been a principal urge behind some of these writings. The growing demands of power politics, too, are responsible for at least some analyses, emanating from well-defined aims and assumptions. Of Pakistani scholars, most have been concerned, quite understandably, with asserting the personality of their new nation and giving it a distinctive character.

The reasons for this state of affairs are varied. Once Pakistan has taken a definite political direction and acquired real stability, no doubt greater attention will be paid to matters of learning. As things are at present, however, one cannot see any real signs of a tradition of historical scholarship and research emerging. An authoritarian regime cannot be conducive to the free growth of learning and thought. But the malaise is deeper. Lack of academic effort must be held principally responsible for the tasks unaccomplished. Indo-Pakistani scholars tend to accept too uncritically historical judgment and evidence. They often collect valuable data most laboriously but neglect to evaluate their relative significance and thus fail to marshal their arguments effectively and sharply. Their studies consequently often are valuable but seldom definitive. Unless, therefore, the basic attitude toward history is altered and a faculty of criticism developed, the writing of history in Pakistan will remain, as in India, subservient to foreign scholarship. There are ten universities in Pakistan now, in addition to numerous colleges, yet there is hardly a well-developed school or institute for historical research in the country. Generally the better research done by Pakistani scholars such as Qureshi, Sayeed, and Choudhury was done outside Pakistan, because of lack of resources and proper academic organization within the country. The *Journal of the Pakistan Historical Society* periodically lists research being done in the universities, but one sees little of it come to print. Book manufacture in Pakistan, in any case, is of too poor a quality to inspire scholars to write; those who have worthwhile manuscripts attempt to find publishers abroad, who are more elusive than available.

Allowance, of course, must be made for the fact that developing countries, with their limited resources, initially must pay greater attention to technological advancement and technical studies. Yet no country can afford to neglect the study of history without undertaking the risk of losing its sense of balance and direction. An important task of the Pakistani historian may well be to make his own people history-minded.[30]

30. For additional titles which relate to Pakistan, see the essay on India, by Robert I. Crane, in this volume, pp. 357-395.

# CEYLON

## K. W. Goonewardena

"THERE IS NO ISLAND in the world, Great Britain itself not excepted, that has attracted the attention of authors in so many distant ages and so many different countries as Ceylon," said Sir James Emerson Tennent, the British administrator and historian in 1859.[1] It could also be mentioned that no other island in the world has such a long and continuous history. The recorded history of Ceylon goes back over two thousand years to about the time when the Buddhist missionary Mahinda—sent by the Emperor Asoka of India—arrived with several other *bhikkhus* or monks. The Pali canon (containing the teachings of the Buddha) which Mahinda brought with him came to include, before long, an introduction containing a history of Buddhist events up to the bringing of the doctrine to Ceylon. The historical tradition thus begun seems to have been continued in order to relate the progress of Buddhism in the island thereafter. To this tradition we owe the *Dipavamsa* (compiled in the fourth or fifth century A.D.) and the *Mahavamsa*[2] (compiled in the fifth or sixth century A.D.). Before taking up these histories or sources for further consideration, however, it is necessary to describe the various chronological divisions into which the island's history has been divided.

The period prior to the Aryan settlements of the fifth or sixth century B.C. falls into the category of prehistory. Even thereafter we are on a firm historical footing only from about the third century B.C. The history of the island from this time on has been subdivided into various periods. The first, extending to the eleventh century, is an era generally referred to as the Anuradhapura Period—named after the capital city of Anuradhapura. It is itself often further subdivided into the Early

1. *Ceylon: An Account of the Island, Physical, Historical and Topographical,* I (London), p. xxiii.
2. *Dipavamsa,* ed. and trans. into English by Hermann Oldenberg (London, 1879); *Mahavamsa,* ed. and trans. into English by Wilhelm Geiger (London, 1912); reprinted with addendum by Garrett C. Mendis (Colombo, 1950).

and Late Anuradhapura Periods. There is no important break in the economic, social, or religious spheres, or even in the political, to justify this subdivision. The fact that the *Mahavamsa* ended its story about A.D. 300 and a new chronicle, the *Culavamsa* (Part I),[3] continued the narrative from that point, seems to have been solely responsible for this subdivision. It has, however, been found convenient by historians faced with a millennium and a half of Anuradhapura history.

From about the eleventh century to the thirteenth, a much shorter time, is designated as the Polonnaruva Period, after the capital city for most of that era. This has more justification than the Early or Late Anuradhapura Periods. It was marked by an extraordinary degree of South Indian and, probably, Malaysian influence.

From the thirteenth century (*ca.* A.D. 1232) to the coming of the Europeans is a period which has been subdivided once again on the basis of capital cities. Up to about the end of the first quarter of the fourteenth century we speak of the so-called Dambadeniya Period. Thereafter, in a time of extreme political disunity, there were capitals at Yapahuva, Jaffna, Kurunegala, Rayigama, Gampola, and Kotte. Periods of history have been assigned to most of these capitals. But the spans concerned are far too brief, the hegemony exercised from these capitals far too limited, to deserve such periodization. A Kotte Period can, however, be spoken of with justification. Kotte was the most powerful political unit of the time and exercised at least nominal overlordship over the rest of the country from the early fifteenth to about the mid-sixteenth century. Moreover, the literary achievements of this period have carved out for Kotte a special niche in the country's cultural history.

There were thus the Anuradhapura, Polonnaruva, and Dambadeniya periods; a period of great political instability which might be called the Rayigama-Gampola Period, and, finally, the Kotte Period. With some justification many of these periods could be further subdivided into what could still be considered as broad chronological divisions. Nevertheless, with regard to the nature of the sources and the economic and cultural situation such demarcations—mainly derived from political history—are of little value. Therefore, for most purposes it is convenient to consider the pre-sixteenth-century period as a unit.

Of the sources for the period up to 1500 none are more important

3. *Culavamsa*, ed. and trans. into English by Wilhelm Geiger in 2 vols. (reprinted Colombo, 1953).

than the historical chronicles and other related literary works. As already noted, the earliest of the surviving historical chronicles of Ceylon is the *Dipavamsa*, compiled in Pali in the fourth or fifth century A.D. A fuller and far better account of the events covered by this work is given in the *Mahavamsa* (fifth or sixth century A.D.), which also was written in Pali, the language of the Buddhist scriptures. The *Mahavamsa* and its continuation, the *Culavamsa*,[4] came to be regarded as *the* chronicle of the history of the Sinhalese people. The historical tradition which had begun as a record of Buddhist events has developed in the *Mahavamsa* into a record of important secular events also. It contains an account of the kings of Ceylon from earliest times down to the early fourth century A.D., arranged chronologically. But the main interest of the chronicler is in the work done for Buddhism and, in particular, for the welfare of the Buddhist sect to which he belonged. Thus he minimizes the importance of certain new sects and schools of thought which had won much support in the country towards the close of the period. The inclusion of legendary, mythical, and miraculous elements detracts from the value of the work, but such elements are virtually confined to the history of the centuries before the Christian era. In most sections, however, the account is sober and factual, and inscriptional evidence has established this fact. As the great German scholar Wilhelm Geiger once remarked, "Not what is said but what is left unsaid is the besetting difficulty of Sinhalese history."[5] Information on economic and social history given in the *Mahavamsa* is far too meager for the purposes of the historian.

Two later authors continued the *Mahavamsa* down to their own times—the first, down to the last quarter of the twelfth century, and the second, down to the last quarter of the eighteenth. Though they also called their works the *Mahavamsa*, these books came to be popularly known as the *Culavamsa*, Part I and Part II respectively. The first part of the *Culavamsa*, composed in the thirteenth century, comes closest to modern ideas of writing history. There is much information

4. See notes 2 and 3 above. For a discussion of the historical value of these chronicles, see Geiger's introduction and comments in the *Mahavamsa* and *Culavamsa* editions. For sources in general, see also Hem C. Ray, ed., the University of Ceylon *History of Ceylon* (1 vol. in 2; Colombo, 1959-60), I, 46-73. The *Vamsatthappakasini*, ed. by George P. Malalasekera (2 vols., London, 1935-36), is a commentary (not later than the tenth century) on the *Mahavamsa* which, by mentioning some of the ancient sources of the *Mahavamsa*, has helped to enhance the value of that work.

5. *Culavamsa*, I, 5.

relating to economic and social history, and most of the reigns of kings are dealt with in a sober and impartial manner. But often where the occasion calls for it there are graphic descriptions such as will be suggested by the following sentence: "In their insatiability and money lust they squeezed out the whole people as sugar cane in a sugar mill, by levying excessive taxes."[6] The great degree of accuracy in these accounts (proved by confirmatory inscriptional evidence) can be ascribed to the fact that the author's sources were not merely monastic records but also court annals. Referring to the great Vijayabahu I (A.D. 1059-1114) the author says: "From the time that he was yuvaraja, the wise Prince, that best of men, had seventeen years chronicled in writing."[7] The second part of the *Culavamsa*, though not so valuable as the first, is nevertheless an important source of history. Together, the *Mahavamsa* series constitutes a unique, uninterrupted source for the history of the island down to the close of the period.

Many other literary sources in Pali and Sinhalese have survived the ravages of time. Some are histories of great religious monuments such as the *Thupavamsaya*, or of relics, such as the *Dathavamsa*. These accounts give an unexpected amount of incidental information valuable for history. The *Dambadeni-asna* deals with the reign of Parakramabahu II (1236-1271) and has references to arts and crafts which are of much historical interest. The *Rajavaliya*,[8] or "The Lineage of Kings," a chronicle with a strong secular tone, attempts to cover the history of the island from earliest times to the late seventeenth century. The accounts are usually more sketchy than those in the *Mahavamsa* series, though a good deal of the material is different from that found in the latter. The *Rajavaliya* still awaits a competent editor. There is also an important category of as yet unedited sources known as *Vittipot* and *Kadayimpot*, encyclopedic accounts of local or provincial history, containing information on boundaries, land-holdings, families, and important historical events within the respective territorial divisions. The *Sandesa* poems are another important historical source for the topography of the fourteenth and fifteenth centuries and for much incidental information on the life of the period. These poems are in the nature of instructions to a messenger—usually a bird—sent to some

6. *Culavamsa*, I, 229-30.
7. *Ibid.*, p. 209.
8. Trans. Ben Gunasekera (Colombo, 1900). Where no English translation of literary sources exists, no publication details will be given.

distant place. The route to be taken and the sights that the messenger is likely to see on his journey are described by the poet; hence the information on topography and on some aspects of the life of the period is valuable. Of Tamil literary sources only two or three of importance can be noted. The *Yalpanavaipava-malai* (trans. by C. Brito [Colombo, 1897]) was composed in the early eighteenth century. It seems to contain a few genuine historical traditions. The *Sekarāsasē-kara-malai* (trans. by V. Sabapati Aiyar [Jaffna, 1902]) is a fourteenth-century astrological work, containing some valuable historical information.

This great variety of literary sources is supplemented by archaeological research. The remains of religious and (the rarely met) secular buildings, of ancient irrigation works, sculptures, and the few specimens of painting that have survived, together with numismatic remains, often give substance and meaning to the written words of the chronicles and other literary sources. Above all, the epigraphic records covering the years from the third century b.c. to the end of this period provide invaluable evidence which has rarely contradicted the information given in the chronicles. Except for the sixth, seventh, and eighth centuries, there is a plethora of inscriptions, varying in length and importance, and hundreds of them have yet to be edited. The epigraphic records[9] have been particularly valuable because some have yielded information on economic and social matters which the monkish chroniclers neglected.

A third body of sources is formed by foreign literary and epigraphical references to Ceylon. There are, for instance, the Indian literary sources such as the *Mahabharata*, and *Manimekalai*, which contain a few references to Ceylon. Chinese court annals and other historical records are also known to have important references to Ceylon, and much can be expected from a systematic examination of such records. The account of Cheng Ho's expedition of A.D. 1432 by his interpreter, Ma Huan, for example, gives much valuable information on events in Ceylon at this period.[10] Two great Chinese travelers, Fa Hsien (fifth

9. About 3,000 inscriptions have been found. Their value in sometimes helping to solve important problems in Indian history has recently been demonstrated by Professor Senarat Paranavitana in his "A Proposed Decipherment of the Indus Script" (a paper read at the Centenary Conference of the Archaeological Survey of India, Dec., 1961).

10. See University of Ceylon, *History of Ceylon* I, 64-68.

century) and Hsuan Tsang,[11] the first of whom spent two years in Ceylon, have left valuable accounts relating to the island. Several ancient Greek and Roman writers have references to Ceylon. Of these the *Periplus of the Erythrean Sea* and Ptolemy's *Geographia* and the *Christian Topography* of Cosmas Indicopleustes are the most important. The Venetian Marco Polo (ca. A.D. 1293), and still more, the great Muslim traveler from Tangiers, Ibn Batuta (A.D. 1344),[12] provide valuable information.

Foreign epigraphic records furnish another extremely important source. They have been useful for checking the accuracy of the Ceylonese sources and for supplementing the latter. The Allahabad Pillar Inscription of King Samudragupta (fourth century A.D.) and a considerable number of South Indian inscriptions of Rajaraja I (A.D. 985-1016), and Rajendra I (1014-1044), among others, may be mentioned.

As regards the publication of sources, the situation is not entirely satisfactory. Almost all the available Ceylonese literary sources have been edited and published in Pali, Sinhalese, or Tamil. But the editing has not been uniformly satisfactory. Many of the most important literary sources[13] have been edited and published in English translation, and these have almost all been competently done. Eduard Mueller's *Ancient Inscriptions in Ceylon* (2 vols.; London, 1883) contained the texts and translations of inscriptions discovered up to that time. A more scholarly type of inscriptional editing and translating began in 1904 with the *Epigraphia Zeylanica* (London, 1912), edited by D. Martino de Zilva Wickremasinghe. Part II of the fifth volume (the last so far published) in this series was published in 1963. But several hundreds of inscriptions still await editing and publishing, as can be inferred from a scrutiny of the *Annual Reports of the Archaeological Survey of Ceylon (Colombo)* for the years from 1890 to the present. Foreign sources that have a bearing on Ceylon history are all known because they have already been published. But it is very probable that among the mass of Chinese chronicles, there may yet be discovered works which will be valuable as sources for the island's history.

11. Samuel Beal, *Buddhist Records of the Western World* (London, 1884) for Fa Hsien; and James Legge, *A Record of Buddhistic Kingdoms* (Oxford, 1886) for Hsuan Tsang.

12. *The Rehla of Ibn Batuta*, trans. Mahdi Husain (Baroda, India, 1953).

13. See University of Ceylon *History of Ceylon* I, 795-97.

How have these sources been utilized? It is convenient to consider at the outset some of the general historical works on this period. The first valuable work of a general nature was Humphrey William Codrington's *A Short History of Ceylon,* published in London for the first time in 1926. It was, as the title suggests, only a sketch, two thousand years of history being encompassed within less than a hundred small pages. In addition to a terse and lucid style, its chief virtue lay in the fact that the author attempted to vouch for many of his statements by rather precise references to sources. A more detailed study was made by Garrett C. Mendis in 1932 in his *The Early History of Ceylon, and Its Relations with India and Other Foreign Countries* (Calcutta). With the publication by the University of Ceylon in 1959 and 1960 of the *History of Ceylon* (hereafter called *University History of Ceylon*) Volume I, Parts I and II, edited by Senarat Paranavitana, the history of this period received sufficient attention for the first time. It was the co-operative effort of about a dozen scholars, who together devoted about a thousand pages of text, maps, diagrams, and plates to set down these two thousand years of history. It has naturally become the standard work of reference for the specialist and other serious students of history. The late C. W. Nicholas and Senarat Paranavitana brought out *A Concise History of Ceylon* in 1961 (Colombo). The *Concise History* was mainly based on the *University History of Ceylon,* but a few important changes were made to take into account the recent research of Professor Paranavitana. This book satisfies the need of the general reader for a reliable and concise account of this period of history.

Evelyn F. C. Ludowyk's *The Story of Ceylon* (London, 1962), which purports to tell the story of Ceylon from the beginning to the present, is a work of quite a different nature and order from the two histories just mentioned, or from Sinnappah Arasaratnam's short, objective *Ceylon* (Englewood Cliffs, N. J., 1964). Ludowyk brings the accomplishments of a literary man to his work and what he says is usually lucidly and expressively—if not colorfully—put. He attempts to simplify and interpret the history of two millennia, and more, in about three hundred pages, and says much that is thought-provoking in the process. On the other hand, it is often not history, but a highly personal reaction to history, the trouble primarily arising out of an attempt to connect present problems to the distant past, and also out of unhistorical attempts "to pick out one clue which will explain them all" (p. 17). Thus *The Story of Ceylon* is a very interesting story, but not quite history.

The outlines of the political history of the period are also established on pretty firm foundations, as can be seen from a study of the *University History of Ceylon*. But certain very important problems still remain unsolved. The political institutions and thought of the period are yet only vaguely known. That there was a large bureaucracy attending to administrative duties even in outlying areas of the kingdom and that local administrative records were kept and that these were periodically checked by the central government are indicated by all-too-rare inscriptions of the type of the Badulla Pillar of *ca.* A.D. 942.[14] But when it comes to a question such as the powers and functions of the *Sabha*, nothing definite is known, although all the evidence suggests that it was a very important institution in the administration. Similarly with regard to political thought, we can conclude, for instance, that kingship was associated with divinity or certain divine attributes in the later centuries of the period; but as to precisely when kings began to claim divine attributes, what particular myths were made use of to foster this idea, why belief in the divinity attached to kingship was not strong enough to prevent frequent usurpations—such questions remain unanswered. Partial answers to some of these problems have been suggested by Senarat Paranavitana in his valuable articles, "Sigiri, The Abode of a God-King," *Journal of the Ceylon Branch of the Royal Asiatic Society* (Colombo) [hereafter *JCBRAS*], n.s. I (1905), 129-83, and in "The God of Adam's Peak," *Artibus Asiae*, Supplementum XVIII (Ascona, Switzerland, 1958).

As regards the religious and cultural history of the entire period, far more is known than regarding any other aspect. This is true because the main interest of the sources—both literary and epigraphical—is religious and cultural. Researchers too have paid more attention to these aspects on account of the wealth of data available. It has to be noted, however, that since the extant records are almost entirely the work of those supporting the orthodox Mahavihare school of Buddhism, little definite is known of the important Mahayanist schools and other dissident sects that sprang up and flourished from time to time. Of popular religious practice, too, research has yet yielded but scant information. Walpola Rahula's *History of Buddhism in Ceylon, The*

14. *Epigraphia Zeylanica*, III (London, 1933), 71-100.

*Anuradhapura Period, 3rd Century B.C.—10th Century A.D.* (Colombo, 1956) was based on a doctoral dissertation for the University of Ceylon. It is the most important general work for the period. Paranavitana has delved into difficult problems connected with popular Buddhism and Mahayanism in valuable contributions such as *The Shrine of Upulvan at Devundara* (*Memoirs of the Archaeological Survey of Ceylon* [Colombo], VI [1953]); "Buddhist Festivals in Ceylon," in Bimala Churn Law, ed., *Buddhistic Studies* (Calcutta, 1931), pp. 529-46; and "Mahayanism in Ceylon," *Ceylon Journal of Science, Section G* (Colombo), II, Pt. 1 (1928), 35-71.

Archaeological remains have been studied by a few enthusiastic scholars who have attempted to fix dates, assess the nature and extent of foreign influences (if any), and arrive at a connected history of art and architecture. Generally speaking, the dating of these remains has not yet reached a very high level of accuracy. To be constrained to allow a couple of centuries for the margin of error indicates this. But it must be admitted that the repair or rebuilding work on the same monuments carried out by successive rulers and their conflicting epigraphic claims have not made the task of the historian easier. Mauryan, Andhra, Gupta, Pallava, Chola, and Pandya influences have been discerned in art and architecture, the South Indian peoples generally influencing the latter part of the period and the North Indians the earlier. It could be said, however, that work of a definitive type on art and architecture has been achieved only in a few specialized monographs on particular aspects. Of the folk art of the time nothing has been written, probably because there are so few traces of it available. Senarat Paranavitana's *The Stupa in Ceylon* (*Memoirs of the Archaeological Survey of Ceylon*, V [1946]) is a study of the historical development of this shrine form. His *Art and Architecture of Ceylon: Polonnaruva Period* (Colombo, 1954), Nandadeva Wijesekera's *Early Sinhalese Painting* (Maharagama, Ceylon, 1959), and Paranavitana's "Sinhalese Arts and Culture," *Journal of the Royal Society of Arts* (London), XCVIII, No. 4822 (1950), may be mentioned among the published work on this subject.

The literary history of this vast period has been tackled by several scholars writing in Sinhalese. There are two competent accounts in English: George Peiris Malalasekera's *The Pali Literature of Ceylon* (London, 1928) and Charles E. Godakumbura's *Sinhalese Litera-*

*ture* (Colombo, 1955). But the history is often a disconnected one because the bulk of the literary works, not only in Sinhalese but also in Pali, Sanskrit, and Tamil, have been lost because of the ravages of time and man.[15]

The economic history of the period has received far less attention than its importance warrants. The first noteworthy work of a fairly general nature was Humphrey William Codrington's *Ancient Land Tenure and Revenue* (Colombo, 1938). Though Codrington gathered a mass of information from varied sources, the material is ill-digested, and uncertainty regarding economic institutions and practices is reflected on almost every page. The *University History of Ceylon* has a more detailed and critical examination of the subject. It has attempted to arrive at the economic institutions and the actual working of those institutions at different times in the period before A.D. 1500. But the position reached is still very unsatisfactory, as can be seen by a comparison of the account of the economic situation and the terminology used to describe economic institutions during the Later Anuradhapura Period (fourth to tenth century A.D.) with the corresponding account for the succeeding period—the Polonnaruwa (eleventh to thirteenth century A.D.)[16] One notices large differences in the economic set-up and terminology, but there are no explanations as to how or when these changes occurred and as to what precise relationship there is between the old institutions and terms and the new. On agriculture little is known beyond the types of crops grown and some idea of the agricultural taxes. The process of cultivating the land and the hard lot of the thirteenth-century farmer is described by Paranavitana (in *University History of Ceylon*, I, pt. 2, 721-22) on the basis of the graphic description in the *Pujavaliya* (*ca.* A.D. 1266). This, however, is information of an exceptional sort. On irrigation activities (which were so closely connected with agriculture) the standard work is Richard Leslie Brohier's *Ancient Irrigation in Ceylon* (3 parts; Colombo, 1934-35). There is no proper history of trade and commerce during this period. All that is known up to the present is set down in the *University History of Ceylon*. One painstaking and valuable piece of research supplies

15. The deliberate destruction of literary works—mainly religious—has been recorded with regard to the reign of Magha (early thirteenth century) and the rule of Rajasingha I and of the Portuguese (sixteenth century).

16. Compare I, i, 352-664 with I, ii, 547-58 and Paranavitana's *Concise History*, pp. 107 ff. with pp. 168 ff.

the essential background for any historical discussion on any aspect of history, including the economic. This is the late C. W. Nicholas' *Historical Topography of Ancient and Mediaeval Ceylon, JCBRAS,* n.s. VI (1959), special number.

The social history of the period is as little known as the economic— and for very much the same reasons: the scattered nature of the data, which are rather rich for some centuries, and very poor or absent in relation to certain others; and the inadequate research done by scholars, who have apparently been discouraged by the nature of the data available. Though the institution of caste, which played such an important part in society, is known, neither its origin nor its development has been traced. On other aspects too, such as slavery, manners and customs, dress and adornments, only bits and snatches of information have been set down by the historian. Wilhelm Geiger's *Culture of Ceylon in Mediaeval Times,* edited by Henry Bechert (Wiesbaden, 1960) though primarily based on the *Culavamsa,* contains the most comprehensive account of Sinhalese society and culture from the fourth to the sixteenth century.

Apart from what already has been mentioned, certain other problems, still unsolved, are of great importance and interest. Of these two may be suggested here. A question which has engaged the attention of a number of scholars has been the causes for the abandonment of the northern and southeastern plains in favor of the southwest of the island from about the thirteenth century. Climatic change, desiccation of the soil, destruction, especially of the great irrigation works, caused by a long period of ruthless warfare and the consequent economic dislocation, a series of natural disasters (floods, famine, drought, pestilence), malaria or some plague of unprecedented magnitude, and, finally, the breakdown of the administrative machinery—these have been from time to time advanced as causes for this shift to the southwest.[17] The breakdown of the administrative machinery necessary for the maintenance of the complicated irrigation system (on which the life-blood of the community depended) was first put forward as the principal cause by Rhoads Murphey in his essay "The Ruin of Ancient Ceylon," in the *Journal of Asian Studies* (Ann Arbor), XVI (February, 1957), 181-200. This view has been generally accepted. But Edmund R. Leach in "Hydraulic Society in Ceylon," *Past and Present* (London),

17. See *University History of Ceylon* I, ii, 712-19.

no. 15 (April, 1959), p. 8, has maintained that large-scale administrative action of the type envisaged by Murphey was not a *sine qua non* for the working of the ancient irrigation system. The abandonment of the two great plains seems to have been the result of a complex set of factors, including economic and political factors as well as natural calamities spread over a long period. With present knowledge, anything beyond such a general and vague conclusion appears unsafe.

Another important question neglected by the historians relates to race relations during the two millennia under review. The chronicles have naturally highlighted the wars and conflicts between the Sinhalese on the one hand and various South Indian peoples on the other. The more silent and positive influences of these peoples and cultures generally have escaped notice. The admixture of races (South Indian, and perhaps Malaysian, with Sinhalese) seems to have been very extensive towards the close of this period—judging by the family names of many members of royalty and the nobility as well as of the commonalty and by the underlying implications of statements in the chronicles. Also, in social and political institutions, arts and crafts, language and literature, as well as in religion, the positive impress of South India is obvious. The historian has yet to pay sufficient attention to this problem.

\* \* \*

The period after the arrival of the Europeans has generally been subdivided into three periods—the Portuguese (1505-1658), Dutch (1638-1796), and British (1796-1948)—on the basis of the European power controlling the island, or part of it. This division may be convenient for various reasons, but it can give a false idea of the shaping of history during these periods. For instance, though their connection with Ceylon began in 1505, the Portuguese did not exercise political authority until from about 1592. Even then the area they controlled was limited and their hold tenuous. In the day-to-day administration, in economic, social, cultural, and religious matters, what was indigenous was far more important than what was Portuguese during this period. The same could be said in relation to the nature and extent of Dutch influences in the subsequent period. The British, however, not only ruled the entire island from 1815 onwards but also brought about such fundamental changes in the economic and social system of the country that there is much justification for naming this period of rule the "British Period." For the purposes of this discussion, therefore, the so-called Portuguese and Dutch Periods could be taken together and the British Period separately.

For the period from about A.D. 1500 to about A.D. 1800, the relevant portions of the *Culavamsa* (Part II) are of little help. Only with respect to the religious and cultural activities of some of the kings do we get a tolerably satisfactory account. The *Rajavaliya* is a little more helpful. There are also a large number of *ola* (palm-leaf) documents recording royal grants, grants made by high officials, or judicial decisions. These can furnish extremely valuable information on administrative, economic, social, and religious matters. But they are dispersed in various collections (public and private) all over the island and few are catalogued or edited. The class of documents known as *Vittipot* and *Kadaimpot* are useful for this period too. Some state documents known as *Lekammiti*, containing registers pertaining to the households, landholdings, and castes of the respective inhabitants and their obligations to the state, are of the greatest importance, but they have hitherto remained virtually untouched by the historian. The Portuguese and the Dutch adopted this system of land and family registers and some of their compilations known as *tombos* have survived to this day. Except for the rather garbled and confused account in the Tamil chronicle, the *Yalpāna-vaipava-mālai*, there are hardly any documents from indigenous sources dealing with the history of the north of the island.

Portuguese and (still more) Dutch sources, on the other hand, contain a mass of invaluable data on many aspects of history. The Portuguese state papers in Lisbon and Goa[18] relating to Asia contain letters and instructions from those cities to Ceylon and replies and reports. Much more detailed, extensive, and reliable, are the papers of the V.O.C. found in the archives in Ceylon, Batavia, and the Hague.[19] The correspondence between the Ceylon government and its superiors at Batavia and in Holland, internal correspondence within the island,

18. On the Portuguese records in Goa see Charles R. Boxer, "A Glimpse of the Goa Archives," in *Bulletin of the School of Oriental and African Studies* (London), XIV, pt. 2 (1952), 299-324.

19. On the Dutch records in the Hague and in Ceylon see K. W. Goonewardena, *The Foundation of Dutch Power in Ceylon, 1638-1658* (Amsterdam, 1958), pp. ix-xi, and Maria W. Jurriaanse, *Catalogue of the Archives of the Dutch Central Government of Coastal Ceylon, 1640-1796* (Colombo, 1943).

and reports on the state of agriculture, on various state projects and reports of investigations into complaints made by the inhabitants or into the causes of rebellions—these and many other V.O.C. records provide a wealth of information on the policy and administration of the Dutch, the reactions of the inhabitants to that administration, and general conditions in Dutch territory. Far more than the Portuguese records, these provide us with information regarding the political, economic, social, and religious conditions in the areas outside European domination in Ceylon, the information being obtained mainly from the reports of spies and ambassadors and also the official correspondence with the Kandyan Kingdom.

Of the Portuguese state documents relating to Ceylon very few have been published or translated into English. Some documents relating to the period from 1539 to 1552 have been published in translation by Mathielde A. H. Fitzler and Paulus E. Pieris as *Ceylon and Portugal: Kings and Christians* (Leipzig, 1927). A few documents relating to the seige of Colombo have been published by Fitzler under the title *O Cerco de Columbo: Ultimos dias do Dominio Portugues em Ceilao* . . . (Coimbra, 1928). There are scattered references to Ceylon in several series of published documents such as *Documentos Remettidos da India* (4 vols.; Lisbon, 1880-93), edited by Raymundo Antoniode Bulhão Pato. Of the Dutch Company's records relating to Ceylon rather more have been published. All the treaties entered into between the Kings of Kandy and the Dutch have been published (*inter alia*) in the series entitled *Corpus Diplomaticum Neerlando-Indicum*, edited by Jan Ernst Heeres (2 vols.; The Hague, 1907-31); J. H. O. Paulusz's *Secret Minutes of the Dutch Political Council, 1762* (Colombo, 1954) contains text and translation of these minutes. Ten of the so-called "Memoirs" or reports handed down to their successors by various governors of Ceylon have been published in Colombo with text and translation, or translation only, between 1908 and 1946 by Sophia Pieters (later Anthonisz), Richard G. Anthonisz, and Edmund Reimers. These constitute a very valuable source of information but are heavily biased and meant to show the authors' actions in the best possible light.

Other European sources for this period are the contemporary or near-contemporary Portuguese and Dutch histories and travelers' accounts and Franciscan and Jesuit correspondence in Portuguese times.

The most useful published Portuguese chronicles are those of Diogo do Couto (edited and translated by Donald Ferguson in *JCBRAS*, XX [1908], 99-445); João Ribeiro (*The Historic Tragedy of the Island of Ceylon*, edited and translated by Paulus E. Pieris [Colombo, 1925]), and of the Jesuit Fernão de Queyroz (*The Temporal and Spiritual Conquest of Ceylon*, edited and translated by Father Simon G. Perera [3 vols.; Colombo, 1930]). Of these, Queyroz's account is the most valuable. The Dutch histories or chronicles are far closer to modern ideas of history, because of their elimination of myths and miracles, than the Portuguese. The *Beschryvinge van de Oostindische Compagnie* of Pieter van Dam (edited by Frederik W. Stapel [6 vols.; The Hague, 1927-39]) is an immense official record of the V.O.C. Though Van Dam was an important official of the Company and had access to all the relevant records, the sections on Ceylon are not satisfactory, as he has made a rather haphazard use of the documents. The Dutch clergyman, Philippus Baldaeus, in his *Naauwkeurige Beschryvinge van Malabar en Choromandel, der Zelver aangrenzende Ryken, en het Machtige Eyland Ceylon* (Amsterdam, 1672), not only gives us the history of the island during the first half of the seventeenth century, but also attempts to recount the ancient history on the basis of the old chronicles and traditions which were revealed to him during his pastoral work in Ceylon. For the later period he utilized his first-hand knowledge of some events, the information provided by contemporaries, and the Company's records, as well as unpublished Portuguese chronicles. Baldaeus' account is reliable on some matters but highly partisan. Besides, he incorporated wholesale other people's work without acknowledgment. François Valentyn, in his great compendium *Oud en Nieuw Oost-Indiën* ... (Dordrecht, 1724-26) wrote on Ceylon in the fifth volume.[20] Up to the mid-seventeenth century he leans heavily on Baldaeus, deliberately changing a turn of phrase or a word here and there to mask the original; for the rest of the century he relied on company records.

The accounts of mercenaries (almost all German) in the Dutch Company's service provide another important source of information. They also often furnish us with more impartial views of the V.O.C.'s

20. On these Dutch histories, see Goonewardena, pp. xiv-xv, and his "Dutch Historical Writing on South Asia" in *Historians of India, Pakistan and Ceylon*, Cyril H. Philips, ed. (London, 1961), pp. 170-82. Baldaeus has been translated by Pieter Brohier ([Dehiwala], 1960).

policies and actions than are found in Dutch writings. On the other hand, there are such astounding errors and misconceptions in some of these accounts that one hesitates to attach much value even to other statements which appear true. In recent years Major Roland Raven-Hart has translated and edited several of these records, from which *Heydt's Ceylon* (Colombo, 1952) may be singled out, if only because Heydt's sketches are unique.

On certain aspects of the economic and social position of the old Kingdom of Kandy, present knowledge is primarily based on Robert Knox's *An Historical Relation of the Island Ceylon* (London, 1681). Knox, who spent nineteen years as a captive in the kingdom in the interior, acquired a pronounced bias. Nevertheless, a critical study reveals that most of his data (though not his opinions) can be accepted.[21]

In spite of the relative abundance of source material for almost all aspects, historical writing on this period has been nearly as limited as for the earlier. The second volume of Sir James Emerson Tennent's *Ceylon: An Account of the Island, Physical, Historical and Topographical* (London, 1859) was the first of the latter-day histories dealing with this period. Till fairly recent times Tennent's work was considered the standard history of the island for the period up to the mid-nineteenth century. But Tennent furnishes only a bare outline, in some sixty pages, of the history of the period now under review. Today his account is of antiquarian interest only.

Of a different nature was William van Geer's *De Opkomst van het Nederlandsch Gezag over Ceilon* (Leiden, 1895), an academic dissertation based on the V.O.C. records at the Hague archives for the period 1638 to 1645. Considering the fact that Van Geer was a Dutchman writing at a time when the Imperial idea was at its height, and when even the existence of relevant Portuguese and Sinhalese sources was practically unknown in the Netherlands, the relatively impartial and scholarly nature of his work evokes admiration—all the more when we note that Ceylonese scholars who utilized his work, were more partial to the Dutch than Van Geer was.[22]

History as a modern discipline was introduced to the English-educated Ceylonese middle class in a British colonial setting in the nineteenth century. Generally speaking, the education which these

---

21. See Goonewardena, "Some Comments on Robert Knox and His Writings on Ceylon," *University of Ceylon Review* (Colombo), XVI (April, 1958), 39-52.
22. See Goonewardena, *The Foundation of Dutch Power*, p. xi.

Ceylonese imbibed and the environment in which they moved led them to look at the past history of the island from the longitude of Greenwich. In the early twentieth century, two Ceylonese scholars reacted against this attitude of denigration of the past. They were Ananda K. Coomaraswamy and Paulus E. Pieris. The former's *Mediaeval Sinhalese Art* (Gloucester, 1908)[23] was an historical and sociological study of the arts and crafts of Ceylon "mainly as surviving in the eighteenth century." It was his thesis that though the arts and crafts of this period were not equal to the ancient standards, they were still worthy of pride. Pieris brought a nationalist viewpoint to his exposition of the relations between the indigenous people and European conquerors. In his *Ceylon: The Portuguese Era, being a History of the Island for the Period 1505-1658* (2 vols.; Colombo, 1913-14) he was at pains to point out that the Ceylonese rulers and peoples were in most matters not more backward than the Portuguese and that in some respects they were indeed superior. The work was based to some extent on a few Portuguese and Sinhalese documents but primarily on Queyroz's *Temporal and Spiritual Conquest of Ceylon.* Pieris' work, therefore, does not stand on the best historical foundations. Moreover, his nationalist bias led him to distort facts at times. However, along with Coomaraswamy he is important in the historiography of modern Ceylon, as they for the first time tried to present the other side of the medal.

Pieris' *Ceylon and the Hollanders 1658-1796* (Tellippalai, Ceylon, 1918) was written in the same rich and forceful style as the previous work, but it was not of the same magnitude. Basing his work almost entirely on that of Van Geer, and covering the same period, Richard G. Anthonisz, a Ceylonese of Dutch descent, published in 1929 his *The Dutch in Ceylon: Early Visits and Settlements in the Island,* I (Colombo). This account is far more prejudiced and pro-Dutch than Van Geer's. The Reverend Robrecht Boudens wrote *The Catholic Church in Ceylon under Dutch Rule* (Rome, 1957) after consulting a large number of manuscripts in Europe and in Ceylon. However, the picture of Dutch persecution of Roman Catholics which he presents is far too exaggerated, because in practice Dutch religious policy was more tolerant than their proclamations and edicts would suggest.

Two London University doctoral dissertations by K. W. Goone-

---

23. The full title was *Mediaeval Sinhalese Art, being a Monograph on Mediaeval Sinhalese Arts and Crafts, Mainly as Surviving in the Eighteenth Century, with an Account of the Structure of Society and the Status of the Craftsman.*

wardena (1953) and Sinnappah Arasaratnam (1956) together covered the eventful period from 1638 to 1687. They were published at Amsterdam in 1958 as *The Foundation of Dutch Power in Ceylon, 1638-1658* and *Dutch Power in Ceylon, 1658-1687* respectively. Practically every relevant Dutch record in the Hague archives was consulted in the writing of these two monographs. They indicate the type of detailed and comprehensive study which can be made of the seventeenth and eighteenth centuries and the extent to which the "other side of the story" can be ferreted out from the Dutch records themselves.

Everything considered, the work done so far is far from satisfactory. Very little is known about the internal history of the Kandyan Kingdom even for the period 1638 to 1687, on which the most detailed work has been done in relation to the coastal territories. Only some vague generalizations and a few details relating to the economic history of the period have been made. Codrington's *Ancient Land Tenure and Revenue in Ceylon* is of some value in this connection. On social and cultural history little is known. But Coomaraswamy's *Mediaeval Sinhalese Art* is valuable not only for the history of arts and crafts but also for information on the social life of the artists and craftsmen. As for religion, hardly anything has been written on Hinduism and Buddhism—the major religions—though with regard to Christianity there is Boudens' work and James Emerson Tennent's *Christianity in Ceylon* (London, 1859).

\* \* \*

British rule over Ceylon prevailed from 1796 to 1947. Between 1796 and 1815, however, the Kandyan Kingdom continued to exist as an independent state in the interior of the island. The sources for a history of that kingdom during these two decades are of the same types as those mentioned in relation to its earlier history. The only difference is that British records, instead of Dutch or Portuguese, now supplement such Kandyan records as have survived.

The sources for the British period as a whole are far more detailed and extensive than for any other. More records have survived because since the nineteenth century ever-increasing attention has been paid to the maintenance and preservation of documents for administrative and historical purposes. Moreover, the processes and action of administration have increasingly developed in a formal and impersonal manner, necessitating more paper work than in previous centuries.

The major government records are to be found at the Public Record Office in London and the Government Archives and Public Record Office in Colombo. Of these records the most noteworthy are the letters and despatches which passed between the Ceylon administration and the Imperial government. The minutes of the Executive and Legislative Councils and the Sessional Papers, the correspondence of departments and their annual reports, the diaries and reports of Government Agents in charge of provinces—these constitute other important official documents.

Documents to be found in private collections, and in the archives of foreign Christian missionary societies which operated in Ceylon provide other valuable sources. English language newspapers, of which the *Observer* (Colombo, founded in 1834) and the *Times* (Colombo, founded in 1846) are the most important for they often reflect points of view different from those in the official records. Closer still to the opinions and interests of the mass of the people were the Sinhalese and Tamil newspapers which made their first appearance in 1862 with the Sinhalese *Lakminipahana* (Colombo). Unlike the English-language newspapers, which till recent times concentrated on economic and political questions, the Sinhalese and Tamil newspapers were preoccupied with religious, cultural, and social matters. As source material the indigenous language newspapers are thus particularly important because those were the matters which were least touched upon in the official records. The reactions of the people to British rule and to the many attendant changes that were brought about can also be noticed in these sources.

The British began writing on various aspects of the history of Ceylon quite soon after their occupation of the island. These writings can be considered as historical works as well as sources. Religious and political considerations made some writers utterly lack the sympathy necessary for an understanding of the subject peoples—let alone for an understanding of the administration and policies of the Kandyan rulers. These writers, following the example official propaganda, built a picture of an indigenous government and society which were rotten or barbarous in every way; the British conquest and administration were viewed as being, in almost every respect, a blessing for the people. The Reverend James Cordiner, the first Colonial Chaplain in Ceylon, in *A Description of Ceylon: Containing an Account of the Country, Inhabitants, and Natural Productions* (2 vols.; London, 1807), was one of the originators of this tradition. The tradition was continued by F. W. Bennett, *Ceylon and its Capabilities* (London, 1843); the Reverend James Selkirk, *Recollections of Ceylon* (London, 1844); Charles Pridham, *An Historical, Political and Statistical Account of Ceylon and its Dependencies* (2 vols.; London, 1849); and Sir George Barrow, *Ceylon Past and Present* (London, 1857). Sir James Emerson Tennent, in his *Ceylon*, was not quite so uncritical as the others, but he agreed with their attitude up to a point. And as his work came to be accepted as the standard authority on the history of Ceylon up to the mid-nineteenth century, he may be said to have given a stamp of authority to the tradition, which thus survived into the present century.

On the other hand, the nineteenth century also saw at least one British writer who succeeded in maintaining an impartial attitude to a surprising degree. This was Henry Marshall, whose *Ceylon: A General Description of the Island and its Inhabitants, with an Historical Sketch of the Conquest of the Colony by the English* (London, 1846), was full of apposite arguments to show that parallels could be found from European and British history, and sometimes from British conduct in Ceylon, for the actions and attitudes of the Kandyan ruler and his subjects. Reference should also be made to John Davy's *An Account of the Interior of Ceylon, and of Its Inhabitants* (London, 1821) and to the soldier-administrator Major Thomas Skinner's *Fifty Years in Ceylon: An Autobiography* (edited by Annie Skinner, London, 1891) as being works in which the aim is to understand rather than condemn the native people and their past.

Most of the nineteenth-century writers thought it necessary to give an account not merely of political history but also of economic, religious, and social history. Anthony Bertolacci's *View of the Agricultural, Commercial and Financial Interests of Ceylon* (London, 1817) is in a rather special category because of the great interest shown in the economic history of early British times and the scholarly nature of the work. Most of the writings of the time also reflect an interest in natural history. But one trouble with some writers, such as Pridham, was that they incorporated without acknowledgment information from previous accounts.

Documents published by historians for historical purposes are quite few and are usually confined to those published in the *Journal of the Ceylon Branch of the Royal Asiatic Society*, *The Ceylon Antiquary and Literary Register* (Colombo), and *The Ceylon Historical Journal* (Colombo). In 1923 Lewis J. B. Turner's *Collected Papers on the History of the Maritime Provinces of Ceylon, 1799-1805* was published in Colombo. *The Colebrooke-Cameron Papers: Documents on British Colonial Policy in Ceylon 1796-1833* (2 vols.; London, 1956), edited by Garrett C. Mendis, contains a valuable collection of official documents including the reports of W. M. G. Colebrooke and Charles Hay Cameron, whose recommendations brought about a radical change in the administration of the island. Most recently there appeared the valuable *Diaries in Ceylon, 1908-1911: Records of a Colonial Administrator, Being the Official Diaries Maintained by Leonard Woolf while Assistant Government Agent of the Hambantota District, Ceylon, during the Period August 1908 to May 1911*, edited by Leonard Woolf as a whole number of *The Ceylon Historical Journal* (IX [July, 1959 to April, 1960], [1962]).

A striking feature of the recent historiography is the overwhelming attention paid to political and constitutional matters. Till comparatively recent times, historians elsewhere in the world too often concentrated on political and constitutional history. These aspects of history appeared prominently before the eyes of people—historians included. Furthermore, the sources for a study of constitutional history were more readily available in print. Of the studies of note which deal with a considerable period, Lennox A. Mills's scholarly *Ceylon under British Rule, 1795-1932* (London, 1933) deserves special mention. Mills's claim that "the greater part of the book is almost entirely based upon my own investigations" was fully justified. The book is remarkable also for the degree of impartiality maintained throughout. Paulus E. Peiris, in his *Tri Simhale—The Last Phase 1796-1815* (Colombo, 1939), made a careful study of the British records and attempted to show that the last ruler of Kandy was not the monster of cruelty that he was depicted to be, and that British conduct in relation to this kingdom was not entirely creditable. His *Sinhale and the Patriots* (Colombo, 1950) was another attempt to present the other side of the picture—this time in relation to the great rebellion of 1817-18. In both these cases, however, Pieris veered toward an extreme. Colvin R. de Silva's *Ceylon under the British Occupation, 1795-1833* (2 vols.; Colombo, 1941-

42) was originally a thesis presented for the Ph.D. at London University. Its chief value lies in the sections on administrative and economic history. *The Dominion of Ceylon—The Development of Its Laws and Constitution* (London, 1952) compiled by Sir (William) Ivor Jennings and H. W. Tambiah, Sir Charles Collins's *Public Administration in Ceylon* (London, 1951), and the late I. de S. Weerawardena's *Government and Politics in Ceylon, 1931-1946* (Colombo, 1951) may be mentioned among the valuable contributions to political, constitutional, and administrative history.

The field of economic history has been rather neglected. Bertolacci made a laudable examination of the very early economic history of the period, and Mills provided a penetrating review of nineteenth-century economic developments. Colvin R. de Silva gave us a more detailed economic study than any of his predecessors, but the period he covered —1795 to 1833—was a rather short one. The history of the coffee industry—the main source of the island's revenue during most of the nineteenth century—has been studied in some detail by Ian H. Vanden Driesen in two articles in *The Ceylon Historical Journal*, III (July, October, 1953), 31-61, 156-72. Similar work in relation to the main plantation crops of the later nineteenth century and the twentieth has been done by S. Rajaratnam in articles in the *Ceylon Journal of Historical and Social Studies* ([Peradeniya], IV [June, December, 1961], 1-20, 169-202) and in the *University of Ceylon Review*, XX (April, 1962), 96-124. H. A. de S. Gunasekera's *From Dependent Currency to Central Banking in Ceylon: An Analysis of Monetary Experience 1825-1957* (London, 1962) is valuable because of its analysis of economic change during the period.

The attention paid by historians to the social and religious history of this period has been even less. Ralph Pieris' useful work, *Sinhalese Social Organization: The Kandyan Period* (Colombo, 1956), deals with the social system of the later Kandyan Kingdom on the basis, primarily, of data left by nineteenth-century British investigators. *Ceylon in Early British Times* (Colombo, *ca.* 1914), by John P. Lewis, is an interesting and unique work in which the writer attempted to give some idea of the social life of the British community in Ceylon during the early nineteenth century. On education Hugh A. Wyndham's *Native Education: Ceylon, Java, Formosa, the Philippines, French Indo-China, and British Malaya* (London, 1933), though rather sketchy, is of some value as a comparative study. Ranjit Ruberu's *Education in Colonial Ceylon for the Period 1796-1834* (Kandy, 1962) covers one of the few gaps that was left in the first four decades of British rule.

Of the aspects of economic and social history that have been ignored, one of the most important relates to the life of the peasantry, who constituted over three-fourths of the total population. The history of peasant farming and the impact of plantation agriculture and capitalist enterprise in general, and of new legal and administrative systems on the mass of the people—such subjects have been hardly touched upon.[24] There seem to be at least two main reasons for this situation. One is that the study of such aspects of history was considered relatively unimportant (not only in Ceylon) until quite recent times. The second is that their proper study required a knowledge of the indigenous languages, and historians, both European and Ceylonese, were usually ill-equipped in this respect. Of late, this situation has begun to change because the disdainful attitude of the English-educated Ceylonese towards indigenous languages is disappearing under the pressure of recent political, social, and cultural changes.

The postindependence era (1948 onwards) has received scant attention from scholars, though a fair amount of tendentious, propagandistic pieces of journalism have been published. William Howard Wriggins' *Ceylon: Dilemmas of a New Nation* (Princeton, 1960) can be considered the only scholarly history relating to this period. It is primarily concerned with the revolutionary change in the politics and general development of Ceylon after the General Elections of 1956. Particularly striking is the degree of impartiality, sympathy, and understanding which the author brings to bear on an era and on subjects which most foreigners and Ceylonese cannot yet discuss dispassionately.

\* \* \*

At this juncture it may be appropriate to make a few general remarks on the historiography of Ceylon in modern times. We have seen some ways in which the question of periodization has been approached, but there is yet another type of periodization which stems from the

24. Bertram Hughes Farmer's *Pioneer Peasant Colonization in Ceylon: A Study in Asian Agrarian Problems* (London, 1957), though the work of a geographer, contains a short history of colonization policy in Ceylon between 1815 and 1953. Farmer is the author of *Ceylon, a Divided Nation* (London, 1963).

experience of European history. This is the division into ancient, medieval, and modern. The Ancient Period is generally accepted as being the same as the Anuradhapura Period, although Geiger in his *Culture of Ceylon in Mediaeval Times* seems to have confined it to the Early Anuradhapura Period only. The Mediaeval Period is usually accepted as being from the eleventh century to A.D. 1505. But no fundamental features differentiate this period from the earlier period in the manner in which the Mediaeval Period in European history is differentiated from the Ancient. Furthermore, the coming of the Portuguese did not usher in the Modern Period of Ceylon's history, as is usually assumed. It was only in British times (in the 1830's) that modern administrative, economic, and social influences came to affect indigenous society in a radical manner.

Another introduction from the experience of European history is the use of the term "feudal" to describe the political, economic, and social systems of the country before the Modern Period. But when the chiefs were servants of the king who could be dismissed from their offices and deprived of lands and titles at will, and who often were transferred from one administrative region to another, and where the people held their land of the king and could render military service only to him or on his behalf, the use of the word "feudal" to describe political, economic, or social relationships is bound to prove misleading and unsatisfactory.

Another aspect of the historiography of Ceylon merits consideration. This relates to certain underlying attitudes common to the majority of historical works on the period after the coming of the Westerners. These attitudes can most conveniently be considered by reference to the texts most widely used till very recent times. Codrington's *A Short History of Ceylon*, first published in 1926, was perhaps not meant to be a secondary school textbook, but it was soon put to that use. It was followed by the Ceylonese Jesuit, Father Simon G. Perera's *History of Ceylon for Schools* (Colombo, 1932), which soon became the most generally used text. Another schoolbook series less widely used was entitled *Our Heritage*, written by Garrett C. Mendis and Sidney A. Pakeman (Colombo, 1937). For all practical purposes, no other textbooks were used up to the University Preliminary level. (Recently Pakeman has written a more advanced work, *Ceylon* [London, 1964]).

On analysis, a striking feature common to all these works is a significant bias in favor of the Portuguese, the Dutch, and the British. It is not present throughout these works, and later editions show it in reduced measure, but it exists in sufficient degree to attract notice. A few examples can be noted here. The killing of a large number of new Christians by Sankili, the Hindu ruler of Jaffna in the mid-sixteenth century, is rightly described as a "massacre" in all these books (Codrington, 1947 ed., p. 103; Perera, 1951 ed., p. 56; Pakeman and Mendis, 1942 ed., p. 131). But the slaughter by the Portuguese of large numbers of Buddhist monks and laymen, who in 1557 protested (some peacefully and some wielding sticks and stones) at the apostasy (under Portuguese influence and pressure) of the Kotte king, is either ignored (as by Codrington) or is made to look as innocuous as possible. Perera (p. 34) says, "But others were incensed and rose in mutiny which the Portuguese repressed so sternly that many went over to Mayadunne" (the opponent of the Portuguese). Pakeman and Mendis (p. 131) say: "The Portuguese further roused the hostility of the people by putting to death a number of members of religious sects on account of a tumult at Kotte directed against them." The murder of King Bhuvaneka Bahu by a Portuguese soldier in 1551, according to the evidence (particularly of the contemporary Portuguese records and of Queyroz), appears to have been a deliberate action planned by the Portuguese authorities themselves. But all these writers suggest that it was done on the instigation of Mayadunne, the Sinhalese hero of the time (Codrington, p. 98; Perera, p. 27; Pakeman and Mendis, p. 127). Then again, the use of passive constructions to admit the ruthless actions of a European power and the active voice to describe similar acts of the indigenous ruler provide interesting evidence on the tendentious use of language. Perera (p. 73 of pt. 2 of the 1951 ed.) rightly notes that the rebellion of 1817-18 was "suppressed so ruthlessly that English writers blush to relate it." Codrington (p. 177), however, uses the following phraseology to describe the same thing: "The suppression of the rebellion entailed great devastation, especially in Uva." Ten pages earlier he had used, quite correctly, the uninhibited words "massacre" and "butchered" to describe the fate of some British prisoners of war in 1803 at the hands of the Kandyan ruler. This tradition of British and Ceylonese writers setting down the actions of the colonial powers in a more favorable light than the facts warrant has survived to the present. A notable example is the introduction to *The Colebrooke-Cameron Papers* (1956) by Garrett C. Mendis (coauthor of the *Our Heritage* series).

It is pertinent at this point to consider why Ceylonese writers such as Mendis and Perera have adopted such a seemingly unnatural approach to colonial history. The bane of modern Indian historical writing was something quite different—a narrow, violent, nationalistic attitude. That was nevertheless more natural than the attitude often displayed by Ceylonese writers (which must not be confused with impartiality). When, however, it is noted that the religio-cultural impact of the West on Ceylon was far more extensive and intensive than on India, the attitude does not appear altogether strange. The fact is that since British times, if not earlier, a great religio-cultural debate has been going on in the island. Those who adopted Western dress, manners and customs, language, and often religion, felt constrained to defend and justify their actions before the eyes of the traditionalist majority. Such justifications, moreover, would naturally evoke the applause of the rulers, even if they did not bring more tangible rewards. On account of such considerations and the influence of the Anglicized and Christianized educational system, they began to assert the superiority of everything Western and the corresponding inferiority of what was traditional. Thus it was that even a man such as James de Alwis, who unlike other English-educated Ceylonese was a scholar of Sinhalese also, is found declaring in 1867 that "the British Government is the humble instrument which God has selected for the dissemination of his Gospel throughout the world" and refers to its "duty to help the benighted natives."[25]

The great scholar Ananda K. Coomaraswamy was revolted by this attitude and wrote in 1908 (*Mediaeval Sinhalese Art*, p. xxxxv): "The 'educated' Ceylonese of today, after on the one hand, a century of foreign government, and of education in which national culture has been completely ignored, and, on the other hand, an equal period of subservient and obsequious imitation of foreign manners, have little reason to be proud of their present achievement in the Art of Living. Evidence of shallow thought is everywhere to be seen in an exaltation of the present age at the expense of the past." This "educated" Cey-

---

25. *Papers Laid before the Legislative Council of Ceylon, 1867*, pt. 11 (Colombo, 1868), p. 168. For the expression of this attitude in the propaganda histories written in Sinhalese, see C. E. Godakumbura, "Historical Writing in Sinhalese," in *Historians of India, Pakistan and Ceylon*, Philips, ed., pp. 82-85.

lonese attitude was further stiffened because a counter-attack against it had made itself felt since the early twentieth century. The literati used the indigenous language press and pamphlets for an uncritical adulation of the ancient past. All the ills of the day were ascribed to the coming of the Europeans and attendant consequences.

Generally speaking, the sharpness of this debate has been modified in recent times. The nationalist movement and post-independence developments made the very Westernized group substantially modify their views. And the greater dissemination, and increasing acceptance, of ideas relating to the scientific study of history have made the traditionalist group tone down their attitude somewhat. But sniping and skirmishing on the religio-cultural historical front has not yet ceased.

Although an old conflict seems to be on the way toward a compromise solution, a new one on a communal basis shows signs of developing. There had always been a certain underlying tendency for the Sinhalese to assume that Dravidian influences on them, and on Ceylon in general, were of little account. On the other hand, the tendency amongst the Tamils had been to minimize Sinhalese influences in history, particularly in relation to the northern peninsula, where, at one time, they had an independent Tamil kingdom. These tendencies had seldom assumed significant proportions, and on such questions as the influence of the Tamil language on Sinhalese, or the later Tamilization of place names which were once Sinhalese, there had been much mutual give and take. But—doubtless reflecting current political attitudes—the dormant tendencies have recently been brought more to the surface, if one is to judge by some of the present controversies through journalistic channels. Fortunately, no historical works of note have yet reflected this type of bias in any marked way.

# BURMA

## *Hugh Tinker*

ALONG WITH South Africa and Eire, Burma must be accounted as a failure of the Commonwealth concept. Perhaps in all three cases, among the reasons for this failure we may detect a narrow, introspective nationalism which never looked beyond its own confines. A survey of historical writing and the historical tradition in Burma appears to lend support to this view. We may look in vain for that sense of wider horizons which can be found in Indian historical writing: whether in the imperialist vein of Lyall or Curzon, or among nationalist historians such as K. M. Panikkar or C. S. Venkatachar. The history of Burma has been set down by two groups of scholars: monks and officials. The monastic tradition of scholarship was, of course, indigenous: though one might argue that it has a Western counterpart in the school of Christian missionary writers (mainly American) who form an important source of knowledge on the changing mores of the peoples of Burma. The official tradition flourished under the Burmese kings and continued as the main seedbed of historical research during the British period.

However, the first important historical work with which we ought to be concerned belonged to neither the official nor the monastic group. U Kala, author of the *Maha Yazawin Gyi* ("Great Chronicle") was an independent writer who, coming from a wealthy family, compiled his study as an attempt at exact scholarship. He drew upon earlier chronicles for his source material, combining critical judgment with a fine prose style. He treated the history of Burma from its legendary origins down to the early eighteenth century.[1] U Kala provided the basis for the next major history, the *Hman Nan Yazawindaw Gyi* or "Great Royal Glass Palace Chronicle." This was the combined work of

1. U Kala produced three versions of his history: The Great Chronicle, *Maha Yazawin Gyi*, the Middle Chronicle, *Yazawin Lat*, and the Little Chronicle, or *Yazawin Gyok*. The Great Chronicle runs to twenty volumes, of which the second volume was published by the Burma Research Society (Rangoon) in 1932.

a group of scholars who prepared their history at the request of the reigning king, Bagyidaw. They conducted their labors in one of the halls of the king's palace: that is, in the Glass Palace. The main editor was a learned abbot, the Monywe Sayadaw. This chronicle continued U Kala's account down to 1821 to the eve of the first disastrous war with the British. The editors consulted temple inscriptions in order to validate certain dates and also made use of Pali sources. As a work of exact and detailed scholarship, the Glass Palace Chronicle stands out from the majority of Asian fable-chronicles. But its attention is focused almost exclusively upon the activities of the rulers, as forming the only significant theme in history: a view which was to be re-echoed in almost all subsequent writing.[2] The penultimate king of Burma, Mindon, ordered that the Glass Palace Chronicle be continued to include events after 1821. The *Dutiya Maha Yazawin*, or "Second Chronicle," was begun in 1867. The first seven volumes formed a detailed account down to 1854; the last three volumes carried through the narrative to 1869. Once again the editors were mainly monks, together with royal officials (including two Atwinwuns, officials of the privy council).

After the royal dynasty was overthrown, a former court official, U Tin of Mandalay, compiled a history of the rulers from the eighteenth-century conqueror, Alaungpaya, down to the last king of all, Thibaw. This became known as *Konbaung Set*, and was published at Mandalay in 1905.

As we shall discover, the Burmese chronicles served, to a large extent, as the source material of British historical writing on Burma. However, the first European accounts of Burma which deserve our attention came from the pens of Catholic missionaries, concerned mainly to render an account of their labors to their own church. Father Sebastien Manrique went to minister to the renegade Portuguese who exercised power in the then independent principality of Arakan. His *Itinerario de los missiones del India oriental* was published in Rome in 1694.[3] The light which is shed upon Arakan is incidental to Man-

2. The volumes of *Hman Nam Yazawindawgyi* were published at Mandalay in the following order: III, 1907, II, 1908, and I, 1921. An English version of a small portion of this history was translated by Gordon H. Luce and Pe Maung Tin: *The Glass Palace Chronicle of the Kings of Burma* (London, 1923).

3. In English: *Travels of Fray Sebastien Manrique, 1629-1643* (2 vols.; Hakluyt Society, London, 1927), trans. Charles Eckford Luard. Drawing upon this work, Maurice Collis wrote his delightful historical pastiche, *The Land of the Great Image* (London, 1943).

rique's missionary purpose; but the next great Catholic study of Burma was also the first European attempt at a comprehensive analysis of Burmese history, social custom, religion, and law. Father Vicentius Sangermano—like Manrique, an Italian—lived in Burma from 1783 to 1808, at the time when the Konbaung dynasty was at the height of its power and expansion. His work came to the attention of British Orientalists, was translated by William Tandy, and was published as *A Description of the Burmese Empire* in 1833.[4] It remains one of the primary works upon Burma for this period.

Toward the end of the eighteenth century, a succession of British envoys visited the Burmese court in the vain attempt to establish some form of mutual understanding. The first regular diplomatic mission was led by Captain Michael Symes; and his official report—later published—forms a historical study of a high order. Symes combined accurate observation with a sensitivity to the Burmese outlook. *An Account of an Embassy to the Kingdom of Ava Sent by the Governor-General of India in the Year 1795* was published in London in 1800.[5] After the first Anglo-Burmese war, diplomatic relations were opened up through a British Resident at the Burmese Court. The first Resident, Captain Henry Burney, was also a considerable scholar. His influence at court was exerted to save one of the princes from his royal brother's wrath; for this action, Burney secured a mention in the *Dutiya Maha Yazawin*, the only Englishman whose name is mentioned in the Chronicles. Burney drew the attention of Western scholars to the value of the Burmese histories. He contributed numerous papers to the newly founded *Journal of the Asiatic Society of Bengal* (Calcutta),[6] and he collected and preserved a number of historical manuscripts. He appears to have drafted studies for a major history, but he never carried this intention into effect. The task of negotiating a commercial treaty between Burma and Great Britain was given to John Crawfurd, a scholarly servant of the British East India Company: a by-product of his mission was another survey of society, government, economic life,

4. The work was printed in Rome, but published in London by John Murray. The edition is extremely rare, and Sangermano's work is known mainly through the reissues (edited by John Jardine) of Rangoon (1885) and London (1893).

5. Symes produced another valuable account of a second mission, which lay in the India Office Library until discovered by D. G. E. Hall. See Hall, *Michael Symes: Journal of His Second Embassy to the Court of Ava in 1802* (London, 1955).

6. For example, "Some Account of the Wars between Burmah and China...," VI (1837), 121-49, 409-51, 542-59.

and custom, which has become a basic document in the history of Burma.[7] The first half of the nineteenth century was a period when British officials in Asia, in the course of very active careers, produced scores of studies of high scholarly quality. In Burma, perhaps none is so valuable as Henry Yule's *A Narrative of the Mission Sent by the Governor-General of India to the Court of Ava in 1855* (London, 1858). The importance of the book may be summarized under three heads. First, it contains a complete, unexpurgated account of the conduct of negotiations. Second, it provides a wealth of background material (including statistical economic material). Third, it includes large numbers of finely drawn plates. Among these are pictures, plans, and elevations of the temple complex of Pagan; though more than a century has intervened, these have never been superseded.

Yule received invaluable assistance in preparing his book from the chief of his mission, Major (later Sir) Arthur Phayre, to whom must be ascribed the fashioning of Burmese history as we know it today. Phayre received his education at a leading British school, but he left for the East as a youth, and he returned to England only after a quarter of a century on the frontier of the Indian empire. His scholarship was his own. During his nearly forty years in Burma he wrote but little. Yet he was celebrated even among the Burmese for his knowledge of their country. King Mindon loved to engage him in scholarly argument, and the king presented Phayre with copies of the *Yazawin* compiled under his direction. In retirement, Phayre embarked on a systematic study of different aspects of Burmese history, his definitive *History of Burma; from the Earliest Times to the End of the First War with British India* was published (London) in 1883. Phayre set Burmese history in a mold in which it broadly remains at the present day. He drew up a king-list which has been accepted by all later scholars, apart from modifications recently proposed by Gordon H. Luce for rulers of Pagan, 1044-1287. He laid down the periodization ("Pagan Period," "Shan Period," etc.) which is still accepted. He gave us a scheme of nomenclature for the Konbaung dynasty. And in general he took over the Burmese tradition that the scope of history is related to the activities of the rulers to the virtual exclusion of any consideration of the activities of the ruled.

7. Crawfurd, *Journal of an Embassy from the Governor-General of India to the Court of Ava, in the Year 1827* (2 vols.; London). The present writer has seen only an edition dated 1834, but Yale University's Beinecke Library holds the edition of 1829.

With the extension of British rule in Burma, Christian missionary enterprise gained a wider field, and the missionary contribution to historical writing expanded. The wife of the pioneer American missionary, Ann Judson, produced a notable work: *An Account of the American Baptist Mission to the Burman Empire* (London, 1823). Among a succession of biographies of Judson, we need only mention the first: that of Wayland.[8] Bishop Bigandet maintained the Catholic historical tradition,[9] while a Protestant missionary trend that was to assume a major part in shaping history is indicated by the appearance of studies emphasizing the rôle of minority peoples—often of frontier tribes—of which *The Loyal Karens of Burma*, by Donald M. Smeaton (London, 1887), is a pioneer example.

The contribution of British officials to historical writing continued. Much of this was a by-product of administration and law. One of the most valuable sources to the historian—as to the anthropologist and archaeologist—is the *Gazetteer of Upper Burma and the Shan States* compiled by Sir James G. Scott and J. P. Hardiman, and issued in five volumes (Rangoon, 1900-1901).[10] Taw Sein Ko, a Sino-Burman, and the government archivist, produced *Selections from the Records of the Hlutdaw* [royal council] (Rangoon, 1889) and later *Burmese Sketches* (Rangoon, 1913). John Jardine, a learned judge, wrote his *Notes on Buddhist Law, with Translations* (Rangoon, 1882-83) and did much to promote studies of the Burmese legal system. A former minister of King Thibaw, Kinwun Mingyi, U Gaung, compiled *A Digest of the Burmese Buddhist Law Concerning Inheritance and Marriage* in two volumes (Rangoon, 1902-9). A member of the Chinese consular service, Edward H. Parker, deputed to assist in demarcating a frontier with China, produced a study of the historical background, *Burma, with Special Reference to Her Relations with China* (Rangoon, 1893). This rare work has long been unobtainable, and a reissue would be welcome. John Nisbet, a forest officer, in *Burma under British Rule—and Before* (2 vols.; London, 1901), gave an account of society, government, and

---

8. Francis A. Wayland, *A Memoir of the Life and Labors of the Rev. Adoniram Judson* (2 vols.; Boston, 1853).

9. For example, Rt. Rev. Paul A. Bigandet, *An Outline of the History of the Catholic Burmese Mission, from the Year 1720 to 1887* (Rangoon, 1887).

10. Scott, before he entered the administration, worked in Burma as a journalist and schoolmaster. Under the pseudonym "Shway Yoe" he wrote *The Burman, His Life and Notions* (London, 1882). This has been reissued, with an introduction by John K. Musgrave, Jr., in paper covers (New York, 1963).

economic life—particularly under the kings—which covers a wide field. The first years of British rule in Upper Burma were the subject of *The Pacification of Burma*, by Sir Charles Crosthwaite (London, 1912), who as Lieutenant-Governor had been largely responsible for instituting the new administrative pattern. Among other autobiographical accounts of this period of British rule, Sir H. Thirkell White's *A Civil Servant in Burma* (London, 1913) is useful in understanding administrative growth. *Yün-nan...*, by Henry Rudolph Davies (London, 1909), provides a wealth of information on Burma's borderland, arising out of a quasi-official survey expedition. The study of archaeology was also begun, under government auspices, by Emil Forchhammer and Charles Duroiselle.

If this review of historical writing and activity down to World War I appears haphazard and individualistic, the reason is that no systematic attempt to approach the subject was possible when there was no forum for discussion and no school of teaching or research. The foundation of the Burma Research Society in 1910 did bring together all those in Burma concerned to introduce more light into the study of the past, of language, and of aspects of sociology. The society built up a learned library and began to publish a journal. However, systematic historical research, and the creation of an academic standard, was due mainly to the foundation of the University of Rangoon in 1920. This institution comprised two colleges: University College, which attempted to reproduce the values of Oxford and Cambridge, and Judson College, which stood for the American missionary educational mode. Within the new department of history, D. G. E. Hall was the first professor. His earlier works were in the field of foreign relations: *Early English Intercourse with Burma, 1587-1743* (London, 1928) and *The Dalhousie-Phayre Correspondence* (London, 1932), mainly an account of the British occupation of Lower Burma and relations with Mindon. Walter Sadgren Desai, his coadjutor, with his *History of the British Residency in Burma, 1826-1840* (Rangoon, 1939), also worked in the diplomatic field. Among Burmese graduates of the new department, outstanding work was done by (Miss) Ma Mya Sein, whose *Administration of Burma: Sir Charles Crosthwaite and the Consolidation of Burma* (Rangoon, 1938) drew upon British and Burmese materials. (This is another work which is almost unobtainable and which deserves to be reprinted.)

All these writers belonged to the University College or Oxbridge stream; Judson College also made contributions to historical research, notably through the young American, John Leroy Christian, whose *Modern Burma* (Berkeley, 1942) provides a broad conspectus of development under Imperial rule, with some emphasis upon foreign relations.[11] Yet the most brilliant of the Rangoon University historians of the interwar years was a man who (to the regret of his friends) steadfastly refused to publish in any extended form the fruits of his research: Gordon H. Luce. Luce was the first scholar to insist that the ancient and medieval history of Burma must be based firmly upon Chinese historical writing and upon inscriptions: Pali, Mon, and Burmese. Himself a master of languages, he insisted upon language studies among his students, to whom he imparted the new interpretation of Burmese history which he was establishing. Some of his conclusions appeared—almost in note form—as papers in the *Journal of the Burma Research Society*: (hereafter, *JBRS*) among these may be mentioned "The Economic Life of the Early Burman" (XXX), "Burma Down to the Fall of Pagan" (XXIX), and "Burma's Debt to Pagan" (XXII). This journal provided the chief vehicle for the growing body of scholarly work; among authors who will not be mentioned elsewhere in this survey were John A. Stewart, "Some Authorities for the History of Burma" (XIII) and R. R. Langham Carter, "The Burmese Army" (XXVII).[12]

To mention these names is to recall that the contribution of British civil servants to historical development was still important. Indeed, the standard history of Burma, appearing at this time, was the work of a British official: Godfrey Eric Harvey's *History of Burma from the Earliest Times to 10 March 1824, the Beginning of the English Conquest* (London, 1924) maintained the tradition of naming historical studies by super-length titles! It also perpetuated the Phayre approach in focusing upon the activities of rulers. But it incorporated another half-century of research, and in a series of appendixes it ran the gamut of Burmese life and thought. A strangely ill-organized book, it is not easy meat for the student, but it still remains the standard history of

11. An expanded version of *Modern Burma* was issued as *Burma and the Japanese Invader* (Bombay, 1945). Christian was killed while serving as an American army officer in Burma.

12. The Burma Research Society issued a volume reproducing many of the major papers by Luce, and others, as *Fiftieth Anniversary Publications*, no. 2 (Rangoon, 1960). This is invaluable for libraries unable to secure copies of the original journal.

Burma.[13] A more radical break with tradition was achieved by John Sydenham Furnivall, the other scholar-official of the time. Although his better-known books were published later, the present writer would be prepared to argue that his earliest work was also his most original contribution to historical development. *An Introduction to the Political Economy of Burma* (Rangoon, 1931; 3rd ed., 1957) was an analysis of the traditional village economy of Burma, reconstructed by reference to *sittans*, original revenue reports, and leading to an exposition of the reasons for the disintegration of the rural economy under British rule.

Among works of a "background" historical nature to appear in the interwar years we may notice examples of different *genres*. Francis Kingdon Ward's *In Farthest Burma* (London, 1921) is a typical excursus by this prolific author: an account of a botanical expedition which is highly informative upon border society and history. *A Burmese Arcady*, by Colin M. D. Enriquez (London, 1923), is a quasi-historical account of the people of the border. Scholars may question the credentials of this army major, writing largely for his own pleasure, but he has observed much that the scholar in his library has never seen. With *Burma and the Karens*, by Sir San C. Po (London, 1928), we pass into a world of political-polemical history which has to be closely evaluated. Harold Fielding-Hall, in *The Soul of a People* (London, 1920), tried to portray the life of the ordinary Burman and created an "image" of Burma which was widely accepted.

All these studies derive from the pens of men working in Burma, whether Burman, British, or Indian. Only one serious work can be cited from outside: *Territoires et populations des confins du Yunnan*, a series of anthropological and historical studies by Chinese scholars, edited by J. Siguret, and published at Peking in 1937. Although this collection was intended to support Kuomintang territorial claims along the frontier, nevertheless it was an authoritative and objective work.

In retrospect, the period between the two World Wars appears as the high noon of historical studies of Burma. The postwar years are something of an afterglow. The British defeat in Burma led to a spate of journalistic writing, most of which may be ignored. Godfrey Eric Harvey's *British Rule in Burma, 1824-1942* (London, 1946) was a

13. Although Harvey's *History* has long been out of print, like so many of the basic materials on Burmese history, an abridged version was made for use in schools: *Outline of Burmese History* (Calcutta, 1926; reprinted 1929, 1947, 1954). This should not be passed over by the advanced student.

form of indictment of the failures in British administrative policy which would have been more impressive if less obviously hastily written. Certain publications issued by the (British) Burma government from Simla were of value to historians: particularly, *Burma Under the Japanese Occupation* (2 vols.; 1943-44), and *The Burma Handbook* (1943), which contains a useful range of topographical and quasi-historical information. The "Burma Pamphlets" series, published by the Indian branch of Oxford University Press (Madras) during the war years, also contained much that was scholarly in content. We may instance H. N. C. Stevenson, *The Hill Peoples of Burma* ("Burma Pamphlets," no. 6), which is the best short introduction to these neglected but important minority peoples. Although published after the war, Ian Morrison's *Grandfather Longlegs: The Life and Gallant Death of Major H. P. Seagrim* (London, 1947) is a work of on-the-spot reporting of the wartime Karen resistance movement which has a higher value as historical record than most works of this nature.

When Rangoon University reopened after the liberation of Burma, it was in many ways an entirely different institution from that which had flourished from 1920 to 1942. In the new Burma, there was no real place for either British or American missionary scholarship, although Gordon H. Luce remained, living near the university campus as the *saya*, or master, of the Rangoon history school. There was an atmosphere of impatient nationalism, and the general attitude was aptly summarized by the Prime Minister, U Nu, when he declared, "Our true history lies ahead." It will have become apparent that, by contrast with India or Ceylon, Burma had not been sufficiently exposed to the liberal, European tradition to have evolved its own school of historians, capable of constructing a synthesis of Eastern and Western views of historical scholarship. To a dangerous extent, the study of history had depended upon foreigners, who now had very largely departed from the scene.

There were a few last sparks from the ashes of official and missionary writing. F. S. V. Donnison, who had been Chief Secretary to the (British) Government of Burma, wrote a brief but cohesive study of British administration: *Public Administration in Burma* (London, 1953). As a member of the team of historians working under the direction of J. R. M. Butler to produce the official histories of the war, Donnison also was responsible for *British Military Administration in the Far East* (London, 1956), which quotes extensively from British official documents, both "in the field" and in Whitehall, and which greatly assists toward an understanding of the evolution of contemporary British policy. A good deal of incidental light is also cast on developments within the nationalist movement. The *doyen* of Burmese studies, John Sydenham Furnivall, originally produced his *Colonial Policy and Practice: A Comparative Study of Burma and Netherlands India* (London, 1948) as a contribution towards the formulation of postwar British policy. Its influence has, of course, extended far, and has largely created the widely held view that British rule produced both political and economic disintegration in Burma and was largely responsible for the emergence of a plural society in which the different communities regarded themselves as separate, and often opposed in purpose. This is hardly the place to attempt a reasoned criticism of Furnivall's thesis: sufficient to say, that along with much that is polemical and even misleading, there is a substratum of vitally useful historical data, particularly with regard to economic history. Furnivall went on writing until he died at a great age, and some of his later work is repetitive. His last book, *The Governance of Modern Burma* (New York, 1958), was a somewhat formalized account of administration and political development, but it does contain a cogent explanation of the military coup of 1958 which historians will find worth taking into consideration.

The missionary tradition was worthily represented by James Russell Andrus, a former professor of Judson College, whose *Burmese Economic Life* was published by Stanford University Press in 1948. This is largely an account of the Burmese economy before World War II. It might perhaps be argued that John F. Cady (at one time a teacher of history at Judson College, but now at Ohio University in the United States) should be included in this group. Cady's *A History of Modern Burma* (Ithaca, 1958) is an attempt to break away from the history of rulers and their wars, and to discover something of the history of the people. His first chapters provide a conspectus of Burma during the latter days of the kings, forming, perhaps, the best general statement on Burmese history. The greater part of the book is an account of the establishment of British rule and the rise of the nationalist movement. This is, at times, somewhat overdetailed, so that no general view of problems and trends emerges. The book ends with a brief outline of the history of the transfer of power in 1948. This work is likely, for many years, to remain the standard history of modern Burma.

D. G. E. Hall, the first professor of history at Rangoon University, also became, in 1949, the first Professor of South East Asian History at London University. His own main contribution has been in the wider field of regional history: *A History of South-East Asia* (London, 1955). Under his supervision, a number of studies were completed by young postgraduate students from Burma. At least one of their Ph.D. theses should be mentioned: Dr. Thaung's "British Interest in Trans-Burma Trade Routes to China, 1826-1876" (1954). Among other studies, completed after Hall's retirement, two works may be noted. Soe Yan-kit produced a study of "Anglo-Chinese Diplomacy regarding Burma, 1885-1897" (1960) which utilizes both Chinese and British official documentary sources. She has contrived to illustrate most vividly how British and Chinese diplomats maneuvered behind smokescreens of misunderstanding, and she shows how the actual border situation frequently bore only a casual likeness to the assumptions made in high-level diplomatic exchanges. Asha Ram's thesis, "Constitutional and Political Development in Burma, 1923-1936" (1961) presents, for the first time, an analysis of political development during the experimental period of Dyarchy which relates the twists and turns of political leaders to ideological and sociological determinants. Two Ph.D. theses have been published recently. Damodar P. Singhal's *The Annexation of Upper Burma* (Singapore, 1960) gives a detailed account of the Anglo-Burmese negotiations before the third Anglo-Burmese war, and shows how British policy changed from non-intervention into active intervention. Usha Mahajani, *The Role of Indian Minorities in Burma and Malaya* (Bombay, 1960), is mainly a study of the political rôle of the Indian community. First, in association with the Indian National Congress, they provided a model for Burmese and Malayan nationalist leaders to follow; but later, as indigenous nationalism became militant, the Indians found themselves the special target for nationalist chauvinism. Miss Mahajani's study is infused with a somewhat ambiguous anti-colonial approach; Dorothy Woodman's *The Making of Burma* (London, 1962) also exhibits an anti-colonial bias which occasionally affects her judgment. This extremely long book falls into three sections, of which the last describes the evolution of a British frontier policy in the Shan and Kachin hills, the counter-imperialism of Chinese frontier policy, the attempts to arrive at an agreed boundary, and the final achievement of agreement between Communist China and independent Burma. Miss Woodman has undertaken extensive research, and includes quotations from many British official documents. As a source book, *The Making of Burma* is of considerable value.

Finally, we must consider the contribution to a deeper knowledge of their national history made by Burmese scholars in the years since independence. Two scholars who are not strictly historians have nevertheless widened the area of understanding of Burmese culture. Htin Aung's *Burmese Law Tales* (London, 1962) shows the significance of the legal tradition in society and government. Hla Pe's commentary on a famous Burmese drama *Konmara Pya Zat*, I (London, 1952) and his *Burmese Proverbs* (London, 1962) similarly help to illustrate Burmese history from literature. A journalist and lawyer, Maung Maung, has written widely upon recent Burmese history. *Burma in the Family of Nations* (Amsterdam, 1956) is largely an account of Anglo-Burmese relations. Composed with wit and a sense of balance, it is marred by many loose statements and doubtful conclusions. His later work, *Burma's Constitution* (The Hague, 1959), is actually a political history of the twentieth century, with emphasis upon the years immediately before independence. It contains supposedly "inside information" about the rôles of the various Thakin leaders. On his return from a sabbatical year at Yale University, Maung Maung was invited by General Ne Win to compile a new constitution to replace that promulgated in 1947 and abrogated by the military. This product is not likely to be as liberal as Maung Maung's literary compositions.

Little has emerged from the academic stream. A project was initiated for a series of histories under the auspices of an Historical Commission (following the Glass Palace Chronicle precedent!) but this has yielded little fruit. The first work expected to be published by the commission was a definitive study of the Pagan Period by Gordon H. Luce, "Old Burma." This has been in manuscript since 1955 but, at the time of writing, no announcement of publication has appeared.[14] Two London-trained younger historians, Than Tun and Yi Yi, have produced a number of original papers, which have appeared in *JBRS* and elsewhere. But the prospects are not hopeful: the atmosphere of a military regime is particularly inauspicious for objective scholarship.

14. But see the contents of the *Bulletin* of the Burma Historical Commission (Rangoon), I, pt. 1 (June, 1960): "Inscriptions of Burma," portfolio I, plates 1 and 2, ed. and trans. by Pe Maung Tin and Gordon H. Luce.

# MALAYSIA

## C. Mary Turnbull

BEFORE THE TWENTIETH CENTURY the Malay Penin-
sula was little more than a geographic unit, lacking political cohesion or
a common historical heritage. By 1914 all the present states of
Malaya and Singapore had fallen under some form of British
control, with the over-all supervision of a colonial governor in
Singapore, but the peninsula remained in 1945 an untidy conglomera-
tion of Crown Colony, Federated, and Unfederated States, with no sense
of nationhood. By 1945 the Malays, many of whom were themselves
fairly recent arrivals, were outnumbered by Chinese and Indian immigrants, who swarmed into the country in the late nineteenth and early
twentieth centuries. Malaysia as a political unit is even more recent in
origin, a creation in fact of 1963. As late as the end of World War II
none of the three Borneo protectorates, with their predominantly Dayak
populations, was under direct British rule. North Borneo was governed
by the Chartered North Borneo Company, Sarawak by the Brooke
family, and the tiny state of Brunei (not a unit in Malaysia, but to be
treated as such in this essay) by its Malay Sultan. The former Malaya
and the present Malaysia are the artificial—and almost accidental—
legacies of British rule, not an area with a common ancient tradition
temporarily overlaid by colonial rule. This has affected historical writing about the region.

British settlement in Malaya began in 1786, when the East India
Company acquired the uninhabited island of Penang, off the northwest
coast of the peninsula, as a trading station and potential naval base, but
the Company had already been in possession of a factory at Bencoolen
in West Sumatra for more than a century. This occupation did not
inspire any descriptive or historical writing until the appearance of
William Marsden's *History of Sumatra* (London, 1783). While
Marsden dealt with the immigration of the Minangkabau Malays to
the peninsula, he made little attempt to trace the history of Sumatra

before the days of European contact. His main concern was to describe the country and the interests of the European powers. "History is only to be prized as it tends to improve our knowledge of mankind," he claimed.

This interpretation of history as meaning a comprehensive description of the existing state and condition of a country, with a recital of past events mainly to show how a present situation had been created, set the tradition to be followed by the earliest of British Malayan historians, Thomas Stamford Raffles and John Crawfurd. As officials of the East India Company in Penang, these political and literary rivals played prominent rôles in the temporary British occupation of Java during the Napoleonic War, which inspired Raffles to publish his *The History of Java* (2 vols.; London, 1817), and Crawfurd his *History of the Indian Archipelago* (3 vols.; Edinburgh, 1820). Despite its more pretentious title, the latter was mainly a study of Java too, and the short chapter on the Malay Peninsula was a mere sketch. The accounts of the past prior to European times made up only one section of the two histories, appearing, like Marsden's, in the latter half. As administrators, men of action and empire builders, Raffles and Crawfurd were typical of their generation in looking forward to the future rather than back into the past. Raffles, it is true, was a diligent Malay scholar, who saw much to admire in past Oriental traditions, but his major preoccupation was to show the maladministration of the Dutch and the improvements that enlightened British rule could bring. Had he lived, Raffles might have delved more deeply and written more widely about the Malayan past, but he died in 1826, soon after his return to England. Unhappily he dealt an unintended blow to the future study of Malayan history, for his priceless collection of Malay manuscripts, so assiduously collected during his years in the East, perished when the ship on which he embarked for his final voyage to England was destroyed by fire.

Contemptuous of traditional Asian society, Crawfurd criticized even more vehemently the cruelty and rapacity of early European—and especially Dutch—colonial rule in the archipelago, and condemned the monopoly of the great trading companies, including his own employers, the English East India Company. His ideal was to elevate an effete and degenerate Oriental society through free trade, European settlement, and the spread of Christianity and Western civilization. This was the underlying theme of his *History of the Indian Archipelago*, and was to be seen in his many later works, his accounts of his visits to Burma, to Siam and Cochin China,[1] and his writings on India.

The next thirty years were a period of prolific writing, but produced no works which could compare in merit or ambition of conception with the histories of Marsden, Raffles, or Crawfurd. This was partly the result of political circumstances. The Anglo-Dutch treaty of 1824, in splitting the old Johore-Lingga empire into separate British and Dutch spheres of interest, divorced the British from direct contact with Java, Sumatra, Celebes, and the islands of the archipelago with ancient traditions, and this isolation was intensified by the trading restrictions imposed by the Culture System in Java after 1830. The British were cut off too from the hinterland of the Malay states by the East India Company's rigid non-intervention policy and were confined to the Straits Settlements, to the modern flourishing seaports of Singapore and Penang, and to the decaying settlement of Malacca. After 1833, when the Company lost its monopoly of the China trade and with it its interest in the Straits Settlements, there were no officials of more than mediocre caliber, and the tradition of scholarship, which was so strong in continental India in that generation, was not extended to the Eastern settlements. Most of the writings on the area in the second quarter of the nineteenth century were personal adventure stories and narratives, useful raw materials for later histories but not themselves works of historical analysis. There were many books of trade and travel, outstanding among them being George Windsor Earl's *The Eastern Seas* ... (London, 1837), which first inspired James Brooke to embark on his expedition to Borneo. There were innumerable accounts by naval officers of expeditions undertaken to suppress piracy, the most important being the works of Captain the Hon. Henry Keppel: *The Expedition to Borneo of H.M.S. Dido* (2 vols.; London, 1845), and *A Visit to the Indian Archipelago, in H.M. Ship Mæander* (2 vols.; London, 1853). And there were countless works by missionaries and naturalists, most of them repetitive in their descriptions of scenery, pirates, tigers, and local customs.[2]

1. *Journal of an Embassy from the Governor-General of India to the Courts of Siam and Cochin China: Exhibiting a View of the Actual State of Those Kingdoms* (London, 1828); and *Journal of an Embassy from the Governor-General of India to the Court of Ava, in the Year 1827* (2 vols.; London, 1829). These works come outside the scope of this essay. They are discussed in this volume in the essay on Burma by Hugh Tinker, p. 451.

2. Constance Mary Turnbull, "Bibliography of Writings in English on British

Apart from those who published full-scale books, less ambitious writers found an outlet for their talents in the *Journal of the Indian Archipelago and Eastern Asia*, edited in the Straits Settlements from 1847 to 1859 by James Richardson Logan, one-time planter, newspaper editor, law agent, and ethnologist. Priority was given in this serious-minded journal to scientific enquiry, exploration, geography, and language study, which make dull reading at the present day and have been largely superseded by more accurate technical information. But many articles on contemporary problems and early administration are invaluable for the historian. These, too, reflect the preoccupation with current events rather than historical analysis. James Low, one of the Company's senior officials in the Straits, claimed that he had been given access to official documents to produce his series of articles entitled, over-importantly, "An Account of the Origin and Progress of the British Colonies in the Straits of Malacca."[3] It was a disjointed chronicle of facts about administration, set in a highly biased account of events in Kedah in Low's time, which was certainly not derived from government documents and ran counter to general official and non-official opinion on the subject in the Straits Settlements. More useful and less pretentious was the series of official records collected and reprinted in most volumes of the *Journal* by Thomas Braddell under the title "Notices of Pinang"[4] and "Notices of Singapore."[5] Braddell, who began life in the Straits as a sugar planter and became the first Attorney-General of the Crown Colony in 1867, intended to compile a history of the Settlements. This collection of papers was all that ever appeared, but it is invaluable since many of the original documents have long since vanished or disintegrated.

The dramatic adventures of James Brooke in Sarawak, the false charges of inhumanity leveled against his dealings with the Dayaks,

Malaya, 1786-1867," in Lennox A. Mills, "British Malaya, 1824-1867," *Journal of the Malayan Branch of the Royal Asiatic Society* (hereafter, *JMBRAS*; earlier, *Journal of the Straits Branch of the Royal Asiatic Society*; hereafter, *JSBRAS*) (Singapore), XXXIII, 3 (1960), gives a comprehensive list of such works. When citing Malaysian journals, issue numbers rather than months of issue will be given. If page numbers are not given, the article cited constituted the entire number of that journal.

3. *Journal of the Indian Archipelago* (Singapore), III (1849), 599-617; and IV (1850), 11-26, 106-18, 360-79.

4. *Ibid.*, pp. 629-44, 645-63; V (1851), 1-14, 93-119, 155-72, 189-210, 292-305, 354-66, 400-29; VI (1852), 18-32, 83-93, 143-72, 218-38, 521-44, 618-35; n.s. II (1857), 182-203.

5. *Ibid.*, 1st ser., VII (1853), 325-57; VIII (1854), 97-111, 329-48, 403-19; IX (1855), 53-65, 442-82.

the controversy, the Commission of Enquiry, and the complete exoneration which followed, fathered a considerable body of literature. Much of this took the form of scurrilous pamphlets of ephemeral interest. More important were the compositions of Brooke's many friends and admirers, who hastened to publish his letters and papers and to produce panegyric biographies and accounts of the achievements of the Brooke regime in Sarawak. John C. Templer edited the *Private Letters of Sir James Brooke, Rajah of Sarawak, Narrating the Events of His Life, from 1838 to the Present Time* (3 vols.; London, 1853), which were published with Brooke's permission, despite the fact that they were often frank to the point of indiscretion. In 1876, eight years after Sir James's death, Gertrude Le Grand Jacob published *The Raja of Sarawak* (2 vols.; London), a long, detailed, careful account by a biographer who had visited Sarawak and made a painstaking study of all the available written material. It was followed three years later by another sympathetic, thorough biography, *The Life of Sir James Brooke* (Edinburgh, 1879), by Sir Spenser B. St. John, who became Sir James's secretary in 1848 and spent many years in the service of the Brookes in Sarawak.

The most important book on Malaysia which Brooke's story inspired at that time was *The Indian Archipelago: Its History and Present State* (2 vols.; London, 1853), by Spenser St. John's brother, Horace. A professional writer, Horace St. John had read all the printed sources available in English and Dutch. His history was not primarily a description of existing conditions, after the fashion of the earlier nineteenth-century works. It was history in the more modern sense, but it dealt sketchily with the pre-European Malay world and was avowedly an account of "the progress of European trade and conquest in the Asiatic Archipelago." St. John reflected at its most extreme the complacent mid-century satisfaction with recent changes in Imperial administration and the contempt for the Oriental organizations of society which nineteenth-century European colonialism sought to replace. "Their imbecility is as incurable as their despotism is ferocious. They deserve only ruin."

Meanwhile, in the peninsula the movement to transfer the Straits Settlements from the East India Company to the direct rule of the Crown provoked a good deal of writing. Braddell and Crawfurd produced pamphlets in favor of the transfer, tracing the past development of the Settlements, describing their present condition, and suggesting a framework for future administration.[6] But the major work which this movement inspired was written by the newspaper editor, John Cameron, whose *Our Tropical Possessions in Malayan India* (London, 1865) was the most comprehensive, well-balanced, and fair account of the Indian regime in the Straits Settlements produced in the nineteenth century. It has been reissued with a new introduction by Wang Gungwu (Kuala Lumpur, 1965).

The transformation of the Straits Settlements into a Crown Colony in 1867 led to the appointment of Colonial Office cadets and officials, who were to develop an interest in local traditions and languages, as their counterparts did in other parts of the Empire in the late nineteenth century. The extension of British control into the Malay hinterland after 1874 established young Englishmen in positions of authority and isolation from their fellow countrymen. Some of them produced vivid pictures of their Malay background, sometimes in autobiographical, sometimes in semi-fictional form.[7]

A Straits Branch of the Royal Asiatic Society was formed in Singapore in 1878, and from that time to the present day—with the exception of the Japanese Occupation period—the society has issued a regular *Journal*.[8] The nineteenth-century issues carried few historical articles, and most of the contributors were officials who chose to describe the geography, plants, animals, and way of life of the particular state in which they were stationed. There were some translations from Malay chronicles, beginning in 1880 with Hugh Low's translation of the "Book of Descent of the Sultans of Brunei."[9] From 1882 William E. Maxwell produced a series of translations from Malay and Dutch works on Perak,[10] and in 1890 printed a Romanized version of "The Ballad of Raja Haji," with a translation from a Dutch account of that warrior's attack on Malacca in 1784.[11] Other officials published translations

6. Braddell, *Singapore and the Straits Settlements Described* (Penang [1857]); Crawfurd, *Memorandum on the British Settlements in the Straits of Malacca* (London, 1858).

7. For example, Sir Frank A. Swettenham's *Malay Sketches* (London, 1895) and *The Real Malay* (London, 1900); and the many books by Sir Hugh Clifford, based upon his early experiences in Pahang, notably: *Studies in Brown Humanity* (London, 1898); *In a Corner of Asia* (London, 1899); *Bush-Whacking, and Other Sketches* (Edinburgh, 1901); *In Court and Kampong* (London, 1897); *The Further Side of Silence* (London, 1916); and *Malayan Monochromes* (London, 1913).

8. In 1923 the society changed its name to the Malayan, and in 1965 to the Malaysian, Branch of the Royal Asiatic Society.

9. *JSBRAS*, V (1880), 1-35.

10. "The History of Perak from Native Sources," *JSBRAS*, IX (1882), 85-108; *ibid.*, XIV (1884), 305-21; "The Dutch in Perak," *ibid.*, X (1882), 245-68.

11. *Ibid.*, XXII (1890), 173-224.

and accounts based on Dutch and Malay sources,[12] but these were isolated contributions, and there was no attempt to produce a coherent history of the Malay states. The one venture into more general history, A. M. Skinner's "An Outline History of the British Connection with Malaya" (*JSBRAS*, X [1882], 269-80), was—as its name implied—a mere sketch, a bare summary of facts and dates of administrative history in the nineteenth century, with a shaky outline of British commercial activities in previous centuries.

Like the histories written by his fellow-officials, Skinner's work aimed to provide background knowledge for young officials. This idea was developed systematically by Richard J. Wilkinson, who edited two series of *Papers on Malay Subjects* (1st series, Kuala Lumpur, 1907-11; 2nd series, 1912-27), which were intended as textbooks for civil service cadets and used as such up to the very end of British rule in Malaya. They were concerned mainly with Malay life and society, customs, literature, and law; but the first series included five volumes of Malay history, and the second series contained historical notes on Negri Sembilan. In 1920 Wilkinson revised the historical volumes of the *Papers* and incorporated the work done by former officials on isolated aspects of Malay history, in order to produce his *A History of the Peninsular Malays* (Singapore, 1920), a short work, but the first attempt to write a coherent history of the indigenous population.

Meanwhile, pride in the progress of imperialism in the late nineteenth century was reflected in the growing interest in recording British achievements in Malaysia. While the area did not provide the same examples of spectacular heroic endeavor as other parts of the Empire, the adventures and character of Raffles and Sir James Brooke attracted writers of the then fashionable school of biographies of "Great Founders of the Empire." Of these the most careful and weighty was Demetrius Charles deK. Boulger's *The Life of Sir Stamford Raffles* (London, 1897). Boulger based his study on India Office records which had hitherto not been used, and although at times he allowed admiration for his subject to color his judgment, this solid, worthy biography remained for more than half a century the standard work on Raffles' life. It was a fitting complement to Lady Sophia Hull Raffles' eulogistic

12. Notably D.F.A. Hervey's translation from the Dutch of "Valentyn's Account of Malacca," *JSBRAS*, XIII (1884), 49-74B; *ibid.*, XV (1885), 119-38; *ibid.*, XVI 298-301; *ibid.*, XXII (1890), 225-46; and Martin Lister's "The Negri Sembilan, Their Origin and Constitution," *ibid.*, XIX (1887), 35-53.

tribute to her husband, *Memoir of the Life and Public Services of Sir Thomas Stamford Raffles* (London, 1830), and superior to Hugh Edward Egerton's *Sir Stamford Raffles: England in the Far East* (London, 1900), or to the Reverend John A. Bethune Cook's *Sir Thomas Stamford Raffles, Founder of Singapore, 1819* (London, 1918), which appeared to celebrate the colony's centenary. Writing in the same spirit as Boulger, Sir Spenser B. St. John produced a slighter biography in his *Rajah Brooke: The Englishman as Ruler of an Eastern State* (London, 1899). Ten years later Charles A. Bampfylde, former Resident of Sarawak and friend of Rajah Charles Brooke, collaborated with a professional writer, Sabine Baring-Gould, to produce *A History of Sarawak under its Two White Rajahs, 1839-1908* (London, 1909), a solid work based upon official correspondence handed over to them by Sir Charles Brooke and revealing a great deal about the latter's character. Strangely enough, little interest was shown in Francis Light, founder of Penang, a more shadowy character than either Raffles or Brooke, but the man who was responsible for the establishment of British influence in Malaysia. Archibald Francis Steuart produced a brief account, *The Founders of Penang and Adelaide: A Short Sketch of the Lives of Francis and William Light* (London, 1901), but it was not until 1948 that the first biography appeared, Harold P. Clodd's *Malaya's First British Pioneer: The Life of Francis Light* (London). This careful little study failed to bring Light to life, and it is doubtful if sufficient sources will ever be discovered to produce a convincing portrait of this important figure in Malaya's history.

In the opening years of the twentieth century reminiscences of earlier times in the Straits Settlements became popular reading. The fashion was set by Charles B. Buckley's *An Anecdotal History of Old Times in Singapore* (2 vols.; Singapore, 1902). From 1884 to 1887 Buckley, as editor of the Singapore *Free Press*, reprinted articles from early editions of the newspaper. When he decided to publish these in book form and to bring the story up to the end of Indian rule in 1867, he revised the original selections in the light of comments from some of the former merchants and officials then living in retirement in England. His book has been hailed as one of the outstanding authorities on nineteenth-century Singapore, since the newspapers on which it was based are not available to historians working outside Malaya, but it should be accepted with caution, for Buckley does not quote his sources, and the truth has often become warped by the defective memory and prejudice of old men. The same reliance on personal reminiscences and the same taste for the anecdotal form of history are to be found in the volumes produced by enthusiastic residents of Singapore at the time of the city's centenary. In *One Hundred Years of Singapore* (2 vols.; London, 1921) the editors, Walter W. Makepeace, Gilbert E. Brooke, and Roland St. John Braddell, invited prominent citizens to contribute articles on every aspect of European life and to record memories of the past. A companion volume, *One Hundred Years' History of the Chinese in Singapore* (London, 1923), by Song Ong Siang, followed the anecdotal pattern. It concentrated upon giving information about individuals and families, and failed to give any composite picture of Chinese activities in Singapore or the hinterland.

The earliest attempt to write a full-scale history of the British impact on Malaya was made by Sir Frank A. Swettenham, one of the first colonial cadets and subsequently Resident General, High Commissioner for the Federated Malay States, and Governor of the Straits Settlements. In the first edition of his *British Malaya* ... (London, 1906) Swettenham covered the whole period of British rule, but concentrated upon British activities in the Malay states in the last quarter of the century, drawing heavily from his own long and colorful experience. His interpretation of British policy, particularly in the initial period of intervention in the hinterland, has since been disputed in the light of official documents, but his highly personal account has a warmth which is lacking in later more academic histories, and a permanent value in reflecting the character and motive force behind some of the leading figures in the story.[13]

Before World War I no dispassionate "professional historian" ventured into the field of Malaysian history. Interest in the Empire was confined mainly to the Dominions, and the study of Crown Colonies was neglected. It was left to the young Canadian scholar, Lennox A. Mills, who had no personal connections with Malaya, to break new ground with his "British Malaya, 1824-1867," *JMBRAS*, III, 2 (1925).[14] The work was based on the first thorough examination ever made of the Straits Settlements documents housed in the India Office Library in London. Careful and detailed, this pioneer study remains

13. Revised editions were published in London in 1929 and 1948.
14. Reprinted as *JMBRAS*, XXXIII, 3 (1960).

today the standard work on the East India Company's administration in the Straits Settlements and its connections with the Malay states.

The other work of outstanding importance in the interwar years came from the pen of another North American professional historian, Rupert Emerson, in *Malaysia: A Study in Direct and Indirect Rule* (New York, 1937). Emerson's term "Malaysia" embraced the Malay Peninsula and the then Dutch East Indies, and his book was primarily concerned with comparing the history and working of the political systems created by the British in the peninsula and the Dutch in the archipelago. Based not upon original archival material but on books, reports, parliamentary papers, and the impressions of a year spent in the field in Southeast Asia, Emerson's book is a refreshing and acute study of permanent value. While the author's interest was in the contemporary scene rather than the past, his account of the development of British administration in the Malay states from the earliest days of intervention remains the most lucid, concise, and perceptive study which has yet appeared in print. Although the book was concerned with politics and administration rather than economic development, Emerson recognized the economic revolution which had taken place in Malaya. As an American he was highly critical of European Imperial economic exploitation and more realistic than his British contemporaries in recognizing the inconsistency of the political façade of Malay rule divorced from economic power. While he sometimes failed, as an outsider, to appreciate colonial attitudes, particularly in the earlier part of the nineteenth century, he was free of many of the inborn assumptions that hampered British colonial writing. Although his book was concerned, for instance, primarily with political systems rather than personalities, his attitude to Raffles was stimulating. He was less blinded by Raffles' contributions to the Empire, more conscious of his personal ambition, his quest for glory, and his capacity for intrigue.

An important economic study of commerce and industry, labor and social services, which complemented Emerson's picture of the political situation in prewar Malaya, was produced by Lennox A. Mills in *British Rule in Eastern Asia* ... (London, 1942), which was published after the fall of Singapore to the Japanese but completed before the collapse. It was particularly welcome as an up-to-the-minute study and yet free from the emotionalism which rapid defeat was to engender.

While writers and historians in Britain showed no interest either in the present condition or past history of this trouble-free corner of the Empire in the 1930's, the many years devoted by officials on the spot to Malay studies began to bear fruit in that peaceful decade. Under the influence of Sir Richard O. Winstedt, who was by then President of the Malayan Branch of the Royal Asiatic Society, the *Journal* became more and more devoted to historical writing. In addition to innumerable short articles, histories appeared of all the major Malay states, many of them written by Winstedt himself. His "A Malay History of Riau and Johore," comprising the Jawi text of the *Tuhfat al-Nafis* with a summary in English, and his "History of Johore (1365-1895)," both of which appeared in 1932,[15] were followed two years later by "A History of Perak," written jointly with Richard James Wilkinson.[16] Then came Winstedt's short "A History of Selangor,"[17] and his "Negri Sembilan: The History, Polity and Beliefs of Nine States,"[18] Anker Rentse's short "History of Kelantan,"[19] W. Linehan's "A History of Pahang,"[20] and Winstedt's "Notes on the History of Kedah."[21] These dealt with each state in isolation, using Malay sources and treating the subject from a Malay standpoint. In the midst of all this activity, Winstedt brought out his full-scale "History of Malaya,"[22] the first comprehensive account of the peninsula from early times, which attempted to weave European activities into the Malayan background. And in 1939 he produced "A History of Malay Literature,"[23] which is of considerable interest to the historian since the line between fact and legend is so nebulous in Malay annals.

No attempt was made to produce translations at that time of the major Malay chronicles. Winstedt edited the romanized text of the *Sejarah Melayu*,[24] but John Leyden's *Malay Annals* (London, 1821) remained the only English translation of this earliest and finest of Malay histories. The *Hikayat Abdullah*, the autobiography of Abdullah bin Abdul Kadir Munshi, one-time secretary to Raffles, a unique and delightful commentary on European activities in the Straits Settlements in the early nineteenth century from a Malay's viewpoint, ap-

15. *JMBRAS*, X, 2 and 3 (1932).
16. *Ibid.*, XII, 1 (1934).
17. *Ibid.*, 3, pp. 1-34.
18. *Ibid.*, pp. 37-114.
19. *Ibid.*, 2, pp. 44-61.
20. *Ibid.*, XIV, 2 (1936).
21. *Ibid.*, 3, pp. 155-89.
22. *Ibid.*, XIII, 1 (1935).
23. *Ibid.*, XVII, 3 (1939); rev. ed., *ibid.*, XXXI, 3 (1958).
24. *Ibid.*, XVI, 3 (1938).

peared in an uninspired translation by William G. Shellabear, *The Autobiography of Munshi Abdullah* (Singapore, 1918). The only other versions in English extant at that time were John Turnbull Thomson's *Translations from the Hikayat Abdullah bin Abdul Kadir, Munshi* (London, 1874), selections apparently based on a draft by Abdullah; and short extracts translated by Thomas Braddell for the *Journal of the Indian Archipelago*.

It has become fashionable in the last decade to argue that the history of Southeast Asia in the past has been written from an exclusively Europe-centric point of view, but no such criticism could be leveled at the corpus of historical writing produced by Sir Richard Winstedt and his colleagues before the war. In fact their exclusive concentration on the Malay world sparked off a reaction and kindled an interest on the one hand in pre-Muslim Malaya and on the other in the part played by non-Malays, and particularly the Chinese, in the nineteenth and twentieth centuries.

Roland (later Dato Sir Roland) St. John Braddell led the way in tracing the early history of the peninsula as revealed in literary sources. Grandson of the first Attorney-General and himself a prominent lawyer, he already had contributed much to the study of the Malayan past. The introductory chapter to his *The Law of the Straits Settlements* (Singapore, 1915)[25] brought up to date the only other attempt to trace the legal history of the Settlement, which appeared as a historical preface to J. W. Norton Kyshe's *Cases Heard and Determined in Her Majesty's Supreme Court of the Straits Settlements* (Singapore, 1885). This latter work provided an invaluable account of the early conflicts between judiciary and executive, based upon Penang court records which have since disappeared, but it was printed in a limited edition and is difficult to come by nowadays. Braddell was also one of the three editors of *One Hundred Years of Singapore* and contributed the most entertaining and vivid chapters to be found in those volumes.

From 1935 onwards, in a series of articles, "An Introduction to the Study of Ancient Times in the Malay Peninsula and the Straits of Malacca,"[26] he challenged the commonly accepted framework of the

25. Copies of this early limited edition are almost unobtainable, and a second edition was printed in two volumes in 1931-32.

26. *JMBRAS*, XIII, 2 (1935), 70-109; *ibid.*, XIV, 3 (1936), 10-71; *ibid.*, XV, 3 (1937), 64-126; *ibid.*, XVII, 1 (1930), 146-212; *ibid.*, XIX, 1 (1941), 21-74.

history of the peninsula in pre-European times. Historical geography in Malaysia presents many problems. Archaeological remains are few, and the first indigenous history of the peninsula is the sixteenth century *Sejarah Melayu*. The historical geographer has to rely on foreign sources, on Chinese histories from the fifth century A.D. onwards, on Arab and Persian records from the ninth century, on references in various Indian writings, occasional clues in Javanese and Siamese, and some dangerously ambiguous testimony in Western classical literature. The first clear European description was Tomé Pires' *Suma Oriental*, written between 1512 and 1515.[27] In the nineteenth century there was some sporadic writing on the historical geography of the peninsula, but the first work of any pretensions was Colonel G. E. Gerini's *Researches on Ptolemy's Geography of Eastern Asia* (London, 1909), a large tome, ingeniously argued, but now completely out of date. Braddell's articles had their faults. He had to rely solely on often untrustworthy translations, and he sometimes displayed a lawyer's tendency to argue weak points over-energetically. Nevertheless, he provided a noble pioneer study in a difficult and obscure field, stimulated discussion in Malaya, and pointed out the need to correlate the work of sinologists and Indian historians.

These researches into the literary evidence relating to Malaya's early history coincided with the first systematic attempt to investigate the archaeological remains of the peninsula. In 1934-35 Horace G. Quaritch Wales explored the route across the Isthmus of Kra, working on the theory that Indian traders and colonists, coming in large numbers to Northern Malaya and Southern Thailand in the first millennium of the Christian era, opened up trading routes across the peninsula and evolved more highly developed states as they moved eastwards. He himself was to modify his theory in the light of subsequent experience, and his book *Towards Angkor* (London, 1937) abounds with specious reasoning which needs to be read with caution. In a second expedition he carried out extensive and energetic field work on ancient sites in Kedah to support his theory and published his initial findings in "Archaeological Researches on Ancient Indian Colonization in Malaya," *JMBRAS*, XVIII, 2 (1940), 1-85.

In the field of modern Malayan history, the preoccupation of Winstedt and some of his colleagues with the Malay world appeared

27. *Suma Oriental*, edited by Augusto Cortesão, Hakluyt Society, 2nd ser., LXXXIX-XC (London, 1944).

growingly unrealistic to those officials of the Malayan Civil Service who were dealing with Chinese affairs. Winstedt treated the Selangor Civil War, for instance, as a purely Malay dynastic struggle, with no mention of the influential Capitan China and no indication that the key to the conflict lay in economic conditions and the dissensions of the Chinese miners. By the 1930's a small group of able Chinese-speaking officials, notably Mervyn L. Wynne, S. M. Middlebrook, Victor W. W. S. Purcell, and Wilfred L. Blythe, began to seek to redress the balance, but little of their research work appeared in print before the Japanese overran Malaya.

On the eve of the invasion late in 1941 much had already been accomplished in investigating the past by officials and by private individuals resident in Malaya. Individual histories of all the major states, relying largely on Malay sources, had been produced. A beginning had been made both in field work and the literary study of ancient times, and the stimulus given to examine the rôle of the Chinese in nineteenth- and twentieth-century Malaya. But this activity was confined to a small group of enthusiasts. With the exception of Mills and Emerson, no professional historian or economist had shown any interest in Malayan affairs. Among the residents the habit of writing long memoirs was dying out. In the early and mid-nineteenth century there was a wealth of valuable books and articles about contemporary Malaya; by the early twentieth century this source had dried up into a trickle of reminiscences of the type written by Sir Laurence Guillemard, governor from 1919 to 1927, and named so aptly *Trivial Fond Records* (London, 1937). There were no local historians and no institution of higher learning to produce them, other than the Raffles College of Arts and Sciences, founded in Singapore in 1928.

In the Borneo territories historical writing was almost extinct. A few articles on North Borneo appeared from time to time in the *Journal of the Straits Branch of the Royal Asiatic Society*,[28] and occasional, mediocre volumes were produced about Sarawak, chiefly at the hands of the female members of the Brooke family, such as Sylvia Brooke's *The Three White Rajas* (London, 1939). British Malaya slumbered peacefully, content with economic prosperity and undisturbed by nationalist aspirations.

The Japanese invasion, the rapid collapse of the colonial administra-

---

28. Notably W. H. Treacher's "British Borneo: Sketches of Brunai, Sarawak, Labuan and North Borneo," XX (1889), 13-74; *ibid.*, XXI (1889), 19-121.

tion, and the three and a half years of occupation that followed destroyed this complacency and awakened the interest of the outside world in Malaya. The first fruits of the shock brought by the defeat was the small book, *Malayan Postscript* (London, 1942) by Ian Morrison, correspondent of *The* (London) *Times*. This was journalism at its best, the most vivid picture produced of the Malayan campaign, and despite the brevity of his stay and the speed with which he wrote his book, Morrison succeeded in giving a more acute portrayal of the colonial background than appeared subsequently in many longer and more pretentious works.

Morrison's summing up was fairer than the impressions to be drawn from the American writer, Virginia McLean Thompson's *Postmortem on Malaya* (New York, 1943). Writing in the full heat of battle, Miss Thompson condemned Britain for not providing sufficient military protection and failing to unite Malayans as a nation and to make them eager to resist the Japanese by her "purely economic form of imperialism." It was an unrealistic study in the context of the early 1940's, lacking the balance of Emerson or the impartiality of Mills, and as Sir George Sansom detected in his Foreword to the book at the time, the author showed "a certain tendency to act as prosecutor rather than as judge."

The humiliation of military defeat led to heart-searching and bitter recriminations. The official war histories and the memoirs of the military commanders involved, have sought mainly to apportion blame for the spectacular disgrace, and an impartial analysis of the military campaign in its political background remains to be written. The Australian Commander, Lieutenant General H. Gordon Bennett's *Why Singapore Fell* (Sydney, 1944), and the British military leader, Lieutenant General Arthur E. Percival's pallid *The War in Malaya* (London, 1949) reveal the personal animosities among the leaders and the divisions in the structure of the high command, which constituted one of the most fundamental weaknesses of the British defense system in Malaya. This is forcibly confirmed in the official British war history, Major General Stanley Woodburn Kirby's *The War Against Japan*, I (London, 1957),[29] which provides a frank, forthright analysis of one of the most controversial situations in British military history, and draws the con-

29. *The War Against Japan* is designed as a five-volume study, of which three volumes have so far appeared. The first volume is entitled *The Loss of Singapore*.

clusion that the loss of Malaya was inevitable before the first shot was fired in the campaign.

The journalistic approach of Frank Owen in his *The Fall of Singapore* (London, 1960) and of other similar books has added little of value to an understanding of the situation. Much more interesting is the account of the Malayan campaign from the Japanese point of view by the Japanese leader, Colonel Masanobu Tsuji, published in 1951 in Japan under the title *Shonan, the Hinge of Fate*, and as an English translation, *Singapore: The Japanese Version* (Sydney, 1960). The book bristles with factual errors, and is misleading about the Malayan political background and the impact of the Japanese upon the country, but it is unique in showing the planning behind the Japanese attack and the attitude of Japan toward the occupation of Malaya.

No thorough study has as yet been made of Japanese administration in wartime Malaya, but Willard H. Elsbree's concise analysis, *Japan's Role in Southeast Asian Nationalist Movements, 1940 to 1945* (Cambridge, Mass., 1953), which is based partly on Japanese documents and newspapers, fitted Malaya neatly but briefly into the context of Japanese policy in Southeast Asia.

The most convincing guide to Malayan opinion toward the British regime before and immediately after the war is the chapter on "Nationalism in Malaya," by Thomas H. Silcock and Ungku Abdul Aziz in *Asian Nationalism and the West*, edited by William L. Holland (New York, 1953). This penetrating study by two economists, one of whom is a Malay whose formative years were spent during the Japanese occupation, traces the origins of nationalism against the background of economic development and immigration of prewar days. The book is important in stressing the impact upon the rapid growth of Malayan nationalism of the failure of immediate British postwar policy, an aspect which has been neglected by most writers in their concern with the spectacular defeat at the hands of the Japanese in 1941. The authors tell the story of Malayan Union, Federation, and the early stages of the Communist Emergency up to 1952. This well-written and fair judgment should be read in conjunction with, and in some respects as a corrective to, Lennox A. Mills's good short chapter on Malaya in Mills and associates, *The New World of Southeast Asia* (Minneapolis, 1949), and to give life to the bare bones of British policy and administration as described in F. S. V. Donnison's *British Military Administra-*

*tion in the Far East, 1943-46* (London, 1956), an official history, for which the author had access to confidential government documents.

The relatively amicable spirit in which both British and Malayan political leaders approached the question of independence did not encourage the growth of polemical nationalist literature, as in other colonial territories, and most of the political writing of the 1950's was concerned with the Communist Emergency. The place of the Malayan Communist movement in the context of Southeast Asia is shown clearly in Jack H. Brimmell's sound and weighty study *Communism in South East Asia: A Political Analysis* (London, 1959), and an excellent description of the origin and growth of the militant Communist movement in Malaya is given in Gene Z. Hanrahan's *The Communist Struggle in Malaya* (New York, 1954). A little of the social background and the attitude of the terrorists is portrayed in Lucian W. Pye's *Guerilla Communism in Malaya: Its Social and Political Meaning* (Princeton, 1956), although this survey was carried out during a brief stay in the country and based on interviews with surrendered terrorists through interpeters. The personal experiences of police officers and soldiers have been recounted in several books. None attained the interest or the literary merit of Frederick Spencer Chapman's *The Jungle Is Neutral* (London, 1949), which described the author's experiences in the Malayan jungle during World War II, and in doing so gives a unique picture of the activities of the Communist guerillas that is relevant to the Emergency period as well.

Many journalists contributed their impressions of the struggle. Most of their productions are likely to be of no more than ephemeral interest, but Vernon Bartlett's *Report from Malaya* (London, 1954) gives a concise analysis of the situation and offers a more favorable impression of the administration of the High Commissioner, Sir Gerald Templer, than the bitter criticism levied by Victor W. W. S. Purcell in his *Malaya: Communist or Free* (London, 1954). Purcell repeats his anti-Templer line in *The Revolution in Southeast Asia* (London, 1962), a book concerned more with the present condition and future of Southeast Asia and lying outside the scope of this essay.

Factually accurate accounts of the stages in constitutional development and the achievement of independence are to be found in Rupert Emerson's *Representative Government in Southeast Asia* (Cambridge, Mass., 1955) and Jess Norman Parmer's chapter on Malaya in *Govern-*

*ments and Politics of Southeast Asia,* edited by George Kahin (Ithaca, 1959, rev. ed., 1964), which brings the story up to the establishment of Malaysia. Lennox A. Mills has provided a longer study, raising more controversial issues, in *Malaya: A Political and Economic Appraisal* (Minneapolis, 1958), an interesting work which was completed at the time when the Federation gained its independence. A dispassionate consideration of the whole conflict must await the impartial historian's attempt to fit the story of the Malayan Communist Emergency into the political, economic, and social background of the country. An official history of the Emergency already has been commissioned by the Federation government.

The absence of acrimonious dispute in the attainment of independence meant that Malaya alone of the former colonial territories of Southeast Asia experienced no abrupt break with a previous generation of European scholars. On the contrary, not only was the historical enquiry which was interrupted by the war continued, but local historians were trained in Western methods and have invariably followed Western techniques. The founding of the University of Malaya in 1949 brought a new body of professional historians on the scene, and students trained at the university have tended to concentrate upon diplomatic and political history, using English language sources and British archives. With the departure of the former overseas officials from the mid-1950's, the Malayan Branch of the Royal Asiatic Society became more and more dominated by the professional historian and its journal was almost exclusively devoted to historical articles. During these years the journal's editor, Carl A. Gibson-Hill, a zoologist and anthropologist, turned more and more to the study of Malaya in the nineteenth century. He contributed many detailed and witty articles to the journal, but died tragically in 1963 without having published any major historical work. In 1960 the University of Malaya (Singapore Division) launched the *Journal of Southeast Asian History* with an emphasis on Malayan history. In the last few years the *Journal of the South Seas Society* (Singapore), which was started in 1940 to deal with subjects of interest to the overseas Chinese, has extended its field to incorporate articles in English as well as Chinese.

Some of the lines of research pursued before the war were taken up quickly afterwards by their former authors. Braddell concluded his series of articles on early history,[30] and Quaritch Wales continued his report with "Further Work on Indian Sites in Malaya," *JMBRAS*, XX, 1 (1947), and "Recent Malayan Excavations and Some Wider Implications," *Journal of the Royal Asiatic Society* (London, 1946), pp. 142-49. By that time he was beginning to abandon his ideas about the supposed evolution of Indian cultural influence as it penetrated from West to East, but he still played down local differences, which he attributed not to indigenous influences but to successive waves of Indianization. He developed this wave theory in "Culture Change in Greater India," *ibid.* (1948), pp. 2-32, and in *The Making of Greater India: A Study in South-east Asian Cultural Change* (London, 1951).

Meanwhile, an important advance had been made in the study of Indian influence in Southeast Asia with the publication of George Coedes' important work, *Histoire ancienne des états hindouisés d' extrême-orient* (Hanoi, 1944; 2nd ed., *Les états hindousés d'Indochine et d'Indonésie*, Paris, 1948; rev. ed., 1964) which provided the first comprehensive history of the Malay Peninsula before the arrival of the Europeans and put Southeast Asia in perspective in relation to India and China. Indian scholars have naturally tended to stress the Indian impact on early Southeast Asia.[31] To redress this Western and Indian viewpoint of an Eastern trade dominated by Indian, Arab, and Persian traders, the Malayan Chinese historian Wang Gungwu used Chinese sources to build up a picture of Chinese trade in the South China Sea from the third century B.C. to the tenth century A.D. in "The Nanhai Trade," *JMBRAS*, XXXI, 2 (1958). This valuable short account was followed by the publication of Paul Wheatley's *The Golden Khersonese . . .* (Kuala Lumpur, 1961), which sought to trace the historical geography of the Malay Peninsula up to the eve of European intrusion at the beginning of the sixteenth century, using mainly early Chinese sources, supplemented by classical European, Indian, and Arab evidence. Wheatley gives extensive translations from his materials, and his ambitious study should provide a fresh starting ground for scholars to investigate and challenge his conclusions. O. W. Wolters' *Early Indonesian Commerce and the Origins of Srivijaya*, which is to be published shortly by Cornell University Press (Ithaca),

30. *JMBRAS*, XX, 1 (1947), 161-86; *ibid.*, XXII, 1 (1949), 1-24; *ibid.*, XXIII, 1 (1950), 1-36; *ibid.*, 3, 1-35; *ibid.*, XXIV, 1 (1951), 1-27.

31. In particular Kallidai Kurichi Nilakanta Sastri, for example in *South Indian Influences in the Far East* (Bombay, 1949).

breaks entirely new ground and is expected to open up fresh perspectives in the early Malay world. Some of his conclusions have appeared in articles and in the second edition of D. G. E. Hall's *A History of South-East Asia* (London, 1964). They show the importance and power of East Sumatra as the center of a Malay commercial empire, which owed comparatively little to Indian influence.

It is obvious that in order to unravel the secrets of the peninsula in ancient times, literary study will have to be supplemented by many years of meticulous field work, not only in Malaya but in South Thailand and Burma. In 1957 the University of Malaya revived archaeological work on some of Quaritch Wales's sites, and in the following year Alastair Lamb embarked on a detailed investigation of one of Wales's temples in Kedah, which in the course of the next two years was completely taken to pieces and reconstructed. Lamb described his findings in detail in his handsomely illustrated *Chandi Bukit Batu Pahat* (Singapore, 1960),[32] in which he challenged Wales's wave theories, dating the building as late as the eleventh century and tracing much purely Indonesian and non-Indian influence in its design.

The immediate postwar years witnessed the revival of studies of the Malay states by Malayan Civil Service officials. In 1949 Mervyn C. (later Haji Mubin) Sheppard produced "A Short History of Trengganu," *JMBRAS*, XXII, 3 (1949), 1-74. That same year John M. Gullick published his "Sungei Ujong," *ibid.*, 2, 1-69, and in the next few years produced a number of studies on the Malay states in the nineteenth century, notably "A Careless Heathen Philosopher?" (a study of Sultan Abdul Samad of Selangor), *JMBRAS*, XXVI, 1 (1953), 86-103; "Captain Speedy of Larut," *ibid.*, 3; and *A History of Selangor, 1742-1957* (Singapore, 1960).

Others devoted themselves to the translation of outstanding Malay texts. A. E. Coope produced a good translation of *The Voyage of Abdullah* (Singapore, 1949), Munshi Abdullah's short but invaluable description of his voyage from Singapore to Kelantan in 1838. A few years later Charles C. Brown published his definitive translation and commentary, "Sějarah Mělayu or 'Malay Annals,' " *JMBRAS*, XXV, 2 and 3 (1952), to be followed by Anthony H. Hill's excellent translation and commentary, "The Hikayat Abdullah," *ibid.*, XXVIII,

---

32. Also published as "Report on the Excavation and Reconstruction of Chandi Bukit Batu Pahat, Central Kedah," *Federation Museums Journal* (Kuala Lumpur), n.s., V (1960).

3 (1955). These translations represent only the beginning of the vast task which needs to be done before the rich store of Malay historical and literary writing, which is revealed in John C. Bottoms' excellent survey of "Malay Historical Works" in *Malaysian Historical Sources*, edited by Kennedy G. Tregonning (Singapore, 1962), can be placed at the disposal of the historian.

The earlier research into Chinese affairs began to bear fruit soon after the war. Wilfred L. Blythe published his useful "Historical Sketch of Chinese Labour in Malaya," *JMBRAS*, XX, 1 (1947), 64-114, and after his retirement in 1953 he embarked on a thorough study of Chinese secret societies in Malaya in the nineteenth and twentieth centuries. This work, which has not yet been completed, is planned as a two-volume survey, based on official archives in Malaya and London, tracing the background of the Chinese immigrants in their homeland in South China and bringing the story up to postwar times. Blythe is well equipped to deal with the modern period through his own personal experience as a Chinese affairs official, and through his special access to secret government documents. Both Wynne and Middlebrook died in captivity during the Japanese occupation, but their work was taken up by other historians. John Gullick completed Middlebrook's manuscript on the important Capitan China of early Kuala Lumpur in "Yap Ah Loy, 1837-85," *JMBRAS*, XXIV, 2 (1951), a study of Chinese activities in Selangor which added an extra dimension to Winstedt's picture of Malay civil strife in that state. In the same way Mervyn L. Wynne's *Triad and Tabut*... revealed the extent of Chinese influence in the Malay states and their rôle in drawing the British into intervention in Perak. Wynne's study of the origin and development of Chinese and Muslim secret societies in Malaya from the beginning of the nineteenth century up to 1935 was printed by the Singapore government in 1941 as a secret and confidential book, for the use of the officials of the Chinese Protectorate and the special branch of the police force. While the book had no literary pretensions, it was a thorough and honest working document, invaluable for the new light which it threw on the early history of the societies. The official ban on its circulation was lifted in 1957. The few surplus copies were distributed to libraries and institutions of learning, but it has not been reprinted and is not readily available. Leon Comber, himself a Chinese-speaking former police official, made extensive use of the work for his *Chinese Secret Societies in Malaya: A Survey of the Triad Society from 1800 to 1900* (Locust Valley, N. Y., 1959), and in fact his book adds little to Wynne's material, although he supports Blythe in challenging some of Wynne's arguments about the origin of the societies.

Western writers have been drawn to the study of Southeast Asia at the close of the eighteenth and the early nineteenth century, at a time when the region played an important part in European affairs. Before the war Cyril Northcote Parkinson wrote his detailed *Trade in the Eastern Seas, 1793-1813* (Cambridge, 1937), and the companion volume, *War in the Eastern Seas, 1793-1815*, was published in London in 1954. The opening chapters of Vincent T. Harlow's *The Founding of the Second British Empire, 1763-1793*, I (London, 1952), provide an admirable background to the East India Company's early search for a base in the Eastern seas, but unfortunately the author died before completing the second volume, which would have covered the founding and early years of Penang. Many books and articles have been published on the East India Company and the China trade, which are of indirect interest in the early story of the Straits Settlements,[33] and several studies have appeared in the last decade describing the Company's activities in Southeast Asia, and particularly in Java, during the Revolutionary and Napoleonic Wars. In particular, John S. Bastin and Harold R. C. Wright have contributed useful articles on the period to the *Journal of the Malayan Branch of the Royal Asiatic Society*[34] and have published several valuable books, notably Bastin's *Raffles's Ideas on the Land Rent System in Java, and the Mackenzie Land Tenure Commission* (The Hague, 1954), *The Native Policies of Sir Stamford Raffles in Java and Sumatra: An Economic Interpretation* (London, 1957), *Essays on Indonesian and Malayan History* (Singapore, 1961), and Wright's *East-Indian Economic Problems of the Age of Cornwallis and Raffles* (London, 1961). Kennedy G. Tregonning's *The British in Malaya: The First Forty Years, 1786-1826* (Tucson, 1965) concentrates upon fitting the Straits Settlements, and in particular Penang, into the context of the China trade.

33. Notably Cyril H. Philips, *The East India Company, 1784-1834* (Manchester, 1940); and Michael Greenberg, *British Trade and the Opening of China, 1800-42* (Cambridge, 1951).

34. Bastin, "Sir Stamford Raffles's and John Crawfurd's Ideas of Colonising the Malay Archipelago," *JMBRAS*, XXVI, 1 (1953), 81-85; Wright, "The Freedom of Labour under Raffles's Administration in Java, 1811-16," *ibid.*, pp. 104-12; Bastin, "Raffles and British Policy in the Indian Archipelago, 1811-1816," *ibid.*, XXVII, 1 (1954), 84-119.

British relations with the Malay states, and in particular the question of intervention, have absorbed several writers. Nicholas Tarling's painstaking "British Policy in the Malay Peninsula and Archipelago, 1824-1871," *JMBRAS*, XXX, 3 (1957), involved a thorough investigation into India Office records. His more recent *Anglo-Dutch Rivalry in the Malay World, 1780-1824* (Cambridge, 1962) is also based upon original documents and provides an expansion of Harry J. Marks's *The First Contest for Singapore, 1819-1824* (The Hague, 1959), a clear and detailed account of the Anglo-Dutch diplomatic tussle.

Two of the most important books on Malayan history, both concerned with the apparently dramatic change in British policy towards the Malay states in 1874, appeared within twelve months of each other: Cyril Northcote Parkinson's *British Intervention in Malaya, 1867-1877* (Singapore, 1960) and Charles Donald Cowan's *Nineteenth Century Malaya: The Origins of British Political Control* (London, 1961). Both works challenge the viewpoint held by Swettenham and his contemporaries that it was the anarchy and inhumanity of Malay rule which finally impelled the British to intervene. Parkinson, in a vivid, highly readable account, if at times perhaps overwhelming in its wealth of detail, tells the story from the angle of the men on the spot, using Straits government documents available in Singapore. But he shows how British action in Malaya fitted in with expansionist policies in Europe in the 1870's. The point is stressed more strongly by Cowan, who in his scholarly work, based upon Colonial Office documents in London, argues that fear of German intrigue in Selangor provoked the final decision to reverse the time-honored non-intervention policy. This view has been disputed by Tarling in the light of his study of the East India Company's commitments in the Peninsula in the 1820's,[35] an argument which he develops further in his *Piracy and Politics in the Malay World: A Study of British Imperialism in Nineteenth Century South East Asia* (Melbourne, 1963).

Further studies of British policy in the peninsula in the nineteenth century have been made in a number of doctoral dissertations. Chai Hon Chan's *The Development of British Malaya, 1896-1909* (London, 1964) has already been published, and others should appear in print shortly. W. David McIntyre's dissertation on British policy in West

35. Tarling, "Intervention and Non-intervention in Malaya," review article, *Journal of Asian Studies* (Ann Arbor), XXI (Aug., 1962), 523-27.

Africa, the Malay Peninsula, and the South Pacific between 1870 and 1876, revealed that the apparent "forward movement" in British colonial policy at that time was much more haphazard and less co-ordinated than had been assumed. Eunice Thio's dissertation on British policy in the Malay states from 1880 to 1902 is being extended to 1909 in the light of material in British archives opened up since her work was first written. Emily Sadka is broadening her study of Hugh Low's administration as Resident of Perak to cover the whole of the British Resident system. My own dissertation on the movement to transfer the Straits Settlements from the East India Company to colonial rule is being expanded as a general history of the Straits Settlements and the Malay hinterland between 1830 and 1873. These studies should supplement the work of Parkinson, Cowan, and Tarling to present a composite picture of British policy and administration in the peninsula from 1830 to 1909. In the meantime various aspects of the authors' work have been published in the form of articles.[36]

Borneo has offered an almost untouched field for historians in the postwar years. Graham Irwin's lucid and well-written *Nineteenth Century Borneo: A Study in Diplomatic Rivalry* (The Hague, 1955) was based upon Dutch and English records and gives a fair and well-balanced treatment of Anglo-Dutch rivalry. Kennedy G. Tregonning used the hitherto neglected records of the British North Borneo Company to write his *Under Chartered Company Rule: North Borneo, 1881-1946* (Singapore, 1958), revised and brought up to date as *A History of Modern Sabah, 1881-1963* (Singapore, 1965). This interesting study of the first use of the commercial company as an instrument in British colonial expansion in the nineteenth century might profitably be linked with the experiences of the more important chartered companies in the African colonies, to provide a general survey of what was in some ways a revival of the practice of earlier centuries, and in some ways a new departure in policy.

Two histories of the Brooke family in Sarawak appeared in the same year, P. S. Robert Payne's *The White Rajahs of Sarawak* (London,

36. Sadka, ed., "The Journal of Sir Hugh Low, Perak, 1877," *JMBRAS*, XXVII, 4 (1954); Thio, "The Extension of British Control to Pahang," *ibid.*, XXX, 1 (1957), 46-74; Turnbull, "Governor Blundell and Sir Benson Maxwell," *ibid.*, XXX, 1 (1957), 134-63; Turnbull, "Communal Disturbances in the Straits Settlements in 1857," *ibid.*, XXXI, 1 (1958), 96-146; Turnbull, "The Johore Gambier and Pepper Trade in the Mid-nineteenth Century," *Journal of the South Seas Society*, XV, 1 (1959), 43-55; and McIntyre, "British Intervention in Malaya," *Journal of Southeast Asian History*, II, 3 (1961), 47-69.

1960), a useful, straightforward account, and Sir Steven Runciman's *The White Rajahs: A History of Sarawak from 1841 to 1946* (Cambridge, 1960). To invite an eminent medievalist to write the history of Brooke hegemony in Sarawak appeared at first sight singularly appropriate, since the adventures of Sir James Brooke and the highly personal administration of his successors were an unlikely anachronism in the modern world. But the book is strangely disappointing, largely because the drama, color, and excitement of the Brooke saga died with the first ruler. The public life of Rajah Charles and his successors settled into a quiet groove of peaceful development and routine administration, which is largely unchronicled.

The real interest in the story of Sarawak since the mid-nineteenth century lies in the subtle disintegration and change of society under Western rule. It is this type of history which is so difficult to write, involving as it does patient and meticulous investigation into scattered and scanty sources of evidence, with no attraction of quick returns. This is true not only of Sarawak, but of all the Malaysian territories, where there is a dearth of social and economic history. As long ago as 1906 Walter W. Skeat and Charles O. Blagden hoped that their massive *Pagan Races of the Malay Peninsula* (2 vols.; London, 1906), would provide the stimulus for a systematic study of all the races in the peninsula. The aspiration remained unfulfilled. Their own work is still the standard text on the aborigines of Malaya. A few articles about aborigines were published before the war, but afterwards anthropological study among them was discouraged during the Emergency. The *Introduction to the Malayan Aborigines* (Kuala Lumpur, 1952) by Peter Williams Hunt, then Commissioner for Aboriginal Affairs, was not an academic study and was described all too accurately by the author as "a somewhat horrid child of necessity, very hurriedly put together for the information of the Security Forces." With the official ending of the Communist Emergency, some field work is being done in scattered aspects of aborigine life and customs, but there is no likelihood of any large-scale study being published in the near future. Meanwhile continual assimilation of aborigine communities into the general rural population is taking place, and the opportunity for studying these tribes may soon be lost forever.

Among the other communities, sociologists in the last decade have been working on detailed projects which will be invaluable to the social historian of the future. The last few years have seen the publication of a number of careful studies about the urban Chinese community, for instance,[37] and the extension of study to the rural Chinese has begun with William Newell's *Treacherous River: A Study of Rural Chinese in North Malaya* (Kuala Lumpur, 1962). But the historian writing about the Chinese community in the early nineteenth century, before the days of the Chinese Protectorate, has little on which to work, apart from the superficial impressions of Europeans, most of whom could speak no Chinese. The Chinese community itself has no early records, and it is only possible to reconstruct a shadowy picture from law reports, from petitions, and from other scattered sources of information. The works of Victor W. W. S. Purcell, *The Chinese in Malaya* (London, 1948) and *The Chinese in Southeast Asia* (London, 1951), which are the only attempts to produce a complete picture of the history of the Chinese in the area, reveal the lack of early materials and concentrate on twentieth-century activities. Despite the inherent difficulties, there is scope for building up an impression of social life among the Chinese community during the nineteenth century, and a beginning has already been made by the social anthropologist, Maurice Freedman.[38]

The prospect of applying the concepts of social anthropology to re-create the indigenous Malay society of past centuries is more promising. Patrick E. de Josslin de Jong has traced the socio-political structure inherited from Sumatra in his comparative study *Minangkabau and Negri Sembilan* (The Hague, 1952), and one of the most important books on Malayan history to appear in the last few years is John M. Gullick's admirable *Indigenous Political Systems of Western Malaya* (London, 1958). This gives a clear description of the social conditions as well as the political framework of those states which were to experience the first impact of British intervention. The Malaysian Sociological Research Institute has recently begun publication of a series of works on the history and practice of Islam in Malaysia, including S. Q. Fatimi's *Islam Comes to Malaya* (Singapore, 1963), and a different

37. Notably, A. J. A. Elliott, *Chinese Spirit-Medium Cults in Singapore* (London, 1955); Maurice Freedman, *Chinese Family and Marriage in Singapore* (London, 1957); and T. Barrington Kaye, *Upper Nankin Street, Singapore* (Singapore, 1960).

38. Freedman, "Colonial Law and Chinese Society," *Journal of the Royal Anthropological Institute* (London), LXXX, 1 and 2 (1950), 97-125; "Immigrants and Associations: Chinese in Nineteenth-Century Singapore," *Comparative Studies in Society and History* (The Hague), III (Oct., 1960), 25-48; "Chinese Kinship and Marriage in Early Singapore," *Journal of Southeast Asian History*, III, 2 (1962), 65-73.

viewpoint can be seen in M. A. Rauf's *A Brief History of Islam, with Special Reference to Malaya* (Kuala Lumpur, 1964).

Difficulties with source material face the historian who tries to trace economic development in Malaya, or even in the Straits Settlements, before the late nineteenth century. Lilian C. A. Knowles's admirable work, *The Economic Development of the British Overseas Empire* (3 vols.; London, 1924-36) concentrated on the Dominions and contains only a brief, though clear, section on Malaya in the first volume of the series. It was only after World War II that historians began to examine the economic development of Malaya in depth. Wong Lin Ken's "The Trade of Singapore," *JMBRAS*, XXXIII, 4 (1960), and his *The Malayan Tin Industry to 1914, with Special Reference to the States of Perak, Selangor, Negri Sembilan and Pahang* (Tucson, 1964) are welcome as the fruit of much painstaking and intricate research in an obscure field. An outline of the latter work appears as one paper in *The Economic Development of South-East Asia: Studies in Economic History and Political Economy*, edited by Charles Donald Cowan (London, 1964), which contains other useful studies on Malayan economic history.[39] The economic historian of the future should have an easier task to reconstruct a convincing picture of twentieth-century Malaysia because of the wealth of statistics and official records, the abundance of newspapers, and the interest in contemporary economic and sociological studies. Already several sound and valuable economic surveys have appeared. George Cyril Allen and Audrey G. Donnithorne in their *Western Enterprise in Indonesia and Malaya: A Study in Economic Development* (London, 1957), which is more reliable on Malaya than on Indonesia, go back to the 1880's but lay stress on economic development since 1945. Jess Norman Parmer's *Colonial Labor Policy and Administration . . .* (New York, 1960) provides a careful and well-balanced analysis of official policy in the Malayan rubber plantation industry up to the time of the Japanese victory. The author does not set out to describe actual living conditions on the estates, but a vivid insight into social conditions and problems is given in a smaller book by Robert N. Jackson, *Immigrant Labour and the Development*

---

39. Notably Francis E. Hyde, "British Shipping Companies and East and South-East Asia 1860-1939"; Jess Norman Parmer, "Chinese Estate Workers' Strikes in Malaya in March 1937"; and T. E. Smith, "Immigration and Permanent Settlement of Chinese and Indians in Malaya: and the Future Growth of the Malay and Chinese Communities."

*of Malaya, 1786-1920* (Kuala Lumpur, 1961), which treats of both the Indian and Chinese communities. *The Political Economy of Independent Malaya: A Case Study in Development* (Singapore, 1963), edited by Thomas H. Silcock and Ernst K. Fisk, provides a valuable collection of studies on modern economic development. Wong Lin Ken's "The Economic History of Malaysia: A Bibliographic Essay," *Journal of Economic History* (New York), XXV (June, 1965), 244-62, discusses in detail the material published on this aspect and reveals the gaps that need to be filled before any historian can attempt a comprehensive account of the economic history of Malaysia. It lists forty unpublished theses.

Investigation into social and economic backgrounds raises the vexed question of Europe-centric and Asia-centric history, a battle of words which—perhaps significantly—has largely been waged by expatriates,[40] while local historians have continued to concentrate upon traditional Western history and metropolitan colonial policy.[41] Despite the heat it has generated, the quarrel is largely academic when applied to nineteenth- and twentieth-century colonial rule in Malaysia. As Damodar P. Singhal has written, "In the commonwealth of historians there are no national compartments,"[42] and in a period when the activities of colonial rulers and indigenous peoples were so intertwined, it is the task of both local and Western historian to analyze the impact of colonialism upon existing society. This involves not so much a difference of interpretation as a difference of emphasis, curbing the temptation to concentrate upon official policies which are fully documented, at the expense of the more difficult study of Asian society.

The attack upon supposedly Europe-centric history is more valid in considering the earlier centuries of European contact in the Malay Peninsula and the archipelago. The new approach was fathered by Dutch administrator-scholars, in particular Jacob Cornelis van Leur and B. J. O. Schrieke. Schrieke was the first historian to make a general

40. John S. Bastin, *The Western Element in Modern Southeast Asian History* (Kuala Lumpur, 1960); Damodar P. Singhal, review article on Bastin's "Western Element," *Journal of Southeast Asian History*, I, 2 (1960), 127-33; John R. W. Smail, "On the Possibility of an Autonomous History of Modern Southeast Asia," *ibid.*, II, 2 (1961), 72-102; Kennedy G. Tregonning, review of D. G. E. Hall, ed. *Historians of Southeast Asia* (London, 1961), *ibid.*, 3 (1961), pp. 114-15.

41. See *Papers on Malayan History* (Singapore, 1962), edited by Kennedy G. Tregonning: a selection from papers submitted to the first International Conference of Southeast Asian historians, Singapore, Jan., 1961.

42. Singhal, review article on Bastin's "Western Element."

survey of native trade in Indonesia, but his *Shifts in Political and Economic Power in the Indonesian Archipelago in the Sixteenth and Seventeenth Century,* which was first published in Dutch in 1925, did not appear in an English translation until thirty years later.[43] Van Leur, writing in the 1930's, attacked previous interpretations of Indonesian history as being written too exclusively from the point of view of European military and economic operations, whereas Western activities barely touched the surface of life in the region. Van Leur was killed in the Battle of the Java Sea, and his work, like Schrieke's, did not become available in English until 1955.[44] But he left a strong influence upon the later works of Schrieke and upon William Frederick Wertheim,[45] while no historian after his time could treat of the early centuries of Western influence in the Malay world without constantly bearing in mind the superficial nature of such contact against a highly complicated background.

The latest work on the subject, M. A. P. Meilink-Roelofsz' *Asian Trade and European Influence in the Indonesian Archipelago between 1500 and about 1630* (The Hague, 1962), which is based on a wealth of archival material, including Dutch East India Company records, Portuguese writings, and English sources, which were not available to Van Leur, challenges some of the economic aspects of Van Leur's and Schrieke's studies, but continues the tradition of tracing the impact of European influence upon Southeast Asian trade from the Asian viewpoint. She sets out to compare native trade in Indonesia before and after the coming of the Europeans, and the first half of her book, which concentrates upon Malacca, gives an excellent picture of the state of trade and society in that port at the time when the Portuguese first appeared on the scene. This is one of the most outstanding contributions to appear in recent years in historical writing on the early modern period in the Malay Peninsula and archipelago. The study of six-teenth-century Malacca is particularly welcome in view of the tragic death in 1956 of the young British historian, Ian A. MacGregor, who had carried out an immense amount of research on the Malayan Pen-

43. Schrieke, *Indonesian Sociological Studies* (The Hague, 1955).

44. Van Leur, *Indonesian Trade and Society: Essays in Asian Social and Economic History* (The Hague, 1955).

45. Wertheim, *Indonesian Society in Transition: A Study in Social Change* (The Hague, 1956), and "Early Asian Trade: An Appreciation of J. C. Van Leur," *The Far Eastern Quarterly* (Ann Arbor), XIII (Feb., 1954), 167-73.

insula in Portuguese times, but had published only a few articles.[46] Up to the present time no other historian has taken over the large body of papers representing his uncompleted research.

The early activities of all the European powers can be examined only in the context of Southeast Asia as a whole, and present political boundaries are meaningless before the end of the eighteenth century. There is no work on the early days of the English East India Company to compare with the impressive corpus of Dutch historical writing, but David K. Bassett is expanding his Ph.D. dissertation to produce a book, "British Trade in Eastern Asia, 1602-1682." This will deal principally with British commerce in the archipelago, with supplementary chapters on the opening of British trade in Siam, Cambodia, Formosa, Tongking, China, and Japan. Bassett already has published several articles on various aspects of the subject.[47] He has also written articles and essays concerning British interest in the present territories of Malaysia, which began only in the eighteenth century.[48]

Political independence has done much to break down the comparative isolation of the several countries of South East Asia. The different paths which they had followed while the region was divided into separate spheres of European interest now converge, and this tendency has been reflected in the number of works published in the last decade which treat Southeast Asia as a distinct region and a historic entity. The fullest exposition of the Malaysian territories' place in the historical development of Southeast Asia is given by D. G. E. Hall in his fine and comprehensive *A History of South-East Asia* (London, 1955),

46. MacGregor, "Notes on the Portuguese in Malaya," *JMBRAS*, XXVIII, 2 (1955), 5-47; "Johore Lama in the Sixteenth Century," *ibid.*, pp. 48-126; and "Europe and the East," in *The New Cambridge Modern History*, ed. Geoffrey R. Elton (Cambridge, 1958), II, 591-614.

47. Bassett, "Dutch Trade in Asia," *Journal of the South Seas Society*, XIV, 1 and 2 (1958), 110-18; "English Trade in Celebes, 1613-1667," *JMBRAS*, XXXI, 1 (1958); "The English East India Company in the Far East, 1623-1684," *Journal of the Royal Asian Society*, April, 1960, pp. 32-47, and Oct., 1960, pp. 145-57; "The Amboyna Massacre," *Journal of Southeast Asian History*, I, 2 (1960), 1-19; and "English Relations with Siam in the Seventeenth Century," *JMBRAS*, XXXIV, 2 (1961), 90-105.

48. Bassett, "European Influence in the Malay Peninsula, 1511-1786," introductory chapter to new edition of Lennox A. Mills, "A History of British Malaya, 1824-1867," *JMBRAS*, XXXIII, 3 (1960), 9-35; "The Surrender of Dutch Malacca, 1795," *Bijdragen de Taal- Land-, en Volkenkunde* (The Hague), CXVII (iii/1961), 344-58; "Thomas Forrest, an Eighteenth Century Mariner," *JMBRAS*, XXXIV, 2 (1961), 106-21; and "British Commercial and Strategic Interest in the Malay Peninsula in the Late Eighteenth Century," in John S. Bastin and Roelof Roolvink, eds., *Malayan and Indonesian Studies* (Oxford, 1964).

which has been expanded and brought up to date in a second edition (London, 1964). Brian Harrison's *South-East Asia: A Short History* (London, 1954; 2nd ed., 1963) is admirably lucid and concise. Bertie R. Pearn's *An Introduction to the History of South-East Asia* (Kuala Lumpur, 1963) is a clearly written summary, but designed, like Victor Purcell's *South and East Asia Since 1800* (Cambridge, 1965), rather as an advanced school text. John F. Cady in his *Southeast Asia: Its Historical Development* (New York, 1964) treats the Malaysian territories briefly but has a thought-provoking section on the later colonial period. Charles A. Fisher's *South-east Asia: A Social, Economic and Political Geography* (London, 1964) is a stimulating new approach, which sets political development against the geographical background. While Malaysia remains firmly in the Commonwealth, since the very conception of the union she has been forcibly brought into the affairs of her neighbors by Indonesian aggression and the Philippine's claims to Sabah. It is likely that modern histories of Malaysia will continue to put her more and more in the Southeast Asian context.

A few new biographical studies have appeared since the war, but Malaysia is not a promising field for biography, since there have been few outstanding personalities either among the indigenous leaders or Westerners. Emily Hahn has produced racy and lively biographies of the most colorful British characters, *Raffles of Singapore* (New York, 1946) and *James Brooke of Sarawak* (London, 1953). Charles E. Wurtzburg's *Raffles of the Eastern Isles* (London, 1954), put together after his death from voluminous papers which he had collected to write Raffles' life story, is a praiseworthy labor of love and provides much new material. It is the latest, most comprehensive, and most ambitious of the many biographies of Raffles, but it is not a definitive work. Despite the large body of literature on the life of Raffles which already exists, the enigma of his complex personality and the excitement of the times in which he lived still offer scope for a biography of outstanding literary merit and human interest.

The peaceful transition to independence in Singapore and the Federation has drained potential drama from the lives of national leaders and discouraged the writing of political biography. The overnight transformation from political agitator into statesman of the first Malayan Prime Minister, Tengku Abdul Rahman, as a result of his overwhelming victory at the 1955 elections, has so far proved the sole incentive to the writing of biography, but as Harry Miller's lively and readable *Prince and Premier* ... (London, 1959) shows, it is as yet too early to produce more than a journalistic impression.

Work has begun on the preparation of documents and private papers as the basis for historical research in Malaysia. Charles Donald Cowan has edited two collections, "Early Penang and the Rise of Singapore, 1805-1832," *JMBRAS*, XXIII, 2 (1950), and "Sir Frank Swettenham's Perak Journals, 1874-1876," *ibid.*, XXIV, 4 (1951). Emily Sadka has edited "The Journal of Sir Hugh Low, Perak, 1877," *ibid.*, XXVII, 4, (1954). John S. Bastin has produced *The British in West Sumatra, 1685-1825* (Kuala Lumpur, 1965), a selection of annotated documents from the East India Company records, and is preparing two volumes of documents on Malaya from 1786 to 1957. Kennedy G. Tregonning is the editor of the useful series of essays on historical material, *Malaysian Historical Sources*. Contemporary documents, which will be of use to the political and legal historian of the future, have been collected by Reginald Hugh Hickling in *Malayan Constitutional Documents*, I (Kuala Lumpur, 1958).

The legal historian will also be helped by the invaluable work edited by Lionel A. Sheridan, *Malaya and Singapore, the Borneo Territories* (London, 1961), being Volume IX of *The British Commonwealth: The Development of its Laws and Institutions*. Sheridan wrote on the constitutions of the Federation and Singapore, while Hickling dealt with the states of the Federation and the Borneo territories. Sheridan and Hickling treated the historical background only briefly, however, and no legal history has been produced in recent years to supplement or supersede the historical introductions of Kyshe and Braddell.

While so much work is being undertaken on detailed projects of Malaysian history, it is unlikely that any definitive and comprehensive history of the whole area will appear for some time. There have been several postwar histories of Malaya: Gerald P. Dartford's *A Short History of Malaya* (London, 1957), Francis Joseph Moorhead's *A History of Malaya and Her Neighbours* (2 vols.; London, 1957-63), Joseph Kennedy's *A History of Malaya* (London, 1962), and Neill J. Ryan's *The Making of Modern Malaya: A History from Earliest Times to the Present* (Kuala Lumpur, 1963). These are all advanced school books, rather than works of interest to the scholar. A more ambitious work, Kennedy G. Tregonning's *A History of Modern Malaya* (Singapore, 1964), although dealing predominantly with British administration, attempts to view historical development from the Malayan standpoint. John S. Bastin and Robin W. Winks have cooperated to produce an organic body of readings, *A History of Malaysia: Selected Readings* (Kuala Lumpur, 1965). A number of scholars have combined to produce a book of essays on *Malaysia*, under the editorship of Wang Gungwu (London, 1964). It contains historical papers by Bassett, Lamb, McIntyre, Turnbull, and Winks. The most stimulating all-round study of the modern development of the Malayan society is John M. Gullick's *Malaya* (London, 1963), to which the author brings his talents and experience as a historian, colonial civil servant, and businessman.

The most satisfactory complete history remains that of Sir Richard Winstedt, who has revised and enlarged his *History of Malaya*, first published in 1935 (Singapore, 1962). This is fitting, for Sir Richard remains the doyen of Malaysian historiography. Some of his theories have been superseded, and modern scholars have delved more deeply into many aspects of history with which he has dealt. But there is no scholar in the Malaysian field today with an equal breadth of interest. *Malayan and Indonesian Studies* (Oxford, 1964), a *festschrift* edited by John S. Bastin and Roelof Roolvink, presented to him to mark his eighty-fifth birthday, reveals the extent to which Malayan historians are indebted to his achievements. It is also a proof of the activity and widespread interest in many varied aspects of Malaysian history, and a healthy augury for the future of Malaysian historiography.[49]

49. Although Singapore is no longer a unit of Malaysia, it is treated as such in this essay.

# COMMONWEALTH LITERATURE: DEVELOPMENTS AND PROSPECTS

*Joseph Jones*

INTERPRETATIONS OF British Commonwealth literature derive much of their significance from one of the prime facts of modern history: British migration, over a period of nearly four centuries, into virtually all parts of the globe. This, for wide-ranging motives, has taken place from the time of the Armada to the time of the Blitz and, on a less spectacular scale, still continues. Extensive and protracted migration works changes slowly but inevitably in the character of migrants; and as their interests and modes of expression are modified, new literatures slowly evolve, conditioned by the eras in which the migrations took place, the ease or difficulty of settlement, the attention or lack of attention by the mother country, and much else. Thus over varying periods of time—in some instances more than a century, in others less than half—there have been emerging several streams of literature in English, separate from that of the United Kingdom or the United States, streams which only in our generation are beginning to receive general attention. Much of this literature is still unknown even to literary experts, other than those in close touch with localized publication. Within the past decade, however, a number of Commonwealth authors have come into world prominence; and it would appear that Commonwealth literature, conceived on quite a broad scale, is a threshold subject of increasing concern.

Why, one may ask, should the study of Commonwealth literature be of special importance just now? First of all, of course, because it is becoming so rapidly apparent as a new field. But there is likewise the growing importance of the Commonwealth itself in world affairs, a trend dictated by the crises developing over the thirty years since the

Statute of Westminster. We may now suppose that the Commonwealth, whatever strains and stresses it is fated to undergo, will not diminish in importance during the next thirty. From an historical viewpoint less immediate, there is the desirability of seeing beginnings and national evolutions as a series of linkages, especially between English-speaking peoples in many different sections of the world. Throughout the liberal arts today, moreover, there is to be noted a tendency toward unification in the study of such branches as history, geography, anthropology, folklore, literature, and art—best seen in the "area studies" programs, into which the Commonwealth enters prominently. Finally, the impact of new writers themselves, in mounting numbers, not only draws current attention but begets interest in origins.

Properly developed, the study of Commonwealth literature should afford insights not always obtainable through the reading of colonial and Commonwealth history.[1] While no one could deny the importance of extensive historical writing on colonies, colonialism, and the movements toward independent status of former colonies, it is also useful to be able to view the colonial question from still another perspective, the personal one, contained in those unofficial, unpolitical documents which appeal to common humanity. The record of what has happened to the person—or, say, the family group or the small community—in a colonial setting needs to be considered alongside whatever the facts of political and economic history have to tell us of the colony. There is no substitute for the understanding we receive from reading the early writings of a people, especially such as enable us to see the individual apart from the mass. To the historical account such reading adds a depth and coloring that otherwise is in danger of being missed; the person himself returns to remind us, "I was not the mere segment of an -ism; I was flesh and blood."

The social historian and literary historian do work, of course, very closely together, each requiring assistance from the other. But in such a time as ours when "colonialism" has become a shibboleth of shame—when ideological battles are being waged in all quarters over what this much-bandied word really means, or ought to mean—surely the colonial experience needs to be made available for interpretation and reinterpre-

1. The following four paragraphs are a restatement of ideas expressed by this writer at a National Conference on Education at Durban, South Africa, in July, 1960. See "British Commonwealth Literature," in *Education and Our Expanding Horizons* (Durban, 1962), 401-11.

tation in as complete and compelling a way as possible. In pointing out distinctions between, let us say, the seventeenth-century "colonialism" of Massachusetts Bay and the nineteenth-century "colonialisms" of Auckland, Sydney, Vancouver, or Johannesburg, one must inevitably demonstrate the complexity of successive or even of concomitant colonialisms and the human responses to them. Critics of colonialism as an abstraction are only too prone to assume uniformity of intention and result, a fallacy which systematic study of colonial literatures will quickly disprove. It is no small task for the student of Commonwealth literature to see to it that British colonial experience, as refracted through literature, does become available and remain so. The handful of pioneering studies at present in existence serve to suggest how much is waiting to be done.

At the same time, there are those who feel already that separation between English and American and Canadian or any other literature in English is artificial and ought to be abandoned. Although this is a defensible position, there would seem at the present time more to be lost than gained by insisting upon immediate abandonment of categories. The comparatively late emergence of American literature as a separate study, or branch, has been productive of more than a little benefit both to scholarship and criticism (though it may have had its occasionally narrowing effects as well). With reference to the ancestral literature of England, it has made us aware of some similarities and differences that might otherwise have escaped us, and has brought authors to our attention who might otherwise have remained unknown. We still have much to learn about South Africa, say, or New Zealand, that can best be learned against the national background. A few classifications, at least, may serve as channels of transmission, as devices to remind us of how wide, after all, the field of literature in English actually is.

Still, one may suspect that in the long run the designation "Commonwealth literature," like a radioactive isotope, will prove to have possessed only a limited lifetime. If so, it behooves us to make the wisest use of it we can while it is still radioactive. The term is a semantic improvement upon "colonial literature," and if it continues to carry political connotations (and how can it escape them?) at least they are less restrictive than nationalistic connotations. But doubtless we should look forward to a time when the simple adjective "English," shorn of any binding geographic associations, will be used to describe whatever is produced, no matter when or where produced, in the English language. It should not be our intention, therefore, to attempt imposing the label "Commonwealth literature" in a permanent, inflexible sense. In any event we can be reasonably sure that within whatever future broadening of outlook that takes place, there will still be much attention paid to national literatures per se. Let us think, then, of the study of Commonwealth literature as an intermediate stage between such local history and criticism as already are available, and the final, far-off integration under the one simple head of "English."

These preliminary reflections imply that before one begins thinking too exclusively about the literature of the Commonwealth he should survey for himself the whole of which it is a part: the sum-total which can be expressed only by the phrase "literature in English." That this is not the same thing as "English literature" becomes evident when one considers that the original constellation is now already a galaxy, with new relations to be charted, many new things to be learned, and possibly some old ones to be unlearned. A few hints, at least, may be offered by way of uncovering some problems.

Approaching "literature in English" even from the mere quantitative, statistical side, one will quickly discover that the entire product down to, say, 1760—the accession-year of George III—is a minor fraction of the whole, and that even when he moves his marker as far down as 1900 he will have come roughly only about half-way through the accumulated bulk. This is in itself revealing. It suggests, first—with reference to the arbitrary date 1760—the enormous productivity of the nineteenth century, which saw American literature in impressive amounts being added to the burgeonings of the Romantic and Victorian eras in Britain. The real surprise, however, comes after 1900. Even when it is conceded that much appearing during the past sixty years still remains relatively untouched by the erosions of time, the developments of our own century are little short of amazing. It is not only science-technology that has proliferated in our lifetime; literature—still viewed in purely the quantitative sense—shows likewise a startling expansiveness. And it is instructive to observe how great a proportion of such writing, though of course linguistically still English, is not British. However much American literature may have helped swell the total in the nineteenth century, American and the several Commonwealth literatures taken together are a far more influential factor in the twentieth.

English literature—the literature of England, or Great Britain—is quite naturally the conceptual base from which we must begin. English departments proceed upon this premise, and it is a sound one, so long as they *do* proceed and not merely vegetate on it. There are various interpretations through which this same conceptual base, in relation to other writing in English, is subject to modification. One of these, which we might call the "English-classics-with-distant-echoes" interpretation, is already sufficiently tarnished—American literature having long since proved itself no mere echo. This is not to say that the study of Milton or Beowulf or Spenser or Fielding is a waste of time: far from it. But it is simply a fact of cultural history that the old monopoly of study within the literature of England alone has been invaded as completely as that study in itself invaded the monopoly of the ancients. It was inevitable that this should happen. The golden voices are still golden, but they are by no means the only ones in the choir.

A second interpretation—still acceptable, if not pushed too far—would assign to the literature of England the rôle of central energizer. But it was not invariably so, and the energy it supplied was not always creatively productive. Witness the long line of complaints, since the beginnings of the nineteenth century, that "imitation" of British models served to debilitate the expression of "national" subject-matter, ideals, etc.—a critical motif constantly recurring in many quarters, expressed perhaps most insistently by Americans between the War of 1812 and the Civil War, by Australians during the late nineteenth-century movement for Federation, a little later by Rabindranath Tagore, and within recent years by West Indians. There is, however, self-evident truth in the assumption of a parent-stem—an assumption once-removed, it should be noted, from the "classics" concept.

The idea of co-operative agency, of catalysis, takes us a step farther. It supposes a maturity of local culture giving rise to creative expression which, while it is recognizably local and "independent," remains quite definably within the hegemony of the parent literature. Though it does not necessarily draw upon the bank-account of English literature, it still trades upon its credit. Within this century, the "credit" has become more and more Anglo-American, and indeed may have begun spreading even beyond these limits. But the pervasive presence of

British literary tradition in one way or another is inescapable, and he would be a wild man indeed who desired to escape it or imagined that he could.

Britain, moreover, has long functioned not only as model, energizer, or catalyst for literature in the colonies and Commonwealth, but as purveyor and audience; and to this we must add again the rôle of the United States. Throughout the last century and in fact throughout much of this one, publication and reception of extra-British literature was the function of British presses and journals. Undeniably this tended towards commercial monopoly and the discouragement of local publication, but it also proved at times the only logically effective outlet. This was not merely parental condescension, although that no doubt may have entered in. Writers from the Empire and Commonwealth had things to say that a British public wanted to hear and still wants to hear. A friend of Samuel Butler's, for example, illustrated this when he told Butler that *Erewhon* had in it "the sound of a new voice"—the kind of new voice being heard as late as the special number of the *Times Literary Supplement* for August 10, 1962, entitled "A Language in Common." The ties of "home" about which it is so easy to be humorous have done more to engender and nourish literature in English than some of us may realize. American literature itself frequently benefited from the same kind of stimulus: the overseas reputation of many of the major figures between Washington Irving and Mark Twain, and beyond, bolstered by overseas publication, played a decisive rôle in their literary fortunes.

All this sounds elementary, as most assuredly it is. Yet it is easy in the hue-and-cry after autochthony to forget or conveniently to ignore elementary truths. Indeed it seems difficult, at times, to avoid applying such labels as "derivative," "over-influenced," etc., when the question of stylistic influence is really less important than that of content. We should take for granted the imitativeness of a poet like the younger Oliver Goldsmith and get on with what he has to tell us about the Canadian frontier.

Having said this much, let us return now to the year 1760 to see what more can be made of what lies on the hither side. India, about this time, was passing convulsively but inexorably into what was to be the British Empire. The American Colonies, on the other hand, were already girding to pass out of it, and might easily have taken

Canada along. The West Indies were isolated sugar plantations only. New Zealand and Australia were on the verge of being "discovered," in an effective political sense. South Africa was to remain Dutch until near the close of George III's reign; most of sub-equatorial Africa was virtually unknown. By and large, the outposts of empire—unwittingly enough, at times—were being fixed while the bulk of literature in English still remained to be written.

Before 1760, however, the yet-unrealized Empire had already left its mark, as the work of Shakespeare, Milton, Dryden, Swift, Defoe, and others will attest. By the time of Samuel Daniel's *Musophilus* (London, 1599), which closed the sixteenth century by lamenting dolefully the scarcity of anything notable in English literature (one thinks of similar laments still to come, but this time from the colonies), Britain already had made tenuous contacts with much of what was to be the Empire and finally the Commonwealth. Voyage-literature, colonization-literature, adventure-literature, even themes for poems and heroic tragedies, offered appeals of varying emphasis to the British public from the mid-sixteenth century onwards. Literary imagination often outran painfully plodding fact, as in *The Tempest* or *Aureng-Zebe*. In a sense, then, a scrap or two of Shakespeare and more than a scrap of Defoe belongs to the Caribbean; of Dryden to the "gorgeous East"; of Swift to *Terra Australis Incognita*. The authors were thinking long thoughts. That portion of North American literature in English beginning about 1585 is already claimed for special study by Americanists, though two centuries elapsed before the Treaty of Paris, and nearly three before the British North America Act. It embraces Elizabethans, Jacobeans, Cavaliers and Roundheads, Augustans, early Romantics.

International free-trade among writers in English has in fact been going on for generations, as a few examples may show. Major John Richardson, the earliest Canadian novelist of note, ended his days (miserably, it must be added) in New York City; his Nova Scotian contemporary, Thomas Chandler Haliburton, spent most of his later life in England, from whence, about the same time, Susanna Strickland Moodie and Catherine Parr Traill had emigrated. Britain sent Macaulay and Edwin Arnold to India, receiving Thackeray and Kipling in return. The colonial Americans Freneau and Hamilton are to be associated with the West Indies; the later West Indians Claude McKay and W. Adolphe Roberts, conversely, with the United States. From

South Africa Roy Campbell and William Plomer migrated to England; more recently, Dan Jacobson, Frank Templeton Prince, Ralph Nixon Currey, and others, with more extensive expatriation yet to be expected for a special set of reasons. Australia and New Zealand provided, similarly, figures such as Henry Handel Richardson and Katherine Mansfield; Anglo-American exchanges took James and Eliot to England, bringing Auden and Aldous Huxley to America, and so forth. Customarily seen in terms of single-line migrations, such movements as these perhaps might be considered, to some profit, in their totality.

Anticipating a roll-call of the several separate Commonwealth literatures, we should perhaps try to search out, first, a few aspects of experience which we might expect to see reflected throughout the whole range. From the beginning, there has been the continual subjection to the accidents of European history: the colonial occupation of one spot or another in the pawn-row of international chess. Likewise, there has occurred the wholesale introduction of Europeans into alien surroundings—animal, vegetable, mineral, uniform at least in their quality of strangeness: the "bush," the "veldt," the "backwoods." This, naturally, has been of great significance. In nearly every instance, also, there has been an encounter with some primitive people or other, variously intelligent and capable, variously amenable to slavery and peonage or else intractable. All this has put a high premium upon adventure-type literature, with special attractions for the escape-story and juvenile fiction. The association of such writing with a country, from the early stages of its history, tends to stereotype attitudes and to render acceptance of serious literature more difficult, as (Ralph) Olive Schreiner's preface to *The Story of an African Farm* (2 vols.; London, 1883) makes clear:

> It has been suggested by a kind critic that he would better have liked the little book if it had been a history of wild adventure; of cattle driven into inaccessible 'kranzes' by Bushmen; "of encounters with ravening lions, and hair-breadth escapes." This could not be. Such works are best written in Piccadilly or in the Strand: there the gifts of the creative imagination, untrammelled by contact with any fact, may spread their wings.[2]

These and other circumstances, often enough economic, have produced special attitudes, sometimes rather morbid ones. From easily bred feelings of inferiority, coupled perhaps with nostalgia, there has been spawned at one time or another the "colonial complex," begetting in

2. (Reprint ed., London, 1953), pp. 15-16.

its turn the "colonial cringe." Such attitudes grew more readily and lingered longer in places like the West Indies or New Zealand than in Australia; in Canada they were intensified and prolonged, no doubt, by the proximity of the United States. (The writings of Joseph Howe are of special interest in this respect.) Later, on the other hand, there has occurred in most places a rediscovery of the native people by the European intellectual, or his descendant, who in questioning his own values begins to find wisdom in the primitive—possibly, now and then, more than is actually there, or at least more than is transferable. Laurens van der Post's studies of the Kalahari Bushmen, and the Jindyworobak movement in Australia, illustrate such tendencies. Including Maori poems "for the first time, in a New Zealand anthology" (1960), Thomas Allen Curnow remarks that such poems represent a significant part of "our commonly diffused consciousness of ourselves as New Zealanders."[3] Atavistic as they may be, these new attitudes serve to reveal lost opportunities not only social but aesthetic. The richness of primitive oral rhetoric, which might have done its part in helping rejuvenate a jaded poetry, was ignored or patronized as naïve, just as native folklore and mythology were attacked as superstition.

Movement, a broad linking (and limiting) factor of the first magnitude, shows subdivisions of its own dynamics: movement *toward*, in the primary thrusts of discovery and exploration; pulsative movement *back and forth* and *within*, as in colonial trade, dispersals into the hinterland, and counter-migrations from hinterland to town and city. Motivations for all this are even more multiplex: economic enticement or the pressure of hardship; vague restlessness, frustration, or adventurousness; punishment for crime; self-exile; political persuasion or religious zeal or religious persecution; military or civil service; scientific curiosity—and who knows what else? Finally, there is movement *away from*—the particular kind of most concern to literature being intellectual and artistic expatriation. Much of the literature of the colonies and Commonwealth is imbued with movement. The journey as a *motif* is apparent in the very titles themselves of such works as Katherine Mansfield's "The Voyage," Henry Handel Richardson (Ethel Florence Lindesay Richardson Robertson's) *The Way Home* (London, 1925, being the second part of *The Fortunes of Richard Mahony*), Uys Krige's *The Way Out* (London, 1946), or George Lamming's

3. Curnow, ed., *The Penguin Book of New Zealand Verse* (Harmondsworth, 1960), p. 20.

*The Emigrants* (London, 1954). Tom Collins (Joseph Furphy's) *Such is Life* (Sydney, 1903) and Rolfe Boldrewood (Thomas Alexander Browne's) *Robbery Under Arms* (3 vols., London, 1888) cross and recross portions of Australia, with Patrick White's much later *Voss* (London, 1957) set to exploration as its symbolic key.

Contact with languages other than English is another important general consideration. English of course collided on many fronts with native languages, most of which exerted little conscious influence upon literature because they lacked written tradition. Exceptions must be made of Sanskrit and Maori, the latter at least partly because the Maori and the *pakeha* met at a time when colonizing manners had begun to improve, slightly, over what they had been.

The British in India and New Zealand, then, made sincere and fruitful attempts to accept and explore indigenous tradition. In Australia virtually nothing of that sort happened until very late, nor did it to any extent in North America or the Caribbean or Africa. It would appear that the Maori alone, among all the primitive peoples touched and at length transformed by Anglo-Saxon penetration, had the good fortune almost from the beginning to be listened to attentively and appreciatively by such a man as Sir George Grey, whose *Polynesian Mythology and Ancient Traditional History of the New Zealand Race* (London, 1855) preserved much that would otherwise have been swept away in the Maori wars a few years later. At the same time, the remaining results of linguistic impacts are sufficient to provide in many places a rich field of study: borrowings, creolizations, and so forth.

The story is quite a different one when it involves a competition between English and another European language. French in Canada and Afrikaans in South Africa maintained themselves successfully within what became politically subordinate groups, producing (and continuing to produce) in each instance parallel literatures of their own, resting upon fierce political passions which only larger minds transcended. These languages in themselves, along with the folkways of their speakers, provided no little local color for coeval literature in English. It is altogether probable, moreover, that the competitive presence of English, with the weight of its literary tradition, has served to stimulate literary production in the other languages of Canada, India, South Africa, or Malaya. Within the linguistic family circle itself, Scottish—particularly in Canada and New Zealand—enjoyed considerable vogue overseas. Australian "slang" has been the one variation of English in Commonwealth countries most often singled out for comment, although the English of the West Indies may come more and more into prominence if the plentitude of writing in that area continues.

At the outset, understanding of the colonies by those outside them was gained very slowly and imperfectly. Expression from the new lands destined to be politically English and English-speaking came first from the discoverers and explorers, whose writings frequently have more appeal than those of their immediate successors, the exploiters. Nearly all such early writing, however, suggests to its chief audience— the "home" population—a proto-society as against an establishment, a searching for life rather than an operating within what has already been defined. Travel literature from the earlier periods tends to confirm this, although later travelers usually offer modified and more evenly balanced estimates—traveler-interpreters like Anthony Trollope, for example, who surveyed in various works practically the whole Empire. Interpretation of a still more authentic kind has come also in varying amounts through a type of personality one might once have called the "colonial sage"—wise men of national and often international reputation whose opinions were generally worth listening to: Benjamin Franklin the archetype, with Thomas Chandler Haliburton and Stephen Leacock from Canada, Rabindranath Tagore and Mahatma Gandhi from India, Muhammad Iqbal from Pakistan, J. E. K. Aggrey from West Africa, Paul Kruger from South Africa, and from Australia and New Zealand—still active into the 1960's in a green old age— Walter Murdoch and Oliver Duff.

Few of the men just named, and even fewer of the earlier types, could properly be called professional authors; and until the professional author makes his appearance, or tries to do so, literary production remains sporadic and amorphous, literary tradition unfixed. We must look to him for the beginnings of continuity. In the eyes of the local author, or would-be author, what has the situation been? Pretty consistently, throughout the whole colonial phase and on into the Commonwealth, all too grim. He (or she) has had a reading population insufficient at best to support the work of authors limited by local boundaries. More disheartening than this, however, has been overwhelming competition from overseas or (as in Canada) from across the border. Ships and trains carried books easily, cheaply, and quickly enough. Through most of the nineteenth century the great British publishing houses dominated the scene so completely that effective colonial publication was all but prohibited; books were printed in the colonies, to be sure, by newspaper firms, religious presses, very occasionally by academic presses—often as not at the author's expense—but this hardly constituted publishing in the true sense. Local periodicals commonly struggled only a brief time before they perished. And though the occasional author may actually have profited from the opportunity of reaching a wider audience, continued overseas publication had its disadvantages.

The authors' complaints that one finds during the first half-century or so of post-revolutionary American literature show up at later dates throughout the Commonwealth, but they are of familiar tone. Emerson's "courtly muses of Europe," to whom he insisted America had listened too long, were made very cheaply accessible by the widely practiced operation of book-piracy, to the detriment of English and American authors alike, as well as Canadian (who suffered from literary competition on both sides of the Atlantic, in addition to being victimized by piracy). The struggle for print still goes on, as always in any author's career, but it is not quite the heartbreaking affair it once was. Publishing is on a much firmer footing; periodicals survive considerably longer; outlets generally are easier, if still not exactly lucrative. Such conditions, of course, are far from uniform.

For the remainder of this discourse, now, we shall be looking briefly at the chief separate components of Commonwealth literature: the literatures of Canada, India-Pakistan-Ceylon, the West Indies, South Africa, Australia, New Zealand. The reader is asked to remember that not very much detail can be offered and not very many names mentioned. A short list of references has been appended to suggest the further reading necessary to a more comprehensive view of the subject. It should never be forgotten that the student of any one of these several literatures needs to keep an eye upon the others, and even more upon the development of British and American literature, both as parallels and as parts of the grand design.

Canada, quite close to "Home," with a long-developing bent towards political and social conservatism, made slow and uncertain starts toward cultural independence throughout most of the latter nineteenth century. No little of its earliest cultural tone was set by émigré American loyalists, scarcely given to hyperprogressivism. Thomas Chandler Haliburton in his humorous "Sam Slick" sketches berated the Nova Scotian "blue-noses" for their apathy, just as his compatriot Joseph Howe expressed for decades his anxieties about Canada's future. For that matter, Canadian writers still satirize their countrymen for what they view as indolence or immaturity. There is much in Canadian literature, on the other hand, that emphasizes strenuosity; a common-man's bard like Alexander McLachlan a hundred years ago was evangelizing for physical if not always intellectual progress.

Before Haliburton, appearing in the 1830's, creative writing had little to show. Two immigrant sisters far to the west of the Maritime Provinces, however, were beginning to chronicle their experience as backwoods settlers about the time "Sam Slick" appeared. These were Susanna Strickland Moodie and Catherine Parr Traill. By mid-century a few poets had begun to publish, and poetic drama (Charles Mair and Charles Heavysege were its principal proponents) was later to be occasionally attempted. Local history and the historically oriented description or character sketch have long been favored by Canadians, with religious narrative both Catholic and Protestant forming an interesting and important historical motif.

Literary nationalism in the 1860's was a minority movement. The preconfederation years (before 1867) show the rather perfervid beginnings of a Canadian fiction, owing much to Walter Scott, which was obliged to wait until the 1890's before gaining any very great momentum. The work of Gilbert Parker, Stephen Leacock, "Ralph Connor" (Charles W. Gordon) and others, continuing for the most part as semi-romantic, preceded that of post-World War I novelists such as Frederick Phillip Grove and Morley Callaghan, who turned more resolutely towards realism to present a picture of austerity not without overtones of hope and courage. The success of Hugh MacLennan's *Barometer Rising* (New York, 1941) foreshadowed a florescence of talent and demonstrated at the same time the continuing suitability of the local theme for fiction. Today, both historical and social fiction have well-established traditions and continue to appear, laced occasionally with comedy and satire. Psychological involvement has long since entered the novel. There is comparatively little experimentation, although the work of Malcolm Lowry—especially *Under the*

*Volcano* (New York, 1947)—is being studied and praised. The names of Thomas H. Raddall, Robertson Davies, Mazo de la Roche, and Ethel Wilson—to mention but a few—are prominent in contemporary Canadian fiction.

Following the later nineteenth-century poetry of Charles Sangster, Archibald Lampman, Duncan Campbell Scott, Bliss Carman, and Charles G. D. Roberts—landscapists and rural environmentalists for the most part, rather close to painting in their basic interests and impulses—on through Marjorie Pickthall and the now older generation of Earle Birney, Roy Daniells, Edwin J. Pratt, and others—there has been a steady if not always spectacular succession of Canadian poets, both popular and academic. Nature as power, often as adversary, has consistently interested the later Canadian poets; this may be seen most dramatically in the work of Pratt. The current scene, with a number of established and still rising reputations, reveals an inevitable shift towards urban themes and introspection. One finds recurring in the anthologies such names as those of James Reaney, Patricia K. Page, Louis Dudek, and A. M. Klein. It is clear that in poetry, and in fiction as well, writers are now active in all sections of Canada: the Pacific coast and the prairie mid-region as well as Ontario, Quebec, and the Maritimes.

Poets are being supported, moreover, by such superior critics as A. J. M. Smith (himself a poet) and Northrop Frye, and by a constantly enlarging and improving body of periodical criticism. Both poetry and criticism have begun turning away from ostensibly national issues, far more than fiction has. Rigorous interpretation, now the rule, seeks to avoid local bias and sets high standards of measurement. It has become the current task of criticism to separate out of the very considerable mass of total Canadian publication such works as will constitute a valid canon. Bibliographers, anthologists, and academic specialists in Canadian literature (courses in the subject are beginning to appear with some frequency) carry on their part of the work with enthusiasm, aided in no small measure by the newly established journal *Canadian Literature* (Vancouver), the founding of which in 1959 may be taken as a landmark not altogether dissimilar to the founding of *American Literature* some thirty years earlier. After protracted hesitation and scepticism, Canadian literature may be said to have asserted, confidently, its self-identity. And such assertion belongs, with that of most other Commonwealth literature, largely though not entirely to the second quarter of the twentieth century.

The Asiatic components of the Commonwealth, principally India, Pakistan, and Ceylon, possess an extensive literary heritage of their own with an introduced English tradition of varying strength now running parallel. Whereas Canada was a largely unpopulated wilderness, India—pulled into the Imperial orbit at about the same time—contained millions of people, great amounts of rather easily available wealth, and extensive literary treasure which it became one of the first duties of cultivated Englishmen (Sir William "Asiatic" Jones, whose biography, *Oriental Jones, 1746-1794* [Bombay, 1964], has been written by Garland H. Cannon; Sir Charles Wilkins; and other early orientalists) to make accessible or at least to begin that task. The problem in India was not so much that of pioneering a land as administering it. Under the Macaulayan system of education introduced in the late 1830's, English became at length well known—available to a large enough segment of the population to attract writers who natually followed European modes, with encouragement by British publication.

By the time the philosopher-poet, dramatist, and critic Rabindranath Tagore received the Nobel Prize in 1913 (Kipling having received it a few years earlier, in 1907), there had been some sixty years or more of Indo-Anglian writing to parallel that of Englishmen who used India as a background for fiction (as did Philip Meadows Taylor in *Confessions of a Thug* [London, 1839], or Robert Edward Forrest in *The Touchstone of Peril* [New York, 1886]) or more frequently for history or autobiography. Both Thackeray and Kipling came from India, though only an early and minor part of Thackeray's work reflects his origin. Kipling remains one of the chief interpreters of the imperialistic era, with his stories rather more than his poems still useful and enjoyable as part of the long record of social attritions. Sir Edwin Arnold became a late-nineteenth century apostle of Asiatic religions in such widely read transmutations as *The Light of Asia* (London, 1879) and *Pearls of the Faith* (London, 1883). Among Indians themselves who performed somewhat the same function for the West were the brothers Ghose (Manmohan and Aurobindo), several members of the Dutt family, Sarojini Naidu, and of course Tagore and Gandhi. In these and others the facts of bilingualism and biculturalism are evident; whether or not such links are finally to be lost it is at present impossible to predict.

In their efforts at heroic tragedy, epic, and elaborate philosophic verse, some among the older Indian figures of this century—Sri Aurobindo, for example, or Sarojini Naidu—seem to hark back rather consciously to romanticism. Yet in remembering that they are heirs to a double tradition—to two sets of classics, Indian and British, in both of which the romantic is so often dominant—we can better understand this. Aurobindo undertakes in such pieces as *Ilion: An Epic in Quantitative Hexameters* (Pondicherry, 1957) or *Savitri* (2 vols.; Pondicherry, 1946-51) the sort of thing for which Sir William Jones late in the eighteenth century sketched out an "argument": a vast philosophic epic entitled "Britain Discovered: An Heroic Poem" it was to have been, commingling Indian with ancient Mediterranean mythology and prophesying current affairs affecting both East and West, to Britain's then rather obvious advantage. (*Savitri* has been examined at length by Prema Nandakumar, in *A Study of 'Savitri'* [Pondicherry, 1962].) In our time, it seems almost as if Sri Aurobindo has resurrected Jones's unrealized purposes; as if a hiatus of a century and a half has disappeared. Gandhi drew much of his idealism, similarly, from earlier sources; so did Tagore. Yet there are moderns, both in verse and prose (P. Lal, Sudhin Ghose, Joseph Furtado, and others) who in the name of Joyce, Eliot, or Pound reject the older tradition.

It is too early to venture much about English writing in Pakistan, whence since the 1930's there have emerged various translations and interpretations of the poet-sage Muhammad Iqbal, with historical, biographical, and general interpretative works alongside small quantities of poetry and fiction. The culture-conflict of East and West appears in the poetry of the critic Shahid Suhrawardy and of the late Miss Mumtaz Shah Nawaz. Some of the distinguished tradition of Bengali writing may very well carry over into what still is to come from Pakistanis. Current Pakistani novelists include Ahmed Ali, Ahmad Abbas, Muhammad Habib, and Firoz Khan Noon.

In Ceylon, says Miss Yamine Dias-Bandaranaike, a special student of the subject, "English literature did not flourish ... [but] rather it was confined to translations of Sinhalese classics, to journalism, to literary classification, research and criticism and to the more intimate belles-lettres such as diaries and letters."[4] The best-known of the diaries relate to social life or sports and date mainly from the nineteenth century, but now and then one encounters such an item as Leonard Woolf's recently published *Diaries in Ceylon, 1908-1911* ... (Colombo, 1962). The same kinds of activity mark much of both Indian and Pakistani literature in English. Journalism, in particular, is a strong influence.

The painful period of separation and uneasy readjustment between India and Pakistan, beginning during the late 1940's and continuing today, has naturally turned writers toward current politics and social issues, just as internal strife has affected the literature of South Africa (where, incidentally, the problems of the sizable Indian minority occasionally receive attention from writers in English: Alan Paton, for instance, has written on behalf of the Indians in Natal, and Mohandas Gandhi's *Satyagraha in South Africa* [Triplicane, 1928], is an Indian classic.) To the theme of Anglo-Indian conflict of modern versus traditional (so often Kipling's) there has been added that of Moslem-Hindu violence. Conventions in fiction, as a result, have moved sharply away from the older exoticism and historicism in the direction of social realism, polemics, and satire. Village life is now being sympathetically explored, along with that of the more ebullient cities; regionalism is an active force, though perhaps more so in poetry than fiction. Socially, India seems still well adapted to the picaresque and to the family-chronicle novel. Fiction has thus far retained its position in the face of challenge from drama and film; and it is to be noted that women writers, who formerly were more likely to be found among the poets, have come into prominence as novelists—among them, Santha Rama Rau, Ruth Prawer Jhabvala, and Kamala Markhandaya. While no contemporary poet of the stature of Tagore has as yet emerged, much poetry is being written and translated. But it is fiction that continues chiefly the function of liaison, in the hands of a number of capable novelists and story-writers. The names of Aubrey Menen, John Masters, R. K. Narayan, Mulk Raj Anand, and Raja Rao, for example, are becoming known to a widely distributed public.

If English does survive as an effective common link among a number of Asian countries both in the Commonwealth and apart from it—

4. On "Ceylon," in Alan L. McLeod, ed., *The Commonwealth Pen: An Introduction to the Literature of the British Commonwealth* (Ithaca, 1961), p. 113.

and there are those who confidently expect that it will—there is a literary tradition of rather long standing, still very much alive, from which much good writing is yet to come. We may expect that both Indian and Pakistani literature will continue to be descriptive of the meeting of alien ideologies both within themselves and from without, subordinating the confrontations of man with nature to those of the dialogues among differing traditions in art, religion, and philosophy. Such writing does much to enrich and vary the texture of the whole.

The West Indies, not altogether unlike India and other parts of the Orient, came into prominence in the eighteenth century only after British competition with other colonial powers. Slavery, coupled with the highly organized mercantilism of which it was a leading part, restricted British society to a small "planter" group among whom literature may have been patronized but was seldom produced. The 1815 diary of Lady (Maria Skinner) Nugent (London, 1939) and the *Journal of a West India Proprietor* (London, 1834) by "Monk" (Matthew Gregory) Lewis are representative of what can only vaguely be described as the "beginnings" of West Indian literature, and they are really not even that. Possibly a better case could be made for that neoclassical poetic curiosity *The Sugar-Cane* (London, 1764), by Dr. James Grainger. Other books about the Caribbean—travel-works, histories, and the like—appeared at intervals, but no coherent body of writing organically associated with the West Indies existed until the 1940's and '50's, when there arose a generation (still at work) to repudiate what it considered the over-gentility and dilettante imitativeness of a few earlier figures, mostly poets, belonging to the 1920's. (These earlier writers may be briefly examined through J. E. Clare McFarlane's *A Literature in the Making* [Kingston, 1956].) There is still an aura of exoticism about West Indian writing, to which the local vernacular English—in drama and fiction especially—contributes a fair bit.

The later, more "native" poets include Claude McKay, Philip M. Sherlock, and Derek Walcott; the novelists, Walter Adolphe Roberts, Roger Mais, Vic Reid, John Hearne, George Lamming, Samuel Selvon, and Edgar Mittelhölzer. Several of these write in more than one medium, and there are the beginnings of a drama movement (being fostered especially through the efforts of Errol Hill), together with a small body of criticism associated with the magazines *Focus* (Mona, founded 1943) *Bim* (Bridgetown, Barbados, founded 1942), and *Kyk-Over-Al* (Georgetown, British Guiana, founded 1945). The West Indian writer of later vintage is restless, sometimes querulous, ambitious to establish himself, along with his people, in the general English-speaking consciousness. In the brief time he has been at work, he has done remarkably well, and may do even better.

South Africa, which has endured a long series of upheavals and reconstructions, has shared with Canada the kind of early history conducive to historical fiction and historical subjects in verse. Multilingual and multiracial, with a native population far out of proportion to that in any part of the Commonwealth outside the Orient, operating upon a religious basis derived originally from the same sources as American puritanism, coming suddenly from agricultural rags to mineral and industrial riches, South Africa has generated divisions faster than irresolute unifying forces could oppose them. British rule, beginning in the early nineteenth century, was one such division imposed abruptly from outside, and in a few years was countered by the treks into the interior which laid the basis for later literary heroics. The Boer War, frequently interpreted as the culmination of numerous lesser injustices, created further rifts which sixty years of attempted co-operation, marked by economic progress equaled nowhere else in Africa, could not heal. Finally, the dogma of apartheid, with its curious logical contradictions which its adherents somehow manage to explain to themselves, proved to be the ultimate division which recently has separated South Africa from virtually the rest of the world. Against this background we should expect to find a literature of tension; and such it is.

British advocates of the native population against Dutch commando rule appear quite early in such missionary figures as John Philip and Thomas Pringle. There is hardly more than a scattering of English poetry and no memorable fiction in either English or Afrikaans before the work of Olive Schreiner, beginning in the 1880's. For a sustained literary movement, in fact, it is necessary to wait until the 1920's, although stories from such writers as William Charles Scully and Perceval Gibbon, together with the earlier poetry of Francis Carey Slater, are some relief from a general barrenness. Afrikaans, meanwhile, had begun to develop a literature of its own, and despite the limited demand for Afrikaans books there has been a steady increase in the amount of creditable work in that language, with poetry well ahead of fiction or drama.

Afrikaans was used for the title of a magazine in the mid-1920's which brought together, for a short time only, the "*Voorslag* [Whiplash] Group": Roy Campbell, William Plomer, and Laurens van der Post. *Voorslag* lasted only a few numbers, but it had the effect of whiplashing, for a time, a fresh note of independence into South African literature. During the same decade the fiction of Sarah Gertrude Millin and Pauline Smith went far toward redeeming the early promise of Olive Schreiner that had not been fulfilled. It was Campbell, however, who proved at length to be the gadfly-genius of his generation; for vigor of language and prodigality of imagery, Campbell's neo-Byronism was, and still is, a poetic force of first magnitude.

A second efflorescence, coming after World War II, brought many more writers into prominence. Among the earliest was the bilingual poet-narrator Uys Krige (a younger link with the *Voorslag* writers), whose World War II escape narrative *The Way Out* appeared in London in 1946 (new ed., Capetown, 1955). Both Alan Paton, beginning with *Cry, the Beloved Country* (New York, 1948), and Peter Abrahams emphasized in their fiction the mounting crisis of racialism, which had been aggravated though by no means initiated by the Afrikaner Nationalists who came to power in 1948. Herman Charles Bosman, on the other hand, used in his stories (*Mafeking Road* [Johannesburg, 1947]) the rural Afrikaner without the same depth of sociopolitical involvement as Paton and Abrahams, or of Harry Bloom and Nadine Gordimer, though Miss Gordimer is not invariably thus involved. Neither is Dan Jacobson or Jack Cope, two others of a surprisingly numerous group of novelists active over approximately the past fifteen years. In Anthony Delius, Guy Butler, Sydney Clouts, Frank Templeton Prince, Ralph Nixon Currey, and a group of still younger poets, South African poetry in English continued what had been begun by Slater, Campbell, and Plomer.

These promising prospects, it may well be, are to be blunted by the increasing expatriation of South African intellectuals, although expatriation by no means always turns a writer's attention away from his homeland. All the *Voorslag* writers, for example, left South Africa at fairly early stages in their careers. Most to be feared is that the consequences of political fanaticism—censorship, a decline in the quality of a manipulated education, and a continued darkening of the mind—may cut short what has been one of the most fascinating and vital literary upthrusts of our time.

In Australia and New Zealand the sense of distance and isolation has played a strong rôle in forming the national outlook, even though the links with Britain have remained consistently firm. Both Canada and South Africa were geographically and economically closer. The early days in "the Antipodes" were rough-and-ready, with ex-convicts, bushrangers, whalers, sealers, and at length gold-seekers all adding complications to an economy which it was assumed (as it had been assumed in South Africa) must remain for an indefinite period agricultural. Nor were the proper methods of agriculture, special to the area, at first well understood. Pastoralism at length succeeded best, creating a landholding group known as "squatters" served by a habitually mobile set of workers and making common cause as a conservative "country" party. Gold-discovery weakened the squatters' hegemony, however, and further challenges rose in the form of trade unionism and the rapid growth of commercially minded cities. Henry Handel Richardson's three volumes of *The Fortunes of Richard Mahony* (London, 1917-29) are an instructive chronicle in this respect; so, for a later generation, is Patrick White's *The Tree of Man* (New York, 1955). The revolutionary tone in the work of Francis Adams (both verse and prose) appears later in the poetry and poetic theorizing of Bernard O'Dowd. Political and social radicalism have been in fact from the beginning a persistent theme in Australian writing. Hardship and "mateship" (as a necessary condition of survival) go hand in hand through many a chronicle.

Newspaper journalism, particularly in Australia, proved crucial to the development of literature. Through *The Bulletin* (still published), beginning in 1880, Sydney gave to virtually all of the then populated Australian continent an outlet, a forum, a sense of direction to literary effort. Remarkably soon after its beginnings it had achieved status as the "Bushman's Bible," and for a critical period it served as a rally-point, encouraging and concentrating virtually all the leading talents of the day and wielding wide authority through its "Red Page" criticisms: perhaps the best example in Commonwealth literature of a "school" phenomenon as distinguished from a coterie. Melbourne formed something of a center, also, but in a less concentrated way; and there were other newspapers and hopeful but early-doomed magazines. In New Zealand a less resolute attempt at literary nationalism in the 1890's fluttered briefly and expired.

In and through *The Bulletin*, the fiction of Marcus Clarke, Rolfe Boldrewood, Henry Lawson, Price Warung (William Astley), and Tom Collins (Joseph Furphy), found a public, limited as it may have been. Lawson and Furphy, in particular, had the gift of intimate, incisive penetration into everyday character that has not departed from Australian fiction (the novel has stayed remarkably close to Australian life); and Furphy deepened the dimensions of a speculative humor that enhances the work of both. The early days of the convict system and of the first flush of gold mining were made subjects of fiction. New Zealand writers were not infrequent *Bulletin* contributors. Lawson, A. B. ("Banjo") Paterson, and a numerous group of "bush balladists" (whose precursor was Adam Lindsay Gordon) provided the poetic stock-in-trade, though the work of Christopher Brennan, an early symbolist and one of Australia's most powerful and original poets, was also welcomed by the "Red Page" critic-editor A. G. Stephens. If by reason of its preoccupations with nature-description and rural mores, earliest Canadian poetry can be said to have tended towards the Wordsworthian, the earliest Australian, by contrast, tended towards the Byronic: it glorified action and created restless, high-strung heroes. Hugh McCrae and Shaw Neilson, along with Brennan and O'Dowd were of a middle generation between the bush-balladists and modernists like R. D. FitzGerald, Kenneth Slessor, and A. D. Hope.

As in virtually all the rest of the Commonwealth, women in Australia came also to play a prominent part in literature, but with a few exceptions like Mary Gilmore, were heard from comparatively late. The novel has done well in the hands of Katherine Susannah Prichard, Mrs. Aeneas Gunn, Miles Franklin, Henry Handel Richardson, Eleanor Dark, Henrietta Drake-Brockman, Kylie Tennant, Mary Durack, and others. Judith Wright, on the other hand, shares poetic honors with Mary Gilmore, Rosemary Dobson, and not so very many more. With the recent advent of Ray Lawler as a playwright (preceded in the 1940's by Douglas Stewart with a series of verse-plays) and such novelists as Patrick White, Randolph Stow, and Hal Porter (again, a series of predecessors—Xavier Herbert, Vance Palmer, Frank Dalby

Davison, Leonard Mann, to make the list brief, are to be noted)[5] the fortunes of Australian literature continue to mount. That such a quarterly as *Meanjin* (Melbourne), founded in Brisbane in 1940, and that chairs of Australian literature are being founded in some of the universities, suggest a well-advanced stage of maturity.

New Zealand, too, has received late attention through the work of two women novelists, Sylvia P. Ashton-Warner and Janet Frame. The establishment of a firm literary tradition in New Zealand, most critics would agree, cannot be dated earlier than the 1930's and some would place it later. But to assign so late a date to a general emergence is not to say that nothing worth considering appeared earlier. Herbert Guthrie-Smith's *Tutira, The Story of a New Zealand Sheep Station* (Edinburgh, 1921), for one exception, in time will undoubtedly take its place among the universally acknowledged classics of natural history. A hundred years ago Frederick Edward Maning's *Old New Zealand* (Auckland, 1863), published as by "A Pakeha Maori," and Samuel Butler's *A First Year in Canterbury Settlement* (London, 1863) virtually began New Zealand belles-lettres with two highly readable books, Maning's having the edge over Butler's.[6] These followed almost a century of sporadic writing about New Zealand, chiefly voyagers' chronicles and a few narratives of exploration and early settlement. An isolated monument of nineteenth-century philosophical verse, having now somewhat the same doubtful status as Heavysege's *Saul* (Montreal, 1857) in Canadian literature after enthusiastic praise from contemporaries, is Alfred Domett's *Ranolf and Amohia* (London, 1872). The still uncollected political poems of Crosbie Ward, an early editor of the Lyttelton *Times*, belong to the extensive tradition of Victorian parody and burlesque. Apart from these, most recognized New Zealand writers lived well down into the twentieth century, indicating the recency of the main body of New Zealand literature relative, say, to that of Canada or Australia.

The one writer most frequently and easily associated with New

5. The varied concerns of these writers, geographically and socially, are to be seen in White's *The Aunt's Story* (London, 1948) and Stow's *To the Islands* (London, 1958), both psychological studies; Herbert's *Capricornia* (Sydney, 1938), which deals boldly with the Queensland outback; Palmer's *The Swayne Family* (Sydney, 1934)—a chronicle novel, as its title suggests; Davison's study of animal life in *Man-Shy* (Sydney, 1931); and Mann's *Flesh in Armour* (Melbourne, 1944), a war novel.

6. Butler took numerous hints from his New Zealand experience in the writing of *Erewhon* (1872).

Zealand, Katherine Mansfield, became an early expatriate and finished her short but highly distinguished career overseas. Within her lifetime, two other novelists of some note—William Satchell and Jane Mander —began publishing, with scant success. The depression and war years brought out a good deal of problem-fiction, by John A. Lee, Robin Hyde (Iris Guiver Wilkinson), John Mulgan, Dan Davin, and Frank Sargeson (who is generally regarded as the key figure among modern New Zealand novelists). Of fiction in present-day New Zealand, Professor Joan Stevens—in an estimate which tends if anything towards overmodesty—has this to say:

New Zealand writing, New Zealand publishing, have taken an upward turn. With literary fund support for some new work and for some reprints of our "classics," interest in our own literature is rising steadily. Equally important are the greater opportunities to novelists who wish to publish overseas. . . . The quality of the items in this rising tide of production varies, naturally enough, nor can any final assessment be made of books so new and so near to us in time. Posterity will sort them out; meanwhile we can read them, and argue.[7]

Early New Zealand poetry has even less to offer than early fiction. For the most part, the genteelism already noted among earlier poets in the West Indies was the dominant note. Again, as with the novel, we assign to the depression and war years a revived and redirected activity, supported by *Landfall* (Christchurch), *The New Zealand Listener* (Wellington), and private presses, which may at times receive inducement to publish through assistance from a national literary fund. (Mention of the *Listener* brings to mind the fact that in New Zealand, as in most of the other Commonwealth countries, broadcasting has been made a much more vital force in the advancement of literature and of culture generally than it has been in the United States.) The poets Eileen Duggan, R. A. K. Mason, A. R. D. Fairburn, and Denis Glover are among the pioneering moderns, accompanied by Allen Curnow and Charles Brasch, whose rise belongs mainly to the 1940's, and by James K. Baxter, of the 1950's. Several recent collections display the considerable production of recent decades, and the surveys by Curnow accompanying his anthologies are models of their kind. Two independent critics, Eric H. McCormick and M. H. Holcroft, have done full-length works on New Zealand literature. These and other critics,

7. Stevens, *The New Zealand Novel, 1860-1960* (Wellington, 1962), p. 95.

not unlike the contemporary Canadians, are severe and selective. To the outsider or even the casual visitor, it might appear that New Zealand writers more often than not are at odds with their country. Expatriation, or the urge towards expatriation, has been a strong subject; New Zealanders treat it with a strength second only to the obvious insistency of South Africans, and for much less compelling reasons. Unfulfilled expectation—disillusioned utopianism, perhaps—is to be heard as an undertone to much of the poetry: the kind of rebelliousness to be found earlier this century in the literature of the American Midwest. Such critical ferment, more than likely, is a sign of vigor, an immediate forerunner of noteworthy achievement, although the reader might wish at times that a few more writers had followed the advice of Baxter:

> Ride easy, stranger:
> Surrender to the sky
> Your heart of anger.

One might state, as a general proposition, that Commonwealth criticism becomes more and more determined to establish standards of judgment independent of conscious nationalistic involvements. But this will not be true, in all likelihood, of certain younger literatures which as yet are scarcely out of the cradle: West, Central, and East African; Malaysian; Philippine, Hawaiian, and other Pacific components (if we are to view them without political ties). Such criticism as does develop may find itself confined within rather narrow circles: all the more reason, consequently, for encouragement of a wide study and for careful reading by all groups of one another's productions.

The literary history produced out of such conditions is likely to err on the side of caution or else over-inclusiveness and special pleading. In three instances, literary historians already have had the opportunity of revising an earlier volume (as W. C. Desmond Pacey in his *Creative Writing in Canada: A Short History of English-Canadian Literature* [Toronto, 1952]) or (as Eric H. McCormick in New Zealand and Henry Mackenzie Green in Australia)[8] of producing a comprehensive effort based upon earlier publications of lesser scope. All these serve well as descriptive accounts; Green's, the largest by far, is the least inhibited in its judgments—a circumstance owing something to the personality of the historian, but something also to the general tenor of

8. For full citations of the works of these and subsequent scholars discussed in this essay, see footnote 9.

Australian criticism. As pioneering efforts, holding to the task of explaining what actually does exist, they have not indulged themselves in a great amount of close analysis or in the luxury of discarding all but a handful of "major" figures (as in the last volume of the recent *Oxford History of English Literature*). Single volumes, on the other hand, making no pretense of being full literary histories, have performed such functions: Tom Inglis Moore's *Six Australian Poets* (Melbourne, 1942), Desmond Pacey's *Ten Canadian Poets* (Toronto [1957]), Arthur L. Phelps's *Canadian Writers* (Toronto, 1951), Airini Elizabeth Woodhouse, ed., *New Zealand Farm and Station Verse, 1850-1950* (Christchurch, 1950), or Charles Brasch, ed., *Landfall Country: Work from Landfall, 1947-61* (Christchurch, 1962).

From the various subdivisions of Africa as well as the West Indies there are as yet no integrated literary histories, though these quite possibly might be attempted from the rather surprising amount of periodical material and monographs already available. In this direction, South Africa is the one most chargeable for neglecting her responsibilities and opportunities; there should have been, by now, at least some systematic attempt to bring together the earlier and more recent literature in English, but with the exception of Miller and Sergeant's work on poetry, this has hardly even been begun. A literary history depends heavily upon a previous substratum of lesser effort—but protracted and persistent effort—in journals and single studies. South African periodicals have remained so thin and short-lived, and so much effort has been channeled into the great debate over racialism, that conditions have been unfavorable to the appearance of a historian who could or would disengage himself. South African English poetry, as Guy Butler's collection demonstrates, has nothing to apologize for, and there is a considerable tradition in fiction. One feels, despite this, that it might be easier to supply the lack of a history for the West Indies, or perhaps even for West Africa, than for South Africa, where the need is greater. Some promise is held out by a journal such as *English Studies in Africa* (Johannesburg), but when one compares its scope and content with that of *Canadian Literature, Meanjin,* or *Landfall,* he is made quickly aware of the need for harder and longer-sustained labor which, under the deplorable conditions currently obtaining, we would be unrealistic to expect.

At the present stage, introductions to anthologies, especially of poetry, belong in any assessment of Commonwealth literary history. One may cite such comprehensive and incisive commentaries as those by Guy Butler (mentioned above), A. J. M. Smith (*The Book of Canadian Poetry* [3rd ed., Toronto, 1957]) and Allen Curnow (*The Penguin Book of New Zealand Verse* [Harmondsworth, 1960]), to demonstrate their value. Authoritative critical prefaces to reprints appear increasingly in series such as the New Canadian Library (Toronto) and Sirius Books (Sydney).

The necessarily oversimple, foreshortened survey-accounts attempted in this essay suggest in themselves the need for scholarly attention which, if signs do not fail, may not be so very long in coming. Only the first stages can be said to have been undertaken: the bringing together of some estimate of separate national achievements into literary histories—of Canada, Australia, New Zealand—all within quite recent years, with less comprehensive work in other places. But the basic material is now clearly revealed; accessibility is the comparatively easy problem still to be solved. When this material does become accessible—Canadiana outside Canada—as in the Harvard, Yale, and Rochester university collections; Australiana outside Australia—as in the University of California (Los Angeles), Pennsylvania State University, Yale, and University of Texas collections; and so forth—it will be used: the sheer multitude of North American students, both undergraduate and graduate, is a predictable guarantee of that. Such undeveloped and potentially fruitful resources cannot long remain overlooked, more especially when so much of the older terrain already bears multiple tracings and retracings fast deepening into ruts. This same older terrain, at the same time, remains to be brought into relationship with the new—a task in itself of no small proportion and challenge, one that must involve not only North Americans but scholars in literally the entire world whose primary interest lies in English.

The necessary assistance to these fresh endeavors may be best provided, one is led to believe, by carefully laid plans to plot the ground and ensure, in so far as may be possible, that Commonwealth literature is made properly accessible. This presupposes a good deal of co-operation on the part of scholars themselves and of the world complex of libraries in which they work. More specifically, there will be need for ready and accurate data in the form of single reports and widely inclusive union lists to determine where, and in what depth, library holdings exist. Gaps must be noted—in newspaper and periodical files, for instance—and steps taken to fill them. We shall require, soon enough, reliable lists of theses and dissertations. In one sense, this may be regarded as provision for a new field of study; in another, it is merely a catching-up on developments that have been rapidly outdistancing general awareness.

Returning now to the literature itself, what developments, in the briefest terms, may we reasonably anticipate? Of all varieties of prophecy, literary prophecy is fortunately the most precarious—fortunately, because it is always a happy event when a true genius or possibly more than one genius appears to upset calculations. We have observed that Canada, Australia, South Africa, New Zealand, and the West Indies have all experienced, within less than a full generation, enlargements of great promise in creation as well as in critical scholarship. Younger writers and critics surely have already seen much to encourage them.

Other areas of the Commonwealth are commencing to show limited amounts of publication in English which in all probability will increase: in Africa, first of all the Rhodesias, where there have been occasional poets and writers of fiction since the early part of this century; then Ghana, Nigeria, and Kenya. African writing in English may be expected to multiply itself in ratio to improved systems of education coupled with the intense nationalisms now sweeping the continent. There may well be some spectacular books of Afro-English poetry and fiction, before the end of the century, to match or surpass those of the Africans Amos Tutuola, Chinua Achebe, or Cyprian Ekwensi. In South Africa, on the other hand, the future is quite uncertain. Emigration of English-speaking people among the professional classes has already reached proportions which would alarm a less egomaniacal government; and for those who by necessity remain, prospects seem increasingly dark. Catastrophe is impending in South Africa which could easily involve neighboring nations. All this, at the same time, is certainly exciting subject matter; and what may be bad for writers as persons may not necessarily prove so for literature.

For quite different reasons, several of the relatively few West Indian writers have emigrated, and it is too soon to forecast what effect this may have upon the recent West Indian upsurge. The difficulties encountered by the attempted Federation may not affect writing immediately, but—as in Africa—much may depend upon advances in education. Will the breakdown of the Federation bring retardations? Quite possibly, though the future of West Indian literature may come to depend more upon education than upon politics.

The inherited momentum of English in India, Pakistan, and Ceylon may be expected to carry for some years. If it carries past current waves of linguistic nationalism, the amount of interesting fiction now appearing regularly will probably increase rather than diminish. About Anglo-Indian poetry and drama it is not so easy to predict, though one would hope for at least some original activity as well as increased refinements in the art of translation. From Malaya and Hong Kong, as well, it may not be too much to expect comparatively few but highly interesting works.

Canada, Australia, and New Zealand form, of course, the irreducibly British core of the Commonwealth. Theirs is the preponderance both of writers and readers, though Africa potentially could some day tip the balance. In these countries the picture is one of confidence in a continued acceleration of good writing and in a rapid increase of special study. Within the past few years new scholarly and critical magazines have been founded, new professorial chairs created, new courses of study proposed and adopted, all in the interest of promoting literary studies from primarily national points of view. We may anticipate that the reading and criticism of Commonwealth literature, with the gradual extension of its academic study into a recognized branch, will continue to provide new insights and a strengthened sense of cultural community-within-diversity for coming generations, whatever their race or nationality, whose mother tongue in the coming space age will still be English.[9]

9. The works cited in this essay were chosen for illustrations only and are not to be taken as forming a composite list. With the reference volumes already mentioned, however, and a few others added here, one may begin finding his way about. A guide is now in preparation; an early draft has been distributed privately as Joseph J. Jones and R. T. Robertson, *Resources for the Study of Commonwealth Literature in English* (Austin, 1959). Serial lists of acquisitions by the libraries of the Commonwealth Institute, Institute of Commonwealth Studies, and Royal Commonwealth Society (all in London) are always fruitful. *CBCL Newsletter* (for the Conference on British Commonwealth Literature, affiliated with the Modern Language Association of America) contains short lists and review-notices. Much more comprehensive coverage including annual bibliographies (already carried by *Canadian Literature* [Vancouver] and *Australian Literary Studies* [Hobart]) is anticipated in the *Journal of Commonwealth Literature,* scheduled to begin publication under the auspices of the University of Leeds late in 1965. On several fronts there is a need for such comprehensive bibliographical aids

as Reginald E. Watters, ed., *A Check List of Canadian Literature and Background Materials, 1628-1950* (Toronto, 1959).

In addition to Henry M. Green's two-volume *History of Australian Literature* (Sydney, 1962), Cecil H. Hadgraft's single volume *Australian Literature: A Critical Account to 1955* (London, 1960), will be found useful, as well as a still later one, *The Literature of Australia* (Harmondsworth, 1964), edited by Geoffrey Dutton. The new *Literary History of Canada: Canadian Literature in English*, Carl F. Klinck, ed. (Toronto, 1965), is similarly by numerous hands; Pacey's *Creative Writing in Canada* was revised in 1961. Eric H. McCormick's *New Zealand Literature* (London, 1959) is also an updating of an earlier work, rendered necessary by increased activity over two decades.

Russel B. Ward's *The Australian Legend* (London, 1958) is one of numerous special critical studies, as is Montague Harry Holcroft's New Zealand trilogy, *Discovered Isles* (Christchurch, 1950), or John Pengwerne Matthews' *Tradition in Exile: A Comparative Study of Social Influence on the Development of Australian and Canadian Poetry in the Nineteenth Century* (Toronto, 1962), a ground-breaking exploration of Canadian-Australian motifs and parallels. The symposium-type book is illustrated by Julian Park, ed., *The Culture of Contemporary Canada* (Ithaca, 1957); Milton Singer, ed., *Introducing India in Liberal Education* (Chicago, 1957); Alan F. McLeod, ed., *The Pattern of Australian Culture* (Ithaca, 1963), or McLeod's *The Commonwealth Pen* (in which the essays, rather uneven in quality, are introductory only; the bibliographies are so impressionistic and fragmentary that they had best be disregarded). Among other anthologies see: for Canada, Ralph Gustafson, ed., *The Penguin Book of Canadian Verse* (Harmondsworth, 1958); Carl F. Klinck and Reginald E. Watters, eds., *Canadian Anthology* (Toronto, n.d.); and Robert Weaver, ed., *Canadian Short Stories* (Toronto, 1960). For Africa, see Gerald Moore and Ulli Beier, eds., *Modern Poetry from Africa* (Harmondsworth, 1963); Gerald Moore, *Seven African Writers* (London, 1962); Peggy Rutherfoord, ed., *Darkness and Light: An Anthology of African Writing* (London, 1958); John Snelling, ed., *A New Anthology of Rhodesian Verse* (Oxford, 1950); Langston Hughes, ed., *An African Treasury* (London, 1961); and David Wright, ed., *South African Stories* (London, 1960). For Australia, see Harry P. Heseltine, ed., *Australian Idiom: Contemporary Prose and Poetry* (Melbourne, 1963); Tom Inglis Moore, ed., *A Book of Australia* (London, 1961); Tom Inglis Moore and Douglas Stewart, eds., *Poetry in Australia* (2 vols.; Berkeley, 1964); Walter Murdoch and Henrietta Drake-Brockman, eds., *Australian Short Stories* (London, 1951); and John Thompson, Kenneth Slessor, and Robert Guy Howarth, eds., *The Penguin Book of Australian Verse* (Harmondsworth, 1958). For New Zealand, see Robert McD. Chapman and Jonathan F. Bennett, eds., *An Anthology of New Zealand Verse* (London, 1956); Daniel M. Davin, ed., *New Zealand Short Stories* (London, 1953); Thomas Allen Curnow, ed., *The Penguin Book of New Zealand Verse*; and Charles Brasch, ed., *Landfall Country* (previously mentioned). General collections are Margaret J. O'Donnell, ed., *An Anthology of Commonwealth Verse* (Glasgow, 1963), and Timothy O'Keeffe, ed., *Alienation: A Symposium* (London, 1960).

Close attention to a combination of history and anthology can be made to yield a reasonably fair picture for Canada, Australia, and New Zealand; for the remainder it is not quite so easy. K. M. Srinivasa Iyengar's *Indian Writing in English* (New York, 1962) fills, at least in part, a long-felt need; but John E. Clare McFarlane's *A Literature in the Making* (Kingston, 1956) is for the West Indies hardly more than a preliminary sketch.

# APPENDIX: AN AMERICAN
# REPORT

IN THE UNITED STATES the field of British Empire-Commonwealth history is growing rapidly but this growth is not immediately apparent. Indeed, one finds scholars who refer to "the decline" of Imperial history, and their view is given misleading support by the fact that several major universities have failed to replace, at least in traditional ways, major scholars in the field upon their retirements. Since one motive for editing the present volume lay in the hope that an historiographical assessment might correct an impression of decline where it is illusory and help allay the decline where it is real, a brief summary of the changing nature of British Empire-Commonwealth scholarship in this country should prove useful.

As university catalogues and syllabi from courses offered in the field through the early 1950's indicate, British Empire-Commonwealth history as taught in the United States has shown three marked tendencies. Imperial studies were chiefly administrative, constitutional, and geographical, with the history of exploration and of war playing slightly smaller rôles. Courses were constructed along Whiggish lines, the history of each then-member of the Commonwealth being traced chronologically from settlement to independence, in succession, usually beginning with Canada and ending with India, creating the impression that the chief significance of such studies lay in the progressive, basically similar, and generally natural paths to independent status taken by each nation. There was a noticeable lack of comparison with other Imperial structures or of regard for the effect of imperialism on the indigenous peoples of the areas acquired. Narrative rather than analysis dominated. People (and their administrations) rather than problems were studied or memorized.

This type of course has so fallen into decline as virtually to be extinct. The growth of analytical, locally based studies, has broken the once broadly based field into regional units. Increased specialization in graduate schools has meant that few younger scholars today are qualified to speak with any authority on all areas of the former Empire. The growth of the Commonwealth itself has made it impossible for us to pursue the Whiggish path over twenty and more separate national histories. A general shift away from chronological to topical approaches in most teaching of history also has had an effect.

More important, however, has been the rapid growth in the United States of area studies programs. A similar but slower growth has taken place in Britain (the United States having established lectureships in African history, for example, well ahead of the creation of such posts at the School of Oriental and African Studies in 1948-52). Southeast Asian, South Asian, African, and Caribbean study centers dot the American academic landscape: many of these programs tend to be oriented toward the British units within their areas. South Asian history as taught tends to be Indian history, and on the basis of most course descriptions as listed in 1964 university catalogues only a minority of the South Asian programs attempt to deal very extensively with the pre-European period. Most of the South Asian and African study programs devote extensive study to units of the British Empire-Commonwealth.

The "decline" in British Imperial history, then, is largely one of semantics. As shown by Dexter Perkins' and John L. Snell, Jr.'s report on *The Education of Historians in the United States* (New York, 1962), growth in the number of courses in English-British Commonwealth history has failed to keep pace with growth in other fields, and student enrollment in existing courses is falling even further behind. But the number of courses touching upon, or even centering upon, units or problems directly relating to the Empire and the Commonwealth has grown rapidly, and the number of scholars committed to such transmuted forms of Imperial history has more than kept pace with the general growth of the academic profession. (English history, on the other hand, is in a decline that is not illusory. In those institutions where British Imperial history is not recognized as a separate entity, but limited to a portion of one semester in English history courses, ill-met by administrative and budgetary necessities, Imperial studies have tended to share in the English decline.) There are, in fact, more students than ever before studying units of the Empire and Commonwealth. The old flag no longer flies, but new flags appear yearly on the old flagstaff.

By virtue of their libraries and the presence of interested faculty, there are several universities where Empire-Commonwealth history may be pursued to good effect in the United States. Although the earlier giants of the profession in this country (e.g., George Louis Beer, Robert Livingston Schuyler, and John Bartlet Brebner at Columbia, Paul Knaplund[1] at Wisconsin, or Alfred LeRoy Burt at Minnesota) are no longer teaching, major research continues. Duke University, with its Center for Commonwealth-Studies, initially supported by the Carnegie Corporation, provides an integrated program of scholarship relating directly to the Commonwealth. Interest continues strong at the University of California at Los Angeles, Chicago, Columbia, Harvard, Minnesota, Northwestern, Rochester, Wisconsin, Yale, and elsewhere.

Late in 1961 the editor distributed to 159 universities and colleges in the United States a questionnaire concerning the nature of their Empire-Commonwealth instruction. He received replies from 71 institutions; 13 of these replies were not usable. On the basis of the 58 remaining replies, a composite of the non-area studies courses can be drawn. On the whole this mountain of labor produced the smallest of molehills, so the statement will be restricted to a bare outline.[2]

The oldest continuing courses are at St. Lawrence University, Ohio Wesleyan University, and the state universities of Colorado, Iowa, North Carolina, and Wisconsin. Of the 46 courses offered, 7 were begun between 1914 and 1939, 23 between 1939 and 1952, and 16 since 1952. All but 7 of these courses were initiated by their present teachers, and we may assume that personal enthusiasm for the subject counted as heavily as administrative desire that it be taught, and that several of the courses may lapse when the present teachers retire. Of the 44 universities offering work in the field, 15 were in New England and the Middle Atlantic states (where the bulk of American institutions are located), 9 were in the South, 11 were in the Middle West, and 9 were in the Far West. Approximately 1,500 students each year register for an undergraduate course in Empire-Commonwealth history; slightly over half of those who do so are taking their degrees in history. All but eight of the courses show an increase in enrollment,

1. Knaplund wrote a pleasant fragment of autobiography in *Moorings Old and New: Entries in an Immigrant's Log* (Madison, 1963).
2. For an earlier survey of *Colonial Studies in the United States during the Twentieth Century* see Lowell J. Ragatz's monograph of that title (Washington, 1934).

although generally not as rapidly as other courses in the same department. Advanced degrees were being pursued in the field at twenty-six of these universities, with the great majority of doctorates being written at seven institutions: the University of California in Los Angeles, Columbia University, Duke University, Harvard University, the University of Minnesota, the University of Wisconsin, and Yale University.[3]

Unfortunately few of the teachers enjoyed the scholar's basic need: the ability to concentrate within a chosen field, even if widely defined. Half the instructors taught nine-hour "teaching loads," while a quarter taught twelve-hour loads, and two grappled with fifteen-hour programs; only three taught as little as six hours. While all but seven of the teachers were trained in history as a discipline, only sixteen of them received their training in the field of Empire-Commonwealth history, the majority having gravitated to it from other fields. Three of the instructors were Canadian-born, one each came from New Zealand, Australia, and the United Kingdom, and the rest were American-born Only eight had received advanced training in Commonwealth universities. The rest had received their graduate degrees from twenty-three different American institutions, with Harvard, California, Columbia, Wisconsin, and Yale predominating in that order. Only five devoted themselves exclusively to Commonwealth areas; the rest taught in tandems ranging from Renaissance and Reformation studies to Far Eastern history, with the usual combination being English or Modern European history; nine combined their Imperial interest with American history, usually of the colonial period.

Well over half the scholars teaching in the field had carried out research in the United Kingdom, and the majority had visited Canada, but other units of the Commonwealth generally were not known at first-hand. Seven each had visited India and New Zealand, six Australia, four Ireland, and only four South Africa. (On the other hand, the area studies programs supplied, of course, a large number of scholars who had worked at length in the area of their interest.) Between them the group had written 59 books and 161 articles.

Those most active in the field were asked to comment on the major

3. Scholars who are otherwise unable to obtain titles mentioned in this volume can do so through inter-library loans from any of these institutions. The editor has checked each title listed in these essays against the Yale University Library's card catalog and has found that Yale has all but seventy-two of the books. One may assume that the other libraries are of approximately equal strength.

problems, as they saw them, in teaching Empire-Commonwealth history. They listed a variety of problems which were both mechanical (inadequate textbooks, sparsity of "readings" collections and of course books, lack of bibliographical tools and of paperback materials for use in the classroom, and of historiographical appraisals) and substantive (prejudice against studying "colonialism," remoteness of the areas involved to most students, the implicit Whig interpretation of much early history in the field, and both too little and too much present-mindedness in such courses). From these remarks three points emerged on which there was consensus.

Mechanically, Empire-Commonwealth courses are lacking in the types of teaching aids American instructors are accustomed to using, aids which are widely available for most fields. But steps to remedy these needs are well in progress, ranging from new collections of source materials for course use to original and interpretative paperback volumes intended for American classrooms. A second area of agreement was, as one reply put it, that "there is no sense in teaching a course in Commonwealth history that ends, because of lack of suitable materials on recent developments, in 1955. The last five years and the last five months must be studied." American historians as a group clearly are more present-minded in their approach than scholars from many nations, and the teacher of British Empire-Commonwealth history shares this tendency. Keeping abreast of current developments, as well as the flood of new literature, makes specialization even more intense in this country. A third area of agreement was that area studies programs have not encroached upon Commonwealth studies; rather, they have strengthened general interest in the subject, although redirecting it and providing an interdisciplinary framework. In some institutions even the more traditional Empire-Commonwealth courses have grown in size simply because students in adjacent area studies programs have wished at least one course which provided an overview.

Where stands Empire-Commonwealth history in the United States? Healthy, changed, and changing. We can no longer afford to mark time to the metrical feet of Kipling; the questions we now ask have changed. As Alistair Cooke wrote in *The Manchester Guardian* recently, "This generation [of American students] either does not know or does not care whether or not Britain 'owned' India or set her free. The splendour of the Commonwealth achievement, so fairly insisted on by British statesmen at the United Nations, is an alien theme, producing a yawning silence among college audiences." Or, as one noted American scholar wrote in response to the questionnaire, "The questions asked by the British Empire historians in the old tradition are no longer of interest to students of young historians. (Who cares what the origins of the Statute of Westminister were?)." But many care about other problems which arise fully as legitimately from Imperial studies, and others continue to find interest in the older questions when they are presented in a new guise.

Today the emphasis in history teaching in the United States increasingly is on interdisciplinary techniques, on comparative (or at least parallel) problems between diverse units of one empire or between similar units of different empires, and on theoretical or conceptual models. One undergraduate course which has enjoyed some success along these lines makes no attempt to survey the broad history of the Empire and Commonwealth but focuses upon four disparate problems: the reasons for the British presence in selected areas through a series of case studies in motives for annexation; the treatment accorded the indigenous peoples by different contact groups at different times; the nature of political expression, especially through emerging party structures, in each indigenous society; and the emergent foreign policies of independent Commonwealth members. This course draws upon other disciplines, beginning with certain models derived from historians and social scientists as they relate to nationalism (Kohn, Shafer, Deutsch, Hayes, Potter, Kedourie, Dia, Hartz), colonialism (Adam, Smith, Mun, Durham, Moon, Knorr, Perham, Etzioni), imperialism (Hobson, Schumpeter, Lenin, Strachey, Panikkar, Greene, Fieldhouse, Koebner, Halevy, Mansergh, Robinson and Gallagher), and racialism (Maunier, Gossett, Elkins, Tannenbaum, Freyre, Dollard). The students then seek to apply these models to selected societies, usually Canada, Australia, the Maori, South Africa, Sierra Leone, India, Malaya, and the West Indies. There are dozens of other themes which could be pursued as effectively, of course, including economic ones. The point is that themes and geographical units must be limited, or courses will sink under the burden of attempting to survey an impossibly large area and time span.

Under whatever rubric and by whatever organization, however, one may safely say that interest in the meaning, in the experience, and thus in the history of the British Empire and of the Commonwealth is growing, not only abroad but in the United States as well.

# INDEX

This index lists all authors, titles of books and journals, and place names. It does not list titles of articles, which may be found by referring to the journals in which they appeared. The index was prepared with the assistance of Mrs. Margaret Singleton. The titles of unpublished dissertations, theses, and articles are not indexed, although their authors are.